INTRODUCTION

The "Elkins' Tax Guide 2019 Edition" was updated as of October 30, 2018. This Guide includes a **separate 92-Page Section** that discusses all provisions of the "Tax Cuts and Jobs Act (TCJA)." This lets readers see those provisions all in one place without going through the entire text of the Guide. Also, all provisions of the TCJA are incorporated into the text of the 24 Chapters of the Guide.

Included in the discussion of the Tax Cuts and Jobs Act (TCJA), among other provisions, are details of the: (1) 20% deduction under Section 199A; (2) Business interest expense limitation; (3) Repatriation tax; (4) Participation exemption; (5) Global Intangible Low Tax Income (GILTI); (6) Foreign Derived Intangible Income (FDII); and (7) Base Erosion and Anti-Abuse Tax (BEAT). The TCJA allows a deduction of up to 20% on qualified business income of passthrough entities such as sole proprietorships, partnerships, and S-corporations for tax years beginning after Dec. 31, 2017. The Guide includes a clear description of qualifications for the 20% deduction and examples of how it is computed. And the same can be said for the other six provisions mentioned above. Also, any IRS proposed regulations applicable to these and other provisions of the TCJA are shown, and a "link" is provided to access the proposed regulations.

Every effort has been taken to make the Elkins' Tax Guide easy to understand. The intent was to write the book in plain, understandable English, trying to make the complicated tax laws and regulations easier to grasp. The contents of the Guide are cross-indexed to other Sections and Chapters in the Guide that may provide further explanations without readers having to search for the information. In addition, the Guide includes "links" that readers can "click on" and their computer will take them directly to PDFs of applicable IRS forms, publications, court cases, and proposed regulations. Of course, this can only be done if you have the Kindle version of the Guide, but the links are shown in the printed version, so all you have to do is type in the links on your computer.

If you need help with your taxes or you just have a tax question, please feel free to contact Chad Elkins, CPA, in Chicago at (703) 217-6646. You can also contact Chad through his website and on Yelp at:
https://www.elkinscpa.com   or   https://www.yelp.com/biz/chad-elkins-cpa-chicago?start=20

Chad Elkins has his own CPA practice in Chicago. He is Certified Public Accountant (CPA), and in addition to having his own practice for several years, he has had experience working for the U.S. Tax Court and the Tax Division of the U.S. Department of Justice. Chad graduated with an MBA from the University of Notre Dame, and he passed all parts of the CPA exam the first time he took it with outstanding scores. The CPA exam is considered the most difficult professional exam, with the CPA designation regarded as the most difficult professional license to obtain.

CONTENTS

TABLE OF CONTENTS

2018 Taxes

Chapter 1 – Income Tax

Income tax is paid on taxable income, which is adjusted gross income (AGI) less either the standard deduction or itemized deductions in 2018. AGI is gross income less certain allowable deductions, known as "above the line deductions." Gross income is the total of all earnings (both earned and unearned) received during the year, including investment earnings, except gross income does not include non-taxable social security benefits and non-taxable income generated by municipal bonds and municipal bond funds.

Taxable income is subject to ordinary income tax **(See 2018 Ordinary Income Tax Brackets Below)** and includes both earned and unearned income. Earned income is subject to both ordinary income tax and payroll tax (FICA). Unearned income is generally subject to ordinary income tax but not payroll tax. Long-term capital gains and qualified dividends are subject to capital gain tax rates instead of ordinary income tax rates, but are not subject to payroll tax. In addition, the 0.9% Medicare surtax and the 3.8% net investment income tax are additional taxes that may be imposed on certain high-income earners. Also, some taxpayers may be subject to the alternative minimum tax (AMT). **(See Chapter 2, "Payroll Tax (FICA)"); (See Chapter 4, "Earned Income"); (See Chapter 5 "Unearned Income"); (See Chapter 6, "Capital Gains and Losses"); (See Chapter 10, "Net Investment Income Tax"); (See Chapter 11, Deductions in Determining Adjusted Gross Income"); (See Chapter 23, "Alternative Minimum Tax')**

Filing Status
The applicable filing status for taxpayers is one of the following: single; married filing jointly; head-of-household; surviving spouse; or married filing separately. The Tax Cuts and Jobs Act (TCJA) eliminated personal exemptions as a deduction in determining taxable income in 2018. Personal exemptions were suspended for tax years 2018 – 2025 but are scheduled to return in 2026. In 2017 and prior years, taxpayers and their dependents were each entitled to a personal exemption in determining taxable income. The personal exemption in 2017 was $4,050 for each eligible individual, but the personal exemption was subject to phase-out when a taxpayer's adjusted gross income (AGI) reached certain high income thresholds.

Standard Deduction
Under the Tax Cuts and Jobs Act (TCJA), the standard deduction is almost doubled in 2018 compared to what is was in 2017. The standard deduction in 2018 is $24,000, $18,000, and $12,000 for married filing jointly, head of household and single taxpayers, and is adjusted for inflation for tax years 2019 – 2025, before returning to the previous lower rates in 2026. Taxpayers can deduct either the standard deduction or itemized deductions from AGI in determining taxable income in 2018. The applicable standard deduction in 2018 for each filing status is the following: **(See Chapter 12, "Itemized Deductions")**
- Single under 65 - $12,000; age 65 or over, blind or disabled - $13,600
- Married filing jointly under 65 - $24,000; one age 65 or over, blind or disabled - $25,300; both age 65 or over, blind or disabled - $26,600
- Surviving spouse under 65 - $24,000; age 65 or over, blind or disabled - $25,300

- Head-of-household under 65 - $18,000; age 65 or over, blind or disabled - $19,600
- Married filing separately - $12,000; age 65 or over, blind or disabled - $13,300
    - * Amount included in the above for each person age 65 or over, blind or disabled - $1,600 (Single and Head-of-household)
    - * Amount included in the above for each person age 65 or over, blind or disabled - $1,300 (Married filing jointly, Surviving Spouse and Married filing separately)
- A dependent child's standard deduction is total earned income plus $350, up to a maximum of $12,000
- The standard deduction for a dependent who is age 65 or over, blind or disabled is total earned income plus $350, up to a maximum of $13,600

A surviving Spouse is a qualifying widow(er) with a dependent child. **(See Chapter 3, "Surviving Spouse")**

Definition of Blind – You can't see better than 20/200 in your better eye with corrective lenses, or your field of vision is 20 degrees or less.

If your 65th birthday is on Jan. 1, 2019, you are considered 65 on the last day of 2018.

Filing Requirements

Taxpayers must file a tax return if their "gross income" is more than the standard deduction, even though they may not owe any income tax. Married taxpayers are required to file a tax return if their combined gross income is more than the standard deduction for a joint return, provided they lived in the same home, did not file separate returns, and neither spouse is a dependent of another taxpayer who has income other than earned income in excess of $500 (indexed for inflation).

Filing Thresholds for 2018:
- Single under age 65 - $12,000; over 65 - $13,600
- Married filing jointly under 65 - $24,000; one over 65 - $25,300; both over 65 - $26,600
- Surviving spouse under 65 - $18,000; over 65 - $19,300
- Head-of household under 65 - $18,000; over 65 - $19,600
- Married filing separately - taxpayer must always file a return regardless of the amount of gross income
- Dependent children must file a return if they have:
    - Unearned income of more than $1,050,
    - Earned income of more than $12,000, or
    - Unearned and earned income together totaling more than the larger of (1) $1,050, or (2) total earned income plus $350 (up to $12,000)

An individual is required to file anyway if he owes: self-employment tax (has net earnings from self-employment of $400 or more); social security or Medicare taxes not withheld from tip income; tax on a qualified retirement plan or IRA; has received advanced Earned Income Tax Credit payments; or has wages of $108.28 or more as an employee of a church or church organization that is exempt from employer Social Security and Medicare taxes (must file Schedule SE). **(See Chapter 2, "Payroll Tax"); (See Chapter 4, "Tips"); (See Chapter 5, "Distributions from Retirement Plans and Traditional IRAs"); (See Chapter 17, "Self-Employment Tax"; & "Ministers and Employees of Religious Organizations")**

2018 Ordinary Income Tax Brackets:

Under the TCJA, reduced tax rates are effective for tax years 2018 – 2025 (indexed for inflation beginning in 2019), before expiring on January 1, 2026. The 7 tax brackets are: 10%; 12%; 22%; 24%; 32%; 35%; and a top rate of 37%.

Married Filing Jointly or Qualified Surviving Spouse

If Taxable Income Is:	The Tax Is:
$0 - $19,050	10%
$19.051 - $77,400	$1,905 + 12% of the amount over $19,050
$77,401 - $165,000	$8,907 + 22% of the amount over $77,400
$165,001 - $315,000	$28,179 + 24% of the amount over $165,000
$315,001 - $400,000	$64,179 + 32% of the amount over $315,000
$400,001 - $600,000	$91,379 + 35% of the amount over $400,000
$600,001 +	$161,379 + 37% of the amount over $600,000

Head of Household

If Taxable Income Is:	The Tax Is:
$0 - $13,600	10%
$13,601 - $51,800	$1,360 + 12% of the amount over $13,600
$51,801 - $82,500	$5,944 + 22% of the amount over $51,800
$82,501 - $157,500	$12,698 + 24% of the amount over $82,500
$157,501 - $200,00	$30,698 + 32% of the amount over $157,500
$200,001 - $500,000	$44,298 + 35% of the amount over $200,000
$500,001 +	$149,298 + 37% of the amount over $500,000

Single Taxpayers

If Taxable Income Is:	The Tax Is:
$0 - $9,525	10%
$9,526 - $38,700	$952.50 + 12% of the amount over $9,525
$38,701 - $82,500	$4,453.50 + 22% of the amount over $38,700
$82,501 - $157,500	$14,089.50 + 24% of the amount over $82,500
$157,501 - $200,000	$32,089.50 + 32% of the amount over $157,500
$200,001 - $500,000	$45,689.50 + 35% of the amount over $200,000
$500,001 +	$150,689.50 + 37% of the amount over $500,000

Married Filing Separately

If Taxable Income Is:	The Tax Is:
$0 - $9,525	10%
$9,526 - $38,700	$952.50 + 12% of the amount over $9,525
$38,701 - $82,500	$4,453.50 + 22% of the amount over $38,700
$82,501 - $157,500	$14,089.50 + 24% of the amount over $82,500
$157,501 - $200,000	$32,089.50 + 32% of the amount over $157,500
$200,001 - $300,000	$45,689.50 + 35% of the amount over $200,000
$300,001 +	$80,689.50 + 37% of the amount over $300,000

Filing Your Return

Individual tax returns for 2018 are due by no later than April 15, 2019. Individual taxpayers can avoid the late filing penalty by filing Form 4868, "Application for Automatic Extension of Time to File," by April 15, 2019, which provides a 6-month extension to October 15, 2019. However, filing Form 4868 doesn't provide you with an extension to pay, i.e. you must pay the taxes you think you owe when you file Form 4868 or you will be subject to interest and penalties for failure to pay on time. The due date for partnership tax returns for tax years beginning after Dec. 31, 2015 is March 15th of the following year for calendar year partnerships or the 15th day of the third month following the close of the fiscal year for fiscal year partnerships, but Form 7004 can be filed to request a 6-month extension. S-corporation tax returns are due by March 15th, but Form 7004 can be filed to get a 6-month extension. Tax returns for C-corporations are due by April 15, 2019. Taxpayers can make a payment to the IRS for taxes owed without the need of a bank account or credit card at over 7,000 7-Eleven stores nationwide. 7-Eleven stores provide a receipt after accepting the cash and the payment usually posts to a taxpayer's account within two business days – there is a $1,000 payment limit per day and a $3.99 processing fee. **(See Chapters 18, "Partnerships"); (See Chapter 19, "Corporations")**
www.irs.gov/pub/irs-pdf/f4868.pdf www.irs.gov/pub/irs-pdf/f7004.pdf www.irs.gov/pub/irs-pdf/i7004.pdf

There are four situations where you should not file an amended return: (1) you made a math error. The IRS computers will find this and make the correction for you; (2) you failed to attach your W-2 form; (3) you want to claim a net operating loss (NOL); and (4) you claimed a moving expense deduction for which you were not eligible. If you took the deduction because you expected to meet the time test, but failed to do so (and the reason for failure is not an IRS-acceptable excuse), you can avoid the need to file an amended return by simply adding the deducted amount as income to your current return. **(See Chapter 4, "Wages and Salaries"); (See Chapter 8, "Net Operating Loss"); (See Chapter 9, "Exclusions from Taxable Income")**
www.irs.gov/pub/irs-pdf/f1045.pdf www.irs.gov/pub/irs-pdf/i1045.pdf

You can change your tax withholding by completing a new Form W-4. You can use the IRS "Withholding Calculator" available on the IRS website, fill out a new Form W-4, print it out online and then give it to your employer so they can withhold the correct amount from your pay. If you move, you should notify the IRS by sending Form 8822, "Change of Address." You can download the form from the IRS website or order it by calling 800-829-3676. If you were married or divorced and changed your name, be sure to notify the Social Security Administration (SSA) before you file your tax return. If the name change on your tax return doesn't match SSA records, the IRS will flag it as an error and that can delay your refund. You can inform the Social Security Administration (SSA) of a name change by filing Form SS-5, "Application for a Social Security Card," and provide a recently issued document as proof of your legal name change. Form SS-5 is available on the SSA's website, by calling 800-772-1213, or at local SSA offices. Your new card will have the same Social Security number (SSN), but will show your new name.
www.irs.gov/pub/irs-pdf/fw4.pdf www.irs.gov/pub/irs-pdf/f8822.pdf
http://famguardian.org/taxfreedom/Forms/Emancipation/ss-5.pdf

For adopted children without Social Security numbers, the parents can apply for an Adoption Taxpayer Identification Number (ATIN) by filing Form W-7A, "Application for Taxpayer Identification Number for Pending U.S. Adoptions," with the IRS. The ATIN is a temporary number used in place of a SSN on the tax return. Form W-7A is available on the IRS.gov website or by calling 800-TAX-FORM (800-829-3676). If you adopted your spouse's children after getting married and their names are changed, you'll need to update their names with the Social Security Administration (SSA). www.irs.gov/pub/irs-pdf/fw7a.pdf

It is highly recommended that if you decide to file a paper tax return with the IRS (amended returns have to be paper filed) or send other correspondence to them by mail to use registered or certified U.S. mail. Taxpayers can prove the timely delivery of physical documents to the IRS by using registered or certified U.S. mail and some private delivery services. The IRS rule is that the date of mailing is considered the date of filing for tax returns and other documents, so you better get an electronic receipt to prove the date of mailing, just in case you have to. IRS Notice 2016-30 updated the list of approved private delivery services: FedEx, UPS, and DHL satisfy the "date of mailing equals the date of filing rule."
www.irs.gov/pub/irs-drop/n-16-30.pdf

Refunds

Individual taxpayers can e-file their tax returns and request that their refunds be split-up and directly deposited into up to 3 accounts in banks, credit unions, and mutual funds by using Form 8888. Also, a tax refund can be paid directly to an IRA. You can check on your refund by using the IRS's online "Where's My Refund?" tool. Some 2018 tax refunds may be delayed, in particular for taxpayers who claim either the earned income credit or the refundable child tax credit. Starting with 2016 returns, the IRS must wait until Feb. 15th to send refunds to taxpayers who claim these two refundable credits. Also, the rise in identity theft is causing the IRS and state tax authorities to spend additional review time to protect against fraud. **(See Chapter 13, "Earned Income Credit"; & "Additional Child Tax Credit")**
www.irs.gov/pub/irs-pdf/f8888.pdf

Beginning on Jan. 1, 2015 the IRS started limiting the number of tax refunds electronically deposited into a single financial account or pre-paid debit card to three. This limitation is part of an effort by the IRS to combat fraud and identity theft, including fraud committed by unscrupulous tax preparers. As a result, the fourth and subsequent refunds to the same account or pre-paid debit card will automatically be converted to a paper refund check and mailed to the taxpayer. In addition, the taxpayers involved will receive a notice informing them that their account has exceeded the direct deposit limits and that they will receive a paper refund check in approximately four weeks. The IRS has said that the limitation could affect some taxpayers, such as families in which the parent's and children's refunds are deposited into a family-held bank account. Taxpayers in this situation should make other deposit arrangements or expect to receive paper refund checks. The direct deposit limit is intended to prevent criminals from easily obtaining multiple tax refunds. The new limitation will also protect taxpayers from preparers who obtain payment for their tax preparation services by depositing part or all of their clients' refunds into the preparers' own bank accounts. Direct deposits must only be made to accounts bearing the taxpayer's name. Tax preparer fees cannot be recovered by using Form 8888 to split the refund or by preparers opening a joint bank account with taxpayers.

If you are a due a refund, you generally must file a tax return to claim the refund, and you must file a tax return to claim the refund within 3 years from the date the return is due (including extensions) to get the refund. For example, if you are due a refund for tax year 2014, and you don't file a tax return claiming the refund until 2018, you will generally not be entitled to receive the refund. The law generally provides for interest on your refund if it is not paid within 45 days of the date you file your return claiming the refund. Publication 556, "Examination of Returns, Appeal Rights, and Claims for Refund," has more information on refunds. If you receive a refund check that is smaller than expected, you can cash it and then work with the IRS to resolve the difference. If, however,

the check is larger than expected, don't cash it. Instead, follow the instructions on the notice accompanying the check.
www.irs.gov/pub/irs-pdf/p556.pdf

New Indexing Method for Cost of Living Adjustments (COLAs) – Effective for 2018 and subsequent years, the TCJA reduces all cost of living adjustments (COLAs) that are applicable throughout the Internal Revenue Code. COLAs for tax rate thresholds, standard deduction amounts, and other amounts for inflation are reduced by converting indexing to chained CPI-U (C-CPI-U) rather than using the consumer price index (CPI) in effect in 2017 and prior years. The new method uses "chained CPI," which assumes consumers look for substitute items rather than absorbing rising prices during periods of inflation. Chained CPI will generally result in smaller annual increases. The difference between the old and new method is quite small in a single year but will get quite large over time due to the effect of compounding. The change to chained CPI for inflation indexing is effective for tax years beginning after 2017 and will remain in effect after 2025 – it is not subject to the sunsetting provisions that apply to most of the other individual tax provisions under the TCJA.

What Happens to Non-Filers
If a taxpayer doesn't file a tax return and pay the taxes owed when due, the IRS can take several steps, including filing a substitute tax return for the taxpayer, and the IRS Collection Division can start the collection process, which can include a tax levy, tax lien, or garnishment of wages.

Extended Time to File Administrative Claim or Bring Suit for wrongful Levy – The TCJA extends the time for individuals and businesses to file an administrative claim with the IRS or bring a civil action suit for wrongful levy by the IRS from 9 months to 2 years. Additionally, if an administrative claim for the return of property is made within the 2-year period, the 2-year period for bringing suit is then extended for 12 months from the date of filing the claim or for 6 months from the disallowance of the claim by the IRS, whichever is shorter. The change applies to levies made after Dec. 22, 2017, and on or before that date, if the previous nine-month period hadn't yet expired.

Tax Information – The IRS provides the following sources for forms, publications, and additional information.
- *Tax Questions:* 1-800-829-1040 (1-800-829-4059 for TTY/TDD)
- *Forms and Publications:* 1-800-829-3676 (1-800-829-4059 for TTY/TDD)
- *Internet:* www.irs.gov
- *Small Business Ombudsman:* A small business entity can participate in the regulatory process and comment on enforcement actions of the IRS by calling 1-888-REG-FAIR.
- *Treasury Inspector General for Tax Administration:* You can confidentially report misconduct, waste, fraud, or abuse by an IRS employee by calling 1-800-366-4484 (1-800-877-8339 for TTY/TDD). You can remain anonymous.

Chapter 2 – Payroll Tax (FICA)

The Federal Insurance Contributions Act (FICA) provides for the payment of Old Age Survivor and Disability Insurance (OASDI) and Medicare taxes on salaries of employees that are reported on Form W-2 by employers. OASDI is also known and better known as the "Social Security" tax. The FICA tax, also known as the payroll tax, is the total of the Social Security tax and the Medicare tax imposed on employees' wages and salaries (earned income). Employees are required to pay a 6.2% Social Security (OASDI) tax and a 1.45% Medicare tax on their wages and salaries – a total of 7.65%, which is matched by their employer, so the total payroll tax is 15.3%. However, there is a cap on salaries and wages that are subject to the Social Security tax, which is $128,400 in 2018 ($127,200 in 2017). There is no cap on wages and salaries that are subject to the Medicare tax. Therefore, the payroll tax on employees' wages and salaries that are more than $128,400 is only 2.9% in 2018, which is the total of the employee's and employer's share of the Medicare tax. **(See Chapter 5, "Social Security Benefits"; & "Medicare Premiums")**
www.irs.gov/pub/irs-pdf/p15.pdf

Employers are required to withhold income taxes and payroll taxes from employees' salaries, and they must use Form 941, "Employer's Quarterly Federal Tax Return," to submit quarterly payments to the IRS. The quarterly payments include the income taxes and payroll taxes withheld from employees' salaries, plus the matching share of payroll taxes paid by employers. Small employers, i.e. those whose annual liability for withheld income taxes and payroll taxes are less than $2,500 a year may use Form 944, "Employer's Annual Federal Tax Return," to submit payments to the IRS.
www.irs.gov/pub/irs-pdf/f941.pdf   www.irs.gov/pub/irs-pdf/i941.pdf   www.irs.gov/pub/irs-pdf/f944.pdf

Self-employed/independent contractors whose earned income may or not be reported on Form 1099-MISC must pay self-employment tax, which is also payroll tax (FICA), equal to 15.3% in 2018. There is no withholding from compensation paid to self-employed persons – they have to compute and pay self-employment taxes on Form 1040, Schedule SE. The self-employment tax is 92.35% of net self-employment income multiplied by the self-employment tax rate of 15.3% (12.4% Social Security and 2.9% Medicare) on self-employment income over $400. Net earnings from self-employment less than $400 in a year are excluded from the self-employment tax. Employees who have wages of $128,400 in 2018 reported of Form W-2 on which they pay FICA are not subject to Social Security tax on any self-employment income. **(See Chapter 17, "Self-Employment Tax")**
www.irs.gov/pub/irs-pdf/f1040sse.pdf

Beginning in July 2016, an employer that uses a certified payroll agent won't be liable for undeposited payroll taxes due to the agent's malfeasance. Prior to 2016, employers that used payroll agents were responsible for undeposited payroll taxes even if it was the agent's fault. The IRS certifies payroll agents who post a bond, submit audited financial statements, and pay an annual fee of $1,000. Most employers who withhold income taxes and payroll taxes from employees' salaries must use Form 941, "Employer's Quarterly Federal Tax Return," to submit payments to the IRS. Businesses that miss payroll tax deposits will be notified by mail by the IRS when records show that their payroll tax deposits have declined. This is a new initiative by the IRS. If a business has missed any deposits, the IRS will pursue collection of the unpaid amounts. **(See Chapter 4, "Wages and Salaries")**

Federal Unemployment Tax (FUTA)

In addition to their matching share of payroll tax (FICA), employers also have to pay Federal Unemployment Tax (FUTA) and state unemployment insurance. For 2018, the FUTA tax rate is 6.0%. The tax applies to the first $7,000 employers pay to each employee as wages during the year. The $7,000 is the federal wage base. The state wage base may be different. Generally, you can take a credit against the FUTA tax for amounts you paid into state unemployment funds. The credit may be as much as 5.4% of FUTA taxable wages. If employers are entitled to the maximum 5.4% credit, the FUTA tax rate after the credit is 0.6%, so employers have to pay $42 per employee in 2018. Employers are entitled to the maximum credit if they pay their state unemployment taxes in full, on time, and on all the same wages as are subject to FUTA tax, and as long as the state isn't determined to be a credit reduction state. In some states, the wages subject to state unemployment tax are the same as the wages subject to FUTA tax. However, certain states exclude some types of wages from state unemployment tax, even though they're subject to FUTA tax (for example, wages paid to corporate officers, certain payments of sick pay by unions, and certain fringe benefits). In such a case, employers may be required to deposit more than 0.6% FUTA tax on those wages.

The FUTA tax is generally computed and deposited quarterly by employers. However, if an employer's FUTA tax liability for any calendar quarter is $500 or less, they don't have to deposit the tax. Instead, they may carry it forward and add it to the liability figured in the next quarter to see if they then must make a deposit. If the FUTA tax liability for any calendar quarter is over $500 (including any FUTA tax carried forward from an earlier quarter), employers must deposit the tax in that quarter. Employer's report their FUTA tax annually on IRS Form 940 "Employer's Annual Unemployment (FUTA) Tax Return," in January of the following year. Self-employed/independent contractors that receive Form 1099-MISC are not subject to the FUTA tax. www.irs.gov/pub/irs-pdf/f940.pdf www.irs.gov/pub/irs-pdf/i940.pdf

In years when there are credit reduction states, employers must include liabilities owed for credit reduction with their fourth quarter deposit. They may deposit the anticipated extra liability throughout the year, but it isn't due until the due date for the deposit for the fourth quarter, and the associated liability should be recorded as being incurred in the fourth quarter. See the Instructions for Form 940 for more information.

The Federal Unemployment Tax Act, with state unemployment systems, provides for payments of unemployment compensation to workers who have lost their jobs. Most employers pay both a federal and a state unemployment tax. For a list of state unemployment agencies, visit the U.S. Department of Labor's website at workforcesecurity.doleta.gov/unemploy/agencies.asp. Only the employer pays FUTA tax; it isn't withheld from the employee's wages. Services rendered to a federally recognized Indian tribal government (or any subdivision, subsidiary, or business wholly owned by such an Indian tribe) are exempt from FUTA tax, subject to the tribe's compliance with state law.

In order to determine whether you (the employer) must pay the FUTA tax, use the following three tests. Each test applies to a different category of employee, and each is independent of the others. If a test describes your situation, you're subject to FUTA tax on the wages you pay to employees in that category in 2018: (1) General test – You're subject to FUTA tax in 2018 on the wages you pay employees who aren't farmworkers or household workers if you paid wages of $1,500 or more in any calendar quarter, or you had one or more employees for at least some part of a day in any 20 or more different weeks or; (2) Household employees test – You're subject to

FUTA tax if you paid total cash wages of $1,000 or more to household employees in any calendar quarter in 2018. A household employee is an employee who performs household work in a private home, local college club, or local fraternity or sorority chapter; (3) Farmworkers test – You're subject to FUTA tax on the wages you pay to farmworkers if you paid cash wages of $20,000 or more to farmworkers during any calendar quarter in 2018, or you employed 10 or more farmworkers during at least some part of a day (whether or not at the same time) during any 20 or more different weeks in 2018. **(See Chapter 17, "Domestic Workers")**

0.9% Medicare Surtax

Under the Tax Cuts and Jobs Act (TCJA), the 0.9% Medicare surtax added by the Affordable Care Act is still in effect. The 0.9% surtax is added to the 1.45% Medicare tax paid by certain high-income earners. High income earners are those with wages and self-employment income above $200,000 single; $250,000 married filing jointly; and $125,000 married filing separately (not indexed for inflation). There is no employer match for this tax. Therefore, high income employees have to pay a 2.35% Medicare tax on any income earned above the applicable thresholds. For self-employed taxpayers, the surtax is added to the 2.9% Medicare tax paid on self-employment income of high income earners, so they have to pay a 3.8% Medicare tax on any income above the applicable thresholds. **(See Chapter 24, "Taxes on High-Income Earners, Insurance Providers, and Other Entities")**

Employers are required to withhold the additional Medicare surtax on wages it pays to an employee in excess of $200,000, even though an employee may not be liable for the additional Medicare surtax because, for example, the spouse had no income. Any withheld Medicare tax not owed will be credited against the total tax liability shown on the tax return. If an individual knows they will be above the limit because of their spouse's wages, the additional tax still won't be withheld until their wages reach $200,000. In this case, the employee can adjust his/her W-4 to have additional taxes withheld. The stated thresholds for high income earners are "not indexed for inflation." Employees may only claim a refund of the additional Medicare surtax on their tax return if they have not received repayment or reimbursement from their employer. Flow-through business income from an S-corporation is not subject to the 0.9% Medicare surtax. If you owe the 0.9% Medicare surtax, you must file Form 8959 with your tax return. **(See Chapter 4, "Earned Income")**
www.irs.gov/pub/irs-pdf/f8959.pdf   www.irs.gov/pub/irs-pdf/i8959.pdf

Domestic Workers

Domestic workers are considered employees and not independent contractors. Domestic household help includes nannies, maids, senior caregivers, housekeepers and other domestic workers. Nannies, babysitters, and other domestic workers are considered household employees if they are in charge of what work is done and how it is done, which is usually the case. It doesn't matter whether they work full-time or part-time, or whether they were hired through an agency or from a list provided by an agency or association. It also doesn't matter whether they are paid for the job or on an hourly, daily or weekly basis. If the person working for you doesn't have his or her own company and is not an employee of an agency or another firm that provides services to you and others throughout the week or month, then he or she is probably your employee, and you are the employer. On the other hand, plumbers, electricians, etc. that you occasionally hire are independent contractors and not employees.

You have to give a Form W-2 to any household employee to whom you pay at least $2,100 in 2018 ($2,000 in 2017). Although you are not required to withhold federal income taxes from these employees' wages, you are required to withhold their share of payroll taxes (FICA), and you are required to pay the other half of payroll taxes

and the FUTA tax (this is sometimes referred to as the "Nanny Tax"). Once a household employee's 2018 wages reach $128,400, you aren't required to pay or withhold Social Security tax, but you are still required to continue withholding Medicare tax. These taxes are accounted for on Schedule H which must be filed with your tax return, and you have to have an employer identification number (EIN). Schedule H helps you calculate the amount of payroll tax you owe, which is based on the total amount of wages paid to applicable household employees. Once you complete Schedule H and know the total amount of household payroll taxes for which you're liable, enter the figure on the "Other Taxes" Line of Form 1040 and include it as part of your personal income tax bill for the year. In addition to giving Form W-2 to applicable household employees to whom you pay at least $2,100, you have to submit the information to the Social Security Administration on Form W-3.
www.irs.gov/pub/irs-pdf/f1040sh.pdf (www.irs.gov/pub/irs-pdf/i1040sh.pdf

If you prefer, you can pay a household employee's share of payroll taxes from your own funds instead of withholding from the employee's wages. Any payroll taxes paid by you on behave of your employee(s) must be included in the employee's wages for income tax purposes. However, it is not counted as wages subject to payroll taxes.

Domestic household help wages are not subject to payroll taxes (FICA) if they are paid to any of the following individuals, even if the wages are $2,100 or more during the year: a spouse; a child who is under the age of 21; a household employee who is under the age of 18 at any time during the year unless providing household services is the employee's principal occupation – providing household services is not considered to be a "student's principal occupation;" or your parent unless your parent cares for a child for which both of the following conditions apply: the child is under 18 and has a physical or mental condition that requires personal care by an adult for at least four continuous weeks during the calendar quarter when services are provided. Also, wages paid to a spouse, a child who is under the age of 21, or your parent are not subject to FUTA. **(See Above, "Federal Unemployment Tax (FUTA)"); (See Chapter 4, "Wages and Salaries")**

Chapter 3 – Determining Filing Status and Dependency Exemptions

Generally, your filing status is: "Single" if you are unmarried and have no dependents; or "Married filing jointly" if you are married and either have or don't have any dependents. All other filing statuses are discussed in this Chapter.

Head of Household

To claim "head-of-household" status, you must either be unmarried (not a surviving spouse), or not live with your spouse during the last 6 months of the year while still considered married, and you must pay more than ½ of the cost of maintaining a home as a household, which is the principal place of abode of a "qualifying child" or another person that can be claimed as a dependent. If you can claim head-of-household while still married, the other spouse must file as "married filing separately." Maintaining a household includes paying for: mortgage interest, property taxes, rent, utilities, upkeep of home and repairs, property insurance, food consumed on premises, and other household expenses. It does not include the cost of: clothing, education expense, medical treatment, vacations, life insurance, transportation, and food consumed off-premises. Temporary absences from the home due to education, business, military service, vacation, or illness do not affect the ½ year rule so long as the home is continuously maintained during the absence. If a qualifying dependent dies, then the ½ year rule does not apply if the taxpayer maintains a household for that person until the time of death. **(See Below, "Qualifying Child for the Dependency Exemption")**

A grandparent who is the primary care giver of a qualifying grandchild or grandchildren can claim head-of-household filing status on his or her tax return if he or she maintains a household for them, and he or she is raising them instead of the parent(s).

A taxpayer does not have to live in a household maintained for an elderly parent in order to claim head-of-household status (this is the only exception) if the taxpayer is otherwise entitled to claim the parent as a dependent. **(See Below, "Other Persons Qualifying as Dependents")**

Under the Tax Cuts and Jobs Act (TCJA), the due diligence requirements for claiming the Earned Income Tax Credit, the Child Tax Credit, the Additional Child Tax Credit, and the American Opportunity Education Tax Credit is expanded to include "Claiming Head of Household." Effective for tax years beginning after December 31, 2017, the TCJA expands the due diligence requirements to paid tax preparers to cover determining eligibility for a taxpayer to file as head of household. A penalty of $500 (adjusted for inflation) will be imposed if a paid tax preparer fails to answer required due diligence questions regarding a taxpayer's eligibility to claim head of household status in 2018. **(See Chapter 13, "Earned Income Tax Credit"; "Child Tax Credit"; "Additional Child Tax Credit"; & "American Opportunity Tax Credit")**

Surviving Spouse

You can file as a surviving spouse, using joint return tax rates, for 2 years following the death of a spouse if you have a dependent child. Your filing status is "Single filing as a Surviving Spouse," not head-of-household. Also, a surviving spouse is entitled to use the $500,000 home sale gain exclusion on the sale of a principal residence for 2 years after the death of a spouse. **(See Chapter 9, "Home Sale Gain Exclusion")**

Married Filing Separately

Both spouses must either itemize or claim the standard deduction when filing as "married Filing separately." In general, filing separate returns in any state – both common law and community property states – will not be beneficial. In fact, about 95% of married people are better off filing jointly. Yet, it's possible that filing as married filing separately may result in a lower combined tax for a married couple in certain situations. However, each specific situation is unique. If you file as "married filing separately," the following conditions apply: **(See Below "Marital Status and Divorce"); (See Chapter 1, "Standard Deduction"); (See Chapter 12, "Itemized Deductions")**

- Up to 85% of Social Security benefits are subject to tax regardless of your taxable income. **(See Chapter 5, "Social Security Benefits")**
- You cannot claim: (1) the IRA deduction for a non-working spouse; (2) the American Opportunity Education Credit or the Lifetime Learning Credit; (3) Dependent Care Credit; and (4) Earned Income Credit, unless you lived apart for the last 6 months of the year (custodial spouse can claim head-of-household in this case). **(See Chapter 11, "IRA Contributions"); (See Chapter 13, "Earned Income Credit"; "Child and Dependent Care Credit"; & "Education Credits")**
- If separate returns are filed, you have 3 years to amend to a joint return. But you can't file a joint return and amend to separate returns.

Although it is a rare situation, some people should not file joint tax returns. That was the lesson learned in a recent Tax Court case (Nicole Ryke). Nicole's husband, a lawyer and self-employed, had a "long history of failing to pay his debts when due." Nicole (a doctor) became aware of this when they purchased a home before marrying in 2004. She did not know the specifics of her husband's financial past, but she was aware that he had a low credit score and outstanding student loans. So, they had separate credit cards and the mortgage on the house was exclusively in Nicole's name. They filed joint returns from 2004 to 2012. Nicole's husband took the documents to their accountant who prepared the returns. When the returns came back Nicole's husband asked her to sign them, which she did. She thought he was sending in the balances due, which he wasn't. In 2011 she learned about some of the balances due when her husband asked her to make a payment of $53,502 for 2007 and 2008. She thought that was it, but it wasn't. In 2014, she learned that $55,859 was still due for 2009 and 2012, and after consulting with an accountant they began filing separate returns in 2013, but they were still married with four children.

Nicole ended up in Tax Court, with an innocent spouse claim for $55,859. The Court decided against her, because "She had reason to know that her husband was not paying the amount of tax owed each year and had actual knowledge of the outstanding tax liabilities. The fact that she did not know the details of those outstanding liabilities was unfortunate, but the Court considered it immaterial. She had reason to know about the full extent of the liabilities, and the fact that she lacked actual knowledge did not release her from the tax liabilities. There is a seven factor test involved with filing for "innocent spouse relief," which are: (1) marital status; (2) economic hardship if relief is not granted; (3) knowledge or reason to know that the tax liability would not be paid; (4) legal obligation to pay the outstanding income tax liability; (5) receipt of a significant benefit from the unpaid income tax liability; (6) compliance with income tax laws; and (7) mental and physical health. Although the Judge found that most of the factors were neutral or slightly favored relief, the overwhelming factor was the third one "knowledge or reason to know that the tax liability would not be paid." Nicole's husband is a bankruptcy attorney, and should have known better. By having Nicole file jointly with him, he was putting more of the family's income in the hands of the IRS. The couple did not live in a community property state, which would introduce another set of complications. https://www.ustaxcourt.gov/UstcInOp/OpinionViewer.aspx?ID=11348

The following are some other situations in which filing separately may be appropriate. However, they are just "guidelines" that may not apply in all similar situations. In addition, they generally apply only to common law states.

- Significant Deductions – If you and your spouse have a large disparity in your respective incomes (the greater the disparity, the more pronounced the effect) and you have potential significant itemized deductions you can take depending on your adjusted gross income (AGI), i.e. you and your spouse have unequal AGIs and you need to itemize significant deductions that are tied to the amount of AGI, it may be better to file separately. For example, medical expenses have to total more than 7.5% of AGI to be deductible (10% in 2019). If you and your spouse together have a combined AGI of $300,000, both of you together need to spend more than $22,500 in medical expenses in order for any of them to be deductible. But if your spouse alone has an AGI of $250,000 and you have an AGI of $50,000, you only need $3,750 in medical expenses to qualify for the deduction if all of these medical expenses are yours. So, if you make less than your spouse, it might make sense in this case to file separately if you have a significant amount of medical bills. However, keep in mind that both of you have to itemize deductions if you file separately. **(See Chapter 12, "Medical Expenses")**

- Divorce – If you are getting a divorce, you can still file jointly until the divorce is final. However, you are considered divorced for the entire year in the year the divorce is finalized. It usually makes sense to file jointly as long as you can. However, in an acrimonious divorce environment, agreeing on how to split the refund when filing jointly, as well as getting your spouse to sign the paperwork, including the tax return, may be difficult. Also, some spouses may choose to file separately regardless of the results. Therefore, paying more taxes might be worth it to you in this predicament. **(See Below, "Marital Status and Divorce")**

- Capital Gains and Dividends – Having a large amount of capital gains and dividends is another situation where unequal incomes between you and your spouse may be conducive to filing separate tax returns. Because, in 2018 the tax on capital gains and qualified dividends is 20% instead of 15% when joint income exceeds $479,000 ($470,700 in 2017). If you are the one with all or most of the capital gains and qualified dividends, it might make sense to file separately. For example, if you earn $120,000 and your spouse earns $415,000 and you are the one with all the capital gains and dividends, the capital gains will probably be taxed at 20% if you file jointly. But, if you file separately the capital gains and qualified dividends will be taxed at the lower rates of 0% or 15%. **(See Chapter 6, "Capital Gains and Losses")**

- The Government May Take Your Spouse's Refund – The government might take your spouse's refund if he or she owes the government money. This may happen because your spouse has delinquent unpaid student loans, unpaid government guaranteed loans or unpaid Small Business Administration loans, or unpaid child support. Also, your spouse might have unfiled tax returns or owe money due on prior filings. In this case, you may want to file separately in order to protect your refund from being taken by the government for your spouse's unpaid debts, because if you file jointly the government can take the entire amount of the joint refund. **(See Chapter 8, "Child Support Payments")**

- Unearned Income – If you have a lot of portfolio unearned income and your spouse doesn't, it might make sense to file separately in order to avoid the 3.8% net investment income (NII) tax implemented by

13

the Affordable Care Act. Unearned income includes dividends, interest, capital gains, rental income, and passive income. The 3.8% NII tax kicks in on unearned income when you and your spouse make more than $250,000 combined, but the threshold for married filing separately is $125,000. If you and your spouse's combined income is more than $250,000, but your income is less than $125,000 and you are the one with the unearned income, filing separately may be best. **(See Chapter 10, "3.8% Net Investment Income Tax); (See Chapter 5, "Portfolio Income")**

Married Filing Separately and Community Property – In community property states (California, Arizona, Idaho, Louisiana, Nevada, New Mexico, Texas, Washington, and Wisconsin) each person must report ½ of community income on each spouse's separate tax return, unless they lived apart for the whole year and did not transfer any income between them, except for payments solely for child support purposes. Community income generally includes income earned by both spouses and any income received from community properties during the year. In other words, a married couple has to add their separate earned incomes together and each spouse has to report ½ of the total amount on their separate tax returns. Also, taxes withheld from their separate earned incomes has to be added together and each spouse has to report ½ of the total amount on their separate tax returns. Form 8958 "Allocation of Tax Amounts" is used to split community income and taxes withheld between the spouses. During the year of divorce, each spouse is taxed on ½ of community income for the part of the year before the divorce is final, unless they lived apart for the whole year. Self-employment income, including a partner's distributive share of partnership income is not considered to be community income. Also, awards for personal injuries sustained by only one spouse is not considered community income, except for the portion of the award intended to compensate for lost wages during the marriage.

The general rule is that anything you bring into a marriage is your separate property, and anything acquired by either partner after marriage is community property. But property inherited or received as a gift by only one spouse during marriage is considered separate property. However, all property is presumed to be community property, unless and until the party claiming the separate property can prove it by a preponderance of the evidence. The way to preserve an asset's separate status is not easy, but keeping good records helps, and you can have a prenuptial or postnuptial agreement specifying those assets.

Generally, you are not responsible for paying tax on community income if all five of the following conditions exist: (1) you did not file a joint return for the year; (2) you did not include an item of community income in gross income on your separate return; (3) the item of community income you did not include is one of the following: (a) wages, salaries, and other compensation your spouse (or former spouse) received for services he or she performed as an employee; (b) income your spouse derived from a trade or business he or she operated as a sole proprietor; (c) your spouse's distributive share of partnership income; (d) income from your spouse's separate property (use the appropriate community property law to determine what is separate property); (e) any other income that belongs to your spouse under community property laws; (4) you establish that you did not know of, and had no reason to know of, your spouse's (or former spouse's) community income; and (5) under all facts and circumstances, it would not be fair to include any community income in your gross income. Form 8857 "Request for Innocent Spouse Relief" can be used to request relief from a tax liability arising from community property laws.
In reality, if you do not have any knowledge of your spouse's income, it is impossible for you to comply with the community property requirements when filing your tax return.

Marital Status and Divorce

You are considered married for filing purposes even if you are separated under a provisional decree of divorce or separate maintenance that has not been finalized. Spouses who have received an interlocutory or temporary divorce decree are deemed to still be married for tax purposes even if they lived apart for the whole year. However, even if still married, a parent can file as "head-of-household" if he or she did not live with the other spouse during the last 6 months of the year, and meets the other requirements to file as head-of-household. It is important to notify the IRS that separate residences have been established. When a divorce is finalized at any time during a year, both persons who are party to the divorce are considered unmarried for the entire year. Usually the custodial parent can claim the children as dependents; however, the decree of divorce should say who can claim the kids as dependents. If you can't agree with your ex-spouse, you can arrange to alternate years claiming the kids by using Form 8332. If you and your spouse obtain a divorce in one year for the sole purpose of filing tax returns as unmarried individuals, and at the time of divorce you intend to remarry each other in the next year, you and your spouse must file as married individuals. If you obtain an annulment, which holds that no valid marriage ever existed, you must file amended returns for all tax years affected by the annulment that are not closed by the statute of limitations. **(See Above, "Head of Household"); (See Below, "Qualifying Child for the Dependency Exemption")**

If you are getting a divorce, but your divorce has not yet been finalized, you must file a joint return in order to be able to claim: the IRA deduction for a non-working spouse, the Education Credits, the Dependent Care Credit, the Elderly and Disabled Credit, and the Adoption Credit. Also, the Earned Income Credit can't be claimed unless you lived apart for the last 6 months of the year, and exclusion of interest on U.S. Savings Bonds for education purposes can't be claimed unless you lived apart for the whole year. If a joint return is filed while a couple is still considered married, the IRS will accept an amended return (Form 1040X) claiming a refund filed by a divorced taxpayer that is signed by only one of the former spouses, and issue a check in the name of the spouse that filed the 1040X, but the IRS will determine the amount of the refund by re-computing the taxpayer's share of the joint liability and the taxpayer's contribution toward the joint liability using the IRS allocation method. Separate returns can be amended to a joint return within 3 years, but a joint return cannot be amended to separate returns. **(See Above, "Married Filing Separately"); (See Chapter 13, "Elderly and Disabled Credit"; & "Adoption Credit")**

No gain or loss is recognized on the transfer of property between spouses during marriage, or any transfer of property between former spouses incident to divorce (even if the transfer is a bona fide sale), or when the transfer occurs within one year after the date the marriage ceases. A transfer of property to a third party on behalf of a former spouse can also qualify for non-recognition of gain, if required by the divorce agreement. The basis of property transferred in a divorce is always the transferor's adjusted basis of the property, which is an exception to the "Gift Tax" rule of lower of fair market value (FMV) or the adjusted basis of property. **(See Chapter 5, "Alimony and Separate Maintenance"); (See Chapter 11, "Alimony/Separate Maintenance); (See Chapter 21, "Estates and Trusts"); (See Chapter 22, "Estate and Gift Tax")**

In the nine "community property states," property is generally owned concurrently between spouses. In the rest, referred to as "common law states," courts must determine an equitable distribution of the spouses' property between them. In the 41 common law states, the courts decide what is fair, reasonable, and equitable division of assets. A court may decide to award a spouse anywhere from none to all of the property value. The courts focus on factors such as how long the marriage lasted, what property each party brought into the marriage, the earning power of each spouse, the responsibilities of each spouse in raising their children, the amount of retraining needed to make a spouse employable, the tax consequences of the asset distribution, and debt allocation. If the couple signed a prenuptial agreement or an agreement during the marriage, they have more control over how the property is divided.

In the end, equitable distribution is considered fair, but not necessarily equal. Almost all states require the parties to disclose all material information needed to allow them to negotiate and agree upon the division of marital property. Therefore, for a property settlement, a schedule of assets with tax considerations for each asset should be prepared. To ensure they comply with the full disclosure requirement, the divorcing couple should inventory all property, including intangible assets such as advanced degrees, goodwill, and patents, that can result in substantially increased income in future years. Consideration of intangible assets in property settlements is becoming more important as courts express an increased willingness to either classify the intangibles as property subject to distribution or to require spouses to pay for reimbursement.

For both spouses to qualify for the home sale gain exclusion after divorce, the divorce instrument must require them to co-own the principle residence, even if only one spouse occupies the residence. Otherwise, the non-occupying former spouse may not qualify for the 2 out of 5-year rule required in order to exclude gain from the sale of the home. If only one spouse gets to keep the home, he or she can include in his or her time of ownership any time that the home was owned by the former spouse even if title had been in the other spouse's name, but he or she must live in the home at least 2 years to be eligible for the home sale gain exclusion – if he or she remarries, the exclusion can be up to $500,000 as long as the new spouse lives in the home for at least 2 years prior to the date of sale. Title need not be shared with the new spouse in order to qualify for the exclusion. **(See Chapter 9, "Home Sale Gain Exclusion")**

IRA's can be transferred from one spouse to another in a divorce agreement without any tax consequences. Retirement plans transferred or split in a divorce require a formal written agreement per the divorce settlement. A qualified domestic relations order (QDRO) allows an employee's retirement plan to pay benefits to an ex-spouse named as an alternate payee. A QDRO relates to a legal separation, marital dissolution, or family support obligation. When a plan participant has remarried before receiving benefits, a QDRO can be useful in stipulating that survivor benefits are payable to the ex-spouse. Otherwise, the second spouse is entitled to receive survivor benefits.

Qualified Domestic Relations Order (QDRO) – A key issue in separation, divorce, and other domestic relations proceedings is whether and how to divide a participant's interest in a retirement plan. This is a recurrent issue in divorce proceedings. It is a key issue because the interests of participants in employer-sponsored retirement plans usually are their largest assets, and the receipt of retirement payments are taxable both to the participant and the ex-spouse named as an alternate payee. A qualified domestic relations order (QDRO) allows an employee's retirement plan to pay benefits to an ex-spouse named as an alternate payee. A QDRO relates to a legal separation, marital dissolution, or family support obligation. The alternate payee can elect the form in which to receive benefits, generally under either a "shared payment" or "separate interest" approach. The former divides payments by amount or percentage; the latter provides an interest in the plan benefits that allows the alternate payee to elect how to receive benefits.

A QDRO is a domestic relations order under state law that creates or recognizes an alternate payee's right to receive all or a portion of the benefits payable to a participant under a retirement plan. QDROs may relate to the provision of child support, alimony payments, or marital property rights for the benefit of one or more of these parties. Plan administrators are not required to follow the terms of domestic relations orders unless they are QDROs. A plan administrator is initially responsible for determining whether a domestic relations order is a QDRO. A plan administrator can provide a CPA access to the plan and participant benefit information sufficient to help prepare a QDRO if the plan administrator determines that the disclosure request is being made in connection with a domestic relation proceeding.

A distribution of a participant's interest in a qualified retirement plan to an alternate payee that is made without a properly executed QDRO will create taxable income for the participant. However, if the distribution to an alternate payee is made pursuant to a properly executed QDRO, there are generally no tax consequences for the participant. The alternate payee will not be taxed on the funds until he or she withdraws them from the retirement plan, and the 10% early withdrawal penalty will not apply to these withdrawals. Also, an alternate payee who is a spouse or ex-spouse can roll over the distribution to his or her individual retirement account (IRA) without tax consequences if the rollover is done within 60 days of receiving the QDRO distribution. The plan administrator is required to withhold 20% of the distribution for federal tax purposes if the payment is made directly to the spouse or former spouse. This can be avoided by having the plan administrator transfer the funds directly to the trustee of his or her IRA. **(See Chapter 9, "Rollovers from Qualified Retirement Plans and Traditional IRAs")**

The Retirement Equity Act of 1984 resolved the disparity between ERISA and state law by allowing qualified retirement plans subject to ERISA to segregate assets for the benefit of one or more "alternate payees" through a qualified domestic relations order (QDRO). The consequences of not preparing a QDRO that satisfies these requirements can be financially harmful for one or both spouses, primarily because of the tax consequences. A lawyer who practices family law usually takes the lead in drafting the QDRO, but the lawyer usually requires the services of CPAs for their financial expertise to ensure an equitable division of retirement assets between the divorcing spouses without triggering negative tax consequences. A shared-payment QDRO should set the date when payments to the alternate payee may begin. Since defined contribution and defined benefit plans have differing benefit mechanisms, the considerations in splitting them differ. Both types of plans can offer the separate-interest or the shared-payment approach to split the benefits. When a plan participant has remarried before receiving benefits, a QDRO can be useful in stipulating that survivor benefits are payable to the ex-spouse. Otherwise, the second spouse is entitled to receive the survivor benefits.

Dependents

In accordance with the Tax Cuts and Jobs Act, the deduction of a personal exemption for taxpayers and their dependents in determining taxable income is eliminated in 2018. Personal exemptions are suspended for tax years 2018 – 2025. However, determining who are qualified dependents and who can claim them is important for other purposes, including who is eligible for the Earned income Tax Cred (EITC), the Affordable Care Tax Credit, head-of-household filing status, liablility for individual mandate penalties, and repayment of advance premium tax credits. **(See Below, "Head of Household"); (See Chapter 1, "Filing Status"); (See Chapter 13, "Earned Income Tax Credit"); (See Chapter 24, "Affordable Care Act (ACA)")**

Qualifying Dependent Child – The uniform definition of a "qualifying dependent child" provides that all of following must be satisfied: (1) relationship to the taxpayer – must be a son, daughter, adopted child, stepchild, foster child, or a descendent of any them such as your grandchild. Also, a brother, sister, half-brother, half-sister, step brother, step sister or a descendant of any of them such as a niece or nephew; (2) same principal place of abode as the taxpayer for more than one-half (½) of the year (except for temporary absences for school or military service); (3) age under 19, or under age 24 if a full-time student at least 5 months of the year; and (4) child must be younger than the individual claiming him/her as a qualifying child, or the qualifying child must be permanently and totally disabled. Permanently and totally disabled qualifies at any age if the dependent is permanently and totally disabled at any time during the calendar year. Also, for the "relationship" test, a stepchild still remains your stepchild after a divorce. You can't claim a child as a dependent if the child provides more than one-half (½) of his own support.

Support includes all amounts spent for food, lodging, clothing, medical expenses, education, recreation, transportation, and similar necessities. Student loans in the name of the student are considered to be support for which the child pays. However, if a child receives a scholarship, it is not considered support. A child that is born or dies during the year will be considered as living with the taxpayer for the entire year if the taxpayer's house was the child's home for the entire time he was alive.

- Definition of permanently and totally disabled—both of the following apply: (1) he or she cannot engage in any substantial gainful activity because of a physical or mental condition; and (2) a doctor must determine that the condition has lasted or can be expected to last continually for at least a year or can lead to death.
- Temporary absences for school or military service means that the child's official permanent residence is the taxpayer's residence even if the child is away from home all year.
- A person is not entitled to the dependency exemption for a child who is not a U.S. citizen or a resident of the U.S. or a contiguous country.

Under the tiebreaker rules, if the parents are divorced, separated under a written separation agreement, or lived apart at all times during the last 6 months of the year, the child is the dependent of the parent with whom the child resides the longest during the year (custodial parent). This is determined by using the counting-nights rule (where the child sleeps), whether or not the parent is present, or if the child is in the company of the parent when not at the parent's residence (such as on vacation). A child who is in the custody of one or both of his or her parents for more than one-half of the calendar year and receives more than one-half of his or her support from the parents is considered the qualifying child of the custodial parent, who is the parent with whom the child resides the longest during the year. For the noncustodial parent to claim the child as a dependent, the custodial parent must sign Form 8332 releasing the custodial parent's claim. **(See Above, "Marital Status and Divorce")**

If divorced, the divorce decree may specify which parent is the custodial parent and which parent is entitled to claim a child as a dependent. However, the formalities don't always control. In one recent court case, the divorce decree designated the father as the custodial parent, but there was no mention of which parent was entitled to claim the child as a dependent. The subject child lived with the mother for more than ½ of the year, and the court allowed the mother to claim the child. The fact that the divorce decree designated the father as the custodial parent wasn't controlling, because he did not have the requisite physical custody to be the custodial parent, and no waiver (Form 8332) was required in order for the mother to claim the child. If the custodial parent uses Form

8332 to release his or her claim to the noncustodial parent, the noncustodial parent can then take the child tax credit and the education credits (no matter who pays the education expenses), but in this case, the actual custodial parent, who released his or her claim to the noncustodial parent, is still entitled to claim the dependent care credit, the Earned Income Tax Credit (EITC), and head-of-household status. Also, Form 8332 can be used by the custodial parent to notify the noncustodial parent that the custodial parent is revoking a signed release of his or her claim to the noncustodial parent. In Johnson v. Commissioner, the Tax Court stated that the test as to primary physical custody between divorced parents as to dependency allowances is based on the comparative number of nights children spend with each parent as opposed to the comparative amount of time parnts spend with the children.

www.irs.gov/pub/irs-pdf/f8332.pdf   https://www.ustaxcourt.gov/UstcInOp/OpinionViewer.aspx?ID=11668

If no parent claims a qualifying child as a dependent, another individual may claim the child as a dependent if that individual is otherwise eligible to claim the child, and has a higher adjusted gross income for the taxable year than any parent eligible to claim the child.

Other Persons Qualifying as Dependents – Other persons besides a "qualifying child" may qualify as a taxpayer's dependent if they satisfy all of the following : (1) the taxpayer provides more than ½ of their support, i.e. food, shelter, clothing, medical, dental, education, etc. (see definition of ½ support for a qualifying child, above) – Social Security benefits used for support count toward the ½ support test only if the Social Security benefits are taxable; (2) the taxpayer has a specified relationship with the person (mother, father, etc.) or if not a relative, the person was a member of the taxpayer's household for the entire year; (3) the person is a U.S. citizen; (4) the person meets the gross income test; and (5) the person meets the joint return test – does not file a joint return with his or her spouse unless the return is filed only to collect a tax refund and neither spouse would have owed tax if they had filed separate returns. Also, a person cannot be a dependent of another person who is not required to file a return for the year or files solely to claim a refund of taxes withheld. In accordance with the Tax Cuts and Jobs Act, the gross income test for the 2018 tax year is the following: the person has gross income of less than $4,150 (adjusted for inflation in subsequent years). **(See Above, "Qualifying Dependent Child"); (See Chapter 1, "Personal Exemption")**

- Gross Income Test – Gross income includes gross receipts from rental property (do not deduct expenses); partner's share of gross income of a partnership (not net income); all unemployment compensation; and certain scholarship and fellowship grants – not tax-exempt scholarships received by degree candidates used for tuition, books, etc. Gross income does not include nontaxable Social Security benefits and tax-free income generated by municipal bonds. NOTE: Gross income for the purpose of this test is not necessarily the same as gross income for taxable income purposes. **(See Chapter 1, "Filing Requirements"); (See Chapter 4, "Earned Income")**
- Dependent Parent – If an elderly parent does not qualify as your dependent simply because he/she had too much gross income ($4,050 or more), the parent can still be counted as your dependent for medical expenses deduction purposes – you can deduct the medical expenses as an itemized deduction. If a dependent parent lives with you and requires continual care, and you work, you can claim the "dependent care tax credit" for the cost of the care provided. You cannot deduct the rent paid to provide a home for an elderly parent; however, the amount paid for the rent counts toward determining the ½ support test. **(See Chapter 12, "Medical Expenses"); (See Chapter 13, "Child and Dependent Care Credit")**

19

- <u>Multiple Support Agreement</u> – If no taxpayer provides more than ½ of the support for a dependent, a multiple support agreement (Form 2120) can be used to allow any individual who provides more than 10% of the support to claim the person as a dependent. More than ½ of the support must be provided by persons providing at least 10% of the support, and all of them must sign the multiple support agreement, and Form 2120 must be filed. For example, if more than one sibling provides more than ½ of the support for a dependent parent, a multiple support agreement can be executed, and who claims the parent as a dependent can be rotated from year to year. The same is true for a dependent child.

Proposed Changes to the Definition of Dependents – The IRS issued proposed regulations for dependents on Jan. 19, 2017. The proposed changes would apply to tax years beginning after the date the regulations are published as final in the Federal Register; however, in the meantime, taxpayers can apply the proposed regulations to any open tax years. The proposed regulations provide that, if a child meets the definition of "qualifying child" for more than one taxpayer, and the child is not treated as a qualifying child of one of the taxpayers under the tiebreaker rules, then the child is also not treated as a qualifying child for purposes of the Earned Income Tax Credit (EITC). Therefore, if otherwise eligible, that taxpayer could claim the EITC for childless taxpayers. **(See Chapter 13, "Earned income Tax Credit")**

Dependency rules: The proposed regulations would update the regulations to address several aspects of the dependency rules. These include: the relationship test; the definition of "principal place of abode" and "temporary absence" for purposes of the residency test; the definition of "student" for the age test; the definition of "support" for the support test; the treatment of noncitizen adopted children; the calculation of adjusted gross income on a joint return for purposes of the tiebreaker rules; the requirements for noncustodial parents who claim a dependency exemption; and the rule that an individual is not a qualifying child of a person if that person is not required to file a tax return and either does not file a return or files a return solely to obtain a refund. The proposed regulations provide that a legally adopted individual of a "taxpayer" is treated as a child by blood of the taxpayer (formerly this provision referred to "individual" rather than "taxpayer"). The IRS recognizes that the use of the word "taxpayer" instead of individual may limit the recognition of relationships through adoption to only those situations where the taxpayer claiming the dependency exemption is the person who adopted the child. The IRS notes that this would make the results of legal adoption under tax law different from that under nontax law, and the IRS believes Congress did not intend to limit the treatment of adopted children in this way. Therefore, the proposed regulations would substitute "person" for "taxpayer" in this situation, so that any child legally adopted by a person or any child placed with a person for legal adoption by that person is treated as a child by blood of that person for purposes of the relationship tests.

https://s3.amazonaws.com/public-inspection.federalregister.gov/2017-01056.pdf
https://www.gpo.gov/fdsys/pkg/FR-2017-01-19/pdf/2017-01056.pdf

Kiddie Tax

The kiddie tax applies to unearned income of qualified dependent children under the age of 19, and to unearned income of qualified dependent children under the age of 24 who are full-time students (at least 5 months in a year). Unearned income is income from sources other than wages and salary, such as dividends, interest and capital gains. Under the Tax Cuts and Jobs Act (TCJA), for tax years 2018 – 2025, all of the income (both earned and unearned) of a dependent child is added together; the child's standard deduction (if any) is then subtracted from the child's total income (the standard deduction is the child's earned income + $350 up to a maximum of $12,000);

if any earned income is left after subtracting the standard deduction, it is taxed at the ordinary income tax rates for a single individual; and the remaining unearned income that exceeds $2,100 is then taxed at the kiddie tax rates. A child's kiddie tax rates for his/her unearned income are the rates applicable to estates and trusts for interest and ordinary dividends, which are the following in 2018: $0 - $2,550 (10%); $2,551 - $9150 ($255 + 24% of the amount over $2,550); $9,151 - $12,500 ($1,839 + 35% of the amount over $9,150); and $12,501 + ($3,011.50 + 37% of the amount over $12,500). A child's kiddie tax rates for capital gains and qualified dividends are the following: $0 - $2,600 (0%); $2,601 -$12,700 (15%); $12,701 + (20%), which are the long-term capital gain rates for estates and trusts.

In 2017, the first $1,050 of a child's unearned income was tax free; the next $1,050 of unearned income was taxed at 10%; and any unearned income over $2,100 was taxed at the parents' highest tax rate. Any earned income of a child, after the allowable standard deduction, was taxed at the child's tax rate (ordinary income tax rate for a single individual).

The kiddie tax rates apply if the following conditions are met:
- At least one parent is alive at the end of the year.
- The child or student does not file a joint return.
- The child lives with their parents for more than ½ of the year (college students away at college counts as living with their parents).
- The child or student's earned income was not more than ½ of his/her support. Support includes all amounts spent for food, lodging, clothing, medical expenses, education, recreation, transportation, and similar necessities. Student loans in the name of a qualified student are considered to be support for which the student pays. However, if a student receives a tax-free scholarship, it is not considered support. If a child or student's earned income is more than ½ of his/her support, then the child or student is not considered to be a dependent and the kiddie tax does not apply.
- The child or college student falls under one of the following age-related rules: (1) age 17 or younger at year end; (2) age 18 at year end and doesn't have earned income that exceeds ½ of his or her support; and (3) age 19 to 23 at year end, a full-time student and doesn't have earned income that exceeds ½ of his or her support. When considering the child's age at the end of the tax year, a birthday on January 1st of the next year doesn't bring the child to the next age level for the tax year.

For purposes of the kiddie tax, unearned income includes taxable scholarships or grants that are reported on a dependent student's tax return. Taxable scholarships or grants permit the funds to be used for room and board or other unqualified expenses.

- **Example** – Jim (age 17) who is a dependent child, has $2,000 of earned income from delivering newspapers and $8,000 of interest and ordinary dividends in 2018. His standard deduction is $2,350 ($2,000 of earned income + $350), so he has no taxable earned income left over. After subtracting the standard deduction, he has $7,650 of unearned income ($2,000 + $8,000 = $10,000 – $2,350 = $7,650). Therefore, Jim has to pay a kiddie tax of $975 on $5,550 of unearned income at the applicable kiddie tax rates. The tax is computed as follows: $7,650 – $2,100 = $5,550 taxable unearned income; the tax is $255 + 24% of the amount over $2,550 = $975 ($255 + $720 = $975).

21

By using some tax planning, a child's earned income can be inflated to an amount that is more than ½ of his/her support, even if it is not actually used for the child's support. This includes reasonable wages that self-employed parents can pay a student/child for services performed by the child. As a result, a contribution by the child to his/her own IRA using earned income could reduce taxable income and thereby reduce or completely eliminate the kiddie tax. Also, the child may be able to take an education tax credit which will offset the kiddie tax. However, this can only be done when the parent cannot claim a student/child as a dependent. Students could also invest in tax-free investments, including Section 529 plans, which are not included in income. **(See Chapter 11, "Child's IRA"); (See Chapter 13, "Education Credits")**

Reporting a Child's Unearned Income – There are two different ways to report a dependent child's unearned taxable income: the parents can report it on their tax return by attaching Form 8814 to their Form 1040, or a dependent child can report it on his/her separate tax return by attaching Form 8615 to his/her Form 1040.

In order for the parents to report their child's unearned income on their tax return the child must: (1) qualify as a dependent; (2) have income from interest, dividends, or capital gain distributions totaling less than $10,500; (3) not otherwise be required to file a separate tax return; and (4) not have made any estimated tax payments, had a prior year over-payment applied to estimated taxes or had any backup withholding on income. The amount of the kiddie tax will be the same whether its reported on the parents' return or the child's separate return. However, most people choose to file a separate return for their child to report the tax. Reporting a child's unearned income on the parents' return will not only increase the parents' taxable income, it can phase-out certain deductions and credits that the parents would otherwise be eligible for. Election to include a qualifying child's income on the parents' return is made by attaching Form 8814 for each child to the parents' return. A child's income must be reported on the parent's return with the greater taxable income, if they are filing as "married filing separately," unless the parents are not living together, in which case the return of the custodial parent must be used. If the custodial parent has remarried, the stepparent is treated as the child's other parent and their joint return is used. **(See Above, "Marital Status and Divorce")**

www.irs.gov/pub/irs-pdf/f8814.pdf   www.irs.gov/pub/irs-pdf/f8615.pdf   www.irs.gov/pub/irs-pdf/i8615.pdf

Same-Sex Couples

On June 26, 2015 the Supreme Court ruled in Obergefell v. Hodges that the Constitution guarantees the right to same-sex marriage. Although there was resistance to this decision in some states, the decision made same-sex married couples subject to the same tax rules as any other married couple. Before the Supreme Court Decision, The Treasury Department and the IRS had already determined that two same-sex persons that were "legally" married in jurisdictions that recognized same-sex marriages were treated as married for federal tax purposes beginning in 2013. The Supreme Court ruling doesn't apply to registered domestic partnerships, civil unions, or similar relationships.

www.supremecourt.gov/opinions/14pdf/14-556_3204.pdf

Legally married same-sex couples had to file their federal tax returns using either the "married filing jointly" or "married filing separately" filing status beginning with tax year 2013. For tax year 2012, and all prior tax years, same-sex spouses who filed an original tax return on or after Sept. 16, 2013, generally were required to file using joint or married filing separately status. For tax years 2011 and earlier, same-sex couples who filed their returns could choose to amend their federal tax returns to file using a married filing separately or joint filing status, i.e.

Individuals who were in same-sex marriages in prior years could (but are not required to) file original or amended returns choosing to be treated as married for federal tax purposes for all open years under the statute of limitations. As a result of this ruling, couples in which one same-sex spouse wishes to adopt the other spouse's child may lose out on the Adoption Tax Credit, because the credit isn't available when adopting a spouse's child.

In September 2013, the IRS set-forth procedures employers could follow for filing refund claims for overpaid FICA and income taxes paid on employer-provided benefits for same-sex spouses that are now tax-free. There were two streamlined administrative procedures for making adjustments or claiming refunds. Under the first method, employers could reimburse its employees for the amount of over collected payroll and income tax withholding for the same-sex spouse for the first three quarters of 2013, and adjust Form 941 for the fourth quarter. Under the second method, employers that had not reimbursed or repaid employees by Dec. 31, could file Form 941-X (amended return). **(See Chapter 2, "Payroll Tax"); (See Chapter 4, "Wages and Salaries")** www.irs.gov/pub/irs-pdf/f941x.pdf   www.irs.gov/pub/irs-pdf/i941x.pdf

In September 2016, the IRS finalized regulations that redefine the way the tax Code looks at the marital status of taxpayers for purposes of the income, estate, gift, excise, and payroll taxes. The new regulations went into effect on September 2, 2016. The regulations make it clear that terms in the tax Code relating to marriage include same-sex spouses as well as opposite-sex spouses. According to the IRS, there are over 200 provisions in the tax Code and regulations that include the terms spouse, marriage, husband and wife, husband, and wife. The regulations state the following: For federal tax purposes, the terms spouse, husband, and wife means an individual lawfully married to another individual. The term husband and wife means two individuals lawfully married to each other. A marriage of two individuals is recognized for federal tax purposes if the marriage is recognized by any state, possession, or territory of the United States in which the marriage is entered into, regardless of where the couple resides. Also, a provision provides that two individuals entering into a marriage under the laws of a foreign country are married for federal tax purposes if the relationship is recognized as a marriage under the laws of at least one state, possession, or territory of the United States. However, the IRS makes it clear that the regulations do not apply to individuals, including same-sex couples, who have chosen to enter into a registered domestic partnership, civil union, or other relationship that is not specifically a "marriage under state law," even if the marriage option is available. But the IRS stopped short of specifically referring to same-sex marriages or mandating the use of gender-neutral terms in the tax code.

The new regulations are generally favorable to same-sex couples, but some of them will be hit with the marriage penalty for the first time, where a higher tax is imposed on a married couple filing jointly than if they filed separately as single taxpayers.

> **Special Procedures for Same-Sex Couples Estates** – Section 3 of the 1996 Defense of Marriage Act (DOMA) was ruled unconstitutional by the 2013 U.S. Supreme Court decision in the case of U.S. v. Windsor. Under Section 3 of DOMA, same-sex marriage was not recognized for any federal purposes, including the filing of joint tax returns and the unlimited marital estate tax deduction. Two years later, the Supreme Court in Obergefell v. Hodges, went a step further and held that, under the Fourteenth Amendment, same-sex couples have a fundamental right to marriage. Due to the Supreme Court's decisions, the IRS issued Notice 2017-15, which provided for special administrative procedures that same-sex married couples should use to recalculate the transfer-tax treatment for property transferred to spouses before provisions of DOMA were invalidated by the

Supreme Court. According to the notice, to the extent that the applicable exclusion amount from estate or gift tax was applied to a transfer between spouses that did not qualify for the marital deduction for federal estate or gift tax purposes at the time of the transfer because of DOMA, taxpayers are permitted to establish that the transfer qualified for the marital deduction and recover the applicable exclusion amount, even if the statute of limitation for the original return has expired. If the limitation period has expired, the notice allows the taxpayer to recalculate the taxpayer's remaining applicable exclusion amount as a result of recognizing the taxpayer's marriage to the taxpayer's spouse. The notice similarly provides relief for generation-skipping transfer (GST) tax purposes by allowing taxpayers to recalculate their available GST exemption. The taxpayer must recalculate the taxpayer's remaining applicable exclusion amount, in accordance with IRS forms and instructions, on either Form 709 or Form 706 and put a notation on the top of the Form that it is being "FILED PURSUANT TO NOTICE 2017-15."

The taxpayer must also attach a statement supporting the marital deduction claim and detailing the recalculation of the taxpayer's exclusion amount as directed by the IRS in its forms and instructions. Also, if applicable, the taxpayer should recalculate his or her available GST exemption in accordance with the instructions for filing Forms 706 or 709 and report the available GST exemption based upon that recalculation, and the taxpayer should put the same notation on the top of the Form as for the estate or gift tax relief that it is being "FILED PURSUANT TO NOTICE 2017-15." Moreover, the taxpayer should attach a statement that the taxpayer's allocation of GST exemption in a prior year is void pursuant to Notice 2017-15 and a copy of the computation of the resulting exemption allocation(s) and the amount of exemption remaining available to that taxpayer.

U.S. Citizens Living Abroad

U.S. citizens and residents living and working abroad are required to file a federal income tax return. This includes people with dual citizenship. U.S. citizens living abroad qualify for an automatic two-month extension to June 15th to file their tax returns, including those serving abroad in the military. Taxpayers' worldwide income should be reported on their tax returns, and they may qualify for the Foreign Earned Income Exclusion or the Foreign Tax Credit. Some taxpayers may need to file Form 8938, "Statement of Specified Foreign Financial Assets," with their tax returns if they have money deposited in foreign bank accounts, and they may also need to file Schedule B, "Interest and Ordinary Dividends," with their tax returns to report interest and dividends earned on foreign assets. Form 8938 is in addition to the "Report of Foreign Bank and Financial Accounts" (FBAR) which has to be filed with the Treasury Department, but not with their tax return. Many Americans living abroad qualify for the foreign income exclusion up to an amount of $104,100 in 2018 ($102,100 in 2017), including the "housing exclusion."

What should you do if you're a dual citizen of the U.S. and another country, living abroad and not compliant with U.S. taxes? Under the IRS's Offshore Voluntary Disclosure Program (OVDP), you may be able to become compliant and get some penalty relief if you come forward and agree to pay income taxes on foreign earned income not reported in prior years. As a U.S. citizen you are required to pay income taxes on your worldwide income, even if you live in another country. However, if you are paying taxes in the country where you live, you may have a Foreign Tax Credit you can claim on your U.S. tax return. **(See Chapter 9, "Foreign Earned Income Exclusion"); (See Chapter 13, "Foreign Tax Credit")**

Expatriate Reporting – Taxpayers who have relinquished their U.S. citizenship or ceased to be lawful permanent residents of the U.S. in 2018 must file a dual-status alien tax return, attaching Form 8854, "Initial and Annual Expatriation Statement," and a copy of Form 8854 must also be filed separately with the Internal Revenue

Service, Philadelphia, PA 19255-0049, by the due date of the tax return, including extensions. (See Aliens below for how to file a dual-status alien tax return). Taxpayers who decide to give up their U.S. citizenship could owe an exit tax if the average income tax they've owed for the past 5 years prior to their expatriation exceeds $165,000 in 2018 ($161,000 in 2017) or they have $2 million or more of net worth. Such taxpayers will be treated as having sold all of their assets at fair market value (FMV) on the day before their expatriation and will be taxed on the profit from the deemed sale that exceeds an exemption amount of approximately $700,000. www.irs.gov/pub/irs-pdf/f8854.pdf   www.irs.gov/pub/irs-pdf/i8854.pdf

Aliens

Foreign persons are considered domiciled in the U.S. when they are physically present and have the intent to remain in this country indefinitely. In theory, a person can attain U.S. domicile as soon as they arrive onto U.S. soil. However, sometimes a foreign person could spend decades here and arguably not have the intent to be considered domiciled in this country. Factors that the IRS and the courts usually look at during their review and consideration of visa status include: owning or renting a home here; presence of family members; club memberships; statements in legal documents such as wills and trusts concerning domicile status; location of doctors and physicians; locations of cemetery plots; and other things that show severance of ties to their home country. **(See Chapter 22, "Transfer Taxes Applicable to Aliens Domiciled in the United States")**

Aliens who are present in the U.S. are considered resident aliens for U.S. income tax purposes if they meet one of three tests: the "green card" test; the substantial presence test; or the first-year election test. Resident aliens who satisfy one of these three tests must file Form 1040 and report all of their worldwide income on Form 1040. Non-resident aliens must file A U.S. tax return only if they have any U.S. source income to report, and if they do, it must be reported on Form 1040NR, "U.S. Nonresident Alien Income Tax Return."

- Green Card Test – An individual generally meets this test if he or she has been issued an alien registration card, also known as a "green card" (although it is not actually green).
- Substantial Presence Test – An individual generally meets this test if he or she doesn't hold an A, F, G, J, M, or Q visa and is physically present in the United States for at least 31 days during the current calendar year and 183 days during a three-calendar-year period that includes the current year. The 183 days test is determined by taking the sum of all the days present in the current year, plus one-third of the days present in the first preceding year, plus one-sixth of the days present in the second preceding year.
- First Year Election – You can make a choice to be treated as a resident alien for income tax purposes from the time of your arrival in the U.S. even if you don't meet either of the above tests if you are: (1) present in the U.S. during the election year for a period of 31 days; (2) your days of presence in the U.S. during the election year are 75% or more of the total days between the beginning of the earliest 31 consecutive day period of presence in the U.S. and December 31st; and (3) you will be a resident alien under the substantial presence test for the immediately following year. If you make the "first year election," you will be considered a dual-status alien (See Below).

If you are present in the U.S. and don't meet one of the three tests, you are considered a non-resident alien. Non-resident aliens only have to report their U.S. income, not their worldwide income, on Form 1040NR. Also, certain individuals are considered exempt individuals. Exempt individuals are those whose days in the U.S. are not counted toward the substantial presence test. Exempt individuals are considered non-resident aliens for U.S. tax purposes until they are no longer exempt individuals, or until they receive permanent residency status. www.irs.gov/pub/irs-pdf/f1040nr.pdf www.irs.gov/pub/irs-pdf/i1040nr.pdf

Alien diplomats (A or G visa holders), teachers or trainees (J or Q visa holders), students (F, J, M or Q visa holders) and professional athletes who are temporarily present in the U.S. are considered exempt individuals for a period of time and, therefore, must file form 1040NR to report any U.S. source income they may have. Alien diplomats usually don't have any U.S. source income to report. Salaries of employees of foreign governments are excluded from U.S. source income. Teachers and trainees who have been in the U.S. for no more than two calendar years out of the last six calendar years are considered non-resident aliens for those two years, but if they are present in the U.S. for at least 183 days in the third year they are in the U.S., they will be considered resident aliens for U.S. tax purposes. Students who are present in the U.S. during no more than five calendar years are considered non-resident aliens for those five years, but if they are present in the U.S. for at least 183 days in the sixth year they are in the U.S., they will be considered resident aliens for U.S. tax purposes. Teachers, students, and professional athletes can refute resident alien status after their exempt period expires if they can establish that they do not intend to reside permanently in the U.S. and are, therefore, dual-status aliens by filing Form 8843. www.irs.gov/pub/irs-pdf/f8843.pdf

- Non-resident alien students must file form 8843, in addition to Form 1040NR while they are considered exempt.
- Resident alien students filing Form 1040 are not eligible for the Earned Income Tax Credit ("Not valid for employment" is on their Social Security card).
- If one spouse is a U.S. citizen or resident alien and the other spouse is a non-resident alien, they can elect to file a joint return and treat the non-resident alien spouse as a U.S. resident.
- Immediate family members of an exempt person are also considered exempt individuals under the same rules.

Dual-Status Aliens – A dual-status alien is both a non-resident alien and resident alien in the same year. Dual-status applies to individuals making the "first-year election" to become resident aliens for tax purposes in the year of the election. This applies to individuals who first arrive in the U.S. too late during the year to pass the substantial presence test, or they are exempt individuals during the first part of the year, so they are generally classified as non-resident aliens for the entire year, unless they make the "first year election" choice (See Above). Dual-status can also apply to teachers or trainees, students, and professional athletes whose exempt status has expired and they remain in the U.S. if they can establish that they do not intend to reside permanently in the U.S. (Form 8843 must be filed). In addition, if you leave the U.S. to re-establish your residence in your native country after you have met the substantial presence test, your residency termination date is generally December 31st of the year you leave. So, you are considered a U.S. resident for the entire calendar year. However, you can claim dual-status for the year you leave if you meet the following conditions: you are not a U.S. resident during any part of the following year; and you establish that after you left the U.S. your tax home was a foreign country and you had a closer connection to that country.

When filing as a dual-status alien, you cannot use the standard deduction and, if married, you can't file a joint return. You must file Form 1040NR or Form 1040NR-EZ and write "Dual-Status Return" across the top of the return. You must include Form 1040 with your 1040NR return to show "worldwide" income and deductions for the

part of the year that you were a resident alien, and write "Dual-Status Statement" across the top of the Form 1040.
www.irs.gov/pub/irs-pdf/f1040nre.pdf www.irs.gov/pub/irs-pdf/i1040nre.pdf

Aliens are generally required to obtain a certificate of compliance, also known as a sailing or departure permit, before leaving the United States by filing Form 1040-C. Visiting students and teachers are not required to get a certificate of compliance as long as their employment income is authorized by the Immigration and Naturalization Service.
www.irs.gov/pub/irs-pdf/f1040c.pdf www.irs.gov/pub/irs-pdf/i1040c.pdf

Individual Tax Identification Number (ITIN) Procedures – Individuals who don't have a Social Security number and, therefore, need an "individual tax identification number" (ITIN) must supply original documents, such as passports or birth certificates, or certified copies of these documents from the issuing agencies. Acceptable identification documents include passports, national identification cards, visas issued by the U.S. State Department, U.S. or foreign military identification, U.S. or foreign driver's licenses, civil birth certificates, medical and school records, and certain other documents. Certifying Acceptance Agents (CAAs) can verify the authenticity of identification documents for ITIN applicants and their spouses and do not need to send the original documents to the IRS. But ITIN applications for dependents must still be submitted with original documents. Taxpayer Assistance Centers are set up where documents can be reviewed so taxpayers do not have to part with their original documents.

ITINs will eventually expire unless renewed. Under the Protecting Americans from Tax Hikes Act of 2015 (PATH Act), any ITIN issued prior to 2013 or that hasn't been used for tax years 2013, 2014, and 2015 will no longer be valid for use in filing 2016 – 2018 tax returns. So, individuals that had expiring ITINs and who needed to file a tax return for 2016 – 2018 tax years needed to renew their ITIN. The renewal process usually takes about 7 weeks but can take as long as 9 – 11 weeks. Individuals affected by this new policy can renew their ITINs by filing Form W-7. The renewal box on the form must be checked and original identifying documents, such as birth certificates or passports, must be submitted with Form W-7.
www.irs.gov/pub/irs-pdf/fw7.pdf www.irs.gov/pub/irs-pdf/iw7.pdf

Federal Disaster Loss Relief

On Sept. 29, 2017, the "Disaster Tax Relief and Airport and Airway Extension Act of 2017" (Act) was passed, which provides temporary tax relief to victims impacted by 2016 and 2017 qualified disasters. 2016 qualified disasters are major disasters declared by the President of the United States under Section 401 of the Robert T. Stafford Disaster Relief and Emergency Assistance Act in calendar year 2016. 2017 qualified disasters include Hurricanes Harvey, Irma, and Maria and the California wildfires. These disasters were declared by the President of the United States under Section 401 of the Robert T. Stafford Disaster Relief and Emergency Assistance Act in calendar year 2017. Following are details of relief under the Act:
https://docs.house.gov/billsthisweek/20170925/HR_____.pdf

Early Withdrawals from Qualified Retirement Plans – The Act eliminates the 10% penalty on early withdrawals of up to $100,000 from qualified retirement plans, including 401(k)s, 403(b) governmental plans, IRAs and tax-sheltered annuities for victims of presidentially declared disasters. These "qualified disaster distributions" are defined as distributions from an eligible retirement plan made on or after Jan. 1, 2016, and before Jan. 1, 2018, to an individual whose principal place of abode at any time during the calendar year 2016 or who resided in the affected areas in 2017 and sustained an economic loss by reason of the events that gave rise to the Presidential disasters. Such withdrawals are normally included in income in the year in which they are distributed. The Act allows the withdrawals to be re-contributed back to retirement plans at any time over a 3-year period without any tax consequences and allows taxpayers to spread out any income inclusion amounts resulting from the withdrawals ratably over a 3-year period. Also, qualified withdrawals aren't treated as rollover distributions, which are generally subject to 20% withholding. The Act also allows the re-contribution of certain retirement plan withdrawals made for home purchases or construction, which were received after Feb. 28, 2017 and before Sept. 21, 2017, where the home purchase or construction was cancelled on account of Hurricanes Harvey, Irma, or Maria (without tax consequences). With respect to retirement plan loans, the Act: increased the maximum amount that a participant or beneficiary can borrow from a qualified employer plan from $50,000 to $100,000. **(See Chapter 5, "Distributions from Retirement Plans: Traditional IRAs & Qualified Retirement Plans")**

Employee Retention Tax Credit for Employers – The Act provides a new "employee retention credit" for "eligible employers" affected by Hurricanes Harvey, Irma, and Maria. Eligible employers are generally defined as employers that conducted an active trade or business in a disaster zone as of a specified date (for Hurricane Harvey, Aug. 23, 2017; Irma, Sept. 4, 2017; and Maria, Sept. 16, 2017), and the active trade or business on any day between the specified dates and Jan. 1, 2018, were rendered inoperable as a result of damage sustained by the hurricanes. In general, the credit is equals to 40% of up to $6,000 of "qualified wages" with respect to each "eligible employee" of such employer for the tax year. Therefore, the maximum credit per employee is $2,400 ($6,000 × 40%).

- **Example** – Employer Y is an eligible employer in the Hurricane Harvey disaster zone. Y has two eligible employees, A and B, to whom Y pays qualified wages of $4,000 and $7,000 respectively. Y is entitled to a total credit of $4,000; $1,600 for the wages paid to A ($4,000 × 40%) and $2,400 for $6,000 of the wages paid to B ($6,000 × 40%).

An eligible employee with respect to an eligible employer is one whose principal place of employment with the employer was in the Hurricane Harvey, Irma, or Maria disaster zones. Qualified wages are wages paid or incurred by an eligible employer to an eligible employee on any day after the specified dates (See above) and before Jan. 1, 2018. An employee cannot be taken into account more than one time for purposes of the employee retention tax credit. So, for instance, if an employee is an eligible employee of an employer with respect to Hurricane Harvey for purposes of the credit, the employee cannot also be an eligible employee with respect to Hurricane Irma or Hurricane Maria. An eligible employee cannot be "related" to an employer. **(See Chapter 13, "Employee Retention Tax Credit for Employers Affected by Hurricanes Harvey, Irma and Maria")**

Eased Casualty Loss Rules for Disaster Loss Victims – The Act eliminated the requirement that personal casualty losses must exceed 10% of AGI to qualify for a deduction, and eliminated the requirement that taxpayers must itemize deductions in order to claim casualty losses—it does so by increasing an individual taxpayer's standard deduction by the amount of the taxpayer's net disaster loss. However, the Act increased the $100 per-casualty loss floor from $100 to $500 for qualified disaster-related personal casualty losses. The Act provides that Code Sec. 56(b)(1)(E), which generally disallows the standard deduction for alternative minimum tax (AMT) purposes, does not apply for the portion of the standard deduction attributable to the amount of the net disaster loss.

Under the Act, individual disaster loss victims in the hurricane affected areas may elect to claim a casualty loss in the tax year immediately preceding the tax year in which the disaster occurred. **Victims have six months after the due date for filing their tax return for the year in which the disaster occurred to make the election, and they have 90 days after that to revoke the election.** Taxpayers make the election by deducting the disaster loss on either an original or an amended tax return for the prior year, and by including an election statement on the return indicating they are making a Section 165(i) election and the name or description of the disaster and the date or dates of the disaster that caused the claimed loss. **(See Chapter 12, "Casualty, Disaster, and Theft Losses")**

Charitable Deduction Limitations Suspended for Disaster Loss Victims – For qualifying charitable contributions, the Act: Provides an exception from the overall limitation on itemized deductions for certain qualified contributions; Temporarily suspends the majority of the limitations on charitable contributions in Code Sec. 170(b); and Provides for eased rules governing the treatment of excess contributions. "Qualified contributions" must have been paid during the period beginning on Aug. 23, 2017, and ending on Dec. 31, 2017, in cash to an organization described in Code Sec. 170(b)(1)(A), for relief efforts in the Hurricane Harvey, Irma, or Maria disaster areas. Qualified contributions must have been substantiated, with a contemporaneous written acknowledgement that the contribution was or is to be used for hurricane relief efforts, and the taxpayer must make an election for the Act to apply. For partnerships and S-corporations, the election is made separately by each partner or shareholder. **(See Chapter 12, "Charitable Contribution Deduction")**

Special Rule on "Earned Income" for Earned Income Tax Credit (EITC) and Child Tax Credit Purposes – The Act provides that, in case a "qualified taxpayer's" earned income, which includes the applicable dates shown below, is less than the taxpayer's earned income for the preceding tax year, then the taxpayer may elect, for purposes of the EITC and the Child Tax Credit, to substitute the earned income for the preceding year for the earned income for the current tax year in computing the EITC and the Child Tax Credit for the current year. For Hurricane Harvey, a "qualified taxpayer" is one whose principal place of abode on Aug. 23, 2017 was located either in the Hurricane Harvey disaster zone, or in the Hurricane Harvey disaster area and the individual was displaced from their principal place of abode by reason of Hurricane Harvey. Similar definitions apply for Hurricanes Irma (using a Sept. 4, 2017 date) and Hurricane Maria (using a Sept. 16, 2017 date). In the case of joint filers, the above election may apply if either spouse is a qualified individual. **(See Chapter 13, "Earned Income Tax Credit"; & "Child Tax Credit")**

Other Relief Provided by the IRS in Federally Declared Disaster Areas
The IRS provides relief by giving extensions of time to file tax returns and make payments to businesses and individuals in parts of Texas and Florida, as well as Puerto Rico and the U.S. Virgin Islands affected by Hurricanes Harvey, Irma and Maria; and to victims of the California wildfires. The relief applied to, among other situations, individuals who had returns on valid extensions due Oct. 16, 2017, and businesses whose returns were on valid extensions and were due Sept. 15, 2017. Both had until Jan. 31, 2018, to file. Also, tax-exempt organizations in the affected disaster areas that had a filing due date before Jan. 31, 2018, were allowed more time to file their returns. The IRS gave tax-exempt organizations until Jan. 31, 2018 to file, and it said the relief applied to both the original and extended due dates in this period.

www.irs.gov/pub/irs-drop/rp-16-53.pdf www.irs.gov/pub/irs-pdf/f4684.pdf www.irs.gov/pub/irs-pdf/i4684.pdf
www.irs.gov/pub/irs-pdf/f1040x.pdf   www.irs.gov/pub/irs-pdf/i1040x.pdf

Employees were allowed to forgo their vacation, sick or personal leave in exchange for cash payments the employer makes, before Jan. 1, 2019, to charitable organizations providing relief for the victims of Hurricanes Harvey, Irma, and Maria. Under this special relief, the donated leave will not be included in the income or wages of the employees, and employers will be permitted to deduct the cash payments as business expenses.

Owners and operators of low-income housing projects in the affected hurricane areas were allowed to offer temporary housing to qualified disaster victims, but they were not required to do so. For those who did this, special rules are applied as spelled out in Revenue Procedure 2014-49 and Revenue Procedure 2014-50. file:///C:/Users/timel/Downloads/MHFA_1040830.pdf www.irs.gov/pub/irs-drop/rp-14-50.pdf

Notice 2017-56 offers relief to residents of Puerto Rico and the U.S. Virgin Islands who evacuated or couldn't return because of Hurricanes Irma or Maria. Most individuals can otherwise lose their status as "bona fide residents" of Puerto Rico or the U.S. Virgin Islands for tax filing and reporting purposes. Notice 2017-56 extended the usual 14-day absence period to 117 days, beginning Sept. 6, 2017 and ending Dec. 31, 2017, for the presence test for residency under the tax rules. An individual who was absent from either U.S. territory on any day during the 117-day period were treated as leaving or being unable to return to the relevant U.S. territory as a result of Hurricane Irma and Maria on that day. There were some exceptions to the general 183-day presence test that requires individuals to be in the location where they claim residence for 183 days during the tax year. Generally, residents can include up to 14 days within the 183-day period because of a declared disaster. Nevertheless, because of the catastrophic damage caused by the monster storms to Puerto Rico and the U.S. Virgin Islands, the Federal Emergency Management Agency issued Notices of a Presidential declaration of a major disaster for both territories, and 117 days of absence are allowed.
www.irs.gov/pub/irs-drop/n-17-56.pdf

In the case of a federally declared disaster, an affected taxpayer can call 866-562-5227 to speak with an IRS specialist trained to handle disaster-related issues. You can find other hurricane preparedness tips and more information about hurricane preparedness on the National Weather Service web site. The IRS has a disaster loss workbook, Publication 584, which can help taxpayers compile a room-by-room list of belongings. Photographs can help an individual prove the fair market value of items for insurance and casualty loss claims. Ideally, photos should be stored with a friend or family member who lives outside the area.

If you are a victim of a disaster such as a flood, hurricane, tornado, forest fire, etc. you should check the IRS's "Disaster Assistance and Emergency Relief for Individuals and Businesses" website to find the latest information about any tax relief for victims of various disasters. The IRS normally gives expanded tax relief to victims of any area designated by the Federal Emergency Management Agency (FEMA) as a federal disaster area. You can also find the latest list of federal disaster areas on the FEMA website. Victims of a disaster in an area declared eligible for federal disaster relief may be entitled to tax relief such as being allowed more time to file tax returns, or relief from penalties usually applicable to delinquent filers. The IRS has the authority to extend filing deadlines, as well as to abate penalties for actions they can't extend.
www.Fema.gov/news/disasters.fema

The goal of the IRS Disaster Relief Resource Center for Tax Professionals is to provide resources and assistance to members of the impacted payroll and practitioner community. As a result of recent natural disasters, many payroll and practitioner businesses and their clients have suffered significant losses.
www.irs.gov/tax-professionals/disaster-relief-resource-center-for-tax-professionals

Expensing Certain Citrus Replanting Costs – The Tax Cuts and Jobs Act (TCJA) includes a special rule for replanting costs paid or incurred after December 22, 2017, but not more than 10 years later – until December 22, 2027, for citrus plants lost or damaged due to a casualty such as freezing temperatures, disease, drought, or pests. Such replanting costs may be deducted by a person other than the affected taxpayer, but the affected taxpayer must have at least a 50% equity interest in the replanted citrus plants and the other person must own the remaining equity interest in the replanted citrus plants, or the other person must have acquired all of the affected taxpayer's equity interest in the land on which the citrus plants are located when damaged and replanted on that land. Any accounting method change must follow the automatic change procedures in Rev. Proc. 2018-32 as modified.

Chapter 4 – Earned Income

Gross income is the total of all income (both earned and unearned) received during the year, including investment earnings, except gross income does not include non-taxable social security benefits and non-taxable income generated by municipal bonds and municipal bond funds. All income received by taxpayers is either taxable or non-taxable and is either active or passive. Active (non-passive) income means taxpayers materially participate and includes both earned and unearned income. Adjusted gross income (AGI) is gross income reduced by certain deductions referred to as "above-the-line deductions." Taxable income is AGI less either the standard deduction or itemized deductions. **(See Chapter 1, "Income Tax"); (See Chapter 9, "Exclusions from Taxable income"); (See Chapter 12, "Itemized Deductions")**

Earned income (wages and salaries) is active income and is generally subject to both ordinary income tax and payroll tax. Unearned income is either subject to ordinary income tax or capital gain tax, but not payroll tax. Payroll tax is the total of Social Security and Medicare taxes. Self-employment tax is the same as payroll tax for self-employed/independent contractors whose income is reported on a Form 1099 rather than on Form W-2. In addition to ordinary income tax and payroll tax, earned income of certain high-income earners may be subject to the 0.9% Medicare surtax. **(See Chapter 2, "0.9% Medicare Surtax"); (See Chapter 17, "Self-Employment Tax")**

These are types of compensation that may or may not be considered earned income:

- Repayment obligation determines if loans and advances are wages – In general, payments made to employees for services they'll perform or complete in the future are considered taxable wages. However, advances are not considered taxable compensation if employees are legally obligated to repay the advanced amounts by signing a note or an agreement.
- Advances for expenses aren't taxable wages – Advances given to employees to cover business expenses are not taxable wages if the advances are for expenses under an "accountable plan." **(See Chapter 15, "The Accountable Plan")**
- Vacation and other time-off are generally included in wages – Payments to employees for vacation time, holiday pay, sick pay, maternity or paternity leave, military leave, and disability pay are considered taxable wages.
- Gifts, awards, and prizes are sometimes considered wages – Prizes and awards presented to employees are considered taxable wages based on the theory that they are presented to them in return for an employee's performance or services. Gifts of property are treated no differently than monetary gifts. However, Christmas gifts are not considered taxable wages only if the gifts are items of property having a nominal value (for example, a turkey or ham) – this is limited to property and doesn't apply to gifts of cash, no matter how nominal. Also, employee achievement awards of tangible personal property that are awarded due to an employee's length of service (including retirement), productivity, or safety achievement that average $400 or less are not considered taxable wages ("qualified" plan awards). Also, other awards to employees that are considered "nonqualified" plan awards of no more than $400 are not considered taxable wages. Up to $1,600 in total awards, both qualified and nonqualified, received by an employee in a year are exempt from taxable wages for both income and payroll tax purposes. **(See Chapter 8, "Awards for Recognition of Achievements"; & "Employee Achievement Awards")**

Wages and Salaries

Wages and salaries, including bonuses, and cash awards are reported as taxable income on Form W-2 if you are an employee, and on Form 1099-MISC if you are self-employed/independent contractor. Salaries reported on Form W-2 are subject to both ordinary income tax and payroll tax withholding. Compensation reported on Form 1099-MISC is not subject to withholding, but nevertheless is subject to both income tax and self-employment tax. However, in some cases, earnings by self-employed persons may not be reported on a Form 1099, but such unreported earnings are still subject to income and self-employment taxes. **(See Chapters 2, "Payroll Tax"); (See Chapter 17, "Self-Employed/Independent Contractors")**

www.irs.gov/pub/irs-pdf/fw2.pdf   www.irs.gov/pub/irs-pdf/iw2w3.pdf   www.irs.gov/pub/irs-pdf/f1099msc.pdf   www.irs.gov/pub/irs-pdf/i1099msc.pdf   www.irs.gov/pub/irs-pdf/f1040.pdf   www.irs.gov/pub/irs-pdf/i1040gi.pdf   www.irs.gov/pub/irs-pdf/f1040a.pdf   www.irs.gov/pub/irs-pdf/i1040a.pdf

Employers should have a Form W-4 on file for each employee in order to calculate federal and state tax withholdings from salaries reported of Form W-2. A legal and acceptable Form W-4 should only contain the employee's demographic information, marital status, and the number of exemptions, with an area for an additional dollar amount of withholding and a box to check if the employee is exempt from withholding. There is no expiration date for W-4s, so employers can rely on the latest one they have on file, i.e. employees are not required to turn in a new Form W-4 every year. There is no minimum or maximum number of times employees are allowed to change their W-4. If an employer does not have a valid W-4 on file for an employee, the employer is required to use "Single, with 0 exemptions." The W-4 is a federal document, and most states – but not all – accept the federal W-4 for state income tax withholding purposes.

www.irs.gov/pub/irs-pdf/fw4.pdf

Employers must use Form W-3 to transmit their employees' W-2 Forms to the Social Security Administration (SSA), and Form 1096 to transmit all 1099 Forms to the IRS. Employers are required to provide Forms W-2 to their employees by January 31st. In past years, employers had until February 28th to transmit Forms W-2s to the SSA for paper returns and until March 31st for e-filings and they could get one automatic 30-day extension and request an extra 30 days. However, beginning in 2017 for the 2016 tax year, W-2s must be transmitted to the SSA by Jan. 31st, matching the date that they have to be provided to employees, and the IRS will grant only one 30-day extension to employers, and only in a limited set of circumstances, such as natural disasters or fire that destroy an employer's books and records. To get a 30-day extension, employers will be required to submit a Form 8809, with an explanation of the reasons for requesting the extension and signed under penalty of perjury. Also, only the last four digits of Social Security numbers have to be shown on W2s sent to employees, but the full Social Security number has to be included on the copy the SSA gets. These rules will also eventually apply to certain other information returns such as 1099s and 1098s. Employers that have to file 250 or more information returns, such as 1099-MISC Forms, must file electronically. The SSA strongly suggests that employers transmit Form W-3, along with all their Forms W-2 electronically instead of on paper. For employers that issue hand-written 1099-MISC Forms to workers, copy A of Form 1099-MISC must be printed in red drop-out ink in order to be properly processed by the IRS. When filing on paper, a separate Form 1096 is required for each 1099 form type being submitted to the IRS (Example: if filing both 1099-MISC forms and 1099-INT forms, two 1096 forms are required).

www.irs.gov/pub/irs-pdf/fw4.pdf   www.irs.gov/pub/irs-pdf/f1096.pdf   www.irs.gov/pub/irs-pdf/f8809.pdf

If you do not receive your W-2 or 1099-MISC by Feb. 14, contact your employer. If your employer still doesn't provide you with your W-2 or 1099-MISC, contact the IRS for assistance at 800-829-1040. You must provide your employer's name, address and phone number, dates of employment, and estimate of wages earned and federal tax withheld, if applicable, and when you worked for that employer based on information from your final pay stub or leave-and-earnings statement. After contacting the IRS, you can then use Form 4852, "Substitute for Form W-2 or 1099-MISC," to file your tax return. Attach Form 4852 to your return, estimating income and withholding tax as accurately as possible. If you have trouble contacting the IRS, you may still estimate your income and withholding tax by attaching Form 4852 to your return. If you receive your missing W-2 or 1099-MISC after you file your return, and the information is different from what was reported on your return, you must file an amended return (Form 1040X).
www.irs.gov/pub/irs-pdf/f4852.pdf

Tips

Tips are earned income subject to both ordinary income tax and payroll tax. The value of non-cash tips, such as tickets, passes, or other items of value is considered income subject to tax. You must include in income all cash tips you receive directly from customers, tips added to credit cards, and your share of any tips received from tip-splitting arrangements with fellow employees. If you receive $20 or more in tips in any one month, you should report all the tips to your employer who is required to withhold income tax and payroll tax from tip income. An employee is responsible for paying income tax and his/her share of payroll tax on unreported tips by completing Form 4137, "Social Security and Medicare Tax on Unreported Tip Income," and filing it with Form 1040. It's a good idea to keep a running daily log of your tip income. **(See Chapter 1, "Filing Requirements")**
www.irs.gov/pub/irs-access/f4137_accessible.pdf

As of January 1, 2014, the IRS required that automatic service charges on large parties would be treated differently than tips. In order to be considered a tip, the IRS cites the following factors: the payment must be free from compulsion; the customer must be able to determine the amount of the payment without restriction; the payment cannot be negotiable or dictated by the employer; and the customer should generally have the right to decide who receives the payment. Beginning in January 2014, the IRS will classify money that wait staff receive from automatic service charges as regular wages, from which the employer must withhold federal taxes and FICA, and the servers will receive the compensation in their paychecks, not at the end of their shifts as they normally would for regular tips. Some restaurant owners and managers will continue levying automatic service charges on large groups – typically 18 or 20 percent, but others are dropping it.

Severance Pay

Severance pay is income subject to both ordinary income tax and payroll tax withholding. In March 2014, the Supreme Court ruled that severance pay packages and payments that are given to involuntarily laid-off workers are taxable not only as income, but also with regard to payroll tax (FICA). The Supreme Court decision overturned a Sixth Circuit Court of Appeals decision in the case of United States vs. Quality Stores that concluded severance payments qualifying as supplemental unemployment compensation were excluded from the Internal Revenue Code's statutory definition of wages, and therefore, were not subject to payroll taxes (FICA).

Noncash Compensation

Noncash compensation for the performance of services is considered earned income subject to both ordinary income and payroll taxes unless the recipient is subject to a substantial risk of forfeiture and the compensation is nontransferable, in which case taxation occurs when the risk is extinguished and the property is transferable. The amount of compensation is determined as follows: the property's fair market value (FMV) less any amount paid for the property. A recipient is subject to substantial risk of forfeiture if rights to the property's full enjoyment are conditioned upon the future performance of substantial services by any individual.

Property Transferred to a Taxpayer in Exchange for Services

The fair market value (FMV) of property transferred to a taxpayer in exchange for services is taxable earned income subject to both ordinary income and payroll taxes, including the cash surrender value of a life insurance contract transferred in exchange for services. **(See Chapter 5, "Cash Surrender Value of a Life Insurance Policy")**

Bartering

Bartering to get products or services results in the fair market value of the goods and services exchanged having to be reported as taxable earned income subject to both ordinary income and payroll taxes by both parties. Barter dollars or trade dollars are identical to real dollars for tax reporting purposes. Income from bartering is taxable in the year it is performed. Rules for reporting barter transactions may vary depending on which form of bartering takes place. Generally, you report this type of business income on Form 1040, Schedule C, or other business returns such as Form 1065 or Form 1120S.

Organized barter exchanges function primarily as the organizer of a marketplace where members buy and sell products and service among themselves. Whether this activity operates out of a physical office or is internet-based, a barter exchange is generally required to issue Form 1099-B, "Proceeds from Broker and Barter Exchange Transactions," annually to their clients or members and to the IRS. **(See Chapter 6, "Form 1099-B: Proceeds from Broker and Barter Exchange Transactions"); (See Chapter 14, "Business Structures")**
www.irs.gov/pub/irs-pdf/f1099b.pdf   www.irs.gov/pub/irs-pdf/i1099b.pdf

Distributable Share of Partnership Income

The distributable share of partnership income to both general partners and limited partners is reported to taxpayers on Schedule K-1, Form 1065. The distributable share of partnership ordinary and business income and guaranteed payments reported to general partners on Schedule K-1 is considered earned income that is subject to both ordinary income tax and self-employment tax (payroll tax). However, any income distributed to limited partners is subject to ordinary income tax, but not self-employment tax, because it is considered passive income. Any other income reported on Schedule K-1 is generally considered unearned income not subject to self-employment tax. When partners are considered passive partners, which includes limited partners, income distributed to them may be subject to the 3.8% net investment income (NII) tax, which is only applicable to high income earners. However, any income considered passive is not subject to self-employment tax. **(See Chapter 5, "Unearned Income"); (See Chapter 7 "Passive Income and Losses"); (See Chapter 10, "3.8% Net Investment Income Tax"); (See Chapter 18, "Partnerships")**

Employer Provided Vehicle

An employer provided vehicle is taxable to the employee if the employee uses the vehicle for personal use. An appropriate amount should be included on an employee's W-2 as earned income subject to both ordinary income and payroll taxes. The amount to be included is calculated based on how much an employee would have to pay for a comparable vehicle in an arms-length transaction. The amount to be included on an employee's W-2 is computed by using one of these methods: **(See Chapter 15, "Employer Provided Vehicle")**

- **The Commuting Rule** – If the only personal use of an employer-provided vehicle is commuting to and from work, the employer can use the commuting rule, which provides that the deemed value of each one-way commute is $1.50, and either the deemed value has to be included in the employee's wages or the employee can reimburse the employer for the amount.

- **The Cents-Per-Mile Method** – The cents-per-mile method is based on the IRS standard business mileage rate (54.5 cents per mile in 2018). In order to use the cents-per-mile method, a particular vehicle must meet one of the following tests: (1) used 50% or more for business purposes during the year; (2) generally used each workday to transport at least three employees to and from work in an employer sponsored commuting vehicle pool; or (3) must be driven by employees at least 10,000 miles per year. Employees must either reimburse the employer at the 54.5 cents per mile rate for all personal miles driven in an employer-provided vehicle, or the amount has to be added to the employee's taxable income reported on his/her Form W-2. If the employer does not provide the fuel for the car, the rate is reduced by 5.5 cents per mile. The cents-per-mile rate includes the value of maintenance and insurance. If the employer does not pay for maintenance and/or insurance and the employee is required to pay for those costs, then the amount included in the employee's income has to be reduced by a portion of those expenses incurred by the employee, who must provide receipts. The cents-per-mile method can be used only if the employer provided vehicle's fair market value (FMV) when first made available to employees in 2018 does not exceed $15,600 for a passenger automobile ($15,900 in 2017) and $17,600 for a truck or van ($17,800 in 2017). These requirements will exclude a lot of vehicles, so the cents-per-mile rule is very restrictive. **(See Chapter 15, "Vehicle and Other Transportation Expenses")**

- **The Lease Value Rule** – The annual lease value method is different from the other methods, because instead of calculating the employee's personal use of the vehicle, the rule provides that the employer has to calculate how much of the vehicle's FMV can be included in the employee's income as a working condition fringe benefit. This is done by calculating the FMV of the vehicle, and based on that amount, calculating the FMV of the business and personal use of the vehicle. The fair market value (FMV) has to be determined on the first date the vehicle is available for use by employees. The annual lease value does not include the cost of gasoline, so the employer can either add to or subtract from (depending on whether the employer or employee furnishes the gasoline) the value of the employee's personal use of the vehicle based on the fair market value of gasoline or use a rate of 5.5 cents per mile.

- **The Fleet-Average Valuation Method** – The fleet-average valuation method can be used by employers maintaining a fleet of at least 20 automobiles – the FMV of each vehicle is determined to be equal to the average value of the entire fleet, i.e. the fleet average value is the average of the FMV of all automobiles used in the fleet. The maximum FMV amounts for using the fleet-average valuation rule in 2018 cannot exceed $20,600 for a passenger car ($21,100 in 2017), and $23,100 for a truck or van ($23,300 in 2017). The employer has to calculate how much of the fleet-average value of the vehicle used by an employee will be included in the employee's income as a fringe benefit. This is done by calculating the FMV of the business use of the vehicle by the employee.

Police officers, firefighters, and public safety officers who are permitted to drive their official vehicles home are exempt from including this benefit in income. However, the vehicles must be clearly marked by insignia or words.

Virtual Currency

Virtual currencies like Bitcoins are not recognized as legal tender in any jurisdiction. Nevertheless, general tax principles that apply to property transactions also apply to transactions using virtual currency. This means that wages paid to employees using virtual currency are taxable earned income that must be reported on an employee's Form W-2, subject to both ordinary income and payroll taxes. Payments using virtual currency made to independent contractors and other service providers are taxable and self-employment tax rules are applicable. **(See Chapter 6, "Virtual Currency")**

Payments to employees and contractors using virtual currency, like Bitcoins, must be valued in dollars as of the time of payment on Form W-2 or Form 1099. If you pay someone in Bitcoins, how do you withhold income and payroll taxes? You have to send the IRS money from something else. You either pay the employee with Bitcoins and some cash and withhold plenty of the cash, or you sell some of the Bitcoins to get money to pay the IRS.

The IRS suspects that Bitcoins and similar virtual currencies are being used for tax evasion. Therefore, the IRS recently signed a contract with a company called Chainalysis that has software that can analyze and track Bitcoin transactions with the company's Reactor tool. The software is supposed to help the IRS track the use of Bitcoins for trade in not only illicit goods such as drugs and ransomware payments, but also to uncover its use for concealing wealth from tax authorities.

Working Interests in Oil and Gas Ventures

Earnings from working interests in oil and gas ventures (not royalties) are considered taxable earned income to the owners and is, therefore, subject to both ordinary income and payroll taxes. Profits are subject to self-employment tax even if you aren't actively running the operation and you have a minimal ownership interest.

Donation of a Female Donor's Eggs to a Recipient

The Tax Court ruled in *Perez v. Commissioner, 144 T.C. 4 (2015)* that compensation received by a female donor of her eggs to a female recipient was taxable income to the donor. "Egg donation" is where a female donor is supplied with hormones that increase her egg production, and the eggs are then removed, fertilized in a laboratory, and ultimately implanted in an intended recipient female. Donating eggs is a selective, painful, and lucrative process for women between the ages of 21 and 30 who are nonsmokers and have no family history of cancer or personal history of infertility or mental disorders. Despite the painful process, egg donation has become increasingly popular among young women who need money for college or other reasons, because a qualified donor can be paid as much as $50,000 for her eggs. The contract that the donor signed stated that Perez was not selling her eggs, but instead she would be compensated whether or not she produced any useable eggs. Therefore, the Tax Court only had to decide whether she was receiving compensation for her "services" or for damages from physical injury resulting from the prolonged painful process. The court ruled that the compensation received by Perez was for "services" rendered. As a result, the amounts paid to Perez, and presumably to all future egg donors,

represented taxable income subject to both ordinary income and payroll taxes.
www.ustaxcourt.gov/InOpHistoric/perezdiv.holmes.TC.WPD.pdf

Differential Pay to Reservists Called to Active Duty

Differential wage payments made by businesses to reservists called to active duty are considered taxable earned income, but the differential wage payments are not subject to payroll tax or FUTA. Small employers with 50 or fewer employees who pay differential pay to reservists called to active duty can claim a tax credit equal to 20% of the differential wages up to $20,000 a year for each employee. Beginning in 2016, the credit applies to employers of any size, not just employers with 50 or fewer employees. **(See Chapter 13, "Credit for Employer Differential Wage Payments")**

Damages Received for Job Discrimination

Damages received for discrimination after loss of a job is taxable income, but how it is taxed depends on the kind of damages collected. Lost wages collected are considered earned income subject to both ordinary income tax and payroll tax. However, payments for emotional suffering from discrimination are punitive or compensatory damages that are considered unearned income. And the tax law treats you as receiving 100% of the settlement, even if the defendant issues a separate check to the lawyer for his cut. However, attorney fees for discrimination awards are deductible in determining adjusted gross income as an above-the-line deduction, so they won't affect how much taxes you have to pay. **(See Chapter 5, "Unearned Income"); (See Chapter 11, "Attorney Fees Paid in Connection with Unlawful Discrimination")**

Royalties from Book Sales –Royalties from book sales and publications are usually reported on Form 1099-MISC, and are considered taxable earned income subject to both ordinary income and self-employment taxes. **(See Chapter 5, "Royalty Income")**

Chapter 5 – Unearned Income

Unearned income is active income of various kinds that is generally subject to ordinary income tax, but not payroll tax, unless there is an exception. Unearned income includes portfolio income such as interest and dividends, but "qualified" dividends are subject to capital gain tax rates instead of ordinary income tax rates. Also, portfolio income may be subject to the 3.8% net investment income (NII) tax which is applicable only to certain high-income earners. **(See Chapter 6, "Capital Gains and Losses"); (See Chapter 10, "3.8% Net Investment Income Tax")**

Portfolio Income:

Interest
Interest income is unearned income subject to ordinary income tax that is reported on Form 1099-INT:
www.irs.gov/pub/irs-pdf/f1099int.pdf   www.irs.gov/pub/irs-pdf/i1099int.pdf

- Interest on U.S. savings bonds are not taxable until redeemed. However, a taxpayer can elect to report the interest earned each year, and the election can be revoked at any time.
- Interest on original issue discount (OID) investments is taxable annually based on deemed interest rates as determined in the prospectus of each individual investment instrument.
  www.irs.gov/pub/irs-pdf/f1099oid.pdf
- Interest payable on a Certificate of Deposit (CD) is taxable if the CD is in a taxable account. However, rolling over the proceeds of the CD when it matures is not a taxable event.
- Contributions made to a traditional IRA in a year can be withdrawn in the same year without penalty, but you must pay tax on the interest earned. Excess contributions to both traditional and Roth IRAs are subject to a 6% excise tax each year until they are withdrawn or treated as being contributions for a later year. **(See Chapter 9, "Contributions to Qualified Employee Retirement Plans"); (See Chapter 11, "IRA Contributions")**
- Interest earned on tax-exempt municipal bonds and tax-exempt bond funds is non-taxable for federal income tax purposes, but it is usually taxable on state income tax returns. **(See Chapter 8, "Interest on Municipal Bonds and Tax-Exempt Municipal Bond Funds")**

Dividends
Dividends are reported to taxpayers on Form 1099-DIV – including mutual fund dividends. Ordinary dividends are taxed at ordinary income tax rates. "Qualified" dividends are taxed at capital gain tax rates. **(See Chapter 6, "Qualified Dividends")**
www.irs.gov/pub/irs-pdf/f1099div.pdf   www.irs.gov/pub/irs-pdf/i1099div.pdf

Constructive Dividends
Constructive dividends distributed to shareholders in the form of loans (no intent to repay); forgone interest on a below market loan made by a shareholder; sale of corporate assets to a shareholder for less than FMV, etc. are considered unearned income to the recipients. These are usually related to small closely held corporations, not labeled as dividends, and taxed at ordinary income tax rates.

Imputed Interest

Grandparents, for example, can lend money to a grandchild to buy a home, start a business, or for any other purpose. If there is no interest charged, or the interest is below the applicable federal rate for the term of the loan, the lenders must report "imputed" interest which is subject to ordinary income taxes even though no funds are received. However, there are two conditions where imputed interest does not have to be reported on the lenders' tax return: (1) the amount of the loan does not exceed $10,000, and (2) the amount of the loan does not exceed $100,000 and the borrower's total "investment income" for the year does not exceed $1,000. It is important to put any loan of this kind in writing and include important loan terms – interest rate if any, repayment schedule, and what happens if there is a default on the loan. If the loan terms are formalized in writing, the lender can write-off the loan if the grandchild fails to repay it, but without a valid promissory note, the IRS may try to claim that the grandparents merely made a "gift" of the money which could be taxable to the grandparents. **(See Chapter 22, "Estate and Gift Tax")**

Earnings on Uniform Transfer to Minors Custodial Accounts (UTMA)

Earnings on uniform transfer to minors' accounts (UTMA) are usually interest or dividends that are taxable to the minor child. In 2018, parents can make a "gift" of up to $15,000 to each dependent child ($30,000 if a married couple and gift-splitting is used) and deposit the funds into one of these custodial accounts. However, keep in mind that the "kiddie tax" may affect the taxation of earnings from these accounts. The kiddie tax applies to the earnings in a UTMA for children under 19 or under 24 if a full-time student. A custodial account comes under the child's legal control when he/she reaches the age of majority under applicable state law. **(See Chapter 3, "Kiddie Tax"); (See Chapter 22, "Exemption for Lifetime Taxable Gifts and Estates")**

Royalty Income

Royalty income is taxed at ordinary tax rates, and is reported to the taxpayer on Form 1099-MISC, which is then reported on Schedule E, Form 1040. 15% depletion is allowed on amounts reported in box 2 of Form 1099-MISC for oil and gas royalties. Royalties paid for use of trademarks must be capitalized.
www.irs.gov/pub/irs-pdf/f1040se.pdf www.irs.gov/pub/irs-pdf/i1040se.pdf

Royalties from book sales, are considered taxable earned income subject to both ordinary income tax and self-employment tax. **(See Chapter 4, "Royalties from Book Sales")**

Other Unearned Income:

Unemployment Compensation
Unemployment compensation is taxable income, but is not considered wages subject to payroll tax.

Requisition of Property by the Government
Requisition of property by the government in exchange for payment is taxable unearned income, i.e. if the government takes part of your land for road widening and you receive a payment, it is taxable.

Jury Duty Pay

Jury duty pay is considered taxable compensation, but it is not subject to payroll tax. If employers allow employees to keep their jury duty pay, then the employees' payroll tax obligations apply only to their regular wages. Jury duty pay is reported as "Other Income" on Form 1040.

Class Action Settlement

Funds received from a class action settlement are generally taxable unearned income, because damages received for any type of injury other than personal physical injury or sickness are taxable. Legal fees incurred by business entities in recovering awards are generally deductible, and in 2017 such legal fees were generally deductible by individuals as miscellaneous itemized deductions subject to the 2% AGI floor. But in 2018, the legal fees are not deductible by individuals because the Tax Cuts and Jobs Act eliminated miscellaneous itemized deductions subject to the 2% floor as an itemized deduction. **(See Below, "Personal Injury Awards Associated with Nonphysical Injuries"); (See Chapter 8, "Personal Injury Awards as a Result of Physical Injuries"); (See Chapter 12, "Legal Expenses"; & "Miscellaneous Itemized Deductions Subject to the 2% AGI floor")**

Prizes

Prizes won or awarded are taxable unearned income reported as "Other Income" on Form 1040. However, cash awards are non-taxable income if they are: (1) in recognition of past achievements of the recipient in religious, charitable, scientific, educational, artistic, literary, or civic fields; and (2) the recipient was selected without any action on his/her own part to enter a contest. This does not apply to prizes received by employees from their employers. **(See Chapter 8, "Awards for Recognition of Achievements"; & "Employee Achievement Awards")**

If you play the state lottery and win $50,000, and you expect to be in a much lower tax bracket next year, you cannot wait until the next year to cash in the lottery ticket and declare the income on next year's tax return. You must declare the income in the year you win the lottery, because the money's yours for the asking.
It makes no difference if you hold off until next year to collect your prize.

Distributable Share of S-Corporation Income

The distributable share of income to shareholders/members of S-corporations is taxable income that is reported to them on Schedule K-1, Form 1120S, but the income is not subject to self-employment tax. Although, any wages paid to shareholders/members has to be reported on Form W-2 and is subject to both ordinary income and payroll taxes. When S-corporation shareholders are considered passive shareholders, the distributable share of S-corporation income to them may be subject to the 3.8% NII tax for high income earners. **(See Chapter 4, "Earned Income"); (See Chapter 7 "Passive Income and Losses"); (See Chapter 10, "3.8% Net Investment Income Tax"); (See Chapter 19, "Compensation of S-Corporation Shareholders/Employees"; & "Implementation of the 3.8% Net Investment Income Tax")**

Distributable Net Income from Estates and Trusts

Beneficiaries' pro rata share of Distributable Net Income (DNI) from estates and trusts is taxable income that is reported to them on Schedule K-1, Form 1041, which is then included on the appropriate 1040 forms and schedules. Classes of income retain their original character in the hands of the beneficiaries. Generally, all distributions are considered unearned income not subject to payroll tax. Classes of income received by beneficiaries include dividends, rental income, etc., and can include some tax-exempt income which is non-taxable income. Some distributions may be subject to the 3.8% NII tax, e.g. dividends and rental income. **(See Chapter 6, "Capital Gains and Losses"); (See Chapter 8, "Nontaxable Income"); (See Chapter 10, "3.8% Net Investment Income Tax"); (See Chapter 21, "Net Investment Income Tax Applicable to Estates and Trusts")**

When an estate or trust distributes appreciated assets to beneficiaries, they generally keep the same tax basis that the trust or estate had in the property, which in the case of an estate is generally the stepped-up basis of the assets to their FMV at the time of the decedent's death. **(See Chapter 22, "Basis of Property Inherited or Gifted")**

Online Fantasy Sports Leagues

Participation in online fantasy sports leagues has grown enormously in the past decade, including fantasy football, baseball, hockey, and basketball. These leagues and college tournament bracket contests operate under the "Unlawful Internet Gambling Enforcement Act (UIGEA) of 2006." This act sets forth the criteria that must be met for an online game not to be illegal gambling or a game of chance, but instead considered a game of skill. To be consistent with fantasy sports leagues being defined as not gambling, operators should report participants' prize money as taxable unearned income using Form 1099-MISC, typically in Box 3 – Other Income, which is reported as other income on Form 1040. Form W-2G, "Certain Gambling Winnings," should not be used to report this income. **(See Below, "Gambling Winnings")**

There are three possible methods of reporting fantasy sports leagues winnings on Form 1099-MISC: (1) the gross method – the site operator reports the total of all winnings for the year if the player wins $600 or more; (2) the net method – the site operator reports the total of all winnings for the year and subtracts the entrance fees from the winning contests only when the net amount the player wins is $600 or more; and (3) the cumulative net method – the site operator reports the player's total winnings less all entrance fees for the year, regardless of whether the participant received a prize. The IRS concluded in a letter ruling that the net method must be used and entrance fees should be netted only against winnings from that particular contest, and entrance fees for losing contests should not be deducted against winnings from other contests.

Disability Income

Disability payments paid by disability insurance for lost wages, etc. may or may not be taxable. If plan premiums were paid by the employer or the premiums were paid by the employee with pre-tax dollars as part of a cafeteria plan, and the cost of the premiums were not included in the employee's taxable income, the disability payments are taxable unearned income to the employee. If an employee paid the premiums with after tax dollars, the disability payments are non-taxable to the employee. If the premiums were paid jointly by the employer and employee with after tax dollars, only the disability payments covered by the employer's premium payments are taxable based on the percentage of the total premiums paid.

If an employee retired due to a disability, the pension payments received are considered wages subject to both ordinary income tax and payroll tax until the employee reaches the minimum retirement age (the age eligible to receive a pension if not disabled). After reaching the minimum retirement age, the pension is no longer reported as taxable wages subject to payroll tax, but instead is reported as unearned pension income. **(See Chapter 4, "Earned Income")**

Personal Injury Awards Associated with Nonphysical Injuries

Personal injury awards associated with nonphysical injuries are taxable unearned income to the recipient. And, even though personal injury awards for physical injuries (say, broken bones from an accident) are generally non-taxable, awards for emotional distress related to a physical injury (Appeals Court decision Murphy, D.C. Cir.) are taxable, except that damages paid for medical care attributable to emotional distress are excluded from taxable income. Punitive damage awards associated with both physical injury or sickness and nonphysical injury are taxable, whether awarded by law suit or agreement. In addition, a portion of contingent fees paid to attorneys may be included in your income, if the recovery amount includes punitive damages. The amount of contingent fees paid to attorneys is taxable based on the percentage of punitive damages compared to the amount of total damages recovered for an injury, and the tax law treats you as receiving 100% of the settlement, even if the defendant issues a separate check to the lawyer for his cut. The contingent fees paid to attorneys that are taxable to you were deductible by you as a miscellaneous itemized deduction subject to the 2% floor in 2017. But in 2018, the contingent fees are not deductible by you because the Tax Cuts and Jobs Act eliminated miscellaneous itemized deductions subject to the 2% floor as an itemized deduction. **(See Chapter 8, "Personal Injury Awards as a Result of Physical Injuries"); (See Chapter 14, "Legal Expenses"; & "Miscellaneous Itemized Deductions Subject to the 2% AGI Floor")**
www.cadc.uscourts.gov/internet/opinions.nsf/BF025959E283DF168525744000455520/$file/05-5139b.pdf

However, there's an exception in the case of worker's compensation payments for personal injuries. Unlike other payments, injuries don't have to be physical to be non-taxable. Thus, nonphysical mental and emotional injuries covered by worker's compensation are considered non-taxable. And what's more, even retirement payments can be tax-free, if they are received under the worker's compensation act. **(See Chapter 8, "Workers' Compensation")**

You have more flexibility to reduce taxes on nonphysical injuries if you settle, especially if you negotiate with an eye on the tax rules. A settlement agreement might say all the cash is for a nontaxable physical injury, while a court verdict might attribute some of it to taxable punitive damages or interest. You can influence how your recovery is taxed by how you deal with these issues.

Cash Surrender Value of a Life Insurance Policy

Even though life insurance payments to beneficiaries as a result of the death of the insured person is non-taxable income, the cash surrender value of a life insurance policy is taxable unearned income to a certain extent. The owner of a surrendered policy must include in unearned income the difference between the proceeds and the total premiums paid on the policy. This also applies to universal life insurance policies where the premiums are more than the cost of the insurance, where part, even most of the premiums go to cash reserves, i.e. the owner does not have to pay tax on the part of the premiums that went to cash reserves. Surrender of a life insurance policy is reported to the taxpayer on Form 1099-R, which shows the total proceeds and the taxable portion.
www.irs.gov/pub/irs-pdf/f1099r.pdf   www.irs.gov/pub/irs-pdf/i1099r.pdf

- Owners of universal life insurance policies can make partial withdrawals, or receive a loan tax-free from the reserves, unless the withdrawals are more than the cost of the policy premiums paid.
- No medical expense deduction is allowed for payment of medical expenses with money from a withdrawal of the cash surrender value of a life insurance contract. Instead, the amount is not included in income and the investment in the contract is reduced by that amount. **(See Chapter 12, "Medical Expenses")**

When an original owner surrenders a policy, the owner's taxable income is reduced by the amount of any premiums paid. However, if the original owner sells the policy to a third party, the original owner's basis is not equal to the full amount of premiums paid, but instead the cost basis consists of the cumulative premiums paid into the insurance contract plus a subjective "cost of insurance" or "provision of insurance."

- **Example** – An owner pays $64,000 in premiums over 8 years, and surrenders the policy for $78,000. During the 8 years, he pays $10,000 in "cost-of-insurance" charges. If he surrenders the policy, he has $14,000 of ordinary income ($78,000 - $64,000). However, if he sells the policy to a 3rd party investor for $80,000, he has $26,000 in taxable income ($14,000 in ordinary income, plus $12,000 long-term capital gain) – calculated as follows: the cost basis drops from $64,000 to $54,000 ($64,000 - $10,000 in "cost-of-insurance"). Therefore, even though the seller received just $2,000 above the cash surrender value ($80,000 - $78,000), the total gain is $26,000 ($80,000 - $54,000 adjusted basis).

Cancellation of Debt

Cancellation of Debt (COD) of $600 or more is generally considered taxable unearned income, and must be reported on Form 1099-C, Box 2 - "discharge of indebtedness," which a lender is required to send to the taxpayer. Cancelled debt is reported as "Other Income" on Form 1040. When a taxpayer receives a Form 1099-C and does not include the cancelled debt in income, the IRS will issue a statutory notice of deficiency. If a taxpayer disagrees that it is COD income, the taxpayer has the right to file suit in the U.S. Tax Court to contest the amount of income alleged to result from a discharge of indebtedness. A number of factual situations can result in the lender canceling the balance of the debt and sending Form 1099-C to the taxpayer. The 1099-C form itself won't have a direct impact on your credit scores. However, whatever behavior led you to receive the 1099-C likely will be affecting your credit. For example, say you didn't pay your debt and it was sent to collections. Having an account in collections can have a negative effect on your credit.
(See Chapter 9, "Cancellation of Debt Excluded from Income")
www.irs.gov/pub/irs-pdf/f1099c.pdf   www.irs.gov/pub/irs-pdf/i1099ac.pdf

What if you get a 1099-C for a debt you paid? First, contact the issuer of the 1099-C and ask them to make the necessary correction. They will need to send you a corrected 1099-C in time for you to file your taxes. If this doesn't work, the IRS has a dispute process you can use. This requires you to contact the IRS and let them know you wish to submit a complaint about an incorrectly issued 1099-C. They will provide you with Form 4598 that you will have to attach to your tax return, along with any additional documentation that supports your claim.
https://irs-form-4598-instructions.pdffiller.com

Debt is deemed to be cancelled at the time it is determined that it will never be repaid, and until Nov. 8, 2016, there was a 36-month testing period where if a creditor had not received any payment from the debtor by the end of such testing period, there was a presumption that the loan had been cancelled; thus triggering the Form 1099-C filing requirement. However, beginning on Nov. 8, 2016, the 36-month testing period for filing Form 1099-C was removed by the IRS, because it was concerned that the rule led to taxpayer confusion and didn't increase tax compliance by debtors or provide the IRS with third-party information that could be used for taxpayer compliance. www.federalregister.gov/documents/2014/10/15/2014-24392/removal-of-the-36-month-non-payment-testing-period-rule

One example of cancellation of debt is when a taxpayer doesn't pay his or her credit card bill and negotiates with the credit card company to reduce the amount to settle the credit card debt. However, debt discharged in bankruptcy has no tax consequences to an individual, because it should be excluded from a debtor's gross income (Internal Revenue Code Par. 108(a)(1)(A)). However, it is common when a debt is discharged in bankruptcy for the debtor to receive a Form 1099-C. When this happens, the debtor should file Form 982, "Reduction of Tax Attributes Due to Discharge of Indebtedness," advising the IRS that the debt was discharged in bankruptcy. www.irs.gov/pub/irs-pdf/f982.pdf https://cdn2.hubspot.net/hub/49162/file-19359013-pdf/docs/instruction-for_1099c-and-982-form.pdf

Is it really cancellation of debt? While the issuance of Form 1099-C is an identifiable event, it is not necessarily determinative of an intent to cancel the debt. Form 1099-C is not always prepared correctly, and it is difficult for the taxpayer to get the lender to correct it. For example, in many cases there is a genuine dispute with the creditor as to the amount of the debt, and the debt is resolved for less than was deemed to be owed, but the creditor considers the unpaid amount as cancelled debt. For example, it is possible that a Form 1099-C was issued after a compromise between a debtor and creditor on a disputed debt amount, which would be a creditor's loss on a debt owed by a solvent debtor, not cancellation of debt. In this case, the taxpayer should take prompt action in an attempt to have the lender correct the Form 1099-C. Failing that, the best alternative is to file a U.S. Tax Court petition. Also, a creditor can rebut the presumption that a debt has been cancelled by showing significant, bona fide collection activity or other facts and circumstances that indicate the debt has not been cancelled.

In a recent court decision (the case of William and Elaine Reed), the court ruled against a bank that had issued the Reeds a 1099-C for COD income, and then filed a lawsuit to try to collect the past due debt, plus interest. In ruling against the bank, the court stated that it is inequitable to require a debtor to claim COD income as a component of the debtor's gross income on which income taxes were paid, while still allowing the creditor, who had reported to the IRS and the debtor that the indebtedness was cancelled, to try to collect it from the debtor. The Reeds argued that the bank had thrown in the towel when it issued the 1099-C. The bank, relying on IRS guidance at the time, argued that the 1099-C was not an admission that the debt was no longer due, but rather an effort to be in compliance with reporting requirements. The court agreed with the Reeds.

A lender who acquires a taxpayer's property through foreclosure, repossession or abandonment should send the taxpayer Form 1099-A, which is the form used by the taxpayer to calculate gain or loss and any ordinary income from disposition of the property.
www.irs.gov/pub/irs-pdf/f1099a.pdf

In June 2016, the IRS issued final regulations regarding how discharge of indebtedness affects grantor trusts, disregarded entities and their owners. Basically, the rules state that the responsibility for any discharge of indebtedness by these entities lies with their owners. For example, if a partnership holds an interest in a grantor trust or a disregarded entity, any discharge of indebtedness is the responsibility of each individual partner to whom the income is allocable. Also, the insolvency and bankruptcy exclusions applicable to discharge of indebtedness are available only to any individual owners that qualify for the exclusions. **(See Chapter 9, "Cancellation of Debt Excluded from Income")**

Gambling Winnings
Gambling winnings of casual gamblers are taxable unearned income, and are reported as other income on Form 1040. Gambling losses can be taken to the extent of gambling winnings on Schedule A as a miscellaneous itemized

deduction "not subject" to the 2% floor. And the expenses of gamblers can be included as part of their losses in tax years 2018 – 2025 as set forth the Tax Cuts and Jobs Act (TCJA). For instance, an individual's expenses in traveling to and from a casino are expenses that can offset gambling winnings beginning in 2018. But the expenses of gamblers were not allowed as part of their losses in 2017 and prior years. However, gamblers cannot have a loss, i.e. the amount of a gambler's losses are limited to the amount of their winnings in a year, and excess losses cannot be carried forward to future years. Also, gambling winnings for the casual gambler will not necessarily be brought to zero by equal gambling losses, because the losses are only deductible as an itemized deduction. The combined gambling losses of a husband and wife who file a joint return can be deducted against the couple's combined gambling winnings. **(See Chapter 12, "Gambling Losses")**

A professional gambler's winnings and losses are shown on Schedule C, and therefore, any profit is subject to ordinary income tax and self-employment tax. In a 2011 Tax Court decision (Mayo vs. Commissioner), the court held that while gambling losses are limited to the extent of gambling winnings, any non-loss expenses of a professional gambler – items like meals, lodging, travel expenses, admission fees and handicapping data – are not subject to the limitation. Thus, a professional gambler can reduce his winnings to zero by his losses, and then further deduct any non-loss business expenses on Schedule C, generating a net loss from the activity. Professional gambler status is hard to achieve. Casual gamblers cannot become professional gamblers in the eyes of the IRS simply by gambling frequently. Strict requirements include the ability of the gambler to show activities being treated in a business-like manner using plans, strategies, and schedules.
www.irs.gov/pub/irs-aod/aod201106.pdf

The IRS says it's permissible for casual gamblers to simply keep a record of their net win or loss amounts on a daily basis as long as it is at the same gambling establishment, i.e. this is considered one gambling session. However, gamblers cannot offset gains and losses on different days against each other. Gambling at different gambling establishments during the same day are considered separate gambling sessions for purposes of offsetting gains and losses. If the casual gambler then reports the sum total of the net winnings from all winning sessions as gross income on Form 1040 and keeps track of the sum total of the net losses from all losing sessions (and expenses beginning in 2018) for purposes of applying the losses-cannot-exceed-winnings limitation to his Schedule A itemized deductions, the IRS will consider that close enough to the theoretically required recording of each win or loss from each spin of the slot machine, etc. **(See Chapter 12, "Gambling Losses")**
www.irs.gov/pub/irs-pdf/fw2g.pdf   www.irs.gov/pub/irs-pdf/iw2g.pdf

Presumably the IRS will consider this concept of recording all the net wins and losses from all the taxpayer's gambling sessions sufficient recordkeeping for both casual gambling and for professional gambling as well. Reporting an amount of gross income equal to the sum total of the net winnings from all days you had winnings will probably keep you out of trouble with the IRS, assuming the amount reported as income equals or exceeds the sum total of any amounts reported as income on Forms W2G submitted to you by gambling establishments. Whether you are an amateur or professional gambler, you must adequately document the amount of your losses and expenses in order to claim them. The following information should be kept in a log: (1) the dates of your losses; (2) name and address of the gambling establishment; (3) if possible, the names of other persons present with you at the gambling facility; and (4) the amount lost (record the number of the table played and keep statements showing casino credit issued to the player).

For most types of gambling at a legitimate gaming facility, the facility will issue you a Form W-2G if you win $1,200 or more in a gambling session (formerly $600) or 300 times the original wager. A gaming facility must give you a W-2G if you receive: $1,200 or more in gambling winnings from bingo or slot machines; $1,500 or more in proceeds (the amount of winnings minus the amount of the wager) from keno; and more than $5,000 in winnings (reduced by the wager or buy-in) from a poker tournament. Gambling wins of $5,000 or more may require withholding of taxes before payout. The "information reporting period" for a gaming facility is either a "calendar day" or a "gaming day" as long as that period is applied uniformly by the payor to all payees during the calendar year. A payor may adopt a different information reporting period from one calendar year to the next, but may not change the information reporting period in the middle of a calendar year. Changes to a payor's information reporting period from one calendar year to the next must be implemented on Jan. 1st. Reportable gambling winnings for bingo and slot machine play are not determined by netting the wager against the winnings, but reportable gambling winnings for keno are determined by netting the wager in that one game against the winnings from that game.

Gambling losses can offset all gains from wagering transactions, not merely gambling winnings, i.e. raffle, lottery, and horse race winnings are treated as gambling winnings that can be offset by gambling losses, and the cost of a losing raffle ticket paid to a charity is a gambling loss, not a charitable contribution. Gambling winnings include cash winnings and the fair market value (FMV) of prizes such as cars and trips. However, a prize or contest award that is won without an entry fee or other consideration is not gambling income. Complimentary items received from a casino as an inducement to gamble are gambling gains from which the casual gambler can deduct gambling losses (and expenses beginning in 2018). However, a casual gambler could not deduct any expenses beyond the amount of any losses that offset the value of any complimentary items received and his or her gambling winnings in 2017 and prior years. For example, in Lakhani vs. Commissioner, the court ruled that a recreational horse racing gambler's argument that his portion of the track's "takeout expenses" represented non-loss business expenses rather than gambling losses, and were thus deductible without limitation was invalid.

Alimony and Separate Maintenance
The Tax Cuts and Jobs Act (TCJA) does not require any change in the tax treatment of alimony under divorce or separation agreements executed before December 31, 2018. The Tax Cuts and Jobs Act (TCJA) eliminates the deduction of alimony payments and the inclusion in income by the recipients required under divorce or separation instruments that are (1) executed after December 31, 2018, or (2) instruments executed before December 31, 2018 that are modified after that date if the modification specifically states that the TCJA treatment of alimony payments now applies. Also, this change is a permanent part of the tax code and doesn't sunset at the end of 2025, as do many of the provisions in the TCJA.

Alimony payments are reported as income on Form 1040 in 2018. The payer spouse can deduct alimony payments as an above-the-line deduction on Form 1040 in 2018. Alimony or spousal support and separate maintenance received is taxable unearned income to the recipient and is deductible by the payer, as opposed to child support, which is non-taxable. Alimony payments do not have to be received under a final decree of divorce or separate maintenance, but must be under a written instrument, such as a separation agreement (an oral understanding will not do), requiring one spouse to make payments of support to the other spouse. Thus, alimony can be paid even though the couple continues to be married for tax purposes. The divorce or separation agreement should clearly state that required alimony payments are not child support. If the divorce decree states that spousal maintenance ends when a child moves out of the ex-spouse's home, the payments should be considered child support, not alimony. A lump sum payment made to settle obligations pursuant to a divorce isn't deductible as alimony, even if the court orders an ex-spouse to pay a lump-sum payment to a former spouse. Also, the transfer of property from one spouse to the other is not considered alimony. Only annual cash payments or cash equivalents can be considered alimony. **(See Chapter 3, "Marital Status and Divorce"); (See Chapter 8, "Child Support Payments"); (See Chapter 11, "Alimony/Separate Maintenance")**

- In the Mudrich v. Commissioner case, Paul Mudrich agreed to split a $250,000 bonus with his soon-to-be ex-wife. The Tax Court found that because the bonus agreement was not a divorce or separation instrument, the payment to Lauri (soon-to-be ex-wife) pursuant to the bonus agreement was not alimony. There was no evidence that the bonus agreement ever became an order in the divorce proceeding, nor was it a written separation agreement. It's not enough to simply give money to your ex-spouse to qualify for an alimony deduction. The payment must be part of a legally valid divorce or separation agreement. http://www.ustaxcourt.gov/ustcinop/opinionviewer.aspx?ID=11265

Indirect alimony includes making mortgage payments and paying real estate taxes on a residence a former spouse is occupying. The payer spouse must be the owner of the residence; if they are joint owners – ½ is treated as alimony. When the payer spouse owns the residence, he or she may be entitled to deduct the mortgage interest and real estate taxes as itemized deductions if the house qualifies as either a principal or secondary residence. It qualifies as a secondary residence if at least one of the payer spouse's children is living in the house. Indirect alimony also includes: (1) maintaining life insurance payments for a former spouse, or for the payer spouse if the payee spouse is the beneficiary and owner of the policy; and (2) paying medical or other expenses of a former spouse – payee spouse must include the payments in income and deduct the medical expenses as itemized deductions. Medical payments made directly to a 3rd party must be documented in writing in order to be considered alimony. Payments do not qualify as alimony/separate maintenance if both spouses still live in the same household (a one-month overlap is OK).

Legal expenses arising from a divorce are usually considered non-deductible personal expenses, unless they are related to obtaining (collecting) alimony or separate maintenance or can be shown to be tax advice related to obtaining or paying alimony/separate maintenance (NOTE: the Tax Cuts and Jobs Act eliminates miscellaneous itemized deductions subject to the 2% AGI floor as an itemized deduction beginning in 2018). But if one spouse is required to pay the other spouse's legal expenses, that may be considered alimony. However, paying an ex-spouse's attorney fees won't qualify as alimony if the divorce decree doesn't state that the liability to make the payments is terminated at the ex-spouse's death. **(See Chapter 12, "Legal Expenses"; & miscellaneous itemized deductions subject to the 2% AGI floor")**

Whether or not required payments, including part of a payer's pension payments, to a former spouse are considered alimony depends to a large degree on when the payments will cease in accordance with the divorce agreement. If the payments are to cease upon the death of the recipient spouse, then it is probably alimony. If the payments are to continue to be paid to the recipient's estate after death, it is probably not alimony. This is especially important in community property states when pension payments to an ex-spouse are required to be paid each year before the payer retires (based on the present value of ex-spouse's share).

Alimony has been a frequent topic in the Tax Court where the cases often are concerned with ambiguous agreements. A payment may arguably qualify as alimony and it also arguably may not. One of the most common things in a divorce agreement is a lack of a provision that payments terminate on the death of the recipient. If payments don't terminate on death, is it more of a property division rather than alimony? The quirk is that just because the agreement doesn't say payments terminate on death doesn't mean that the payments continue after death. That will sometimes depend on state law and will not be readily apparent.

Recapture Provisions – When the divorce or separation agreement designates all or a portion of any required payments as a "property settlement," such payments are not includable in the recipient's gross income as alimony. And no gain or loss is recognized on the transfer of property resulting from a divorce. However, the "recapture provisions" prevent alimony from being disguised as property settlement payments, by stating that a reduction of $15,000 in alimony payments during the first 3 post-separation years results in recapture of property settlement payments as alimony. Recapture can occur only in the 3rd calendar year after payments begin and should be reported on Form 1040 as income from alimony—cross out "received" and write in "recapture." Exceptions are death or remarriage before the end of the 3rd year. Payments made pursuant to a temporary support order are not subject to recapture – the entire amounts are included as alimony.

Social Security Benefits

Social Security recipients get a 2% cost-of-living adjustment in their monthly benefit starting in January 2018. Annual Social Security benefits are reported on Form SSA-1099, Box 5. Up to 85% of social security benefits, including Tier 1 Railroad Retirement Benefits (reported on Form RRB-1099-R), are taxable unearned income. Zero to 85% of your social security benefits are taxable depending on how much other income you have. If your "provisional income" exceeds the base amounts of $25,000 (single, head-of-household, and married filing separately) and $32,000 (married filing jointly), up to 50% of your benefits are taxable. If your provisional income exceeds the base amounts of $34,000 (single, head-of-household, and married filing separately) and $44,000 (married filing jointly), up to 85% of your social security benefits are taxable. If you are married filing separately, and you did not live apart for the whole year, each spouse has to pay ordinary income tax on 85% of their social security benefits no matter how much other income they have, i.e. the provisional income rules do not apply. Provisional income = Modified Adjusted Gross Income (MAGI) + ½ of social security payments received in the current year. MAGI = Adjusted Gross Income (AGI), less social security payments received in current year + higher education expense deductions + deduction for interest on qualified student loans + tax exempt interest income. **(See Chapter 2, "Payroll Tax")**
www.irs.gov/pub/irs-pdf/p915.pdf#page=20

Workers' compensation payments that reduce Social Security benefits are treated as a Social Security benefit received during the year and, therefore, are indirectly taxable (Box 5 of Form SSA-1099 is the taxable amount – not reduced by any amount, such as a workers' compensation offset, shown in Box 3), i.e. workers' compensation paid in lieu of Social Security benefits is taxable ordinary income. **(See Chapter 8, "Workers' Compensation")**

The full retirement age for Social Security (SS) benefits has been 66 years of age for a long time, but under the TCJA, the full retirement age gradually increases to 67 years of age for Americans born after 1954. If you were born in 1955, your full retirement age is 66 and 2 months; 1956 – 66 and 4 months; 1957 – 66 and 6 months; 1958 – 66 and 8 months; 1959 – 66 and 10 months; and 1960 or later – your full retirement age is 67. Your SS benefits will be reduced if you decide to start taking SS benefits before your full retirement age. For example, if your full retirement age is 66 in 2018, and you decide to start taking Social Security (SS) benefits at age 62, you will receive 75% of your full benefit payments. If your full retirement age is 66 and 4 months, and you decide to start taking SS benefits at age 62, you will receive 74.2% of your full benefit payments. If you work and are at full retirement age, you can earn any amount without your SS benefits being reduced. If you are younger than full retirement age when you start receiving SS benefits, $1.00 is deducted from your benefits for each $2.00 of earned income above $17,040 in 2018 ($16,920 in 2017). However, the benefit reductions are not truly lost if you earn more than $17,040 in 2018, i.e. your benefit will be increased at full retirement age to account for the benefits withheld due to earlier earnings. If you reach full retirement age during 2018, $1.00 is deducted for each $3.00 earned above $45,360 in 2018 ($44,880 in 2017) until the month you reach full retirement age, so you won't lose any benefits if you make $45,360 or less before you reach full retirement age in 2018. If you work for more than one employer in 2018, and Social Security taxes of more than $7,979 ($128,700 x 6.2%) are withheld from your wages in the taxable year, the excess may be claimed as a credit on Line 65 in the "Payments" section of Form 1040.

The Social Security wage base is $128,700 in 2018 ($127,200 in 2017). The maximum Social Security benefit an individual can receive per month in 2018 is $2,788 or $33,456 for the year. You have to have $1,320 of earned income in order to earn one Social Security quarter of credit in 2018, so earning $5,280 anytime during 2018 will net you the maximum four quarters of credits for the year. You need 40 quarters of coverage to qualify for Social Security retirement benefits (10 years).

The tax treatment of the "repayment of Social Security benefits as a result of overpayment" depends on the amount. Any repayment of benefits must be subtracted from the gross amount of Social Security benefits received in 2018, regardless of whether the repayment was for a benefit you received in 2018 or in an earlier year. If the repayment is more than your total benefits in 2018, you may be entitled to a credit as long as the benefits had been included in gross income in an earlier year.

Individuals who misplace their SSA-1099 can obtain a replacement by setting up an online Social Security account where they can print the form. You can go to www.socialsecurity.gov/myaccount to establish an online account.

Social Security Spousal Benefits

When you file for your Social Security retirement benefits, your spouse may also be eligible for an additional benefit based on your earnings, even if your spouse has never worked and never paid Social Security taxes. But the spouse must be at least age 62 or any age if caring for a qualifying child (a child who is under age 16 or is disabled and receiving Social Security disability benefits). The spousal benefit can be as much as one-half of your benefit based on the spouse's age. However, if the spouse begins receiving benefits before full retirement age (probably 66) the spouse will receive a reduced benefit. If a spouse is eligible for a Social Security retirement benefit based on his or her own earnings, and that benefit is higher than the spousal benefit, then he or she will receive the higher benefit.

Newly divorced individuals share rights to their former spouses' Social Security benefits, and they don't have to wait for their exes to apply for those benefits before they can apply for the benefits themselves. For example, if your ex-husband has not applied for his Social Security benefits, but can qualify for benefits and is age 62 or older, you can start receiving benefits if you have been divorced for two or more years. For divorced persons, the Social

Security spousal benefit is equal to one-half of a former spouses' full retirement age benefit, but only if the spouse applies after reaching full retirement age (probably 66). The divorced former spouse gets only 35% of their exes' Social Security benefit if he or she applies at age 62, which is the earliest age for eligibility.

Social Security Disability Benefits

Social Security disability benefits are taxable to the same extent as regular Social Security benefits. However, Social Security disability income (SSDI) received by a child as a result of a parent's disability is usually not taxable to the child. Because it can take years to receive SSDI benefits, most people receive a lump-sum amount, which includes back payments. Paying tax on this amount in one year is a mistake—the IRS allows taxes on this lump-sum payment to be spread over previous tax years using the current year's tax return, without having to file amended returns.

Taxpayers who get a Social Security disability benefit will receive a Form SSA-1099 each year they receive benefits. If you get a lump-sum payment when you receive your first Form SSA-1099, the form should show in Box 3 the exact amount of your lump sum that was accrued in previous years – each year will be listed separately alongside the total amount paid. The lump-sum payment can be spread over previous years on the current year's tax return, using prior years' income amounts. The formula for doing the computation is highly technical and confusing and may have to be done by a tax professional. However, if your income is about the same for each of the years over which your lump-sum SSDI benefits are spread, you most likely will pay the same taxes as if all of the lump-sum benefits are allocable to the year in which the lump-sum benefits are received.

The maximum monthly amount of income that you can still earn while collecting Social Security disability benefits in 2018 is $1,180 ($1,170 in 2017), unless you are blind, then the maximum monthly amount is $1,970 (also $1,950 in 2017).

Workers' compensation paid in lieu of Social Security disability benefits is taxable. By law, workers compensation payments offset Social Security disability benefits dollar for dollar, and therefore, are taxable to the same extent as Social Security payments when this occurs. **(See Chapter 8, "Workers' Compensation")**

Beginning Oct. 3, 2015, the IRS stopped withholding payments of Social Security disability benefits from taxpayers for unpaid taxes.

Conversion of Traditional IRAs to Roth IRAs

A Rollover from a traditional IRA to a Roth IRA is taxable unearned income reported on Form 1099-R as a distribution for the current year, and taxpayers are taxed at their highest regular tax rate on the amount converted, but the 10% penalty imposed on early withdrawals does not apply. The conversion may occur directly, through a trustee-to-trustee transfer, or indirectly, via a distribution to the taxpayer that he or she must deposit into a Roth IRA within 60 days. The distribution must happen in 2018 to qualify as a 2018 rollover or conversion, but the deposit may take place in 2019, as long as it occurs within 60 days of the distribution. Married taxpayers filing separately are not allowed to make a conversion of a traditional IRA to a Roth IRA. **(See Below, "Distributions from Retirement Plans: Traditional IRAs and Qualified Retirement Plans")**

www.irs.gov/pub/irs-pdf/f1099r.pdf   www.irs.gov/pub/irs-pdf/i1099r.pdf

Under the Tax Cuts and Jobs Act (TCJA), for tax years beginning after Dec. 31, 2017, you cannot undo your decision to rollover a traditional IRA to a Roth IRA and re-characterize the Roth IRA back into a traditional IRA and recoup the taxes paid on the conversion. For 2017 and prior years, if you converted a traditional IRA to a Roth IRA, you had until October 15th to undo your decision and recoup the taxes paid. And, if you had already filed your 2017 tax return, you could amend it. For example, if you converted to a Roth and owed 25% tax on the amount converted and the Roth lost value in the meantime, you could save the taxes paid by re-characterizing the Roth IRA back into a traditional IRA by 10/15/2018 (due date of the 2017 tax return including the allowed 6-month extension). But no more beginning with the 2018 tax year.

Taxpayers with MAGIs of more than $100,000 who are eligible to convert a traditional IRA to a Roth in 2018 may not be eligible to contribute to the Roth annually because the MAGI thresholds for contributing to a Roth in 2018 are between $120,000 - $135,0000 (single and head-of-household), and between $189,000 - $199,000 (married filing jointly). However, some high-income investors can get around contribution limits through what's known as a "back-door" Roth IRA, where you contribute to a nondeductible traditional IRA, then immediately convert it to a Roth. In this regard, as long as you act before any earnings accumulate, you won't owe any tax, unless you have other traditional IRAs. For example, suppose you contribute $5,000 to a traditional IRA then immediately convert it to a Roth, but you have another traditional IRA that holds $95,000 in contributions. Because the $5,000 represents just 5% of the new total of $100,000, only 5% or $250, of the $5,000 conversion would be tax-free. **(See Chapter 11, "Roth IRA")**

Three factors to consider when contemplating a Roth conversion are: Tax rate differential; use of outside funds to pay the income tax; and the time horizon. Because if the taxpayer's current and future tax rates are the same, and the income tax liability is paid with funds inside the IRA, the taxpayer is in the same economic position when converting to a Roth IRA as if no conversion took place. However, a taxpayer who uses outside funds to pay the income tax liability on a Roth conversion is in a better economic position than if the income tax liability is paid with funds inside the IRA. The time horizon is critical, because the longer the funds can grow in a tax-exempt environment, the better the economic result.

 Reasons Not to Convert to a Roth IRA – (1) You expect to be in a lower tax bracket during the traditional IRA withdrawal period (after age 70 ½) than in the year of conversion; (2) your AGI in the year of conversion will be higher, which could put you in a higher tax bracket and affect the amount of Social Security benefits taxed; and (3) the 7 ½ % (10% starting in 2019) of AGI floor for including medical expenses as an itemized deduction will be higher, which might result in no medical expense deduction as part of your itemized deduction. Also, converting to a Roth may increase your Part B Medicare insurance premium. **(See Chapter 12, "Medical Expenses")**

 Reasons to Convert to a Roth IRA – Converting a traditional IRA to a Roth IRA is a hedge against higher income taxes in the future, due either to a general elevation of the tax rate structure or to the taxpayer moving into a higher tax bracket during the traditional IRA withdrawal phase. Converting is not really a mechanism for taking advantage of diminished investment values in your traditional IRA due to the decline in the stock market, unless the decline has resulted in your investments being depressed to the extent that the current value of your tax-deferred retirement account is less than the contributions originally contributed to the account, at which point the amount converted to the Roth IRA will never be taxed. You will have the opportunity for the retirement account to grow from then on and be distributed free of any future income tax; and you will have the ability to retain the funds in the Roth IRA indefinitely beyond retirement which provides a very effective means for accumulating assets to pass on to your heirs free of future income tax. Heirs will be subject to required minimum distribution (RMD) rules when they inherit Roth IRAs, but they will not owe income tax on the funds they withdraw. **(See Below, "Required Minimum Distributions")**

Even if your IRA account has not declined to the extent that the current value is less than the contributions originally made to the account, you might decide at some point to convert the total amount of contributions originally made to traditional IRAs to a Roth IRA, and thus, take advantage of the reasons set forth above in favor of conversion.

2017 Traditional IRA Converted to a Roth and Re-Characterized back to a Traditional IRA (NOTE: This can no longer be done beginning in 2018) – You don't want to pay taxes before changing your mind, if possible. No formal election is required for the re-characterization. However, the taxpayer must notify the trustee of each IRA involved in the trustee-to-trustee transfer by the due date of the tax return, including the allowed 6-month extension. The process is simple: ask your IRA administrator to re-characterize the account, then file an amended return with the IRS and you'll get a refund of the taxes you paid. Then, you can reconvert to a Roth after 30 days and report the amount as 2019 income. The only exception to re-characterization by October 15th is in the case of fraud – if you convert your traditional IRA into a Roth and invest the funds in a company that turns out to be defrauding its clients, the IRS will grant you relief past the October 15th due date to elect to undo the conversion.

When an entire traditional IRA is converted into a Roth IRA and subsequently re-characterized, the process is relatively simple – the entire Roth is transferred back to a traditional IRA, including any gains or losses that occurred during the temporary conversion period. However, when the original conversion is added to an existing Roth account, the re-characterization must include a pro rata share of the gains or losses of the entire account.

- **Example** – You convert $100,000 of Z corporation stock that is in a traditional IRA to a Roth IRA and add it to an already existing $400,000 Roth IRA account that is invested in a moderately aggressive mutual fund, making the total in the Roth after the conversion $500,000. After the conversion, Z corporation stock declines 30% to $70,000, while the rest of the Roth account increases 20% to $480,000. You want to re-characterize the Z corporation stock conversion, because it triggered ordinary income tax on $100,000 but is now worth only $70,000. However, in this case, you can't re-characterize just the Z corporation stock. Instead, you must re-characterize a pro rata share of the entire account – the account balance started at $500,000 on the conversion date but is now worth $550,000 ($70,000 + $480,000), so in the aggregate it is up 10%. Therefore, you have to re-characterize $110,000 – all of the Z corporation stock worth $70,000 and another $40,000 of the investments that were in the Roth IRA before the conversion ($70,000 + $40,000 = $110,000). But this would be a very disadvantageous move, so what do you do?

What you should have done with the $100,000 of Z corporation stock in the traditional IRA was to convert it into a stand-alone second Roth IRA, instead of mixing it with the first Roth IRA. If it then declines, you can re-characterize only the $70,000 – the actual value of the entire second Roth IRA and leave the first IRA worth $480,000 untouched. Since it is more favorable to re-characterize a particular investment that has gone down in value after a Roth conversion, it is now a standard best practice to do new conversions to stand-alone Roth IRAs whenever there is a chance of material decline and a possibility of the need to re-characterize. You can always merge the Roth IRAs into one Roth IRA after the re-characterization window has passed.

Conversion from Pre-Tax Qualified Plans to Roth Qualified Plans

Just like rollovers From traditional IRA's to Roth IRA's, rollovers from traditional qualified plans to Roth qualified plans are included in taxable income (reported to taxpayer on Form 1099-R) as a distribution for the tax year, and taxpayers are taxed at their highest regular tax rate on the amount converted in the year of conversion. However, the 10% penalty imposed on early withdrawals does not apply. Participants in 401(k) plans with in-plan Roth conversion features may make transfers to a Roth 401(k) at any time. Also, participants in eligible state and local government 457(b) and 403(b) plans (but not plans of nonprofit organizations) are allowed to convert and contribute amounts to Roth accounts (applies to the Federal Thrift Savings Plan). However, the plans must be amended to permit these rollovers before they can happen.

While the tax-free nature of a Roth 401(k) plan can be appealing, just like Roth IRAs, when you convert your pre-tax 401(k) to a Roth 401(k), you can't change your mind and re-characterize the conversion when the market value in the Roth 401(k) declines after the conversion. Also, unlike a Roth IRA, required minimum distributions (RMDs) that don't apply to Roth IRAs (until they are inherited), apply to Roth 401(k) plans. When you reach the age of 70 ½, you must start taking RMDs from Roth 401(k) plans each year, just like pre-tax 401(k) plans. Also, you must satisfy the RMD requirement from each qualified plan and cannot elect to take your total RMDs from just one plan. However, you can avoid taking RMDs from Roth 401(k) plans by simply rolling over the Roth 401(k) plan to a Roth IRA before you reach age 70 ½. This may seem like a "no-brainer," but there are other considerations. For example, creditor protection is not as strong with an IRA as it is with a 401(k) plan.

Distributions made from a taxpayer's designated Roth account to both the taxpayer and to an eligible retirement plan in a direct rollover are excluded from income and are allocated as follows: the contribution amounts are allocated first to the direct rollover, rather than being allocated pro rata to the taxpayer and to the retirement account. Also, the taxpayer can direct the allocation of the contributions and earnings that are included in the distribution to multiple designations, applying the same allocation rules that apply to distributions from other types of accounts. This is a taxpayer friendly rule that was recently adopted by the IRS, eliminating the requirement that each disbursement from a designated Roth account that is directly rolled over to an eligible retirement plan be treated as a separate distribution from any amount paid directly to the employee. **(See Chapter 9, "Rollover Distributions from Roth Accounts")**

Distributions from Retirement Plans: Traditional IRAs and Qualified Retirement Plans

Distributions from traditional IRAs, qualified retirement plans, defined benefit plans, and other retirement plans (reported to taxpayers on Form 1099-R) are taxable unearned income. This includes qualified employee retirement and pension benefit plans—401(k), 403(b), and 457(b) plans; SEPs, SIMPLEs, and defined benefit plans, as well as traditional IRAs. You are required to start receiving required minimum distributions (RMDs) from these plans by April 1st following the year you turn 70 ½, or pay a penalty. A "qualified" retirement account, including an IRA, is creditor protected under State law and in bankruptcy. However, qualified accounts are not protected from the IRS. There is a 10% penalty for early withdrawals from qualified retirement accounts before age 59 ½ unless the withdrawals are a series of equal annual payments over the taxpayer's lifetime. However, disabled persons can make withdrawals before age 59 ½ without having to pay the penalty. Also, effective for distributions after 2015,

federal public safety officers will be allowed to make withdrawals at the age of 50 without having to pay the 10% penalty. The definition of public safety officers also includes nuclear materials couriers, United States Capital police, Supreme Court police, and diplomatic security agents. Individuals making early withdrawals before age 59 ½ may be able to report the 10% penalty directly on their 1040 tax return but in some cases they may have to file Form 5329 with their tax return to pay the 10% penalty. **(See Below, "Required Minimum Distributions"); (See Chapter 9, "Rollovers from Qualified Retirement Plans and Traditional IRAs")**
www.irs.gov/pub/irs-pdf/f5329.pdf   www.irs.gov/pub/irs-pdf/i5329.pdf

Traditional IRAs – The 10% penalty for early withdrawals can be avoided if an early distribution is: (1) to pay medical insurance premiums for a person who received unemployment compensation for 12 consecutive weeks; (2) to pay qualified higher education expenses for the IRA owner, spouse, child or grandchild, including graduate level courses – qualified expenses include tuition, fees, textbooks, supplies, and room and board for at least a ½ time student; (3) to pay for medical expenses of the IRA owner, spouse or a dependent; (4) due to the death or disability of the participant; or (5) is to pay a first-time homebuyer's expenses up to a $10,000 limitation – to qualify as a first-time homebuyer, the taxpayer must not have had an ownership interest in a principal residence during the two-year period ending on the date that the new home is acquired, and the distribution must be used to pay for qualified acquisition costs before the close of the 120ᵗʰ day after you receive the funds. Form 5329 is used to claim an exemption from the 10% penalty. **(See Chapter 12, "Medical Expenses")**

Reservists and National Guard members called to active duty can withdraw money from their IRAs, 401(k), and 403(b) retirement plans without paying the 10% penalty, but the money has to be returned to the plan within two years after active duty ends to avoid paying the penalty. They must be called to active duty for at least 179 days or more to qualify. If you served on active duty after 12/31/2007, you are eligible for retroactive tax relief if you've already paid a penalty. You can claim a refund from the IRS. A divorce-related transfer will not trigger the 10% penalty after the IRA owner has started taking a series of equal payments before age 59 ½, even though the transfer lowered the payout amount to the IRA owner. If you alter a series of pre-59 ½ equal payments due to financial need, all prior withdrawals will be hit with the 10% penalty. **(See Chapter 3, "Marital Status and Divorce")**

A portion of a traditional IRA distribution may be excluded from taxable income if a taxpayer has made nondeductible contributions to the IRA in certain years, which should be shown on Form 8606. The excluded portion is not subject to the 10% penalty if the taxpayer withdraws the money before age 59 ½. **(See Chapter 11, "IRA Contributions")**

You cannot take a loan from your IRA account. If you have a short-term cash need, you can withdraw funds from your IRA account, but the identical amount of funds withdrawn must be returned to the same IRA account within 60 days or the distribution will be taxed, and you will also have to pay the 10% early withdrawal penalty.

Qualified Retirement Plans – 401(k), 403(b), and 457(b) Plans – The 10% penalty for early withdrawals from a 401(k) or another qualified retirement plan can be avoided if it is: to pay for deductible medical expenses; is due to a participant's separation from service after the calendar year in which the participant has reached age 55; is due to the death or disability of the participant; or in case of another hardship such as: inability to pay for medical care expenses; to prevent eviction or foreclosure from a principal residence; to pay burial expenses for a deceased parent, spouse or child; or to pay repair damages to a residence that qualifies for a casualty loss deduction without regard to the over 10% itemized deduction floor. Diabetics don't automatically qualify as being disabled – the illness must be to the degree that prevents the person from engaging in gainful activity. The employee must have exhausted all other resources, including other distributions and non-taxable loans from pension plans to qualify for the hardship determination. Form 5329 is used to claim an exemption from the 10% penalty. **(See Chapter 12, "Medical Expenses"; & "Casualty, Disaster, and Theft Losses")**

The IRS has issued final regulations clarifying the rules regarding the tax treatment of payments from qualified retirement plans for accident and health insurance. The final regulations effective Jan. 1, 2015, state that amounts held in qualified plans that are used to pay accident or health insurance premiums are taxable distributions except for certain exceptions. One exception, is for retired public safety officers and certain federal employees. Beginning in 2007, Retired Public Safety Officers (Policemen and Firemen) can exclude up to $3,000 of otherwise taxable distributions from a government retirement plan for amounts withheld and paid directly to a health insurance company to pay premiums for accident or health insurance coverage, or long-term care insurance. A former public safety officer is not eligible for the exclusion unless the former employer's retirement plan offers the election. They can't claim the exclusion by paying the medical premiums themselves. The amount shown in Box 2a of Form 1099-R does not reflect this exclusion. Instead, the amount withheld is shown in Box 5 of Form 1099-R. Premiums may be for the retired public safety officer, spouse, or dependents. At the end of June 2015, Congress passed the Trade Priorities and Accountability Act of 2015 which permits early penalty free withdrawals from qualified retirement plans for certain federal law enforcement officers, federal firefighters, customs and border protection officers, and air traffic controllers.

A taxpayer can take a loan from a 401(k) or another qualified retirement plan, but not from an IRA. The loan cannot be for more than ½ of the account balance up to a maximum of $50,000, and it must be repaid in 5 years in equal payments over the 5-year period. However, if a taxpayer losses his/her job, the loan must be repaid within 60 days.

In 2017, the IRS announced that 401(k)s, 403(b)s, and 457(b)s and similar employer-sponsored retirement plans can make loans and hardship distributions to victims of Hurricanes Harvey, Irma, and Maria and members of their families. This is similar to relief provided last year to victims of Hurricane Matthew. Participants in these employer-sponsored retirement plans may be eligible to take advantage of streamlined loan procedures and liberalized hardship distribution rules. Retirement plans can provide this relief to employees and certain members of their families who live or work in the hurricane disaster areas that are designated for individual assistance by the Federal Emergency Management Agency (FEMA). To qualify for this relief, hardship withdrawals must be made by Jan. 31, 2018. Though IRA participants are barred from taking out loans, they may be eligible to receive distributions under liberalized procedures.

Defined Benefit Plans – The IRS has issued new distribution regulations for "defined benefit plans" to permit participants to elect to receive split benefits of monthly annuity payments together with a lump-sum payout without disqualifying the plan. This will enable participants to receive a portion of the plan benefits as a separate stream of monthly payments while taking the remainder in a single, lump-sum payment. The new rules encourage participants to utilize these split options by changing the minimum present value requirements for plan distributions to allow plans to simplify the treatment of certain optional forms of benefits that are paid partly in the form of an annuity and partly in a more accelerated form. Defined benefit plans are allowed to apply actuarial assumptions on interest rates and mortality benefits only to the portion of the distribution being paid in a lump sum. The partial annuity portion of the benefit is determined using the plan's regular conversion factors. It is believed that these new rules better serve plan participants against the possibility of outliving their retirement benefits.

Railroad Retirement Plans – Just like traditional IRAs, a portion of "Railroad" retirement and other plans with employee after tax contributions may be excluded from taxable income. The excluded amount must be computed using the "simplified method," where the amount of employee after tax contributions are divided by the expected number of payments to determine the excluded portion applicable to each payment. Railroad employee after tax contributions are shown in box 3 of Form RRB-1099-R (railroad pensions). The expected number of payments for computing the excluded amount is based on the taxpayer's age at the starting date of the "Annuity" (retirement age). The expected number of payments using the simplified method are: ages 55 and under, 360 payments; ages 56–60, 310 payments; ages 61–65, 260 payments; ages 66–70, 210 payments; ages 71 and over, 160 payments. In the case of an annuity payable based on the life of more than one individual (survivor annuity), the expected number of payments is based on the combined ages of the annuitants: 110 and under, 410 payments; 111–120, 360 payments; 121–130, 310 payments; 131–140, 260 payments; 141 and over, 210 payments. **(See Above, "Traditional IRAs")**

- **Example** - Assume that the after-tax contributions shown in box 3 of Form RRB-1099-R is $50,000, and the taxpayer retires at the age of 65 (no survivor annuity) – divide $50,000 by 260 = $192 per month; therefore, the amount of each annual payment that is excluded from taxable income after the taxpayer's retirement is $2,304 ($192 X 12).

Federal Disaster Loss Relief – On Sept. 29, 2017, the "Disaster Tax Relief and Airport and Airway Extension Act of 2017" was passed, which provides temporary tax relief to victims in disaster areas in 2016 and 2017. The Act eliminates the 10% penalty on early withdrawals of up to $100,000 from qualified retirement plans, including 401(k)s, 403(b) governmental plans, IRAs and tax-sheltered annuities for victims of presidentially declared disasters. These "qualified disaster distributions" are defined as distributions from an eligible retirement plan made on or after Jan. 1, 2016, and before Jan. 1, 2018, to an individual whose principal place of abode at any time during the calendar year 2016 or who resided in the affected areas in 2017 and sustained an economic loss by reason of the events that gave rise to the Presidential disasters. Such withdrawals are normally included in income in the year in which they are distributed. The Act allows the withdrawals to be re-contributed back to retirement plans at any time over a 3-year period without any tax consequences and allows taxpayers to spread out any income inclusion amounts resulting from the withdrawals ratably over a 3-year period. Also, qualified withdrawals aren't treated as rollover distributions, which are generally subject to 20% withholding. The Act also allows the re-contribution of certain retirement plan withdrawals made for home purchases or construction, which were received after Feb. 28, 2017 and before Sept. 21, 2017, where the home purchase or construction was cancelled on account of Hurricanes Harvey, Irma, or Maria (without tax consequences). With respect to retirement plan loans, the Act: increased the maximum amount that a participant or beneficiary can borrow from a qualified employer plan from $50,000 to $100,000. of Hurricanes Harvey, Irma, and Maria that occurred in 2017. **(See Chapter 3, "Federal Disaster Loss Relief")**

Required Minimum Distributions

A taxpayer must begin taking Required Minimum Distributions (RMDs) from traditional IRAs and qualified retirement plans no later than April 1 of the year following the year in which he/she turns age 70 ½. RMDs from traditional IRAs and other qualified retirement plans are reported to the taxpayer on Form 1099-R. There is a penalty for failure to take Required Minimum Distributions, which is a tax equal to 50% of the amount the RMD exceeds actual distributions taken by the taxpayer during the year. RMDs are taxable income, except for the nontaxable portion. A nontaxable portion, in the case of traditional IRAs, is based on any nondeductible contributions you may have made to your IRAs in certain years. Qualified defined benefit pension plans are not included in the computation of annual RMDs.

If you reach age 70 ½ in 2018, you can either take your first RMD by the end of 2018 or delay it until April 1, 2019. However, if you take your 1st RMD after the end of 2018, you will have to take your 2nd RMD by Dec. 31, 2019, which means that you will be taxed on two RMDs in the same year. After the first RMD, you must take your RMDs by Dec. 31st every year. For determining the first year a taxpayer has to take a RMD, the IRS specifically states to use your age on your birthday in the year you turn 70 ½. For example, if your birthday is between Jan. 1st and June 30th, the first year of your initial RMD is the year when you turn age 70. But if your birthday is between July 1st and Dec. 31st, the first year of your initial RMD is the year when you turn age 71.

- **Exception** – if you continue working after age 70 ½, and you don't own over 5% of the business that employs you, you can put off taking RMDs from that employer's plan for as long as you keep working (but the exception only applies to your current employer's plan, not to IRAs or former employers' plans).

Annual RMDs are calculated in accordance with IRS actuarial tables. Your RMD is always based on your IRA and qualified retirement plan account balances at the end of the previous year. The best way to determine your annual RMD requirement is to use a RMD calculator. Several RMD calculators are available online and can be found by doing a web search. Using a RMD calculator will tell you what your RMD should be for the current year. If you have multiple IRAs, you're supposed to figure the RMD for each account separately, but you don't have to take a withdrawal from each account. You can take the required amount from any IRA or combination of IRAs. In reality, you can simply add the account balances of all your IRAs, including SIMPLE IRAs and SEPs, as of the end of the prior year, and divide it by your life expectancy factor – use an RMD calculator. However, RMDs must be figured separately for each of your 401(k)s, 403(b)s, and other retirement accounts. Do not combine a 401(k) account with other 401(k) accounts or with your IRAs when determining RMDs. Also, even though RMDs are based on your account balances at the end to the previous year (2017), the non-taxable portion (if any) is always based on your account balances at the end of the current year (2018).

- **Example** – Suppose your traditional IRA and SIMPLE IRA account balances were $376,696 on Dec. 31, 2017. Therefore, your RMD for 2018 is $14,215 (using RMD calculator based on account balance of $376,696 on 12/31/2017). The balance of your nondeductible IRA contributions, including those made for 2019 from Jan. 1, 2019 through April 17, 2019, is $15,494. Your traditional IRA and SIMPLE IRA account balances are $374,471 on Dec. 31, 2018. Therefore, the nontaxable portion of your RMD for 2018 is $567 ($374, 471 + $14,215 = $388,686; $15,494/$388,686 = .03986 X $14,215 = $567). The taxable portion of your RMD for 2018 is $13,648 ($14,215 - $567 = $13,648).

If your husband or wife is more than 10 years younger than you and the sole beneficiary of one, but not all, of your IRAs, you'll need to use different life expectancy factors for different accounts.

You can take RMDs in cash or in kind, meaning in stock. The option you use depends on what's in your account and what you want to do with it. You don't have to sell stock to meet your obligation, but be sure that if you're taking out stock, you use the fair market value (FMV) of the stock to figure your RMD. The stock you take out has a zero basis, so be sure to hold onto the stock for more than one year to qualify for the tax-favored long-term capital gain rates, because what you paid for the stock in the IRA and the time you had it in the IRA account doesn't count.

Required minimum distributions (RMDs) from IRAs and qualified retirement accounts cannot be put into a Roth IRA account. However, if you don't need to spend the distributions you can use the RMD to pay the tax due on a Roth conversion, i.e. retirees can use their current unwanted RMD to pay the taxes due upon converting their traditional IRA to a Roth. And once converted there will no longer be an RMD requirement.

If you miss an RMD, you can escape the 50% penalty by asking the IRS to waive it. This can be done where there is a reasonable cause for the failure, such as an illness or bad advice from the financial institution with which you hold your account. You must complete Form 5329 (lines 50 and 51), and on line 52 enter "RC" and the amount you want waived. Subtract this amount from the total shortfall. Attach a statement to the form indicating the reason why you think the penalty should be waived. You need only pay the penalty on any portion of the shortfall you do not ask the IRS to waive. The IRS will review your waiver request and inform you of whether it is granted. The IRS generally is liberal in granting such a request.
www.irs.gov/pub/irs-pdf/f5329.pdf   www.irs.gov/pub/irs-pdf/i5329.pdf

Tax-Free Distributions for Charitable Purposes – Taxpayers who are required to take RMDs can take tax-free distributions of up to $100,000 from traditional IRAs for charitable purposes, and these distributions can go to qualified charitable organizations in lieu of RMDs (reported on Form 1040 – write "QCD"). The money must go directly from the IRA trustee to the charity (You can't receive the distribution and then donate it to the charitable organization). This provision was made permanent by the "Protecting Americans from Tax Hikes Act of 2015." Taxpayers who have already taken their RMDs can't return their IRA payouts to the IRA trustee to be used as a tax-free distribution directly to a charitable organization. A special rule treats transferred amounts as coming first from taxable funds, instead of proportionately from taxable and nontaxable funds, as would be the case for regular RMDs. Not all charities are eligible. For example, donor-advised funds and supporting organizations are not eligible recipients. Taxpayers who take advantage of the up to $100,000 tax-free distributions from their IRAs are not allowed a charitable itemized deduction for the contribution. **(See Chapter 12, "Tax-Free Distributions from IRAs for Charitable Purposes")**

Qualified Longevity Annuities (QLAC) – Final regulations issued in July 2014 permit a traditional IRA owner to enter into a Qualified Longevity Annuity Contract (QLAC) and exclude the premium paid for the QLAC from his or her IRA account balance(s) that are used to determine his or her annual Required Minimum Distribution (RMD) after reaching age 70 ½. The premiums paid for QLACs are limited to the lesser of $125,000 (adjusted for inflation in $10,000 increments), or 25% of the participant's IRA account balance at the date of payment of the premium. In fact, this provision applies not only to IRAs, but also to account balances in 401(k)s, 403(b)s, and eligible government 457 plans, as well as to IRAs (but not to Roth IRAs or defined benefit plans). IRA accounts are aggregated for the percentage limit, but employer plans are considered separately. However, for the dollar limit, IRAs and employer plans are all aggregated together. The fair market value of a QLAC is the premium paid on the date of purchase which counts toward the QLAC limit. The contract must state that it is intended to be a QLAC. The regulations apply to QLACs purchased on or after July 2, 2014, and to existing annuity contracts converted to QLACs.

- **Example** – Suppose a taxpayer who turns age 70 ½ in 2017, has an IRA account balance of $500,000 at the end 2016, so his RMD for 2017 would be $18,248. However, if the taxpayer uses 25% of the balance in his IRA ($500,000 X 25% = $125,000) to purchase a Qualifying Longevity Annuity Contract (QLAC) paying a premium of $125,000 for the QLAC, then his RMD for 2017 would be reduced to $13,686 from $18,248. Which means the taxpayer would only have to pay taxes on an RMD of $13,686, rather than $18,248 in 2017 (a tax savings of about $1,150 in 2017).

QLACs are annuities that begin at an advanced age, usually 80 or 85, allowing participants to hedge against the risk of outliving their retirement savings. QLACs are required to begin distributions no later than the first day of the month following the purchaser's 85th birthday, but can provide for an earlier starting date. Participants are allowed to exclude the value of the QLAC from the account balance that is used to determine RMDs. QLACs cannot be invested into variable or index type annuities, and they can have a return of premium death benefit before and after income starts. QLACs must not provide any commutation benefit, cash surrender right or similar feature; however, the IRS is authorized to create exceptions. If the sole beneficiary is a surviving spouse, the spouse is permitted to receive a life annuity, provided it does not exceed 100% of the annuity the participant received. However, the final regulations include a special exception that would allow a plan to comply with any applicable requirement to provide a qualified pre-retirement survivor annuity. To encourage retirees to purchase QLACs without worrying that they may not receive their investment back, the final regulations permit a QLAC to provide for a single-sum death benefit to be paid to a beneficiary in an amount equal to the excess of the QLAC premium payment over the payments made to the participant (in other words, a return of premium). If the QLAC is providing or will provide a life annuity to a surviving spouse, it may also provide a return of premium after both the participant and spouse die. A return of premium payment must be paid no later than the end of the calendar year following the calendar year in which the participant dies or the surviving spouse dies, whichever applies. If the participant dies after the annuity beginning date, the return of premium is treated as a RMD for the year in which it is paid and is not eligible for rollover. A non-spouse beneficiary may receive a reduced annuity, but a non-spouse beneficiary would not receive an annuity if there is a return of premium feature.

Since QLACs are often purchased many years before its payments are scheduled to begin, the regulations require annual reporting to the IRS and the participant. The reports must begin in the calendar year in which the premiums are first paid and end with the earlier of the year the participant for whom the contract was purchased turns 85 or dies. However, if the participant who dies has a surviving spouse as the sole beneficiary, reporting must continue until the year the spouse's distributions commence or the spouse dies, if earlier.

Distributions from "Nonqualified" Tax Deferred Annuities

Distributions from "nonqualified" tax deferred annuities are usually taxable unearned income reported on Form 1099-R. Nonqualified tax deferred annuities are issued by insurance companies, and are generally funded with voluntary contributions that have already been taxed, and the owner of the annuity must start receiving equal periodic payments over 5, 10, 20 years, etc. before the already taxed contributions will be taken into account.

Unlike qualified employee retirement plans and traditional IRAs, these contracts do not require a person to start receiving required minimum distributions or substantial equal periodic payments by age 70 ½. However, like qualified plans there is a 10% early withdrawal penalty prior to age 59 ½ unless payments are made because of disability or other permissible reasons. Regardless, most nonqualified annuities allow annual penalty free withdrawals of up to 10% of the value each year prior to maturity. There is no penalty if the payment is from an annuity contract under a qualified personal injury settlement or from an immediate annuity, which is a single-premium annuity where the starting date is no more than one year from the date of purchase.

Loans taken from nonqualified tax deferred annuities are treated just like cash withdrawals. If you borrow against the contract, you are taxed in the same way as if you'd taken a distribution. This distribution is taxable to the extent that the cash value of the contract exceeds your contributions (the premiums paid into the contract). If the insurance contract was purchased after August 13, 1982, withdrawals are considered interest only, which is taxed as ordinary income. If the contract was purchased before Aug. 14, 1982, the withdrawals are usually considered principal first and, therefore, may not be taxable.

When substantially equal periodic payments begin ("Annuitization"), the nontaxable portion of each payment is computed by using the "General Rule" method—dividing the contributions (principal) by the "total expected return" to get a percentage, which is used to compute the nontaxable portion of each annual equal payment. Annual equal payments are computed by dividing the total expected return by either the fixed number of years over which payments will be received, or if for life, by the multiple found in the Treasury (IRS) Tables.

- **Example** – The multiple for age 62 is 22.5. Therefore, equal annual payments for life are computed by dividing the total expected return by 22.5. The Small Business Jobs Act allows an owner of a nonqualified annuity to split up the contract by taking a portion of the benefits as a separate stream of annuity payments (must be for 10 years or more, or over the lives of one or more individuals) while leaving the remaining balance of the contract untouched. The remaining balance of the contract will continue to accumulate earnings on a tax-deferred basis. This provision applies to payouts after 12/31/2010.

If you want to move the tax deferred annuity to another insurance company, you can do so tax free via a "Section 1035 exchange" (it must be a direct exchange in order to avoid being taxed). Cashing out a policy triggers tax, even when the funds received are used to purchase an annuity from another insurance company. Also, you can't exchange on a tax-free basis an annuity contract for a life insurance contract or endowment policy. Some annuities cannot be passed on to heirs because payments cease at the owner's death. However, other annuities have guaranteed payouts, which means that amounts that have not been paid to the owner will be paid to named beneficiaries. Annuity payments made to beneficiaries are taxable in the same way as they would have been had they been made to the contract owner before death.

IRAs and Retirement Plans Inherited by Beneficiaries

Traditional IRA's, Roth IRA's, and qualified retirement plans inherited by beneficiaries are taxable unearned income to beneficiaries based on the same amount as they would have been taxable to the original owner. However, taxable distributions received by a beneficiary who is under age 59 ½ are not subject to the 10% penalty. Also, individuals who inherit a traditional IRA partly funded by nondeductible contributions should take care in reporting taxes owed, by filing Form 8606 to show that taxes have already been paid on the nondeductible contributions.

(See Above, "Traditional IRAs"); (See Chapter 21, "Beneficiaries of Estates"); (See Chapter 22," Basis of Property Inherited or Gifted")
www.irs.gov/pub/irs-prior/f8606--2015.pdf   www.irs.gov/pub/irs-prior/f8606--2015.pdf

A surviving spouse beneficiary who inherits a traditional IRA or a qualified retirement plan can keep it separate as an inherited IRA, or can roll-it-over into an IRA or qualified retirement plan in his or her own name. Whether a surviving spouse should keep the IRA separate as an inherited IRA or roll it over and treat it as his/her own depends on the circumstances. A surviving spouse who is under age 59 ½ and who keeps a traditional IRA in a separate inherited IRA can take penalty-free distributions from it, and for RMD purposes must follow beneficiary rules, meaning he/she must start to take RMDs by the end of the year after the year of the decedent's death and base the RMDs on the surviving spouse's life expectancy. However, if the traditional IRA is rolled over and treated as his or her own, then the account cannot be tapped penalty free until the spouse reaches age 59 ½. In this case the surviving spouse can name new beneficiaries and would not start RMDs until reaching age 70 ½. The rollover election is available whether or not the decedent had begun taking IRA distributions. If the decedent was required to have taken a RMD in the year of death but had not already done so, the surviving spouse, although electing to roll it over and be the owner of the IRA, must take the RMD in that year for the decedent (but only in that one year). NOTE: The rollover option can be used by the spouse for part of the IRA, i.e. the rollover need not be all or nothing. A partial rollover allows the surviving spouse under the age of 59 ½ to access some of the funds in the inherited non-rolled-over account without any early distribution penalty. **(See Above, "Required Minimum Distributions")**

A non-spouse beneficiary has two options for liquidating an inherited traditional IRA or a qualified retirement plan. The first and least desirable option is to liquidate it within five years (the 10% penalty does not apply), i.e. the distribution is taxable to the beneficiary in the year received as "income in respect of a decedent" and must be distributed to the beneficiary by the end of the 5th year following the year of death. During those 5 years no distribution is required, but it would most likely be tax advantageous to take annual distributions to keep from having to pay taxes on the total amount of the distributions all in the same year.

The second option is the "stretch option," in which a non-spouse beneficiary can make the choice to take the distributions over his or her life expectancy. A designated or "NAMED" beneficiary (other than a surviving spouse) who inherits an IRA from a relative can roll it over in a trustee-to-trustee transfer to an "Inherited IRA", and utilize the beneficiary's life expectancy (Life expectancy is determined by looking at the IRS tables in Appendix C of IRS Publication 590). The stretch option was not available for inherited employee retirement plans before 2010. However, beginning in 2010, a non-spouse beneficiary who inherited a qualified employee retirement plan (401(k), 403(b), or governmental 457 plan) must have been allowed to rollover the account to an IRA in a trustee-to-trustee transfer. Before 2010, this requirement was optional (not a plan requirement). However, in order to choose the stretch option, the beneficiary must immediately begin taking yearly RMDs, based on his/her own life expectancy. The beneficiary has to take the first RMD in the next calendar year by Dec. 31 of the calendar year following the year that the deceased died. If the beneficiary misses that date, he defaults back to the five-year rule. The inherited IRA must be set up and maintained in the name of the deceased for the benefit of the non-spouse beneficiary, such as: "Jane Smith IRA, deceased Nov. 16, 2009, FBO John Jones, beneficiary." The election is valid even if the decedent had already begun taking distributions from the IRA or retirement plan. Split inherited IRAs that have more than one beneficiary (co-beneficiaries) must take the distributions over the life expectancy of the oldest beneficiary.

An inherited IRA's beneficiaries must be set by Sept. 30th of the year following the death of the IRA owner, and if just one of the beneficiaries isn't an individual, the IRA must be liquidated using the first option discussed above – within five years for all beneficiaries. This circumstance can arise when the IRA owner names a charity or a college/university as one of the beneficiaries. However, if the charitable beneficiary is paid off from the IRA by Sept. 30th of the year following the death of the IRA owner, the remaining individual beneficiaries can take distributions over the life expectancy of the oldest beneficiary (See above).

If a beneficiary inherits an IRA from someone whose estate was big enough to be subject to the federal estate tax, the beneficiary can get an income tax deduction for the amount of estate taxes paid on the amount of the inherited IRA. For example, you inherit a $100,000 IRA, and the fact that the money was included in your benefactor's estate added $45,000 to the estate tax bill; therefore, you get to deduct that $45,000 on your income tax returns as you withdraw the money from the IRA. If you withdraw $50,000 in one year, for example, you get to claim a $22,500 itemized deduction on Schedule A (Miscellaneous Itemized Deduction Not Subject to the 2% AGI Floor). **(See Chapter 12, "Deduction for Federal Estate Taxes")**

Inherited IRAs are not considered to be retirement funds if inherited by beneficiaries other than a surviving spouse. In Clark v. Rameker, the Supreme Court ruled that inherited IRAs are not exempt assets in bankruptcy, reasoning that they are not retirement funds because no additional money can be invested, withdrawals can begin before retirement and the funds may be used for any purpose without penalty.
www.supremecourt.gov/opinions/13pdf/13-299_6k4c.pdf

Roth IRAs – Inherited Roth IRAs will be tax-free unless the account was established less than five years before, in which case beneficiaries who are not age 59 ½ will pay taxes on any distributed earnings but not on the original contributions, and any distributions represent a return of the contributions first. Also, each separate Roth account has a separate 5 year waiting period. While distributions from Roth IRAs are generally not taxable and are exempt from RMDs during the original owner's life time, beneficiaries other than surviving spouses must immediately start taking RMDs from inherited Roth IRAs over the beneficiary's life expectancy. **(See Above, "Conversion of Traditional IRAs to Roth IRAs"; & "Conversion from Pre-Tax Qualified Plans to Roth Qualified Plans")**

Chapter 6 – Capital Gains and Losses

Long-term capital gains and "qualified" dividends are generally taxed at capital gain tax rates, but ordinary income tax rates (See Ordinary Income Tax Brackets) apply to short-term capital gains and ordinary dividends. However, neither are subject to payroll tax. Net capital losses are generally treated as ordinary loses that can offset ordinary income, but the offset may be limited. The 3.8% net investment income (NII) tax applies to capital gains and qualified dividends of certain high-income earners. Therefore, the highest tax rate on long term capital gains and qualified dividends is equal to 23.8%. **(See Chapter 1, "2018 Ordinary Income Tax Brackets"); (See Chapter 10, "3.8% Net Investment Income Tax")**

Capital Gain Tax Rates

Capital gains are taxable on all capital assets, which includes tangible property, stocks, bonds, and other securities. A taxpayer must hold a capital asset for one year and a day in order to get long-term capital gain treatment (taxed at capital gain tax rates). If not, it will be a short-term capital gain subject to ordinary income tax rates. Under the Tax Cuts and Jobs Act (TCJA), the long-term capital gain rates for 2018 are 0%, 15%, and 20%, broken down as follows:

Married Filing Jointly or Qualified Surviving Spouse

If Taxable Income Is:	The Tax Is:
$0 - $77,200	0%
$77,201 - $479,000	15%
$479,001 and above	20%

Head of Household

If Taxable Income Is:	The Tax Is:
$0 - $51,700	0%
$51,701 - $452,400	15%
$452,401 and above	20%

Single Taxpayers

If Taxable Income Is:	The Tax Is:
$0 - $38,600	0%
$38,601 - $425,800	15%
$425,801 and above	20%

Married Filing Separately

If Taxable Income Is:	The Tax Is:
$0 - $38,600	0%
$38,601 - $239,500	15%
$239,501 and above	20%

Trusts and Estates

If Taxable Income Is:	The Tax Is:
$0 - $2,600	0%
$2,601 - $12,700	15%
$12,701 and above	20%

In 2017, taxpayers in the 39.6% ordinary income tax bracket were subject to a maximum 20% tax on long-term capital gains and qualified dividends. A 15% long-term capital gain tax rate applied to taxpayers in the 25%, 28%, 33%, and 35% ordinary income tax brackets. A 0% rate applied to taxpayers is in the 10% and 15% ordinary income tax brackets.

Reporting Capital Gains and Losses

Capital gains and losses are reported on Form 8949 and then on Schedule D, Form 1040. Capital gains and losses can occur upon the sale or exchange of capital assets, which includes investments, such as stocks, bonds, and other securities, as well as land and other tangible property. However, the sale of personal use capital assets such as your vehicle or your house can incur a capital gain, but generally cannot incur a capital loss. Capital gains are not subject to the payroll tax – this is also true for any income treated as ordinary income, such as short-term capital gains. **(See Chapter 2, "Payroll Tax")**

- Gifts, and property acquired from a spouse (or ex-spouse) includes their holding period. **(See Chapter 8, "Gifts and Inheritances")**
- If you inherit a capital asset, such as a house, you automatically are treated as having held it for more than one year. **(See Chapter 21, "Beneficiaries of Estates")**
- Losses between related parties are disallowed. For example, if you sell 100 shares of stock to your son for $11,000 for which you paid $15,000, you can't claim a loss. And if your son sells the stock to an unrelated party for $16,000, he must claim a $1,000 gain on the sale.
- Capital gain distributions are generally treated as long-term capital gains. **(See Chapter 22, "Basis of Property Inherited or Gifted")**
- Profit from managing oil and gas wells is a capital gain if the persons managing the wells have a stake in the profits upon the sale of the properties instead of receiving a salary for managing the wells. **(See Chapter 4, "Working Interests in Oil and Gas Ventures")**
- Form 8949 is used by an executor of an estate to report the carryover basis of those inherited assets where the estate elected the 2010 estate tax repeal. This provides the basis information should the heir have sold those inherited assets in 2011 or in the future. Heirs should obtain the backup support from the executor spelling out how basis determination was made. **(See Chapter 22, "Basis of Property Inherited or Gifted")**

www.irs.gov/pub/irs-pdf/f8949.pdf   www.irs.gov/pub/irs-pdf/i8949.pdf   www.irs.gov/pub/irs-pdf/f1040sd.pdf www.irs.gov/pub/irs-pdf/i1040sd.pdf

Example of computing net long-term capital gains subject to the 20% capital gain tax rate: When your ordinary taxable income exceeds the thresholds where the 20% capital gain tax rate begins ($479,001 – married filing jointly; $425,801 – single; $452,401 – head-of-household; $239,501 – married filing separately), all of your net capital gains are taxed at 20%. However, if your ordinary taxable income is below the threshold amounts (assuming no gain on collectibles or unrecaptured Sec. 1250 gain is involved), the amount of net capital gains taxed at 20% is the excess of ordinary taxable income and capital gains beyond the thresholds. For example, if joint filers have $390,000 in ordinary taxable income, then their first $89,000 in net capital gains is taxed at 15% ($390,000 + $89,000 = $479,000); any excess net capital gains beyond $89,000 is taxed at 20%.

Capital Gain Rollover to Specialized Small Business Investment Companies – The Tax Cuts and Jobs Act (TCJA) repeals the provision that allowed a taxpayer to defer capital gains from the sale of publicly traded securities by rolling over the proceeds of the sale to purchase interests in a "specialized small business investment corporation" (SSBIC), effective for sales after December 31, 2017. An SSBIC is an investment fund licensed by the U.S. Small Business Administration. And even though the SSBIC program was repealed in 1996, certain grandfathered SSBIC's still exist. **(See Below, "Gain on the Sale of Section 1202 Small Business Stock")**

Form 1099-B: Proceeds from Broker and Barter Exchange Transactions
Form 1099-B (Proceeds From Broker and Barter Exchange Transactions) should be received by taxpayers from brokers when stocks, bonds, mutual funds and other securities are sold, and you must indicate on Form 8949 whether a basis for the securities sold is shown on Form 1099-B, not shown on Form 1099-B, or no Form 1099-B was issued. Brokers that show the gross proceeds from the sale of stocks on Form 1099-B must show the date the securities were purchased, the date the securities were sold, the adjusted cost basis, and whether the gain or loss shown is short or long-term capital gain and wash sale status. Brokers are required to report on Form 1099-B whether the basis of securities sold is reported to the IRS or not reported to the IRS. Generally, if Form 1099-B doesn't report the basis and date of purchase, it means that the broker doesn't have a record of the basis (purchase price) and date of purchase of the securities sold. When this is the case, you, the taxpayer, must be able to come up with a basis (purchase price) and the date of purchase for the securities to put on Form 8949, because if you don't and a zero basis is shown on Form 8949, you will have to pay capital gain tax on the total proceeds of the sale.
www.irs.gov/pub/irs-pdf/f1099b.pdf   www.irs.gov/pub/irs-pdf/i1099b.pdf   www.irs.gov/pub/irs-pdf/i1099b.pdf

Form 8949 has a line to include an adjustment to basis/sales price of the securities and the reason for the adjustment. Adjustments may be necessary for different reasons. For example, in stock-option transactions, the Form 1099-B you receive may underreport your cost basis, causing you to overpay taxes unless you adjust the amount. This can happen because the broker likely won't include a compensation adjustment that can serve to increase your gain or decrease your loss. In this situation and some other situations, you may need to make an adjustment on Form 8949.

The requirement to report the basis by brokers on Form 1099-B was to be carried out in three phases: (1) stocks purchased/acquired on or after 1/1/2011; (2) mutual funds purchased on or after 1/1/2012; and (3) bonds, options and private placements bought on or after 1/1/2013. Phases one and two occurred as planned, but the IRS delayed the effective date of phase three until Jan. 1, 2014, to allow additional time for brokers to deal with the multiple issues involved in accurately reporting the basis of complicated debt instruments and options. And even though typical fixed bonds and most options were covered as of 1/1/2014, reporting on many complicated securities was further delayed until Jan. 1, 2016. Brokers are required to reduce the gross proceeds on securities sales on Form 1099-B by commissions and transfer taxes. Brokers are to determine the customer's basis under the first-in, first-out (FIFO) method as a default. However, if a customer owns mutual funds, the basis is measured according to the "average basis method." As the name implies, the broker computes the average basis by dividing the aggregate cost of the securities by the number of shares the taxpayer purchased.

Brokers are required to offer customers a choice of at least 4 reporting methods for stock sales: first-in, first-out; last-in, first-out; highest-cost, first-out; and specific identification. If a customer doesn't specify, IRS rules specify first-in, first-out as the default—which could increase taxes paid. A customer can switch methods, but only before selling shares, not after. If possible, you should specify highest-cost, first-out, which can minimize taxes on gains. For purposes of computing gain or loss before executing year-end trade tax strategies, an investor should confirm the amount of basis that a broker will be reporting to the IRS for any securities that are sold. An investor must decide what method they are using no later than the settlement date. Stock traded in the over-the-counter market or a national exchange is considered sold on the trade date, rather than the settlement date, unless it is a short sale. In the case of a short sale, gain is realized on the trade date (the stock price falls and a gain results), but a loss is not realized until the settlement date (the stock price rises and a loss results).

Selling Securities at a Loss

Selling securities that have fallen in value since purchase generates a tax loss that can offset realized capital gains as well as up to $3,000 of ordinary income in the current year, and any unused losses can be carried forward to future years. Selling securities at a loss that offsets capital gains can result in a substantial tax advantage. For example: a $17,000 short-term capital loss will offset a $12,000 long-term capital gain, potentially taxed at 20%, resulting in a net $5,000 short-term capital loss that can offset $3,000 of ordinary income, potentially taxed at 37%, and you can carry over the remaining $2,000 loss to the next year to offset capital gains and ordinary income in that year. This is known as "Harvesting Tax Losses." If you forget to carry over a capital loss to the next year, and later discover that they were not used when available to offset capital gains, you can't go back and reclaim those losses and apply them to later years.

Losses are disallowed when you sell securities at a loss and buy the same or substantially similar securities 30 days before or after the sale. This is known as a "wash sale" and applies only to the sale of losers. Wash sale rules are not imposed on recognizing gains and then immediately purchasing the same securities again.

Wash Sale Rules – If you buy the same or substantially similar securities 30 calendar days (not trading days when the market is open) before or after the sale date of losers, a total period of 61 days, the wash sale rules bar use of the loss to offset other capital gains. These rules also apply to an option to sell stock. These rules also bar the use of a loss when you sell stock and then your spouse or some other "related person," such as a corporation controlled by you, buys substantially identical stock within the stated time frames. These rules similarly apply when you use your IRA to quickly repurchase stock sold for a loss. The easiest way to use a loss for this year and retain the stock is simply to sell and then wait more than 30 days before you repurchase. The loss-registering sale can take place as late as the close of trading on the last business day of 2018. Another maneuver can provide an identical tax break. Buy the same amount you already hold, wait at least 31 days, and then sell the original holding. To qualify the loss as a deduction on this year's return, the doubling up must take place by the end of November, so you can sell by the end of this year. Another tactic is "suitable switching" which allows you to bypass the wash sale problem and remain an investor in the same industry, but not the same company. Sell your stock and buy similar shares of a comparable company. For example, you might sell a bank stock and immediately buy the shares of another one.

Capital Gains on Collectibles

Collectibles include art, antiques, gold bullion, gold collectible coins, etc. Long-term capital gains on collectibles are taxed at a maximum rate of 28% rather than the usual 15% or 20% maximum capital gain rates. Here's how it works—if you are in the 32%, 35%, or 37% ordinary income tax brackets you are taxed at 28%, but if you are in the 22% or 24% ordinary income tax brackets, you are taxed at those rates instead of the 28% capital gain rate. Instead of physically owning gold bullion and coins, you can buy shares of an exchange traded fund (ETF) that tracks the value of particular precious metals. However, these ETFs are also considered collectibles that are taxed at the maximum capital gain rate of 28%.

Qualified Dividends

Dividends reported to a taxpayer on Form 1099-DIV – including mutual fund dividends – are taxable income. Ordinary dividends are taxed at ordinary income tax rates, but qualified dividends are taxed at capital gain tax rates—they must satisfy a holding requirement of at least 61 days during the 121-day period that began 60 days before the ex-dividend date. In 2018, taxpayers who are in the 37% ordinary income tax bracket are subject to a maximum 20% tax on qualified dividends. However, qualified dividends may be subject to the additional 3.8% net investment income (NII) tax imposed by the Affordable Care Act (ACA), which would make the highest tax on qualified dividends equal to 23.8% for high income earners. The rates on qualified dividends were made permanent as of 1/1/2013. The 15% rate applies to taxpayers in the 22%, 24%, 32%, and 35% ordinary income tax brackets. The 0% rate applies to taxpayers is in the 10% and 12% ordinary income tax brackets. **(See Chapter 5, "Dividends"); (See Chapter 10, "3.8% Net Investment Income Tax")**

- Capital gain distributions are generally treated as long-term capital gains.
- Undistributed Capital Gains are reported in Box 1a of Form 1099-DIV. The mutual fund will send Form 2439 "Notice to Shareholder of Undistributed Long-Term Capital Gains" showing the taxpayer's share (Box 1a) and any tax paid by the mutual fund in Box 2. The taxpayer can take a credit for his/her share of the tax paid by the mutual fund because the shareholder is treated as having paid that tax. **(See Chapter 14, "Requirement to File Information Returns")**
- Ordinary investment income is taxable. Investment expenses are deductible as an itemized deduction on Schedule A, Form 1040. However, investment expenses are deductible only to the extent of investment income in tax year. The election to treat ordinary dividend income as investment income is made on Form 4952. **(See Chapter 12, "Investment Interest Deduction")**

www.irs.gov/pub/irs-pdf/f1099div.pdf   www.irs.gov/pub/irs-access/f4952_accessible.pdf
www.irs.gov/pub/irs-pdf/f2439.pdf

Carried Interest – Receipt of a capital interest for services provided to a partnership or LLC results in taxable compensation to fund managers. Typically, hedge fund managers guide the investment strategy and act as general partners to an "investment partnership," while their client investors act as limited partners. Fund managers are compensated in two ways. First, to the extent they invest their own capital in the funds, they share in the appreciation of fund assets. Second, they charge their client investors two kinds of annual fees: a management fee which is typically 2%, and a percentage of the fund's earnings and profits, typically 20%, which is usually carried over from year to year until a cash payment is made, usually following the closing out of an investment. This is called "carried interest."

Prior to enactment of the TCJA, "carried interest" was taxed in the hands of hedge fund managers at favorable long-term capital gain rates, provided it was held for at least one year. However, in 2018 and subsequent years, the TCJA states that "carried interest" held by hedge fund managers for less than three years (3-year holding period) will be taxed at short-term capital gain rates instead of at long-term capital gain rates. (Code Sec. 1061, Partnership Interests Held in Connection with Performance of Services, added by Act Sec. 13309(a)). If the 3-year holding period is not met with respect to an applicable partnership interest held by fund managers, their gains will be treated as short-term gains taxed at ordinary income tax rates. Also, the new TCJA statute does not grandfather partnership interests issued prior to the enactment of the TCJA; therefore, fund managers should be aware that this new provision may impact investment partnerships initiated in 2015, 2016 or 2017, i.e. the 3-year holding period requirement will be applicable in the 2018 tax year to "carried interest" on partnership investments going back to 2015.

Mark-to-Market Election
The mark-to-market election is advantageous to securities dealers and traders who incur losses. This Section 475 election for a tax year must be made by the due date of the tax return for the prior year. With the election, all securities positions held in the trading business are treated as if sold at the end of the year at FMV, and all of the deemed gains and losses are treated as ordinary gains and losses on Schedule C (losses are not limited to a $3,000 in a year). Dealers have customers and inventory and are required to use the mark-to-market method of accounting (no election is available). Dealers can obtain capital gain and loss treatment only if they clearly identify securities held for investment as opposed to securities in their inventory for sale to customers. **(See Above, "Selling Securities at a Loss")**

Traders are not investors and are, therefore, treated as carrying on a trade or business, but they do not have inventory or customers. Like investors, traders' gains and losses are considered capital gains and losses unless they make the "mark-to-market election." An important factor distinguishing a trader from an investor involves a number of factors; although an important factor is the volume of the taxpayer's trades during the year. Once the mark-to-market election is made by a trader, the election is in effect from then on unless revoked with the IRS's consent. The IRS frequently challenges whether a taxpayer who chooses the mark-to-market election is a trader.

Futures Contract – A futures contract traded in the U.S. is taxed as if you sold the position on Dec. 31st and bought it right back; an accounting scheme called "mark to market." These paper gains and losses are presumed to be 60% long and 40% short term capital gains. The DB Commodity Index Tracking Fund (DBC), U.S. Oil (USO) Fund and other funds like them are partnerships, and therefore, the paper gains and losses on these funds' future contracts flow through to investors' tax returns via a Schedule K-1.

Incentive Stock Options
A dual holding period applies to incentive stock options (ISO)—you must hold the stock for more than one year after the shares are transferred to you (exercise date), and for more than two years from the date the ISO was granted in order to be eligible for long-term capital gain treatment. No income is recognized when stock options are exercised; instead when the stock is later sold, any gain or loss is treated as a long-term capital gain (basis of stock is exercise price). However, part of the gain may be ordinary income, if the exercise price is less than 85% of the market price on the exercise date. A disqualifying disposition occurs if the taxpayer sales the stock within one year of the date of exercising (or within 2 years from the date of the grant—known as the statutory holding

period), which triggers ordinary income equal to the difference between the exercise price and market price on the exercise date, in which case the basis of the stock would be the market price instead of the exercise price. And, any difference between the sale price and the market price would be capital gain.

Sale of Demutualized Stock
Sale of demutualized stock is stock that a life insurance policyholder receives when the insurer switches from being a mutual company owned by the policyholders to a stock company owned by stockholders. The IRS's longstanding position was that such stock had no tax basis, so that when the shares were sold, the taxpayer owed capital gain tax on 100% of the proceeds of the sale. One federal district court upheld the IRS's position, but a second district court ruled that taxpayers should have some basis in the stock; however, the court didn't say what the basis of the stock should be. Many experts think it's whatever the shares were worth (FMV) when they were distributed to policyholders.

Net Unrealized Appreciation
Net Unrealized Appreciation (NUA) should be elected if you hold a significant amount of your employer's stock in a 401(k) plan and you receive a lump-sum distribution of such stock when you retire or change jobs. This means that you should not roll it over to an IRA, because the money you or your heirs withdraw from the IRA will be taxed as ordinary income. Instead, you should elect net unrealized appreciation (NUA) for sale of appreciated company stock purchased and held in a qualified plan, such as a 401(k) or an employee stock ownership plan (ESOP). This is a special tax treatment that allows an individual who is retiring or changing jobs to take a distribution of company stock and immediately pay ordinary income tax on just the basis of the stock and not the appreciated value (you must take a lump-sum distribution from the plan). In all cases, the appreciated value is not taxed at capital gain rates until the company stock is sold, either immediately or at a later date. The election can be made on your tax return for the year in which the distribution is made or on an amended return. The taxpayer makes the election by attaching an election statement to the tax return and by including the applicable amount of ordinary income as "other income" on Form 1040.

Worthless Securities
You can only take a deduction in the year securities become totally worthless, and then they are treated as a loss from the sale of a capital asset on the last day of that tax year. Also, the loss can only offset up to $3,000 of ordinary income in a year, and the remainder is carried over to future years. The stock's worthlessness must be established by identifiable events sufficient to establish the worthlessness of the securities, including: cessation of the corporation's business; commencement of liquidation; appointment of a receiver; and actual foreclosure. However, a corporation and its securities may be worthless even though the corporation has not dissolved, liquidated, or ceased doing business. It depends on the securities' current liquidation value and the potential value the securities may acquire through the foreseeable operations of the corporation. A security is completely worthless only if both elements of value have disappeared. **(See Above, "Form 1099-B: Proceeds from Broker and Barter Exchange Transactions")**

When an S-corporation's stock becomes worthless, shareholders who are considered passive owners are treated as having disposed of their entire interest in the S-corporation for passive activity loss purposes, allowing the shareholders to deduct all of their suspended passive losses from the S-corporation without regard to the passive activity loss rules. **(See Chapter 21, "S-Corporation Becomes Totally Worthless")**

Section 1244 Small Business Stock

Section 1244 small business stock that becomes totally worthless is deductible as an ordinary loss on Form 4797, and the loss is not subject to the $3,000 limitation on the offset of ordinary income in the current year. To qualify the loss as ordinary, the following requirements must be met: (1) the stock must have been originally issued by the corporation to the individual or partnership in which the individual is an investor; (2) the corporation must not have derived over 50% of its gross receipts from passive income sources during the five years immediately preceding the year of worthlessness; and (3) at the time the stock was issued the amount of capital and paid-in surplus did not exceed $1 million. To be treated as worthless stock, the stock may not be traded on an exchange, and a 90% decline in value does not make it a deductible loss. A Section 1244 loss is treated as a loss on Form 4797 Part II, limited to $50,000 (single) or $100,000 (married filing jointly). Any loss in excess of these limits is reported on Schedule D either as a long or short-term capital loss. **(See Chapter 7, "How to Determine When an Activity is Passive or Active"); (See Chapter 14, "Passive Activities"; & "Sale of Business Property")**
www.irs.gov/pub/irs-pdf/f4797.pdf   www.irs.gov/pub/irs-pdf/i4797.pdf

Gain on the Sale of Section 1202 Small Business Stock

Gain on the sale of Section 1202 Small Business stock that is held more than 5 years, is either totally or partially excluded from taxable income depending on when it was acquired. 50% of any gain is excluded from taxable income on the sale of stock acquired before 2/17/2009. 75% of any gain is excluded on the sale of stock acquired after 2/17/2009 and before 9/28/2010. The Small Business Jobs Act raised the exclusion to 100% of any gain on the sale of such stock acquired after 9/27/2010, and the 100% exclusion was made permanent by the "Protecting Americans from Tax Hikes Act of 2015." Also, the non-taxable gain from the sale of the 100% exclusion does not count as an AMT preference item. To be eligible for the exclusion, the taxpayer must acquire the stock when originally issued (directly or through an under-writer), for money, property other than stock, or as compensation for services provided to the corporation. The non-excluded portion of section 1202 gain is taxed at the lesser of ordinary income tax rates or 28%, instead of the lower capital gain rates. When the stock is issued, a qualified small-business corporation's aggregate gross assets may not exceed $50 million. If at any time before the issuance of the stock, the corporation or any predecessor held gross assets exceeding $50 million, the stock will not qualify. Although qualification of issued stock is not dependent upon keeping under the $50 million asset ceiling subsequent to its issuance, the test will disqualify any subsequently issued stock once the $50 million ceiling is reached. Also, the corporation must use at least 80% of the value of its assets in the active conduct of one or more qualified trades or businesses. Gain excludable under this provision is not used in computing a taxpayer's long-term capital gains or losses. **(See Chapter 23, "Alternative Minimum Tax")**

There is a non-exclusive long list of trades or businesses that do not qualify for the exclusion, including service businesses in health, law, architecture, accounting, and financial services. It is the shareholders' burden to prove qualification for the exclusion. The sale of shares in a specialized small business investment company (SSBIC) may qualify for the exclusion; however, any gain deferred as the result of a rollover from the sale of publicly traded securities is not eligible for the exclusion. A taxpayer may hold qualified stock in more than one corporation and apply the limit separately to each. The amount of gain eligible for exclusion of gain from the disposition of qualified stock of any single issuer for any given tax year is limited to the greater of $10 million ($5 million for married taxpayers filing separately) reduced by the total amount of eligible gains taken in prior tax years, or 10 times the taxpayer's adjusted basis in all qualified stock disposed of during the tax year. This provision is limited to individual investments and not the investments of a corporation. **(See Above, "Capital Gain Rollover to Specialized Small Business Investment Companies")**

Section 1231 – Assets Used in a Trade or Business

Assets used in a trade or business are not capital assets, but they are generally treated like capital assets when sold. For example, stocks and bonds, your personal residence, and your car are capital assets, but property used in a trade or business (property, plant, machinery, and equipment), and tangible investment property, i.e. rental properties are not capital assets. Also, inventory and accounts receivable are not capital assets.

Form 4797 is used to report sales of business property, and even though business assets are not capital assets, any gain on business property and rental property held more than 12 months, that is more than the part that is ordinary income due to depreciation, is Section 1231 gain which is treated as long-term capital gain. Some Section 1231 gain must be recaptured as ordinary income (depreciation, Section 179 expensing, bonus depreciation and amortization). Section 1231 makes available the best of both worlds to businesses with both capital gains and losses. Net gains from the sale or disposal of Section 1231 business property are taxed at long-term capital gain rates, while net losses are taxed as ordinary losses, including business property disposed of at a loss that is held less than one year. If total Section 1231 gains exceed losses for the year then the net gains are treated as long-term capital gains. If total losses exceed gains for the year, then the net losses are treated as ordinary losses which, unlike capital gain losses, are not subject to the $3,000 limitation on offset of ordinary income in the current year. However, Section 1231 losses on business property held more or less than one year that are not fully applied against Section 1231 gains in the same year, are subject to recapture against net Section 1231 gains in previous years. Section 1231 losses for the previous 5 years that have not been applied against net Section 1231 gains by reclassifying the gains as ordinary income, are applied against net Section 1231 gains beginning with the earliest loss in the 5-year period. **(See Above, "Form 1099-B: Proceeds from Broker and Barter Exchange Transactions"); See Chapter 14, "Sale of Business Property")**

When real property such as a building is sold, any depreciation taken after 1986 is straight-line depreciation that is "unrecaptured" Section 1250 gain" that is taxed at 25% instead of being taxed as ordinary income or at capital gain rates (15% or 20%). The gain attributed to depreciation of real property is entered in the "unrecaptured Section" of the Section 1250 Gain Worksheet. **(See Chapter 16, "Modified Accelerated Cost Recovery System (MACRS)")** http://pbsact.com/wp-content/uploads/2014/04/2014-Unrecaptured-Section-1250-Gain-Worksheet.pdf

Supplies regularly used in a trade or business; accounts or notes receivable acquired in the ordinary course of a trade or business; U.S. government publications that you obtain from the government for free or less than the normal sales price; and securities held by a dealer in securities are not capital assets. Gains on the sale of these assets are not treated in accordance with Section 1231; instead any gains are ordinary income reported in Part II of Form 4797. Another example: Profit from a housing developer's sale of land is ordinary income, not capital gain, because the land is held in the ordinary course of business, thus triggering ordinary income. www.irs.gov/pub/irs-pdf/f4797.pdf

Self-Created Intangible Assets

Under the Tax Cuts and Jobs Act (TCJA), self-created intangible assets such as copyrights, literary compositions, musical or artistic compositions, patents, goodwill, etc. are removed from the definition of capital assets effective in 2018. However, transfers of all substantial rights to a patent or an undivided interest in a portion of patent rights by the inventor or a holder of a patent continues to get long-term capital gain treatment under Section 1235 if payments are tied to productivity or are payable periodically over the transferee's use of the patent. A "holder of a patent" means: any individual whose efforts created such property, or any other individual who has acquired an interest in such property in exchange for consideration in money paid to the creator prior to actual reduction to practice of the invention covered by the patent, if such individual is neither: the employer of the creator, or related to such creator.

In 2017 and prior years, a safe-harbor allowed self-created intangibles to be treated as capital assets and the cost of the self-created intangible assets to be amortized over 15 years. **(See Chapter 16, "Amortization of Intangible Assets")**

Qualified Opportunity Zones – In accordance with the Tax Cuts and Jobs Act (TCJA), as of December 22, 2017, the chief executive officer (probably the Governor) of each U.S. state or possession (including the District of Columbia) is allowed to designate a limited number of low-income communities as "qualified opportunity zones." A qualified opportunity zone is the same as the community development entity (CDE) designation for the New Markets Tax Credit. The TCJA provides that investments made in qualified opportunity zones will result in the temporary deferral of capital gains from inclusion in gross income when the capital gains are reinvested in a qualified opportunity fund, and the permanent exclusion of capital gains from inclusion in gross income on sales of such investments when the investments are held for at least 10 years. A qualified opportunity fund is an investment vehicle organized as a corporation or a partnership for the purpose of investing in and holding at least 90% of its assets in qualified opportunity zone property, which includes any qualified opportunity zone stock, any qualified opportunity zone partnership interests, and any qualified opportunity zone business property. The certification of a qualified opportunity fund is done by the Secretary of the Community Development Financial Institutions (CDFI) Fund, effective on the date of enactment. The TCJA states that there is no exclusion from income for investments in qualified opportunity zones made after December 31, 2026. **(See Chapter 13, "New Markets Credit")**

Abandonment of Property

Abandonment of property by voluntary or involuntary action can result in a capital gain depending on whether the taxpayer was personally liable for the debt securing the abandoned property. If the debtor is personally liable for the loan it is a recourse debt, and until foreclosure or repossession procedures are completed, there are no tax consequences, whether the property is personal use or business use property. Abandonment of property is treated as a sale, and the debtor may realize a gain or loss. If a property is abandoned, it is reported by the creditor to the debtor on Form 1099-A (Acquisition or Abandonment of Secured Property). You (the debtor) should use the Form 1099-A to report the abandonment like a sale on your tax return, using Form 8949 and Schedule D. The amount realized from the deemed sale is the lower of the asset's fair market value (FMV) on the date of abandonment or the outstanding debt immediately before the transfer. The amount realized is compared with the debtor's basis in the property to determine capital gain or loss. The gain is taxable whether or not the taxpayer used the property for business or personal purposes unless the gain is on a principal residence, which is usually forgiven. If it is a business use asset, either a gain or loss may result. However, losses on personal use property are nondeductible. **(See Above, "Reporting Capital Gains and Losses"); (See Chapter 9, "Home Sale Gain Exclusion")**
www.irs.gov/pub/irs-pdf/f1099a.pdf

If the debtor is not personally liable for the debt (nonrecourse debt) and abandons personal use property, such as a home or car, the abandonment is treated as a sale in the year of the abandonment. The amount realized on the sale—the outstanding loan balance—is compared with the taxpayer's basis in the property to determine gain or loss. Any loss is nondeductible personal expense. If the property abandoned is business or investment property, the amount of gain or loss is determined in the same way, however a loss is deductible. Generally, there is no cancellation of debt because the debtor is not personally liable for the debt. However, if the debtor retains the collateral and accepts a discount from the creditor for early payment of the debt, or agrees to a loan modification that reduces its principal balance, the amount of the discount or principal reduction is considered cancellation of debt (COD) income. **(See Chapter 5, "Cancellation of Debt")**

Drop in Value of Property – A drop in value of business or investment property, such as real estate, does not create a loss for tax purposes. There has to actually be evidence of a closed and completed transaction, which typically occurs upon the sale of a property before a loss can be claimed by a taxpayer. A closed and completed transaction may occur in the absence of a sale, if a property has been abandoned or becomes totally worthless. Also, a closed and completed transaction can occur in real estate when a recourse mortgage is foreclosed upon, i.e. the fair market value (FMV) of the foreclosed property acts as a "deemed sale;" the borrower can then recognize a gain or loss for the difference between his basis in the property and the property's FMV at the time of the deemed sale; and the lender may pursue the borrower for the excess of the principal amount of the mortgage over the FMV of the property. However, after the taxpayer recognizes a loss in a foreclosure, if the lender chooses to forgive the excess deficiency, the taxpayer has to then recognize cancellation of debt income equal to the excess forgiven. **(See Above, "Reporting Capital Gains and Losses"); (See Chapter 5, "Cancellation of Debt")**

A recourse debt (mortgage) means that not only can a lender seize a property and sell it at auction, but also the lender can pursue the borrower for any remaining deficiency.

Installment Sale

An Installment sale is a sale of property for a gain, with payments after the year of sale, which allows gain to be deferred in direct proportion to the payments that are deferred. Each installment payment under the "note" will include a portion of: return of adjusted basis of the property; gain on the sale; and interest. The objective of an installment sale is to lock in a sale while deferring recognition of income. In reporting gain, two variables are key: basis in the property and the sales price. The basis includes selling expenses and depreciation recapture. "Gross profit" is determined by subtracting the basis from the sales price. Next, gross profit is divided by the contract sales price, which results in the "gross profit percentage." The gross profit percentage is applied to each payment to determine the amount of reportable gain. If the property is a capital asset, the seller recognizes capital gain and ordinary income for depreciation recapture. A sale at a loss does not qualify for an installment sale. **(See Chapter 14, "Sale of Business Property")**

Electing out of deferral of gain on an installment sale – Capital gain is usually recognized as cash received from the buyer, but the taxpayer can elect to recognize the entire gain in the year of sale (not usually advantageous to buyer). NOTE: Installment payments received after 2012 are subject to the tax rates for the year of payment, not the year of sale. Thus, the capital gains portion of payments made in 2013 and later are now taxed at the 20% rate for higher-income taxpayers. **(See Above, "Capital Gain Tax Rates")**

Non-Business Bad Debt

A "non-business bad debt" must be totally worthless and is deducted as a short-term capital loss on Schedule D, and therefore, is limited to offset only $3,000 of ordinary income per year. Also, you can't include any interest that you may have collected had the debt been repaid as part of a non-business bad debt, i.e. only the amount of cash that you actually loaned to the debtor can be included as a bad debt. No bad debt deduction is allowed if you guaranteed a loan as a personal favor to a family member, relative or friend, with no profit motive and without consideration. In which case, no bad debt deduction is available, and the payment under such guarantee will likely be characterized as a "gift." If you claim a loss, you must attach a statement to the tax return describing the loan, relationship to debtor, how you tried to collect it, and why you decided it is worthless. The loss is equal to the creditor's basis in the loan. For a debt to be considered a bad debt, the creditor must have no reasonable expectation of collecting it. The lender must be able to demonstrate that the debt is wholly without value and that the debt became worthless during the tax year for which the lender is claiming the deduction. **(See Above, "Reporting Capital Gains and Losses"); (See Chapter 14, "Business Bad Debts"); (See Chapter 22, "Estate and Gift Tax")**

Deferral Election for Qualified Equity Grants

Code Sec. 83 governs the amount and timing of income inclusion for property, including employer stock, transferred to an eligible employee (excluding most shareholders and officers) in connection with the performance of services. The Tax Cuts and Jobs Act (TCJA) provides that an eligible employee can "elect" to defer for income tax purposes the recognition of income attributable to qualified stock (settled restricted stock units or exercised options) transferred to the employee by a qualified employer after December 31, 2017. A qualified employer is one which offers the benefit to at least 80% of employees working at least 30 hours per week. The employee election applies only to the recognition of income for income tax purposes and not to the recognition of income for FICA and FUTA purposes. An employee's election must be made within 30 days of the earlier of when the stock is substantially vested or first transferable, whichever occurs first. If an employee makes the election, the election defers the recognition of income for income tax purposes for a period up to 5 years (with forced recognition earlier if the corporation goes public or the employee becomes an "excluded employee" (see below). The employee must recognize income for income tax purposes before the end of 5 years if any of the following occurs:

1. The stock becomes readily tradable on an established securities market (public stock offering).
2. The employee becomes an "excluded employee," which is an individual: (a) who is a one-percent owner of the corporation; (b) who is the chief executive officer or chief financial officer of the corporation, including acting as such; or (c) who is one of the four highest compensated officers of the corporation.
3. The employee revokes his or her election (Code Sec. 83(i)(1)(B), as amended by the Act Sec. 13603(a)).

www.irs.gov/pub/irs-drop/rr-04-37.pdf

Virtual Currency

The character of gain or loss from the sale or exchange of virtual currencies like Bitcoins is a capital asset in the hands of the taxpayer. A payment made using virtual currency is subject to information reporting to the same extent as any other payment. The basis of the virtual currency is its FMV on the date of receipt. Thus, the difference between the sales price and the FMV will result in a capital gain or loss upon disposition of the currency. Therefore, if you walk into a Starbucks and pay $5 in Bitcoins for a cup of coffee (Starbucks accepts Bitcoins), you will owe capital gain tax on your $1 profit if you acquired the Bitcoins for $4. Theoretically, you would have to report the tax ramifications for each and every transaction you engaged in using Bitcoins. **(See Chapter 7, "Virtual Currency")**

Chapter 7 – Passive Income and Losses

Passive activity income is taxable at ordinary income tax rates (See Ordinary Income Tax Brackets), and deductions or expenses related to passive income are allowed only to the extent of passive income. Passive losses are only deductible from passive income of other passive activities. Form 8582 must be completed to identify passive income and losses and help determine if passive loss items are deductible. Passive losses disallowed (suspended) can be carried forward to later years and become deductible only when passive income is realized or the passive activity is sold. Passive activity income is not subject to payroll tax. The 3.8% net investment income (NII) tax may apply to passive activity income of certain high-income earners. **(See Chapter 1, "Ordinary Income Tax Brackets"); (See Chapter 2, "Payroll Tax"); (See Chapter 10, "3.8% Net Investment Income Tax"); (See Chapter 14, "Passive Activities")**
www.irs.gov/pub/irs-pdf/f8582.pdf   www.irs.gov/pub/irs-pdf/i8582.pdf

How to Determine When an Activity is Passive or Active (Non-Passive)
The passive activity rules focus on participation in a business activity. In order to determine whether an activity is passive or active (non-passive), there are two key terms: "material participation" and "significant participation." A taxpayer materially participates in an activity if he/she is involved in the operations of the activity on a regular, continuous, and substantial basis, in which case, he/she is participating in an "active" business. Significant participation is a lower standard than material participation and only applies to rental activities which are considered "passive" activities (unless you are a real estate professional). **(See Below, "Rental Income"); (See Below, "Real Estate Professional")**

In order to "materially participate" in an activity you must meet one of six IRS tests that qualifies the business activity as "active" (non-passive activity), and a taxpayer must be prepared to prove that one of the material participation tests has been met in order to be able to deduct losses from the activity against active business income. The six safe harbor provisions that deem material participation are the following:
1. Participated in the activity more than 500 hours during the year;
2. Provided substantially all of the participation by individuals;
3. Participated for 100 hours or more, and this equaled or exceeded all others' participation;
4. Participated for more than 100 hours in several activities and total participation adds up to more than 500 hours annually;
5. Materially participated in the activity for 5 of the 10 previous years; or
6. Provided personal (professional) services to the business and materially participated in any three preceding years.

The passive activity rules apply to: individuals, personal service corporations, closely held C-corporations, partners, and S-corporation shareholders. The rules do not apply to partnerships, S-corporations, or widely held C-corporations. Whether or not an activity is considered passive is determined each year. If a taxpayer has a carryover of a passive activity loss from a prior year, and the same activity generates active (non-passive) income in the current year, the passive activity loss carryover can be used against active income of the same activity in the current year. In general, limited partners are not deemed to materially participate in partnership activities, so their share of partnership income and losses is considered passive. Interests in LLCs and LLPs are not considered limited partnership interests for purposes of the passive-activity loss rules. However, partners of LLCs and LLPs may have to prove material participation in order to claim any resulting losses against non-passive income. **(See Chapter 18, "Limited Liability Partnership"; & "Limited Liability Company"); (See Chapter 19, "Limited Liability Company")**

Suspended Passive Losses

A suspended passive activity loss is deductible against active (non-passive) income upon disposition of a taxpayer's entire interest in the passive activity. There are three tests for a qualifying disposition:

- The disposition must be of your entire interest. A sale of your ownership interest in an activity is a good example of a disposition. A mere change in the form of the entity running the activity is not a disposition.
- The disposition must be a fully taxable event where gain or loss is realized and recognized. A tax-free exchange is not a taxable event because gain is not recognized. Other examples of nontaxable events include gifts, conversion to personal use, transfers to a partnership or corporation, and filing for bankruptcy.
- The disposition must be made to an unrelated party. This means dispositions to third parties and not to a family member, a business controlled by the taxpayer, or other related entity.

(See Chapter 9, "Section 1031 Like-Kind Exchange")

When an S-corporation's stock becomes totally worthless, shareholders who are considered passive owners are treated as having disposed of their entire interest in the S-corporation for passive activity loss purposes, allowing the shareholders to deduct all of their suspended passive losses from the S-corporation without regard to the passive activity loss rules – in other words the suspended passive losses can be deducted from active (non-passive) income. **(See Chapter 19, "S-Corporation Becomes Totally Worthless")**

Rental Income

Rental activities are considered passive activities, regardless of the taxpayer's level of participation, unless the individual is a real estate professional. Rental income and expenses are reported on Schedule E, Form 1040, and rental income is not subject to payroll tax or self-employment tax whether or not you are a real estate professional. Income is the monthly rental revenues received from renters or lessees which may or may not be reported to the owner on a Form 1099-MISC. Advance rental payments are included in income in the year received, but deposits are not included in income until forfeited. Rental income includes improvements made by the lessee if made as a substitute for rent. Lease cancellation payments are included in income in the year received. Expenses allowed to be deducted from rental income include: the cost of insurance; maintenance and cleaning; repairs; supplies; utilities; management fees; mortgage interest paid to banks; real estate taxes; and depreciation. **(See Above, "How to Determine When an Activity is Passive or Active (Non-Passive)"); (See Below, "Real Estate Professional"); (See Chapter 2, "Payroll Tax (FICA)"); (See Chapter 14, "Business Expenses"); (See Chapter 17, "Self-Employment Tax")**

- **Example** – A taxpayer, who was a handyman, was having a tough time paying his monthly rent. He worked out a deal with the landlord to have the rent amount reduced in exchange for doing some maintenance work around the building. The rent offset equaled the value of the services that the handyman provided. Nevertheless, in this Welemin Case, the Tax Court ruled that the handyman owed tax on the "compensation" he received in the form of a rent reduction from the landlord – an indirect form of taxable income or compensation equal to the value of the repair and maintenance services provided by the handyman, and the value of the services he provided was considered rental income to be reported by the landlord. http://ustaxcourt.gov/UstcInOp/OpinionViewer.aspx?ID=11337

The Tax Cuts and Jobs Act (TCJA) brings several important changes that owners of rental properties can take advantage of, because a real property business includes any real property rental, development, redevelopment, construction, reconstruction, acquisition, conversion, operation, management, leasing or brokerage business. In general, rental property owners enjoy lower ordinary income tax rates for tax years 2018 through 2025, and the TCJA retains the existing tax rates for long-term capital gains. And, in accordance with the law that was in effect in 2017 and prior years, you can still deduct mortgage interest and state and local real estate taxes on rental properties. While the TCJA imposes new limitations on deducting personal residence mortgage interest and state and local taxes (including property taxes on personal residences), those limitations do not apply to rental properties, unless you also use the property for personal purposes. In that case, the new limitations only apply to mortgage interest and real estate taxes that are allocable to your personal use and deducted as an itemized deduction. In addition, you can still deduct all of the other standard operating expenses for rental properties, including depreciation, utilities, insurance, repairs and maintenance, yard care and association fees. **(See Below, "Renting Out Part of Your Dwelling Unit")**

The TCJA also changes the way rental income is taxed beginning in 2018. Starting in 2018, taxpayers with qualified business income (including rental income), are eligible to take a tax deduction up to 20% of their "qualified business income" (QBI). Determining whether or not you will be eligible to capture the full 20% deduction on your rental income is based on your "total taxable income" for the year. If your total taxable income is below the thresholds of $315,000 (Married filing jointly) or $157,000 (Single), you can simply take a deduction of 20% of your net rental income. For example, if you are married filing jointly and your total taxable income is $250,000 and your net rental income is $20,000, you get a deduction of $4,000 ($20,000 X 20% = $4,000). It gets more complicated if your total taxable income is above the stated thresholds, but that will be discussed in another chapter of this book. Also, "total taxable income" is not your AGI (adjusted gross income) and it's not just income from your rental property or self-employment activities.

 Deducting Travel Expenses – You can deduct travel expenses necessary to go check on a rental property. Travel expenses include automobile expenses at the standard business mileage rate or actual expenses. The U.S. Tax Court allowed a couple who bought their own airplane to deduct their condo-related trips in their airplane to check on their rental condo, rather than drive five to seven hours or be tied to the only daily commercial flight available. They were allowed to deduct the cost of fuel and depreciation of the airplane on Schedule E for the portion of time used for business-related purposes, even though those costs increased their overall rental loss on the condo. **(See Chapter 15, "Vehicle and Other Transportation Expenses"); (See Chapter 16, "Modified Accelerated Cost Recovery System (MACRS)")**

 Rental Losses – As stated above, rental activities are considered passive (unless you are a real estate professional), and this is still the case under the TCJA. And only real estate professionals are generally eligible for the 20% deduction because they are considered actively participating in the real estate business. Generally, passive losses can only be offset against passive income in a year, but there is an exception for owners who "significantly" participate in managing a rental property (See above). Significant participation is a lower standard than material participation, which means the owner of a residential rental property always meets the significant participation standard (but the active participation standard), even if the owner hires a property manager to manage the property. The exception is that individuals who own and "significantly" participate in the management of residential rental property can offset up to $25,000 of passive losses against non-passive income in any year. If rental expenses are more than rental revenues, then you have a loss.

However, the $25,000 loss allowance is phased-out if the taxpayer's modified adjusted gross income (MAGI) is between $100,000 –$150,000 (Married filing jointly) or $50,000 – $75,000 (Single). Also, married persons must file jointly to take advantage of the entire $25,000 rental loss allowance (the allowance is reduced to $12,500 if filing status is "married filing separately.") Rental real estate losses in excess of $25,000 are allowed just like other passive losses, i.e. to the extent of income from other passive activities. **(See Above, "How to Determine When an Activity is Passive or Active (Non-Passive"); (See Below, "Real Estate Professional")** www.irs.gov/pub/irs-pdf/f1040se.pdf

- **Example** – Suppose your filing status is married filing jointly, and your MAGI is $125,000. Then your rental loss allowance is reduced by 50% to $12,500.

If you buy a house and charge a dependent child one-half of the fair rental value to live in the house, and you pay the real estate taxes and mortgage interest, the house doesn't qualify to be a rental property because you don't charge the child a fair rental value to live in the house. According to the Tax Court, fair rent for a family member may be up to 20% below fair market value in order for a residential property to qualify as a rental property. However, even though the house doesn't qualify as a rental property, you can deduct the real estate taxes and mortgage interest as itemized deductions on your tax return. If you buy a house for an adult child, who is not your dependent, it is considered a "gift" subject to the gift tax, and even if you pay the real estate taxes and mortgage interest on the house, the child can deduct the costs on his/her tax return. **(See Chapter 12, "Itemized Deductions"); (See Chapter 22, "Estate and Gift Tax")**

Other rulings regarding rental income:
- In TC Sum. Op. 2011-122, a taxpayer was allowed to deduct rental property losses for two years when there were no tenants in the property, because the property was held for income-producing purposes and was available for rent.
- In PLR 201143011, the IRS determined that rentals received for billboard space were taxable as real estate rental income rather than personal property rentals.

You cannot write off rental losses against S-corporation income, if you "materially" participate in the S-corporation. Material participation S-corporation income is "not" considered passive. **(See Chapter 19, "Computation of S-Corporation Income")**

Classifying a Vacation Home (Second Home) as a Rental Property – A vacation home is considered a rental property instead of a second home if it rented at fair rental value for 15 days or more during the year, and is used by the owner no more than 14 days or more than 10% of the number of days during the year that the home is rented at a fair rental value, whichever is greater. When a vacation home is used by the owner more than 14 days or more than 10% of the number of days during the year that the home is rented at fair rental value, it is considered a "combination" second home, which means that if the home is rented out 15 days or more during the year, expenses allocated to rental use (including depreciation) are deductible only to the extent of income received from rentals – a loss cannot be taken, but expenses that are not deductible may be carried over to subsequent years. However, the owner can deduct 100% of the property taxes and mortgage interest on the home as itemized deductions. If the home is rented out for 14 days or less during the year, the income received from rentals during the year doesn't have to be reported on your tax return, and likewise no expenses should be reported. Therefore, you need to keep a record of days rented and the number of days used for personal purposes. **(See Above, "Rental Income"); (See Chapter 12, "Real Property Taxes"; & "Home Mortgage Interest Deduction")**

Selling a Rental Property – If you sell a rental property or a vacation home for a gain, all previously un-allowed passive losses from rentals of the property are allowed against the gain. Plus, the excess of any gain resulting from the sale is allowed to offset any other passive losses. However, any depreciation taken has to be recaptured and taxed – the depreciation is entered in the "unrecaptured Section" of the Section 1250 Gain Worksheet in Schedule D and is subject to a top tax rate of 25%. If you sell a vacation (second) home for a loss, the loss is not deductible unless the home qualifies as a rental property. A "combination" second home does not qualify as a rental property (See above). **(See Above, "Classifying a Vacation Home (Second Home) as a Rental Property"); (See Chapter 6, "Reporting Capital Gains and Losses"; & "Form 1099-B: Proceeds from Broker and Barter Exchange Transactions")**

Renting Out Part of Your Dwelling Unit – If you rent out a part of your dwelling unit and live in the other part, you must divide the expenses between the rental portion and the personal use portion and treat them as though they are separate pieces of property. You can use any reasonable method for dividing the expenses. The two most common methods are based on a home's square footage and the number of rooms in the home. If the rental portion of the dwelling is used for less than the entire year, the deductible amount of the expenses for the rental portion of the dwelling is determined by multiplying the total expenses of the rental portion of the property by a fraction, with the denominator being the total number of days the dwelling is used during the year and the numerator being the total number of days the rental portion of the dwelling is rented at fair value. For purposes of this calculation, any day that the rental part of the dwelling is not rented is treated as a personal-use day. If the rental portion is rented out for the entire year, then the second step is not necessary. Owners can deduct the expenses associated with the rental portion, such as home mortgage interest, real estate taxes, and utilities, as rental expenses on Schedule E. The expenses that are allowable for the personal-use portion of the property (mortgage interest and real estate taxes) are taken on Schedule A as itemized deductions. You do not have to divide the expenses between rental and personal-use for the items that relate only to the rental portion, such as painting, repairs, or a second phone line. These expenses are deductible as rental expenses. You are also allowed to claim a depreciation deduction for the rental portion of the dwelling and on furniture and equipment attributable to the rental portion. The $25,000 passive loss limitation applies to the rental portion of the dwelling.

Selling a Principal Residence That Was Initially a Vacation Home or a Rental Property
When you sell a principal residence that was initially a vacation (second) home or a rental property, exclusion of any gain on the sale of the residence attributable to periods the dwelling was used as a vacation (second) home or a rental property after 2008 and then converted to a principal residence is not allowed. The portion of any gain on the sale that is taxable is based on the percentage of time before the sale that the home was used as a vacation home or rental property. A period of absence generally counts as qualifying use as a principal residence if it occurs after the home was last used as a principal residence, but not before it was converted to a principal residence and then sold. **(See Chapter 9, "Home Sale Gain Exclusion")**

- **Example** – Suppose you owned a rental house in 2008 or before, and in 2011 converted it to your principal residence and didn't sell it until 2014. The home qualifies as a principal residence because you lived in the residence for at least 2 of the 5 years before the date of the sale. But any gain related to "nonqualified use" (when the home was a rental property) after 2008 is not eligible for the "home sale gain exclusion;" therefore you must pay capital gain tax on the portion of any gain on the sale that is related to the period 2009–2011. Also, the home sale gain exclusion does not apply to any gain attributable to any depreciation taken on the home after May 6, 1997. So, all of the depreciation taken must be taxed, and recapture of the depreciation is subject to the Section 1231 netting rules, which means that any gain attributable to the depreciation is entered in the "unrecaptured Section" of the Section 1250 Gain Worksheet in Schedule D and is subject to a top tax rate of 25%.

Converting Your Principal Residence to a Rental Property

If you move from your home and turn it into a rental property during the year, you can deduct all expenses related to the rental property to the extent of generating a loss of up to $25,000 for the year against non-passive income. However, you can only deduct the expenses allocable to the months after the property is converted to a rental property (including depreciation).

Selling a Principal Residence That Was Converted to a Rental Property

The IRS has ruled that selling a home that's been converted from a principal residence to a rental property is a complete disposition of a taxpayer's interest in a "passive" activity even though gain is excluded under the home sale gain exclusion law (up to $500,000 for joint filers and $250,000 for singles) if requirements are met. **(See Chapter 9, "Home Sale Gain Exclusion")**

- **Example** – A homeowner buys a residence for $500,000 that is used as a principal residence for more than 2 years. The homeowner then converts it to a rental property, and has a $10,000 loss annually for 3 years (assume the taxpayer's income is too high to allow him to use the $25,000 annual rental loss allowance), before selling it for $600,000. The $100,000 gain is not taxed because of the home sale gain exclusion since the taxpayer met the 2 out of 5-year rule. The taxpayer can deduct the suspended $30,000 loss against non-passive income because there was a complete disposition of the property. However, before deducting any of the $30,000 suspended loss against non-passive income, the taxpayer must first offset the suspended loss against income from any other passive activities. Also, any depreciation on the home that is included in the suspended loss must be recaptured and tax paid on it at a maximum rate of 25%. **(See Above, "Suspended Passive Losses")**

When you have converted a principal residence to a rental property, you may be able to deduct a loss from the sale. But your basis for tax purposes is the lesser of the home's original purchase price (plus any improvements) or its fair market value (FMV) on the date of conversion from a principal residence to a rental property. However, there are parameters for successfully converting a principal residence to a rental property. First of all, you must be serious about renting out the place, and if it is never rented out before you sell it, it may not be considered converted to a rental property. The Tax Court traditionally looks at the following factors to determine a taxpayer's intent to covert a principal residence to a rental property: (1) the length of time the house was occupied by the taxpayer as a principal residence before placing it on the market for sale; (2) whether the taxpayer permanently abandoned all further personal use of the home; (3) any offers to rent; and (4) any offers to sell.

Short-Term Rentals

Short-term vacation home rentals averaging seven days or less do not qualify for the $25,000 loss allowance, even if the property is rented out for the entire year. The number of personal use days and fair rental days is used to determine the tax treatment of expenses incurred and the amount of depreciation allowed for short-term rentals. This is how it works in determining the allowable expenses deductible against rental income – the denominator is equal to the total of the number of personal use days and the fair rental days, and the numerator is equal to the number of fair rental days. So, the expenses incurred for the entire year, such as utilities, repairs and maintenance, and depreciation are allocated based on this formula, except for mortgage interest and real estate taxes, which are deductible anyway as itemized deductions. Personal use days include: use by the taxpayer or relatives including siblings, spouse, ancestors, and lineal descendants. Personal use days even include days when the property is rented to a relative at fair rental value, if the owner retains free access to the unit. Use under house-swapping arrangements are considered personal use days, whether or not a fair rental is charged. However, personal use days do not include days when repairs and maintenance are performed on a substantially full-time basis by the owner, even if other individuals are present who are not repairing or maintaining the property.

Short-term rentals have become very popular in the travel scene, becoming hugely popular with homeowners and travelers alike. Though sometimes overlooked, sales and lodging taxes are an entire class of taxes that expose individuals to a significant liability. Depending on what State the home is located in, short-term rental property owners are sometimes required to collect and remit sales and lodging taxes on the gross rent collected from guests – the same taxes a hotel is required to collect. Short-term in most states is less than 30 days, but there are a handful of states that have 90-day requirements, and a few, such as the popular travel states of Hawaii and Florida, where short-term is defined as up to six months. These taxes are typically 10 percent to 15 percent of the gross rent collected – overnight accommodations are heavily taxed. Sales and lodging taxes are a type of gross receipts tax and are generally not deductible. Further complicating lodging taxes is the fact that there are often different city, county and state taxes that apply to each rental. **(See Above, "Classifying a Vacation Home (Second Home) as a Rental Property")**

A "timeshare" that you own is treated in the same way as a short-term vacation home rental property.

Real Estate Professional

You can avoid the $25,000 passive loss limitation only if you are considered a real estate professional. Also, rental income is not subject to payroll tax or self-employment tax even if you are a real estate professional. You are considered a real estate professional if you materially participate in a real property trade or business, which means that you meet one of the six safe harbor tests that are deemed material participation: participated in the activity more than 500 hours during the year; provided substantially all of the participation by individuals; participated for 100 hours or more and this equaled or exceeded all others' participation; participated for more than 100 hours in several activities and total participation adds up to more than 500 hours annually; materially participated in the activity for 5 of the 10 previous years; or provided personal (professional) services to the business and materially participated in any three preceding years. You have to meet one of the six tests, or you can be considered to materially participate in an activity if, based on all the facts and circumstances, you participate in an activity on a regular, continuous, and substantial basis during the year. And, in addition to meeting one of the tests to demonstrate material participation, you have to spend over 50% of your total working hours and more than 750 hours each year materially participating in real estate activities as a broker, landlord, or builder. Also, if married, you can only count the hours of participation of the spouse seeking to qualify as a real estate professional.

It is a common misconception that qualifying as a real estate professional makes all of a real estate professional's rental activities nonpassive. This is not the case; rather, a person who qualifies as a real estate professional has merely overcome the presumption that all rental activities are passive regardless of the individual's level of participation. In reality, for the real estate professional's rental activities to become nonpassive activities, only those rental activities in which the real estate professional materially participates are nonpassive activities. Importantly, the statute provides that a qualifying real estate professional must establish material participation in each separate rental activity. However, an exception is provided by which the taxpayer may elect to aggregate all interests in rental real estate for purposes of measuring material participation. This election allows a real estate professional to "aggregate all rental activities." This is the Section 469 aggregation election that allows you to treat all of your rental properties as one activity. The election permits taxpayers to group trades or businesses, including rental activities, together to satisfy the material participation standards and avoid characterization as a passive activityn – the election is not just for aggregating rental activities. This election allows you to materially participate in "grouped rental activities" for more than 750 hours during the year, and in doing so, treat all of the rental properties in the aggregated group as nonpassive activities. And the time driving to and from the rental houses (properties) counts toward the 750-hour requirement.

- **Example** - In the Gragg case, the Ninth Circuit considered whether rental losses for real estate professionals are automatically entitled to nonpassive treatment. Charles and Delores Gragg, on their 2006 and 2007 tax returns, asserted they met the requirements for real estate professional status because Delores was a full-time real estate agent, which required more than 50% of her personal service time and 750 hours. The Gragg's deducted the losses they incurred in 2006-2007 from two rental properties in full as nonpassive losses. They did not make the election to group the two properties as a single activity. The nonpassive losses were disallowed because the taxpayer who qualified for real estate professional status was still required to meet the material-participation requirements for each of the rental properties, which would not include her time working as a real estate agent. If a qualifying real estate professional has not made the election to group all of his or her rental activities as a single activity, he/she has 2 options: (1) filing for the election on an amended return if the taxpayer qualifies, or (2) seeking an extension of time to make the election by requesting a private letter ruling. The IRS has the authority to require a regrouping of activities by a taxpayer if it determines that the grouping is not an "appropriate economic unit."

https://cdn.ca9.uscourts.gov/datastore/opinions/2016/08/04/14-16053.pdf

Qualifying as a real estate professional suddenly became much more meaningful to taxpayers with rental income when the 3.8% net investment income tax went into effect, levying an additional 3.8% surtax on, among other items of investment income, all passive income of a taxpayer. Thus, a taxpayer with rental income now has an incentive to qualify as a real estate professional to avoid the 3.8% NII tax. All passive income, including from rental activities, can be (but not always) subject to the 3.8% net investment income tax.

Section 469 Aggregation Election – The Section 469 Election requires the creation of an "appropriate economic unit." All relevant facts and circumstances are considered in determining what comprises an "appropriate economic unit" for the purpose of the 469 Election, and any reasonable method may be used with the following factors given the greatest weight: similarities in types of trades or businesses; the extent of common control and ownership; geographical location; and interdependencies between or among the activities. The election is properly made by filing a statement with the taxpayer's tax return. The statement must provide the names, addresses, types of property (single-family, duplex, etc.) and employer identification numbers (EIN), if applicable, of each of the activities being grouped as a single activity. In addition, the statement must contain a declaration that the grouped activities make up an appropriate economic unit for the measurement of gain or loss.

Even if you qualify as a real estate professional, it may not be possible to materially participate in each property if you have multiple properties, and without material participation, rental losses will be subject to the passive loss limitation ($25,000) on each property. However, the Section 469 aggregation election allows you to convert otherwise passive rental activities to non-passive by grouping them, i.e. treating them collectively as a single activity by combining the participation hours and improving one's ability to achieve the necessary hours for material participation. Without the election, you might be unable to show material participation in all of the activities, although you may be able to show material participation in some of the activities or properties, because it is not an all or nothing election after a taxpayer qualifies as a real estate professional.

A taxpayer's initial Section 469 election is binding for the year it is made and for all future years and can't be changed unless it is clearly inappropriate or there is a material change in circumstances, i.e. a taxpayer can revoke the 469 Election only when a material change in the taxpayer's facts and circumstances occurs. Taxpayers are allowed to file a late Section 469 election after filing their original tax return by attaching a statement to their amended tax return. Taxpayers filing a late 469 Election must include the following on their amended return: an explanation of why the election was not timely made; designation of the tax year for which the taxpayer seeks to make the late election; a declaration that the representations are made under penalties of perjury; and a statement at the top of the return declaring "FILED PURSUANT TO REV. PROC. 2011-34." The individual or individuals who sign must have personal knowledge of the facts and circumstances related to the election. Thus, taxpayers that qualify for the 469 Election and have timely filed all previous tax returns and consistently reported the income or loss as aggregated can avail themselves of this revenue procedure as long as they have "reasonable cause" for the failure to make the election on their original tax return. The taxpayer will be treated as having timely filed a required tax or information return if the return is filed within six months after the due date, including extensions. Reasonable cause generally means the exercise of ordinary business care, and a taxpayer must prove that failure to file a timely return was not the result of carelessness, reckless indifference, or intentional failure. To revoke the election in a subsequent year, the taxpayer must file a statement with the tax return for the year of revocation containing a declaration that the taxpayer is revoking the election and an explanation of the nature of the material change.

There are downsides to a 469 Election. One downside is that any suspended losses on a single property will not be freed up unless a complete disposition is made of all properties under the election. The ability to make this election underscores how proactive attention to each real estate activity before year's end may help determine whether such an election is advisable.

The IRS has agreed with recommendations in a government report urging the Agency to increase its examinations of individual tax returns that report losses from rental real estate activities.

Chapter 8 – Non-Taxable Income

Non-taxable income is either tax-free compensation or other payments that are specifically exempted from taxable income by law or regulation, but may be taxable or partially taxable at ordinary income tax rates under certain circumstances. Non-taxable income is generally not subject to payroll tax, but there are exceptions. In some cases, tax-free income is actually reported on a Form 1099, but a code on the Form indicates the exemption. **(See Chapter 14, "Where Payments Are Reported on Form 1099-MISC")**

Combat Pay Earned by Military Personnel

Combat pay of enlisted military personnel, including non-commissioned officers, is tax-free. Part of military officers' combat pay is tax-free – limited to the maximum salary of a non-commissioned officer. This covers all compensation for any month the individual served in a combat zone or was hospitalized as result of wounds, disease, or injury in a combat zone. Combat pay is shown in Box 14, Form W-2 and is not included in Box 1, Form W-2. See Publication 3, "Armed Forces' Tax Guide" for details. **(See Chapter 4, "Wages and Salaries")**
www.irs.gov/pub/irs-pdf/p3.pdf

The Tax Cuts and Jobs Act (TCJA) grants combat zone benefits to military personnel performing services in the Sinai Peninsula of Egypt, retroactively effective to June 9, 2015. Benefits include limited tax-free income, excise tax exclusions, surviving spouse benefits, and tax return filing extensions. This provision is scheduled to sunset at the end of the 2025 tax year.

State Paid Veterans Bonuses and Payments for Combat Service

State paid veterans' bonuses are tax-free. State payments for combat service are tax-free, even if paid to a dependent.

Social Security Death Benefit

The $255 death benefit paid by Social Security when a person dies is tax-free. **(See Chapter 5, "Social Security Benefits")**

Payments to Volunteer Fire Fighters and Medical Responders

Payments to volunteer fire fighters and emergency medical responders are tax-free.

Clergy Furnished Housing

Clergy furnished housing or an allowance for housing is income tax-free, but "self-employment tax (FICA)" must be paid on the FMV of the housing or the housing allowance." **(See Chapter 2, "Payroll Tax"); (See Chapter 17, "Self-Employment Tax"; & "Ministers and Employees of Religious Organizations")**

Awards for Recognition of Achievements

Cash awards are tax-free if they are in recognition of past achievements of the recipient in religious, charitable, scientific, educational, artistic, literary, or civic fields; and the recipient was selected without any action on his/her part to enter a contest. **(See Chapter 4, "Earned Income")**

Employee Achievement Awards

Employee achievement awards provided by employers to employees are tax-free. However, the Tax Cuts and Jobs Act (TCJA) limits tax fee employee achievement awards and other employee awards such as length of service awards to tangible personal property effective for tax year 2018 and subsequent years. This includes watches, golf clubs, and other tangible personal property. Normally, the value of such items cannot exceed $1,600 in a year. The purpose of this change is intended to eliminate disguised compensation to employees. In 2017 and prior years, such awards to employees could include certain intangible items, such as vacations, meals, lodging, tickets to events, and gift certificates. But no more beginning in 2018. **(See Chapter 4, "Earned Income")**

Interest on Municipal Bonds and Tax-Exempt Municipal Bond Funds

Interest earned on municipal bonds and tax-exempt municipal bond funds is tax-free for federal income tax purposes, but may be taxable for state income tax purposes. **(See Chapter 5, "Interest")**

Interest Earned on Tax-Exempt Housing Bonds

Interest earned on tax-exempt housing bonds issued by state and local governments is tax-free. To help veterans buy homes, Congress authorized states to issue qualified veterans' mortgage bonds under which interest payments are tax-free. Certain dates for the completion of military service before 1977 are removed, and the eligibility period is reduced from 30 to 25 years after separation from service.

Stock Dividends

Stock dividends are tax-free, unless the shareholder has the option to take cash or property instead of stock, or it is a preferred stock dividend. **(See Chapter 5, "Dividends"); (See Chapter 6, "Qualified Dividends")**

Child Support Payments

Child support payments are tax-free to the recipient, and are not deductible by the payer. In order to be considered child support payments, the divorce agreement must tie the payments to an event related to a child, i.e. reaching a specified age, graduating from school, leaving the household, marriage, etc. If payments are for both alimony and child support, child support takes priority over alimony when the total required amount is not paid. **(See Chapter 5, "Alimony and Separate Maintenance"); (See Chapter 11, "Alimony/Separate Maintenance")**

Long-Term Care Insurance Benefits

A qualified long-term care insurance contract is treated as an accident and health insurance contract. Thus, amounts (other than dividends or premium refunds) received under such a contract are treated as amounts received for personal injuries and sickness and are treated as reimbursement for expenses actually incurred for medical care. Since amounts received for personal injuries and sickness are generally not includable in gross income, benefits received under qualified long-term care insurance are generally not taxable. But there is a limit: Long-term care benefits paid by long-term care insurance policies to taxpayers are not included in income except for amounts that exceed the beneficiary's total qualified long-term care expenses or $360 per day, whichever is greater. **(See Below, "Personal Injury Awards as a Result of Physical Injuries or Sickness"); (See Chapter 4, "Earned Income"); (See Chapter 5, "Disability Income"); (See Chapter 12, "Medical Expenses")**

Rebates Received from Purchases of Tangible Assets

Rebates received resulting from purchases of tangible assets are tax-free. Also, credit card rebates are tax-free, even though they may be claimed as a charitable contribution if so directed. Awards generated by business-owner reward cards used for the purchase of equipment used in a business should reduce the basis of the equipment by the value of the awards. **(See Chapter 12, "Charitable Contribution Deduction"); (See Chapter 16, "Personal Property")**

Property Damage Payments

Payments from insurance companies for property damages are tax-free if the settlement merely pays for the cost of fixing, for example, your car or house, even if you get back more than you paid for the car or house, and you have not claimed a casualty loss deduction for damage to the property. If you get back more than you paid to fix your house, the excess will be treated as a reduction in the purchase price. If the damage is to your business, the same rules apply although a recovery in excess of your basis may be taxed at the 15% or 20% capital gain tax rate. **(See Chapter 6, "Capital Gain Tax Rates"; & "Reporting Capital Gains and Losses"); (See Chapter 12, "Casualty, Disaster, and Theft Losses")**

Workers' Compensation

Worker's Compensation payments for job-related injuries or illness are tax-free. Payments must be made under the authority of a law or regulation that provides compensation for on-the-job injuries or illness. Workers' compensation payments that reduce Social Security benefits are treated as a Social Security benefit received during the year and are indirectly subject to income tax but not payroll tax (Box 5 of Form SSA-1099 is the taxable amount – not reduced by any amount, such as a workers' compensation offset, shown in Box 3). Workers' compensation paid in lieu of Social Security disability benefits is taxable. By law, workers compensation payments offset Social Security benefits dollar for dollar, and therefore, are taxable to the same extent as Social Security payments when this occurs. **(See Chapter 5, "Social Security Benefits"; & "Social Security Disability Benefits")**

Federal Disaster Loss Relief

Payments received from a charity or government agency to cover personal living expenses resulting from a federal declared disaster are tax-free, as are grants made under the Disaster Relief Act to pay for housing, transportation, medical expenses, personal property, and funeral expenses. However, if a grant reimburses a casualty loss, no casualty loss deduction can be claimed to the extent of the reimbursement. Also, reimbursements from other sources intended to help with repairs or reconstruction of a personal residence and its contents lost in a federal disaster area are tax-free, and no loss deduction can be taken to the extent of the reimbursements. Any cancellation of a federal disaster loan under the Robert T. Stafford Disaster Relief and Emergency Assistance Act is also treated as a reimbursement of a casualty loss and no deduction can be taken to the extent of the reimbursement. **(See Chapter 3, "Federal Disaster Loss Relief"); (See Chapter 12, "Casualty, Disaster, and Theft Losses")**

Qualified Distributions from Roth IRAs

Qualified distributions from Roth IRAs that include any earnings are tax-free, and are penalty free if you are age 59 ½ or older. If you are under age 59 ½, and have owned a Roth account for at least 5 years, distributions that include any earnings are also tax-free and penalty free if you: have a disability; are a qualified new home buyer; or are using the funds to pay for a child's college expenses. Also, each separate Roth account has a separate 5-year waiting period. Otherwise, if you withdraw earnings before the age of 59 ½, you'll pay income tax on the earnings (but not payroll tax) plus a 10% penalty. But to the extent any distributions represent a return of the owner's contributions, the penalty would not apply, and you can withdraw the amount of your contributions at any time, for any reason, without having to pay tax or a penalty, and any distributions represent a return of the owner's contributions first. **(See Chapter 5, "Conversion of Traditional IRAs to Roth IRAs"; & "Distributions from Retirement Plans and Traditional IRAs")**

Foster Care Income

Payments received by foster care providers is tax-free income. The payments come from a state's (or a political subdivision of a state) foster care program to care for foster care individuals placed in providers' homes by an agency of the state, or an agency licensed by the state. Payments made for additional care because an individual has a physical, mental, or emotional handicap, defined as difficulty-of-care payments, are also tax-free – limited to payments for 10 qualified foster care individuals under the age of 19 or five individuals age 19 or older per foster care home. Effective for payments made on or after Jan. 3, 2014, the IRS announced that it will treat qualified Medicaid waiver payments as difficulty-of-care payments that are tax-free, regardless of whether the care provider is related to the eligible individual. Qualified Medicaid waiver payments are defined as "payments made by a state or political subdivision thereof, or an entity that is a certified Medicaid provider, under a Medicaid waiver program to an individual care provider for nonmedical support services provided under a plan of care to an eligible individual (whether related or unrelated) living in the individual care provider's home." Taxpayers may also use this guidance for tax years still open under the normal statute of limitations period.

Qualified Scholarships and Grants

Qualified scholarships and grants received by an individual who is a candidate for a degree are tax-free. Qualified scholarships are used to pay for tuition and course-related fees, books, supplies, and equipment required for courses. On the other hand, some scholarships or grants are considered taxable if the terms of a scholarship or grant permits the funds to be used to pay for room and board or other non-qualified expenses, but they are not subject to payroll tax. However, tuition reductions received for teaching, research, or services required as a condition of receiving a grant or scholarship are usually taxable for income tax purposes but not for payroll tax (FICA) purposes, except tuition reductions received by teachers' aides and individuals who have armed services obligations after graduation as a condition of receiving the scholarship are totally tax-free. National Health Services Corps and Armed Forces Health Professions Scholarships were made permanently tax-free by the American Taxpayer Relief Act of 2012.

Free and partially free tuition provided to a faculty member or school employee for undergraduate studies is tax-free to the recipient. This also applies to tuition reductions for spouses, dependents, former employees who have retired or left on disability, widows and widowers of former employees, and a child under age 25 whose parents have died. Tuition reductions for graduate courses are also tax-free if it is in addition to payments for teaching, research, or providing other services.

Gifts and Inheritances

Gifts and inheritances are totally tax-free to the beneficiaries, except for inherited retirement accounts, traditional IRAs and tax-deferred annuities, which are taxable unearned income to beneficiaries based on the same amount as they would have been taxable to the original owner. The basis of a gift of property to a beneficiary is the lower of

FMV or the adjusted basis of the property. The basis of inherited property is usually the stepped-up basis to FMV on the date of the decedent's death. Cash you receive as a gift or inheritance is tax-free to you, unless it is a gift or an inheritance of a retirement account or an IRA. (NOTE: gifts and inheritances may be taxable to the benefactors or benefactors' estates). **(See Chapter 21, "Estates"); (See Chapter 22, "Basis of Property Inherited or Gifted"; & "Estate Tax Return")**

If you receive a gift or inheritance that is not an IRA or retirement account, start with the assumption that it isn't taxable to you and therefore, you don't have to do anything. However, if you're concerned about proving that something is a gift or inheritance, file Form 3520. In any case, File Form 3520 if you receive either of the following during the year: (1) more than $100,000 from a nonresident alien individual or foreign estate that you treated as a gift or bequest, or (2) more than $14,375 from foreign corporations or foreign partnerships (including foreign persons related to such foreign corporations or foreign partnerships) that you treated as gifts.
www.irs.gov/pub/irs-pdf/f3520.pdf   www.irs.gov/pub/irs-pdf/i3520.pdf

You are required to report bequests on Form 3520 when you actually or constructively receive them (report bequests as gifts in the year you actually receive them or the year you could have acquired title in your name, whichever occurs first). In this regard, the penalty for reporting a bequest late is 5% of its value for each month the gift is not reported (capped at 25%). However, no penalty applies if the IRS is convinced the failure to report was due to reasonable cause and not willful neglect.

Life Insurance Proceeds

Life insurance proceeds received by a beneficiary in a lump-sum payment are tax-free. However, if installments are received by the beneficiary, part of each installment may be taxable as interest income – divide the lump-sum amount payable at death by the number of installments to be paid, and include anything paid over the excluded part per installment as interest subject to income tax. But for a surviving spouse who receives installments, up to $1,000 of interest per year is considered tax-free income. **(See Chapter 5, "Interest")**

Life insurance policies with an accelerated death benefit clause allows lifetime distributions for those who are terminally ill (someone with a condition expected to result in death within 24 months) or chronically ill. Such payments to a terminally ill person are tax-free, as well as payments to a chronically ill person for long-term care expenses. Payments made to chronically ill individuals on a per diem basis without regard to care costs are tax-free income up to a set dollar amount ($340 per day). If benefits exceed this limit, the excess is tax-free to the extent used to pay for long-term care services. Insurance companies that pay long-term care insurance benefits are required to provide claimants with a Form 1099-LTC, Copy B that reports payments made under a long-term care insurance contract. **(See Chapter 12, "Long-Term Care Insurance Premiums")**
www.irs.gov/pub/irs-pdf/i3520.pdf   www.irs.gov/pub/irs-pdf/i1099ltc.pdf

With or without an accelerated death benefit clause, it may be possible to sell a life insurance policy to pay for long-term care. Proceeds from the sale of a life insurance policy paid to a terminally ill individual are tax-free. Proceeds paid to a chronically ill individual are tax-free to the same extent as accelerated death benefits.

Life Insurance Borrowings – Where borrowings on a life insurance policy exceed the cash value of the policy and the insurer cancels the policy, the borrower owes income tax on the difference between his total debt and his investment in the policy.

VA Pensions or Allowances

VA pensions or allowances for personal injuries, sickness, or death resulting from active service in the armed forces or foreign service are tax-free. This includes payments to eligible survivors of deceased service members, such as proceeds from government life insurance.

- Payments under the Dept. of Veterans Affairs Compensated Work Therapy (CWT) Program are tax-free. These are service connected disability payments that some veterans receive as a result of certain conditions they have due to active military service. Service connected disability payments can range from 10% to 100% depending on the severity.
- Part of a VA pension may be taxable when part of the pension is based on years of service, such as a disabled career service person who retired from military service. Report the amount that is based on years of service as earned income subject to income and payroll taxes and exclude the portion based on a service connected disability.
- Education and training allowances paid by the VA are tax-free. Any deductible education expenses or education tax credits that you're entitled to must be reduced by VA allowances. **(See Chapter 11, "Tuition and Fees for Higher Education"); (See Chapter 13, "Education Credits")**
- If a veteran qualifies for retroactive disability compensation, any taxable retiree pay, or a percentage thereof, that he or she has already received may be designated as tax-free disability compensation, and the veteran is eligible for a refund of the taxes already paid on the amount designated as disability compensation (not limited to the usual 3 year statute of limitations). In some cases, a retired service member receiving taxable retirement benefits may later receive a determination that he or she is retroactively eligible for a service connected disability, in which case the portion of retirement benefits attributable to the disability is retroactively reclassified as tax-free income.

Personal Injury Awards as a Result of Physical Injuries or Sickness

Personal injury awards as a result of physical injuries or physical sickness are tax-free. However, punitive damages awarded in addition to personal injury awards are taxable for income tax purposes, but not for payroll tax purposes. For example, if you receive a legal settlement from an insurance company as a result of your injury in a car accident, the settlement is tax-free to you because it is compensation for a personal physical injury. However, if any part of the settlement is for punitive damages, that part is considered taxable income. In addition, payments for medical treatment, including counseling (treatment of emotional trauma related to physical injury), are tax-free. Payments for medical expenses are tax-free, and what constitutes "medical expenses" is surprisingly liberal. For example, payments to a psychiatrist or counselor qualify, as do payments to a chiropractor or physical therapist. And many nontraditional treatments count too. But, a portion of contingent fees paid to your attorneys may be taxable to you, if the recovery amount includes punitive damages, which are taxable. **(See Above, "Workers' Compensation"); (See Chapter 5, "Personal Injury Awards Associated with Nonphysical Injuries"); (See Chapter 12, "Legal Expenses")**

- Example – A college campus security officer was injured in a car accident unrelated to his job. The injuries forced him to go on disability temporarily. But the school fired him, and he sued based on employment

discrimination. Eventually, the parties settled the case and the security officer received a tidy amount. However, in Rajcoomar v. Commissioner, the Tax Court ruled that no part of the payout represented compensation for physical injury, so the entire settlement was taxable compensation.
http://ustaxcourt.gov/UstcInOp/OpinionViewer.aspx?ID=11314

Damages for Emotional Injuries – Damages for emotional injuries are taxable. Physical symptoms caused by emotional distress – say, headaches – are generally taxable, but it's fuzzy and much litigated. The IRS says that in order for physical injuries to be tax-free, they must be visible. Example: If in settling an employment dispute you receive $50,000 extra because your employer gave you an ulcer, is an ulcer physical or is it merely a symptom of your emotional distress? Many plaintiffs end up taking aggressive positions on their tax returns, claiming damages of this nature are tax-free. But that can be a losing battle if the defendant issues a Form 1099 for the entire settlement. This means it can behoove you to try to get an agreement with the defendant about the tax issues. If you sue your employer for sexual harassment involving rude comments or even fondling, that's not physical enough for the IRS. Taxpayers routinely argue in Tax Court that their damages are sufficiently physical to be tax-free, but the IRS usually wins these cases.

U.S. Savings Bond Redemptions Used for Higher Education Expenses

U.S. Savings Bond redemptions used for qualified higher education expenses or for contributions to 529 Qualified Tuition Plans and Coverdell education savings accounts are tax-free if they are Series EE or I U.S. Savings Bonds issued after 1989 to an individual who has reached the age of 24 before the date of issuance. If you plan to use them for your children's education, the bonds have to be owned in the parent's name. The children can be named as a beneficiary on the bond, but they can't be named as co-owner. Savings bonds issued in 1990 or later have a final maturity of 30 years after the purchase date. That means the first maturities of savings bonds that qualify for the education tax exclusion are in 2020. Of course, you can cash them in any time before maturity and the interest earned on them is tax-free if used for higher education expenses. Married persons must file jointly to claim tax-free interest on U.S. Savings Bonds unless they lived apart for the whole year. You must file Form 8815 or optional Form 8818 when the Savings Bonds are redeemed. Redemptions can be used for the taxpayer, spouse, and dependents. If the savings bond redemptions are used to fund contributions to a 529 plan, the funds must be deposited into the 529 plan within 60 days of redemption and in the same tax year as the redemption. The 529 plan administrator will require the receipt of Form 1099-INT or the account statement issued by the redeeming institution. **(See Chapter 11, "Tuition and Fees for Higher Education"); (See Chapter 13, "Education Credits")**
www.irs.gov/pub/irs-pdf/i1099ltc.pdf www.irs.gov/pub/irs-pdf/f8818.pdf

You must know both the total redemption amount and the interest earned to put on Form 8815. In 2018, tax-free redemptions are subject to phase-outs beginning at modified adjusted gross incomes (MAGI) of $119,550 (married filing jointly & surviving spouse); and $79,700 (single & head-of-household).

Damages Paid for Wrongful Imprisonment

Beginning with tax year 2016, all compensation that a person receives for being wrongfully incarcerated is tax-free. For previous years, such compensation was considered tax-free only if the compensation received by the individual was based on injuries incurred while in prison. However, individuals who treated such amounts taxable in prior years can request a refund of the taxes paid by filing Form 1040X, submitting supporting documentation, and writing "Incarceration Exclusion PATH Act" on the top of their Form 1040X.

Identity Theft Protection Services

When victims of data breaches receive free identity protection services from an organization that suffered a data breach, the value of those identity protection services is tax-free. This applies to anyone whose personal information may have been compromised in a data breach, including customers, employees, and others.

Distributions from ABLE Accounts

The Achieving a Better Life Experience Act (ABLE) creates tax-favored savings accounts for individuals with disabilities and their families for tax years beginning January 1, 2015. Contributions to the accounts are not deductible and can be made by the person with the disability (the "designated beneficiary"), parents, family members or others. In 2017, the annual contribution was limited to the amount of the annual gift-tax exclusion ($15,000 in 2018; $14,000 in 2017).

The Tax Cuts and Jobs Act (TCJA) increases the annual ABLE contribution limit for tax years 2018 – 2025 to more than $15,000 in 2018, by allowing the disabled beneficiary or others to contribute an additional amount equal to the lesser of the beneficiary's compensation for the current year or the poverty level for a one-person household for the preceding year ($12,060 in 2017). Therefore, a designated beneficiary with no compensation in 2018 could have $27,060 contributed ($15,000 + $12,060) to his/her ABLE account in 2018 (indexed for inflation beginning in 2019). The TCJA also allows the designated beneficiary of the ABLE account to claim the "Savers Tax Credit" in an amount equal to 10% to 50% of the annual contributions to his/her account based on the filing status and adjusted gross income (AGI) of the designated beneficiary, limited to a maximum credit of $1,000. In addition, tax-free rollovers are allowed from 529 Plans to ABLE accounts, either for the benefit of the disabled transferor or for a disabled family member, effective as of December 22, 2017 through December 31, 2025, and the rollovers count toward the annual ABLE contribution limit. Contributions to ABLE accounts are reported on Form 5498-QA and distributions are reported on Form 1099-QA. **(See Below, "Distributions from Qualified Tuition Programs – 529 Plans"); (See Chapter 13, "Savers Credit")**
www.irs.gov/pub/irs-prior/f1099qa--2015.pdf   www.irs.gov/pub/irs-prior/f1099qa--2015.pdf

Distributions from ABLE accounts that are used for a disabled person's expenses are tax-free. Allowable expenses are for basic living expenses to help a beneficiary improve his/her quality of life, including expenses for housing, transportation, job training, and even for such items as smartphones that can help, for example, autistic people navigate and communicate better. The expenses don't have to be medically necessary. Distributions (earnings only) for nonqualified purposes are subject to income tax, but not payroll tax, and a 10% penalty is payable. The ABLE Act allows families to set aside money in accounts to be used for a disabled person's expenses without risking the loss of government benefits. The beneficiary must have become blind or disabled before age 26 to qualify for an ABLE account. ABLE accounts are administered by the states, and the "Protecting Americans from Tax Hikes Act of 2015" allows individuals to set-up ABLE accounts in any state, not just in the state of their residence. However, the law allows families to open just one account per beneficiary (individuals can choose the state program that best fits their needs). Distributions from ABLE accounts are reported on Form 1099-QA.

Generally, a disabled person with more than $2,000 in personal assets is ineligible for Medicaid and Supplemental Social Security benefits. However, money held in an ABLE account is generally exempt from the $2,000 limit on personal assets for individuals who wish to qualify for government benefits such as Medicaid and other federal means-tested programs, or in determining the amount of any benefit or assistance provided under those programs, although special rules and limits apply for Supplemental Security Income (SSI) purposes. With an ABLE account, a disabled person can have up to $100,000 in assets before their savings affect their ability to qualify for most federal benefit programs. Rollovers to another ABLE account for the individual or a disabled sibling are limited. When the disabled person dies, amounts left over in an ABLE account goes to the state to recover its Medicaid costs and any other costs paid-out for the benefit of the deceased. However, any money left after the state takes its share goes to a designated beneficiary, who would owe income tax on the amount received, but with no penalty. See ABLE Accounts – Tax Benefit for People with Disabilities and Publication 907, "Tax Highlights for Persons with Disabilities."

www.irs.gov/pub/irs-pdf/p907.pdf www.irs.gov/government-entities/federal-state-local-governments/able-accounts-tax-benefit-for-people-with-disabilities

Distributions from Coverdell Education Savings Accounts

The Coverdell Education Savings law was made permanent as of Jan. 1, 2013. A Coverdell works just like a Roth IRA – you are allowed to make an annual non-deductible contribution to a specially designated investment trust account each year. An individual can contribute a maximum of $2,000 to a Coverdell Education Savings Account each year to an unlimited number of beneficiaries, but the contributions are not deductible. Contributions must be made by the tax return filing date and are reported on Form 5498-ESA. Distributions from Coverdell Education Savings Accounts are tax-free if used to pay for qualified primary, secondary, and postsecondary (higher) education expenses. Distributions are reported to the taxpayer on Form 1099-Q, which should show the tax-free earnings portion of each distribution. In 2017 and 2018, the maximum contribution of $2,000 per student to a Coverdell account is phased-out between MAGIs of $190,000 - $220,000 (married filing jointly) and $95,000 - $110,000 (all others).

www.irs.gov/pub/irs-access/f5498e_accessible.pdf www.irs.gov/pub/irs-pdf/i5498e.pdf
www.irs.gov/pub/irs-access/f1099q_accessible.pdf www.irs.gov/pub/irs-pdf/i1099q.pdf

Unlike 529 Plans, Coverdells allow you to self-direct your investments, just like you might do for your IRA. Funds from Coverdells can be withdrawn tax-free to pay expenses for grades K through 12 and for college expenses, while 529 plans are limited to college expenses. This feature is appreciated most in families planning to send their children to private grade schools which can cost a lot. Qualified education expenses include: tuition; fees; tutoring; books; supplies; related equipment; room and board; uniforms; transportation; computers; and special needs services. Also, distributions from Coverdell's to Qualified Tuition Programs (529 Plans) are tax-free. Contributions for a beneficiary can be made each year to both to a Coverdell plan and a 529 plan. Individuals receiving military death benefits can disregard the contribution limitations for Coverdell Savings Accounts, and can contribute the full amount of the death benefits to a Coverdell.

You cannot claim education credits for the same expenses paid for with Coverdell distributions and 529 Plan distributions. Also, any expenses paid with tax-free scholarships and VA education assistance cannot be claimed with Coverdell distributions and 529 plan distributions. Any distributions (earnings only) not used for education expenses are taxable unearned income, plus an additional 10% penalty, that should be reported as "Other Income" on Form 1040. Only earnings are subject to taxation and the 10% penalty. A contribution cannot be made to a beneficiary after he reaches age 18, unless he is a special needs beneficiary. Any assets remaining in the account when the designated beneficiary reaches age 30 must be withdrawn within 30 days. **(See Below, "Distributions from Qualified Tuition Programs (QTPs) – 529 Plans"); (See Chapter 13, "Education Credits")**

Taxpayers that have Coverdell accounts are allowed to make only one tax-free rollover each year, no matter how many Coverdell accounts they own. However, as with IRAs, you can make unlimited trustee-to-trustee transfers between Coverdell accounts each year because such direct transfers are not considered to be distributions or rollovers. **(See Chapter 9, "Rollovers from Qualified Retirement Plans and Traditional IRAs")**

Distributions from Qualified Tuition Programs (QTPs) – 529 Plans

A 529 Plan (QTP) is an education savings plan operated by a state or educational institution designed to help families set aside funds for future education costs, and beginning in 2018, the Tax Cuts and Jobs Act (TCJA) allows distributions of up to $10,000 per year from a 529 Plan for a child to attend public or private (secular or religious) elementary or secondary schools. For 2017 and prior years, distributions from 529 plans could only be used for qualified higher education expenses. Distributions from 529 Plans are not allowed for home schooling expenses; however, out-of-pocket expenses may be deductible if state law defines a home school as a type of private school. Tax-free rollovers are allowed from 529 Plans to ABLE accounts, either for the benefit of the disabled transferor or for a disabled family member, effective as of December 22, 2017 through December 31, 2025, and the rollovers count toward the annual ABLE contribution limit. 529 plan distributions are reported on Form 1099-Q, which should show the tax-free earnings portion of each distribution. **(See Above, "Distributions from ABLE Accounts")**

Contributions to Qualified Tuition Programs (QTPs, or 529 Plans) are not deductible, and distributions from the plans are tax-free if used for qualified education expenses. Qualified higher education expenses include graduate school (tuition and fees, books, room and board, supplies, and computer equipment). Computer equipment and technology was added as qualified expenses by the "Protecting Americans from Tax Hikes Act of 2015." 529 funds can be used at any eligible educational institution meeting accreditation standards. Contributions to 529 plans must be made by December 31st each year. Before 2015, an IRS rule allowed only one investment allocation change per year for 529 plans, but beginning in 2015 investment allocations can be changed twice a year. Nearly every state now has at least one 529 plan available. 529 plans are usually categorized as either savings plans or prepaid tuition plans. **(See Chapter 11, "Tuition and Fees for Higher Education"); (See Chapter 13, "Education Credits")**

- A savings plan works much like a 401(k) or IRA by investing your contributions in mutual funds or similar investments. You have available what you contributed plus the earnings on it (which may vary depending on the success of your investments). There are usually no boundaries for selecting a plan. For example, if you are in Illinois, you can select a plan from Michigan, even if your child eventually goes to a school in California. Savings plans may be used at any private and out-of-state colleges.

- A prepaid tuition plan allows families to buy "units" of tuition at a rate close to today's prices, and the units are cashed in when the student attends school. You can prefund the cost of tuition at a public college or university within your state, and you receive what you have paid for, which will likely cover only part of the tuition at the school your child chooses to attend. Also, if you use a prepaid 529 tuition plan available from private institutions, your state of residence is irrelevant. You can prepay tuition at any of more than 270 private colleges and universities.

There are two ways to invest in a 529 plan: directly with the 529 Plan manager, or through a financial advisor. 529 plans are subject to the same requirements as distributions from Coverdell Education Savings Accounts. The Act permits refunds of tuition fees paid with amounts distributed from a 529 account to be treated as qualified expenses if the refunds are re-contributed to a 529 account within 60 days. **(See Above, "Distributions from Coverdell Education Savings Accounts")**

The best part about a 529 Plan is that no amount accumulated in the plan will be included in the gross income of a designated beneficiary or a contributor to the plan with respect to any distributions or earnings under the program. What's more, there is asset protection for 529 plans, preventing them from being obtained by creditors in the case of an account owner's personal bankruptcy. For financial purposes, a 529 plan is treated as a parental asset. This means only 5.64% of the account's value is included in the financial aid formula (a child's assets are included at 20%).
www.irs.gov/pub/irs-pdf/f1099q.pdf www.irs.gov/pub/irs-pdf/f1099q.pdf

Anyone can be a 529 account owner and anyone can be named a beneficiary. The only requirements for being a beneficiary are that the person must be a U.S. citizen and have a Social Security number. There are absolutely no age restrictions for a participant. For example, if a beneficiary decides to go back to school later in life, the assets are there for them because there is no time limit for keeping funds in a 529 plan. However, if you realize you won't be able to use all of the funds in a 529 account and decide to close it, the income earned on the contributions will be taxable unearned income, in addition, there is a 10% penalty on the income withdrawn. If your child wins a scholarship and you can't use the amount accumulated in the 529 plan to pay for college expenses, normally you would owe income taxes and a 10% penalty on the earnings portion of any 529 withdrawals that are not used for qualified education expenses. But there is an exception for tax-free scholarships, i.e. you can withdraw up to the amount of the scholarship without being subject to the 10% penalty (you still have to pay income taxes on the withdrawal). However, you should ensure that the money and the 1099 Form reporting the withdrawal is sent to the student who is in a lower tax bracket than you. If you withdraw money from a 529 plan to use for other than education expenses, then change your mind and return the money to the same 529 plan, it isn't a tax-free rollover because the money was not transferred to a different 529 plan for the same beneficiary or to a different beneficiary's 529 plan. Thus, the withdrawal is taxed, but you won't have to pay the 10% penalty.

Many states don't cap annual contributions to 529 plans. But in your lifetime, you can put up to a total of $250,000 into a single 529 plan without having to file a Gift Tax return. However, you should consider limiting your annual contributions to the annual allowable Gift Tax exclusion for a single beneficiary ($15,000 or $30,000 in 2018, if married and gift-splitting is used) in order to avoid Gift taxes. Also, according to the 5-year averaging rule a donor can contribute up to $75,000 in a year to a beneficiary; $150,000 if a married couple, and average it over 5 years with no gift tax consequences (however, a gift tax return must be filed, and the election for 5-year averaging must be made on the donor's Gift tax return). A 529 plan is the only investment vehicle allowing five years of tax-free gifts in a single year. However, giving the maximum in one year, 2018, will wipe out your 2018 and 2019 gift tax exclusion and most of it for 2019-2022. One child can be the beneficiary of numerous accounts, and if a beneficiary chooses not to go to college, plan assets can be transferred to another close relative without penalty. You can transfer assets among family members with no tax repercussions. Also, multiple family members and friends can give to the same 529 plan account to help create larger education funds. **(See Above, "Gifts and Inheritances");** **(See Chapter 22, "Exemption for Lifetime Taxable Gifts and Estates")**

Many states allow a state tax deduction for withdrawals from a 529 plan, imposing no waiting period on 529 withdrawals and allowing account holders to deduct contributions from their state income taxes regardless of how long the money is held in the account. This tax loophole can lower your state income tax bill, i.e. let's say a child attending school in the fall plans to pay his/her tuition out of pocket. Rather than paying the school directly, the family instead adds funds to an existing or newly opened 529 account in the student's name and then withdraws the funds shortly thereafter to cover the tuition payment. This allows the family a deduction in the amount of the contribution on their state income tax return, assuming their state offers a tax break and their plan has no waiting time limit for withdrawals. For example, Illinois allows residents to deduct up to $20,000 per year in contributions for a couple filing jointly, and has a flat income tax rate of 5%. So, if a family contributed $20,000 to one of the state's 529 plans and then withdrew it for tuition in the fall, they would gain a tax break of $1,000 ($20,000 x .05). There is no waiting period for withdrawals in 34 states.

Taxpayers should consider rolling over children's UTMA investments into a 529 Plan to avoid paying taxes on those investments under the kiddie tax rules. For 2018, the kiddie tax is applicable to dependents under age 19 or under age 24 if a full-time student. There are no tax implications if you are rolling over cash from A UTMA to a 529 plan. However, if the UTMA holds appreciated securities, they must be sold (only cash can be contributed to a 529 Plan), and your child will be taxed on the gains, if any, under the kiddie tax rules. Contributors to 529 plans, such as grandparents who don't want to owe estate taxes but also worry they might have unexpected costs, such as health care, have a useful option. Although 529 contributions remove assets from an estate, the giver can take back account assets if the money is needed (although they will have to pay a 10% penalty on funds taken back). **(See Chapter 5, "Earnings on Uniform Transfers to Minors Custodial Accounts"); (See Chapter 3, "Kiddie Tax")**

Parents or grandparents can make tuition payments directly to an education institution without using up their gift tax exclusion. Grandparents can also take their required minimum distributions (RMDs) from their IRA accounts and transfer those funds to a 529 plan, where the funds can continue to grow tax-deferred.

Also, it might be prudent to split education savings between a 529 plan and a second type of account, such as a child's IRA in the child's name. This would allow for investment changes when needed. A child's IRA can be used for education expenses without triggering early-withdrawal penalties and it isn't reported as an asset on financial applications, thus avoiding the risk of a smaller aid package. One option is a Roth IRA, which allows tax-deferred growth for educations costs. However, in order to be able to establish an IRA in the child's name, contributions to the IRA must come from the child's earnings. But parents can pay children for household services as long as the wage is reasonable for the work performed.

529 plan distributions that exceed qualified education expenses in a year can be partially taxable on the earnings only.

- **Example** – Total qualified education expenses = $8,300; tax-free scholarship = $3,100; QTP distribution = $5,300 of which $950 are earnings. Adjusted qualified expenses: $8,300, minus $3,100 (scholarship) = $5,200. $5,200 divided by $5,300 = .98 X $950 = $932. Therefore $18 is taxable QTP earnings ($950 minus $932 = $18)

Airline Miles
Airline miles received for making purchases on credit cards or frequent flier miles earned for taking trips are tax-free. But consumers technically owe taxes on miles they receive for opening a bank or credit card account. Miles earned for making purchases on a credit card can be used or donated to a charity, and if donated to a charity it is a

deductible charitable contribution provided substantiation rules for written acknowledgment from the charity are followed for amounts of $250 or more. **(See Chapter 12, "Non-Cash Contributions")**

- Personal use of airline frequent flier miles or other in-kind promotional benefits attributable to a taxpayer's business or official travel are tax-free to the employee.
- Mutual funds that offer a promotion that awards airline miles for the purchase of shares lowers the basis in the shares that the investor purchases by the value of the miles acquired.

Airline miles received for opening up a bank account or received as a sign-up bonus for getting a credit card are technically taxable, but unless the recipient receives a 1099-MISC, the reality is that not reporting this as income is likely to be overlooked. In the past, a Form 1099-MISC has not been required to be issued unless the payer has paid a recipient at least $600 during the year in rents, services, prizes and awards, and usually not that many miles are paid to open an account that would exceed the $600 mark. However, in the case of Shankar v. Commissioner the Tax Court sided with the IRS by deciding that the value of an airline ticket redeemed with "Thank You Points" received from opening an account with Citibank was taxable. Shankar received 50,000 thank you points from Citibank in 2009. Citibank reported this as "other Income" of $668 on Form 1099-MISC, but Shankar did not report the income on his tax return. The IRS introduced evidence that Shankar redeemed the points to purchase an airline ticket valued at $668.

www.ustaxcourt.gov/InOpHistoric/ShankarDiv.Halpern.TC.WPD.pdf

Citibank brought this on itself by issuing Form 1099-MISC to customers who receive frequent flyer miles – called "Thank You Points" – for opening accounts. Not all banks agreed with Citibank's position. When Citibank announced the practice in 2012, American Express explained that they treat the miles more like a rebate, just as airlines do (those miles are generally considered tax-free). Most tax professionals are saying that the issue would not have even been raised if not for the issuance of Form 1099-MISC by Citibank to its customers. However, from now on if you receive a Form 1099-MISC for receiving frequent flyer miles from a bank and you use the miles to purchase an airline ticket, most likely you will have to pay taxes on the value of the miles received.

Employer Provided Tax-Free Benefits

Employer provided tax-free benefits: An employer provides tax-free benefits to employees either directly or makes payments for the benefit of employees to third parties that are tax-free to the employees. Also, employees can elect to have part of their salaries excluded from their gross income on a pre-tax basis for benefits funded through a cafeteria plan. Following are certain employer provided tax-free benefits:

Employer Educational Assistance Programs – Educational assistance of up to $5,250 provided annually by an employer to an employee is tax-free income to the employee (including graduate school tuition assistance). This provision was made permanent as of Jan.1, 2013. This does not include educational assistance benefits to employees' spouses or dependents.

Dependent Care Benefits – Under the Dependent Care Assistance Program (DCAP), employer paid dependent care benefits up to $5,000 annually ($2,500 if married filing separately) are provided tax-free to employees. Employers must show the total amount of dependent care benefits provided to an employee during the year in Box 10 of Form W-2. **(See Chapter 13, "Child and Dependent Care Credit")**

Group Term Life Insurance – The cost of employer provided group term life insurance up to $50,000 in coverage is tax-free to an employee. In addition, the cost of employer provided group term life insurance on the life of an employee's spouse or dependents is tax-free to the employee if the amount of the coverage doesn't exceed $2,000. These exemptions are not available to highly paid and key employees unless the plan meets the nondiscrimination tests of eligibility.

The cost of additional employer provided insurance coverage of more than $50,000 on the life of an employee must be included in earned income subject to both ordinary income and payroll taxes.

Long-Term Care Coverage – Contributions by employers to provide coverage for long-term care services to employees are generally tax-free to employees. However, if the contributions are made through an employee's cafeteria plan, they must be included in the employee's taxable income subject to both income and payroll tax, reported in Box 1, Form W-2. **(See Chapter 4, "Earned Income"); (See Chapter 12, "Long-Term Care Insurance Premiums")**

Transit Benefits – The Tax Cuts and Jobs Act (TCJA) eliminated the bicycle commuter benefit for tax years 2018 – 2025. Before 2018, businesses were able to offer employees up to a $20 tax-free subsidy per month for biking to work. However, beginning in 2018, businesses can continue to provide the $20 benefit to employees, but it will be considered taxable income to employees for tax years 2018 – 2025.

The Tax Cuts and Jobs Act raises the transit benefit for transit passes and parking from $255 per month in 2017 to $260 per month in 2018; and likewise raises the parking benefit from $255 per month to $260 per month in 2018. However, the TCJA disallows any employer deduction for qualified transportation benefits provided to employees after 2017, including employee buses, van pools, subway or transit cards, and parking fees (unless the expenses are necessary for ensuring the safety of employees). Employees are still able to take advantage of pre-tax transit benefits. However, for tax years 2018 – 2025, employers will no longer be able to directly subsidize their employees for the transportation benefits without the subsidies being considered taxable income to employees and not deductible by employers.

Cell Phones – The cost of employer provided cell phones is a tax-free fringe benefit to employees. When an employer provides an employee with a cell phone primarily for non-compensatory business reasons, the business and personal use of the cell phone is exempt from the employee's taxable income. **(See Chapter 18, "Listed Property")**

Adoption Assistance – The cost of Employer paid adoption assistance in connection with the adoption of an eligible child is tax-free to employees, but the payments are "subject to payroll tax." In 2018, the exclusion from taxable income is limited to $13,810 per child. However, since the exclusion is per child, the maximum exclusion depends on the number of children adopted. If you adopt two children in 2018, the maximum exclusion is $13,810 x 2 or $27,620. If you adopt four children, the maximum exclusion is $13,570 x 4 or $55,240. The amount excludable from an employee's taxable income begins to phase-out for taxpayers (families) with modified adjusted gross incomes (MAGI) of $207,140, and is completely phased-out when MAGI is $247,140. **(See Chapter 2, "Payroll Tax (FICA)")**

Employees may take full advantage of both the tax credit and tax exclusion for employer provided benefits – just not for the same expenses. **(See Chapter 13, "Adoption Credit")**

Athletic Facilities – The cost of employer provided athletic facilities is tax-free to employees, if it is an employer-operated gym or other athletic club located on the employer's premises. It must be used primarily by employees, their spouses, and their dependents.

If an employer pays for a fitness program provided to employees at an off-site athletic club or facility, the value of the program should be included in employees' taxable income and is also subject to payroll taxes. When an employer provides benefits under a wellness program at no cost to employees that enables employees to earn cash awards or gym memberships, etc., the benefits are considered taxable wages and are subject to payroll taxes. If employees make pre-tax contributions to help pay for the wellness program and the employer later reimburses them for some or a portion of the amounts they paid as a reward for participating in the program, the reimbursements by the employer are considered taxable wages subject to payroll taxes. **(See Chapter 4, "Earned Income")**

De Minimis Fringe Benefits – The cost of de minimis fringe benefits provided by employers to employees is tax-free. This includes qualified employee discounts (up to 20% of retail); no-additional cost services; holiday gifts worth less than $25; employer-provided clothing such as polo shirts and caps with the company logo if employees are prohibited from wearing the clothes when off duty; occasional parties or picnics for employees and guests; occasional tickets for theater or sporting events; etc. **(See Chapter 15, "Entertainment Expenses")**

Employer Furnished Meals and Lodging – In 2017 and prior years, the following benefits were in effect for employer furnished meals and lodging: Employer furnished meals and lodging are tax-free to the employees and 100% deductible by the employers when the employers furnish the meals and lodging on the employer's business premises, and the meals and lodging are furnished for the convenience of the employer, and not for the convenience of the employee. The meals furnished to employees must be during working hours. However, if work duties prevent an employee from eating during working hours, a meal qualifying for the exemption can be provided to the employee immediately after working hours. The exemption applies to meals provided "in kind" by the employer. It does not apply to cash meal allowances provided by employers to employees, i.e. such allowances usually have to be included in employees' earned income subject to income and payroll taxes to the extent that such allowances are considered compensation. The employer must require employees to accept employer furnished lodging as a condition of employment. Therefore, an employee must be required to live in the lodging to be able to perform the duties of employment in order for the value of the lodging to be exempt from taxable income. In addition to employer provided meals and lodging, the value of small de minimis food items and soft drinks provided by an employer is tax-free. Also, occasional meals provided in kind or occasional cash received from the employer by an employee to buy dinner to allow the employee to work overtime is tax-free. The same treatment may be extended to food and drinks provided by the employer to employees and their guests at picnics and parties.

Under the Tax Cuts and Jobs Act (TCJA), meals provided to employees by an employer during working hours, including meals provided at on-premises dining facilities and for the convenience of the employer, that were tax-free to employees and 100% deductible by employers in 2017 and prior years, including de minimis food and beverages, have been reduced to being 50% deductible by employers for tax years 2018 – 2025, and will be nondeductible starting in 2026 (The TCJA doesn't mention anything about lodging expenses). However, an employer has the choice of including the cost of employee provided meals and de minimis food and beverages in employees' taxable income and then taking a 100% tax deduction for the meals and de minimis items in 2018 – 2025.

Net Operating Loss (NOL)

Under the TCJA, the 2-year net operating loss carryback that was available in 2017 and prior years is eliminated, except for farmers, effective for 2018 and subsequent years. However, the TCJA allows an indefinite carryforward of a NOL, but a NOL carryforward can be used only against 80% of a subsequent year's taxable income. The rules for pre-2018 NOLs remain the same – they can be carried back 2 years and forward 20 years. There is no taxable income limit for usage of pre-2018 NOLs.

Computation of a NOL – The NOL deduction is computed on Schedule A of Form 1045, "Application for Tentative Refund." Schedule B of Form 1045 is used to calculate the actual amounts to be carried forward. Form 1045 can be attached to your annual income tax return, but it can also be filed separately. Form 1045 must be filed within one year of the end of the tax year generating a NOL. When a partnership or S-corporation incurs a NOL, it passes through to the individual partners or shareholders (owners). Taxpayers can deduct from a current year's taxable income NOLs carried over to the current tax year from previous tax years (80%). www.irs.gov/pub/irs-pdf/f1045.pdf   www.irs.gov/pub/irs-pdf/i1045.pdf

NOLs carried forward from other years to the current year do not reduce income subject to self-employment tax (the self-employment tax must be paid no matter what). An NOL claimed on a joint return can be used to offset the joint income on prior or future joint returns. However, if a taxpayer was single in the year the NOL occurred, then it can only be used to offset that person's income in other years.

A NOL can apply to self-employed persons, farmers, individuals whose casualty losses exceed income, and partnerships and S-corporations. Individual taxpayers can have a NOL, including losses from employment, business losses, losses from rental property, and business casualty and theft losses. Passive activity losses cannot be treated as part of a NOL, since they are subject to other rules. If a taxpayer invests in a business in which he/she is not an active participant, then the investor cannot share in any operating losses of the business for NOL purposes. However, if the business goes into bankruptcy, the investor can claim a capital loss, which can be offset against the capital gains. However, only $3,000 of net capital losses can be offset against earned income in a tax year, and any remaining capital losses are carried over to the next year. So, only $3,000 in capital losses in any year can be used in the computation of NOLs. The at-risk rules limit the deductibility of losses in computing NOLs to the amount that was actually invested or at risk, which must be computed on Form 6198, "At-Risk Limitations," with the result being used to compute the NOL on Form 1045. The "Hobby Loss" rules may also limit the deductibility of business losses for computing NOLs, if the activity is conducted more as a hobby rather than a business.

Determining a NOL for a year is not a simple calculation. You have to know what qualifies in figuring a NOL. A NOL is the excess of allowable deductions over gross income for the year. The starting point for determining whether an individual taxpayer has a NOL is, "adjusted gross income" (AGI), minus itemized deductions or the standard deduction. If the result is a negative number, you may have a NOL. But further computations and adjustments must be made, including: **(See Chapter 11, "Deductions in Determining Adjusted Gross Income"); (See Chapter 12, "Itemized Deductions")**

- If an individual itemizes deductions, all itemized deductions, such as charitable donations, deductible medical expenses, mortgage interest, real estate taxes, etc. must be added back.
- All above-the-line deductions in determining AGI such as contributions to traditional IRAs, alimony/separate maintenance, health savings accounts (HSA), self-employed individual retirement accounts, etc. must be added back. **(See Chapter 11, "Deductions in Determining Adjusted Gross Income")**
- All of the above listed itemized deductions, and above-the-line deductions that must be added back, can be used to offset non-business income, which includes interest income, dividends, annuity income, and non-business capital gains. This means that if the total of all of these non-business deductions is more than non-business income, NOL is increased (which means the difference must be subtracted).
- Non-business capital losses (those arising outside your trade or business) can only be used against non-business capital gains, which means that net capital losses must be added back. **(See Chapter 6, "Reporting Capital Gains and Losses")**
- Expenses of rental property can be used to offset business income, which includes rental income (whether net rental income is a gain or a loss). Therefore, nothing has to be added back or subtracted. **(See Chapter 7, "Rental Income")**
- Exclusion of gain from Section 1202 small business stock must be added back. **(See Chapter 6, "Gain on the Sale of Section 1202 Small Business Stock")**
- Net operating losses (NOLs) carried forward from a different year must be added back.

If the current tax year doesn't have a NOL (computed on Form 1045), NOLs carried over from other years can be 80% deducted on Form 1040. Therefore, 80% of NOLs carried over from other years can be deducted in computing taxable income for the current year.

Chapter 9 – Exclusions from Taxable Income

Exclusions from taxable income are generally excluded by law or regulation. However, there are exceptions, i.e. some usual exclusions may be taxable or partially taxable at ordinary income tax rates under certain circumstances. In some cases, excluded income is actually reported on a Form 1099, but a code on the Form indicates the exclusion. **(See Chapter 1, "2018 Income Tax Brackets"); (See Chapter 14, "Where Payments Are Reported on Form 1099-MISC")**

State and Local Tax Refunds

State and local tax refunds are generally excluded from taxable income. State and local tax refunds are included in 0taxable income only when the refunds were beneficial to a taxpayer in a prior year, i.e. the state and local taxes were deducted as an itemized deduction and resulted in reduced taxable income in a prior year. **(See Chapter 12, "Itemized Deductions")**

Reimbursements for Medical Expenses

Reimbursements for medical expenses are generally excluded from taxable income. Reimbursements for medical expenses are included in taxable income only when the reimbursements were beneficial to a taxpayer in a prior year, i.e. the medical expenses were deducted as an itemized deduction and resulted in reduced taxable income in a prior year. Any reimbursements received in excess of your medical expenses may be partially taxable only if your employer paid all or part of your health insurance premiums; in which case, a proportional part of the excess reimbursements would be included in taxable income for the portion of your health insurance premiums paid by your employer. **(See Chapter 12, "Itemized Deductions")**

Loans from Retirement Plans

Loans to employees from their retirement plans are excluded from taxable income if the total amount of the loan doesn't exceed the smaller of $50,000 or 50% of the borrower's account balance. Most loans must be paid back in full within five years, but loans used to purchase or construct a principal residence can have a longer repayment period. **(See Chapter 5, "Distributions from Retirement Plans: Traditional IRAs and Qualified Retirement Plans")**

Direct Payments of Tuition and Medical Costs

Payments by parents or grandparents for a child's tuition and medical costs that are made directly to the providers (e.g. university, school, hospital or doctor) are excluded from the child's income, and the direct payments don't reduce the annual gift tax exclusion allowable to the parents or grandparents for the benefit of the children, i.e. such direct payments are not considered "gifts." **(See Chapter 22, "Gift Tax Exclusion")**

Reduced Tuition for Graduate Students

Tuition waivers for graduate students are excluded from taxable income if you are a graduate student who teaches or does research in exchange for tuition. Some estimates place the value of that waived tuition as high as $50,000 a year.

Reverse Mortgage

A reverse mortgage is a loan where the lender pays you in a lump sum or with monthly payments, while you continue to live in your home. The amount you receive is excluded from income because reverse mortgages are considered loan advances and not income. With a reverse mortgage, you retain title to your home. Depending on the plan, a reverse mortgage becomes due with interest when you move, sell your home, reach the end of a pre-selected loan period, or die. Any interest (including original issue discount) accrued on a reverse mortgage is not deductible until you actually pay it, which is usually when you pay off the loan in full. Your deduction may be limited because deductible interest is generally limited to that of a home equity loan.

A reverse mortgage loan is available to homeowners who are at least 62 years old. Borrowers don't repay the loan until the last borrower dies or moves from the home as long as they live in the home, take care of it and pay their real estate taxes and homeowner's insurance. But reverse mortgages tap into the home's equity and reduce it. Not only do homeowners take on the principal loan amount, but they also pay for interest, mortgage insurance premiums and monthly servicing fees — all of which are added to the loan amount monthly. Origination and closing costs also are often added to the loan balance.

Rollovers from Qualified Retirement Plans and Traditional IRAs

Rollovers from qualified employee retirement plans – 401(k), 403(b), and 457(b) plans; SEPs; SIMPLEs; and traditional IRAs (reported to taxpayer on Form 1099-R) are excluded from taxable income. Rollovers can be made to IRAs or designated employer retirement plans. Rollovers can be either direct or indirect. If indirect, a 20% withholding tax is required, and deposits to another IRA or to a new employer plan must be made within 60 calendar days (not business days). The taxable and non-taxable portions of distributions from 401(k), 403(b), and 457(b) plans can be directed into separate accounts, which, for example, allows taxpayers to rollover only the taxable portion of the total distribution back into an employer plan of a new employer and rollover the non-taxable portion of the distribution to a Roth account (Roth conversion), thus minimizing the tax consequences of the conversion. Also, the "Protecting Americans from Tax Hikes Act of 2015 (PATH)" allows tax-free rollovers from employee retirement plans (401(k)s, etc.) to SIMPLE IRAs, provided the plan has existed for at least 2 years (applies to distributions made after enactment of PATH on 12/18/2015). **(See Chapter 5, "Distributions from Retirement Plans: Traditional IRAs and Qualified Retirement Plans")**

Effective Jan. 1, 2015, taxpayers are limited to one indirect IRA rollover per year. This means one indirect rollover per year for all of a taxpayer's IRA accounts, rather than one indirect rollover per year for each IRA account. This …rule does not affect an IRA owner's ability to transfer funds directly from one IRA to another IRA in a trustee-to-trustee transfer. It only affects indirect transfers where the IRA owner actually receives the check, and then redeposits into another IRA account within 60 days. IRA owners can have an unlimited number of direct transfers between IRA accounts in trustee-to-trustee transfers during the year. In addition, this change does not affect rollovers from defined-contribution accounts (401(k), 403(b), and 457(b) plans) to an IRA, or to Roth conversions. Also, Effective Jan. 1, 2015, transfer of funds from 401(k), 403(b), and 457(b) plans are permitted to have the earnings and contribution portions of transferred funds directed to separate accounts – this applies whether it is a partial or a total transfer, and whether it is a direct transfer of funds or an indirect rollover. Plan administrators may have to revise plan language to reflect this change.

Beginning in 2016, if a taxpayer misses the 60-day rollover deadline, the IRS will grant automatic waivers of the 60-day rollover rule when the "sole reason" for missing the deadline is that the financial institution made an error. The following requirements must be met in order for a taxpayer to receive an automatic waiver: (1) the financial institution must have received the funds before the expiration of the 60-day rollover period; (2) the taxpayer must have followed all procedures required by the financial institution for directly depositing the funds into an eligible retirement plan within the 60-day rollover period; and (3) the taxpayer must have given instructions to the institution to deposit the funds into an eligible retirement plan and, solely due to the financial institution's error, the funds were not deposited into an eligible retirement plan as directed within the 60-day rollover period. Automatic approval is then granted if the funds are deposited into an eligible retirement plan within one year from the beginning of the 60-day rollover period and, if the financial institution had deposited the funds as originally instructed, it would have been a valid rollover.

The IRS also established a "self-certification" option for taxpayers who missed the 60-day rollover period for rollovers occurring on or after Aug. 24, 2016. Under this option, taxpayers must have missed the deadline due to one or more of the following reasons: the distribution check was misplaced; the distribution was deposited into and remained in an account the taxpayer thought was an eligible retirement plan; the taxpayer's principal residence was severely damaged; a member of the taxpayer's family died; the taxpayer or a member of the taxpayer's family was seriously ill; an error was committed by a financial institution; the taxpayer was incarcerated; restrictions were imposed by a foreign country; a postal error occurred; the distribution was made on account of a levy under Sec. 6331, and the proceeds of the levy have been returned to the taxpayer; or the party making the distribution to which the rollover related delayed providing the information that the receiving plan or IRS required to complete the rollover despite the taxpayer's reasonable efforts to obtain the information. Also, the contribution to the plan or IRA was made as soon as practical after the reason or reasons for missing the deadline that had prevented the taxpayer from making the contribution. This condition is considered satisfied if the contribution is made within 30 days after the reason occurred. The taxpayer can send a written self-certification letter to a plan cadministrator or an IRA trustee. A taxpayer must use either the model letter provided within Rev. Proc. 2016-47 (word for word) or may use a letter that is substantially similar in all material respects. Once received, a plan administrator or IRA trustee may rely on the taxpayer's self-certification unless he or she possesses actual knowledge to the contrary, but must report the late rollover to the IRS. The mere act of the taxpayer's completing the self-certification is not a waiver by the IRS of the 60-day rollover requirement. However, the taxpayer may report the contribution as a valid rollover unless later informed otherwise by the IRS. In an examination, the IRS may consider whether a taxpayer's contribution meets the requirements of the waiver. The taxpayer should keep a copy of the self-certification letter in his or her files so it can be produced in the case of an audit. https://www.irs.gov/pub/irs-drop/rp-16-47.pdf

If you hold a significant amount of your employer's stock in a 401(k) plan, you probably should not roll it over to an IRA at retirement or when you change jobs, because the money you or your heirs withdraw from the IRA is taxed as ordinary income. Instead, you should elect "net unrealized appreciation" (NUA) for sale of appreciated company stock purchased and held in a qualified plan.
(See Chapter 6, "Net Unrealized Appreciation")

Rollover Distributions from Roth Accounts
Distributions made from a taxpayer's designated Roth account to both the taxpayer and to an eligible retirement plan in a direct rollover are excluded from income and are allocated as follows: the contribution amounts are allocated first to the direct rollover, rather than being allocated pro rata to the taxpayer and to the retirement account. Also, the taxpayer can direct the allocation of the contributions and earnings that are included in the distribution to multiple designations, applying the same allocation rules that apply to distributions from other

types of accounts. This is a taxpayer friendly rule that was recently adopted by the IRS, eliminating the requirement that each disbursement from a designated Roth account that is directly rolled over to an eligible retirement plan be treated as a separate distribution from any amount paid directly to the employee. **(See Chapter 5, "Conversion from Pre-Tax Qualified Plans to Roth Qualified Plans")**
www.irs.gov/pub/irs-drop/n-14-54.pdf

Foreign Earned Income Exclusion

The Foreign earned income exclusion is reported on Form 2555. In 2018, up to a maximum of $103,900 of foreign earned income ($284.66 per day) can be excluded from taxable income. The total amount of foreign earned income you can exclude, includes the foreign "housing exclusion." The maximum "housing exclusion" is computed by deducting the "base housing amount" – which is 16% of $103,900, or $16,624 in 2018 – from your total housing expenses – which is limited to 30% of $103,900, or $31,170 in 2018. The base housing amount is 16% of the maximum exclusion amount (computed on a daily basis), multiplied by the number of days in the applicable period that fall within the taxable year. The base housing amount of $16,624 computed on a daily basis is $45.55 per day, and the limit on housing expenses of $31,170 is $85.40 per day. However, if a qualified individual spends all of 2018 abroad, and spent the maximum allowable for housing expenses of $31,170, then his or her maximum housing exclusion would be $14,546 ($31,170 minus $16,624), which leaves the remaining $89,354 available for the foreign earned income exclusion. But here's the deal, the maximum allowable housing expenses of $31,170 is based on the three most expensive foreign cities, which are Hong Kong, Moscow, and Geneva. There are lower maximums for other foreign cities which can be found on the IRS Website, and those maximums must be used if you are living in those cities and the computations must be adjusted accordingly. If the limitation on housing expenses is higher for 2018 than for 2017, the IRS has said that qualified taxpayers can apply the 2018 limitations to their 2017 tax year. **(See Chapter 12, "Foreign Source Income Taxes"); (See Chapter 13, "Foreign Tax Credit")**
www.irs.gov/pub/irs-pdf/f2555.pdf   www.irs.gov/pub/irs-pdf/f2555ez.pdf   www.irs.gov/pub/irs-pdf/i2555.pdf
Notice 2017-21   Notice 2016-21

The housing exclusion applies only to amounts considered paid for by your employer and included on your Form W-2, or to amounts paid with self-employment earnings. In the case of married taxpayers, each spouse may compute the exclusions separately, if both earn foreign income. To qualify, a taxpayer's home must be in a foreign country, and must either meet the bone fide resident test or physical presence in a foreign country test: The bone fide resident test requires a taxpayer to be an uninterrupted resident of a foreign country for one entire calendar year (Jan 1 – Dec 31). The physical presence test requires 330 full days of physical presence in a foreign country during 12 consecutive months. After meeting one of the tests, you can leave temporarily and still qualify, and part-years will then qualify. The bona fide residence test or physical presence in a foreign country test can be waived if taxpayers had to leave a foreign country because of war, civil unrest, or similar adverse conditions in that country. The IRS website has complete list of qualifying countries. **(See Chapter 3, "U.S. Citizens Living Abroad")**
www.irs.gov/pub/irs-drop/rp-12-21.pdf

Combat-Zone Contract Workers Qualify for Foreign Earned Income Exclusion – Certain U.S. citizens or resident aliens, specifically contractors or employees of contractors supporting the U.S. Armed Forces in designated combat zones, now qualify for the foreign earned income exclusion. The Bipartisan Budget Act of 2018, changed the tax home requirement for eligible taxpayers, enabling them to claim the foreign earned income exclusion even if their "abode" is in the United States. The new law applies for tax year 2018 and subsequent years. Therefore, these taxpayers, if eligible, will be able to claim the foreign earned income exclusion on their income tax return for 2018. Under prior law, many otherwise eligible taxpayers who lived and worked in designated combat zones failed to qualify because they had an abode in the United States. Publication 54, "Guide for U.S. Citizens and Resident Aliens Abroad," will be revised later this year to reflect this clarification. www.irs.gov/pub/irs-pdf/p54.pdf

Foreign Earned Income is Subject to Payroll Tax – The maximum foreign earned income exclusion includes the "housing exclusion." You must claim the housing exclusion before claiming the rest as the "foreign earned income exclusion," and both are considered foreign earned taxable income paid by your employer. However, even if you can exclude foreign earned income from U.S. income taxes, you still must pay payroll taxes on the income if you work for an American employer, which includes the U.S. government, a U.S. corporation, or a foreign affiliate of an American employer (10% or more American ownership), and they are required to withhold payroll taxes (FICA) based on the amount of the foreign earned income exclusion. However, if you are a consultant or contractor (compensation reported on Form 1099-MISC), you must pay self-employment tax. If you work in a country with which the U.S. has a social security agreement (Europe, Australia, Japan, etc.), you may have to pay social security taxes to that country, but not to both the U.S and that country. **(See Chapter 2, "Payroll Tax")**

HR 6081 stops the practice of some U.S. government contractors from using offshore shell companies to avoid paying payroll taxes (FICA) and unemployment taxes (FUTA). Therefore, such foreign subsidiaries of U.S. companies performing services under a contract for the U.S. government are considered U.S. employers and thus are required to withhold and pay payroll taxes (FICA).

Cancellation of Debt Excluded from Income
Discharge of indebtedness is considered excluded from taxable income under certain circumstances, which are: insolvency, bankruptcy, a disaster, qualified farm indebtedness, and discharge of qualified student loans. **(See Chapter 5, "Cancellation of Debt")**

Insolvency – Insolvency occurs when a taxpayer's liabilities exceed his/her assets, including retirement accounts, annuities, and home, in which case the taxpayer is considered insolvent and may declare insolvency or bankruptcy. The taxpayer has the burden of proof in establishing insolvency. For example, to determine insolvency, you have to compile a list of all of your assets and all of your debts the day before you default on a debt. Your list of assets must include the fair market value (FMV) of a principal residence, a vacation home, and your pension plan. If you arrive at a negative number after subtracting all of your debts from all or your assets, you are considered insolvent to that extent. For example, if your assets, including the vacation home you are defaulting on, total $500,000, and your debts, including the balance of the mortgage on your vacation home and your credit card debt total $720,000, then you are insolvent to the extent of $220,000. If cancellation of debt totals $250,000, you would be required to pay taxes on only $30,000 ($250,000 less $220,000).
- **Example** – If you receive a Form 1099-C in the amount of $100,000 from the bank that held the mortgage on your vacation home three years after you defaulted on the loan, you can exclude the $100,000 from your taxable income if you can show that the amount of your insolvency exceeded the remaining balance of the loan stated on the Form 1099-C. Referring to the situation above, you may have to prove that you have already paid taxes on the $30,000.

Form 982, "Reduction of Tax Attributes Due to Discharge of Indebtedness" should be filed if you default on a rental property or any other property, and you can show you are insolvent. Bankruptcy requires a taxpayer to be under the jurisdiction of the court, but not insolvency. Cancellation of debt (COD) excluded from income as a result of insolvency is generally limited to the amount of insolvency, but that does not necessarily apply to bankruptcy. However, for both bankruptcy and insolvency, certain losses, credits, and the basis of property must be reduced by the amount excluded from income. The order of the required reductions is in accordance with certain "tax attributes." A taxpayer may elect to initially apply all or part of the required reductions to the basis in depreciable assets or to real property held as an investment.
www.irs.gov/pub/irs-pdf/f982.pdf   https://cdn2.hubspot.net/hub/49162/file-19359013-pdf/docs/instruction-for_1099c-and-982-form.pdf

In the Newman case, the Tax Court ruled that a taxpayer could exclude COD income due to an overdraft of a bank account under the insolvency provisions. In 2008, the taxpayer opened a bank account at Bank of America, deposited over $8,800 in funds, including a check for $8,500 drawn on his Wells Fargo bank account, and withdrew $8,000. The Wells Fargo check did not clear, and the taxpayer never repaid the funds. In 2011, Bank of America provided the taxpayer with a Form 1099-C, Cancellation of Debt, reporting $7,875 of COD Income. The court ruled that since Bank of America had not received any payments in 36 months, the debt was presumed canceled in 2011 under the 36-month nonpayment testing period rule and the taxpayer had COD income that year. But the court also found the taxpayer to be insolvent in 2011 and therefore the COD income was excluded from income. However, it should be noted that the Newman Case was ruled in June 2016, but that beginning on November 8, 2016, the 36-month testing period for filing Form 1099-C was repealed by the IRS, because it was concerned that the rule lead to taxpayer confusion and didn't increase tax compliance by debtors or provide the IRS with third-party information that could be used for taxpayer compliance.
(See Chapter 5, "Cancellation of Debt")
http://www.ustaxcourt.gov/USTCInOP/OpinionViewer.aspx?ID=10844

In the Schieber case, the Tax Court ruled that a married couple's interest in their retirement account was not considered an asset for purposes of the COD insolvency test, and therefore, the taxpayers could exclude a portion of the income from their retirement account in determining COD excluded from income. According to the court, the retirement account could not be used to immediately pay any income tax due to the discharged debt and therefore was not an asset for purposes of the test.
http://www.ustaxcourt.gov/ustcinop/opinionviewer.aspx?ID=11118

Bankruptcy – Cancellation of Debt (COD) is excluded from income when discharge of indebtedness is granted in a bankruptcy case, which includes Chapter 11 reorganizations; Chapter 7 liquidations; and Chapter 13 bankruptcy. The bankruptcy exclusion is applicable only if granted by a court order or in a court-approved plan. When debt is discharged in bankruptcy, the bankruptcy exclusion rules govern, even if one of the other exclusions, such as insolvency, could have been applied. This is important since the required reduction of tax attributes differs depending on which COD income exclusion applies.

Smith v. United States – In Smith v. United States, the Supreme Court declined to review a decision of the Ninth Circuit Court of Appeals where the court, now in accord with nine other Courts of Appeal, held that income

tax liability may not be discharged in bankruptcy after the IRS has prepared a Substitute Tax Return.
https://cdn.ca9.uscourts.gov/datastore/opinions/2016/07/13/14-15857.pdf
www.justice.gov/sites/default/files/osg/briefs/2017/01/25/16-497_smith_opp.pdf
www.irs.gov/pub/irs-utl/2013_NTF_Dealing_with_SFRs.pdf

If the insolvency or bankruptcy indebtedness exclusions are used, and COD is not considered taxable income, the basis reductions do not occur immediately, but instead at the start of the next year, and any gain on the subsequent sale of the assets as a result of the "reduction in basis due to tax attributes" is recaptured as ordinary income. Some tax attributes are business related, such as a "net operating loss" (NOL). A common attribute for individuals is the basis of property. Thus, the excluded income is offset by reducing the basis of property owned by the debtor. This reduction delays the recognition of the cancellation of debt income, but generally ensures that the income will be recognized on the sale of the property unless any gain is excluded under the "gain on sale of a principal residence" rules. Tax attributes have to be reduced for most exclusions due to discharge of indebtedness, but not on exclusions for qualified student loans.

Qualified Real Property Indebtedness – The IRS issued Rev. Rul. 2016-15 to clarify when a real estate developer can exclude COD income under the "qualified real property business indebtedness exclusion." The revenue ruling states that real property that a taxpayer develops and holds for lease in its leasing business is "real property used in a trade or business" for purposes of Sec. 108(C)(3)(A), and thus can qualify for the COD exclusion while real property that a taxpayer develops and holds primarily for sale to customers in the ordinary course of business is not "real property used in a trade or business" for purposes of Sec. 108(C)(3)(A) and does not qualify for the COD exclusion.
www.irs.gov/pub/irs-drop/rr-16-15.pdf

Home Sale Gain Exclusion
Gain on the sale of a principle residence is excluded from taxable income if the taxpayer qualifies for the home sale gain exclusion of $500,000 (married filing jointly), or $250,000 (single). Any gain above the $500,000 and $250,000 thresholds is subject to capital gain tax. Taxpayers cannot deduct a loss on the sale of a principal residence for any reason. A Surviving Spouse may use the joint return $500,000 home sale gain exclusion for 2 years following the date of death of a spouse. A surviving spouse is allowed the stepped-up basis for the deceased spouse's ½ share of the home. A taxpayer may have only one principal residence at a time – usually the one occupied more of the time. Factors in establishing a principal residence: place of employment; location of recreational clubs; address used on driver's license; and voter registration. Proceeds from a home sale should be, but are not always, reported on Form 1099-S (Proceeds from Real Estate Transactions), which shows the date of closing and gross proceeds from the sale. The home sale gain exclusion doesn't apply to any furniture or other personal property you might sell with the home for a profit. Count any profit on those items as reportable income in the year of sale. Also, you can't deduct any loss on the sale of any furniture and personal items, as you didn't originally buy them to make a profit or earn income. Nor can you reduce the profit from the sale of a home by a loss suffered from a sale of furniture; the furniture sale is a separate transaction.
www.irs.gov/pub/irs-pdf/f1099s.pdf   www.irs.gov/pub/irs-pdf/i1099s.pdf

Exclusion of gain does not require the home to be used as a principal residence at the time of sale, but only as a principal residence for 2 years (24 full months or 730 days) out of a 5-year period, and you cannot have gone through a sale in which you excluded gain from the sale of a home during the prior two years before the sale of the current home. Otherwise, you cannot exclude any gain unless there is: a change in employment requiring a change in location; change in health requiring money for a cure, diagnosis or care; or "unforeseen circumstances," such as: death; termination of employment; divorce/separation; a job change reducing the ability to pay for the home; birth of a baby; damage from a disaster; taking of property; or other qualified reasons (hardships). In which case, exclusion of gain is prorated based on the number of days lived in the home over a 2-year period, divided by 730 days, times the maximum exclusion ($250,000 or $500,000). NOTE: Persons who move to a nursing home because they can't take care of themselves only have to live in their principal residence for one out of five years preceding the sale in order to get the maximum exclusion.

A marriage that results in a large, combined new family is considered an "unforeseen circumstance" that allows a taxpayer to benefit from the capital gain exclusion on the sale of a principal residence, even though the taxpayer owned the house for less than 2 years (a larger house with more bedrooms is needed). Also, In Letter Ruling 201628002, the IRS ruled that the unexpected birth of a child counted as an unforeseen circumstance, which allowed the taxpayers to exclude gain from the sale of their principal residence without meeting the normal two-out-of-five-year requirement. At the time the taxpayers purchased the two-bedroom, two-bath condo, they had one child. The second bedroom was used as the child's bedroom, a home office, and a guest room. The wife unexpectedly became pregnant with a second child, and the family moved to a larger residence. The IRS determined the suitability of the condo materially changed and ruled that the gain on the sale was excludable. Other hardship exceptions are available, but must be proven to the satisfaction of the IRS, usually through the letter ruling process. For both spouses to qualify for the home sale gain exclusion after divorce, the divorce instrument must require them to co-own the principle residence, even if only one spouse occupies the residence. Otherwise, the non-occupying former spouse may not qualify for the 2 out of 5-year rule. www.irs.gov/pub/irs-wd/201628002.pdf

The five-year ownership and use test period is suspended for certain individuals working outside of the country – members of the uniformed services, foreign service, intelligence community, and peace corp. These taxpayers may extend the running time of the 5-year ownership and use requirement for a maximum of 10 years (taxpayer and/or spouse). Employees of federal contractors do not qualify for the extension. Other U.S. citizens living abroad have to pay capital gains tax when they sell a house in the United States. They do not qualify for the $250,000/$500,000 gain exclusion. Unmarried co-owners of a residence can exclude each of their share of gain on the sale of a principal residence (other than gain allocated to nonqualified use of the home) as long as they used the home as their principal residence for at least 2 of 5 years preceding the date of sale. Therefore, one co-owner may qualify to exclude his $250,000 share of the gain and the other may not.

You can add the following to the purchase price of the home (basis): closing costs from the original purchase and from any refinancing or equity line loans secured by the property that were made over the course of the ownership; capital improvements made to the residence such as a new roof, windows, landscaping, etc. You can't include costs for painting or basic maintenance. You can deduct the following from the selling price of the home: realtors' commissions, closing costs and any agreed upon costs to fulfill the contract. You can also deduct advertising expenses and certain repairs if they were made within 90 days of the sale and clearly for the intent of marketing the property. The sale of vacant land is not included in the sale of a home unless: (1) it is adjacent to land where the home is located, and (2) taxpayer owned and used it as part of the main home.

The exclusion of gain does not apply to any gain attributable to any depreciation taken on the home after May 6, 1997. Recapture of depreciation resulting from such gain is subject to the Section 1231 netting rules. If there is a net Section 1231 gain, the gain attributed to the depreciation is entered in the "unrecaptured Section" of the 1250 Gain Worksheet in Schedule D – the gain is subject to a top tax rate of 25%. If the house is sold, any depreciation claimed for a home office must also be recaptured as unrecaptured Section 1250 gain (LT capital gain taxed @ 25%). If you sell a home at a loss, you cannot claim a loss on your tax return. However, if you took home office depreciation, you may be able to take a portion as a loss – Example: purchase price $100,000; sale price $85,000; business use 10%; depreciation taken $10,000; recognized loss $500 ($8,500 – [$9,000]). **(See Chapter 16, "Residential and Nonresidential Real Property"); (See Chapter 17, "Home Office Expenses")**

The new Housing Act tightens the "home sale gain exclusion," i.e. it disallows the exclusion of gain from the sale of a principal residence attributable to periods the dwelling was used as a vacation home or a rental property or other nonqualified use, and then converted to a principal residence – effective for sales and periods of nonqualified use after 2008. The portion of the profit that is taxable is based on the percentage of time before the sale when the home was used as a second home or rented out. The portion of profit that is taxable does not include a period of absence that occurs after the home was last used as the principal residence.

Forgiveness of Mortgage Debt on a Principal Residence
Forgiveness of Mortgage debt on a principal residence was originally unavailable in 2017, because the "Debt Forgiveness Relief Act" was only extended through 2016 by the "Protecting Americans from Tax Hikes Act of 2015." But in February 2018, it was retroactively extended to the 2017 tax year by the Bipartisan Budget Act of 2018, and it was also made available in 2018.

In accordance with the Debt Forgiveness Relief Act, up to $2 million, or $1 million (married filing separately) in mortgage debt is forgiven and excluded from taxable income. However, even if you are entitled to mortgage debt forgiveness, you may still receive a Form 1099-C (Cancellation of Debt) from the mortgage company. If this happens, in order to claim mortgage debt forgiveness, you will need to complete Form 982 and check the appropriate box to tell the IRS that you're entitled to an exclusion from taxable income for the cancelled debt. Foreclosure on a home can result in income to the owner that is forgiven, if at the time of foreclosure the fair market value (FMV) of the encumbered property is less than the outstanding debt. Also, a "short sale" can result in forgiven income to the owner. A short sale in real estate occurs when the outstanding loans against a property are greater than what the property is worth and the lender agrees to accept less than what is owed to permit a sale of the property (home) that secures the note. This benefit also covers an agreement or "work-out" with the lender to make payments lower. **(See Chapter 5, "Cancellation of Debt")**
- **Example** – Lender forgives $100,000 of taxpayer's current $325,000 mortgage debt + $4,500 of interest in arrears, thus both the $100,000 and the $4,500 are excluded from taxable income.
www.irs.gov/pub/irs-pdf/f1099c.pdf www.irs.gov/pub/irs-pdf/i1099ac.pdf www.irs.gov/pub/irs-pdf/f982.pdf

Another option to take advantage of mortgage debt forgiveness is called "deed in lieu of foreclosure" in which the homeowner vacates the residence and turns it over to the lender in exchange for debt forgiveness. In this case, the Mortgage Debt Forgiveness Act allows some of the debt to be excluded from taxable income, and allows most of the gain from the sale of the home (whether foreclosure action is now or years later in the case of a "mortgage workout") to escape tax through the home sale gain exclusion. Abandonment of a property is also disposition of a

111

property that can result in discharge of indebtedness that is forgiven when the property is a principal residence. Forgiveness of mortgage debt income also includes refinancing up to the amount of the old mortgage principal. However, forgiveness of mortgage debt does not include home equity loans not used for home improvements. Also, mortgage debt forgiveness does not include debt on a second home or rental property.

- Forgiveness of mortgage debt reduces the basis of a principal residence by the amount of the debt forgiven and not included in income, but not below zero. However, this does not normally hurt the homeowner, because the sale of the residence is usually sheltered by the "home sale gain exclusion." A taxpayer must live in a home 2 out of 5 years in order to take advantage of the home sale gain exclusion, but no period of ownership or use is needed to obtain mortgage debt forgiveness. **(See Above, "Home Sale Gain Exclusion")**

- You can have a principal residence short sale that produces a capital gain – say you paid $190,000 for a home that you sell for $250,000; it is a short sale because you have first and second recourse mortgages that total $280,000; but for IRS purposes you have a $60,000 capital gain ($250,000 sale price, $190,000 basis = $60,000 gain). However, the $60,000 gain is probably tax exempt, thanks to the home sale gain exclusion (but not for a rental property or a vacation home).

- Home owners who took advantage of the run-up in real estate prices to do a "cash out" refinancing in which funds were not put back into their home but instead were used to pay off credit card debt, etc. are excluded from the mortgage debt forgiveness program.

- In some states, some personal residence mortgages can be nonrecourse. When these residences are sold in a short sale, the transaction is treated for tax purposes as a sale for a price equal to the nonrecourse loan balance. The actual sale price is irrelevant, so there is no cancellation of debt (COD) income because the nonrecourse mortgage obligation is deemed to be fully satisfied in the short sale. A tax gain is triggered if the nonrecourse loan balance exceeds the property's basis, which is probably tax exempt, thanks to the home sale gain exclusion.

A lender who acquires a taxpayer's property through foreclosure, repossession or abandonment should send the taxpayer Form 1099-A, which is the form used by the taxpayer to calculate gain or loss and any ordinary income from disposition of the property.
www.irs.gov/pub/irs-pdf/f1099a.pdf

Home Affordable Refinance Program (HARP) – Note: The Home Affordable Refinance Program (HARP) is scheduled to expire on December 31, 2018. If Freddie Mac owns your mortgage and you are timely with your mortgage payments but unable to refinance because you have little or no equity in the home, you may be able to refinance to a lower interest rate or more stable mortgage through the federal Home Affordable Refinance Program (HARP). HARP is designed for homeowners who have not been able to refinance due to a decline in the value of their home. Freddie Mac's implementation of HARP may help you obtain a monthly payment you can afford, and may result in one or more of the following: (1) a reduction in your interest rate and or your monthly principal and interest mortgage payment; (2) a fixed-rate mortgage in place of an adjustable-rate, interest only, or balloon/reset mortgage; or (3) a reduction in the term of your mortgage (e.g. from 30 to 15 years).

Forgiveness of Student Loans
Under the Tax Cuts and Jobs Act, Federal and private student loan forgiveness due to death or permanent disability is excluded from taxable income for tax years 2018 – 2025 (this includes forgiveness in the event of death

if there is a cosigner on the loan). In 2017 and prior years, forgiveness of student loans due to death or disability was considered taxable unearned income, and a Form 1099-C was issued to the benefactor.

Forgiveness of qualified student loans made by a governmental agency or a qualified public benefit corporation, where a student is required to work for a specific period of time in certain professions, is excluded from income (does not apply to private or non-governmental loans). Also, forgiveness of student loans to certain medical professionals under state loan repayment or forgiveness programs, as implemented by the Affordable Care Act (ACA), with the intent to provide increased availability of health care services in underserved or health-professional-shortage areas is excluded from income. **(See Chapter 5, "Cancellation of Debt"); (See Chapter 14, "Requirement to File Information Returns"); (See Chapter 24, "Affordable Care Act")**

Section 1031 Like-Kind Exchange

The Tax Cuts and Jobs Act eliminates like-kind exchanges other than for "real property" effective beginning in tax year 2018. However, like-kind exchanges for other than real property that were in progress as of December 31, 2017, are protected, i.e. they can proceed until finalized. 1031 like-kind exchanges of other than real property that were allowed through 2017, included exchanges of vehicles, equipment, livestock, other business property, and even Intangibles (trademarks, trade names, etc.) – except for goodwill. Like-kind exchanges of real property does not include transfers of buildings constructed on owned land, sold to investors, and then leased back. Also, you cannot apply Section 1031 to any personal use real property such as your residence.

Form 8824 must be filed when there is a Section 1031 like-kind exchange. Like-kind or Section 1031 exchanges are used by owners who would otherwise have a large gain on the sale of investment or business real property they have held for years. The exchange of like-kind real property means the exchanged properties must be of the same nature or character – the grade or quality of the properties is not relevant. For example, in a real estate for real estate exchange, it can be an apartment building for raw land. Like-kind real estate can be: vacant land; commercial rental property; commercial property; industrial property; 30-year or more leasehold interest property; farm property; or residential rental property. The replacement property must be identified within 45 days from the sale of the relinquished property, and the exchange must be completed within 180 days. Also, the replacement property must be of equivalent or higher in value, the cash invested in the replacement property must be equal to or greater than the cash received from the sale of the relinquished property, and the debt placed or assumed on the replacement property must be equal to or greater than the debt on the relinquished property. After the transfer, the business nature of the transaction must remain intact. There is no law written, but several Tax Court cases have stated that the replacement property should be held for at least two years after the exchange.

www.irs.gov/pub/irs-access/f8824accessible.pdf   www.irs.gov/pub/irs-pdf/i8824.pdf

Property used primarily for personal use, like a primary residence or a second home (vacation home), does not technically qualify for Section 1031 like-kind exchange treatment, even though a vacation home may be considered an investment property for other purposes. However, there is a "safe harbor" where vacation homes can be considered like-kind exchange property. The safe harbor for vacation homes is: (1) both the relinquished and replacement properties must be owned by you for at least 2 years immediately before (relinquished property) and immediately after (replacement property); and (2) for each of those years, the dwellings must be rented at FMV for at least 14 days, and your personal use of the properties can't exceed the greater of 14 days or 10% of the days the property is rented out at fair market value. **(See Chapter 7, "Classifying a Vacation Home as a Rental Property")**

In most cases, a Section 1031 exchange requires a "Qualified Intermediary ("QI") to facilitate the exchange, because the seller cannot receive or control the net sale proceeds – the proceeds must be deposited with a QI (within 45 days, you can identify to the QI up to three possible replacement properties). Since there is no entity that oversees or regulates QIs, it is crucial in selecting a QI that you verify the experience of the company and the security measures it will provide for the exchange funds held in its possession during the exchange period. A QI is a company that is in the full-time business of facilitating Section 1031 tax-deferred exchanges. The QI enters into a written agreement with the taxpayer where the QI transfers the relinquished property to the buyer, and transfers the replacement property to the taxpayer pursuant to an exchange agreement. The QI holds the proceeds from the sale of the relinquished property in a trust or escrow account in order to ensure the taxpayer never has actual or constructive receipt of the sale proceeds. Disqualified persons to be QIs are persons who have acted as the taxpayer's employee, attorney, accountant, investment banker or broker, or real estate agent or broker within the two-year period preceding the date of the transfer.

No gain or loss is recognized in a Section 1031 like-kind exchange of business or investment real property, except to the extent of "boot" received – money, other property, or a transferred liability (mortgage). If you receive any cash or other property in addition to the like-kind property, then gain, but not loss, is recognized equal to the lesser of the boot received or the gain realized, and the gain is subject to long-term capital gain treatment. No loss is ever recognized to any extent. The basis of the replacement property is the same as the adjusted basis of the property relinquished, increased by any gain recognized and decreased by any boot received; or if you pay an additional amount for the replacement property, the basis of the replacement property is the same as the adjusted basis of the relinquished property, plus any cash paid. A replacement property can be purchased from a related party only if the replacement property was held by the related party for at least two years before the exchange, and the relinquished property was held by you at least 2 years immediately before the exchange. There are exceptions for dispositions following the taxpayer's death, involuntary conversions, and transactions whose principal purpose was not tax avoidance.

- **Example** – You exchange an apartment building with worth $900,000, but with a tax basis (after depreciation) of $300,000 for unimproved land worth $1,000,000, and in addition you receive a cash payment of $200,000 (boot). You realize capital gain on the exchange of $200,000 (limited to the boot received). Therefore, the basis of the replacement property is $300,000 ($300,000 basis of relinquished property + $200,000 gain recognized - $200,000 boot received).
- **Example** – You exchange your vacation home that qualifies for like-kind exchange treatment under the "safe harbor" for another vacation home that qualifies under the "safe harbor." The relinquished vacation home is worth $600,000 with a tax basis of only $200,000. You find another home worth $700,000 that you would like to own. So, you swap your old vacation home (the relinquished property) for the new one (the replacement property) and throw in $100,000 cash in the trade. As long as you meet the aforementioned usage guidelines for both properties, you can pull off a tax-deferred 1031 exchange and thereby avoid any current income tax hit. Your basis in the replacement property is $300,000 ($700,000 - $400,000 gain rolled over from the relinquished property), or figured another way, the basis of the replacement property is still $300,000 ($200,000 basis of relinquished property + $100,000 cash paid).

The basis of the relinquished property is adjusted for any depreciation taken on the property before the exchange takes place.

To qualify for a Section 1031 exchange, a taxpayer must be able to support that their "intent" at the time of the purchase was to hold the property for business or investment purposes. Some factors the IRS may review to determine intent are: purpose for which the property was initially acquired; purpose for which the property was subsequently held; purpose for which the property was being held at the time of sale; the extent of advertising, promotion and soliciting buyers for the sale of the property; listing of property with brokers; the extent of improvements, if any, made to the property; frequency, number and continuity of sales; extent and nature of the transaction; and the ordinary course of business of the taxpayer. If you are a dealer in real estate, such as a house flipper, you do not qualify for the 1031 exchange deferral, because your intent is to develop the property and hold it for resale, not to hold it for investment. Whether a taxpayer intends to hold a property for resale or investment can be a critical issue if an exchange is challenged by the IRS, and sometimes proving such intent can be difficult. Although the intent with respect to a property can change over time, the intent during the period prior to the exchange is what matters most. Solid evidence such as documentation and establishing clear facts and circumstances is extremely important.

Reverse 1031 Exchange – A reverse 1031 exchange represents a tax deferment strategy when for a variety of reasons, the replacement property must be purchased before the relinquished or old property is sold. It is more complex than a forward or regular 1031 exchange and requires careful planning. To date, the statute and regulations do not address reverse exchanges; however, a safe harbor for using these transactions has been established. The Tax Court's recent decision in Estate of Bartell, 147 T.C. No. 5 (2016), alleviates some of the uncertainty that taxpayers and practitioners face when structuring a reverse like-kind exchange intended to qualify for nonrecognition treatment under Sec. 1031. In its decision, the Tax Court rejected the IRS's position that a QI the taxpayer engaged to take legal title to the replacement property was required to assume the benefits and burdens of ownership of the property to facilitate a valid 1031 exchange. Moreover, the Tax Court held that existing case law did not limit the time a QI may hold title to the replacement property before the exchange must occur.
www.ustaxcourt.gov/UstclnOp/OpinionViewer.aspx?ID=10868

1031/721 Exchange - An umbrella partnership real estate investment trust, usually referred to as an UPREIT or a 1031/721 exchange, can provide virtually the same tax-deferred benefits to real estate investors that a like-kind exchange provides when they contribute their investment real estate property into a new ownership structure that includes an operating partnership with a REIT. Investors can effectively dispose of real estate and acquire an interest in a REIT on a tax-deferred basis by taking advantage of the UPREIT strategy. An UPREIT is basically structured as a two-step process. The first step uses a 1031 exchange and then a subsequent exchange of the money into a REIT. It involves selling the relinquished property and structuring a 1031 exchange. However, instead of searching for suitable replacement property, the investor would identify and acquire a fractional interest (tenant-in-common interest) in real estate that the REIT has already designated. This completes the 1031 exchange portion of the transaction. The second step is to contribute the fractional interest into the operating partnership after a holding period of 12 to 24 months as part of a 721 exchange (tax-deferred contribution into a partnership). The investor receives an interest in the operating partnership in exchange for his or her contribution of the real estate and is now effectively part of the REIT.

Section 1033 Condemnation and Involuntary Conversion

Exchanging a property as a result of a condemnation or an involuntary conversion for another property results in an exclusion from taxable income. The rules for a Section 1033 involuntary conversion exchange relate to property that has been disposed of as a result of destruction, theft, condemnation, or threat of condemnation. An involuntary conversion may be either direct or indirect. A direct involuntary conversion is where a property is converted directly into a similar property, and exclusion from income as a result of a direct conversion is mandatory. An indirect involuntary conversion is where property is converted into cash or dissimilar property. The exclusion of income from an indirect conversion is elective and time periods and other steps need to be complied with in order to receive exclusion from tax treatment. There is no requirement under Section 1033 that a third-party accommodator – such as a qualified intermediary (QI) – be used to hold the conversion proceeds as is required in a Section 1031 tax-deferred exchange. Also, there is no requirement that the replacement property be identified within a certain period of time, like in a Section 1031 like-kind exchange. **(See Above, "Section 1031 Like-Kind Exchange")**

Property is involuntarily converted when the following events occur:
- Property is destroyed by fire, earthquake, hurricane, or some other catastrophic event.
- Property is stolen, which is usually personal property.
- Property is seized – usually without any compensation.
- Condemnation of property occurs when the government exercises its power of eminent domain, which must be compensable and involuntary.
- Condemnation occurs through a sale due to the threat of a requisition or condemnation. The property owner must be aware of the threat and must reasonably believe that a condemnation is likely to occur.

The two most common kinds of indirect involuntary conversions are destruction and condemnations through eminent domain. If the property is real estate, the replacement property must be "like kind" to the relinquished property. For other property, the replacement property must meet a narrower "similar or related in service use" standard, i.e. if an item of equipment is destroyed, such as power generator, the similar or related in service or use standard generally requires that the replacement property be a power generator. For an involuntary conversion, the replacement period is much longer than for a Section 1031 exchange. For business or investment real property, a calendar-year taxpayer has until December 31st three years after the start of the replacement period to acquire the replacement property. Therefore, for a condemnation completed in March 2015, the replacement period would end on December 31, 2018. For property other than real estate, the replacement period is generally two years instead of three years. If an involuntary conversion has occurred through destruction or the government exercising its power of eminent domain, the funds from the insurance company or from the governmental entity are often not immediately paid to the taxpayer; therefore, the law provides that the replacement period does not start until the taxpayer has received cash equal to the taxpayer's basis in the destroyed or condemned property.

There is no concept of debt replacement or boot in a Section 1033 exchange like there is in a Section 1031 exchange. For example, in an involuntary conversion, if a taxpayer's unencumbered property worth $500,000 is condemned, the taxpayer can replace it with property worth $500,000 that is acquired with a down payment of $200,000 and a $300,000 mortgage. Thus, the taxpayer can walk away with $300,000 in cash and not be required to pay any tax on the transaction. For both a Section 1031 exchange and a Section 1033 involuntary conversion, the replacement property cannot be acquired from a related party. But for a Section 1031 exchange, a number of exceptions are available that are not available for a Section 1033 conversion. Undoubtedly, the most important exception is that for purposes of a 1031 exchange, the replacement property can be purchased from a related party if both the relinquished and replacement properties were held by the taxpayer and the related party for at least two years – this exception is not available for a 1033 exchange.

For a Section 1033 involuntary conversion, the taxpayer has the option of not electing exchange status, i.e. not to defer any income. Generally, the election to defer tax on an exchange is made by not reporting the income on the taxpayer's tax return for the year for which tax would otherwise be due. Also, involuntary conversions that produce a tax loss are not subject to the involuntary conversion exchange rules.

Contributions to Qualified Employee Retirement Plans
Salary reduction pre-tax contributions made by employees to qualified employer retirement plans are excluded from taxable income, but are "subject to payroll tax (FICA)." Employer matching contributions are not subject to either income tax or payroll tax. Most of the key dollar ceilings for contributions to retirement plans that were applicable to the 2017 tax year remained the same for the 2018 tax year. **(See Chapter 2, "Payroll Tax (FICA)")**

Contributions to retirement plans fall into two basic broad categories – defined contribution plans and defined benefit plans. Defined contribution plans are more popular than defined benefit plans, in fact defined benefit plans make up only about 10% of retirement plans that are in effect today. Defined contribution plans include a broad range of plans including cash or deferred arrangement plans (401(k), 403(b), and 457(b) plans); employee stock ownership (ESOP) plans; Keoghs; and two types of plans popular with small businesses – SIMPLE and SEP plans. Contributions to qualified defined contribution plans - 401(k), 403(b), and 457(b) plans, SEPs, and SIMPLEs can be made by both employees and employers. These plans are pre-tax or salary reduction retirement plans where employee contributions are excluded from federal income tax. For all qualified plans, the maximum annual compensation taken into account for contributions is increased from $400,000 in 2017 to $405,000 in 2018. Retirement plan contributions are reflected on Form W-2, Box 12 and each type of plan is allocated a different Code.

You can continue contributing to a retirement plan (including SIMPLEs) after age 70 ½ if you are still working, even though you must take RMDs from IRAs and any other retirement plans except for the one you continue making contributions to while working. However, if you own 5% or more of the company you continue working for, you must also take RMDs from that plan. **(See Chapter 5, "Required Minimum Distributions")**

    401(k), 403(b), and 457(b) Plans – 401(k)s are retirement plans offered by corporations to their employees (Roth 401(k)s are a subgroup that has a different tax treatment); 403(b)s are retirement plans for employees of public education entities and most other nonprofit organizations; 457(b)s are retirement plans for state and municipal employees, as well as employees of qualified nonprofits; and the Thrift Savings Plan (TSP) is a retirement plan available to federal employees. All of these plans basically work the same way. You decide how much you want to contribute, and your employer puts the money into your individual account on your behalf. The investment happens through payroll deductions. You decide what percentage of your salary you want to contribute on a pre-tax basis, and that amount comes out of your paycheck and goes into your account automatically. Part-time employees who work 1,000 hours or more during the year should be allowed to participate in 403(b) retirement plans, if not, the universal availability rules applicable to these plans are not being followed. **(See Chapter 5, "Qualified Retirement Plans – 401(k), 403(b), and 457(b) Plans")**

Most employers make matching contributions, such as 50 cents for every dollar you contribute up to a certain percentage of your salary (perhaps 3% to 6%). Employee salary deferrals are immediately 100% vested. When an employee leaves employment, he or she is entitled to those deferrals, plus any investment gains (or minus losses) on the deferrals. The tax deferral limit for employee contributions is $18,500 in 2018 ($18,000 in 2017). The catch-up contributions for those over 50 is $6,000 in 2017 and 2018, or a total of $24,500 in 2018. The annual additions to an individual's plan in 2018 cannot exceed the lesser of 100% of the participant's compensation or $55,000 ($61,000 including catch-up contributions). Investments made with your money is up to you. You can usually choose among a variety of mutual funds that the plan offers. The significant advantage over a SIMPLE plan is that the only eligible employees are those who are age 21 and who work 1,000 hours or more in their first 12 months of employment. They become eligible on the following January 1 or July 1, so most part-time or seasonal workers never enter the plan. Employer's matching contributions are in addition to the employee limits – maximum contribution limit in 2018 is $36,500 ($55,000 – $18,500). You can borrow from these plans, but the maximum amount is limited to (1) the greater of $10,000 or 50% of your vested account balance, or (2) $50,000, whichever is less. You cannot roll over funds from a 401(k) to a 403(b)-non-profit plan.

The threshold amount for highly compensated employees in 2017 and 2018 is annual compensation of $120,000. Every year, all 401(k) plans must pass a discrimination test, which means that the average contributions of highly compensated employees, as a group, to 401(k) plans cannot exceed the average contributions of non-highly compensated employees, as a group, by more than about 2%. If this threshold is exceeded and the employer fails to correct the imbalance by refunding some of the contributions made to the plan by highly compensated employees, the plan could lose its tax-qualified status. This test is not applicable to SIMPLEs, SEPs, and Keoghs. Even if a plan passes the discrimination test, it must also satisfy the "top-heavy" test. A defined contribution plan is top heavy when the aggregate value of the plan accounts of "key" employees exceeds 60% of the aggregate value of the plan accounts of all employees in the plan. A key employee is: a more than 5% owner of the employer; a more than 1% owner of the employer with annual compensation greater than $120,000; and an officer (key employee) with annual compensation greater than $175,000 in 2018. If a plan is top-heavy, the allocation made to a participant in a defined contribution plan must satisfy certain minimum benefit standards, i.e. the allocation of a "non-key" employee must not be less than 3% of compensation for the entire plan year. Elective deferrals made by a non-key employee in a 401(k) plan do not count toward the 3% minimum. Generally, if the employee's allocation is a least 3%, no further contribution is required to satisfy the top-heavy rules.

Your employer may include a Roth 401(k) or Roth 403(b) feature in your retirement plan. However, contributions to Roth plans are made with after-tax dollars, so they won't reduce your current taxable compensation as do traditional retirement plans with pre-tax contributions. The advantage of a Roth feature in your employer retirement plan is that you can withdraw funds later on (generally after age 59 ½) free from federal taxes. You may find this appealing if you expect to be in a higher tax bracket during your retirement years. If you are eligible to make a Roth conversion from an employee plan, the new law allows you to rollover your retirement plan directly into a Roth IRA (although you will owe federal taxes on the amount converted).

401(k) and similar plans are required to file an annual report with the Federal Government, in which information about the plan and its operation is disclosed to the IRS and the U.S. Department of Labor. Depending on the number and type of participants covered, 401(k) and similar plans must file one of the following forms: Form 5500 – Annual Return/Report of Employee Benefit Plan; Form 5500-SF – Short Form; or Form 5500-EZ – Annual Return of One-Participant (Owners and Their Spouses) Retirement Plan. Most one-participant plans (sole proprietor and partnership plans) with total annual assets of $250,000 or less are exempt from the annual filing requirement. However, regardless of the value of the plan's assets, a final report must be filed when the plan is terminated. www.dol.gov/agencies/ebsa/employers-and-advisers/plan-administration-and-compliance/reporting-and-filing/form-5500) www.irs.gov/pub/irs-pdf/i5500ez.pdf

Plan Loans – If an employee stops making payments on a retirement plan loan before the loan is repaid, a deemed distribution of the outstanding loan balance generally occurs. Such a distribution is generally taxed as though an actual distribution occurred, including being subject to a 10% early distribution tax and the deemed distribution isn't eligible for rollover to another eligible retirement plan. However, in certain circumstances (for example, if an employee terminates employment), an employee's obligation to repay a retirement plan loan is accelerated and, if the loan is not repaid, the loan is cancelled and the amount in the employee's account balance is offset by the amount of the unpaid loan balance, referred to as a loan offset.

For retirement plan loan offset amounts which are treated as distributed in tax years beginning after Dec. 31, 2017, the TCJA provides that the period during which a qualified plan loan offset amount may be contributed to another eligible retirement plan as a rollover contribution is extended from 60 days (in 2017 and prior years) to the due date (including extensions) for filing the tax return for the tax year in which the plan loan offset occurs. For this purpose, a qualified plan loan offset amount is a plan loan offset amount that is treated as distributed from a qualified 403(b) or 457(b) retirement plan solely by reason of termination of the plan or the failure to meet the repayment terms of the loan because of an employee's separation from service, whether due to layoff, cessation of business, termination of employment, or otherwise.

Length of Service Award Programs for Public Safety Volunteers – Under the Tax Cuts and Jobs Act (TCJA), for 2018 and subsequent years the TCJA increases the aggregate amount of length of service awards that may accrue under 457 plan rules for bona fide volunteers (volunteer firefighters and prevention services, emergency medical services, and ambulance services, including services performed by dispatchers, mechanics, ambulance drivers, and certified instructors) from $3,000 in 2017 and prior years to $6,000 with respect to any year of service, with cost of living adjustments beginning in 2019. Also, if the plan is a defined benefit plan (see below), the limit applies to the actuarial present value of the aggregate amount of length of service awards accruing with respect to any year of service. Actuarial present value is calculated using reasonable actuarial assumptions and methods, assuming payment will be made under the most valuable form of payment under the plan, with payment commencing at the later of the earliest age at which unreduced benefits are payable under the plan or the participant's age at the time of the calculation. For 2017 and prior years, any 457 plan that solely provided length of service awards to bona fide volunteers or their beneficiaries, on account of qualified services performed by the volunteers, was not treated as a plan of deferred compensation.

Saving Incentive Match Plans (SIMPLEs) – SIMPLE plans are pre-tax salary reduction retirement plans for employers with 100 or fewer employees with at least $6,000 in compensation. The SIMPLE is the least expensive to

install because it is free. You simply set up IRAs for each eligible employee. However, the deferral is limited to $12,500 in 2017 and 2018, but for those over age 50 the catch-up provision adds $3,000 or a deferral limit of $15,500 in 2017 and 2018. Contributions must be made by April 15th, even if an extension has been requested. All employees are eligible no matter the age or number of hours worked, so even part-time employees can become eligible. Employers must make either matching contributions or non-elective contributions at a maximum of 3%, but can be as low as 1%. All contributions must be fully vested. Employers can establish a SIMPLE by using Form 5304-SIMPLE. Once a SIMPLE plan has been adopted, no other plan can be adopted during the plan year. After terminating a SIMPLE plan, no other plan can be adopted until the following year. SIMPLEs and SEPs are popular with small employers who can't afford the expense or effort of establishing a 401(k) plan. Even a sole proprietor using Form 1040, Schedule C, can set-up a SIMPLE IRA. Contributions to the SIMPLE are deductions in determining adjusted gross income (AGI) that reduce taxable income, but do not reduce Schedule C net income that is subject to self-employment tax. **(See Chapter 2, "Payroll Tax (FICA)"); (See Chapter 5, "Traditional IRAs"); (See Chapter 17, "Self-Employment Tax")**
www.irs.gov/pub/irs-pdf/f5304sim.pdf   www.zillionforms.com/2016/I668407267.PDF

Simplified Employee Pension IRA (SEP) – A SEP allows employees to make contributions on a tax-deferred basis to IRAs. Employees actually setup the accounts by using Form 5305-SEP that can also accept employer contributions. The deferral limit for employee/employer contributions is $55,000 in 2018. All contributions are immediately vested, and employee withdrawals are permitted without penalty. All employees who are age 21, and have performed services during 3 of the immediately preceding 5 years and receive $550 in compensation are eligible. Contributions by employers must be made for all employees who qualify (the same percentage of salary must be contributed for each employee). You have until October 15th of the following year to make contributions to a SEP or Keogh plan, but you must establish the plan by Jan. 1, 2018, in order to make contributions for the 2018 tax year. **(See Chapter 5, "Traditional IRAs")**
www.irs.gov/pub/irs-pdf/f5305sep.pdf

Keoghs – Keoghs are tax-deferred retirement plans for self-employed persons (similar to SEPs). Self-employed individuals can contribute as much as $55,000 to a Keogh in 2018. Contributions are subject to deduction limits, i.e. taxable income.

Employee Stock Ownership Plan (ESOP) – An ESOP is a stock bonus plan or a combination stock bonus plan and money purchase plan that is designed to invest primarily in qualifying employer stock. An ESOP provides similar benefits of other company funded retirement plans (e.g. 401k) – tax deductible contributions for the employer and tax deferred growth of investments for employees. An ESOP is funded by employer contributions of stock in the corporation or allows you to buy shares of stock as an investment plan option. To companies, the ESOP is a means to increase productivity, as well as a qualified retirement plan. To employees, the ESOP is a company funded retirement plan and an incentive to affect their own personal wealth. The ESOP trust is the direct owner of the company stock, not the employees. Employees are beneficial owners, and thus, do not have the same rights as direct owners of the stock. Only the plan committee can sell ESOP shares. ESOPs provide liquidity and diversification of employees' investments, promote employee productivity, and increase the company's cash flow. The theory behind an ESOP is that people work best when they work for themselves. Numerous studies have all concluded that ESOPs increase company performance. Required information disclosure is limited to the employee account balance. ESOPs must comply with all the requirements imposed on defined contribution plans and cannot be integrated with Social Security.

Defined Benefit Plan – Defined benefit plans are employer-sponsored retirement plans where in the private sector, they are usually funded exclusively by employer contributions. In the public sector, defined benefit plans usually require some employee contributions. In general, the annual benefit for a participant cannot exceed the lesser of: 100% of the participant's average compensation for the highest 3 consecutive calendar years, or $220,000 for 2018 ($215,000 for 2017). Defined benefit plans offer tax incentives both to employers and to participating employees. For example, your employer can deduct all of the contributions made to the plan, and you generally won't owe tax on those contributions until you begin receiving distributions from the plan when you retire. A defined benefit plan guarantees you a certain benefit when you retire. How much you receive generally depends on factors such as your salary, age, and years of service with the company. **(See Chapter 5, "Defined Benefit Plans")**

Retirement benefits are based on a formula. This formula can provide for a set dollar amount for each year you work for the employer, or it can provide for a specified percentage of earnings. Many plans calculate an employee's retirement benefit by averaging the employee's earnings during the last few years of employment (or, alternatively, averaging an employee's earnings for his or her entire career), taking a specified percentage of the average, and then multiplying it by the employee's number of years in service. Also, many defined benefit plan formulas reduce pension benefits by a percentage of the amount of Social Security benefits you can expect to receive.

Many defined benefit plans allow you to choose how you want your benefits to be paid. Payment options include: a single life annuity – you receive a fixed monthly benefit until you die and no further payments are made to your survivors; a qualified joint and survivor annuity – you receive a fixed monthly benefit until you die and your surviving spouse will continue to receive benefits (in an amount equal to at least 50% of your benefit) until his or her death; or a lump-sum payment – you receive the entire value of your plan in a lump sum and no further payments are made to you or your survivors.

Self-Directed Retirement Plan – Self-directed retirement plans can be very risky due to the possibility of involvement in a prohibited transaction. In fact, the main culprit in a self-directed retirement plan gone wrong is the dreaded prohibited transaction. In a recent real-life example, an accountant lost a sizable portion of his retirement account by using a self-directed 401(k) plan where he became a disqualified person who executed a prohibited transaction for the plan. What Is a Prohibited Transaction? Code Section 4975 imposes a tax on a disqualified person who participates in a prohibited transaction. A disqualified person includes a plan fiduciary, a person providing services to a plan and an employer whose employees are covered by a plan. The following are considered prohibited transactions: sale or exchange, or leasing of any property between a plan and a disqualified person; lending money or other extension of credit between a plan and a disqualified person; furnishing of goods, services, or facilities between a plan and a disqualified person; transfer to, or use by or for the benefit of a disqualified person of the income or assets of a plan; an act by a disqualified person who is a fiduciary whereby he deals with the income or assets of a plan in his own interest or for his own account; or receipt of any consideration for his own personal account by any disqualified person who is a fiduciary from any party dealing with the plan in connection with a transaction involving the income or assets of the plan.

Nonqualified Deferred Compensation Plan – A nonqualified deferred compensation plan (NQDC plan) is generally an arrangement, other than a qualified employer plan, such as a 401(k) plan, in which an employer agrees to pay compensation in the future to an employee. A special timing rule applies to a NQDC plan, in that compensation deferred under the plan may be subject to payroll tax (FICA) when the employee has a vested right to the compensation. The special timing rule benefits both employers and employees, because at the time the deferred compensation is taken into account for payroll tax purposes under the special timing rule, the employee is often still employed and has wages in excess of the wage base limit for purposes of calculating the Social Security tax. Therefore, under the special timing rule the employer and employee may pay little or no additional Social Security tax on the deferred compensation. If the employer does not apply the special timing rule, then in accordance with the general rule, the payroll tax is imposed when the compensation is paid, which may trigger adverse tax consequences. Once the deferred compensation is taken into account for payroll tax purposes under the special timing rule, the compensation and related earnings are then free from any additional payroll tax when actually paid to the employee. This is referred to as the "nonduplication" rule.

Employee Tax-Advantaged Spending Accounts

Contributions to employee tax-advantaged spending accounts are usually made via an employer's cafeteria plan which provides employees the opportunity to receive health insurance, disability, dependent care, and other benefits by making salary reduction contributions on a pre-tax basis that are excluded from taxable income and not subject to payroll tax. Tax-advantaged spending accounts include Health Reimbursement Arrangements (HRAs); Health Savings Accounts (HSAs); and Flexible Spending Accounts (FSAs). An employer's contributions to tax-advantaged spending accounts for the benefit of employees are also non-taxable and not subject to payroll tax. Distributions from tax-advantaged spending accounts are non-taxable if used to pay for qualified expenses. **(See Chapter 8, "Employer Provided Tax-Free Benefits")**

In order for large employers (50 or more full-time equivalent employees – FTEs) to be in compliance with the Affordable Care Act (ACA), they can't use stand-alone tax-advantaged spending accounts to assist their employees with health insurance premiums, but instead, such plans must be "integrated" with group health insurance plans offered to employees. So, in 2018, large employers have to pay a penalty if they directly pay the premiums for health insurance coverage that employees purchase on their own, or they reimburse employees for health insurance premiums using stand-alone Health Reimbursement Arrangements (HRAs), unless the HRAs are set-up to only cover excepted insurance benefits, e.g. dental, vision, disability, long-term care, accident-only coverage, etc. However, Qualified Small Employer Health Reimbursement Arrangements (QSEHRAs) were signed into law by the "21st Century Cures Act" in December 2017, and this allows small employers (fewer than 50 FTE employees) to use stand-alone Health Reimbursement Arrangements (HRAs) to assist their employees with out-of-pocket health insurance premiums and medical costs and not be subject to the penalty. **(See Chapter 24, "Excise Tax on Employers That Reimburse Employees for Health Insurance")**

The Affordable Care Act (ACA) excludes over-the-counter medications, except for insulin and over-the-counter medications prescribed by a physician, from qualified medical expenses for purposes of reimbursement and tax-free distributions from employee tax-advantaged spending accounts. This does not apply to non-drug health care expenses such as medical devices, eye glasses, contact lenses, bandages, and diagnostic devices such as blood sugar test kits, co-pays and deductibles. **(See Chapter 24, "Affordable Care Act (ACA)")**

Health Reimbursement Arrangement (HRA) – Health Reimbursement Arrangements (HRAs) are employer-sponsored plans that are owned by the employer. The employer sets allowances for employees to spend on healthcare and contributes money to HRAs on a pre-tax basis on behalf of their employees to use for qualified medical expenses. There is no limit to the amount of money an employer can contribute to an employee's HRA. When money is added to an HRA, it belongs to the employer until a qualified medical expense is incurred. No funds are expensed until eligible medical expenses are reimbursed. However, the employer specifies the categories of medical expenses that an HRA will cover, i.e. if an employer decides to cover doctor's visits and prescriptions, but not dental or vision, the HRA can be set-up that way. Additionally, HRAs allow annual rollover of unused dollars for use in subsequent years. If an employee leaves a company without spending all the money in the HRA, the employee usually losses access to that money. However, employers may allow employees to have access to their HRAs after retirement.

HRA plans that are setup to only cover excepted benefits (dental, vision, long-term care, etc.) are exempt from the Affordabke Care Act (ACA) integration requirements. Also, retiree HRAs are exempt from the ACA rules, including the annual limit prohibition and the preventive care requirements. In this regard, retirees can put the value of unused sick leave into HRAs at retirement if doing so is mandatory under the plan, and then use the value of the unused sick leave tax-free for medical insurance premiums and expenses. Thus, stand-alone HRAs that provide benefits for retirees (including pre-tax reimbursement of individual major medical coverage) are permissible under the ACA. However, such arrangements are considered group health plans and will preclude eligibility for premium tax credits for the individuals. Thus, retirees must be offered the opportunity to opt out of such arrangements in order to give the retirees the opportunity to seek a premium tax credit subsidy by acquiring insurance through the government Exchanges.

Qualified Small Employer Health Reimbursement Arrangement (QSEHRA) – A qualified small employer health reimbursement arrangement (QSEHRA), or small business HRA, is an employer funded tax-free health benefit that allows small businesses with fewer than 50 full-time or full-time-equivalent (FTE) employees to reimburse their employees for individual health care expenses. QSEHRAs were signed into law by the "21st Century Cures Act" in December 2017. Most stand-alone health reimbursement arrangements (HRAs), which is an HRA that is not offered in conjunction with a group health plan, have been prohibited since 2014 by the Affordable Care Act (ACA). However, the 21st Century Cures Act (Act) allows small employers that do not maintain group health plans to establish stand-alone HRAs that are called QSEHRAs, effective for plan years beginning on or after Jan. 1, 2017. Like all HRAs, a QSEHRA must be funded solely by the employer. Employees cannot make their own contributions to an HRA, either directly or indirectly through salary reduction contributions. Specific requirements apply, including a maximum benefit limit and a notice requirement. For 2018, the maximum reimbursements cannot exceed $5,050 for those with self-only coverage and $10,250 for those with family coverage. In 2017, the QSEHRA contribution limits were $4,950 annually for self-only employees and $10,000 annually for family coverage. For employees who become eligible for the QSEHRA midyear, the limits must be prorated to reflect the total amount of time the employee is eligible. For example, an employee who is eligible for the QSEHRA for 6 months in 2018 can receive up to $2,524.98 through the benefit that year.

In order to calculate whether a QSEHRA provides affordable coverage in accordance with the Affordable Care Act (ACA), employees have to determine whether the premium for the QSEHRA offered by their employer costs 9.56% or less of their household income in 2018. If the QSEHRA's premium meets that cost standard, the employee has affordable coverage and doesn't qualify for a premium tax credit. However, if the premium costs more than 9.56% of their household income, employees may be eligible for a premium tax credit. **(See Chapter 24," Qualified Small Employer Health Reimbursement Arrangement (QSEHRA)")**

Health Savings Account (HSA) – Health Savings Accounts (HSAs) are individual bank accounts that belong to the account holders (employees) that allow for tax-free reimbursement of eligible medical expenses. With an HSA, anyone (employees, employers, and third parties) can contribute to the account. To be eligible to contribute to an HSA, employees must have an HSA-qualified high-deductible health plan (HDHP). A qualified HDHP is a healthcare plan that satisfies certain requirements with respect to minimum deductibles and maximum out-of-pocket expenses. It must cover, on average, at least 60% of the cost of all medical expenses paid by employees and dependents. HDHPs offered by employers to their employees can't be only for excepted benefits (vision, dental, long-term care, etc.). But not all high-deductible policies are HSA-eligible. The policy must make everything (all types of expenses) subject to the same deductible. Some plans, for example, aren't eligible because they have a separate deductible for prescription drugs. HDHPs being sold today generally meet minimum essential coverage requirements, and employers usually offer a HSA alongside a HSA-qualified HDHP through a cafeteria plan. If an employer offers an HSA, but not a qualified HDHP, then employees must have a HDHP that they purchase on their own before they are eligible to contribute to the employer's HSA.

Employees' contributions (other than pre-tax contributions) to HSAs are deductible as an above-the-line deduction on their tax return, but contributions are usually pre-tax. The maximum allowable contributions in 2018 are $6,850 for family coverage ($6,750 in 2017), and $3,450 for self-only coverage ($3,400 in 2017). In addition, taxpayers who are age 55 or older can make an additional $1,000 catch-up contribution each year. If you have an HSA-eligible policy for only the first few months of 2018, your contribution is limited based on the number of months you have the policy, but if you have an HSA-eligible policy on December 1, 2018, you can make the full year's contribution even if you didn't have the policy for the full year. However, in that situation, you must keep an HSA-eligible policy for all of 2018 in order to avoid a penalty. Contributions to HSAs can't be used to pay for health insurance premiums except for: long-term care insurance; COBRA coverage; health care coverage while receiving unemployment compensation under federal or state law; and Medicare if you are age 65 or older. **(See Chapter 11, "Contributions to a Health Savings Account (HSA")); (See Chapter 24, "Affordable Care Act")**

For 2018, a high deductible health plan (HDHP) must have an annual deductible that is not less than $2,700 family coverage ($2,600 in 2017), and $1,350 for self-only coverage ($1,300 in 2017) where the maximum out of pocket expenses cannot exceed $13,300 for family coverage ($13,100 in 2017) and $6,650 for self-only coverage ($6,550 in 2017). However, a plan will not fail to qualify as a HDHP merely because it has no deductible for the preventive care health services required by the Affordable Care Act (ACA). Preventive services include a long list of shots, screening tests, and counseling services. In addition to a HDHP, an eligible individual may be covered by another health insurance plan that provides permitted or "excepted" coverage. Other permitted or "excepted" insurance covers only accidents, disability, dental care, vision care, or long-term care.

Distributions from HSAs (including interest earned on the accounts) are excluded from income and payroll taxes if the distributions are made for qualified medical expenses. Distributions are reported on Form 1099-SA. Non-qualified distributions from an HSA are taxable and in addition a 20% excise tax (penalty) is applicable. However,

once an account holder reaches age 65 or 66 (Medicare eligibility age), becomes disabled, or dies, withdrawals for non-medical purposes are subject to income tax only, with no penalty.
www.irs.gov/pub/irs-pdf/f1099sa.pdf   www.irs.gov/pub/irs-pdf/i1099sa.pdf

HSAs combine the benefits of both traditional and Roth IRAs, in that contributions to an HSA are 100% excludable from taxable income and the funds can be used tax-free for qualified medical expenses at any time; there is tax-free accumulation of interest and dividends; distributions for qualified medical expenses are excluded from taxable income; and unused contributions can be carried over indefinitely. Every person who qualifies – has a high deductible health insurance plan – should contribute the maximum amount allowable to their HSA each year before they contribute to any other type of retirement account. After a person retires, their HSA becomes one of their most valuable retirement vehicles because it offers tax-free dollars for one of their biggest expenses – medical care. **(See Chapter 11, "Roth IRA")**

If an employer contributes to an employee's HSA, the employee controls the money immediately and can use the money for any qualified medical expense unless the employer's contributions are restricted to be used only for "excepted benefits" (vision, dental, long-term care, etc.). HSAs and HRAs are not mutually exclusive, i.e. employees can have both types of accounts at the same time if they meet certain requirements. Unlike distributions from a Flexible Spending Account (FSA), distributions from an HSA are not required to be substantiated by the employer or a third party for the distributions to be excluded from taxable income. The determination is subject to individual self-reporting and IRS enforcement.

Flexible Spending Account (FSA) – Contributions to Flexible Spending Accounts (FSAs) are generally salary reduction pre-tax contributions under an employer sponsored cafeteria plan that are excluded from income and payroll taxes, and distributions from FSAs are excluded from taxable income if used to pay for qualified employee medical expenses (Health FSA) and dependent care expenses (Dependent Care FSA). **(See Chapter 8, "Employer Provided Tax-Free Benefits")**

- **Health FSA** – Total contributions to Health FSAs are limited to $2,650 in 2018 ($2,600 in 2017) per individual under the Affordable Care Act. A provision adopted in 2013 permits employers to allow participants who do not use all of the money in a plan year to carry over up to $500 to the next plan year. Prior to 2013 there was no limit on the amount of money you or your employer could contribute to a Health FSA, but there was no carryover provision. Amounts contributed had to be spent on eligible unreimbursed medical expenses by the end of the year or the money was forfeited, unless employers permitted the grace period rule which allowed participants to spend unused amounts in the first two months and 15 days of the next plan year (2 ½ month grace period). The up-to-$500 carryover amount will not count toward the following year's maximum allowable contribution. Any unused amount above $500 will be forfeited. It will be up to the employer to decide whether or not to offer this option. Any plan adopting a carryover provision will have to be amended by the employer, and cannot also permit the 2 ½ month grace period.

  If a Health FSA only qualifies as an "excepted benefit," (dental, vision, long-term care, etc.) it doesn't have to comply with the ACA integration requirements, and the FSA must be structured so that both employer and employee contributions can only be used for excepted benefits. For reservists called to active duty, the law permits, but does not require, amounts left over at the end of the year not to be forfeited, i.e. reservists can get money back, but must pay income taxes and payroll taxes on the amounts recovered. **(See Chapter 24, "Excise Tax on Employers that Reimburse Employees for Health Insurance")**

- **Dependent Care FSA** – Contributions to Dependent Care FSAs are used to pay for childcare and other dependent care expenses while parents or legal guardians are at work and also for qualified adult daycare expenses. A Dependent Care FSA can be used for daycare, before and after school care, summer day camps, and other care costs for dependents under age 13, or for those over age 13 (such as dependent adult parents) who cannot adequately care for themselves while the employee is at work. The person or persons on whom the dependent care funds are spent must be able to be claimed as a dependent on the employee's tax return. The funds cannot be used for summer camps (other than "day camps") or for long-term care for an employee's parents who live elsewhere (such as a nursing home). The maximum Dependent Care FSA contribution for married/family, singles and heads-of-household in 2018 is $5,000, and the maximum contribution for married persons filing separately is $2,500. Married persons can each have an FSA, but their total combined contributions cannot exceed $5,000. Also, the maximum contribution is limited to an employee's earned income for the year, or the spouse's earned income if the employee is married at the end of the year. Employees can be reimbursed only up to the amount they deduct during the plan year for dependent care expenses. **(See Chapter 13, "Child and Dependent Care Credit")**

Advance Refunding Bonds
The exclusion from gross income of interest earned on State and local bonds was applicable to "refunding bonds" with some limitations on advance refunding bonds in 2017 and prior years. However, the TCJA repealed the exclusion from gross income of interest earned on advance refunding bonds for bonds issued after December 31, 2017. A refunding bond is defined as any bond used to pay principal, interest, or redemption price on a prior bond issue (the refunded bond). A current refunding occurs when the refunded bond is redeemed within 90 days of issuance of the refunding bonds. Conversely, a bond is classified as an advance refunding if it is issued more than 90 days before the redemption of the refunded bond. In general, governmental bonds and qualified 501(c)(3) bonds may be advance refunded only one time, while private activity bonds (other than qualified 501(c)(3) bonds may not be advance refunded at all. Proceeds of advance refunding bonds are generally invested in an escrow account and held until a future date when the refunded bond may be redeemed.

Chapter 10 – 3.8% Net Investment Income Tax

The 3.8% net Investment Income (NII) tax was initiated starting in 2013 by the Affordable Care Act (ACA), and was implemented to provide additional revenue for Medicare. The tax is also referred to as the "unearned income contribution tax," because it is imposed on certain unearned income of high-income individuals and it also applies to estates and trusts. High-income individuals are those with adjusted gross income (AGI) above $200,000 single; $250,000 married filing jointly and surviving spouse; $125,000 married filing separately; and $200,000 head-of-household, and the thresholds are not adjusted for inflation. The net investment income (NII) tax is in addition to the regular income taxes and capital gain taxes already paid by high-income individuals. The 3.8% NII tax is computed on Form 8960, "Net Investment Income Tax - Individuals, Estates, and Trusts." **(See Chapter 5, "Portfolio Income"); (See Chapter 24, "Taxes on High-Income Earners, Insurance Providers, and Others")**

The 3.8% NII tax on individuals is on the lesser of "net investment income" or the amount by which modified adjusted gross income (MAGI) exceeds the above stated thresholds for high-income earners. www.irs.gov/pub/irs-pdf/f8960.pdf   www.irs.gov/pub/irs-pdf/i8960.pdf

Modified Adjusted Gross Income (MAGI)
MAGI for purposes of the NII tax is usually identical to adjusted gross income (AGI) for most taxpayers, but if you have excluded foreign earned income and/or foreign housing, it must be added back to AGI to get MAGI. MAGI for this purpose does not include: tax-exempt interest; veterans' benefits; and excluded gain from the sale of a principal residence. However, MAGI does include: lump-sum distributions from retirement plans; conversion of traditional IRAs to Roth IRAs; required minimum distributions (RMD); all distributions from qualified plans, IRAs, and Roth IRAs; and any gain over and above the $250,000/$500,000 exclusion from the sale of a principal residence. **(See Chapter 11, "Modified Adjusted Gross Income")**

Included in Net Investment Income
Net Investment Income (NII) Includes: interest; dividends; gain/loss on the sale of securities; annuity income; royalties; rental income; gain over and above the $250,000/$500,000 exclusion from the sale of a principal residence; income/losses derived in the ordinary course of a passive partnership, S-corporation or other passive trade or business; gain/loss attributable to the disposition of property and equipment held in a passive partnership, S-corporation or other passive trade or business; and gain/loss on the sale of interests in a passive partnership, S-corporation or other passive trade or business. A passive business activity is generally a pass-through entity such as a partnership or S-corporation in which a taxpayer does not materially participate in the management and/or operation of the entity. Losses can be used to offset gains – but not below zero – if both the gains and losses would have been classified as NII. Also, taxpayers are allowed to use prior-year capital-loss carryovers against current capital gains. Suspended passive losses from a former passive activity (after an activity becomes non-passive) are allowed in the calculation of NII, but only to the extent of non-passive income from the former passive activity that is included in income in the current year. In addition, NII includes income attributable to the business of trading in financial instruments or commodities no matter whether the activity is considered a passive or a non-passive activity. **(See Chapter 5, "Portfolio Income"); (See Chapter 6, "Reporting Capital Gains and Losses"); (See Chapter 7, "Passive Income and Losses"); (See Chapter 9, "Home Sale Gain Exclusion")**

NII includes traditional pass-through investment income items (interest, dividends, rental income, royalties, annuity income) allocable to owners/shareholders of all partnerships and S-corporations (whether passive or non-passive); and gains or losses allocable to owners/shareholders of partnerships and S-corporations from dispositions of marketable securities held in partnerships or S-corporations (whether passive or non-passive). **(See Chapter 18, "Partnerships"); (See Chapter 19, "S-Corporation Status")**

Not Included in Net Investment Income

Net Investment Income (NII) does not include: salaries and wages; social security; self-employment income; tax-exempt interest; conversion of traditional IRAs to Roth IRAs; excluded gain from the sale of a principal residence; distributions from qualified plans, IRAs and Roth IRAs (including required minimum distributions (RMDs)); lump-sum distributions from retirement plans; income derived in the ordinary course of a non-passive partnership, S-corporation or other trade or business; gains or losses from the disposition of property and equipment held in a non-passive partnership, S-corporation or other trade or business; and gains or losses on the sale or disposition of an interest in a non-passive partnership, S-corporation or other trade or business. A non-passive partnership or S-corporation is one in which a taxpayer "materially" participates in the management and/or operation of the entity. **(See Chapter 4, "Wages and Salaries"); (See Chapter 5, "Social Security Benefits"; "Conversion of Traditional IRAs to Roth IRAs"; "Distributions from Retirement Plans and Traditional IRAs"; & "Required Minimum Distributions"); (See Chapter 17, "Self-Employed/Independent Contractors")**

- **Example** – For tax year 2017: disposition of passive activity X results in a $20,000 loss to owner A; passive activity Y has a gain of $62,000 to owner A; non-passive activity Z has a gain of $60,000 to owner A; and the sale of marketable securities results in a gain of $8,000 for owner A. Owner A's gain applicable to the 3.8% NII tax is $50,000 ($62,000 minus $20,000 + $8,000). $50,000 of A's overall gain of $110,000 in 2017 is NII.

Net Investment Income is Reduced By

Net Investment Income (NII) is reduced by: allowed itemized deductions (NOTE: in 2018 miscellaneous itemized deductions subject to the 2% AGI floor are no longer deductible). Allowable itemized deductions in 2018 are state and local income taxes and investment interest expenses. **(See Chapter 12, "Miscellaneous Itemized Deductions Subject to the 2% AGI Floor")**

- **Example** – You have a passive interest in a number of investments that generate investment income of $100,000, and the NII tax applies to your investments. State and local income taxes = $10,000 and investment interest expenses = $5,000; Therefore, you are allowed a deduction of $15,000 against NII.

Special Exclusions from Net Investment Income

Special exclusions from Net Investment Income (NII) include: self-rented business property; rental income derived by real estate professionals; and self-charged interest.

Self-Rented Property – A single rental property can qualify as a trade or business if the taxpayer participates in the activity – essentially meaning that self-rental income is not subject to the NII tax. Therefore, if an individual derives rental income from a business activity in which the individual is materially participating, the 3.8% NII tax will not apply.

- **Example** - A business owner/operator, generally for legal liability purposes, holds "business" real estate in one entity and an active trade or business in another entity, with the latter paying rent to the former. The rent that is paid by the business entity to the real estate entity is considered non-passive and, therefore not subject to the NII tax. Also, gain or loss from disposition of the business real estate property would be treated as non-passive, meaning the sale of the property would not be subject to the NII tax. Note: this is not the same thing as individuals with non-business rental property (residential property) in which they "significantly" participate, which is considered passive income, but the owners are allowed to deduct up to $25,000 in rental losses from non-passive income each year.

Real Estate Professionals – Net investment income usually includes "rental income" unless the rental income was derived from a trade or business carried on by a taxpayer who meets the stringent requirements of being classified as a real estate professional. Qualifying as a real estate professional isn't easy, but there is a "safe harbor" for a taxpayer who materially participates in rental real estate activities for more than 750 hours each year, and thus, rental income derived from these rental activities is exempt from the passive loss rules and would not be included in NII. Also, the IRS recognizes that some real estate professionals with substantial rental activities may derive rental income in the ordinary course of a trade or business, even though they fail to satisfy the 750-hour requirement. As a result, the final regulations specifically provide that such failure would not preclude a taxpayer from establishing that rental income and gain or loss from the disposition of real property, as applicable, is not included in NII. Essentially, this means that rental income derived by most real estate professionals is considered non-passive and will not be subject to the NII tax. However, mortgage brokers are specifically not eligible for the special exclusion granted to real estate professionals. **(See Chapter 7, "Real Estate Professional")**

Self-Charged Interest – The IRS added a special rule that permits taxpayers to exclude from NII the amount of interest income equal to a taxpayer's allocable share of interest income that is considered self-charged interest income.

- **Example** – An individual makes a loan to a pass-through entity (S-corporation or partnership) in which the individual materially participates and has a 60% ownership in the entity. If the individual receives $3,000 of interest income from the loan that is reported as interest income on his personal tax return, $1,800 of the interest is considered non-passive and, therefore is excluded from NII under the self-charged interest rule ($3,000 X 60% = $1,800).

Net Investment Income Tax Applicable to Estates and Trusts

An estate or trust is subject to the 3.8% Net Investment Income (NII) tax to the extent of the lesser of: the estate's or trust's undistributed net investment income; or the excess (if any) of the estate's or trust's AGI over the dollar amount at which the highest tax bracket begins for the year ($12,400 for 2018). Grantor trust income flows-through to the grantor; therefore, only non-grantor trusts are required to pay the NII tax. Non-grantor trusts should consider paying distributions to beneficiaries to avoid the 3.8% NII tax, which kicks in for trusts at $12,400 in 2018. The 65-day rule can be used to defer distributions to as late as March 6th of the following year and still have them apply to the current year. Trusts that are subject to the NII tax include: non-grantor trusts; electing small business trusts; non-grantor charitable lead trusts; pooled income funds; cemetery perpetual care funds; qualified funeral trusts; Alaska Native Settlement Trusts; and foreign trusts with U.S. beneficiaries. The NII tax does not apply to common trust funds, real estate investment trusts, designated settlement funds, wholly charitable trusts, other trusts exempt from tax and foreign trusts without U.S. beneficiaries. **(See Chapter 21, "Net Investment Income Tax Applicable to Estates and Trusts")**

Ways Individuals Can Avoid the Net Investment Income (NII) Tax

There are various steps that taxpayers who fall within the parameters of the NII tax can take to reduce their chances of having to pay it, including:

- Buy municipal bonds – The NII tax isn't levied on interest and dividends that are normally excluded from federal income tax, such as interest earned on tax-exempt state and municipal bonds and municipal bond funds. Moreover, tax-exempt interest doesn't count in your MAGI for NII tax purposes, so it could help keep you below the $200,000/$250,000 thresholds.

- Give appreciated property away – Donate appreciated property to your favorite charity and you can deduct the full value of your gift but won't have to recognize the appreciation for purposes of either the capital gains tax or the NII tax. Also, you can give appreciated property to relatives who have income below the $200,000/$250,000 thresholds and let them sell it.

- Loan money to your business – Interest payable as a result of a loan you've made is generally subject to the NII tax, but not if the loan is to your legitimate business.

- Convert your role in a business from passive to active – Income isn't subject to the NII tax if it comes from a trade or business in which you materially participate (other than the trading of financial instruments or commodities). Generally, material participation is working more than 500 hours a year in the business, performing most of the services in the business or demonstrating a consistent work history in the business. However, any salary you earn from working in the business is subject to the self-employment tax, as well as the added 0.9% Medicare surtax on employment earnings above $200,000/$250,000. **(See Chapter 7, "Rental Income"); (See Chapter 14, "Passive Activities")**

- Become a professional realtor – If you can qualify as a real estate professional for purposes of the federal income tax, then you can report your rental income as non-passive, and it will be exempt from the NII tax. **(See Chapter 7, "Real Estate Professional")**

- Section 1031 like-kind exchange – Instead of selling "real" property, execute a Section 1031 like-kind exchange. Any capital gain you would have recognized from a sale is deferred until the final sale of the new property received in the exchange. A Section 1031 exchange defers regular capital gain tax as well as the NII tax. **(See Chapter 9, "Section 1031 Like-Kind Exchange")**

- An Installment sale – When selling an appreciated asset, consider whether you need the income all in one year. The proceeds from an installment sale are hit by the NII tax only when they're received, not at the time of sale. With an installment sale, you can delay the recognition of income, delay the NII tax, or even better avoid it altogether by keeping your annual income under the $200,000/$250,000 thresholds for the NII tax. **(See Chapter 6, "Installment Sale")**

- Sell losers – Under the final rules, net capital losses can be used to offset gains for purposes of the NII tax, if both the gains and losses would have been classified as NII. The final regulations also allow taxpayers to use prior-year capital-loss carryovers against current gains.

Chapter 11 – Deductions in Determining Adjusted Gross Income

Gross income minus the following deductions equals adjusted gross income (AGI). These deductions are known as "above-the-line" deductions that are reported on Form 1040. Above-the-line deductions are deductible even if taxpayers take the standard deduction. Modified Adjusted Gross Income (MAGI) is used to determine certain allowances. **(See Chapter 1, "Standard Deduction"; & "Filing Your Return"); (See Chapter 4, "Wages and Salaries")**

Modified Adjusted Gross Income

In general, Modified Adjusted Gross Income (MAGI) which is used to determine certain allowances is the same as adjusted gross income (AGI) for most people. However, for some people MAGI is AGI increased by certain items that are excluded from gross income, which are: foreign earned income and housing; nontaxable Social Security benefits and tier 1 railroad retirement benefits; tax-exempt interest; U.S. savings bond interest used to pay for higher education expenses; rental real estate losses; passive losses; any overall loss from publicly traded partnerships; and employer provided adoption expenses. Also, MAGI is AGI increased by certain items that are excluded in determining AGI, which are: contributions to traditional IRAs; one-half of self-employment tax; student loan interest; and qualified tuition and related expenses for higher education. **(See Below, "Student Loan Interest"; "Tuition and Fees for Higher Education"; & "Self-Employment Tax"); (See Chapter 5, "Social Security Benefits"; & "Railroad Retirement Plans"); (See Chapter 7, "Passive Income and Losses"; & "Rental Income"); (See Chapter 8, "Interest on Municipal Bonds and Tax-Exempt Municipal Bond Funds"; "U.S. Savings Bond Redemptions Used for Higher Education Expenses"; & "Employer Provided Tax-Free Benefits"); (See Chapter 9, "Foreign Earned Income Exclusion" & "Contributions to Qualified Employee Retirement Plans"); (See Chapter 17, "Self-Employment Tax")**

Educator Expenses

The $250 teacher deduction for supplies was made permanent by the "Protecting Americans from Tax Hikes Act of 2015," and the law expanded the deduction to include professional development expenses. The deduction is not limited to teachers – you are considered an educator and can take the deduction if you are employed at a state-approved public or private school system and hold one of several positions. Up to $250 ($500 if married filing jointly and both spouses are educators, but not more than $250 each) in qualified out-of-pocket expenses can be deducted each year by teachers, instructors, counselors, principals, teachers' aides, and others who are qualified and work in public or private schools and who work at least 900 hours during the school year. Qualified expenses are amounts you paid or incurred for books, supplies, computer equipment (including related software and services), and other equipment and supplementary materials used in the classroom. For courses in health and physical education, expenses for supplies are qualified only if related to athletics. Also, beginning in 2016, the $250 cap is indexed for inflation. However, due to low inflation, the deduction remained at $250 for the 2018 tax year. The deduction is claimed on Form 1040.

Student Loan Interest

The student loan interest deduction was made permanent as of Jan. 1, 2013. A maximum of $2,500 can be deducted each year by a taxpayer. Student loan interest is reported on Form 1098-E when a person pays more than $600 in interest in a year. The deduction is also available for loans used to pay for room and board expenses. However, mixed loans are not eligible for the deduction, i.e. loans that are for other things unrelated to the student loan portion. Phase-out ranges for the deduction in 2018 (also in 2017) are MAGI of: $65,001 – $80,000 (single and head of household); and $135,001 – $165,000 (married filing jointly). You can't claim the student loan interest deduction in 2018 if your MAGI is $80,000 or more ($165,000 or more if you file a joint return). If a parent(s) pays student loan interest for a dependent child, the parent(s) can deduct the interest on their tax return. If a parent pays student loan interest for a child not claimed as a dependent, the IRS treats the payment as a gift to the child, who can then deduct the interest on his/her tax return. If another person makes a student loan payment on your behalf, it's as though you made the payment and you can deduct the interest on your return. Also, if the parents take out the loan or co-sign and make the payments, they can claim the deduction even after the child is no longer a dependent. If the student takes out the loan and defers repayment until he or she is no longer a dependent, he or she can claim the interest deduction on his own tax return even if his parents make the payments, as per the rule that allows the deduction when someone else makes a payment of interest on the behalf of the student. The student is then treated as receiving the payments from the other person and, in turn, paying the interest.

Usually, forgiveness of a student loan is taxable income to the student borrower. However, if the loan is from a government agency, a government-funded education organization, or qualified hospital organization and the loan is cancelled because the student will be working in certain geographical areas or in certain professions (medicine, teaching, etc.), the debt forgiveness is tax-free. **(See Chapter 9, "Forgiveness of Student Loans"); (See Chapter 22, "Estate and Gift Tax")**
www.irs.gov/pub/irs-pdf/f1098e.pdf

Tuition and Fees for Higher Education (Form 8917)
The tuition and fees for higher education deduction was originally unavailable in 2017, because it was only extended through 2016 by the "Protecting Americans from Tax Hikes Act of 2015." But in February 2018 it was retroactively extended to the 2017 tax year by the Bipartisan Budget Act of 2018 and it is also available in 2018.

A tuition and fees deduction of up to $4,000 per student is available for single taxpayers with modified adjusted gross incomes (MAGI) up to $65,000 (up to $130,000 for joint filers), and a deduction of up to $2,000 per student is available for single taxpayers with MAGIs over $65,000 and up to $80,000 (over $130,000 and up to $160,000 for joint filers). No deduction is available for taxpayers with MAGIs over $80,000 for single filers ($160,000 for joint filers). The deduction is not available to married taxpayers filing separately. Tuition and fees must be required for enrollment in an accredited post-secondary institution for the taxpayer, spouse and dependents. Allowable expenses do not include expenditures for room and board or books, supplies and equipment. You must attach Form 8917 to your tax return to claim the deduction. The deduction cannot be taken if one of the available Education Credits is taken. Also, the deduction is reduced by the tax-free earnings portion of any distributions from Coverdell savings accounts and 529 plans (reported on Form 1099-Q) that pay for the same expenses. **(See Chapter 13, "Education Credits")**
www.irs.gov/pub/irs-pdf/f8917.pdf   www.congress.gov/115/bills/hr1892/BILLS-115hr1892enr.pdf

Effective for tax years beginning January 1, 2016, taxpayers can't claim the deduction unless they have a Form 1098-T from the college or university containing information showing the actual expenses paid by the student during the calendar year. Beginning in 2016, colleges and universities are supposed to report tuition and other payments received for students during the calendar year on Form 1098-T. In prior years, they could either report amounts billed or payments received, which made the information confusing and sometimes incorrect. www.irs.gov/pub/irs-pdf/f1098t.pdf

Contributions to a Health Savings Account (HSA)

Health Savings Accounts (HSAs) are individual accounts that belong to employees that allow for tax-free reimbursement of eligible medical expenses. To be eligible to contribute to a HSA, individuals must: participate in a high deductible health plan (HDHP); not be covered by any other health plan except for some "excepted coverages,'" which are dental, vision, etc.; not be eligible for and not enrolled in Medicare; and not be claimed as a dependent on someone else's tax return. However, a plan will not fail to qualify as a HDHP merely because it has no deductible for the preventive care health services required by the Affordable Care Act (ACA). Preventive services include a long list of shots, screening tests, and counseling services. In addition to a HDHP, an eligible individual may be covered by another health insurance plan that provides permitted or "excepted" coverage. Other permitted or "excepted" insurance covers only accidents, disability, dental care, vision care, or long-term care. Beginning January 1, 2016, an individual's eligibility to contribute to a HSA is not affected by his or her receipt of armed service or Veterans Administration (VA) benefits, i.e. an individual is not "ineligible" for a HSA merely because he or she receives hospital care or medical services from the Veterans Administration for a service-connected disability. **(See Chapter 9, "Health Savings Account (HSA)")**

Employees' contributions (other than pre-tax contributions) to HSAs are deductible as an above-the-line deduction on their tax return, but contributions are usually pre-tax. An employer usually offers an HSA-qualified HDHP in conjunction with an HSA that is established through an employer's cafeteria plan. The maximum allowable contributions in 2018 are $6,850 for family coverage ($6,750 in 2017), and $3,450 for self-only coverage ($3,400 in 2017). In addition, taxpayers who are age 55 or older can make an additional $1,000 catch-up contribution each year, and contributions have to be reported on Form 8889. If you have an HSA-eligible policy for only the first few months of 2018, your contribution is limited based on the number of months you have the policy, but if you have an HSA-eligible policy on December 1, 2018, you can make the full year's contribution even if you didn't have the policy for the full year. However, in that situation, you must keep an HSA-eligible policy for all of 2018 in order to avoid a penalty. Contributions can be made by employees, employers, and third parties. Contributions made by employees can be deducted as an above-the-line deduction on their tax returns if they aren't pre-tax contributions. However, contributions to HSAs are usually pre-tax contributions allowed by an employer's cafeteria plan, and therefore not deductible. If annual contributions are not used for qualified medical expenses, then the unused amounts, plus any earnings, carry over indefinitely. They can be used in the future for qualified medical expenses, even if you are no longer covered by a HDHP at the time. And when you die, unused funds can be rolled over to a surviving spouse who can use the account for his/her own purposes.
www.irs.gov/pub/irs-pdf/f8889.pdf www.irs.gov/pub/irs-pdf/i8889.pdf

Contributions to HSAs can't be used to pay for health insurance premiums except for: long-term care insurance; COBRA coverage; health care coverage while receiving unemployment compensation under federal or state law; and Medicare if you are age 65 or older. Individuals have to pay a 20% penalty on withdrawals from HSAs that are not used to pay for qualified medical expenses. You can't contribute to an HSA once you reach 65 years of age, because you have to enroll in Medicare by then. However, you can continue to use the funds built up in your account. Also, if you tap the money for nonqualified expenses (anything besides qualified medical expenses) after you are 65, you won't be penalized, but you will have to pay income taxes on the distributions. Excess contributions to an HSA in a year are subject to an excise tax of 6 percent (amounts in excess of the maximum amounts allowable). Self-employed persons may not contribute to HSAs on a pre-tax basis and may not take the amount of their HSA contributions as a deduction for self-employment tax purposes. However, they may contribute to HSAs with after-tax dollars and take the above-the-line deduction. Contributions can be made until the income tax filing due date, and interest earned on HSAs is tax-free. Individuals are allowed to fund a full year as long as the HSA starts by Dec. 1st of that year. Deductible contributions can be made by eligible individuals or by any other person, including a family member, on behalf of the account beneficiary. Employers' contributions to an HSA are reported on employees' W-2 Forms, Box 12, Code W (employers' contributions are not deductible by individuals on their tax returns, and are also not taxable income to them). Form 8889 is used to report all contributions, deductions, and distributions from HSAs, including employer contributions. Employers that make contributions to HSAs must make comparable contributions to each employee. Unlike distributions from a FSA, distributions from an HSA are not required to be substantiated by the employer or a third party for the distributions to be excluded from taxable income. The determination is subject to individual self-reporting and IRS enforcement.

Distributions from HSAs are reported on Form 1099-SA, and are not taxable if used to pay for qualified medical expenses. Over-the-counter medications are excluded from the definition of qualified medical expenses unless prescribed by a health care professional, or is insulin. Meds purchased from Canada are not eligible for reimbursement from HSAs.
www.irs.gov/pub/irs-pdf/f1099sa.pdf   www.irs.gov/pub/irs-pdf/i1099sa.pdf

Moving Expenses (Form 3903)
Under the Tax Cuts and Jobs Act (TCJA), the deduction for moving expenses is suspended for tax years 2018 – 2025, except for members of the Armed Forces on active duty, including spouses and dependents, who move under official military orders to a permanent change of station. In 2017 and prior years, all taxpayers could claim a deduction for moving expenses incurred in connection with starting a new job if the new workplace was at least 50 miles farther from the taxpayer's former residence than the former place of work.

Under the Tax Cuts and Jobs Act (TCJA), the exclusion from taxable income by taxpayers for qualified moving expense reimbursements by employers is suspended for tax years 2018 – 2025. In 2017 and prior years, all taxpayers could exclude qualified moving expense reimbursements from their gross income and from their wages when the moving expenses were in connection with their employment. Moving expenses were not deductible unless the move was related to starting work in a new location. Unreimbursed moving expenses were deductible by filing Form 3903. Also, moving expenses that were reimbursed by employers (Box 14 of Form W-2) and included in taxable income (Box 1 of Form W-2) were deductible by taxpayers by filing Form 3903. However, it was not necessary to file Form 3903 when moving expenses were reimbursed by employers, and not included in taxable income (Shown in Box 12, Code P of Form W-2), because the non-taxable reimbursements offset allowable moving expenses, and therefore were not deductible by the taxpayer.
www.irs.gov/pub/irs-pdf/f3903.pdf   http://taxmap.ntis.gov/taxmap/pubs/p521-004.htm
www.irs.gov/pub/irs-pdf/fw2.pdf

Allowable moving expenses (by members of the Armed Forces on active duty in 2018) include: cost of packing and moving household goods; storage of household goods for 30 days; cost of transporting a vehicle(s); cost of transporting family members to new location including airfare and by car at a mileage rate of 18 cents per mile in 2018 (17 cents in 2017); the cost to disconnect utilities at your old residence and connect them at your new residence; and one night's lodging at both old and new locations. Meals are not deductible. You can write-off the cost of hiring movers or renting a moving truck plus the cost of one-way travel to your new home for everyone in your household – whether it's by airfare, train, or by car. Also, you can deduct lodging expenses while traveling to your new home. In addition, because your dog is considered property, you can deduct expenses to move your dog.

Nondeductible expenses include: House hunting trips, temporary living expenses at the new location except for one night's lodging expense for everyone in your household; expenses related to the sale, purchase or lease of a residence; mortgage penalties, etc. Job-hunting expenses incurred while looking for your first job after graduating from college are not deductible. However, moving expenses after you get the position are deductible. A delay of up to one year does not jeopardize a deduction for moving expenses. If you move to the new job area within one year, your family may stay in the old residence for a longer period and their moving expenses will still be deductible, even though incurred after one year. There are special rules for foreign moves.

IRA Contributions

A deductible contribution to a traditional IRA is the lesser of taxable earnings, or the maximum allowable contribution, which is $5,500 in 2017 and 2018 ($6,500 if over age 50). Taxpayers can make both deductible and non-deductible contributions which must be made by the filing due date, which for IRA contribution purposes is April 15, 2019 for the 2018 tax year even if you get an extension to file your tax return. Both deductible and non-deductible contributions are limited to taxable earned income (salaries and wages, self-employment income, partnership income etc.). However, alimony and nontaxable combat pay can also be counted (added to taxable earned income). A non-deductible contribution cannot be more than the difference between the maximum allowable contribution and the deductible contribution, and it is still limited to taxable earned income. On a joint return, each spouse can contribute the maximum amount, so long as the combined earned income of both spouses is at least equal to the allowable maximum amount; also, the allowable contribution amounts are doubled, even if one spouse has no earned income – which is a "nonworking spouse IRA." Contributions can be made to both traditional and Roth IRAs in the same year, as long as the total for both does not exceed the maximum allowable contribution for the year. Contributions to traditional IRAs cannot be made once an individual reaches age 70 ½, including the nonworking spouse contribution. If you make non-deductible contributions, you must file Form 8606. Only cash contributions can be made to IRAs, including Roth IRAs. You cannot contribute stock to an IRA, but you can buy stock with cash that you contribute to an IRA. A deductible contribution may be less than taxable earned income, because it can be further limited if you are a participant in an employer retirement plan, even if the plan is available and you decline to participate. **(See Below, "Alimony/Separate Maintenance"); (See Chapter 8, "Combat Pay Earned by Military Personnel")**
www.irs.gov/pub/irs-prior/f8606--2015.pdf   www.irs.gov/pub/irs-pdf/i8606.pdf

The amount of deductible contributions is phased-out based on taxpayers' MAGIs in 2018 as follows:

- Married filing jointly or qualifying widow(er)
  - Neither spouse covered by employer's plan: Any amount – Full deduction

  - Both covered by employer's retirement plan: $101,000 or less – Full deduction
    $101,001 - $120,999 – Partial deduction
    $121,000 or more – No deduction
  - One spouse covered by employer's: $101,000 or less – Full deduction
    plan (covered spouse) $101,001 - $120,999 – Partial deduction
    $121,000 or more – No deduction

- Single and Head-of-household
  - Not covered by employer's retirement plan: Any amount – Full deduction
  - Covered by employer's retirement plan: $63,000 or less – Full deduction
    $63,001 - $72,999 – Partial deduction
    $73,000 or more – No deduction

- Married filing separately
  - Neither spouse covered by employer's plan: Any amount – Full deduction
  - Either spouse covered by employer's plan: $10,000 or more – No deduction

  *If you file separately and didn't live with your spouse at any time during the year, your IRA deduction is determined under the "single" filing status

If an IRA contribution exceeds the maximum amount allowable, the excess can be carried over to succeeding years to the extent that contributions in succeeding years are less than the allowable contributions in those years, or you can have the excess returned (withdrawn) by the filing date – April 15, 2019. Contributions made in a year can be withdrawn in the same year without penalty, but you must pay tax on the interest earned. Excess contributions to both traditional and Roth IRAs are imposed with an excise tax equal to 6% of the lesser of the excess contribution or the fair value of the IRA account at the end of the year. The tax is imposed each year until the excess contribution and its earnings are removed from the account. A taxpayer who has made an excess contribution is required to file Form 5329, and failure to file the form can result in a penalty of up to 25% of the excise tax. The penalty will not apply if the failure is due to a reasonable cause. Taxpayers who mistakenly contribute to a traditional IRA when they intended to make a contribution to a Roth IRA or vice versa can undo the mistake by electing to re-characterize the contribution. The re-characterization must be made by the due date of the tax return, including extensions. **(See Chapter 5, "Traditional IRAs")**
www.irs.gov/pub/irs-pdf/f5329.pdf   www.irs.gov/pub/irs-pdf/i5329.pdf

The following apply to both traditional and Roth IRAs:
- One important aspect of contributions to both traditional and Roth IRAs, as well as qualified retirement plans, is that these contributions qualify for the Savers Tax Credit for lower-income taxpayers. **(See Chapter 13, "Savers Credit")**

- A fellowship or grant type of payment to an individual – such as a grant from the National Institute of Health (NIH) – is not considered earned income and, therefore, cannot be used for funding either a traditional or Roth IRA.

Child's IRA – A child's IRA can be used for college without triggering early-withdrawal penalties, and it isn't reported as an asset on financial applications, thus avoiding the risk of a smaller aid package. One option is a Roth IRA, which allows tax-deferred growth for college. However, in order to be able to establish an IRA in the child's name, contributions to the IRA must come from the child's earnings. Parents can pay children for household services as long as the wage is reasonable for the work performed. It might be prudent to split college savings between a 529 plan and an IRA in the child's name.

Roth IRA – The maximum allowable contribution also applies to Roth IRAs. However, Roth contributions are not deductible, and are not limited by whether or not an individual is a participant in an employer's retirement plan. However, the maximum allowable contribution to a Roth is phased-out in 2018 between MAGIs: $189,000 – $199,000 for married filing jointly; $120,000 - $135,000 for single and head-of-household; and $0 - $10,000 for married filing separately. Also, unlike traditional IRAs, contributions to Roth IRAs have no age limit and, therefore you can make a contribution to a Roth after reaching age 70 ½. Contributions to Roth IRAs generally benefit younger individuals saving for retirement and those who expect their tax bracket to increase in retirement. Individuals receiving military death benefits are allowed to disregard the Roth dollar amount contribution limitations, and start a Roth IRA with the full amount of the death benefits. **(See Chapter 5, "Conversion of Traditional IRAs to Roth IRAs")**

Five reasons to favor a Roth IRA:
1. Having a tax-free account in addition to pre-tax savings gives you more options to reduce taxes in retirement. You'll want to delay paying taxes on your tax-deferred savings in traditional retirement accounts for as long as possible. But it's also possible that you could pay significantly higher taxes if you delay too long and required minimum distributions (RMDs) kick in and force you into a higher tax bracket. With money in different pots, you'll have a chance to run different scenarios and maximize your after-tax retirement income.
2. You can effectively contribute more of your wealth to tax-sheltered accounts every year. A dollar in a Roth is worth more than a dollar in a pre-tax account because the government will eventually take a share of the money in traditional 401(k) and traditional IRA accounts. For example: Having $17,500 in a Roth that won't be taxed again means that the entire account balance belongs to you, while $17,500 in a regular IRA account or 401(k) that will be taxed at the 15% rate is worth only $14,875.
3. A smaller account balance in an after-tax Roth account may make you feel poorer, and thus keep you from wasting more of your hard-earned cash and instead save more of your money. Getting ahead financially is often a game of psychology.
4. You might be able to tap your Roth contributions penalty-free before reaching age 59 ½. With a Roth, contributions can be withdrawn from the account after five years without penalty. This can be handy if you run into an emergency.
5. Many people are better off deferring taxes on their retirement savings for as long as possible because very few people will have an equal or higher tax rate in retirement than they do while working. Having at least part of your retirement savings in a Roth will give you options in retirement.

137

Self-Directed IRA – Nontraditional investments favored by many account holders of "self-directed IRAs" can often result in unexpected taxation. A self-directed IRA (SDIRA) can be formed by an IRA account holder with a custodian (e.g. bank or trust company) that is willing to hold "nontraditional" types of investments. What makes an IRA self-directed is not its legal framework, but rather the fact that the SDIRA's custodian permits a wide variety of investments and maximum control by the account holder. There has been a surge in the use of SDIRAs due to the appeal of investing retirement funds outside of the typical securities market. Nontraditional investments within a SDIRA include real estate, closely held business entities, structured settlements and private loans, trusts holding gold and can include any other investment that is not specifically prohibited by federal law – anything other than life insurance and collectibles. The rules prohibit direct investments in gold bullion unless the gold is held by an independent trustee, because shares in the trust are traded. But if account holders redeem trust shares for physical gold bullion, it will be treated as acquiring a collectible and they will have to pay tax on the full value of the shares exchanged for gold at the 28% tax rate.

If you have a self-directed IRA, you can buy rental property with your IRA. However, there are many restrictions when it comes to owning real estate in an IRA. For example, the rental property can't be leased to someone who is related to you; this would be prohibited and would trigger taxation of the IRA, and the 10% penalty if you're under age 59 ½. Two fundamental legal and tax issues must be considered with any SDIRA investment: first, the SDIRA's investment could raise a prohibited transaction problem, and if the investment is not a prohibited transaction, the second consideration is whether the SDIRA's investment results in current tax to the SDIRA as a result of unrelated business taxable income (UBTI) or unrelated debt-financed income (UDFI). **(See Chapter 9, "Self-Directed Retirement Plan"); (See Chapter 20, "Tax-Exempt Organizations")**

Investments in a traditional IRA do not trigger tax consequences until withdrawals are made, not because IRA earnings grow tax free, but because the types of income that an IRA typically earns are exempt from UBTI rules – buying and selling publicly traded securities (stocks, bonds and mutual funds), as well as dividends and interest income. For this reason, most SDIRA investors are unaware that a SDIRA can be required to file a current year tax return (Form 990-T, "Exempt Organization Business Income Tax Return") and pay tax. The two key triggers for current SDIRA tax consequences are (1) income from a business that is regularly carried on, whether directly or indirectly, and (2) income from debt-financed property. It is common for SDIRA custodians to receive tax documents (e.g. Schedules K-1) and send them to SDIRA owners without mentioning the potential UBTI tax consequences.
www.irs.gov/pub/irs-pdf/f990t.pdf   www.irs.gov/pub/irs-pdf/i990t.pdf

Alimony/Separate Maintenance (Form 3559)
The Tax Cuts and Jobs Act does not require any change in the tax treatment of alimony under divorce or separation agreements executed before December 31, 2018. Alimony payments are an above-the-line deduction on Form 1040. Alimony or Separate maintenance payments to a former spouse are deductible only if you have a written instrument of divorce or separation agreement in place (an oral understanding between the husband and his former wife will not do), so if you pay your ex-spouse before an official agreement is in place, the payments aren't deductible as alimony. You must file Form 3559 with your tax return to claim the deduction. The divorce agreement has to require payments to cease upon the death of the former spouse in order for the payments to be considered alimony. Also, any payments due at death can be alimony. You should be aware of the recapture provisions. **(See Chapter 5, "Alimony and Separate Maintenance")**

The Tax Cuts and Jobs Act (TCJA) eliminates the deduction of alimony payments and the inclusion in income by the recipients required under divorce or separation instruments that are: (1) executed after December 31, 2018, or (2) instruments executed before December 31, 2018 that are modified after that date if the modification specifically states that the TCJA treatment of alimony payments now applies. Also, this change is a permanent part of the tax code and doesn't sunset at the end of 2025, as do many of the provisions in the TCJA.

Alimony Paid by a U.S. Citizen Resident to a Nonresident – Alimony is still deductible by the payer in 2018. However, the payer is required to withhold tax on the alimony payment at a 30% rate, unless the recipient provides the payer with a completed Form W-8BEN, "Certificate of Foreign Status of Beneficial Owner for United States Tax Withholding and Reporting (Individuals)," that states that, pursuant to the treaty between the United States and the recipient's country of residence, a withholding tax rate of less than 30% on the payment is allowed. If the payer has to withhold 30%, the payer should obtain an individual taxpayer identification number from the recipient, in order to complete the appropriate Form 1042, "Annual Withholding Tax Return for U.S. Source Income of Foreign Persons," and Form 1042-S, "Foreign Person's U.S. Source Income Subject to Withholding," at year end, and remit the withholding tax via the Electronic Federal Tax Payment System. www.irs.gov/pub/irs-pdf/fw8ben.pdf www.irs.gov/pub/irs-pdf/iw8ben.pdf

Self-Employment Tax
50% of Self-Employment Tax is deductible. **(See Chapter 17, "Self-Employment Tax")**

Self-Employed Health Insurance Premiums
If you are self-employed, 100% of your self-employed health insurance premiums paid for yourself, spouse, and dependents are deductible in determining AGI, but not in determining net income from self-employment on Schedule C. This includes dental insurance premiums, and some long-term care premiums. It also includes premiums paid for coverage for any child of yours who was under age 26 by the end of the year, even if the child was not your dependent. However, you cannot deduct self-employed health insurance premiums if you participate in an employer subsidized health plan. Self-employed taxpayers can move Medicare premiums from Schedule A, itemized medical expenses, where they may be wasted anyway, to "self-employed health insurance premiums." Flag prior years' tax returns to be amended to include Medicare premiums as self-employed health insurance premiums (above-the-line deduction). **(See Chapter 8, "Medicare Premiums"); (See Chapter 12, "Health Insurance Premiums")**

Besides a sole proprietor, a self-employed individual for purposes of the Medicare premiums deduction can be a person who has self-employment earnings as a partner reported on Schedule K-1, Form 1065, or has wages reported on Form W-2 as a shareholder who owns more than 2% of the outstanding stock of an S-corporation. **(See Chapter 18, "Distribution of Profits and Losses to Partners"); (See Chapter 19, "Computation of S-Corporation Income")**

Self-Employed Retirement Contributions
Self-employed persons can deduct amounts contributed to retirement programs. This includes SIMPLE and SEP IRA contributions which are deductible as an above-the-line deduction. The deductions do not reduce the amount of

income on which self-employed persons have to pay self-employment taxes. **(See Chapter 9, "Saving Incentive Match Plans (SIMPLEs)"; & "Simplified Employee Pension IRA (SEP)")**

Penalty for Early Withdrawal of Savings
The penalty for early withdrawal of savings is deductible. This is forfeited interest and any principal (Box 2 of Form 1099-INT).

Business Expenses of Statutory Employees
Business expenses of statutory employees are deductible on Form 1040, Schedule C. **(See Chapter 12, "Miscellaneous Itemized Deductions Subject to the 2% AGI Floor"); (See Chapter 14, "Statutory Employees"); (See Chapter 17, "Self-Employed/Independent Contractors")**

Business Expenses of State and Local Officials
Unreimbursed business expenses of state and local officials paid on a fee basis are deductible as an above-the-line deduction, and Form 2106 must be filed to report the expenses. This includes unreimbursed employee business expenses of a public official paid or incurred while performing services as an employee of a state or one of its political subdivisions when the official is "compensated in whole or in part on a fee basis by fees paid directly by the public for his services," such as fees for performing wedding ceremonies. In a 2016 ruling, the Tax Court disallowed a county judge's above-the-line deductions for unreimbursed business expenses because the judge was not compensated in whole or in part on a fee basis. The judge had claimed the expenses as an above-the-line deduction because the court was partially funded by fees for case filings and other documents, but the Tax Court disallowed the deductions because the judge did not receive direct payments on a fee basis from the public for any of his services.

Overnight Travel Costs of Reservists and National Guard Members
Overnight travel costs of reservists and National Guard members, such as travel expenses to go to drills and meetings – they must travel more than 100 miles away from home and stay overnight for training – are deductible as an above-the-line deduction. Federal per diem rates for lodging and meals (M&IE) and standard mileage rates, plus parking and toll fees must be used, and Form 2106 must be filed to report the expenses. **(See Chapter 15, "Lodging, Meals and Incidental Expenses"; & "Vehicle and Other Transportation Expenses")**

Business Expenses of Performing Artists
Business expenses of professional artists and performers – like the cost of clown noses and sparkly leotards – are deductible as an above-the-line deduction if those items are used exclusively for performances, and Form 2106 must be filed to report the expenses. Also, Code Sec. 181 permits an owner of a qualified film or television production company to elect to deduct production costs paid or incurred by the owner for the year the costs are paid or incurred, in lieu of capitalizing the costs and recovering them through depreciation. For productions commencing after 1/1/2008, the amount that can be deducted is limited to $15 million. A film or television production is qualified if at least 75% of the total compensation of the production is compensation for services performed in the United States by actors, directors, producers, and other production personnel.

Attorney Fees Paid in Connection with Unlawful Discrimination

Attorney fees paid in connection with damages or awards received resulting from an "unlawful discrimination" claim after a job loss or under the Medicare Secondary Payer Statute are deductible. Deductible attorney fees are limited to the amount of awards received that are included in taxable income as a result of unlawful discrimination. **(See Chapter 4, "Damages Received for Job Discrimination")**

Domestic Production Activities Deduction (Form 8903)

Under the Tax Cuts and Jobs Act (TCJA), the 9% deduction attributable to domestic production activities is repealed for tax years after 2017 (starting in 2018). Following are the provisions regarding the deduction that was in effect for 2017 and prior years.

Per Section 199, Qualified taxpayers are allowed a deduction equal to 9% of the smaller of: (1) adjusted gross income for an individual, estate, or trust, or (2) qualified production activities income (QPAI), defined as the gross receipts from the sale of qualified production property (QPP) minus the cost of the QPP sold and minus any expenses allocable to the QPP. The deduction cannot exceed 50% of Form W-2 wages of the taxpayer's employees for the year. Generally, QPP is tangible personal property manufactured, produced, grown, or extracted substantially within the United States. QPP is property in which the form or function of the property has been changed. Only one taxpayer can take the deduction. When a taxpayer has a contract with an unrelated third party to manufacture the product, the taxpayer must possess the benefits and burdens of ownership during the production process to take the deduction. However, determining which party has the "benefits and burdens" of ownership is often a complex process. The deduction is determined on Form 8903.
www.irs.gov/pub/irs-pdf/f8903.pdf www.irs.gov/pub/irs-pdf/i8903.pdf

Eligible activities center around manufacturing products in the United States, but many other businesses can qualify. In addition to manufacturing, the parameters for qualifying for the deduction are broad but generally have to go beyond mere repackaging to qualify. For example, such activities as software development, producing electricity, producing films, assembling gift baskets, assembling and selling single doses of medicine, making hamburgers, or roasting coffee qualify for the deduction. Domestic production gross receipts (DPGR) can be derived from the following qualifying production activities as long as they are conducted in whole or in significant part within the U.S.: The manufacture, production, growth, or extraction by the taxpayer of tangible personal property. This encompasses all tangible personal property (except land and buildings), computer software, and sound recordings; the production of qualified film; the production of electricity, natural gas, or water; the construction of real property; and the services of architecture/engineering. DPGR resulting from the property produced must be owned by the producer taking the deduction (i.e. the production of property that is owned and under contract by someone else would generally not be eligible).

- **Example** – For the year ended December 31, 2015, Steve Donald Manufacturing Company (a C-Corp) had taxable income, all from qualifying manufacturing activities, of $1 million and paid $100,000 in W-2 wages. Steve Donald will be entitled to a Section 199 deduction of $50,000 due to the 50% limit of W-2 wages. If the W-2 wages had been greater than $180,000, the deduction would have been $90,000 [$1 million X 9%].
- **Example** – Same facts as in Example #1 ($180k W-2 wages), except Steve Donald Manufacturing Company is a S-Corp, with Steve Donald owning 60% and Jack Donald owning 40%. The deduction passes through to the shareholders, with Steve receiving $54,000 and Jack receiving $36,000 of the deduction.

- **Example** – Same facts as Example#2, except that Steve takes a $108,000 distribution and Jack takes a $72,000 distribution. No W-2 wages are paid. A Section 199 deduction cannot be taken because W-2 wages were not paid.

In a technical advice memorandum (TAM 201638022), the IRS National Office of the Chief Counsel determined a taxpayer's substantial renovation, construction, and erection of certain property qualified as the construction of real property under Sec. 199 such that the gross receipts derived from those activities qualified as domestic production gross receipts (DPGR). In reaching its decision, the Chief Counsel determined that the property was "inherently permanent structures."
https://www.irs.gov/pub/irs-wd/201638022.pdf

In past years, about one-third of corporate activities in the U.S. have qualified for the deduction.

Deduction of Living Expenses by Members of Congress
Members of Congress were able to deduct up to $3,000 per year in living expenses while away from their home states or Congressional districts. However, the Tax Cuts and Jobs Act (TCJA) repealed their ability to deduct these expenses beginning with the 2018 tax year.
www.senate.gov/CRSpubs/9c14ec69-c4e4-4bd8-8953-f73daa1640e4.pdf

Chapter 12 – Itemized Deductions

Itemized deductions are shown on Schedule A, Form 1040, and generally can be deducted if they are more than the standard deduction. In 2017, itemized deductions were phased-out at adjusted gross income (AGI) thresholds of: $261,500 - $384,000 (singles); $313,800 - $436,300 (married filing jointly and surviving spouse); $287,650 - $410,150 (head-of-household); and $156,900 - $218,150 (married filing separately). However, under the Tax Cuts and Jobs Act (TCJA), the allowable itemized deductions are not phased-out (the "Pease" limitation is suspended). The AGI phase-out thresholds are suspended for tax years 2018 – 2025 before being scheduled to return on January 1, 2026. **(See Chapter 1, "Standard Deduction")**
www.irs.gov/pub/irs-pdf/f1040sa.pdf

When claiming itemized deductions, they are deductible in the current year when you pay with a check even if the check doesn't clear until January of the next year. Also, paying with a bank credit card counts as a current year deduction even though you don't actually pay the bill until the next year. Bank credit card payments, whether for charitable contributions, medical expenses, or business expenses qualify as 2017 deductions as soon as you authorize the charges, even if the banks don't bill you until 2018, and you don't actually pay the bill until 30 days later. But, if you pay with a retail store credit card, you are allowed to claim a deduction only in the year you pay the bill.

Homeschooling expenses are not deductible, in any circumstances. Also, there is no itemized tax deduction allowable for the installation and maintenance of an alarm system at your home; however, if your place of business happens to be in your home, you can deduct a portion of the alarm system if you claim the home office deduction. **(See Chapter 17, "Home Office Expenses")**

Under the "tax benefit" rule, if you claimed a deduction for an amount that produced a tax benefit to you in the prior year (meaning it reduced the amount of income tax you paid), and you receive a refund of that amount or a portion of that amount in the current year, you must include the recovered amount in income and pay tax on it in the current year. The tax benefit rule usually applies to refunds of state and local income taxes withheld and claimed as an itemized deduction in the prior year. However, if you did not receive any tax benefit in the prior year for a deduction or a portion of a deduction that was refunded to you in the next year, then you don't have to include the recovered amount in income in the next year – for example, you may have claimed the standard deduction instead of itemized deductions in the prior year.

Medical Expenses

Expenditures incurred as a medical necessity and that are not reimbursed by insurance are fully deductible as itemized deductions if they are more than 7 ½ % of adjusted gross income (AGI) in 2018. In 2017, the floor was more than 10% of AGI, until it was retroactively changed by the Tax Cuts and Jobs Act (TCJA) to 7 ½% of AGI. However, the TCJA returns the floor for deducting medical expenses to 10% in 2019.

Medical expenses of a qualifying child can be claimed, even if you can't claim the child as a dependent. Also, medical expenses of a qualifying relative who is not your child can be claimed, even if you can't claim the relative as a dependent due to the gross income test ($4,150 in 2018), but you must furnish more than ½ of the support of the relative, e.g. your mother. You can claim the medical expenses of a supported person who doesn't meet the relationship test if you live in the same household and the other tests are met. **(See Chapter 3, "Dependency Exemptions")**

Medical expenses that are paid with funds from Health Reimbursement Arrangements (HRAs), Health Savings Accounts (HSAs), and Flexible Spending Accounts (FSAs) are generally not deductible, because they are usually funded with pre-tax dollars, or contributions to HSAs are deductible in determining AGI. Also, medical expenses paid with money from a withdrawal of the cash surrender value of a life insurance contract are not deductible – instead, the amount is not included in income and the investment in the contract is reduced by that amount. **(See Chapter 5, "Cash Surrender Value of a Life Insurance Policy"); (See Chapter 9, "Employee Tax-Advantaged Spending Accounts"); (See Chapter 11, "Contributions to a Health Savings Account (HSA)")**

Reimbursements received in excess of medical expenses are not taxable, unless your employer paid all or part of your health insurance premiums, then part must be included in gross income. Reimbursements for medical expenses, received in the next year, are taxable if beneficial to the taxpayer in the prior year.

Deductible Medical Expenses Include the Following:

Travel Expenses – Medical mileage expenses which include round trips to the doctor, dentist, pharmacy, dialysis, etc. are deductible. The medical mileage allowance in 2018 is 18 cents per mile (17 cents per mile in 2017). In addition, the cost of any other necessary transportation is deductible, as is lodging at $50 per night for each of 2 people while away from home – but not meals. Parking and tolls are also deductible. Travel costs may or may not be deductible, i.e. travel costs to accompany a child who needs medical care and to visit a patient if the visitation is recommended as part of the treatment are deductible. It is up to you to show that travel was medically necessary and not just your personal choice.

Health Insurance Premiums – Health insurance premiums paid by a taxpayer, unless paid with pre-tax dollars, are deductible. Medicare Part B premiums are deductible. Premiums that cover more than health insurance and long-term care insurance (e.g. life insurance) are not deductible, unless the separate items can be identified.

Long-Term Care Insurance Premiums – Long-term care Insurance premiums paid in 2018 are deductible based on the age of the taxpayer: $420 age 40 or under; $780 age 41 -50; $1,560 age 51 - 60; $4,160 age 61 - 70; and $5,200 over age 70. Long-term care benefits paid by long-term care insurance policies to taxpayers are not included in income except amounts that exceed the beneficiary's total qualified long-term care expenses or $360 per day in 2018, whichever is greater (this amount did not change from 2017). **(See Chapter 8, "Long-Term Care Insurance Benefits"; & "Life Insurance Proceeds")**

Prescription Medications – The cost of prescription medications are deductible, including birth control pills. Also, if you can get a prescription from a doctor, the cost of some over-the-counter drugs, such as Nexium and Motrin are deductible. Insulin is deductible, even without a prescription. Vitamins and nutritional supplements are not deductible unless prescribed by a physician.

Doctor, Hospital and Other Medical Expenses – Doctor, hospital, and other medical expenses are deductible and include the following:

- Doctor, dentist, chiropractor, physical therapist, optometrist, and acupuncture expenses.
- Laboratory tests, X-rays, and diagnostics.
- All Hospital expenses, including nursing care, tests, most surgeries, medications, and hospital room expenses.
- Ambulance services.
- Cataract and Lasik eye surgery.
- Lap-band surgery to treat obesity.
- Expenses for legal abortions.
- Fertility enhancement treatments.
- Sterilization for birth control.
- The cost of stop-smoking programs.
- Alcohol and drug treatment, including inpatient care.
- Expenses of a rehabilitation facility for substance abuse.
- Mental health therapy.
- Braille books and magazines for visually-impaired persons.
- Special diets if prescribed by a physician to alleviate specific medical conditions. However, even when prescribed by a doctor, certain foods and food supplements – like health shakes – may be non-deductible if they are merely taking the place of other foods. But there are some exceptions, like those for food allergies or celiac disease (See below).
- The cost of weight loss programs to treat obesity or hypertension if prescribed by a doctor, and if a doctor puts you on a special diet, even the extra amount spent for groceries is deductible.
- Gym memberships only as a treatment for a diagnosed disease or condition. The program must be specifically ordered by your doctor.

Medical Devices and Equipment – Eye glasses, contact lenses, hearing aids and batteries, costs associated with guide dogs or other service animals, artificial teeth, artificial limbs, cost and maintenance of wheelchairs, crutches, cost and repair of special telephone equipment for people who are deaf or hard of hearing, oxygen equipment, breast pumps, the cost of a chairlift on the stairs, blood sugar kits for diabetics, pregnancy test kits, needles, bandages, and other medical devices are deductible medical expenses.

Nursing Home Care – Medical services, meals, and lodging in nursing homes, convalescent homes, and special schools for the mentally or physically handicapped that qualify as long-term care are deductible if obtaining medical care is the primary reason for admission. However, if obtaining medical care is not the primary reason for admission (e.g. an assisted living facility), then institutional care that represents medical or nursing care, but not the portion that represents living expenses, is deductible. Medical care is the primary reason for admission if a person is unable to perform at least 2 of 6 specified daily living activities – eating, toileting, transferring, bathing, dressing, and continence due to a loss of functional capacity or requiring substantial supervision to protect the individual from threats to health and safety due to severe cognitive impairment.

Medicare does not pay for long-term care, but will pay for related expenses for a period of at least 90 days. The ways to pay for long-term care expenses are the following: out-of-pocket (personal resources); long-term care insurance; and Medicaid for those who fall below certain income and asset limits. Seniors who move into a retirement community where the entrance fees and the monthly residential fees include assisted living and skilled nursing support as part of what are considered lifetime care benefits may be able to include between 30 to 40 percent of the fees paid as allowable medical expenses.

Education Expenses for Physically or Mentally Impaired Individuals – Education expenses of physically or mentally impaired individuals are deductible if the school provides special education for a diagnosed medical condition and the school has a professional staff competent to provide help for the condition. A child with a special physical, mental, or emotional condition who attends a private school that is able to treat the condition can deduct the cost of tuition, room and board, special counseling, etc. The principle reason for attendance must be for medical care (not education), and the schooling must be recommended by a physician. Examples of conditions a child can have for educational expenses to be deductible as a medical expense are: Dyslexia, Epilepsy, Hearing impairment to learn lip reading; Visual impairment to learn Braille; and Hyperactivity.

Capital Expenditures – Capital expenditures such as removing barriers and adding ramps and railings in the home of a physically handicapped person or special telephone equipment for the hearing impaired are deductible. In theory, expenditures that permanently improve a taxpayer's property as well as providing medical care (e.g. swimming pools and spas) are currently deductible only to the extent that the amount of the expenditure exceeds the increase in the fair market value (FMV) of the residence. However, if an expense is to accommodate a disability, a home improvement is treated as not increasing the value of the home. If a swimming pool is installed to accommodate a person's disability, the cost of heating the pool, pool chemicals, and a proportionate part of insuring the pool area are also treated as medical expenses.

In-Home Long-Term Care – Qualified in-home long-term care expenses required by a chronically ill person under a prescribed plan of care by a licensed physician (diagnostic, therapeutic, rehabilitative, and personal care services) are deductible. A U.S. Tax Court decision held that a person was qualified as a chronically ill individual because she required substantial in-home care and supervision to protect her from threats to her health and safety due to her severe cognitive impairment (dementia, impaired speech, and confusion). The court held that the services provided by the caregivers were necessary maintenance and personal care services to assist her with daily living activities that she required because of her diminished capacity and the risk of falling, and that they were provided pursuant to a care plan prescribed by her physician, and furthermore, the individuals providing the care didn't have to be licensed. Therefore, they were qualified long-term care services, and the payments to the caregivers for their services and the payments to the physician both qualified as deductible medical expenses.

Transgender Surgery – Transgender surgery may be deductible. For example, a man who felt he was a woman trapped in a male body was diagnosed with gender-identity disorder. He tried to deduct $22,000 in medical costs for multiple surgeries, including hormone therapy, sexual-reassignment surgeries, and breast augmentation, in order to become a woman. The U.S. Tax Court allowed the costs of the hormone therapy and sex-change operation – a total of $14,500 – as qualified medical expenses because those procedures helped treat a disease, but the court disallowed the cost of breast augmentation, saying it was nondeductible cosmetic surgery.

Allergy Treatments – Expenditures to treat allergies or other specific conditions may or may not be deductible. The Tax Court allowed a deduction for the extra cost of organic food compared to the cost of regular (chemically treated) food where a doctor prescribed the diet to treat a specific allergy condition. Also, a district court allowed a deduction for the cost of constructing a concrete home for an allergy sufferer. However, the Tax Court denied a deduction for the cost of replacing carpet with wood flooring by a person with allergies.

Alternative Medicine – In Malev v. Commissioner, the Tax Court determined that "alternative" medicine costs (integrative medical costs) are deductible based on a subjective test of whether the individual believed that they may be effective at least where they are of the type that would not be routinely incurred for non-medical reasons. The medical care must take into account not only what is known but what is less understood as well – namely, the role that an individual's state of mind plays in the treatment of disease.
https://www.ustaxcourt.gov/InternetOrders/DocumentViewer.aspx?IndexSearchableOrdersID=222974

Cosmetic Surgery – Cosmetic surgery is deductible only if it is necessary to correct a deformity arising from a congenital abnormality, personal injury resulting from an accident or trauma, or a disfiguring disease.

In vitro fertilization – Costs of in vitro fertilization have generally been held deductible only when necessary to overcome infertility for couples who are unable to conceive naturally. Expenses incurred in fathering children through unrelated gestational carriers via in vitro fertilization of an anonymous donor's eggs using the taxpayer's sperm are not deductible.

Surrogate Parenting – Payments to surrogates are not deductible. However, if the sperm or egg donor is one of the spouses of a married couple, any medical expenses incurred by the donor are deductible if paid by the recipient. Donor expenses include IVF expenses, doctor visits, lab fees, and medication. Additionally, transportation and lodging costs for egg transfer or sperm donation can be deducted for both of the spouses. Also, because signing a contract is usually necessary for surrogate parenting, the legal fees are also deductible. Expenses for the child (once born) are also deductible.

Maternity Clothes – If you have to stock up on maternity clothes – including suits for court or coats for outdoor use – to get you through your pregnancy, that cost is not deductible even if you don't plan to wear them again. Ever.

Fidget Spinners – Fidget spinners were originally designed to be toys, but some doctors and therapists have found that they can be calming for children who are diagnosed with autism, attention deficit disorder (ADD), attention deficit hyperactivity disorder (ADHD) or anxiety. Whether that's enough to qualify the fidget spinner as a medical expense depend on the child and the doctor. A specific diagnosis is necessary and the cure or treatment - like a fidget spinner - must be specifically ordered by the doctor. If your child's doctor advises you to pick up a fidget spinner because it might be helpful or calming, that's not sufficient for purposes of the deduction. However, if your child's doctor "prescribes" in writing a fidget spinner in response to a specific medical condition, like autism, that should qualify as a medical expense.

Expenses generally not deductible as medical expenses are the following:
- Cosmetic surgery.
- Teeth whitening.
- Medicinal marijuana.
-

- Infant formula.
- Condoms.
- Medicine purchased from another country, such as Canada.
- Funeral expenses.
- Vitamins and nutritional supplements.
- Health club dues.
- Marriage counseling.

State and Local Tax Deductions

Expenditures incurred for state and local taxes that are deductible as itemized deductions are capped at $10,000 ($5,000 for married filing separately) for tax years 2018 – 2025 by the Tax Cuts and Jobs Act (TCJA). The definition of state and local taxes includes: property taxes; state, local and foreign income taxes; and sales taxes. There are no AGI thresholds for claiming the allowable state and local tax deduction in 2018. State and local taxes were fully deductible as itemized deductions in 2017.

Prepayments of 2018 state and local taxes in 2017 were prohibited by statute, and the IRS used tax case precedent to prevent prepayments of 2018 taxes in 2017. Therefore, taxpayers were prohibited from deducting 2018 state and local taxes on their 2017 tax returns. In August 2018, the IRS moved to block states from trying to skirt the $10,000 cap on the deduction of state and local taxes. The IRS put the New York, New Jersey and Connecticut tri-state area on notice that the charitable workarounds that New York, New Jersey and Connecticut have approved following the new federal cap on deductions for state and local taxes aren't acceptable to the federal government.

Allowable tax deductions in 2018 include the following:

Real Property Taxes – Real property taxes paid on real estate not used for business are deductible in the year paid. This includes property taxes paid on your principal residence and a vacation home (second home), as well as on unimproved land if the land is considered a personal asset. For example, if you purchase land because you think it would be a good place to build a home and it is also a good investment, you can deduct the property taxes and mortgage interest on the land. Taxes paid on unimproved land that is considered investment property were supposed to be included in miscellaneous itemized deductions subject to the 2% floor in 2017, but the TCJA repealed miscellaneous itemized deductions subject to the 2% AGI floor as an itemized deduction for tax years 2018 – 2025. Deductibility of property taxes is not limited to two properties or houses owned by a taxpayer. In order to be deductible, property taxes must be based on the assessed value of a property. Special assessments or service charges are not deductible. Property taxes paid by the seller of a house for a buyer, and vice versa, that are shown on a closing "settlement statement" when a house is sold are not deductible, but instead the amount of the taxes should reduce the amount realized by the seller and the adjusted basis of the house for the buyer. If you pay the real estate taxes of a relative who is not your dependent, such as a daughter, the relative can deduct the real estate taxes on his/her tax return because your payment is considered a "gift" subject to the Estate and Gift tax. And if the payment is less than $15,000, you do not have to file a gift tax return. **(See Below, "Miscellaneous Itemized Deductions Subject to the 2% Floor"); (See Chapter 22, "Gift Tax Exclusion")**

Unmarried co-owners of a property can allocate property taxes based on any reasonable method such as: the amount of payments during the year or the percentage of home ownership, i.e. if the home is owned 50/50, then each owner can deduct half of the property tax payments regardless of which one actually made the payments. If you pay your property taxes with a credit card, the convenience fee charged by the taxing authority may be deductible. The IRS hasn't said whether this specific convenience fee is deductible as part of your real estate taxes, but the IRS ruled that the convenience fee paid when charging federal income taxes is deductible, but only as a miscellaneous itemized deduction.

Personal Property Taxes – Personal property taxes are deductible if based on the value of the personal property. For example, annual property taxes paid based on the value of your car are deductible, but annual automobile license fees are usually not deductible because they are not based on the value of the car.

State and Local Income Taxes – State and local income taxes are deductible in the year paid. State and local income tax refunds received are taxable in the subsequent tax year only if they gave rise to a tax benefit in the prior year as an itemized deduction that reduced taxable income in the prior year.

Sales Taxes – Deduction of sales taxes are in lieu of state and local income taxes (you can deduct either state and local income taxes, or sales taxes, whichever is more), and this rule was made permanent by the "Protecting Americans from Tax Hikes Act of 2015." Actual sales taxes paid in a year are deductible, or you can use the "Sales Tax Tables" provided by the IRS, which are based on a taxpayer's adjusted gross income (AGI). If the sales tax tables are used, the actual sales taxes paid on large ticket items may be added to the table amounts. Large ticket items include: cars, other motor vehicles, boats, mobile homes, and major home improvements. If the total sales taxes you pay on a motor vehicle is higher than the general sales tax rate, you are allowed to include only the amount of tax that would have been paid at the general sales tax rate. For boats and aircraft, if the sales taxes paid exceed the general sales tax rate, no deduction is allowed for a boat or an aircraft you purchase. The sales tax deduction usually benefits taxpayers who live in states that do not have state income taxes, such as Texas, Washington, and Florida. Nontaxable income items can be added back to AGI in order to maximize your AGI in determining your deductible sales taxes when using the Sales Tax Tables. Nontaxable income items that can be added to AGI include: tax-exempt interest, veterans' disability benefits, nontaxable combat pay, workers' compensation, the nontaxable portion of Social Security/railroad retirement income, and the nontaxable portion of IRA and pension payments.

- **Example** – The Sales Tax Table for Texas is based on the state tax rate of 6.25%, so you have to add the local sales tax of 2.00% to get the total tax rate of 8.25% paid in Texas. Also, if you bought a car, you can add the sales taxes paid on the purchase of the car to the allowable deductible sales taxes obtained from the Sales Tax Tables.

Foreign Source Income Taxes – Income taxes paid on foreign source income are deductible if you do not opt for the "foreign tax credit." However, usually the foreign tax credit is more beneficial to taxpayers. The amount of foreign income taxes that qualify for the deduction is not necessarily the amount of tax withheld by the foreign country – certain adjustments may be required. **(See Chapter 13, "Foreign Tax Credit")**

Home Mortgage Interest Deduction

Home mortgage interest is deductible as an itemized deduction in 2018, except the TCJA suspends the deduction for interest on home equity loans for tax years 2018 – 2025, unless the loan is used to buy, build or substantially improve the home that secures the loan. Therefore, if you take out an equity loan to pay for things like an addition to the home, a new roof or a kitchen renovation, you can still deduct the interest on the loan.

There is no AGI threshold for claiming allowable mortgage interest. Interest on mortgage loans is deductible on two residences – a principal residence, and a second residence or vacation home. A residence is defined as a house, condominium, cooperative unit, mobile home, house trailer, recreational vehicle (RV), or a house boat that has sleeping, cooking, and toilet facilities. However, a house boat is not considered a second home for AMT purposes. There is no requirement that the home be located within the United States. A second home is considered a residence if the number of days it is used for personal use exceeds 14 days or 10% of the number of days during the year it is rented at fair rental value, whichever is greater. **(See Chapter 7, "Rental Income"; & "Classifying a Vacation Home as a Rental Property")**

Deductible mortgage interest is reported by the mortgage company on Form 1098 "Mortgage Interest Statement." In 2018, mortgage interest is deductible on qualifying mortgage loans up to a maximum of $750,000 ($375,000 for married filing separately) on a principal residence, and a maximum of $750,000 on a second residence. The TCJA reduced the maximum loan amount from $1 million to $750,000 effective December 16, 2017 (except in the case of binding contracts scheduled to close in 2017 that actually closed by March 31, 2018), and this change is in effect through tax year 2025. Existing mortgage loans before the effective date of the new law, including refinancing, are still subject to the prior $1 million maximum that was in effect in 2017 and prior years, but no deduction is available for interest on debt beyond $750,000/$375,000 after the expiration of the term of the original indebtedness (if not amortized, then this must be determined based on the earlier of the term of the first refinancing or 30 years).

Married couples are limited to deducting interest on $750,000 in mortgage debt on a home, but two unmarried taxpayers who jointly buy a home are allowed $750,000 in mortgage debt each, for a total of $1.5 million of acquisition indebtedness. The doubling of the amount of the allowable mortgage interest deduction may also apply to a vacation home, where several members of the same extended family might purchase and jointly own a family vacation home.

You can deduct mortgage interest you pay, even if you are not the legal owner of the residence securing the mortgage if you occupy the residence and make the mortgage payments (This does not apply to renters who make rental payments).
www.irs.gov/pub/irs-pdf/f1098.pdf

- When a taxpayer owns a residence that his former spouse lives in and makes the mortgage payments, he may be entitled to deduct the mortgage interest and real estate taxes as itemized deductions if the house qualifies either as his principal or secondary residence. The house qualifies as a second home if at least one of his children is living in the house.
- You are allowed a mortgage interest deduction for a house even though it is never built. Interest is deductible on a loan for 24 months after construction begins or for 24 months after the teardown date if you are replacing an existing structure. IRS regulations on deducting interest on a loan for a home under

construction don't condition deductibility on the house's completion. However, after the 24-month period, the interest paid is nondeductible personal interest.

Forms 1098 filed after Dec. 31, 2016, are required to include more information than they have in the past, which will include: the amount of the mortgage principal at the start of the year, the mortgage origination date, and the address of the property securing the loan. This change is designed to provide the IRS with more information to better audit the accuracy of mortgage interest deductions.

Points – Points paid to purchase a principal residence are deductible in the year of purchase, including loan origination fees that are based on a percentage of the loan amount. However, points paid to purchase a second home (vacation home) are not currently deductible, but instead must be deducted ratably over the term of the loan. Also, points paid to refinance a mortgage must be deducted ratably over the term of the loan. But, if a loan is paid off, you can deduct the balance of the points in the year the loan is paid off, with one exception – if you refinance a loan with the same lender, you have to add the points paid on the latest deal to the left over points from the previous financing and deduct that amount gradually over the life of the new loan. These rules also apply to refinancing a loan on a second home. You can deduct points paid by the seller on your behalf to sweeten the deal when you buy a home.

Increasing the Amount of the Loan When Refinancing – If you refinance your home mortgage and increase the amount of the loan to improve your principal residence, your new mortgage is considered to have two separate parts for tax purposes – the first part equals the refinanced balance from your old loan and is considered home acquisition debt, and the second part in excess of the original loan balance is considered separate home acquisition debt when used to improve the residence. Thus, you may be able to currently deduct the points paid on the second part of the loan.

Mortgage Insurance Premiums – The mortgage insurance premium deduction was originally unavailable in 2017, because the "Protecting Americans from Tax Hikes Act of 2015" extended the deduction only through 2016. But in February 2018, the deduction was retroactively extended through the 2017 tax year by the Bipartisan Budget Act of 2018. However, it is unsure whether the deduction will be available in 2018, because the bill that extended the deduction through 2017 is silent about future deductions, including for 2018. Below are the parameters of the deduction that was in effect through 2017:

Qualified mortgage insurance premiums can be deducted as home mortgage interest. This is Private Mortgage Insurance (PMI) provided by the VA, FHA, and the Rural Housing Administration when required by the terms of the mortgage loan. Mortgage insurance premiums of $600 or more during any calendar year must be reported on Form 1098, "Mortgage Insurance Statement." Allowable mortgage insurance premium deductions are reduced by 10% for every $1,000 by which a taxpayer's AGI exceeds $100,000 and completely phases out when AGI is $110,000 or more. For married taxpayers filing separately, the 10% phase-out applies to every $500 that AGI exceeds $50,000 and completely phases out when AGI is $55,000 or more. If you prepay mortgage insurance premiums that are allocable to periods that extend beyond the year in which they are paid, you must allocate the premiums over the shorter of: the mortgage's stated term, or 84 months, beginning with the month the insurance was obtained.

www.congress.gov/115/bills/hr1892/BILLS-115hr1892enr.pdf

151

Reverse Mortgage – There is no current mortgage deduction when you get a reverse mortgage. A reverse mortgage is a loan where the lender pays you in a lump sum, a monthly advance, a line of credit, or a combination of all three while you continue to live in your home and you retain title to your home. No payments are required, so there is no tax deduction. A reverse mortgage is a bank loan secured by the house. The money received is tax-free and can be used for any purpose (unlike a regular mortgage), including investments. Any interest accrued on a reverse mortgage is not deductible until you actually pay it, which is not until you move or die. When you move or die, the mortgage is paid off from the proceeds of the sale of the house. If the proceeds are greater than the mortgage balance (which includes the interest that has built up), you or your heirs would receive a check for the difference. However, if the proceeds are less than the mortgage balance, you or your heirs may have a tax deduction. You must be at least age 62 to obtain a reverse mortgage. **(See Chapter 9, "Reverse Mortgage")**

Investment Interest Deduction

Investment interest expense is the interest on money borrowed to purchase taxable investments. Investment interest on indebtedness to carry portfolio investments, except for tax-exempt securities, is deductible. Investment interest is the interest you pay on a margin loan used to purchase stock, but you can't use the margin loan to buy a car or tax-exempt municipal bonds. Also, investment expense is only deductible in the current year to the extent of investment income (investment income does not include any capital gains or qualified dividends that enjoy favorable tax treatment). And any amount not deductible in the current year can be carried over to subsequent years. The election to treat "ordinary dividend income" as investment income for this purpose is made on Form 4952. **(See Chapter 6, "Form 1099-B: Proceeds from Broker and Barter Exchange Transactions"; & "Qualified Dividends")**
www.irs.gov/pub/irs-access/f4952_accessible.pdf

Charitable Contribution Deduction

Charitable contributions are generally fully deductible as itemized deductions by most people. The Tax Cuts and Jobs Act (TCJA) increases the maximum deduction for cash donations from 50% to 60% of AGI in 2018. But the maximum deduction for property contributions remains at 50% and is applied before determining allowable cash contributions. Any excess contributions over 60%/50% of AGI can be carried forward for 5 years in the same category. **(See Below, "Cash Contributions")**

The Tax Cuts and Jobs Act (TCJA) repealed a provision that exempted donors from having to substantiate charitable contributions of $250 or more with a contemporaneous written acknowledgment from the donee organization if the donee organization filed a return with the required information. This applies retroactively to contributions made starting in 2017.

Donations of capital gain property (stocks, clothes, household goods etc.) to a public charity are limited to the lesser of fair market value (FMV) or 30% of AGI, unless the contribution is limited to its adjusted basis, in which case it is limited to 50% of AGI. Donation of capital gain property to a private non-operating foundation is limited to 20% of AGI. Cash donations by C-corporations are limited annually to 10% of taxable income. Charitable contributions provide the greatest flexibility of any itemized deduction, because their timing is completely discretionary. Just keep in mind that gifts to charitable organizations are deductible when paid. Pledges don't

152

count, i.e. they are deductible in the year they are fulfilled, not in the year the pledges are made. Last minute donations made with checks count as deductions in 2018 as long as the payments are mailed and postmarked by midnight December 31st. Bank credit card payments, whether for charitable contributions, medical expenses, or business expenses qualify as 2018 deductions as soon as you authorize the charges, even if the banks don't bill you until 2019, and you don't actually pay the bill until 30 days later.

In planning for charitable contributions, one strategy is to accelerate payments by taking care of pledges to schools, churches, religious groups and other charities this year, instead of next year, as well as by donating the entire amount that you expect to give to favorite charities next year before year end to increase itemized deductions this year and reduce taxable income. Some people might even consider borrowing money to accelerate deductions, because the tax savings may be more than the interest expense on a loan. Donating stocks, real estate, or other capital assets owned for more than 12 months that have increased in value can give you a double tax break – you can deduct their full fair market value (FMV) as a charitable donation and you can escape the long-term capital gains tax that you would owe if you sold the items. However, don't make the mistake of donating stocks that are losers. Instead, sell them and donate the proceeds to charity and claim both the charitable deduction and the capital loss. **(See Chapter 6, "Reporting Capital Gains and Losses")**

Any contribution you make to reduce the national debt burden is deductible as a charitable contribution. You should make the payment as a separate check payable to the Bureau of Public Debt and send it to: Bureau of the Public Debt, Department G. P.O. Box 2188, Parkersburg, W.Va. 26106-2188, or you can stick the check in your tax return envelope.

Qualified Charities – Only donations to "qualified" charitable organizations are tax deductible. You can check whether an organization is qualified on a searchable online database available on IRS.gov, which lists most organizations that are qualified to receive deductible contributions. In addition, churches, synagogues, temples, mosques and government agencies are eligible to receive deductible donations, even if they are not listed in the database. Qualified charities include religious organizations such as churches and synagogues; federal, state and local governments; nonprofit schools and hospitals; public parks and recreation facilities; public charities such as United Way, Salvation Army, Red Cross, Boy and Girl Scouts; war veterans' groups; and other qualified charitable organizations. Contributions to domestic tax-exempt, charitable organizations that provide assistance to individuals in foreign countries qualify as tax deductible, provided a U.S. organization has control and discretion over the use of the funds. Certain organizations such as churches or governmental organizations may be qualified to accept charitable contributions that provide assistance to foreign countries. To ensure the deductibility of donations, confirm that the charity is a U.S. based charity. **(See Chapter 22, "Gift Tax Exclusion")**

Nondeductible Contributions – Nondeductible contributions for charitable purposes include:
- contributions to: individuals; political organizations or political candidates; civic leagues; social and sports clubs; labor unions; chambers of commerce; lobbying organizations; homeowners associations; and foreign organizations (with some exceptions).
- Donations to personal fund-raising websites are generally not deductible as charitable contributions because they are usually established for a single individual or a small group of people – this includes contributions made on websites set-up to help with someone's medical expenses or to help a family in need.

- No charitable deduction is allowed for contributions of an interest in a property that is less than the entire interest in the property.
- The value of your time or services, and the rental value of a vacation home that you allow to be used for charitable purposes is nondeductible. Likewise, donation of the use of your timeshare as a prize in a charity's auction is a nondeductible contribution.
- If you receive a benefit because of your cash or other contribution to a qualified charity, such as merchandise, tickets to a ball game, or other goods and services, then you can deduct only the amount of the contribution that exceeds the FMV of the benefit received.
- In Accordance with the Tax Cuts and Jobs Act (TCJA), beginning in 2018, deductions for donations coupled with preferred seating at college sports events are disallowed as a charitable contribution. But in 2017 and prior years, persons who purchased season tickets to college football games or other college sporting events were allowed to claim a charitable contribution deduction. Here's how it worked – if they paid $1,640 to buy tickets to 8 games, and in addition they were required to donate an additional $3,700 to the college or university to be able to buy the tickets, they were allowed to deduct 80% of the $3,700, or $2,960 as a charitable contribution. No more beginning in 2018.
- The cost of raffle, bingo or lottery tickets is not a charitable contribution, but instead is a gambling expense, i.e. a losing raffle ticket paid to a charity is a gambling loss, not a charitable contribution. **(See Chapter 5, "Gambling Winnings"); (See Chapter 20, "Tax-Exempt Organizations")**

Cash Contributions – Cash donations are the most common kind of charitable contribution, and taxpayers are required to have written proof of all cash contributions no matter how small. Proof can be a bank record, credit card statement, or written communication from the charity showing the name of the charity and the date and amount of the contribution. Therefore, it's not a good idea to contribute actual cash currency to a charity without getting a receipt for the donation. For charitable payroll deductions, the taxpayer should retain a pay stub, a Form W-2 or other document furnished by the employer showing the total amount withheld for a charity, along with the pledge card showing the name of the charity. For individual cash donations of $250 or more, there are more stringent substantiation requirements – you must have a written statement from the charitable organization that shows the amount of the donation and a written statement from the organization that says whether any goods or services were provided to the donor in exchange for the gift, i.e. the donor must obtain a contemporaneous written acknowledgment from the charitable organization stating the amount of the donation, and a good-faith estimate of the value of any goods or services the organization provided in exchange for the contribution. If goods or services received consist solely of intangible religious benefits, the contemporaneous documentation must contain a statement to that effect.

- **Example** – in the 2012 Durden case, the U.S. Tax Court denied the Durdens a charitable contribution deduction because the statement from their church did not contain the required statement regarding whether any goods or services were received in consideration for their contributions (most of their individual contributions to the church exceeded $250). The IRS disallowed the deductions even after the Durdens subsequently obtained a second written acknowledgment from their church with the required language, because the statement was after the due date of the return, including extensions, and the Tax Court agreed with the IRS.

www.ustaxcourt.gov/inophistoric/durdenmemo.tcm.wpd.pdf

Following are cash contributions where goods or services are generally provided in exchange for the donations, or that are different than most cash contributions:

- If you purchase tickets or merchandize from a charitable organization or for a charitable purpose, you can deduct the excess of the amount paid over the fair market value (FMV) of the tickets or merchandize received.
- You can deduct $50 a month in qualifying expenses as a charitable contribution for a foreign exchange student living with you. The student must be residing in your home under a written agreement with a qualified charitable organization. If the foreign exchange student lives with you for 15 days or more in a month, that counts as a full month.
- Supporting a foster child is considered a charitable contribution (expenses exceeding reimbursements). **(See Chapter 8, "Foster Care Income")**
- Airline miles earned for making purchases on a credit card can be used or donated to a charity, and if donated to a charity it is considered a charitable contribution deduction provided substantiation rules for written acknowledgment from the charity are followed for amounts of $250 or more. **(See Chapter 8, "Airline Miles")**
- Credit card rebates are not included in gross income, even though they may be claimed as a charitable contribution if so directed. **(See Chapter 8, "Rebates Received from Purchases of Tangible Assets")**

Non-Cash Contributions – For donations of non-cash property, taxpayers must have a paper trail for any donation, no matter how small. For individual non-cash donations of $250 or more, there are more stringent substantiation requirements – you must have a written statement from the charitable organization that shows the amount of the donation, a description of the property given, and a written statement from the organization that says whether any goods or services were provided to the donor in exchange for the gift, i.e. the donor must obtain a contemporaneous written acknowledgment from the charitable organization stating the amount of the donation, and a good-faith estimate of the value of any goods or services the organization provided in exchange for the contribution. For the donation of any type of non-cash contribution of $250 or more, a taxpayer needs a signed receipt from the charity showing a description of the property donated and a statement of the estimated value (taxpayer can prepare the receipt and have the charity sign it). If you have non-cash contributions of more than $500 in a calendar year, you must file Form 8283, providing dates of the contributions, names and addresses of the charitable organizations, and descriptions of the donated property. In addition, if any individual non-cash donation is $500 or more, you must provide the date the property was acquired, how acquired (purchase, etc.), and the cost or adjusted basis of the donated property. To be deductible, used clothing and household items (furniture, electronics, appliances and linens) donated to charity must be in good used condition or better (should be stated on the receipt). There is no fixed formula or method for determining the value of used clothing and household items, but the IRS suggests that you use the value that would be set by a consignment or thrift shop. Both Goodwill and the Salvation Army have online guides. However, a taxpayer may claim a deduction of $500 or more for any single item, regardless of condition, if the taxpayer includes a qualified appraisal of the item with the return. www.irs.gov/pub/irs-pdf/f8283.pdf www.irs.gov/pub/irs-pdf/i8283.pdf

For donations of property, other than vehicles and used clothing and household items, fair market value (FMV) is normally deductible, but there are instances where the allowable deduction must be reduced to the adjusted basis of the property, e.g. the charitable organization sells or disposes of the property before the last day of the taxable year in which the contribution was made. You can deduct the FMV of donated capital gain property unless the charitable organization promptly sells it, in which case you can only deduct the adjusted basis. It's best to use an impartial guideline to establish the FMV of donated property. FMV is generally the price at which property would change hands between a willing buyer and a willing seller, neither having to buy or sell, and both having reasonable knowledge of all the relevant facts. In the case of stocks, the FMV is generally the market value on the date it is donated. Taxpayers are required to obtain a qualified appraisal for an individual non-cash donation, other than stock, with a value of $5,000 or more and attach an appraisal summary to the tax return. A qualified appraisal must be conducted by a qualified appraiser in accordance with generally accepted appraisal standards (consistent with the Uniform Standards of Professional Appraisal Practice).

Donation of ordinary income property (i.e. inventory and short-term capital gain property) is valued at the lesser of FMV or the adjusted basis (essentially your cost). The "Protecting Americans from Tax Hikes Act of 2015" makes permanent the "enhanced charitable deduction for donations of food inventory," which allows individuals and organizations to reduce their taxable income by providing qualifying food inventory to certain charitable organizations. The provision raises the cap to allow small businesses donating wholesome excess food inventory to take the same enhanced tax deduction as C-corporations have been permitted to do since 1976. This deduction is equal to the basis of the food contributed plus one half of the appreciation, not to exceed twice the basis. This amount is treated as a contribution and cost of goods sold is reduced by the basis of the food inventory contributed. **(See Chapter 14, "Enhanced Deduction of Food Inventory")**

The "Protecting Americans from Tax Hikes Act of 2015" makes permanent a provision allowing farmers and ranchers to donate capital gain real property easements for conservation purposes, and to offset up to 100% of the value of the gift from their adjusted gross income in the current year and to carry forward any unused write-off for a full 15 years, potentially zeroing out their tax liability for the next 15 years. Also, non-farmer donors can make a donation of conservation real property and offset up to 50% of the value of the gift from their adjusted gross income in the current year and carry forward any unused write-offs for a full 15 years. How does this work? With a conservation easement a donor gives some or all of the development rights on their land to a government agency or non-for-profit charitable organization, and in turn gets a tax deduction for the gift, which is the difference in the value of the land before and after the easement is in place. The donor still owns the land and can enjoy the land, such as farming and fishing on the land. Conservation easements are a powerful tool to protect land from development. **(See Chapter 17, "Conservation Easements")**

Donation of Motor Vehicles – Allowable charitable deductions for donations of motor vehicles (including automobiles, boats, airplanes, and motorcycles) cannot exceed the gross proceeds, if sold by the charitable organization. The donor can deduct the lesser of the FMV of the vehicle, or what the charitable organization sells it for. The limit on the donation of a motor vehicle to a charitable organization is $500 unless more is provable. As proof of contribution of a motor vehicle by a donor, the charitable organization must complete IRS Form 1098-C, "Contributions of Motor Vehicles, Boats, and Airplanes," and send it to the IRS with a copy to the donor as a written acknowledgment of the donation. The donor must attach the acknowledgment to his tax return. There are potentially severe penalties for fraudulent acknowledgments of vehicle donations or for failing to provide a Form 1098-C or other proper acknowledgment to the donor and to the IRS.
www.irs.gov/pub/irs-pdf/f1098c.pdf   www.irs.gov/pub/irs-pdf/i1098c.pdf

Form 1098-C includes the following information: date the vehicle was sold by the charitable organization, certification that it was sold in an arms-length transaction, gross proceeds from the sale, and a statement that the deductible amount may not exceed the gross proceeds. If the charitable organization actually uses the vehicle (does not sell it), donates it to a needy individual in direct furtherance of its charitable purpose, or sells it for significantly less than FMV to a needy individual, the gross sale proceeds limitation does not apply and you should be able to deduct the FMV of the donated vehicle, but you must have proof of "use" by the organization (a written statement from the organization to that effect). Use by the organization includes: actual use by the organization for their charitable purpose, or donation of the vehicle to a needy person or family in furtherance of its charitable purpose.

- **Example** – You may claim a deduction of the FMV of a donated car to your church if the church gives the car to a needy family and certifies in a letter that the disposition of the car was in furtherance of the church's charitable purpose.

For vehicles with a value of $500 or less, only the general substantiation requirements are required for non-cash contributions. You must have an acknowledgement of the donation from the charitable organization. If the charity sells the vehicle for $500 or less, you can deduct $500 or the vehicle's FMV, whichever is less. For example, if the vehicle has a FMV of $650 and the charity sells it for $350, you can deduct $500. An accepted measure of the FMV of a donated automobile is an amount not in excess of the price listed in an established used vehicle pricing guide, such as Kelley Blue Book or the National Automobile Dealers Association Used Car Guide for a private party sale. Vehicles are an exception to the requirement to have a qualified appraisal of a non-cash donation if the FMV is more than $5,000, as long as the written acknowledgment by the charitable organization states that the vehicle was sold without significant intervening use or material improvement and the donor deducts no more than the amount of the sale proceeds. However, if the vehicle has a claimed value of more than $5,000 and the organization does not sell the vehicle, the appraisal requirements apply.

Instead of donating a vehicle outright to a charitable organization, consider selling it yourself and donating part or all of the proceeds to the charitable organization. While this process may take more effort on your part, it generally leads to the highest return on your vehicle's value, which benefits both you and the charity of your choice. Plus, there is less paper work to worry about.

Volunteer Work For Charitable Organizations – You can't deduct the value of your time spent performing volunteer work for a charity, but you can deduct any unreimbursed expenses incurred doing such work, such as charity related volunteer mileage and any other transportation, lodging, and 50% of meals; however, You can't deduct the cost of meals when volunteering your time to qualified local charitable organizations. The charitable mileage rate in 2018 is 14 cents per mile (also 14 cents per mile in 2017), or you can claim actual expenses attributable to charitable trips – gas, oil, insurance, and repairs (based on the percentage of charitable miles driven compared to total miles driven in the year). Parking and toll fees are deductible in addition to the 14 cents per mile charitable mileage rate for a car. According to the U.S. Tax Court, fees paid to a baby sitter to enable a parent to get out of the house and do volunteer work for a charity are deductible, even though the money doesn't go directly to the charity. The court expressly rejected a contrary IRS ruling. Also, you can deduct the cost of paper, postage, and other out-of-pocket costs incurred while sending out mailings on behalf of a charity – even amounts spent on paper clips and staples. If you're required to wear a uniform or other special clothing, such as a troop leader for the Boy Scouts, you may deduct the cost of the uniforms as long as they're not suitable for everyday wear. In addition, the cost of cleaning uniforms and special clothing counts. Reimbursement for any charitable work expenses should be included in taxable income.

Since there is no standard meal allowance for charitable travel away from home, a taxpayer must keep very good records. You can't deduct the cost of a cell phone, but additional costs for long-distance phone calls are deductible. You can deduct the costs associated with attending a convention on behalf of a charitable organization if you've been designated as an official delegate to the convention. This includes meals and lodging while you're staying at the convention.

- **Example** – If you travel to Africa on a mission trip for your church and you pay for the airfare, you can deduct the cost of the airfare along with meals and other trip expenses you incur as an unreimbursed out-of-pocket expense for the charity if the travel did not have any significant element of personal pleasure, recreation, or vacation. If the cost of the airfare (and other expenses) is $250 or more, you must obtain a written acknowledgment from the charity.
- **Example** – When you host a gathering at your home to promote charitable fundraising, you can deduct the cost of food, beverages etc. as a charitable contribution. However, donating the use of your home for the charitable purpose does not qualify as a deductible charitable contribution. Also, if you donate your mountain condo for 2 nights as a winning prize in a lottery, it is not deductible. The reason for both of the described usages of your home not being deductible is that the contribution of a partial use of property is not a qualifying deductible contribution.

You can't deduct your personal expenses when volunteering your time to groups created to lobby for law changes, homeowner associations, social or sport clubs, civic leagues or chambers of commerce.

Agricultural Research Organizations – The PATH Act allows a tax deduction for charitable contributions to an agricultural research organization made on or after Dec. 18, 2015. The organization must be directly engaged in continuous agricultural research in conjunction with a land-grant college of agriculture, and the organization must commit to spend the contributions on such research within five years.

Tax-Free Distributions from IRAs for Charitable Purposes – Tax-free distributions from traditional IRAs for charitable purposes was made permanent by the "Protecting Americans from Tax Hikes Act of 2015." The provision applies to individuals age 70 ½ or older. The maximum a person can contribute in a year is $100,000, and the contributions must go directly to qualified charitable organizations (you can't touch the money). This is handy for seniors who have paid off their homes and can no longer itemize deductions. For example, to take advantage of this tax benefit, when an individual over the age of 70 ½ takes a required minimum distribution (RMD) of $12,000 from an IRA, he or she can designate that all or part of that amount goes directly to a charity and he/she will have to pay income tax only on the part that doesn't go directly to the charity. Tax-free charitable contributions going directly from your IRA to a charity are not allowable as itemized deductions. Distributions from employer-sponsored retirement plans, including SIMPLE IRAs and SEPs are not eligible for these tax-free distributions. **(See Chapter 5, "Required Minimum Distributions"; & "Tax-Free Distributions for Charitable Purposes")**

Charitable Remainder Trust – If you are thinking about selling your company, a charitable remainder trust is an option that helps reduce your payout to the IRS. Charitable remainder trusts allow you to significantly reduce your tax and ensure that you receive regular income in return for donating cash, securities, or real estate to a charity. Because you are giving assets to charity, you qualify for a charitable deduction.

Federal Disaster Loss Relief

On Sept. 29, 2017, the "Disaster Tax Relief and Airport and Airway Extension Act of 2017" was passed, which provides temporary tax relief to victims of Hurricanes Harvey, Irma, and Maria. For qualifying charitable contributions, the Act provides an exception from the overall limitation on itemized deductions for certain qualified contributions, temporarily suspends the majority of the limitations on charitable contributions in Code Sec. 170(b) and provides for eased rules governing the treatment of excess contributions. "Qualified contributions" must have been paid during the period beginning on Aug. 23, 2017, and ending on Dec. 31, 2017, in cash to an organization described in Code Sec. 170(b)(1)(A), for relief efforts in the Hurricane Harvey, Irma, or Maria disaster areas. Qualified contributions must have been substantiated, with a contemporaneous written acknowledgement that the contribution was or is to be used for hurricane relief efforts, and the taxpayer must make an election for the Act to apply. For partnerships and S-corporations, the election is made separately by each partner or shareholder. **(See Chapter 3 "Federal Disaster Loss Relief")**

Casualty, Disaster, and Theft Losses

The Tax Cuts and Jobs Act (TCJA) eliminated personal theft and casualty losses as an itemized deduction for tax years 2018 – 2025, except for losses in federal disaster areas declared by the President of the United States. However, non-disaster personal casualty and theft losses may be used to reduce personal casualty and theft gains in the same year. Business theft and casualty losses are still deductible in 2018.

In 2017 and prior years, personal casualty and theft losses were deductible as itemized deductions in the year discovered. The aggregate of all losses "not reimbursed by insurance" in a year had to be more than 10% of adjusted gross income (AGI) to be deductible, and in addition, each separate casualty or theft loss had to be more than $100 to be deductible. Personal casualty and theft losses were reported in Section B of Form 4684, and then deducted as an itemized deduction on Schedule A, Form 1040.

Federal Disaster Loss Relief – On Sept. 29, 2017, the "Disaster Tax Relief and Airport and Airway Extension Act of 2017" was passed, which provides temporary tax relief to victims of Hurricanes Harvey, Irma, and Maria. The Act eliminated the requirement that personal casualty losses must exceed 10% of AGI to qualify for a deduction and eliminated the requirement that taxpayers must itemize deductions in order to claim casualty losses—it does so by increasing an individual taxpayer's standard deduction by the amount of the taxpayer's net disaster loss. However, the Act increased the $100 per-casualty loss floor from $100 to $500 for qualified disaster-related personal casualty losses. The Act provides that Code Sec. 56(b)(1)(E), which generally disallows the standard deduction for alternative minimum tax (AMT) purposes, does not apply for the portion of the standard deduction attributable to the amount of the net disaster loss.

Under the Act, individual disaster loss victims in the hurricane affected areas may elect to claim a casualty loss in the tax year immediately preceding the tax year in which the disaster occurred or in the current year, whichever saves you more money. Victims have six months after the due date for filing their tax return for the year in which the disaster occurred to make the election, and they have 90 days after that to revoke the election. Taxpayers make the election by deducting the disaster loss on either an original or an amended tax return for the prior year, and by including an election statement on the return indicating they are making a Section 165(i) election and the name or description of the disaster and the date or dates of the disaster that caused the claimed loss. (See Chapter 3, "Federal Disaster Loss Relief")

Casualty – A total or partial casualty or theft loss is defined as the lesser of the adjusted basis of a property or item, or the difference in its FMV immediately before and after the loss (decline in FMV is provable by necessary repairs) after taking into account any reimbursement from insurance claims. A casualty is the damage, destruction, or loss of property resulting from an identifiable event due to a sudden, unexpected, or unusual cause. Examples include fires, earthquakes, floods, storms, tornados, and hurricanes. Damage or loss of property as a result of progressive deterioration is not considered a casualty, and therefore, is not deductible. In the 2015 Wideman case, the Tax Court ruled that damage caused by faulty construction was not considered a sudden or unusual event and, therefore, the cost of repairs to fix the damage couldn't be claimed as a loss. www.irs.gov/pub/irs-pdf/f4684.pdf   www.irs.gov/pub/irs-pdf/i4684.pdf www.ustaxcourt.gov/USTCInOP/OpinionViewer.aspx?ID=1128

In calculating the allowable casualty loss for a personal car, don't include these items: towing charges, the cost of renting a replacement car, or legal fees to defend against a suit for negligent operation of your vehicle. The deduction is available only to the owner of the damaged property. Thus, even if you get stuck with the bill, there is no write-off for damage or destruction of a car registered in your child's name.

Proving a Casualty Loss – You have to prove two things: (1) that your loss was the result of a casualty event; and (2) the amount of your financial loss. You'll need pictures, newspaper clippings, insurance claims, or other evidence that your property was damaged or destroyed by a casualty event. The trickiest part of claiming a casualty loss is proving the amount of the loss. You can't take into account any ascetic or sentimental value to you; it must be based solely on the facts. You can obtain an appraisal made by a qualified appraiser of the FMV. Instead of obtaining an appraisal, the cost of repairs to the damaged property is acceptable evidence of the loss in value – the repairs must relate only to the damage suffered in the casualty, and must be only those repairs necessary to restore the property to its pre-casualty condition. Damage to an individual's residence or appliances resulting from corrosive drywall made in China can be treated as a casualty loss in the year of payment for the repairs if the taxpayer does not have a pending claim for reimbursement and does not intend to pursue reimbursement. If a taxpayer has a pending claim for reimbursement or intends to pursue reimbursement, he may take advantage of the safe harbor method and claim a loss of 75% of the unreimbursed amount paid during the year for the repairs.

Theft – A Theft includes the illegal taking of money or property – Theft is pretty broad, including the taking of money or property by: blackmail; burglary; embezzlement; extortion; larceny; robbery; and kidnapping for ransom. In the case of misrepresentation, there must be intent to defraud. If you pay hackers a ransom is it tax deductible? Whether personal or business, it probably is, although the type of deduction can vary. The taking of money or property through fraud or misrepresentation probably includes a ransom demand, which would be a theft if it is illegal under state or local law. For businesses, paying a ransom or blackmail is likely to fall into the wide category of business expenses. A theft loss cannot be claimed for unpaid services for which you were never paid.

A theft loss may be deducted in the year it is discovered. However, if in that year there is a reimbursement claim with a reasonable prospect of recovery, the deduction for any part of the loss should be postponed until the year in which the taxpayer is reasonably certain whether any reimbursement will be received. Whether a reasonable prospect of recovery exists at the time of discovery is determined by the facts of each case. Reasonable certainty of whether a reimbursement will be received is determined by examining all the facts and circumstances and can be demonstrated by the taxpayer's settling, adjudicating, or abandoning the claim. However, in the Adkins Case, the U.S. Court of Appeals held that taxpayers did not have to abandon their claim for reimbursement of their theft loss to establish that there was no reasonable certainty of receiving it, so their theft loss was allowed in the year they claimed it.
www.cafc.uscourts.gov/sites/default/files/opinions-orders/16-1961.Opinion.5-5-2017.1.PDF

      Proving a Theft Loss – You have to prove two things: (1) that your loss was the result of illegal taking of your money or property; and (2) the amount of your financial loss. Taxpayers may not claim a theft loss for a decline in the value of stock purchased on the open market due to misrepresentation of the financial status, fraud, or other illegal misconduct by corporate officers, investment churning, and broker risk misrepresentations, i.e. a stock's worthlessness resulting from corporate fraud isn't a theft loss. Losses resulting from "Tax Shelters" are not deductible. In Vincentini v. Commissioner, the court ruled that an investor who thought he was buying tax benefits couldn't claim a theft loss when the investment imploded and the promoters went to jail. Tax shelters are defined by the tax code to include any plan or arrangement having a significant purpose of avoiding or evading federal income tax. The key is whether the tax ramifications are the reason for entering into the transaction.
www.ustaxcourt.gov/InOpHistoric/vincentini.TCM.WPD.pdf
www.ustaxcourt.gov/InOpHistoric/vin2centini.TCM.WPD.pdf

A loss as a result of a Ponzi scheme is allowed if the stock is worthless or has no recognizable value. However, a loss as a result of a Ponzi scheme is not deducted as a "Casualty, Disaster or Theft Loss," but instead is deducted as a "miscellaneous itemized deduction not subject to the 2% floor." **(See Below, "Miscellaneous Itemized Deductions Not Subject to the 2% AGI Floor")**

      Business Casualty, Disaster or Theft Loss – There is no limitation on the amount that can be deducted for business casualty, disaster or theft losses. Business casualty, disaster and theft losses are not an itemized deduction, but instead are deducted on the applicable business form, such as on Schedule C. A total business loss is the adjusted basis of a property or item, even if the FMV of the property is less immediately before the loss. A partial business casualty or theft loss is defined as the lesser of the adjusted basis of a property or item, or the difference in its FMV immediately before and after the loss (decline in FMV is provable by necessary repairs) after taking into account any reimbursement from insurance claims. Business losses (property used in a trade or business) are reported in Section B of Form 4684, and then taken as a loss on Form 4797. However, if property is classified as inventory, the loss is reported as a "miscellaneous itemized deduction not subject to the 2% floor," which are no longer deductible as an itemized deduction in 2018. **(See Chapter 14, "Business Casualty and Theft Losses"); (See Below, "Miscellaneous Itemized Deductions Not Subject to the 2% AIG Floor")**

You must capitalize amounts paid to restore business property resulting from a disaster, including amounts paid "for the repair of damage to a unit of property" even if your casualty loss is ameliorated by insurance.

- **Example** – You have a property damaged by a hurricane that had a 15-year recovery period when placed in service 10 years ago and has been depreciated for 10 years. The cost to repair the property and its remaining basis are both $1 million. In this case, you have two alternatives: (1) you can claim a $1 million casualty loss and depreciate the property's remaining basis of $1 million over 15 years; or (2) instead of claiming a casualty loss, you can deduct the $1 million repair cost and continue to depreciate the remaining basis of $1 million over the remaining 5-year recovery period.

Miscellaneous Itemized Deductions Subject to the 2% AGI Floor

In accordance with the Tax Cuts and Jobs Act (TCJA), the deduction for miscellaneous itemized deductions subject to the 2% of adjusted gross income (AGI) floor is eliminated for tax years 2018 – 2025.

The elimination of miscellaneous itemized deductions subject to the 2% AGI floor will result in some legal fees that were allowable miscellaneous itemized deductions in prior years being non-deductible beginning in 2018, which may be construed as unfair to individuals seeking taxable damages (other than damages for discrimination where the legal fees are deducted as an above-the-line deduction). For example, assume a plaintiff in a law suit related to his employment (other than job discrimination) is awarded $600,000 settlement; the attorney gets one-third of the award on a contingency ($200,000); and the plaintiff has to pay taxes on the full $600,000 settlement without getting any offsetting deduction for the legal fees in 2018, like he or she would have gotten in 2017 and prior years. Another example that may be construed as unfair is when a taxpayer has income from a hobby but can no longer deduct expenses related to the hobby as a miscellaneous itemized deduction in 2018, like he or she could in 2017 and prior years. And there are many other examples where the elimination of miscellaneous itemized deductions subject to the 2% AGI floor can be construed as unfair to taxpayers.

Following is a rundown of the miscellaneous itemized deductions subject to the 2% AGI floor that were deductible in 2017 and prior years, but are no longer deductible in 2018:

Employee Business Expenses – Unreimbursed employee travel and entertainment expenses, and other employee business expenses are deductible. Travel and entertainment expenses are reported on Form 2106, while other employee business expenses are reported directly as miscellaneous itemized deductions, unless an employee has to file Form 2106, in which case other employee business expenses are reported on Line 4 of Form 2106.

Employees who are entitled to reimbursement for expenses from their employers should not use Form 2106 to claim the expenses on their own tax returns. Employees who are under an "Accountable Plan" are entitled to reimbursement of their expenses from their employers. In the Beckey case, the taxpayer was denied a deduction for expenses reported on Form 2106, because the taxpayer failed to prove that the employer would not have reimbursed the expenses. The Tax Court stated: "When an employee has a right to reimbursement for expenditures related to his status as an employee but fails to claim reimbursement, the expenses are not necessary and are not deductible." Additionally, the court provided that "an employee cannot fail to seek reimbursement and convert his/her expenses into the employer's."
http://ustaxcourt.gov/UstcInOp/OpinionViewer.aspx?ID=11143

Employee Home Office Expenses – Employee home office expenses, if necessary and for the convenience of the employer, are deductible. Employees who are allowed to claim home office expenses are not required to file Form 8829 (a worksheet is provided). Instead the expenses are reported directly as miscellaneous itemized deductions, unless an employee has to file Form 2106, in which case the home office expenses (figured on the worksheet provided) are reported on Line 4, Form 2106. Mortgage interest and real estate taxes are fully deductible itemized deductions, and therefore, should not be allocated to home office expenses for an employee. **(See Chapter 17, "Home Office Expenses")**

Hobby Expenses – A hobby is an activity that is deemed not to be a profit-motivated activity or business. Hobby expenses are deductible from adjusted gross income (AGI) as a miscellaneous itemized deduction, but only to the extent of income from the activity (a loss is not allowed). Hobby Income is reported as "other income," on Line 21 of Form 1040. **(See Chapter 14, "Business or Hobby")**

Expenses to Look for a New Job in the Same Line of Work – Expenses to look for a new job in the same line of work are deductible – travel and entertainment expenses, including meals, lodging, and transportation expenses are deductible if the job search takes you away from home overnight (reported on Form 2106). The cost of resumes, employment agency fees, and costs of printing resumes, business cards, postage, and advertising are reported directly as miscellaneous itemized deductions unless you have file Form 2106. You can't deduct job search expenses if there was a substantial break between the end of your last job and the time you began looking for a new job, and Job hunting expenses incurred while looking for your first job don't qualify either. **(See Chapter 15, "Travel and Entertainment Expenses")**

Work Related Education Costs – Work related education costs, but not education costs that qualify a person for a new profession, are generally deductible. The costs of education expenses are generally deductible if the courses taken maintain or improve skills required by the individual's employment or trade or business or meets the express requirements of the individual's employer or the requirements of applicable law. If a college degree or courses taken will qualify an employee for a new trade or business or is required to meet the minimum education requirements for an individual's employment or trade or business, its costs are generally not deductible. However, a court held that a high school teacher's graduate school expenses were deductible, even though the teacher took a year off from teaching to pursue the studies full time and was not on a leave of absence. A suspension for a period of one year or less, after which the taxpayer returns to the same employment or profession, is considered temporary.

Special Work Clothes – Special work clothes not suitable to wear off the job and that are "ordinary and necessary" in relation to your business, such as special protective clothing and safety boots worn by police officers and firemen are deductible. Work clothes, uniforms and costumes qualify if they satisfy a two-step test: (1) required as a condition of employment, and (2) unsuitable for everyday use. However, just because you purchase clothes for business purposes (e.g. suits and ties) doesn't mean they qualify as a deduction. Generally, what you spend to improve your appearance, general health or sense of well-being, are nondeductible personal expenses, e.g. clothes you can wear when you're not at work.

Investment Expenses – Safe deposit boxes, IRA custodial fees, brokers' commissions, fees for investment advice, trust administration fees, subscriptions to investment and financial planning journals, and clerical help and office rent in caring for investments are deductible. Mutual fund expenses are not deductible because they flow through, i.e. the mutual funds report net income (income minus expenses). No deduction is allowed for attending conventions, seminars, or meetings related to income-producing (investment) activities.

Real Estate Taxes Paid on Unimproved Land – Real estate taxes paid on unimproved land that is considered investment property are deductible, if the investment property is purchased primarily to realize appreciation in value. You can deduct expenses related to the land that you can't deduct if the land is considered personal use property, including association dues and maintenance expenses, management fees etc. If you won't receive any benefit by itemizing these expenses, you can capitalize them and add them to the basis of the property. **(See Above, "State and Local Tax Deductions")**

Tax Prepartaion Fees – Fees paid to have a tax professional prepare your Federal and state income tax returns are deductible.

Legal Expenses – Usually, legal fees and expenses incurred by individuals are not deductible, including legal fees related to the collection of punitive damages. However, some legal expenses are deductible as miscellaneous itemized deductions subject to the 2% floor including: (1) Legal fees paid in connection with the preparation of tax returns or in connection with any proceedings involved in determining the extent of your tax liability or in contesting a tax liability; (2) Legal fees for preparing wills and estate planning; (3) tax planning advice, including investment advice (tax advice is not restricted to that provided by attorneys and CPAs, so expenses for advice provided by your accountant and investment advisor may also be deductible); (4) Legal fees paid in connection with a claim for disputed Social Security benefits due to a disability are deductible if the benefits received are taxable, i.e. if only 50% of Social Security benefits are taxable, you can deduct 50% of the legal fees. If you hire an attorney to help you get your Social Security Disability (SSDI) benefits, you can deduct the fees you paid for your attorney when figuring out the taxability of a lump-sum payment; (5) Some legal fees related to divorce are deductible – specifically, you can deduct legal fees related to collecting child support and alimony. However, a payer of alimony or child support may not deduct the cost of legal fees in fighting against paying support. Other divorce related attorneys' fees are not deductible; and (6) Legal expenses may be deductible if they are tied to or related to keeping your job, including fees paid to defend yourself against criminal charges arising out of your trade or business. **(See Chapter 5, "Personal Injury Awards Associated with Nonphysical Injuries"; "Alimony and Separate Maintenance"; & "Social Security Disability Benefits"); (See Chapter 8, "Personal Injury Awards as a Result of Physical Injuries")**

Legal expenses that are deductible elsewhere on your tax return include: (1) attorney fees paid in connection with damages or awards received resulting from an "unlawful discrimination" claim after a job loss or under the Medicare Secondary Payer Statute are deductible as an above-the-line deduction; and (2) Legal fees related to the operation of a business activity are always deductible as a business expense on the applicable form or schedule, e.g. Schedule C. However, some legal fees must be capitalized and added to the basis of assets, i.e. if you are trying to sell your business and spend $50,000 in legal fees, you'll usually have to add the legal fees to the basis of your assets. **(See Chapter 4, "Damages Received for Job Discrimination")**

Fiduciary Bundled Fees – The final regulations apply to tax years beginning after December 31, 2014. Fiduciary Bundled fees that are billed together, where a portion is fully deductible and another portion is subject to the 2% of AGI floor, must be "unbundled," i.e. the costs have to be allocated between costs that are subject to the 2% floor and those that are not. Generally, the portion of a bundled fiduciary fee attributable to investment advice (including any related services that would be provided to any individual investor as part of an investment advisory fee) is subject to the 2% floor. Any fiduciary fee not allocated to investment advice and not calculated on an hourly basis is generally fully deductible, except for (1) payments made to a third party out of the bundled fee that would have been subject to the 2% floor if paid directly by an estate or trust, and (2) separately assessed expenses (in addition to usual or basic fees or commissions) that are commonly or customarily incurred by an individual. If amounts are allocable to investment advice but are not traceable to separate payments, the final regulations allow the use of "any reasonable method" to make the allocation between costs that are subject to the 2% floor and those that are not. **(See Chapter 21, "Final Rules on Bundled Fiduciary Fees for Estates and Trusts")**

Other Miscellaneous Itemized Deductions Subject to the 2% AGI Floor:
- Income tax preparation fees and counsel. The portion of income tax preparation fees related to Schedules C, E, and F are deductible in determining net income on the relevant forms.
- Employer required medical examinations if not reimbursed by the employer.
- Dues and subscriptions to professional journals.
- Professional and trade association dues are deductible, but not social organization dues, such as country club dues, etc.
- Appraisal fees for charitable contributions or casualty losses.
- Union dues and costs.
- Passport fees for a business trip if required and not reimbursed by the employer.
- Professional liability insurance if not reimbursed by the employer.
- Small tools necessary for employment.
- Gifts to business associates or clients – up to $25 per person per year.
- Depreciation of a computer used to manage investments.

Miscellaneous Itemized Deductions Not Subject to the 2% AGI Floor

Miscellaneous itemized deductions not subject to the 2% AGI floor are still deductible in 2018, but there are some changes:

Gambling Losses – Gambling losses to the extent of gambling winnings are deductible as an itemized deduction, and the Tax Cuts and Jobs Act (TCJA) added the expenses of gamblers to be included as part of their losses in tax years 2018 – 2025. But the expenses of gamblers were not allowed as part of their losses in 2017 and prior years. However, gamblers cannot have a loss, i.e. the amount of a gambler's losses are limited to the amount of their winnings in a year, and excess losses cannot be carried forward to the next tax year. Gambling winnings are reported as "other income" on Form 1040. **(See Chapter 5, "Gambling Winnings")**

Disability or Impairment Related Expenses – Disability or impairment related expenses incurred by physically or mentally disabled persons which are necessary to allow them to work are deductible. This includes attendant care services at a place of employment that are necessary in order that a disabled person can work.

Deduction for Federal Estate Taxes – If you inherit a $100,000 IRA that added $45,000 to your benefactor's estate tax bill, you can deduct the $45,000 in estate taxes paid by your benefactor ratably as you withdraw the money from the inherited IRA. **(See Chapter 5, "IRAs and Retirement Plans Inherited by Beneficiaries")**

Ponzi Scheme Losses – Ponzi scheme losses are deductible in the year discovered. Ponzi scheme losses are not subject to the $3,000 annual limitation on capital losses. A Ponzi scheme is one in which a party receives cash or property from investors, reports false investment income amounts to the investors, and appropriates some or all of the investors' cash or property. A qualified loss from a Ponzi scheme is considered deductible when there is evidence of a closed or completed transaction fixed by an identifiable event. This generally occurs when the fraudulent arrangement results in federal or state criminal charges for theft (larceny, embezzlement, robbery or similar offenses), or there is a criminal complaint making such allegations. A complaint must also allege that the perpetrator admitted the conduct, or there must have been a receiver or trustee appointed or its assets must have been frozen. The loss is considered discovered and deductible when charges are brought and guilt is implied. The IRS recently broadened the definition of a qualified loss from a Ponzi scheme in two ways. First, by including schemes in which a civil complaint is brought against the lead figure by a state or federal authority that has not been withdrawn. Second, by making an exception for when a lead figure died and foreclosed all criminal charges. The death of the lead figure must preclude criminal charges against the figure, and assets of the arrangement must be frozen or be placed under a receiver's jurisdiction.

A safe harbor allows investors in a Ponzi scheme to elect to deduct 95% of the amount of their loss in the tax year of discovery as a theft-loss, or 75% of the amount if the investor is pursuing a third-party recovery. The loss includes your unrecovered investment, including any fictitious income you reported in prior years. The "discovery year" is defined as the year in which criminal charges are filed against the lead figures of the Ponzi scheme. Taxpayers not using the safe harbor may deduct their investment in the Ponzi scheme as a theft-loss, including any "phantom" or fictitious income included on prior year tax returns. Income may be considered phantom if it was only constructively received or, if actually paid to the investor it was not actually earned because the promoter of the scheme falsely represented the payment as income when it was actually paid from the capital funds of the investor or investors to perpetuate and conceal the scheme. While a reasonable prospect of recovery may postpone a theft loss deduction, it does not prevent investors from amending prior open-year tax returns to eliminate phantom income reported in those years. **(See Above, "Casualty, Disaster, and Theft Losses")**

Other Miscellaneous Itemized Deductions Not Subject to the 2% AGI Floor:
- Jury duty pay relinquished to your employer (if included in taxable income). **(See Chapter 5, "Jury Duty Pay")**
- Business casualty and theft loses from income producing properties (inventory, etc.). **(See Chapter 14, "Business Casualty and Theft Losses")**
- Unrecovered investment in a decedent's annuity or pension on a decedent's final return. **(See Chapter 21, "Final Return of Decedent")**
- Deductions for amortizable bond premiums.

Chapter 13 – Tax Credits

Refundable tax credits can offset other taxes, i.e. taxes on early distributions from employee retirement plans and IRAs, etc., and are not limited to an individual's tax liability for a year. Non-refundable tax credits are limited to a taxpayer's tax liability for a year. All non-refundable tax credits are allowed against both regular tax and the alternative minimum tax (AMT). If you are subject to the AMT in the current year, you may not receive all of your tax credits, such as the Work Opportunity Credit – The "tentative minimum tax" limits the Work Opportunity Credit and most of the other general business credits, other than the energy credits (the credits can't reduce the tax you pay below the tentative minimum tax). However, any general business credits not allowed may be carried back 2 years and carried forward 20 years in the AMT tax system. **(See Chapter 23, "Alternative Minimum Tax")**

Repayment of the First-Time Homebuyer Credit

Repayment of the first-time home buyer credit is an additional tax payable that is reported on Form 1040 for the repayment of the first-time Homebuyer Credit that was available to taxpayers in 2008. First-time homebuyers who purchased new homes in 2008 were eligible for a credit of 10% of the purchase price up to a maximum credit of $7,500 ($3,750 for married filing separately) which had to be repaid over a 15-year period starting with the 2010 tax year. Repayment of the credit was originally to be reported on Form 5405, "Repayment of the First-Time Homebuyer Credit." However, for the first time in 2011, Form 1040 included a separate line where first-time homebuyers can include a normal installment payment without having to file Form 5405, although Form 5405 still has to be filed in certain circumstances.

www.irs.gov/pub/irs-pdf/f5405.pdf   www.irs.gov/pub/irs-pdf/i5405.pdf

Taxpayers who sell, dispose, or rent out their home before the end of the 15-year repayment period have to repay the entire remaining balance of the credit in the year when the sale or change in use of the home occurs. However, the amount of the repayment should not exceed the gain on the sale of the home to an unrelated 3rd party. In computing the gain, the adjusted basis of the home should be reduced by the balance of the remaining credit still owed. Couples who filed jointly in 2008, when they received the credit, had to file two separate Forms 5405 beginning in 2010 to start repaying the credit. However, couples who filed jointly in 2010 but had a different filing status in 2008, and only one spouse received the credit, had to file just one Form 5405 starting in 2010 for the spouse who received the credit. Couples who received the credit but are no longer living in the house due to separation or divorce are each responsible for immediately repaying the full amount of their remaining half of the credit. If a taxpayer dies, his or her repayment responsibility is immediately excused. **(See Chapter 3, "Marital Status and Divorce")**

Second First-Time Home Buyer Credit – The second first-time home buyer credit was a maximum $8,000 credit for homes purchased after Dec. 31, 2008 and before May 1, 2010 that didn't have to be repaid, but had to be recaptured if the home purchased ceased to be the principal residence of the taxpayer at any time within the 36 month period after the date of purchase. The recaptured amount had to be shown as an addition to the taxpayer's taxable income in the year the property was disposed of or ceased to be the taxpayer's principal residence. The recaptured amount could not exceed the amount of gain from the sale of the home to an unrelated 3rd party. But in computing the gain the adjusted basis of the home had to be reduced by the amount of the credit. Exceptions to credit recapture were: death of the taxpayer; involuntary conversion if the taxpayer acquired a new residence within 2 years; and transfer between spouses incident to divorce. **(See Chapter 6, "Reporting Capital Gains and Losses")**

Refundable Tax Credits:

Earned Income Tax Credit (EITC)

The earned income tax credit (EITC) was made permanent by the "Protecting Americans from Tax Hikes Act of 2015," and is claimed on Schedule EIC, Form 1040. A taxpayer must be over age 24 and below age 65 to claim the EITC. Also, the taxpayer (and spouse, if married) must have a valid Social Security number and be a U.S. citizen or resident alien for the entire year in order to claim the EITC. A taxpayer (or spouse) who is a nonresident alien for any part of the year cannot claim the EITC unless the taxpayer files jointly with his or her spouse who is a U.S. citizen or resident. If they make this election, the couple will be subject to U.S. taxes on their worldwide income. A taxpayer who has an "individual tax identification number" (ITIN) cannot claim the credit even if he or she has dependent children with valid Social Security numbers who would otherwise qualify for the EITC. An ITIN always begins with the number 9, and will have a 7, 8, or 9 in the 4th digit of the number. Also, an individual cannot retroactively claim the EITC by amending a return (or filing an original return if he failed to file) for any prior year in which he did not have a valid Social Security number. Working grandparents raising grandchildren should be aware that they are eligible for the EITC, and that they can correctly claim it if they qualify (they must be under the age of 65). **(See Chapter 3, "Aliens"; & "Individual Tax Identification Number (ITIN) Procedures")** www.irs.gov/pub/irs-pdf/f1040sei.pdf   http://f1040.com/-%20IRS/Worksheets/EIC%20Worksheet%20B%20-%20Lines%2064a%20and%2064b%20.pdf

The maximum credits in 2018 are: $519 (no qualifying children); $3,461 (one qualifying child); $5,716 (two qualifying children); and $6,431 (three or more qualifying children).

In order to claim the EITC, a taxpayer must have some earned income (usually income either from a job or self-employment), and unemployment benefits are not treated as earnings for EITC purposes. But taxpayers who are retired on disability can count as earned income any taxable benefits they receive under an employer's disability retirement plan – these benefits remain earned income until the disability retiree reaches minimum retirement age. An election may be made to include tax-free combat pay, otherwise excluded from income, for EITC purposes. The election is all or nothing—if made, all nontaxable combat pay must be included when making the EITC calculation. Depending on the service member's situation, this may not result in a bigger EITC. There is evidence that few military personnel take advantage of this election, and those who do often do not make the optimal choice when deciding on it. Income earned while a person is in prison or a penal institution does not count for EITC purposes. In the Skaggs case, the Tax Court concluded that a prisoner who was transferred to a state mental health care institution while incarcerated, nevertheless remained an inmate in a penal institution, which meant that income he earned while he was at the state mental health care institution was not earned income for EITC purposes.
http://ustaxcourt.gov/UstcInOp/OpinionViewer.aspx?ID=11221

Taxpayers are not eligible for the EITC in 2018 if they have disqualified investment income of $3,500 or more – both taxable and tax-exempt interest, dividends, net rent, royalty income, net capital gain income, and net passive income that is not self-employment income.

Following are the 2018 maximum credits and phaseout parameters for the EITC:
- No qualifying children: Maximum credit = $519 (7.65% of earned income); Phaseouts: $8,490 – 15,270 (single, head-of-household, or surviving spouse); $14,170 – $20,950 (married filing jointly).
- One qualifying child: Maximum credit = $3,461 (34% of earned income); Phaseouts: $18,660 - $40,320 (single, head-of-household, or surviving spouse); $24,350 – $46,010 (married filing jointly).
- Two qualifying children: Maximum credit = $5,716 (40% of earned income); Phaseouts: $18,660 – $45,802 (single, head-of-household, or surviving spouse); $24,350 – $51,492 (married filing jointly).
- Three or more children: Maximum credit = $6,431 (45% of earned income); Phaseouts: $18,660 – $49,194 (single, head-of-household, or surviving spouse); $24,350 – $54,884 (married filing jointly).

Qualifying children are those under age 19 or under 24 if a full-time student at least 5 months of the year who lives with the taxpayer more than ½ of the year except for temporary absences such as school. Foster children qualify, and children who are permanently and totally disabled qualify at any age. A qualifying child must also have a valid Social Security number. A child who provides more than ½ of his own support may be a qualifying child for purposes of the EITC – this is the only exception to the ½ support dependency exemption definition. **(See Below, "Adoption Credit"); (See Chapter 3, "Qualifying Child for the Dependency Exemption")**

Married persons must file jointly to claim the credit, unless they lived apart for the last 6 months of the year, in which case the custodial parent can claim the credit as head-of-household. If both parents are eligible and they do not file a joint return, the parent with whom the child resided the longest during the year may claim the credit. If the child lived with each parent for the same amount of time, the child will be treated as the qualifying child of the parent with the higher adjusted gross income (AGI). For divorced parents, the parent who has custody of a child for the longer period of time during the year (custodial parent) is entitled to the EITC, regardless of whether he/she can claim the child as a dependent. **(See Chapter 3, "Head of Household"; "Marital Status and Divorce"; & "Dependency Exemptions")**

For tax years beginning after December 31, 2015, taxpayers who file a false EITC claim can be barred from claiming the credit for ten years if they are convicted of fraud and for two years if they are found to have recklessly or intentionally disregarded the rules. The IRS also has math error authority, which permits them to disallow improper EITC claims without a formal audit if a taxpayer claims the credit in a period during which he is barred from doing so due to fraud or reckless or intentional disregard. These rules also apply to the Child Tax Credit, the American Opportunity Tax Credit, and qualification for Head of Household status. **(See Below, "American Opportunity Tax Credit"; & "Child Tax Credit"); (See Chapter 3, "Head of Household")**

Tax preparers must answer due diligence questions on Form 8867, "Paid Preparer's Due Diligence Checklist," and the form must be attached to a taxpayer's tax return. The consequences for a tax practitioner not completing Form 8867 and attaching it to the tax return could be losing IRS e-file privileges, and other sanctions that could include barring them from tax return preparation. Beginning with the 2018 tax year, Form 8867 also applies to the Child Tax Credit/Additional Child Tax Credit, the American Opportunity Credit, and qualification for Head of Household

status. A $500 penalty (adjusted for inflation to in 2018) will apply to tax preparers who fail to comply with the due diligence requirements. The penalty applies separately to each of the four, meaning a tax preparer could conceivably be subject to as many as four penalties for one tax return for failing to exercise due diligence for the EITC, the American Opportunity Credit, the Child Tax Credit and eligibility for head of household status. In addition to completing Form 8867, tax preparers must complete any required Earned Income Tax Credit worksheets in Schedule EIC. Tax preparers must not know or have reason to know that any information used to determine eligibility for, and the amount of the credit is incorrect. Tax preparers must make reasonable inquiries if the information furnished by the taxpayer appears to be incorrect, inconsistent, or incomplete. Tax preparers must document inquiries and responses contemporaneously and retain the information for at least three years. **(See Below, "Additional Child Tax Credit"; "Education Credits"; & "Child Tax Credit"); (See Chapter 3, "Head of Household")**
www.irs.gov/pub/irs-pdf/f8867.pdf www.irs.gov/pub/irs-pdf/i8867.pdf

Federal Disaster Loss Relief – On Sept. 29, 2017, the "Disaster Tax Relief and Airport and Airway Extension Act of 2017" was passed, which provides temporary tax relief to victims of Hurricanes Harvey, Irma, and Maria that occurred in 2017. The Act provides that, in case a "qualified taxpayer's" earned income, which includes the applicable dates shown below, is less than the taxpayer's earned income for the preceding tax year, then the taxpayer may elect, for purposes of the EITC and the Child Tax Credit, to substitute the earned income for the preceding year for the earned income for the current tax year in computing the EITC and the Child Tax Credit for the current year. For Hurricane Harvey, a "qualified taxpayer" is one whose principal place of abode on Aug. 23, 2017 was located either in the Hurricane Harvey disaster zone, or in the Hurricane Harvey disaster area and the individual was displaced from their principal place of abode by reason of Hurricane Harvey. Similar definitions apply for Hurricanes Irma (using a Sept. 4, 2017 date) and Hurricane Maria (using a Sept. 16, 2017 date). In the case of joint filers, the above election may apply if either spouse is a qualified individual. **(See Chapter 3, "Federal Disaster Loss Relief"); (See Below, "Child Tax Credit")**

Additional Child Tax Credit (Schedule 8812, Form 1040)
The additional child tax credit was made permanent by the "Protecting Americans from Tax Hikes Act of 2015 (PATH)." The Tax Cuts and Jobs Act (TCJA) doubled the Child Tax Credit to $2,000 for each "qualifying child" for tax years 2018 – 2025. The Additional Child Tax Credit is the refundable portion of the child tax credit available to 0taxpayers who can't take advantage of the full amount of the credit due to a limited amount of income tax liability. As set forth in the TCJA, the additional child tax credit is 15% of earned income greater than $2,500, up to a maximum of $1,400 per child in 2018. Schedule 8812, Form 1040, "Additional Child Tax Credit," must be filed with your tax return to claim the credit. **(See Below, "Child Tax Credit")**
www.irs.gov/pub/irs-pdf/f1040s8.pdf www.irs.gov/pub/irs-pdf/i1040s8.pdf

Taxpayers who take the foreign earned income exclusion or the foreign housing exclusion are prohibited from also claiming the additional child tax credit. This provision was effective for tax years beginning on or after January 1, 2015. **(See Chapter 9, "Foreign Earned Income Exclusion")**

40% of the American Opportunity Education Tax Credit
This is the refundable portion of the American Opportunity Tax Credit (AOTC), which was made permanent by the "Protecting Americans from Tax Hikes Act of 2015." However, no portion is refundable if the taxpayer claiming the

credit is a child to whom the Kiddie tax can be applied – a person under 19 or under 24 who is a full-time student providing less than ½ of his or her own support, who has a living parent, and does not file a joint return. **(See Below, "Education Credits"); (See Chapter 3, "Kiddie Tax")**

www.irs.gov/pub/irs-pdf/f8863.pdf www.irs.gov/pub/irs-pdf/i8863.pdf

Credit for Federal Excise Tax Paid on Fuels (Form 4136)

This is a refundable credit for federal taxes paid on fuels used for nontaxable purposes. Fuels used that are taxed by the federal government and are eligible for the credit are gasoline, diesel, and kerosene. Anyone who uses these fuels for nontaxable purposes (individuals or businesses) should file Form 4136 to claim the credit. Nontaxable fuel uses include: fueling equipment used in farming; running public transit or school buses; fueling aircraft operated by a museum; and powering off-highway vehicles or stationary equipment. Companies that sell fuels to the federal government are also eligible for the credit. No credit is allowed if the fuel or mixture is produced outside the United States for use outside the United States.

www.irs.gov/pub/irs-access/f4136_accessible.pdf www.irs.gov/pub/irs-pdf/i4136.pdf

The "Protecting Americans from Tax Hikes Act of 2015" specifies that liquefied petroleum gas and liquefied natural gas are eligible for the credit, and that the excise tax credit equivalency for liquefied petroleum gas and liquefied natural gas is approximately 29 cents per gallon for liquefied natural gas and approximately 36 cents per gallon for liquefied petroleum gas, compared to 50 cents per gallon for diesel fuel (effective for fuel sold or used after 2015).

Form 4136 requires taxpayers to provide information about the type of fuel and number of gallons used for nontaxable purposes during the year – each type of fuel has its own tax credit calculation. The amount of the credit for each type of fuel is determined by multiplying the number of gallons used by the applicable rate per gallon provided on the form. The amount of the credit must be entered on Form 1040. Taxpayers who expect their fuel tax credit will exceed their tax liability for any quarter during the year should file Form 8849, "Claim for Refund of Excise Taxes," in order to receive a refund payment from the IRS.

www.irs.gov/pub/irs-pdf/f8849.pdf www.irs.gov/pub/irs-prior/i8849--1994.pdf

Health Coverage Tax Credit (HCTC) (Form 8885)

The Health Coverage Tax Credit (HCTC) expired at the end of 2013, but in June 2015, legislation revived the HCTC, made it retroactive to Jan. 1, 2014, and extended and modified the credit through the end of 2019. The HCTC is available to certain displaced workers whose jobs have been outsourced and who are certified by the Department of Labor as eligible to receive Trade Readjustment Allowances under the Trade Adjustment Assistance program. Others may be eligible because they are 55 years old or older and receive benefits from the Pension Benefit Guaranty Corporation (PBGC). The credit is claimed on Form 8885).

www.irs.gov/pub/irs-access/f8885_accessible.pdf www.irs.gov/pub/irs-pdf/i8885.pdf

Eligible taxpayers can claim the HCTC for the 2018 tax year by filing Form 8885. The IRS continues to work with its partners, the Pension Benefit Guaranty Corporation, the Department of Labor and State Workforce Agencies to ensure that all eligible taxpayers receive this important credit. The IRS expects to begin making payments for the advance monthly program in Jan. 2017, and will provide more information about the enrollment process later on.

Refundable AMT Credit (Form 8801)

Beginning in 2007, taxpayers with old prior year minimum tax credits were allowed to start using the "refundable AMT credit." This allowed a taxpayer to claim the credit, but only if the taxpayer had unused prior minimum tax credits from four or more years earlier. The refundable credit was enacted to give relief to individuals who exercised incentive stock options (ISO) that generated prior year minimum tax credits that lost all or a significant portion of their value in later years due to the loss in value of the stocks. Since the difference between the fair market value (FMV) and the option price is an adjustment item for AMT purposes, these taxpayers paid an increased amount in taxes that generated prior year minimum tax credits for use in later years, when the stocks were sold for a profit. The loss in value of the stocks resulted in these individuals being unable to use any of the sizable amount of accumulated credits to offset their tax liability, and they kept carrying the amount forward to the next year with the same results. Unfortunately for these taxpayers, this meant the credits were of limited benefit if the stock was sold at a loss, i.e. at a lower price than the market price on the day the options were exercised. However, as a result of 2006 legislation, a taxpayer was eligible to receive a refundable AMT credit beginning in 2007 if the prior year minimum tax credit arose from an incentive stock option (ISO) that was exercised before the third immediately preceding tax year. In other words, the AMT refundable credit for tax year 2007 was available for credits generated during 2003 or earlier.

The "AMT refundable credit amount" is the greater of (1) the lesser of $5,000 or the long-term unused minimum tax credit, or (2) 20% of the long-term unused minimum tax credit. Also, taxpayers could use their first-year refundable credit amount for the succeeding four years, and theoretically take the entire refundable credit over a five-year period. The long-term unused minimum tax credit for any taxable year means the portion of the minimum tax credit attributable to the adjusted net minimum tax for taxable years before the 3rd taxable year immediately preceding the current tax year.

- **Example** – In 2013, John has a regular tax payable of $50,000, and a tentative minimum tax of $40,000, so his regular tax exceeds his tentative minimum tax by $10,000; therefore, he is eligible for a regular minimum tax credit of $10,000 (no other credits are available). John has a long-term unused minimum tax credit available of $500,000, so the minimum tax credit allowable for the 2013 tax year is $100,000 (20% X $500,000, which is greater than $10,000). The $10,000 credit – without regard to this provision – is nonrefundable under the regular AMT rules ($50,000 regular taxable income, less the tentative minimum tax of $40,000 computed under the AMT tax system), which reduces John's taxable income to $40,000. Therefore, the additional $90,000 of the credit – allowable by reason of this provision – is treated as a "refundable credit." Thus, John has an overpayment of $50,000 ($90,000 less $40,000) in 2013. The $50,000 overpayment of taxes is allowed as a refund or credit to John. The remaining $400,000 minimum tax credit is carried forward to future taxable years.

To claim the prior year minimum tax credit, including the refundable portion, taxpayers must complete Form 8801, "Credit for Prior Year Minimum Tax – Individuals, Estates, and Trusts." The additional (refundable) credit is limited to the lesser of $30 million or 6% of the AMT credit carry forwards generated in tax years beginning before 1/1/2006 that were not used in tax years ending before April 1, 2008. The minimum AMT credit allowed in a year is not less than the greater of the amount of the AMT refundable credit amount determined for the preceding year or 50% of the unused credit. **(See Below, "Credit for Prior Year Minimum Tax – Individuals, Estates, and Trusts")** www.irs.gov/pub/irs-pdf/f8801.pdf   www.irs.gov/pub/irs-pdf/i8801.pdf

Affordable Care Act (ACA) Premium Tax Credits

In accordance with the Affordable Care Act, premium tax credits are "refundable" tax credits that are only available to individuals eligible to purchase health insurance through the government insurance "Exchanges" (Marketplace). Individuals are generally eligible if they are ineligible for health insurance coverage through an employer or government insurance plan, such as Medicare Part A, and they are within certain income limits. **(See Chapter 24, "Premium Tax Credits")**

www.irs.gov/pub/irs-pdf/f8962.pdf   www.irs.gov/pub/irs-pdf/i8962.pdf

Non-Refundable Tax Credits:

Non-refundable personal tax credits are claimed in the following order: (1) foreign tax credit; (2) child and dependent care credit; (3) elderly and disabled credit; (4) adoption credit; (5) education credits; (6) savers credit; (7) child tax credit; (8) mortgage interest credit; (9) residential energy credits; (10) plug-in electric vehicle credits; (11) credit for prior year minimum tax; and (12) general business credits.

Foreign Tax Credit (Form 1116)

A taxpayer who pays income taxes to a foreign government on foreign source income that is subject to U.S. taxes can either: deduct those taxes as an itemized deduction; or take the foreign tax credit on Form 1116. The foreign tax credit cannot exceed the amount of U.S. tax liability on the foreign income. Therefore, if a taxpayer receives foreign sourced qualified dividends and/or capital gains (including long-term capital gains, unrecaptured Section 1250 gains, and/or Section 1231 gains) that are taxed in the U.S. at a reduced rate, the taxpayer must adjust the foreign source income that is reported on Form 1116, line 1a. Otherwise, the allowable foreign tax credit may be significantly overstated, which can trigger a substantial tax underpayment penalty. Also, interest expense must be apportioned between U.S. and foreign source income. **(See Chapter 12, "Foreign Source Income Taxes")**
www.irs.gov/pub/irs-pdf/f1116.pdf   www.irs.gov/pub/irs-pdf/i1116.pdf

The amount of foreign tax that qualifies for the credit is not necessarily the amount of tax withheld by the foreign country. If you are entitled to a reduced rate of foreign tax based on an income tax treaty between the U.S. and a foreign country, only that reduced tax qualifies for the credit. Also, if a foreign tax redetermination occurs, a redetermination of your U.S. tax liability is required in most situations. Foreign taxes that exceed the credit limitation can be carried back 2 years and forward 5 years. The credit is not allowable for taxes paid to countries the U.S. does not recognize. There is a separate AMT foreign tax credit. **(See Chapter 23, "Alternative Minimum Tax")**

Child and Dependent Care Credit (Form 2441)

The Child and Dependent Care Credit was made permanent as of Jan. 1, 2013. You can claim the credit on Form 2441 for expenses incurred to care for a qualified dependent child under age 13, or dependents of any age, including a spouse or a parent who lives with you for more than ½ of the year, who are disabled (physically or mentally incapable of self-care). To claim the credit, you need to have earned income during the year (this also applies to your spouse). However, it can include expenses allowing you to look for work, so you must be working or looking for work, but you still need to have earned income. And if you are married filing a joint return, both parents must be either gainfully employed or looking for work, but you can claim the credit if one parent is a full-time student or is incapacitated. If you claim the credit for care of a disabled person, you don't have to submit proof of disability with your tax return. But to safeguard your credit, should the IRS ask questions, you should get a certification from the attending physician regarding the nature and duration of the disability.

The maximum dependent care credit is determined on a sliding scale based on a taxpayer's adjusted gross income (AGI). If your AGI is below $15,000, you qualify for a credit of 35% of your dependent care expenses up to $3,000 for 1 dependent, which is a maximum credit of $1,050; or dependent care expenses up to $6,000 for 2 or more dependents, which is a maximum credit of $2,100. The percentage you qualify for falls by 1% for every $2,000 your AGI is over $15,000 until it reaches 20% based on an AGI of $43,000, but the rate is not reduced below 20%. **If your AGI is $43,000 or more, you qualify for a credit of 20% of your dependent care expenses up to $3,000 for 1 dependent, which is a maximum credit of $600; or dependent care expenses up to $6,000 for 2 or more dependents, which is a maximum credit of $1,200.**

Married persons must file jointly to claim the credit, unless they lived apart for the last 6 months of the year, in which case the custodial parent can claim the credit as head-of-household – a custodial parent can claim the credit even if he/she did not provide more than ½ of the cost of maintaining a household for a child. For example, a taxpayer who lived with a qualifying child in the home of another family member can still claim the credit. The credit goes to the custodial parent (parent with whom a dependent child resides the longest during year), even if the other parent claims the child as a dependent. If divorced, the non-custodial parent is not entitled to any credit even if the child resides with him/her for part of the year. **(See Chapter 3, "Head of Household"; "Marital Status and Divorce"; & "Dependency Exemptions")**

The name, address, taxpayer ID or Social Security number of the child care provider must be included on Form 2441, unless it is an exempt organization in which case only the name and address must be shown. The care-taker can be a relative that you pay for the care as long as it is not your spouse; a parent of the child being cared for; one of your dependents; or your own child age 18 or younger regardless of whether he or she is your dependent. If you pay someone to come to your home to care for your dependent, they may be considered a "household employee," and as such, you may be required give them a Form W-2 and withhold payroll taxes from their wages and pay federal unemployment taxes (FUTA). **(See Chapter 2, "Domestic Workers")**

Kindergarten or higher-grade tuition costs don't count as child care expenses, but if taxpayers pay other child care expenses before or after full or half-day kindergarten or elementary school sessions, those expenses are eligible for the credit, and the cost of preschool qualifies for the credit. Expenses incurred for summer day camps and similar programs (soccer and computer camps) qualify for the credit, but expenses for summer school and tutoring programs do not qualify. If a dependent parent lives with you and requires continual care or you have an incapacitated spouse, you can claim the credit based on the cost of the medical care provided to them. However, the medical costs or care costs claimed for the dependent parent or incapacitated spouse can't also be claimed as medical expenses for itemized deductions, which means you may not reach the 7 ½ % requirement for claiming medical expenses for itemized deduction purposes. You have to do the math to see which option is better for you.

If a taxpayer receives "dependent care benefits" under an employer provided dependent care assistance plan such as a Dependent Care flexible spending account (FSA), the amount of employer paid benefits are shown in Box 10 of Form W-2. A taxpayer will owe taxes on those benefits, unless they are used for dependent care expenses. A

taxpayer can only claim a credit for any amount paid for child care expenses that is more than the amount shown in Box 10 of Form W-2. For example, the tax credit applies to as much as $6,000 if you have two or more children under the age of 13; therefore, if the FSA pays $5,000, the difference of $1,000 would be eligible for the tax credit. **(See Chapter 8, "Employer Provided Tax-Free Benefits"); (See Chapter 9, "Flexible Spending Account (FSA)")**
www.irs.gov/pub/irs-pdf/f2441.pdf www.irs.gov/pub/irs-pdf/i2441.pdf

Elderly and Disabled Credit (Schedule R)

The Elderly and Disabled Credit is available to low income persons who are age 65 or older (you don't have to be disabled), or at any age if you are permanently and totally disabled. If you are under 65 and are totally and permanently disabled, you must receive taxable disability income during the year, and you must obtain a physician's certification stating that you cannot engage in gainful activity because of your mental or physical condition and that the condition has lasted, or is expected to last, continuously for 12 months or more or that the condition is expected to result in death. Married persons must file jointly to claim the credit unless they lived apart for the whole year. The credit is computed on Schedule R and reported on Form 1040. **(See Chapter 5, "Disability Income"; & "Social Security Disability Benefits")**

The Elderly and Disabled Credit ranges from $3,750 to $7,500, depending on your income and status. You "do not qualify" for the credit if you are: (1) single, head of household or a qualifying widow(er) with a dependent child, and your adjusted gross income (AGI) is equal to or more than $17,500 and your nontaxable Social Security benefits and other nontaxable pensions are equal to or more than $5,000; (2) married filing jointly, both spouses qualify, and your AGI is equal to or more than $25,000 and your nontaxable Social Security benefits and other nontaxable pensions are equal to or more than $7,500; (3) married filing jointly, one spouse qualifies, and your AGI is equal to or more than $20,000 and your nontaxable Social Security benefits and other nontaxable pensions are equal to or more than $5,000; (4) married filing separately and lived apart for the whole year and your AGI is equal to or more than $12,500 and your nontaxable Social Security benefits and other nontaxable pensions are equal to or more than $3,750.
www.irs.gov/pub/irs-pdf/f1040sr.pdf www.irs.gov/pub/irs-pdf/i1040sr.pdf

Adoption Credit (Form 8839)

The adoption tax credit is available for expenses of adopting a child under 18, but there is an exception to this rule for "Special Needs" children. The maximum credit for qualified adoption expenses in 2018 is $13,810. For a special needs adoption, the full $13,810 credit is allowable, even if it costs less. The adoption credit was made permanent as of Jan. 1, 2013. Form 8839, "Qualified Adoption Expenses," is used to claim the credit, and the taxpayer has to attach certain documents to the tax return, which means that the tax return cannot be e-filed. Documentation of qualified adoption expenses, including any adoption decree or court order, should be retained with copies of the tax return. The credit begins to phase-out for taxpayers with modified adjusted gross incomes (MAGI) of $207,140 in 2018, and completely phases-out for taxpayers with MAGIs of $247,140. **(See Chapter 8, "Employer Provided Tax-Free Benefits")**
www.irs.gov/pub/irs-pdf/f8839.pdf www.irs.gov/pub/irs-pdf/i8839.pdf

For domestic adoptions (children who are U.S. citizens), you may be able to claim the credit even if the adoption is not finalized, but usually the credit is allowed in the year the adoption becomes final even if the expenses are paid in the prior year. The credit is allowed in the year after the adoption if the expenses occur then. If the adoption is unsuccessful, the credit is allowed in the next tax year (you can still get the credit if the adoption is unsuccessful). For foreign adoptions, the credit is allowed in the year the adoption becomes final.

Allowable expenses include adoption fees, court costs, attorney fees, travel expenses (including amounts spent for meals and lodging while away from home), and certain other expenses directly related to legal adoption of an eligible child. You calculate qualified expenses by adding up all the expenses, then subtracting any amounts reimbursed or paid for by your employer, government agency or other organization. Even though the credit is not refundable, you have six years (the year you first claim the credit plus five additional years) to use the credit.

- "Special needs" children means hard to place, not necessarily a disability or medical condition. Often these children are older, waiting to be adopted with brothers or sisters, or have a disability. Another qualification is that a State has determined that the child cannot or should not be returned to the birth parents' home and that the child will not be adopted unless assistance is provided to the adoptive parents.
- As a result of the ruling that married same-sex couples are recognized as married for federal income tax purposes, couples in which one same-sex spouse wishes to adopt the other spouse's child lose out on the Adoption Tax Credit, because the credit isn't available when adopting a spouse's child.
- Generally, if you are married, you must file a joint return to claim the credit. A married person, as well as a single person, may be eligible to file as head-of-household under certain circumstances and claim the credit.
- If your adopted child does not have a Social Security number, you must apply for an Adoption Tax ID Number (ATIN) to begin claiming your adopted child as a dependent. You cannot get the Earned Income Tax Credit (EITC) using the adopted child as a qualifying child until the child has a Social Security number (SSN). However, after receiving the SSN for the child, you can file an amended return claiming the EITC for the qualifying adopted child. **(See Above, "Earned Income Credit")**

www.irs.gov/pub/irs-pdf/f8839.pdf www.irs.gov/pub/irs-pdf/i8839.pdf

Education Credits (Form 8863)
Education credits can be claimed for the taxpayer, spouse, and dependents on Form 8863. Taxpayers can't claim the education credits unless they have either a Social Security number or an Individual Tax Identification number (ITIN), and students for whom the education credits are claimed must have a Social Security number or an ITIN. A person claiming a student as a dependent can claim the credit, not the student. If a third person pays the expenses, the student can claim the credit if the student is not claimed as a dependent, but if the student is a dependent, the person claiming the student as a dependent can claim the credit, i.e. if a student's grandparents pay the expenses, the student's parents are the ones who get to claim the credit. Married persons must file jointly to claim the education credits, unless they lived apart for the last 6 months of the year, in which case the custodial parent can claim the credit as head-of-household. Tuition and related expenses are eligible for the credits, but not room and board. Related expenses include required text books and supplies. Student activity fees are included only if they must be paid to the educational institution as a condition of enrollment. Expenses related to sports, games, or hobbies are not eligible unless part of a degree program. "Course Materials" are added as eligible expenses by the American Opportunity Credit, which includes any other necessary expenses other than room and board. **(See Chapter 3, "Qualifying Child for the Dependency Exemption")**

www.irs.gov/pub/irs-pdf/f8863.pdf www.irs.gov/pub/irs-pdf/i8863.pdf

Allowable tuition and fees are reported on Form 1098-T by educational institutions. And, in accordance with the "Protecting Americans from Tax Hikes Act of 2015," Form 1098-T submitted by colleges and universities for academic periods beginning on or after January 1, 2016, should include the correct taxpayer identification number of the educational institution and should include only the payments actually received from students in the calendar year. In 2017 and subsequent years, taxpayers can't claim the credit unless they have a Form 1098-T from the college or university with the correct taxpayer ID number. In 2015 and prior years, colleges and universities could either report amounts billed or payments received, which made the information confusing and sometimes incorrect. Penalties will be assessed on educational institutions that fail to provide a Form 1098-T with an accurate taxpayer ID number and the amount of payments for tuition, etc. actually received from students (not billed to students) in the 2018 tax year.
www.irs.gov/pub/irs-pdf/f1098t.pdf

The amount of any scholarships and grants received by students is also shown on Form 1098-T. Most scholarships and grants received by students are non-taxable, but some are taxable. A taxable scholarship or grant is one that is used to pay for room and board or other unallowable expenses, and should be shown as taxable unearned income on the student's tax return – allowing the parents, who are claiming the student as a dependent, to claim that amount in determining the amount of the education credits claimed by them. The Educations credits can't be taken for the tax-free earnings portion of any distributions from Coverdell savings accounts and 529 plans shown on Form 1099-Q that pay for any of the expenses shown on Form 1098-T. **(See Chapter 8, "Distributions from Coverdell Education Savings Accounts"; & "Distributions from Qualified Tuition Programs – 529 Plans")**

American Opportunity Tax Credit – The American Opportunity Tax Credit (AOTC) was made permanent by the "Protecting Americans from Tax Hikes Act of 2015." The maximum credit is $2,500 per year for each eligible student for "4 years" of higher education. In addition to tuition, fees, text books, etc., "Course Materials" are added as qualifying expenses for the American Opportunity Credit. Course Materials do not include computers unless the university requires the students to have one. A student must be in a degree program and at least a half (½) time student to qualify for the credit. Students who are still in high school and taking dual college credit courses are not eligible for the credit even if the 1098-T received from the college shows they are at least a ½ time student. The allowable credit is 100% of the first $2,000 of expenses, and 25% of the next $2,000 of expenses, which equals the total allowable credit of $2,500. 40% of the credit is refundable, but no portion is refundable if the taxpayer claiming the credit is a child to whom the "kiddie tax" may be applicable – any person under 19 or under 24 who is a full-time student providing less than ½ of their own support, who has a living parent, and does not file a joint return. The phase-outs for the credit are MAGI: $160,000 - $180,000 (married filing jointly), and $80,000 - $90,000 (single, head-of-household, or qualifying widow(er)) for the 2018 tax year. A taxpayer whose MAGI is greater than $90,000 (single) or $180,000 (married filing jointly) can't claim any of the credit. Those fling as "married filing separately" can't claim the credit. **(See Above, "40% of the American Opportunity Education Credit"); (See Chapter 3, "Kiddie Tax")**

An Individual is prohibited from retroactively claiming the American Opportunity Credit by amending a return (or filing an original return if he failed to file) for any prior year in which the individual or a student for whom the credit is claimed did not have either a Social Security number or an Individual Tax Identification number (ITIN).

Taxpayers who claim a false American Opportunity credit after 12/31/2015 can be barred from claiming the credit for up to 10 years if convicted of fraud, and for 2 years if found to have recklessly or intentionally disregarded the rules. Due diligence applies to tax preparers beginning in 2016. Form 8867, "Paid Preparer's Due Diligence Checklist," must be completed by tax preparers. A $500 penalty (adjusted for inflation in 2018) will apply to tax preparers who fail to comply with the due diligence requirements. Also, in addition to completing Form 8867, tax preparers must complete the American Opportunity Tax worksheet in Form 8863. Tax preparers must not know or have reason to know that any information used to determine eligibility for, and the amount of the credit is incorrect. Preparers must make reasonable inquiries if the information furnished by the taxpayer appears to be incorrect, inconsistent, or incomplete. Preparers must document inquiries and responses contemporaneously and retain the information for at least three years **(See Above, "Earned Income Credit"); (See Below, "Child Tax Credit")**

Life Time Learning Credit – The maximum Life Time Learning credit is $2,000 per year for all qualified students (20% of $10,000) in a family. A person is eligible for the credit even if enrolled in one course of higher education. The Life Time Learning Credit can be taken by anybody, at any age, if they are enrolled in a course of higher education. It is not limited to persons who already have a college degree or don't have a college degree, and does not require them to be trying to get a college degree. For 2018, the MAGI phase-outs for the credit are: $110,000 - $130,000 (married filing jointly), and $55,000 - $65,000 (single, head-of-household or qualifying widow(er)). Those fling as "married filing separately" can't claim the credit. **(See Chapter 3, "Married Filing Separately")**

Savers Credit (Form 8880)

The Savers Credit is for low-income taxpayers who have made elective contributions to tax deferred employee 401(k), 403(b), 457, SIMPLE IRA, and SEP IRA retirement plans, as well as to both traditional and Roth IRAs. You can take the credit regardless of the deductibility of the contributions, i.e. if your traditional IRA contributions are deductible, you can still take the Savers Credit if you qualify. The maximum Savers Credit you can claim is 50%, 20%, or 10% of the first $2,000 you contribute to a retirement account, and any unused credit can be carried forward. To be eligible for the credit a taxpayer must be at least age 18, not a full-time student, and not claimed as a dependent by someone else. The savers credit is reported on Form 8880, "Credit for Qualified Retirement Savings Contributions." In 2018, The MAGI limits for the Saver's Credit are: **(See Chapter 11, "IRA Contributions")**

- 50% Credit: Up to $38,001 (married filing jointly); Up to $19,000 (single and married filing separately); Up to $28,500 (head-of-household)
- 20% Credit: $38,001 - $41,000 (married filing jointly); $19,001 - $20,500 (single and married filing separately); $28,501 - $30,750 (head-of-household)
- 10% Credit: $41,001 - $63,000 (married filing jointly); $20,501 - $31,500 (single and married filing separately; $30,751 - $47,250 (head-of-household)
- 0% Credit: Over $63,000 (married filing jointly); Over $31,500 (single and married filing separately); Over $47,250 (head-of-household)

www.irs.gov/pub/irs-pdf/f8880.pdf

The Tax Cuts and Jobs Act (TCJA) allows the designated beneficiary of an ABLE account to claim the Savers Tax Credit in an amount equal to 10% to 50% of the annual contributions to his/her account based on the filing status and adjusted gross income (AGI) of the designated beneficiary, limited to a maximum credit of $1,000. This change is applicable for tax years 2018 – 2025. **(See Chapter 8, "Distributions from ABLE Accounts")**

Child Tax Credit

The Tax Cuts and Jobs Act (TCJA) doubled the Child Tax Credit to $2,000 for each "qualifying child" for tax years 2018 – 2025, with the refundable portion (Additional Child Tax Credit) equal to 15% of earned income greater than $2,500, up to a maximum of $1,400 per child in 2018. The child tax credit is $2,000 per qualifying child in 2018, but the credit is subject to cost of living increases in 2019 and subsequent years. In 2018, the credit is phased-out at $50 per $1,000 or fraction thereof on incomes over the following thresholds: $400,000 for married couples filing jointly and $200,000 for all others. Also, for tax years 2018 – 2025, the TCJA establishes a new $500 nonrefundable tax credit applicable to qualifying dependents, other than qualifying children, who are U.S. citizens or residents. To be eligible for the maximum $2,000 credit, a child must be issued a Social Security number by the due date of the tax return. In addition to other qualifying dependents, the $500 nonrefundable tax credit applies to a qualifying child under 17 who doesn't have a Social Security number by the due date of the tax return, e.g. a child who has an Individual Tax Identification number (ITIN) instead of a Social Security number is only eligible for the $500 nonrefundable tax credit. An individual cannot retroactively claim the child tax credit by amending a return (or filing an original return if he/she failed to file) for any prior year in which a qualifying child for whom the credit is claimed did not have a Social Security number (SSN) in that year but subsequently obtained a SSN in a future year. Unused credits in a year can be carried forward to future years if not refundable in the current year. The child tax credit is allowed against the Alternative Minimum Tax (AMT), and the refundable portion is not reduced by the AMT. **(See Above, "Additional Child Tax Credit"); (See Chapter 3, "Dependency Exemptions")**

The Child Tax Credit, including the refundable portion (Additional Child Tax Credit), was made permanent by the "Protecting Americans from Tax Hikes Act of 2015." A qualifying child includes your child, foster child, stepchild, grandchild, great-grandchild, brother, sister, stepbrother, stepsister, half-brother or sister, or a descendant of any of these who are under age 17 and lived with you for more than ½ the year. You cannot claim the child tax credit for qualifying children who are age 17 or older. For example, if you can claim your qualifying dependent son who is age 19 as a dependent, you can't claim the child tax credit for him. However, you can claim the $500 nonrefundable credit for other persons qualifying as dependents, such as your mother, father, etc. The person who can claim the child as a dependent is entitled to the child tax credit, e.g. a non-custodial parent who is authorized to claim a child as a dependent can claim the credit. However, individuals who don't have a Social Security number or an ITIN cannot claim the child tax credit. **(See Chapter 3, "Qualifying Child for the Dependency Exemption"; & "Other Persons Qualifying as Dependents")**

Taxpayers who claim a false Child Tax Credit/Additional Child Tax Credit after 12/31/2015 can be barred from claiming the credit for up to 10 years if convicted of fraud, and for 2 years if found to have recklessly or intentionally disregarded the rules. Due diligence applies to tax preparers beginning with 2016. A $500 penalty (adjusted for inflation) will apply to tax preparers who fail to comply with the due diligence requirements. Also, in addition to completing Form 8867, tax preparers must complete any required associated worksheets. Tax preparers must not know or have reason to know that any information used to determine eligibility for, and the amount of the credit is incorrect. Preparers must make reasonable inquiries if the information furnished by the taxpayer appears to be incorrect, inconsistent, or incomplete. Preparers must document inquiries and responses

contemporaneously and retain the information for at least three years **(See Above, "Earned Income Credit";** **"Additional Child Tax Credit"; & "Education Credits")**
www.irs.gov/pub/irs-pdf/f8867.pdf

Federal Disaster Loss Relief – On Sept. 29, 2017, the "Disaster Tax Relief and Airport and Airway Extension Act of 2017" was passed, which provides temporary tax relief to victims of Hurricanes Harvey, Irma, and Maria. The Act provides that, in case a "qualified taxpayer's" earned income, which includes the applicable dates shown below, is less than the taxpayer's earned income for the preceding tax year, then the taxpayer may elect, for purposes of the EITC and the Child Tax Credit, to substitute the earned income for the preceding year for the earned income for the current tax year in computing the EITC and the Child Tax Credit for the current year. For Hurricane Harvey, a "qualified taxpayer" is one whose principal place of abode on Aug. 23, 2017 was located either in the Hurricane Harvey disaster zone, or in the Hurricane Harvey disaster area and the individual was displaced from their principal place of abode by reason of Hurricane Harvey. Similar definitions apply for Hurricanes Irma (using a Sept. 4, 2017 date) and Hurricane Maria (using a Sept. 16, 2017 date). In the case of joint filers, the above election may apply if either spouse is a qualified individual. **(See Above," Earned Income Tax Credit"); (See Chapter 3, "Federal Disaster Loss Relief")**

Mortgage Interest Credit (Form 8396)
If you qualify, you can claim the Mortgage Interest Credit on Form 8396 each year for part of the home mortgage interest you pay each year on your home mortgage. You are eligible for the credit if you are issued a Mortgage Credit Certificate (MCC) through special programs established by state or local governments. Generally, MCCs are issued only in connection with a new mortgage for the purchase of a principal residence and are issued to lower-income individuals to help them afford a home. A qualified home buyer with a MCC is eligible to write off a portion of the annual interest paid on a home mortgage as a special tax credit. While all home owners can claim an itemized deduction for mortgage interest, a taxpayer can go a step further with a MCC. MCC reduces tax liability dollar-for-dollar by a percentage of the mortgage interest paid. The MCC will show the percentage rate to be used to figure your credit. It will also show the certified indebtedness amount and only the interest on that amount will qualify for the credit.

The credit is determined by multiplying the percentage rate (shown on the MCC) by the amount of home mortgage interest paid by you.
- **Example** – The MCC specifies a percentage rate of 15%. So, if you (the taxpayer) pays $4,000 in mortgage interest for the year, and your mortgage loan is equal to or smaller than the certified indebtedness amount shown on the MCC, then you may claim a mortgage interest credit of $600 ($4,000 X 15%), and you can also claim an itemized mortgage interest deduction of $3,400 for the year ($4,000 - $600). **(See Chapter 12, "Home Mortgage Interest Deduction")**

If your mortgage loan amount is larger than the certified indebtedness amount shown on the MCC, you must figure the credit on only part of the interest you paid.
- **Example** – The MCC specifies a percentage rate of 15% and a certified indebtedness amount of $100,000. If your mortgage loan is $150,000, and you paid $7,500 in mortgage interest for the year, then you may claim a mortgage interest credit of $5,000 for the year ($100,000 divided by $150,000 = 66.67% X $7,500 = $5,000).

180

If the MCC specifies a percentage rate that exceeds 20%, then the maximum credit you are allowed cannot be more than $2,000 for the year. Unused credits can be carried forward to the next 3 years or until used, whichever comes first. The current year's credit is used first and then the subsequent years' credits are then used, beginning with the earliest next year. The amount of the credit computed on Form 8396 is shown on Form 1040. www.irs.gov/pub/irs-pdf/f8396.pdf

Nonbusiness Energy Property Credit (Form 5695)
The nonbusiness energy property credit was originally unavailable in 2017. But in February 2018, it was retroactively extended to the 2017 tax year by the Bipartisan Budget Act of 2018. However, it is not available in 2018. The credit is worth up to 10% of the amount paid for allowable energy-efficient home improvements to your principal residence (not a new home) up to a lifetime maximum of $500. The credit is from $50 to $500, but you can take advantage of the credit only if you did not take advantage of at least $500 of the $1,500 aggregate credit offered in 2009 and 2010, or you had not already taken advantage of credits in prior years (since 2005) of $500 or more. The credits are available for: home insulation; exterior doors; exterior windows and skylights; metal and certain asphalt roofs designed to reduce heat loss or gain; electric heat pumps; electric heat pump water heaters; central air conditioning systems; natural gas, propane or oil hot water heaters; stoves that use biomass fuel; natural gas, propane or oil furnaces; natural gas, propane or oil hot water boilers; and advanced main air-circulating fans for natural gas, propane or oil furnaces. Of the combined $500 lifetime allowable credit, there are limits on certain items: a maximum credit of $200 can be claimed for windows and skylights; a maximum credit of $150 can be claimed for water heaters and furnaces; a maximum credit of $300 can be claimed for biomass fuel stoves; and a maximum credit of $50 can be claimed for an advanced main air circulating fan.
www.irs.gov/pub/irs-pdf/f5695.pdf   www.irs.gov/pub/irs-pdf/i5695.pdf
www.congress.gov/115/bills/hr1892/BILLS-115hr1892enr.pdf

Residential Energy Property Credit (Form 5695) – The credit for solar panels and solar energy systems installed in your residence is available in 2017 through the 2019 tax year and then phases out and ends after 2021. But the rest of the credit was originally unavailable in 2017. But in February 2018, the credit for wind turbines, geothermal heat pumps, and fuel cell equipment was retroactively extended to match the availability of the credit for solar panels and solar energy systems (2017 through the 2019 tax year and phasing out through 2021). The credit is worth up to 30% of the total cost of installing certain renewable energy sources in your home and is not restricted to your primary residence (except for fuel cell equipment) and can be claimed for newly constructed homes. However, the home must be located in the United States. You can claim a credit of 30% of the total cost of solar panels and solar energy systems installed in your residence in 2018, and there is no upper limit on the amount of this credit. You can claim the credit for geothermal heat pumps, small wind turbines up to $4,000, and fuel cells in 2017 and 2018. The maximum credit that can be claimed for fuel cells is $500 for each 0.5 kilowatt of power capacity. If your credit is more than the tax you owe, you can carry forward the unused portion of the credit to next year's tax return. Following is the phaseout schedule for the credits available for solar panels and solar energy systems, geothermal heat pumps, wind turbines, and fuel cells:

- 2017 – 30% credit
- 2018 – 30% credit
- 2019 – 30% credit
- 2020 – 26% credit

- 2021 – 22% credit

Qualified Plug-in Electric Drive Motor Vehicle Credit (Form 8936)

Form 8936 allows you to claim a qualified plug-in electric vehicle tax credit for four-wheel, highway-legal cars and trucks that use rechargeable electric batteries. These vehicles are propelled to a significant extent by an electric motor that draws electricity from a battery that has a capacity of not less than 4 kilowatt hours and is capable of being recharged from an external source of electricity, and has a gross vehicle weight of less than 14,000 pounds. The credit is available for both battery-electric and plug-in hybrid passenger cars. The amount of the credit ranges from $2,500 to $7,500 based on the size of the car's battery pack. The minimum pack size is 4 kilowatt hours, and the scale runs from 4 to 16 kilowatt hours. Each additional kilowatt hour over 4 adds an additional $417 to the minimum $2,500 credit available for a vehicle. In general, you can rely on the vehicle manufacturer's certification that a specific vehicle qualifies for the credit and the amount of the allowable credit.

The credit is still available for the 2017 and 2018 tax years, because the phase-out of the credit is based on sales volumes and, therefore, the credit doesn't expire according to an arbitrary calendar date. The expiration date is separate for each manufacturer and comes only after an automaker sells 200,000 qualified vehicles. This is a process that can take several years, given present sales rates for plug-in electric cars. The credit begins to phase out for a manufacturer's vehicles over the one-year period beginning with the second calendar quarter after the calendar quarter in which at least 200,000 qualifying vehicles manufactured by each manufacturer have been sold for use in the U.S. (determined on a cumulative basis for sales after December 31, 2009). Qualifying vehicles are eligible for 50% of the credit in the first two quarters of the phase-out period, and 25% of the credit in the third or fourth quarters of the phase-out period. A vehicle used in a trade or business will be treated as a component of the General Business Credit. The personal use of such a vehicle will be treated as a non-refundable personal tax credit. www.irs.gov/pub/irs-pdf/f8936.pdf   www.irs.gov/pub/irs-pdf/i8936.pdf

Credit for Prior Year Minimum Tax – Individuals, Estates, and Trusts (Form 8801)

You can get a credit for prior year minimum tax based on the alternative minimum taxes (AMT) you had to pay in prior years. The amount of this credit is calculated on Form 8801, "Credit for Prior Year Minimum Tax." The credit is based on tax items that result in "timing differences," between what is allowed by the regular tax system and what is allowed by the alternative minimum tax system, which generates available credits in future years when you do not owe any alternative minimum taxes. Two familiar items that create timing differences between the two tax systems are: depreciation differences between the two tax systems, and the phantom income from exercising incentive stock options (ISOs). AMT credits can only be used in years when your regular tax liability exceeds the "Tentative Minimum Tax" for the year.

There are two ways to claim the prior year minimum tax credit: the "regular credit," which is discussed here, and the "refundable credit" (See above). The first step in determining the amount of your regular credit is to find out how much of your AMT liability from a prior year is eligible for the credit. In order to do this, you have to find out how much of your AMT liability came from timing items, which are the only ones that can give rise to an AMT credit. Timing items are those accounted for in different tax years in the regular tax system and the AMT tax system. For example, the exercising of incentive stock options (ISOs), and the difference between 200% declining balance depreciation allowed in the regular tax system and 150% declining balance depreciation allowed in the AMT tax system. Prior year minimum tax credits can only be used in years when the regular tax liability exceeds the "Tentative Minimum Tax" for the year. The next step is to determine how much of the credit you can use in the current year. Under the regular credit rules, you can begin claiming the credit in the first year after you paid AMT if you are not subject to and are not paying the AMT in the next year – the amount of the credit you can use is limited to the difference between your regular tax liability and the tax calculated under the AMT tax rules. **(See Above, "Refundable AMT Credit")**

www.irs.gov/pub/irs-pdf/f8801.pdf   www.irs.gov/pub/irs-pdf/i8801.pdf

Non-Refundable Business Tax Credits:

The General Business Credit (Form 3800)

The General Business Credit is made up of many separate tax credits, and each separate credit is computed on its own unique IRS form. The general business credits are nonrefundable and are claimed after all other nonrefundable tax credits. If you can claim only one tax credit under the umbrella of the General Business Credit, then you do not have to complete Form 3800, "General Business Credit." However, if you qualify for more than one of the credits that make up the General Business Credit, you must complete Form 3800. Each separate credit is computed on its own particular form before completing Form 3800, and the combined credit is subject to a limitation based on your tax liability for the year. The general business credits are the sum of: (1) the general business credits carried forward to the current year; (2) the amount of the current year's general business credits; and (3) the general business credits carried back to the current year. All general business credits generated can offset both regular tax and AMT (including the R&D tax credit). General business credits are shown on Form 1040.

Following are some of the individual tax credits that make up the General Business Credit:
- Investment Credit, Form 3468 (this consists of the Qualifying Advanced Coal Project Credit; Qualifying Gasification Project Credit; Rehabilitation Credit, and Energy Credits);
- Work Opportunity Credit, Form 5884;
- Research & Development Credit, Form 6765;
- Orphan Drug Credit, Form 8820;
- Disabled Access Credit, Form 8826;
- Credit for Employer Differential Wage Payments, Form 8932
- Renewable Electricity, Refined Coal, and Indian Coal Production Credit, Form 8835;
- New Markets Credit, Form 8874;
- Credit for Small Employer Pension Plan Startup Costs, Form 8881;
- Credit for Employer-Provided Childcare Facilities and Services, Form 8882
- Energy Efficient Homebuilder Credit, Form 8908;
- Alternative Fuel Vehicle Refueling Property Credit, Form 8911;
- Low-Income Housing Credit, Form 8586
- Small Business Healthcare Tax Credit, Form 8941.

www.irs.gov/pub/irs-pdf/f3800.pdf   www.irs.gov/pub/irs-pdf/i3800.pdf

Investment Credit (Form 3468)

The Investment Credit includes: (1) the Qualifying Advanced Coal Project Credit; (2) the Qualifying Gasification Project Credit; (3) the Rehabilitation Credit; and (4) and the Energy Credits.

Qualifying Advanced Coal Project Credit – This credit is 20% of qualified investments in advanced coal projects using an integrated gasification combined cycle, and 15% of qualified investments in other certified qualifying advanced coal projects.

Qualifying Gasification Project Credit – This credit is 20% of qualified investments in qualifying gasification projects that employ gasification technology and the investment amount does not exceed $650 million. The credit is 30% where (1) $350 million of credits are allocated to qualifying projects ("Phase 1 gasification projects"), and (2) an additional $250 million of credits are to be allocated to qualifying projects that include equipment that separates and sequesters at least 75% of such project's total CO_2 emissions ("Phase II gasification projects").

Rehabilitation Credit – Beginning in 2018, the Tax Cuts and Jobs Act (TCJA) eliminates the 10% credit for qualified expenditures on buildings placed in service before 1936. The TCJA retains the 20% credit for qualified expenditures on certified historic structures but specifies that the credit has to be taken ratably over 5 years starting with the date the rehabilitated structure is placed in service. Before 2018, the entire credit could be taken in the year the structure was placed in service. A transition rule is also provided for certain buildings owned or leased at all times on and after January 1, 2018.

The rehabilitation credit applies to costs incurred for rehabilitation and reconstruction of certain buildings. Rehabilitation includes renovation, restoration, and reconstruction. It does not include enlargement or new construction. Also, the credit is not allowed for expenditures with respect to property that is considered to be tax-exempt use property. Before the change by the TCJA, the credit was 10% for buildings placed in service before 1936, and 20% for certified historic structures. The credit was temporally increased for property located in specific disaster areas: 13% for pre-1936 buildings and 26% for certified historic structures. The Increase applied to property located in disaster areas impacted by Hurricanes Katrina, Rita, and Wilma before January 1, 2012.

Energy Credits – The Energy Credits include the following:
- The credit for solar energy property is 30%. Equipment that uses fiber-optic distributed sunlight to illuminate the inside of a structure is solar energy property eligible for the 30% credit. In accordance with the "Protecting Americans from Tax Hikes Act of 2015," commercial and residential solar developers are able to claim an investment tax credit for 5 more years, though the credit gradually phases-down from 30% of qualifying costs to 10%.
- The credit that applies for qualified fuel-cell power plants is 30%.
- In accordance with the "Protecting Americans from Tax Hikes Act of 2015," the wind energy production credit is extended for 5 years – the credit is 100% in 2015 and 2016; 80% in 2017; 60% in 2018; and 40% in 2019.
- The credit that applies to qualified geothermal heat pump property is 10%.

www.irs.gov/pub/irs-pdf/f3468.pdf   www.irs.gov/pub/irs-pdf/i3468.pdf

Work Opportunity Tax Credit (WOTC) (Form 5884)

The work opportunity tax credit (WOTC) was extended for five years through 2019 by the "Protecting Americans from Tax Hikes Act of 2015," and beginning in 2016 is expanded to cover employers who hire "qualified long-term unemployed" individuals, defined as individuals who have been unemployed for 27 weeks or more and received unemployment benefits. The 40% credit for the qualified long-term unemployed is on the first $6,000 in wages paid and is applicable to those beginning work after 2015. Also, the WOTC is available to employers who hire and retain veterans and individuals from other target groups with significant impediments to employment. There is no limit on the number of individuals an employer can hire to qualify for the credit, and there are several steps involved in applying for the credit. The amount of credit employers can claim depends upon the target group, the wages paid to the individual hired in the first year of employment, and the number of hours the individual worked. There is also a maximum tax credit available. In 2017 and 2018, employers can hire eligible employees from the following target groups, other than the qualified long-term unemployed:

- Qualified Food Stamp (SNAP) recipients – Must be age 18 to 39 years old and reside within one of the federally designated Rural Renewal Counties (RCs) or Empowerment Zones (EZs).
- Designated Community Residents – Must be 18 to 39 years old and a member of a family with a place of abode in one of the federally designated Empowerment Zones (EZs), or Rural Renewal Counties (RCs).
- Vocational rehabilitation referred individuals – Must have a disability and have completed, or is in the process of completing rehabilitative services provided by a state-certified agency, an employment network under the Ticket to Work program, or the U.S. Department of Veterans Affairs.
- Ex-felons – Must have been convicted of a felony and hired not more than one year after their conviction or release from prison.
- Supplemental Security Income (SSI) recipients – Must be hired within 60 days of any month in which they were recipients of SSI benefits.
- Summer youth employees – Must be a 16 or 17-year old youth who resides in an Empowerment Zone and works for the employer between May 1 and September 15.
- Temporary assistance for needy families (TANF) recipients – A long-term TANF recipient must be a member of a family that has received TANF benefits for at least 18 consecutive or non-consecutive months and is hired after the family became ineligible for TANF payments during the past 2 years, because a federal or state law limited the maximum time those payments could be made. A short-term TANF recipient qualifies if the individual is a member of a family that received TANF benefits for any 9-month period and the individual is hired within 18 months after the family received the benefits.
- Unemployed veterans target groups: Group 1 – Must be a veteran who is a member of a family that received food stamps for at least a 3-month period and is hired within 15 months after the family received food stamps; Group 2 – Must be a disabled veteran entitled to compensation for a service-connected disability who is hired within one year of discharge from active duty or who has been unemployed for at least 6 months; and Group 3 – Must be a veteran who is hired after being unemployed for at least 4 weeks in the year or for at least 6 months in the year.

Except for unemployed veterans, summer youth employees, and TANF recipients, the credit program is available to employers for qualified wages paid to new employees who are members of the target groups. The maximum credit for the target groups is equal to 25% of first year wages of $6,000 when the employee works 120 hours = $1,500 maximum credit, or 40% of first year wages of $6,000 when the employee works 400 hours = $2,400 maximum credit.

For qualified summer youth employees, the maximum credit is 25% of first year wages of $3,000 when the employee works 120 hours = $750 maximum credit, or 40% of first year wages of $3,000 when the employee works 400 hours = $1,200 maximum credit.

TANF recipients are the only target group that has an available credit for 2 years. Maximum credit for the first year is 25% of first year wages of $10,000 when the employee works 120 hours = $2,500 maximum credit, or 40% of first year wages of $10,000 when the employee works 400 hours = $4,000 maximum credit. Maximum credit for the second year is 25% of second year wages of $10,000 when the employee works 120 hours = $2,500 maximum credit, or 50% of second year wages of $10,000 when the employee works 400 hours = $5,000 maximum credit. Total maximum credit = $9,000.

For unemployed veterans, employers can get a tax credit of up to $5,600 for hiring veterans who have been looking for a job for more than six months, as well as a $2,400 credit for veterans who have been unemployed for more than four weeks but less than 6 months. In addition, it offers a tax credit of up to $9,600 for hiring veterans with service-connected disabilities who have been looking for a job for more than six months, and $4,800 for all veterans with service-connected disabilities who qualified for food stamps. It also provides expanded training and education opportunities for all veterans.

Steps in Applying for the WOTC – For all target groups, qualified wages can be paid by more than one employer, i.e. Temp Agencies qualify. Wages can be paid to aliens who are here legally. Employers begin the process by completing IRS Form 8850, "Pre-Screening Notice and Certification Request for the Work Opportunity Tax Credit," to certify that the hiring is eligible for the credit. Form 8850 must be signed by both the employer and the eligible employee and must normally be submitted to the WOTC Coordinator within the applicable state workforce agency (not sent to the IRS) within 28 days of when the employee starts work. However, employers were granted more time to submit Form 8850 to the state agency for employees that started work from Jan. 1, 2015 to Aug. 31, 2016. In addition, Form 9061 or 9062 must be sent to the state agency with supporting documentation, including birth certificates, drivers' licenses, DD Forms 214, W-4's, parole officer's statements, etc. Then, the WOTC Coordinator within the State Workforce Agency will send the employer Form 9063 (employer cannot take advantage of the credit until they receive this Form). Employers must use IRS Form 5884 to claim the WOTC. The credit can be carried forward 20 years and back one year.
www.irs.gov/pub/irs-pdf/f5884.pdf   www.irs.gov/pub/irs-pdf/i5884.pdf   www.irs.gov/pub/irs-pdf/f8850.pdf
www.irs.gov/pub/irs-pdf/i8850.pdf   www.doleta.gov/business/incentives/opptax/ETA_Form_9061_05_31.pdf
https://wdr.doleta.gov/directives/attach/TEGL/TEGL_09-15_Attachment_3.pdf

Tax-exempt organizations can qualify for the WOTC against their share of payroll tax (FICA) they pay on wages to qualified veterans, provided the veterans are performing services related to the organizations' tax-exempt function. **(See Chapter 20, "Tax-Exempt Organizations")**

Research and Development (R&D) Tax Credit (Form 6765)
The R&D tax credit was made permanent by the "Protecting Americans from Tax Hikes Act of 2015," and is computed on Form 6765, "Credit for Increasing Research Activities." Eligible costs for the credit are "Qualified Research Expenditures," which include qualified wages (W-2), supplies, and contract costs. The net benefit from the R&D tax credit comes out to about 6.5% of all qualified costs, including wages, supplies, and 65% of contract

costs. Unused credits can be carried back one year and forward 20 years. A company getting the credit for the first time can use 4 years of payroll (current year + 3 prior years) to determine the amount of the credit. To qualify for the credit, a company's expenditures must pass each of four tests to be eligible for the credit: (1) technical uncertainty; (2) technological in nature; (3) a new or improved business component; and (4) a process of experimentation. The burden of proof in determining the amount of the R&D tax credit is on the company no matter which method is used. the R&D tax credit generally cannot be used to reduce tax liability below the amount of the taxpayer's tentative minimum tax. This restriction has been a disincentive for any taxpayer with AMT liability. There is an assumed blanket denial by the IRS, because computing the credit can often be a complex process. Therefore, a company will usually benefit from hiring an engineering company specializing in computing the R&D tax credit to compute and document the credit before claiming the credit.
www.irs.gov/pub/irs-pdf/f6765.pdf   www.irs.gov/pub/irs-pdf/i6765.pdf

In July 2014, the IRS issued final regulations that settle the question of whether the sale of a product resulting from otherwise qualifying research and experimental expenditures disqualifies those expenditures from getting the credit. The answer: if expenditures qualify as research or experimental expenditures, it no longer matters, for purposes of the deduction, whether the resulting product is ultimately sold or used in the taxpayer's trade or business. However, consulting firms that receive guaranteed payments generally cannot take the credit. In the Geosyntec Consultants case, the Court ruled that a consulting firm that did environmental studies and natural resource assessments for clients could not take the credit, because the company didn't bear any risk of loss if its research failed. The consulting contracts were on a cost-plus basis, which guaranteed payment to the consulting firm whether or not its research was a success.
http://media.ca11.uscourts.gov/opinions/pub/files/201411107.pdf

There has been continuing disagreement between taxpayers and the IRS for years over whether internal-use computer software qualifies for the credit. Finally, in January 2015, the IRS issued new proposed regulations that taxpayers can rely on for tax years ending on or after January 20, 2015. The proposed regulations provide a clear definition of internal-use software that qualifies for the credit, restricting the definition to software considered especially innovative that is developed for general and administrative purposes. The proposed regulations stipulate that general and administrative functions are limited to "financial management functions, human resource management functions, and support services functions." By narrowing the definition of internal-use software, the IRS is seeking to expand R&D credit eligibility for software development that implements, improves, or expands upon the research and experimentation process.

Calculating the R&D Credit for Controlled Groups – Effective as of April 3, 2015, the IRS issued new regulations that significantly simplify the calculation of the R&D credit for a controlled group. The new calculation can be used for tax years beginning after Dec. 31, 2011. The new regulations eliminate the requirement for a stand-alone credit calculation for each member of a controlled group, and calls for a single calculation of the credit at the group level, and the allocation of the group credit to each member of the controlled group in proportion to each member's Qualified Research Expenditures.

Qualified Small Businesses (QSB) – Beginning in 2016, small start-up firms, defined as qualified small businesses (QSBs), can elect to claim the credit against their payroll tax liability instead of their income tax liability. The payroll tax option is aimed at startups. A QSB is a corporation, including S-corporations, or a partnership that

187

has gross receipts of less than $5 million for the current year, and did not have gross receipts for any tax year preceding the 5-year period ending with the current tax year (year of the election). The credit that may be applied against the payroll tax is the lesser of: the research credit for the tax year; $250,000; or the amount of the total business credit for the tax year, including the research credit that may be carried forward to the tax year immediately after the election year.

For purposes of this provision, the definition of gross receipts adopted by the IRS surprisingly is more inclusive than the definition of gross receipts used by businesses that calculate the R&D credit using the regular R&D credit method. The definition Includes investment income, such as interest income, which may be a limitation to a startup company that had a bank account open for even a brief time before receiving sales derived in the ordinary course of business, perhaps before five years prior to the current tax year. Also, the investment income may cause total gross receipts to exceed the $5 million gross-receipts limitation in the current year even if sales derived in the ordinary course of business are less than $5 million. This inclusive definition of gross receipts seems counterintuitive to the advantageous addition of the payroll tax credit offset, which could be remedied by defining gross receipts more narrowly.

Eligible Small Businesses (ESB) – Eligible small businesses (ESBs) can ignore the tentative minimum tax limitation effective for credits generated beginning Jan. 1, 2016. An ESB is defined as a sole proprietorship, partnership, or a non-publicly traded corporation with average annual gross receipts for the three-year period preceding the tax year of the credit that do not exceed $50 million. For purposes of the gross receipts test, all members of a controlled group of corporations and all members of a group of businesses under common control are treated as a single taxpayer. The gross-receipts test must be met by both the entity and the partners of a partnership and the shareholders of a S-corporation.

Orphan Drug Credit (Form 8820)

Prior to 2018, the Orphan Drug Tax Credit provided a credit of 50% of clinical drug testing costs for drugs being tested under Section 505(i) of the Federal Food, Drug and Cosmetic Act. Under the Tax Cuts and Jobs Act (TCJA), the 50% credit is cut in half to 25% beginning in 2018. Taxpayers that claim the full 25% credit have to reduce the amount of any otherwise allowable deduction for the expenses regardless of limitations under the general business credit. Similarly, taxpayers that capitalize, rather than deduct, their expenses have to reduce the amount charged to a capital account. However, the TCJA gives taxpayers the option of taking a reduced credit that if elected allows them to avoid reducing otherwise allowable deductions or charges to their capital account. The election for the reduced credit for any tax year must be made no later than the time for filing the return for that year (including extensions). Once the reduced credit election is made, it is irrevocable.

The orphan drug credit provides an incentive for pharmaceutical companies to seek treatments and cures for rare diseases affecting Americans. Normally, companies may not be motivated to make a drug for a small population because sales may be insufficient to justify the research and development costs of creating the drug.
www.irs.gov/pub/irs-access/f8820_accessible.pdf

Disabled Access Credit (Form 8826)

If your sales for the prior year were less than $1 million or you had fewer than 30 employees, you may take a tax credit for improvements made to your business property to fulfill the requirements of the Americans for Disability Act. You can take a tax credit of 50% of your expenditures up to a maximum credit of $5,000.
www.irs.gov/pub/irs-pdf/f8826.pdf

Credit for Employer Differential Wage Payments (Form 8932)

Small employers with fewer than 50 employees who pay differential pay to reservists called to active duty can claim a tax credit equal to 20% of the differential wages up to $20,000 a year for each employee. The differential pay is treated as taxable wages subject to income tax withholding, but it is exempt from payroll taxes (FICA and FUTA). A qualified employee is a person who was employed by the employer for the 91-day period immediately preceding the period for which any differential wage payment is made. The credit applies to an employee performing services on active duty in the uniformed services for a period of more than 30 days. The credit was made permanent by the "Protecting Americans from Tax Hikes Act of 2015," and beginning in 2016, the credit applies to employers of any size, not just employers with 50 or fewer employees. **(See Chapter 2, "Payroll Tax")**
www.irs.gov/pub/irs-access/f8932_accessible.pdf

Renewable Electricity, Refined Coal, and Indian Coal Production Credit (Form 8835)

In 2016, the PATH Act removed the 9-year limitation for claiming the credit and allowed the credit to be claimed against the AMT. The 2018 inflation adjustment factor and reference prices are used in determining the availability of the credit for renewable electricity production and refined coal production under section 45. The 2018 inflation adjustment factor and reference prices apply to calendar year 2018 sales of kilowatt hours of electricity produced in the United States or a possession thereof from qualified energy resources and to 2018 sales of refined coal produced in the United States or a possession thereof. The inflation adjustment factor for calendar year 2018 for qualified energy resources and refined coal is 1.6072. Following are the credits available in 2018:

- The credit rate for wind, closed-loop biomass and geothermal facilities claiming the renewable electricity production credit is 2.4 cents per kilowatt hour in 2018. The reference price for electricity produced from wind is 4.85 cents per kilowatt hour. Because the 2018 reference price for electricity produced from wind (4.85 cents per kilowatt hour) does not exceed 8 cents multiplied by the inflation adjustment factor (1.6072), the phaseout of the credit provided in section 45(b)(1) does not apply to such electricity sold during calendar year 2018.
- The credit rate for open-loop biomass, landfill gas, trash, qualified hydropower and marine and hydrokinetic facilities is unchanged at 1.2 cents per kilowatt hour in 2018.
- The credit rate for refined coal production is $7.03 per ton on the sale of refined coal in 2018. The reference prices for fuel used as feedstock within the meaning of section 45(c)(7)(A) (relating to refined coal production) is $49.69 per ton for calendar year 2018. Because the 2018 reference price of fuel used as feedstock for refined coal ($49.69) does not exceed $87.16 (which is the $31.90 reference price of such fuel in 2002 multiplied by the inflation adjustment factor (1.6072) and 1.7), the phaseout of the credit provided in section 45(e)(8)(B) does not apply to refined coal sold during calendar year 2018.

For electricity produced from closed-loop biomass, open-loop biomass, geothermal energy, small irrigation power, municipal solid waste, qualified hydropower production, and marine and hydrokinetic renewable energy, the phaseout of the credit provided in section 45(b)(1) does not apply to such electricity sold during calendar year

2018. The reference prices for facilities producing electricity from closed-loop biomass, open-loop biomass, geothermal energy, small irrigation power, municipal solid waste, qualified hydropower production, and marine and hydrokinetic renewable energy have not been determined for calendar year 2018. www.irs.gov/pub/irs-access/f8835_accessible.pdf   www.irs.gov/pub/irs-pdf/i8835.pdf

New Markets Credit (NMTC) (Form 8874)

The NMTC was extended for five years through 2019 by the "Protecting Americans from Tax Hikes Act of 2015." $3.5 million is allocated to this credit each year from 2015 – 2019. The NMTC is designed to encourage investments, loans, or financial counseling for businesses and real estate projects in low-income communities. Under Code Sec. 45D, taxpayers may claim the credit by making an equity investment in a community development entity (CDE), which in turn will invest the funds in the low-income community. Both individuals and corporations can invest in a CDE. The investment must be acquired at its original issue, either directly or through an underwriter. The Treasury Department allocates credits to the CDEs. Taxpayers may claim a total credit of 39% of the original amount invested. The credit is claimed over seven years: 5% in the first three years, and 6% over the succeeding four years. Because the majority of investments have involved real estate, Treasury and the IRS have issued regulations to encourage investments, primarily as working capital and equipment loans, in businesses that are not involved in real estate. **(See Chapter 6, "Qualified Opportunity Zones")**
www.irs.gov/pub/irs-access/f8874_accessible.pdf   www.irs.gov/pub/irs-access/f8874a_accessible.pdf

Credit for Small Employer Pension Plan Startup Costs (Form 8881)

This credit applies to pension plan startup costs of a new qualified defined benefit or defined contribution plan (including a 401(k) plan, SIMPLE plan, or SEP). If you implement one of these plans in a tax year, you are entitled to a credit of up to $500 for startup expenses which can be claimed on Form 8881. **(See Chapter 12, "Contributions to Qualified Employee Retirement Plans")**
www.irs.gov/pub/irs-access/f8881_accessible.pdf

Credit for Employer-Provided Child Care Facilities and Services (Form 8882)

This credit applies to qualified expenses paid by an employer for employee childcare and childcare services. The credit is 25% of the child care expenditures made by an employer, limited to $150,000 of qualified expenditures. **(See Chapter 11, "Employer Provided Tax-Free Benefits")**
www.irs.gov/pub/irs-access/f8882_accessible.pdf

Energy Efficient Homebuilder Credit (Form 8908)

The Energy Efficient Homebuilder credit was originally unavailable in 2017, but in February 2018 the Bipartisan Budget Act of 2018 reinstated this credit for homes constructed in 2017. Any qualified homes constructed prior to January 1, 2018 are eligible for this credit. Homes constructed on or after January 1, 2018 are not eligible for the credit. Tax credits of up to $2,000 are provided to builders of all new energy-efficient homes, including manufactured homes constructed in accordance with the Federal Manufactured Homes Construction and Safety Standards. Initially scheduled to expire at the end of 2007, the tax credit was extended several times, and expired at the end of 2017.

Newly constructed homes qualify for a $2,000 credit if they are certified to reduce heating and cooling energy consumption by 50% relative to the International Energy Conservation Code (IECC) of 2006 and meet minimum

190

efficiency standards established by the Department of Energy. Building envelope component improvements must account for at least one-fifth of the reduction in energy consumption. Manufactured homes qualify for a $2,000 credit if they conform to Federal Manufactured Home Construction and Safety Standards and meet the energy savings requirements of site-built homes described above. Manufactured homes qualify for a $1,000 credit if they conform to Federal Manufactured Home Construction and Safety Standards and reduce energy consumption by 30% relative to IECC of 2006. In this case, building envelope component improvements must account for at least one-third of the reduction in energy consumption. Alternatively, manufactured homes can also qualify for a $1,000 credit if they meet ENERGY STAR Labeled Home requirements.
www.irs.gov/pub/irs-pdf/f8908.pdf

Alternative Fuel Vehicle Refueling Property Credit (Form 8911)

The Alternative Fuel Vehicle Refueling Property Credit was originally unavailable in 2017, because it was only extended through 2016 by the "Protecting Americans from Tax Hikes Act of 2015." But in February 2018, the Bipartisan Budget Act of 2018 extended the credit through December 31, 2017. However, unless it is extended again, it is not available in 2018. Taxpayers are allowed a 30% credit for the cost of installation of qualified alternative fuel vehicle refueling property, which includes commercial and retail refueling stations placed in service in 2017 – any fuel at least 85% of which consists of one or more of the following: ethanol, natural gas, compressed natural gas, liquified natural gas, liquefied petroleum gas, or hydrogen; any mixture which consists of two or more of the following: biodiesel, diesel fuel, or kerosene and at least 20% of the volume of which consists of biodiesel determined without regard to any kerosene in such mixture; or electricity.
www.irs.gov/pub/irs-pdf/f8911.pdf   www.irs.gov/pub/irs-pdf/i8911.pdf

Low-Income Housing Credit (Form 8586)

The Low-Income Housing Credit is designed to encourage private sector investment in the new construction, acquisition, and rehabilitation of rental housing affordable to low-income households. It offers a dollar-for-dollar reduction in a taxpayer's income tax liability in return for making a long-term investment in affordable rental housing. State agencies award Housing Credits to developers, who then sell the Credits to private investors in exchange for funding for the construction and rehabilitation of affordable housing. These funds allow developers to borrow less money and pass through the savings in lower rents for low-income tenants. Investors, in turn, receive a 10-year tax credit based on the cost of constructing or rehabilitating apartments that cannot be rented to anyone whose income exceeds 60 percent of area median income.

The two components of the program are the "9 Percent Credit" and the "4 Percent Credit." Each state's 9% Housing Credit allocation is subject to a volume cap based on its population that limits the availability of the Credit in each state. In 2018, the state Credit cap is $2.70 times the state's population, with a state minimum of $3,105,000. Volume cap figures are published by the IRS on an annual basis. The 4% component of the program can only be triggered by the use of tax-exempt private activity multifamily Housing Bonds. Housing Bonds and the 4% Housing Credit finance approximately 50% of Housing Credit rental homes every year. Because multifamily Housing Bonds are limited by the Private Activity Bond volume cap, the 4% Credit is not subject to the Housing Credit volume cap. Not only do Housing Bonds make possible the production of substantial numbers of new Housing Credit properties, but they are essential to state efforts to preserve affordable housing.

Affordable Care Act – Small Business Healthcare Tax Credit (Form 8941)

In accordance with the Affordable Care Act, the small Business Healthcare Tax Credit is 50% of all health insurance premiums paid by small employers on behalf of employees (35% for small tax-exempt organizations). In 2018, small employers with up to 10 full-time or full-time equivalent (FTE) employees and average annual wages of $25,900 or less can receive the maximum credit. The credit is reduced on a sliding scale for small employers with from 11 to 25 FTE employees and annual wages from $25,900 to $51,800, and is phased out completely for businesses with more than 25 FTE employees or average annual wages in excess of $51,800. **(See Chapter 24, "Small Business Healthcare Tax Credit")**

www.irs.gov/pub/irs-pdf/f8941.pdf   www.irs.gov/pub/irs-pdf/i8941.pdf

Credit for Employer Social Security and Medicare Taxes Paid on Certain Employee Tips (Form 8846)

This credit is generally equal to an employer's portion of Social Security and Medicare taxes paid on tips received by employees of food and beverage establishments where tipping is customary. The credit applies regardless of whether the food is consumed on or off the business premises. **(See Chapter 4, "Tips")**

www.irs.gov/pub/irs-access/f8846_accessible.pdf

Employee Retention Tax Credit for Employers Affected by Hurricanes Harvey, Irma and Maria (Form 5884a)

On Sept. 29, 2017, the "Disaster Tax Relief and Airport and Airway Extension Act of 2017" was passed, which provides temporary tax relief to victims of Hurricanes Harvey, Irma, and Maria. The Act provides a new "employee retention credit" for "eligible employers" affected by Hurricanes Harvey, Irma, and Maria. Eligible employers are generally defined as employers that conducted an active trade or business in a disaster zone as of a specified date (for Hurricane Harvey, Aug. 23, 2017; Irma, Sept. 4, 2017; and Maria, Sept. 16, 2017), and the active trade or business on any day between the specified dates and Jan. 1, 2018, were rendered inoperable as a result of damage sustained by the hurricanes. In general, the credit is equals to 40% of up to $6,000 of "qualified wages" with respect to each "eligible employee" of such employer for the tax year. Therefore, the maximum credit per employee is $2,400 ($6,000 × 40%).

- **Example** – Employer Y is an eligible employer in the Hurricane Harvey disaster zone. Y has two eligible employees, A and B, to whom Y pays qualified wages of $4,000 and $6,000 respectively. Y is entitled to a total credit of $4,000; $1,600 for the wages paid to A ($4,000 × 40%) and $2,400 for the wages paid to B ($6,000 × 40%).

An eligible employee with respect to an eligible employer is one whose principal place of employment with the employer was in the Hurricane Harvey, Irma, or Maria disaster zones. Qualified wages are wages paid or incurred by an eligible employer to an eligible employee on any day after the specified dates (See above) and before Jan. 1, 2018. An employee cannot be taken into account more than one time for purposes of the employee retention tax credit. So, for instance, if an employee is an eligible employee of an employer with respect to Hurricane Harvey for purposes of the credit, the employee cannot also be an eligible employee with respect to Hurricane Irma or Hurricane Maria. An eligible employee cannot be "related" to an employer. **(See Chapter 3, "Federal Disaster Loss Relief")**

www.irs.gov/pub/irs-pdf/f5884a.pdf   www.irs.gov/pub/irs-dft/i5884a--dft.pdf

Paid Family and Medical Leave Credit

The Tax Cuts and Jobs Act (TCJA) adds a new credit to the general business credit that is available to employers with a written family and medical leave policy for full and part time employees who are on family and medical leave. The credit is temporary – available only for employer years beginning in 2018 and 2019 and won't be available for employer tax years beginning in 2020 or later, unless extended by Congress. The credit is available to employers as long as the amount paid to employees on family and medical leave is at least 50% of their normal wages, and the payments are made in 2018 and 2019. Paid leave provided as vacation leave, personal leave, or other medical or sick leave is not considered family and medical leave.

For payments of 50% of normal wages, the credit is 12.5% of wages paid to employees while they are on leave. If the leave payment is more than 50% of normal wages, the credit is raised by .25% for each 1% by which the leave payment is more than 50% of normal wages. So, if the leave payment is 100% of normal wages, the credit is 25% of an employee's normal wages. The maximum leave payment allowed for any employee for any tax year is 12 weeks.

Employers must have a written policy in place allowing: (1) qualifying full-time employees at least 2 weeks of paid family and medical leave a year, and (2) less than full-time employees a pro-rated amount of family and medical leave. Qualifying employees are those who (1) have been employed by the employer for one year or more, and (2) in the preceding year, had compensation not above 60% of the compensation threshold for highly compensated employees under the qualified retirement plan rules. **(See Chapter 9, "Contributions to Qualified Employee Retirement Plans")**

Tax-Credit Bonds

Tax-credit bonds provide tax credits to investors to replace part of the portion of the interest they have to pay on the bonds. The subsidy or credits are generally determined by reference to the credit rate set by the Department of the Treasury. Qualified tax credit bonds have certain common general requirements, and include clean renewable energy bonds, new clean renewable energy bonds, qualified energy conservation bonds, qualified zone academy bonds, qualified school construction bonds, qualified forestry conservation bonds, and Build America Bonds. The TCJA repeals the authority to issue tax-credit bonds and direct-pay bonds after December 31, 2017, but the repeal does not affect the tax treatment of existing obligations.

The TCJA also repeals the election that allows an issuer of tax credit bonds to receive a payment in lieu of the holder receiving a credit and a provision that permits an eligible taxpayer that holds a qualified zone academy bond to claim a credit against taxable income.

Chapter 14 – Business Structures and Provisions

Operating and managing a trade or business requires knowledge of certain business principals, including: how to claim travel, vehicle, meals and entertainment expenses; depreciation and cost recovery; and how to carry on a business as a sole proprietorship, partnership, or corporation. **(See Chapter 15, "Travel and Entertainment Expenses"); (See Chapter 16, "Property Depreciation and Expensing")**

There are many factors in choosing the proper business structure for your enterprise, which includes income tax rates, Social Security and Medicare taxes, filing deadlines, and liability concerns. A sole proprietorship is a very inexpensive way to get a business started, and if you need to dissolve it, you can just walk away. If you have two or more owners it has to be a partnership instead of a sole proprietorship, unless it is a husband and wife team, and then it can be a sole proprietorship. For a partnership, it makes sense to have an operating agreement or a partnership agreement down on paper, even though it isn't required, rather than have the owners think or assume what their responsibilities are. With a sole proprietorship or a partnership there is no liability protection for the owners. If there are liability concerns, a Limited Liability Company (LLC) provides some legal protection for its members. Forming an LLC requires filing formation documents with the state where you reside. You can form a LLC with one person, or with two or more persons. A one-member LLC is taxed as a sole proprietorship, and a LLC with two or more members is taxed as a partnership, unless S-corporation status is applied for and attained from the IRS. An S-corporation is a pass-through entity that doesn't pay income taxes, and the member(s) don't have to pay self-employment taxes on their pro-rata share of S-corporation income. Thus, the primary benefit of applying for S-corporation status can be some savings on self-employment taxes. **(See Chapter 17, "Self-Employed/Independent Contractors"); (See Chapter 18, "Partnerships"); (See Chapter 19, "Corporations")**

The entity's tax structure shouldn't govern the business strategy. Single-owner LLCs (including a husband and wife team) are taxed as a sole proprietorship and multiple-owner LLCs are taxed as a partnership, so there are no tax consequences per se, unless S-corporation status is obtained through the IRS. However, some states may impose added taxes on LLCs in the form of franchise taxes, in addition to the state and local income taxes. In selecting an entity for your enterprise, you need to go through a decision analysis where you evaluate what the business goals are, who the owners are going to be, what kind of growth you expect, and other factors.

Business or Hobby

For tax purposes, a hobby is an activity that is "not engaged in for profit." If an individual, S-corporation, or partnership does not engage in an activity for profit, deductions for expenses related to the activity are limited to the income from the activity, i.e. you are not allowed to have a loss. This is commonly known as the "hobby loss limitation" and is aimed at activities primarily carried on as a sport, hobby, or recreational activity. To treat the activity as a business, the taxpayer must have a good faith expectation of making a profit. The burden is normally on the taxpayer to prove that an activity is a business, i.e. has a profit motive. However, a test whereby an activity may be presumed to be a business is when it shows a profit for any three years during a consecutive five-year period (two out of seven years for horse breeding and other horse-related activities) – the burden of proof normally shifts to the IRS when this can be demonstrated. If a taxpayer is questioned before this time frame has elapsed, he/she can file Form 5213, "Election to Postpone Determination of Whether an Activity is Engaged in for a Profit" within 60 days of receiving an IRS notice. Filing this form will delay determination of whether an activity is engaged in for profit until the end of the fourth year (sixth year for horses). However, filing this form also extends the statute of limitations for the activity, i.e. if the taxpayer fails to demonstrate that it is a business activity, the IRS can go back 5 years and disallow any prior losses, plus penalties. www.irs.gov/pub/irs-pdf/f5213.pdf

Hobby income is reported as "Other Income," on Form 1040, and is not subject to self-employment tax. In 2017 and prior years, hobby expenses were deductible as a miscellaneous itemized deduction subject to the 2% AGI floor, but only to the extent of income from the activity. Therefore, a loss was not allowed. In accordance with the Tax Cuts and Jobs Act (TCJA), the deduction for miscellaneous itemized deductions subject to the 2% of adjusted gross income (AGI) floor is eliminated for tax years 2018 – 2025. Therefore, a deduction for hobby expenses is no longer allowed in 2018. Some expenses that may be related to a hobby may be deductible anyway, such as mortgage interest and property taxes that are still deductible as itemized deductions. For entities such as limited partnerships, the hobby loss rule applies to tax shelters, which are investments structured to provide favorable tax treatment, and may be used to deny deductions to the partners or shareholders if the entity was set-up primarily to generate large tax losses and not to make a profit. **(See Chapter 12, "Hobby Expenses")**

In addition to the 3 out of 5 year rule to show a profit, the IRS has provided guidance on factors it will use to determine whether a business with a loss is a for-profit venture: (1) is there an intention to make a profit; (2) does the taxpayer depend on income from the activity, i.e. the fact that the taxpayer does not have substantial income or capital from other sources may indicate an activity is for profit; (3) did the losses occur in the start-up phase of the business; (4) has the taxpayer made a profit in similar activities in the past; (5) does the activity make a profit in some years; (6) does the taxpayer carry on the activity in a business-like manner (maintains books and records, separate checking account, etc.); (7) does the taxpayer have expertise or skills involved with the activity; and (8) how much time and effort is expended in the activity. In addition, elements of pleasure or recreation may indicate that the activity is a hobby, but not necessarily. In addition, other considerations should be given to the type of activity and whether it is one that happens to take more time than normal to turn a profit, particularly in a recession economy. Also, it is important to know whether a taxpayer acquired a loan to start up the business or for operating capital. Would anyone operating an activity as a hobby get into debt and personally guarantee a loan just to create a loss?

The business or hobby rule is a gray area as demonstrated by one case where the Tax Court ruled that a racehorse venture that was profitable in just 5 of 30 years was a business, not a hobby. A couple co-owned most of the horses with a professional horse trainer and shared income and expenses with the trainer during the 30 years. The venture had suffered a series of 16 consecutive annual losses during the 30 years, but the Tax Court said the activity wasn't a hobby and the losses were deductible, because the stable was run in a businesslike manner. The couple had made changes to the business plan to emphasize breeding, and they were able to demonstrate they expected the horses to appreciate in value over time. A series of injuries to some of their most promising racehorses was a set-back that had resulted in some of their losses. The fact that the couple was partnering with an "expert" was an important aspect in their favor.

- **Example** – In the Hess case, the Tax Court concluded that the taxpayer did not operate [his] Amway activity in a businesslike manner, and therefore, it was a hobby. The taxpayer reported seven consistent years of Schedule C losses from being a distributor of Amway products. During those seven years, the taxpayer did not seek any outside business advice besides that of his sponsoring distributor; nor was there any overall business plan, invoices to customers, or any financial statements produced for this activity.

The only documentation that the taxpayer maintained was receipts to substantiate expenses. Additionally, the taxpayer was not able to provide support for any of his "two to four distributors" he had added to his downline distributors (distributors recruited by the taxpayer) each year from 2005 to 2010. www.ustaxcourt.gov/UstclnOp/OpinionViewer.aspx?ID=10830

- **Example** – In the Delia case, the Tax Court ruled that the taxpayer's hair-braiding salon business was for profit, and therefore, it was a business. Despite little revenue and substantial expenses (mainly rent), along with a history of losses from 2004 to 2012, the court found that the taxpayer had a profit motive. The taxpayer had entered into a long-term lease for a booth in a shopping mall. The court found that it might have been "prudent for her to have exited this business before she did, but the long-term rental contract posed a serious obstacle." The taxpayer closed her business at the conclusion of the lease agreement. Additionally, the court found that there was no personal pleasure in operating the salon activity. "Although petitioner had a nostalgic fondness for hair braiding, sitting in an empty booth in a shopping mall is not as much fun as (say) riding horses." www.ustaxcourt.gov/ustcinop/opinionviewer.aspx?ID=10768

- **Example** – In the Zudak case, a taxpayer reported $250,000 in wages from his corporate job in 2013, but he also claimed a $32,000 loss for scheduling film festivals at colleges and universities. He didn't have a business plan, kept sloppy records and lacked practical experience in this business. Accordingly, the Tax Court ruled that it was a hobby, not a business. So, if you claim a large loss from an activity in the same tax year you report a high salary, you're likely to have a hard time proving that the activity is a business. http://ustaxcourt.gov/UstclnOp/OpinionViewer.aspx?ID=11293

Professional Blood Donor– In a recent decision, the Tax Court ruled that an individual whose blood type is rare AB negative, and who earned most of her income by selling her blood to a laboratory, is a business. She filed her tax return and claimed hefty business expense deductions for travel, medical insurance, special drugs and high-protein diet foods, and a depletion write-off for the loss of her blood's mineral content and the loss of her blood's ability to regenerate. The IRS argued that all of the deductions should be disallowed, because she didn't carry on a trade or business. In particular, the IRS maintained that the travel expenses she claimed to and from the laboratory were commuting expenses between work and home, and as such were nondeductible. However, the court for the most part sided with the taxpayer by stating that it was precisely for business reasons (to sale of her plasma) that she maintained a special diet and regularly traveled to the lab. The court approved the expenses she claimed for high-protein foods and diet supplements to maintain the quality of her plasma. The court also approved the deductions for home to lab travel. The court said that, "unique to this situation, the taxpayer was the container in which her product was transported to market. Had she been able to extract the plasma at home and transport it to the lab without her being present, such shipping expenses would have been deductible as selling expenses." However, the court disallowed her claim for medical insurance as a business expense, and her claim for a depletion deduction for the loss of her blood's mineral content.

Accounting Method Changes Under the Tax Cuts and Jobs Act (TCJA)
The TCJA includes several accounting method changes that are effective beginning in 2018 that involve the overall method of accounting for a business, and several changes that affect certain types of businesses. Most of the changes are favorable for businesses, and unlike most of the changes involving personal income taxes, the accounting method changes for businesses are permanent. Revenue Procedure 2018-40 outlines how eligible existing small business taxpayers can obtain automatic consent to change accounting methods that are now

permitted under the Tax Cuts and Jobs Act (TCJA). New businesses can simply start using the appropriate method under the TCJA in 2018. A 4-year adjustment period will be allowed if a change in accounting method increases taxable income.

www.irs.gov/pub/irs-pdf/f3115.pdf   www.irs.gov/pub/irs-pdf/i3115.pdf
www.irs.gov/pub/irs-drop/rp-18-40.pdf

Cash Method of Accounting – Effective for the 2018 tax year, the Tax Cuts and Jobs Act (TCJA) allows cash basis accounting for all businesses including C-corporations (except for "tax shelters") provided their average gross receipts (revenues) for the three preceding years are less than $25 million (indexed for inflation beginning in 2019). This is more favorable for businesses than the $5 million threshold that was in effect in 2017 and prior years. The same $25 million threshold also applies to partnerships with C-corporation partners. Control group rules will continue to apply when testing for average revenues for certain related entities. Under cash basis accounting, transactions for revenue and expenses are recorded when the corresponding cash is received or payments are made. Revenue is recognized when payments are received and expenses are recognized when they are paid. Thus, you record revenue only when a customer pays for a billed product or service, and you record a payable only when it is actually paid by the company.

Accrual Method of Accounting – Under the accrual basis of accounting, the "matching principle" governs the recognizing of income in the books for financial accounting purposes. The tax law is largely unconcerned with the matching principle. Therefore, for tax purposes, an accrual basis taxpayer is required to recognize income when "all events" have occurred to fix the taxpayer's right to the income and the amount can be determined with reasonable accuracy, which would be the earlier of three dates: the date on which the income is earned, due, or received. Expenses are recognized when it is established that the company owes the bill regardless of when it is actually paid. Under the Tax Cuts and Jobs Act (TCJA), effective for the 2018 tax year, accrual basis businesses are permitted to defer the reporting of advance payments to the next year, but income deferrals are prohibited beyond the year when the income is recognized on the applicable financial statements.

Inventory Accounting – Beginning in 2018, businesses with inventories that satisfy the $25 million revenue test can now use cash basis accounting and account for their inventories as non-incidental materials and supplies or use their financial accounting treatment for inventories (See above – cash method of accounting). In 2017 and prior years there were two exceptions to the accrual basis accounting requirement: (1) certain small business's average annual gross receipts (based on the prior 3 years) did not exceed $1 million; and (2) businesses in certain industries had annual gross receipts (based on the prior 3 tax years) did not exceed $10 million.

Under the TCJA, producers or resellers with average annual gross receipts of $25 million or less are exempt from the UNICAP rules (Revenue Code Section 263A) with respect to personal property acquired for resale. This exemption applies to both resellers and manufacturers. In 2017 and prior years, a business with $10 million or less in average annual gross receipts were exempt from the UNICAP rule with respect to property acquired for resale.
www.irs.gov/pub/irs-drop/rr-05-53.pdf

Long-Term Contract Accounting – The $25 million threshold applies when defining what a "small contractor" is for purposes of Internal Revenue Code 460 and the long-term contract accounting rules. Businesses that fall under the $25 million average are allowed to use the completed contract method for contracts entered

into during tax years beginning after December 31, 2017. The threshold before 2018 was $10 million. In Shea Homes v. Commissioner, the Ninth Circuit Court of Appeals ruled that developers using the completed contract method should report net income only on completion of the development and not for each home. However, the IRS will not follow that ruling outside of the Ninth Circuit.
www.gpo.gov/fdsys/granule/USCODE-2013-title26/USCODE-2013-title26-subtitleA-chap1-subchapE-partII-subpartB-sec460   www.irs.gov/pub/irs-utl/Construction_ATG.pdf

For accrual basis businesses, the completed contract method is used to recognize all of the **revenue** and **profits** associated with a project only after the project has been completed. This method is used when there is uncertainty about the collection of funds due from a customer under the terms of a contract. This method yields the same results as the percentage of completion method but only after a project has been completed. Prior to completion, this method does not yield any useful information for the reader of a company's financial statements. However, the delay in income recognition allows a business to defer the recognition of related income taxes.

Deferred Revenue/Advance payments – Generally revenue can only be deferred if it is deferred for financial statement purposes. This affects both one-year and two-year deferral items. Essentially, this codifies the IRS position taken in Revenue Procedure 2004-34 on the issue, meaning that for accrual basis businesses advance payments can only be deferred to the next year but, in any case, are prohibited from being deferred beyond the year when the income is shown on the applicable financial statements. Not all financial statements are applicable financial statements, so you will need to review that definition, which has changed from the definition included in Revenue Procedure 2004-34. This deferral change doesn't apply to long-term contract accounting or installment sale reporting.
www.irs.gov/pub/irs-drop/rp-04-34.pdf

Research and Development Expense Accounting – For tax years beginning after December 31, 2021, R&D expenses must be capitalized and amortized over 5 years. The Tax Cuts and Jobs Act (TCJA) specifies that research and experimental (R&E) expenditures and software development costs paid or incurred in tax years beginning after December 31, 2021, should be capitalized and amortized ratably over a 5-year period, beginning with the midpoint of the tax year in which the R&E expenditures are paid or incurred. Also, R&E expenditures paid or incurred outside of the United States should be capitalized and amortized ratably over a 15-year period after December 31, 2021. The "United States" includes Puerto Rico and other U.S. possessions. In the event of abandonment, retirement or disposal of property included in R&E expenditures, no immediate write-off of the unamortized portion is allowed, but instead such property must continue to be amortized over the remaining amortization period. Currently, in 2018, R&E expenditures and software development costs can be expensed in the year in which the expenses are incurred, or a company may elect to defer the expenses and deduct them ratably over a period of not less than 60 months. And, of course, the R&D tax credit is still available in 2018 and subsequent years. **(See Chapter 13, "Research and Development (R&D) Tax Credit")**

At-Risk Rules
The at-risk rules generally apply to trade or business activities engaged in for profit. The at-risk rules limit the deduction of losses to the taxpayer's investment in the activity (the amount the taxpayer could actually lose) and denies losses that exceed the taxpayer's investment. If a taxpayer is denied a loss because of the at-risk rules, the

loss may be carried over for deduction in subsequent tax years when the amount at-risk increases. The at-risk rules apply to individuals, individual partners of a partnership, individual shareholders of an S-corporation, estates, trusts, and certain closely held corporations (more than 50% of the value of outstanding stock is owned directly or indirectly by five or fewer individuals); but do not apply to widely held C-corporations, partnerships, and S-corporations at the entity level. Any loss that is disallowed in a tax year is carried over and treated as a deduction from the amount at risk in the same activity in the next year. If losses from an at-risk activity are allowed, those losses are subject to recapture in later years if the at-risk amount is reduced below zero.

The at-risk rules are applied to partners and S-corporation shareholders before the passive activity loss rules. A loss that is denied under the at-risk rules is not a passive loss. Form 6198, "At-Risk Limitations," is used to compute the deductible loss from an at-risk activity. Form 6198 must be filed if a taxpayer has a loss from any part of an activity covered by the at-risk rules if you are not at risk from some of the investment in the activity. The amount at risk includes:

- The amount of money contributed (whether capital or a loan);
- The adjusted basis (not fair market value) of property contributed to the activity;
- Amounts borrowed for use in the activity, if the taxpayer is personally liable for repayment or the taxpayer pledged property (other than property used in the activity) as security for the loan;
- Income from the activity (or from selling an interest in the activity) – all income ever received or made from the activity.

www.irs.gov/pub/irs-pdf/f6198.pdf   www.irs.gov/pub/irs-pdf/i6198.pdf

If a taxpayer has a loss or makes a withdrawal from a business, the loss or withdrawal reduces the amount at risk. Taxpayers are not at risk for personal services provided, such as accounting services. Even though they have a value, personal services are not treated as a capital contribution. Taxpayers are not at risk with respect to borrowed money from a person who also has an interest in the activity or from someone related to a person with an interest in the activity. A taxpayer is generally not considered at risk for amounts protected against loss through nonrecourse financing (nonrecourse financing is financing for which a taxpayer is not personally liable). However, the at-risk rules are more lenient for real estate activities, i.e. if a taxpayer engages in a real estate activity, the individual is also at risk for qualified nonrecourse financing for which there is no personal liability that is secured by real property used in the activity, and that is loaned by a government or "qualified person" (an unrelated person who is in the business of lending money and who was not the seller of the property). This exception does not apply to amounts borrowed from a person holding an interest in the activity or a person related to the interest-holder.

Recapture Rules – When the amount a taxpayer has at risk in a business, trade or activity is less than zero at the end of the year, a portion of previously allowed losses must be recaptured. The amount to be recaptured is the lesser of (1) the negative at-risk amount, or (2) the total amount of losses, deducted in all previous years after 1978, less any amounts previously added to the taxpayer's income from the activity due to prior allowed losses. The calculated recaptured amount is then added to the income from the activity for the year. If the taxpayer has a loss instead of income at the end of the year, the recaptured amount is not used to reduce the current year net loss from the activity, but instead is carried over and treated as a deduction in the next year.

Passive Activities

Unlike the at-risk rules, which focus on financial contributions to a trade or business, the passive activity loss rules focus on an individual's participation in a trade or business. The passive activity rules apply to: individuals, partners, S-corporation shareholders or members, and personal service and closely held corporations. The rules do not apply to partnerships, S-corporations, or widely held corporations. Active or non-passive participation is when taxpayers "materially" participate in a trade or business. Non-passive income also includes portfolio income which generally includes interest, dividends, royalties, and annuities, although portfolio income derived in the ordinary course of a passive trade or business may be passive income. Passive activity income does not include income from: personal services and covenants not to compete; a working interest in oil and gas property; and intangible property significantly created by the taxpayer. Passive income also does not include income from: "significant participation" rental activities; rental and sale of property developed by the taxpayer; rental of property to a trade or business in which the taxpayer materially participates; rental of non-depreciable property; and equity-financed lending activities and interests in pass-through entities that license intangible property if the taxpayer acquires the interest after the entity creates the property. Anti-abuse provisions prevent active and portfolio income from being converted into passive income and soaking up passive activity losses. **(See Chapter 5, "Portfolio Income"); (See Chapter 7, "Passive Income and Losses")**

Business Expenses

Business expenses are "use or lose." If you spend money on your business, you are required to take the expenses off against your business income in the applicable year, including sole proprietorships that are reported on Schedule C, Form 1040. And, of course, you should have documentation to prove all of your business expenses. When doing your personal income taxes, you have a choice of taking the standard deduction or itemized deductions, even if the itemized deductions are more. This is not the case for business income and deductions. The IRS expects a business to report all income and take all of the ordinary and necessary expenses paid in connection with the business. Business expenses shouldn't be manipulated for any reason, such as obtaining eligibility for the "Earned Income Tax Credit," as that can lead to trouble with the IRS. For personal taxes, the only interest expense that is deductible is mortgage interest. However, for business purposes all applicable interest expenses are deductible, such as interest paid on business loans and credit cards used for business purposes. **(See Chapter 12, "Home Mortgage Interest Deduction"); (See Chapter 13, "Earned Income Credit"); (See Chapter 17, "Self-Employed/Independent Contractors")**
www.irs.gov/pub/irs-pdf/f1040sc.pdf www.irs.gov/pub/irs-pdf/i1040sc.pdf

Start-up and Organizational Costs – In creating a trade or business, sole proprietorships, partnerships, LLCs, and corporations often have certain start-up and organizational costs that are incurred before activities of the trade or business actually begin. Start-up costs and organizational costs for a business had to be capitalized and amortized until 10/22/2004. However, for such expenditures incurred after 10/22/2004, a limited amount of such expenditures can be deducted in the year the business begins.

Sole proprietorships and single-member LLCs, including S-corporations, that are treated as disregarded entities are allowed to deduct up to $5,000 in start-up costs in the year the business begins and to amortize the remainder of the costs over 180 months (15 years) beginning in the month the active business begins. However, if the costs exceed $50,000, the $5,000 deduction is reduced dollar for dollar by the excess of the start-up costs over $50,000. Taxpayers may choose to elect to capitalize and amortize all of the start-up costs. Organizational costs for these entities that do not exceed $5,000 can be deducted in the year the business begins as de minimis expenses. If the organizational costs exceed $5,000 they must be capitalized and are not deductible until the dissolution or termination of the entity. However, if business operations never begin or are abandoned, any expenses incurred before the business is started are not deductible. **(See Chapter 17, "Self-Employed/Independent Contractors")**

- **Example** – Assume entity Y is a single member LLC that is a disregarded entity. Y begins business on June 1, 2014 and incurs $500 of legal expenses for preparation of articles of organization and $500 for state filing fees. Entity Y can deduct the $1,000 of organizational costs in the year the business begins because the costs fall below the $5,000 de minimis threshold.
- **Example** – Assume the same facts as above, except entity Y incurs $5,500 in legal expenses for articles of organization and $500 for state filing fees. In this case, no organizational costs are deductible or amortizable. Y must capitalize the $6,000 of organizational costs, and these costs would be deductible as a loss upon Y's dissolution or termination.

Partnerships and corporations, including S-corporations, can elect to deduct up to $5,000 in start-up costs and up to $5,000 in organizational costs in the year the business begins, but the deductible amount of the start-up costs are reduced dollar for dollar by the excess of the start-up costs over $50,000, and likewise, the deductible amount of organizational costs are reduced dollar for dollar by the excess over $50,000. The remainder of the start-up costs and organizational costs have to be amortized over a 180-month period (15 years) beginning with the month in which the active trade or business begins. Taxpayers may choose to elect to capitalize and amortize all of the start-up and organizational costs. However, if business operations never begin or are abandoned, any expenses incurred before the business is started are not deductible. **(See Chapter 28, "Partnerships"); (See Chapter 19, "Corporations")**

Start-up expenses are the costs of getting started in business before you actually begin doing business. Start-up costs include expenses for advertising, supplies, travel, communications, utilities, repairs, and employee wages. These expenses are often the same kinds of costs that can be deducted when they occur after you open for business. Start-up costs also include the costs of investigating a prospective business before you get it started. For example, start-up costs may include: a market review of potential business opportunities; an analysis of open office spaces, or labor potential in your community; marketing and advertising to open shop; salaries and wages for employees who are being trained plus their instructors; travel and other necessary costs for signing up prospective distributors, suppliers, or customers; and salaries and fees for executives and consultants or for other professional services. Start-up costs do not include deductible interest, taxes, or research and experimental costs.

Organizational costs include costs of legal services to organize a business, such as filing fees with the state to set up a limited liability company (LLC) or corporation; setting up accounting services; and drafting a corporation charter, partnership agreement, by-laws, and terms of stock certificates. Commissions paid in connection with issuing and marketing a partnership interest are considered "syndication" fees and are not deductible. NOTE: For 2010 (one year only), the Small Business Jobs Act raised the deduction limit for start-up costs (sole proprietors, but not corporations or partnerships) to $10,000 and increased the phase-out threshold to $60,000.

- Effective 9/6/2008, taxpayers are considered to have made the election to expense the costs in the year the business begins unless they clearly elect to capitalize the costs.
- Start-up and organizational expenses must be deducted in the year in which the business becomes active. Therefore, even if you do not have any income to report, you must file a tax return to preserve the tax

benefit of these amortizable and otherwise deductible expense items. If you don't report the expenses in the year they are incurred, you will be unable to deduct them against future income in most cases.

- If a taxpayer disposes of a trade or business before the end of the deduction period, any deferred expenses not yet deducted may be deducted to the extent the closing or disposition of the business results in a net operating loss (NOL).
- If you are purchasing an active trade or business, start-up costs include only investigative costs incurred in the course of a general search for or preliminary investigation of the business (costs that help you decide whether to purchase a business). Costs you incur in an attempt to purchase a specific business are capital expenses that you cannot amortize.

Business Interest Expense – Under the Tax Cuts and Jobs Act (TCJA), businesses will generally not be able to deduct business interest expenses, which is considered any interest paid or accrued on indebtedness properly allocable to a trade or business, exceeding the sum of: (1) business interest income; (2) 30% of the adjusted taxable income of the business (without deductions for interest, net operating loss, and for 2018 – 2021 depreciation, amortization and depletion); and (3) the floor-plan financing interest of the business. Indexing for inflation begins in 2019. Any disallowed business interest deduction can be carried forward indefinitely. For S-corporations, partnerships and limited liability corporations that are treated as partnerships for tax purposes, this limit is applied at the entity level rather than at the owner level. The new limitation is effective for tax years beginning after December 31, 2017, so it is effective for the 2018 tax year. The limitation applies to all businesses with average annual gross receipts of greater than $25 million for the prior three tax years. Floor plan financing is a type of short-term loan used by retailers to purchase high-cost inventory such as automobiles. These loans are generally secured by the inventory purchased as collateral and is commonly used in new and used car dealerships.

Businesses, such as utility companies, are not subject to the business interest limitation if they furnish or sell any of the following: electrical energy, water, or sewage disposal services; gas or steam through a local distribution system; or transportation of gas or steam by pipeline.

Taxpayers engaged in a real property business, including a real estate development, construction, rental, management, or brokerage business, among others, may elect to not have the interest limitation apply to their business, and the election is irrevocable. However, when businesses elect not to have the limitation apply, they are required to use the alternative depreciation system for their nonresidential real property, residential rental property, and qualified improvement property. **(See Chapter 16, "Residential and Nonresidential Real Property")**

Taxpayers engaged in the farming business may elect out of the interest limitation, and the election is irrevocable. However, an electing farm business is required to use the Alternative Depreciation System (ADS) – with its accompanying restriction on using bonus depreciation and longer depreciation recovery period – for any asset with a useful life of more than 10 years, including land improvements, barns, and other farm buildings in years beginning after 2017. **(See Chapter 16, "Farm Machinery and Equipment"); (See Chapter 17, "Farmers and Ranchers")**

- Computing the Business Interest Limitation – a taxpayer's deduction for net business interest is limited to 30% of adjusted taxable income, which is taxable income without taking into account:

  o Non-business income, like gains from the sale of assets held for investment

- Business interest expense or business interest income

- Net operating loss deductions

- The 20% qualified business income deduction (the TCJA includes new Code 199A which allows a deduction of 20% for certain pass-through income)

- Depreciation, amortization, or depletion

The limitation does not apply to investment interest. The adjustment for depreciation, amortization, or depletion applies only through 2021, so the limitation will be much more restrictive for capital-intensive businesses for tax years starting in 2022.

The deduction for floor plan interest — which is interest on debt incurred to finance a dealer's purchase of motor vehicle inventory for sale or lease — is not limited. However, most businesses that have floor plan financing will not be able to claim the new 100% bonus depreciation deduction with respect to any of their asset purchases.

- **Example** – Ace Company is a C corporation that has the following items of income and expense during the 2018 tax year:

Gross receipts	150
Interest income	5
Cost of goods sold	(100)
Interest expense	(30)
Depreciation	(10)

Taxable income before
interest limitation   15

Ace Company's interest expense deduction is computed as follows:

Taxable income before interest limitation	15
Add back: net interest expense	30
Add back: depreciation	10
Adjusted taxable income	55
Multiply by 30%	x30%
Business interest expense limitation	17

Therefore, Ace Company's deduction for net interest expense is limited to $17 in 2018, resulting in disallowance of $13 of interest expense ($30 – $17 = $13)

Enhanced Deduction of Food Inventory

The "Protecting Americans from Tax Hikes Act of 2015" makes permanent the "enhanced charitable deduction for donations of food inventory," which allows businesses to reduce their taxable income by providing qualifying food inventory to certain charitable organizations. The provision raises the cap to allow small businesses donating wholesome excess food inventory to take the same enhanced tax deduction as C-corporations have been permitted to do since 1976. This deduction is equal to the basis of the food contributed plus one half of the appreciation, not to exceed twice the basis. This amount is treated as a contribution and cost of goods sold is reduced by the basis of the food inventory contributed. **(See Chapter 12, "Non-Cash Contributions")**

Lobbying Expenses – The Tax Cuts and Jobs Act (TCJA) disallows the deduction for lobbying expenses at the local level after December 22, 2017 – lobbying for legislation before local government bodies (including Indian tribal governments). This exclusion conforms to what were already nondeductible lobbying and political expenditures at all other levels of government in 2017 and prior years. However, expenses associated with other common local government affairs, such as monitoring legislation, attempts to influence rules and regulations, and relationship building at the local government level, are considered deductible as ordinary and necessary business expenses.

Deduction for Penalties – The Tax Cuts and Jobs Act (TCJA) disallows the deduction of fines and penalties related to a violation of law paid to or at the direction of a government or governmental entity on or after December 22, 2017, except for the following 3 exceptions: amounts constituting restitution; certain court-ordered amounts; and penalties on taxes due.

Sexual Harassment – The Tax Cuts and Jobs Act (TCJA) disallows deductions related to any settlement, payout, or attorney fees related to sexual harassment or sexual abuse if such payments are subject to a nondisclosure agreement, effective on or after December 22, 2017.

Other Deductible Business Expenses – In general, business expenses are deductible if they are reasonable costs you would not have incurred if you didn't have your business. A list of common deductible business expenses are: **(See Chapter 12, "Miscellaneous Itemized Deductions Subject to the 2% AGI Floor"; & "Employee Business Expenses")**

- Wages, commissions, and salaries paid to employees. **(See Chapter 4, "Wages and Salaries")**
- Payroll taxes paid on behalf of employees. **(See Chapter 2, "Payroll Tax (FICA)")**
- Non-employee compensation for consultants and subcontractors. **(See Below, "Independent Contractors/Non-Employees"); (See Chapter 17, "Self-Employed/Independent Contractors")**
- Employee pensions and benefit programs.
- Employee fringe benefits.
- Taxes – business and personal property taxes on business assets.
- Insurance – liability, malpractice, workers compensation, and other business-related insurance.
- Accounting, consultation, and bookkeeping fees (including the cost of preparing the business Portion of tax returns).
- Furniture and equipment, including computers.
- Travel and entertainment expenses. **(See Chapter 15, "Travel and Entertainment Expenses")**

- Car and truck expenses, including parking and tolls. **(See Chapter 15, "Vehicle and Other Transportation Expenses"); (See Chapter 16, "Listed Property")**
- Rental of office space, equipment, and storage space.
- Home office expenses. **(See Chapter 12, "Employee Home Office Expenses"); (See Chapter 17, "Home Office Expenses")**
- Legal and professional dues and fees.
- Licenses and professional fees.
- Utilities.
- Continuing education, including seminars and conferences that increase your knowledge and skills.
- Maintenance and repairs.
- Office expenses and supplies.
- Postage, delivery, and freight costs.
- Advertising and promotion, including contributions that result in publicity for the business.
- Bank service charges and fees.
- Annual fees for credit cards used in your business. If your card is used partly for business and partly for personal expenses, pro-rate the fees accordingly.
- Internet and email expenses used for business.
- Subscriptions to professional journals, etc.
- Telephone expenses – you can deduct long distance business calls made from your home even if you don't qualify for an office-in-home. Monthly service charges are deductible for land lines only if you have more than one phone line in your home and it is used for business.
- Cell Phones – if you have a home phone line and need a cell phone for business, you can typically deduct 100% of your cell phone and the accompanying service, otherwise the cell phone expenses will have to be prorated.
- Uniforms and special work clothing.

Requirement to File Information Returns (Form 1099-MISC, etc.)

If you are in business and pay someone for services in the course of your business, and the payments total $600 or more during the year, you must issue a Form 1099-MISC to them. Since the $600 is cumulative, you must keep track of all payments to each service provider. Businesses are required to designate on their returns if they should have filed 1099s to back-up deductions and if they did. There are penalties if you don't issue the 1099s as required. Small businesses, including sole proprietorships, are required to send these information returns (Forms 1099-MISC) to the IRS by Feb. 28, but you can get an automatic 30-day extension by filing Form 8809. However, payees' copies of 1099s must be furnished to them by Jan. 31st. Exceptions to the 1099-MISC reporting requirement include: **(See Chapter 4, "Wages and Salaries")**

- Payments to corporations, except for legal services. For payments after 12/31/2011, businesses were supposed to be required to file a 1099 for all payments aggregating $600 or more in a calendar year to a single payee, including corporations. But the requirement for corporations was repealed.
- Payments for merchandise.
- Payments for telephone and similar services.
- Payments for rent to real estate agents.
- Payments for life insurance, etc.

- The requirement to issue Form 1099-MISC for the payment of services of $600 or more applies only to businesses. It does not apply to individuals – for example if you pay a painting contractor $1,200 to paint your house, you don't have to issue a Form 1099-MISC to the contractor.

www.irs.gov/pub/irs-pdf/f1099msc.pdf   www.irs.gov/pub/irs-pdf/i1099msc.pdf
www.irs.gov/pub/irs-pdf/f8809.pdf

Where payments are reported on Form 1099-MISC:

- Payments of $600 or more to individuals (not corporations) for cleaning office space (Box 7).
- Payments of $600 or more to individuals and exchanges of services between individuals (not corporations), excluding real estate agents, for rentals of office space, machines, etc. (Box 1).
- Payments of $600 or more to an attorney in connection with legal services – gross payments are reported in Box 14. But if payment is made in the course of a taxpayer's trade or business, it is reported in Box 7.
- Royalty Payments from oil and gas royalties, copyrights, trade names, trademarks, etc. of $10 or more to any other person (not corporations, tax-exempt entities, and government entities) – report gross amount before taxes and expenses (Box 2).
- Prizes and awards (Box 3).
- Physicians (Box 6).
- Payers who sell consumer products of $5,000 or more to any buyer (not corporations) on a commission basis for resale other than to a permanent retail establishment must check Box 9 (no dollar amount has to be shown).

Businesses should start keeping adequate records of payments so they are prepared to issue correct 1099s. They should give a Form W-9 to each service provider to which they make payments of $600 or more in order to obtain the name, address, and taxpayer identification numbers of service providers. Penalties for not filing 1099s range from $30 (first-tier) to $250 for intentional disregard of the requirement.
www.irs.gov/pub/irs-pdf/fw9.pdf

Form 1099-K, Merchant Card and Third-Party Payments – Form 1099-K, "Merchant Card and Third-Party Payments" is important if you are in the retail business, restaurant business, etc., and you accept payments with credit cards. It also applies to those selling products on internet sites like eBay and Amazon. Credit card companies are required to provide information about what a business was paid through them by credit or debit cards on Form 1099-K if gross payments exceed $20,000 for the year and when there are more than 200 transactions with the participating payee. If a business accepts credit cards and meets the above criteria, they are going to receive a 1099-K showing the amount of payments they received through charges on credit card(s). Most small businesses just report their net sales on their tax returns; so, by definition there is going to be a mismatch between what is reported on Form 1099-K and the tax returns. Nevertheless, it is a good idea for merchants to make sure that there is enough difference between the amount reported on Form 1099-K (credit card sales) and their total sales so that a reasonable amount of cash sales are included, considering the type of business.
www.irs.gov/pub/irs-pdf/f1099k.pdf   www.irs.gov/pub/irs-pdf/i1099k.pdf

The IRS has begun requiring more information reporting from credit and debit card providers and is using it to match the data it receives from tax returns to safeguard against tax fraud. In IRS Notice 1430, the IRS tells businesses that the name and taxpayer identification number (TIN) submitted by credit and debit card companies on Form 1099-K must match the IRS's other records for the business, i.e. if a payment card processor or third-party settlement organization submits a Form 1099-K with an incorrect TIN or name for you, the payments will be subject to backup withholding. The IRS notice says, "This means the payment card processor or third-party settlement organization will be required to withhold 28% from each payment to you beginning as early as September 2014. If you operate as a partnership or S-corporation, any monies withheld due to an incorrect name or TIN can only be claimed by the partners and shareholders on their individual income tax returns for their share of the withheld amounts. The monies are not refundable to the partnership or S-corporation."

Independent Contractors/ Non-Employees

Payments to non-employees are required to be reported on Form 1099-MISC if payments to any individual are $600 or more in a calendar year. Also, Form 1096 must be filed by the payers. There are deadlines and penalties for incorrect reporting. The following are exempt from reporting requirements for payments to non-employees: (1) reimbursements of expenses under an accountable plan, and (2) payments that are for services outside the U.S. to U.S. citizens, if it is reasonable to believe the amounts will be excluded from income as foreign earned income. **(See Chapter 2, "Payroll Tax (FICA)"); (See Chapter 9, "Foreign Earned Income Exclusion"); (See Chapter 15, "The Accountable Plan"); (See Chapter 17, "Self-Employment Tax")**

Employers who classify workers as independent contractors avoid paying payroll taxes (FICA), federal and state unemployment taxes (FUTA), minimum wages, overtime, worker's compensation, health benefits, 401(k) benefits, as well as income tax withholding. They also escape providing benefits such as vacation pay, sick pay, paid leave, and offering subsidized employee health benefits (complying with the Affordable Care Act). Moreover, workers may be motivated to be misclassified as independent contractors so they can be paid in cash, avoid withholding of taxes, and/or avoid proving immigration status. Workers who are hired in the U.S. have a duty to establish they are here legally. An employee must fill out Form I-9 to verify legal working status, while an independent contractor doesn't have that duty. Also, independent contractors have the ability to deduct certain business expenses that are not available to employees, as well as the ability to set up their own retirement plans. Of course, many workers want to be considered employees so they can get the benefits due employees, such as vacation pay, overtime pay and health insurance. The IRS, the DOL and the state workers' compensation board can object to the status of a worker.
www.uscis.gov/sites/default/files/USCIS/Verification/I-9%20Central/Form_I-9_Employee_Information_Sheet.pdf

There is no bright-line test as to whether a worker is an employee or an independent contractor, but it has been determined that 40.4% of the U.S. workforce is made up of contingent or on-demand workers, who are service providers without secure jobs, and are not considered employees. This not only includes workers who are truly independent contractors, but also agency temps; on-call workers (people called to work when needed); and standard part-time workers. This suggests that some of these people who are paid with a 1099-MISC, instead of a Form W-2 might actually be employees. Another study found that 15% of employers misclassified 3.4 million workers as independent contractors, costing the federal government $1.6 billion. Businesses often hire part-time, temporary, or seasonal workers and classify them as independent contractors when they are actually employees. **(See Above, "Requirement to File Information Returns")**

In making the determination whether a worker is an independent contractor, all factors that provide evidence of the degree of control and independence must be considered. The business relationship that exists with the person performing the services is important. He may be an independent contractor; a common-law employee; a statutory employee; or a statutory nonemployee:

- Independent contractor – payer has the right to control or direct only the result of the work and not the means and methods of accomplishing the result (example: worker performs a job for a set fee or based on invoices submitted instead of by the hour, and also does the same type of work for other payers). Reimbursement of business expenses is pursuant to a contract. A business should have an independent contractor complete a Form W-9. Independent contractors are required to pay self-employment taxes. www.irs.gov/pub/irs-pdf/fw9.pdf
- Common-Law Employee – payer should withhold FICA, pay FUTA, and issue a Form W-2 to the worker. Payer can control what will be done and how it will be done, even when employee has freedom of action. What matters is that employer has the right to control the details of how the services are performed. Employee receives training from the employer and follows a set program or format in performing the services.
- Statutory Employee – certain workers who are independent contractors under the common law rules should, nevertheless, be treated as employees by statute. These include traveling salespersons, insurance salespersons, and individuals who work at home ("home worker") on materials or goods supplied by the payer that must be returned to a person named by the payer if the payer furnishes specifications for the work to be done. Statutory employees are subject to payroll tax (FICA) and income tax withholding, but may report their expenses on Form 1040, Schedule C.
- Statutory Nonemployee – there are two categories: (1) direct sellers, and (2) licensed real estate agents, both of whom are treated as self-employed for federal income tax purposes and have a contract stating as such; therefore, they have to pay self-employment taxes.

Facts that provide evidence of the degree of control and independence fall into three categories: behavioral control, financial control, and the type of relationship of the parties. The IRS has developed 20 factors that are relevant in determining behavioral control, financial control, and the relationship of the parties: control of when, where, and how the worker performs services; training; integration into firm operations; requirement that services are personally performed; control over assistants; length of relationship; work schedule; number of service hours required; location of services; control over technique or sequence; reports to employer; payment method; work-related expenses; tools; work facilities; profit and loss; multiple employers; restrictions on customers and clients; termination of worker; and termination of relationship. A general rule is that "anyone who performs services for a payer (employer) is an employee if the employer can control what will be done and how it will be done." Contractor or employee? – Questions to ask: Does he/she work for someone else as well, does he/she come and go whenever they feel like it (set their own hours), does he/she have all of their own equipment, and does he/she obtain customers on their own?

New guidance issued by the Labor Department is a tougher interpretation of the classification rules for workers under the Fair Labor Standards Act. The new guidance states that contractors can be treated as employees if their work is integral to a firm's business, even if the work is done off-premises, and workers who supply their own tools won't necessarily be classified as contractors. Under the guidance, a permanent or indefinite working relationship suggests that workers are employees, and those who perform work for more than one company aren't necessarily contractors. These rules don't change the income tax standards for worker classification – the IRS will continue to use its standards. However, if the Labor Department tells The IRS that a company's workers are employees instead of contractors, the company may have a hard time convincing the IRS otherwise.

Some businesses automatically treat workers that have a business name and an employer identification number (EIN) as independent contractors, when they should actually be classified as employees. In the past, the IRS has inadvertently overlooked many of these situations in audits because the auditors commonly look for Forms 1099 issued to individuals with Social Security numbers. The worker's business name and EIN may disguise an employer-employee relationship.

Because of the implementation of the Affordable Care Act (ACA), businesses will have yet another reason to misclassify workers, because businesses with 50 or more full-time equivalent (FTE) employees will be required to provide health insurance to their employees or pay a substantial penalty. Therefore, the status of part-time workers could see more scrutiny by the IRS, because classifying workers as independent contractors instead of employees is quickly dispelled when evidence indicates that the work performed by them is substantially similar to the work performed by other workers that are classified as employees. Under the ACA, part-time employees and seasonal workers are included in the calculation of determining whether a business has 50 or more full time equivalent (FTE) employees, but independent contractors aren't included in the calculation. **(See Chapter 24, "Employer Mandate")**

If a person is a worker and receives a Form 1099-MISC from an employer but thinks he's not an independent contractor and should not have to pay self-employment tax because he was previously treated as an employee or is doing the same or similar work as co-workers who are treated as employees, then that person should file Form SS-8 "Determination of Worker Status for Purposes of Federal Taxes and Income Tax Withholding" with the IRS, which is the form to be filed with the IRS to have them determine whether a taxpayer is an employee or a contractor. Employers that do not withhold taxes from "employees" wages may be liable for not only the employer's share of employment taxes but also the worker's share, unless they can prove the worker reported and paid it. Contracts saying workers aren't employees have no tax effect, i.e. the IRS can still reclassify independent contractors as employees. If the IRS reclassifies an employer's independent contractors as employees, they can get some relief on back income taxes not withheld and payroll taxes owed if the misclassification was not intentional. However, if the IRS determines that the employer's conduct was willful, it can be hit with tax deficiencies exceeding 40% of reclassified salaries for the previous three years.
www.irs.gov/pub/irs-pdf/fss8.pdf

Safe Harbor – The safe harbor allows employers to classify certain workers as independent contractors even though they may be common-law employees. It provides that an individual who has not been treated as an employee will not be reclassified if: (1) the employer has consistently treated the worker as an independent contractor and had a reasonable basis for not treating the worker as an employee; (2) the employer did not treat any worker in a similar position as an employee for any prior period; and (3) the employer has filed all required tax returns, including any Form 1099 information returns (1099-MISCs, etc.), in a manner consistent with the worker not being an employee. The safe harbor rule governs employee status only with respect to payroll taxes, and not for other purposes. For example, employees who have been misclassified as independent contractors must be allowed to retroactively participate in a qualified retirement plan. This applies even if the worker has signed an agreement as to his status as an independent contractor and agreeing to forego all benefits. Businesses that don't qualify for this safe harbor relief are eligible for reduced penalties if the misclassification was unintentional.

Voluntary Classification Settlement Program (VCSP) – Under the IRS's VCSP, employers may voluntarily reclassify independent contractors as employees, which limits the resulting payroll taxes they have to pay for their most recent tax year and avoids related penalties and interest for prior years because there is no admission of guilt (the employer is not making a representation as to the proper status of the workers for prior years). To participate in the VCSP, employers must submit an application and agree to prospectively treat their workers or a class or group of workers as employees for payroll tax purposes in future tax periods. In return, employers will pay 10% of the employment tax liability otherwise due for the most recent tax year, which will not be subject to interest or penalties. In addition, the IRS will not conduct an employment tax audit with respect to worker classification for prior years. To be eligible for the Program, a taxpayer can be under an IRS audit other than an employment tax audit. However, a taxpayer is not eligible to participate in the Program if he/she is contesting in court the classification of the class or classes of workers from a previous audit by the IRS or the Department of Labor. Employers whose worker classification has been previously audited must have complied with the results of the audit. Also, employers must have consistently treated workers as nonemployees for the previous three years. Employers can use Form 8952 to apply for the VCSP at least 60 days before they want to begin treating the workers as employees.
www.irs.gov/pub/irs-pdf/f8952.pdf www.irs.gov/pub/irs-pdf/i8952.pdf

The VCSP has been a great success for the IRS – employers that have in the past consistently treated workers as independent contractors have to pay a modest fine, and in turn receive audit protection for prior years, and afterward the workers are treated as employees, get W-2s instead of 1099s and become tax compliant. **(See Chapter 4, "Earned Income"; & "Wages and Salaries")**

Statutory Employees
Statutory employees are employees that usually have payroll taxes withheld from wages, but can deduct expenses on Schedule C instead of Form 2106 (Form W-2 will designate the individual as a statutory employee). In VanZant v. Commissioner, the Tax Court ruled that Laverne VanZant, who received a 1099-MISC from her employer, was a statutory employee and did not have to pay self-employment tax. See Tax Bulletin dated 12/2/2007. Under Code Section 3121(d)(3)(C), a statutory employee includes any individual, other than an officer of a corporation or a common-law employee, who performs services for pay for any person "as a home worker" performing work, according to specifications furnished by the person for whom the services are performed, on materials or goods furnished by such person." An individual is considered to be a home worker if he or she performs services off the premises of the person for whom the services are performed. An individual is not a statutory employee if the services are performed as a single transaction rather than part of a continuing relationship, or if the individual has a substantial investment in the facilities used in connection with the performance of the services.

In the VanZant case, Laverne VanZant worked for Action Learning Systems Inc. (ALS) as an educational consultant for the LA Unified School District – requiring her to visit schools, collect data, and input data into a software template provided by ALS. ALS determined which schools she would service and supplied the material and format for submitting the data. She was also required to attend training at ALS facilities, where she was given a training manual, a CD with a template on it, and instructions on how to collect and input data. She returned the templates

to ALS after the data was entered. The IRS argued that Laverne was not a statutory employee because she did not receive materials or goods from ALS. The U.S. Tax Court said that neither the Code nor the regulations provide guidance on the meaning of "materials" or "goods." It therefore looked to a dictionary for the common definition that materials are typically the "tools or apparatus for the performance of a given task." Here, Laverne was required to use the ALS template to perform her duties, which was a material furnished by ALS. Furthermore, her services were not performed as a single transaction. The court concluded that she was a home worker, and therefore a statutory employee exempt from self-employment taxes.
www.ustaxcourt.gov/InOpHistoric/vanzant.sum.WPD.pdf

Hiring Your Teenage Children to Work for Your Business

You can hire your teenage children to work for your business after school or on weekends, and this strategy may result in tax savings and other potential benefits if the children are treated as official employees. The children are taxed at their lower tax rate, and assuming you reduce your compensation accordingly the family can save income taxes overall. In addition, there are no kiddie tax complications because earned income from employment is exempt from the kiddie tax. The wages paid by the owner to the child are fully deductible by the business, and as an employee, the child is also eligible for certain benefits such as health insurance coverage and participation in retirement plans and other employer-sponsored programs. If a child under 18 is employed by a parent who runs an unincorporated business (self-employed individuals or partners), the child's wages are exempt from federal payroll taxes (FICA). This exemption also applies to FUTA for children up to age 21. **(See Chapter 2, "Federal Unemployment Tax (FUTA)"); (See Chapter 3, "Kiddie Tax")**

The IRS is suspicious of deductions for wages paid to your own children. The deductions will survive scrutiny only if you're able to establish that the children actually render services. Another hurdle is the "reasonableness" requirement. Wages paid to children can't be more than the going rate for unrelated employees who perform comparable tasks. It means that you have to treat your children the same way as any other employee and keep the usual records showing amounts paid and hours worked. You have to give them W-2s, even if their wages are exempt from withholding of income taxes, and use checks drawn on business accounts to evidence the payments. Otherwise, the IRS might contend that the payments exceeded the going rate or that your kids weren't bona fide employees, but merely rendering the token kinds of services that parents expect their children to perform.

Military Service Break – Participation in Employer's Retirement Plan

An employer cannot treat a period of military service as a break in service for purposes of participation, vesting, or accrual of benefits under an employer's qualified retirement plan. In addition, the time allowed for the employee to report back to work or apply for reemployment as well as any time – up to two years – required to recover from an illness or injury must be counted for participation, vesting, and benefit accrual purposes. Therefore, once the employee is reemployed, the employer is required to contribute "make-up" contributions to the plan to cover those periods. Benefits that are contingent on the employee's own contributions or elective deferrals are required to be made up only if the employee actually makes those contributions. **(See Chapter 9, "Contributions to Qualified Employee Retirement Plans")**

Exempt vs. Non-Exempt Employees

Generally, hourly employees are non-exempt, while salaried employees are exempt unless their salaries are less than a certain amount per year. Non-exempt employees are covered by the Fair Labor Standards Act (FLSA), which imposes requirements for overtime pay and other aspects of employment. Exempt employees, on the other hand, are not subject to the FLSA. This means that non-exempt employees generally receive overtime pay for working more than 40 hours in a given week, but exempt employees do not receive overtime pay.

New Overtime Rules – Salaried employees have generally been considered exempt when their annual salaries are over a certain amount, but the parameters were supposed to be changed with the implementation of the "new overtime rules" that were scheduled to go into effect on Dec. 1, 2016:

- On Dec. 1, 2016, the annual salary cap for overtime increased to $47,476, or $913 per week. This is approximately double the previous threshold of $23,660, or $455 per week. This means that any salaried employee who earns under the new threshold will be eligible for overtime pay for time worked over the standard 40-hour work week;
- The threshold for highly compensated salaried employees who generally don't have any executive, or decision-making authority increased from $100,000 annually to $134,000 annually;
- These new salary thresholds will be updated every three years – currently indexed to the Census' 40th percentile of weekly earnings in the lowest region of the U.S. This means that the salary cap for salaried employees being eligible for overtime pay will see further hikes in 2020.

Businesses with revenues of less than $500,000 annually are exempt from the new overtime rules.
What do these new rules mean for various classes of salaried employees if allowed to be implemented? To be considered exempt employees, the following requirements would have to be met:

- Administrative employees – Administrative employees must make at least $913 per 40-hour work week or they will be eligible for overtime pay. Their primary duties consist of office or non-manual work directly related to the management policies or general operations of the employer or the employer's customers. Their Job must require them to exercise discretion and independent judgment over significant matters.
- Executive employees – Executive employees must make at least $913 per 40-hour work week, and their primary duties must consist of management of the company or business. They regularly direct the work of two or more employees, and they have the authority to hire and fire, or have significant influence over the hiring and firing process.
- Computer employees – Computer employees must make at least $913 per 40-hour work week or be paid at least $55.44 per hour. They must apply system analysis techniques and procedures including consulting with users to determine hardware, software, or system functional specifications and design, or modification of computer systems or programs.
- High-dollar employees – Employees who make more than $134,000 per year are generally exempt.

NOTE: In November 2016, a federal judge in Texas blocked the new overtime rules from taking effect as scheduled. The new overtime rules would have extended mandatory overtime pay to more than 4 million salaried workers in the country. The Department of Labor (DOL) strongly disagrees with the Judge's decision and is confident that the new overtime rules are legal, and will probably appeal to the New Orleans, Louisiana-based 5th U.S. Circuit Court of Appeals. We will have to see how this plays out in the implementation of these new rules.

Certain professionals are considered exempt not withstanding any salary requirements. These Exempt professionals include lawyers, doctors, accountants (but not bookkeepers), architects, teachers, registered nurses, actuaries, scientists (but not technicians), pharmacists, engineers who have engineering degrees or the equivalent and perform work of the sort usually performed by licensed professional engineers, and other employees who perform work requiring advanced knowledge similar to that associated with learned professions. Professionally exempt workers must have education beyond high school in fields that are more academic than the skilled trades. Creative professionals are also considered exempt and includes employees whose work requires invention, imagination, originality, or talent. This includes actors, musicians, composers, writers, cartoonists, and some journalists. Determining whether an employee is a creative professional can sometimes be difficult, especially for jobs like commercial artists and journalists.

The wrong classification of an employee's exemption status can sometimes result in an inquiry from the IRS. Therefore, employers should be familiar with the rules, including the new overtime rules that were scheduled to go into effect on Dec. 1, 2016, and know why each employee is classified as exempt or non-exempt.

Business Casualty and Theft Losses

There is no limitation on the amount that can be deducted for business casualty and theft losses. A total business loss is the adjusted basis of the property or item, even if the fair market value (FMV) of the property is less immediately before the loss. A partial business casualty or theft loss is defined as the lesser of the adjusted basis of a property or item or the difference in its FMV immediately before and after the loss (decline in FMV is provable by necessary repairs, etc.). Business losses are reported in Section B of Form 4684 and then taken as a loss on Form 4797. However, if the property is for sale, i.e. inventory or other income producing property, the loss is reported as a miscellaneous itemized deduction not subject to the 2% floor. **(See Below, "Sale of Business Property"); (See Chapter 6, "Reporting Capital Gains and Losses"); (See Chapter 12, "Casualty, Disaster, and Theft losses"; & "Other Miscellaneous Itemized Deductions Not Subject to the 2% AGI Floor")**
www.irs.gov/pub/irs-pdf/f4684.pdf   www.irs.gov/pub/irs-pdf/i4684.pdf

You must capitalize amounts paid to restore business property, including amounts paid "for the repair of damage to a unit of property" resulting from a disaster even if your casualty loss is ameliorated by insurance. Example: you have a property damaged by a hurricane that had a 15-year recovery period when placed it in service 10 years ago and has been depreciated for 10 years. The cost to repair the property and its remaining basis are both $1 million. In this case, you have two alternatives: (1) you can claim a $1 million casualty loss and depreciate the property's remaining basis of $1 million over 15 years; or (2) You don't claim a casualty loss, but you can deduct the $1 million cost of the repairs and continue to depreciate the $1 million remaining basis over the remaining 5-year recovery period.

Excess Business Losses Under the Tax Cuts and Jobs Act (TCJA)

Beginning in 2018, and for tax years 2018 – 2025, the Tax Cuts and Jobs Act (TCJA) restricts the use of excess business losses by individuals if the taxpayer's losses from all trades or businesses exceeds the taxpayer's income from all trades or businesses by more than $250,000 ($500,000 for taxpayers who file joint returns). The $250,000/$500,000 amount is adjusted for inflation in years after 2018. The excess business loss limitation is applied after the passive loss rules. This means that if a loss is disallowed under the passive activity loss rules, income and deductions from that activity would not be included in the excess business loss calculation. Excess business losses aren't allowed for the current tax year but are instead carried forward and treated as part of the taxpayer's net operating loss (NOL) carryforward to subsequent tax years where they can be used to offset 80% of subsequent years' taxable income (starting in 2018, net operating losses can't be carried back to pior years). Under the law in effect in 2017 and prior years, all business losses recognized by individuals could reduce non-business income after the passive loss rules were applied. **(See Chapter 8, "Net Operating Loss (NOL)")**

Several questions exist in regard to this new provision, including how "excess business losses" carried over will be synchronized with the "qualified business income deduction." **(See Below, "20% Deduction Under Section 199A)**

Business Bad Debts

If a debt is in connection with a trade or business, the loss is an ordinary loss and can be deducted against ordinary income. A business bad debt can be totally or partially worthless. However, in order to write off a business bad debt you must have a bona fide business operation (Not a Hobby), and you usually have to be on the accrual basis of accounting. A cash-basis taxpayer can claim a business bad debt only if the amount owed was previously included in gross income, i.e. if you are on the cash basis, you can't have a lack of a sale that was supposed to be for $1,000 and take a $1,000 loss on top of it. But if you are using accrual accounting and had already recorded a sale of $1,000, then you can write off a $1,000 bad debt. Therefore, you can only claim a bad debt deduction for an uncollectible receivable if you had previously included an uncollectible amount in income. However, even if you are on the cash basis you can deduct any expenses related to an invalid sale, such as directly related consulting fees and office supplies and expenses, but you can't write off your time spent on making the sale (your time is worth nothing to the IRS). **(See Above, "Business or Hobby"); (See Chapter 6, "Non-Business Bad Debt")**

To qualify to write-off a business bad debt, you must be able to show that the debt is legitimate, worthless, and can't be recovered from the debtor. This means that you must make a reasonable effort to obtain payment. This doesn't necessarily mean that you have to sue the debtor, but you have to do more than just make one phone call. Your collection efforts should start with phone or email contacts, then the issuance of a series of collection letters. Also, you might consider hiring a collection agency. After exhausting all collection efforts, you may have to send the debtor a Form 1099-C (Cancellation of Debt). **(See Chapter 5, "Cancellation of Debt")**

For partially worthless debts, a bad debt deduction is limited to the amount actually charged off on your books during the year. You don't have to charge off and deduct partially worthless debts annually, so you can delay the charge off until a later year, but you can't deduct any part of a debt after the year it becomes totally worthless. For debts that become totally worthless in the current year, you can deduct the entire amount, less any amount deducted in an earlier year when the debt was only partially worthless. You don't have to have an actual charge-off on your books in order to claim a bad debt deduction for a totally worthless debt, but if you don't and the IRS later rules that the debt is only partially worthless, you won't be allowed a deduction for the debt in that tax year, because a deduction of a partially worthless bad debt is limited to the amount actually charged off.

If you are an employee and make a loan to an employer who fails to pay you back, you may be able to write off a bad debt on Form 2106. **(See Chapter 12, "Employee Business Expenses")**

Sale of Business Property (Form 4797)

Form 4797 is used to report sales and disposal of business property, including rental property and leaseholds. Generally, any gain on Section 1245 depreciable or amortizable personal property and Section 1250 real property, including rental property, used in a trade or business that is held for more than a year and that is more than the depreciation or amortization already taken is Section 1231 gain, which is treated as a long-term capital gain. There are exceptions to the one-year rule: cattle and horses held for draft, breeding, dairy, or sporting purposes must be held for 2 years (24 months) to qualify. Section 1231 makes available the best of both worlds to businesses with a certain combination of capital gains and losses. Net gains from the sale or disposal of Section 1231 property are taxed at capital gains rates, while net losses from the sale or disposal of Section 1231 property and losses on property held for less than one year are taxed as ordinary losses. If total Section 1231 gains exceed losses for the year, then all gains and losses are treated as long-term capital gains. If total losses exceed gains for the year, then all gains and losses are treated as ordinary losses and are entirely deductible for the year, i.e. losses on the disposal of property held more or less than one year that are not fully applied against Section 1231 gains in the same year are fully deductible as an ordinary loss in the year (not limited to $3,000). **(See Chapter 6, "Reporting Capital Gains and Losses"; & "Form 1099-B: Proceeds from Broker and Barter Exchange Transactions")** www.irs.gov/pub/irs-pdf/f4797.pdf   www.irs.gov/pub/irs-pdf/i4797.pdf

- Some Section 1231 gain must be recaptured as ordinary income – generally, Section 1231 gain that must be recaptured as ordinary income is all depreciation, bonus depreciation, Section 179 expensing and amortization that has been taken on Section 1245 personal assets.
- Section 1245 personal assets are: personal property – cars, machinery, livestock, equipment, etc., and also, all intangible property – patents, licenses, franchises, and trademarks. All depreciation and 179 expensing, plus any bonus depreciation taken on personal property is recaptured as ordinary income when the property is sold or disposed of, and all amortization taken on intangible assets is recaptured as ordinary income when sold. **(See Chapter 16, "Modified Accelerated Cost Recovery System (MACRS)")**
- Section 1250 assets are: non-residential real property, residential rental property, and other depreciable real property. Only straight-line depreciation has been allowed on real property since 1986. Any depreciation taken before 1987 that is more than straight-line depreciation is recaptured as ordinary income. All depreciation taken on Section 1250 real property since 1986 is straight-line depreciation that is "Unrecaptured Section 1250 gain." When real property is sold or disposed, all Unrecaptured Section 1250 gain is taxed at 25% instead of being taxed as ordinary income or at long-term capital gain rates (15% or 20%). However, any Section 179 expensing allowed on real estate (Section 1250 assets) that is recaptured is ordinary income.

Non-recaptured Section 1231 losses for the previous 5-year period that have not been applied against net Section 1231 gains by treating the gains as ordinary income are applied against net Section 1231 gains beginning with the earliest loss in the 5 year period.

How to figure capital gains and losses for 2017:

Previous 5-year period:

Net Sec. 1231 gain or (loss)

2012	0	2017 Net Sec. 1231 Gain	$2,000
2013	0	Treated as ordinary income	(700)
2014	($2,500)	Treated as LT capital gain	$1,300
2015	0	in 2017	
2016	$1,800		

Remaining Sec. 1231 Loss ($ 700)

When listed property (cars, trucks etc.) formerly used predominately (more than 50%) in a trade or business is converted to personal use (less than 50% business use), any depreciation that exceeds the amount that would have been allowed under the alternative depreciation system (ADS) as well as any 179 expensing and bonus depreciation taken must be recaptured as ordinary income reported on Form 4797, and added to the basis of the property. The depreciation that must be recaptured is the difference between 200% declining balance (DB) claimed under the general depreciation system (GDS) and straight-line depreciation under ADS. **(See Chapter 16, "Listed Property")**

If you sell or dispose of your car, you may have a taxable gain or a deductible loss. The portion of any gain that is due to depreciation that you claimed on the car will be treated as ordinary income. However, you may not have to recognize a gain or loss if you dispose of the car because of a casualty or theft. For a casualty or theft of a car, a gain results when you receive insurance or other reimbursement that is more than your adjusted basis in the car. If you then spend all of the proceeds to acquire replacement property (a new car or repairs to the old car) within a specified period of time, you do not recognize any gain. Your basis in the replacement property is generally your adjusted basis in the old property plus any additional amount you pay. When you trade in an old car for a new one, the transaction is no longer considered a Section 1031 like-kind exchange (beginning in 2018). **(See Chapter 16, "Trading in a Vehicle")**

In general, no gain, loss, or depreciation recapture is recognized upon conversion of non-listed business property to personal property, but this would be recognized when the property is sold. No depreciation deduction is allowable for property placed in service and disposed of in the same year, and no gain, loss, or depreciation recapture is recognized.

A taxpayer may wish to time the sale of a depreciable asset to coincide with a loss year. Such timing can enable the taxpayer to be hit with a recapture in a year in which the taxpayer's business has an operating loss (which can be used to offset the recapture amount) rather than in a profitable year, when the recapture liability will increase the taxpayer's taxable income and possibly even move the taxpayer into a higher tax bracket.

20% Deduction Under Section 199A

Under the Tax Cuts and Jobs Act (TCJA), a deduction of up to 20% is allowed on qualified business income (QBI) passed-through to taxpayers for tax years beginning after December 31, 2017 and ending on December 31, 2025 (eight years). A qualified trade or business for this purpose is the same as the definition of a qualified business under Section 162, i.e. the primary purpose of the business must be for income or profit and the owner(s) must be actively engaged in the operation of the business. This includes passthrough entities such as sole proprietorships, partnerships, S-corporations, limited liability companies (LLC), and limited liability partnerships (LLP). These types of businesses pay no taxes themselves, but instead profits (or losses) are passed through to the individual owners, partners or shareholders (individual taxpayers) who are active participants in the businesses and pay taxes on their individual tax returns, and in the case of these passthrough entities, the 20% deduction is determined at the owner, partner or shareholder level. And for purposes of this provision individual taxpayers include trusts and estates. Of course, this means that income from passthrough entities that are passive trades or businesses are not eligible for the 20% deduction. Also, there is one exception to the qualified trade or business rule – the 20% deduction is available for rental or licensing of tangible or intangible property to a commonly controlled business (self-rental rule) which will benefit those who are in the business of renting property or providing services to a commonly controlled business. So, what about rental real estate, is it considered a qualified trade or business? Well it depends – if you are in the business of renting or leasing rental property it may be a qualified trade or business depending on what kind and how many properties are being rented or leased, how actively involved you are in the business, the types of rentals, terms of the leases, etc. Therefore, rental real estate businesses may be eligible for the Section 199A deduction.

When taxpayers have passthrough income from a sole proprietorship, partnership, S-corporation or other passthrough entity, their maximum Section 199A deduction is 20% of their qualified business income (QBI) from each of their non-passive, for-profit trades or businesses. An individual taxpayer's qualified business income (QBI) for the tax year is the net amount of domestic qualified items of income, gain, deduction, and loss (determined by taking-into-account only items included in the determination of taxable income) with respect to the taxpayer's business. If the amount of qualified business income for a tax year is less than zero (i.e., a loss), the loss is treated as a loss from qualified businesses in the next tax year. Under the "abrogation rule," profitable trades or businesses can be offset against those with losses. The QBI of each qualified trade or business must be determined separately, i.e. the 20% deduction has to be figured separately for each business. And when a taxpayer's annual taxable income is $315,000 or less for married individuals filing jointly or $157,500 for non-joint filers, the only limitation is that the allowable 20% deduction is either 20% of QBI or 20% of taxable income, whichever is less. The deduction is available to taxpayers that itemize deductions, as well as those that do not.

A taxpayer's taxable income for Section 199A purposes is taxable income on which federal income tax is owed (not taking-into-account any Section 199A deduction that may be available), i.e. all deductions available must be deducted in determining adjusted gross income (AGI), and either the standard deduction or itemized deductions must be deducted in determining taxable income. The 20% deduction is not allowed in computing AGI; instead, it is allowed as a deduction in reducing final taxable income (but not for Section 199A purposes). Also, any interest income, qualified dividends (non-REIT dividends), and capital gains included in taxable income must be deducted in determining taxable income for purposes of computing the Section 199A deduction.

The QBI for each trade or business is the "net amount" of income, gains, deductions, and losses for each business, but excluding reasonable compensation paid by the business to the owner, guaranteed payments to partners of a partnership under Section 707(c), and other allowable payments in accordance with Section 707(a). Specifically, QBI does not include an amount paid to a shareholder/owner of an S-corporation as reasonable compensation (generally included on a Form W-2). Further, it does not include a payment by a partnership to a partner in exchange for services, regardless of whether that payment is characterized as a guaranteed payment or one made to a partner acting outside his or her partner capacity. The Section 199A deduction has no effect on the adjusted basis of a partner's interest in a partnership or a shareholder's basis in S-corporation stock. 20% of any qualified dividends received from: a real estate investment trust (REIT) – other than any portion that is a capital gain dividend; a publicly traded partnership (PTP); and certain cooperatives must be added to QBI for purposes of computing the Section 199A deduction. No QBI deduction is attributable to REIT losses. Qualified publicly traded partnership (PTP) income includes any gain recognized on the sale of an interest in a publicly traded partnership to the extent that gain is characterized as ordinary income under section 751.

W-2 wages reported by a 3rd party that are applicable to more than one trade of business should be allocated to those businesses in the same proportion that total W-2 wages are associated with those businesses.

- **Example** – Ben is a sole proprietor consultant to oil companies who earned net income of $150,000 from his consulting business that is reported on Schedule C, Form 1040. He had no other earned income during the year, but he received $1,000 in qualified dividends and $2,000 in REIT dividends. Ben is single and, therefore, a non-joint filer. His taxable income for filing purposes is $141,000 computed as follows ($150,000 + $1,000 + $2,000 = $153,000 minus $12,000 standard deduction = $141,000). But for purposes of computing his Section 199A deduction his taxable income is $140,000 ($141,000 minus $1,000 in qualified dividends = $140,000). So, Ben's annual taxable income is below the $157,500 cap for a single filer. Ben's qualified business income (QBI) is $150,000. His Section 199A deduction based on his QBI would $30,400 computed as follows: $150,000 X 20% = $30,000 + (20% X $2,000 REIT dividends = $400) = $30,400. His Section 199A deduction based on this taxable income is $28,000 ($140,000 X 20% = $28,000). So, Ben's allowable Section 199A deduction for the year is $28,000, because it is less than the $30,400 based on his QBI. Ben's $150,000 taxable income reported on Schedule C is subject to self-employment tax.

- **Example** – Charles is a 25% partner in a law firm that had net earnings of $800,000; therefore, his share of the annual net passthrough earnings from the partnership is $200,000. Charles' wife also works as an employee for a manufacturing company and she earned a salary of $100,000 for the year. Charles and his wife had no other income. Therefore, their taxable income for both filing and Section 199A deduction purposes is $276,000 computed as follows: ($200,000 + $100,000 = $300,000 minus $24,000 standard deduction = $276,000), which is below the $315,000 cap for joint filers. Charles' QBI is $200,000, so his allowable Section 199A deduction based on QBI is $40,000 ($200,000 X 20% = $40,000), which is less than what it would be based on taxable income, which would be $55,200 ($276,000 X 20% = $55,200). Charles' $200,000 passthrough share of partnership income is reported on Schedule K-1 (1065) and is subject to self-employment tax.

When your taxable income is more than $315,000 (married filing jointly), or $157,500 (non-joint filers), calculating your Section 199A deduction becomes much more complicated. The first thing you need to do is determine if the business from which you receive passthrough income is a "specified service trade of business." A specified service trade or business (SSTB) is any trade or business activity involving the performance of services in the fields of health, law, accounting, actuarial science, performing arts, consulting, athletics, financial services, brokerage services, any business that involves the performance of services that consist of investment and investment managing, trading, or dealing in securities, partnership interests, or commodities, or any trade or business where the principal asset is the reputation or skill of one or more of its owners or employees (excluding engineering and architecture). In determining whether a business is a SSTB, the meaning of the phrase: "the principal asset is the reputation or skill of an owner or an employee" has raised many questions, but it has generally been determined that under the "Kardashian Rule" a truck driver or similar profession would not be considered a SSTB. Also, under the De minimis rule, a business is not a SSTB if it has gross receipts of $25 million or less in a tax year and less than 10% of its gross receipts are attributable to services, or if the business's gross receipts are greater than $25 million in a tax year, and less than 5% of its gross receipts are attributable to services. Pass-through entities must determine whether it is a specified service trade or business (SSTB) and disclose it to the owners, partners or shareholders of the business.

218

Passthrough owners, partners, and shareholders of a SSTB are "ineligible" for the 20% Section 199A deduction when their taxable income is above the thresholds of $415,000 (joint filers) and $207,500 (non-joint filers). However, for owners, partners, and shareholders of a qualified trade or business that is not a SSTB (non-service trade or business) there is no such limitation, i.e. a non-service trade or business can have an unlimited amount of taxable income and still be eligible for the 20% Section 199A deduction.

Taxable Income of a SSTB Over $315,000/$157,500 and up to $415,000/$207,500 – If your passthrough business is a specified service trade or business (SSTB) and your taxable income is over the $315,000/$157,500 threshold, your pass-through deduction is gradually phased-out until taxable income reaches $415,000/$207,500, i.e. it is phased out over the next $100,000 of taxable income for married individuals filing jointly ($50,000 for other individuals). Your maximum Section 199A deduction is determined based on the same rules discussed above for taxable income up to $315,000/$157,500. It is a maximum deduction of 20% of QBI and the same limitations and parameters are still in effect as previously discussed, but in addition your deduction may not exceed the greater of (1) 50% of your share of W-2 wages paid by the business, or (2) 25% of your share of W-2 wages, plus 2.5% of the acquisition cost of qualified depreciable property used in the business. Therefore, if the business has no employees or no qualified depreciable property, no deduction can be taken. However, if the SSTB has employees, your deduction is phased-out by 1% for every $1,000 your taxable income exceeds the $315,000 threshold for joint filers, and by 2% for every $1,000 your taxable income exceeds the $157,500 threshold for non-joint filers and your allowable deduction is completely phased-out when your taxable income reaches $415,000 (joint filers) and $207,500 (non-joint filers).

A taxpayer's share of "W-2 wages" generally equals the sum of wages subject to withholding, plus elective deferrals and deferred compensation paid by a sole proprietorship, partnership, or S-corporation during a taxable year. The acquisition cost of qualified property is the "unadjusted basis" of the property which is either the purchase price or other means of determining the initial basis of the property (determined immediately after acquisition of the property and before any depreciation) upon acquisition of the property by the business. Qualified property is all tangible property that is placed in service by the business and is subject to depreciation and: (1) is available for use in the business at the close of the tax year; (2) is used at any point during the tax year in the production of business income; and (3) the depreciable period of the property has not ended before the close of the particular tax year. The depreciable period is the period beginning on the date the property is placed in service by the taxpayer and ending on the later of either 10 years after the date the property is placed in service or the last day of the last full year of the applicable recovery (depreciable) period for the property. In the case of a trust or estate, rules similar to Code section 199 (as in effect on December 1, 2017) would apply for purposes of apportioning between fiduciaries and beneficiaries any W-2 wages and the unadjusted basis of qualified property.

- **Example** – Jack files a joint return and is a 25% partner in a law firm partnership that is a SSTB. The partnership had net taxable income of $1,500,000 for the year of which Jack's allocable passthrough share is $375,000. The partnership's W-2 wages paid to employees of the partnership are $550,000; so, Jack's allocable share of the W-2 wages is equal to $137,500. The partnership's qualified property is equal to $750,000; so, Jack's allocable share of the partnership's qualified property is $187,500. Jack has no other earned income, but his taxable income includes interest income of $15,000 and qualified REIT dividends of $20,000. Therefore, Jack's taxable income before any Section 199A deduction is $386,000, computed as follows: $375,000 + $15,000 + $20,000 minus $24,000 standard deduction = $386,000. However, his taxable income for Section 199A purposes is $371,000 ($386,000 minus $15,000 interest income = $371,000). Jack's QBI is $395,000 ($375,000 passthrough partnership income + $20,000 REIT dividends = $395,000). Jack's 199A deduction is computed as follows: $371,000 taxable income X 20% = $74,200; $395,000 QBI X 20% = $79,000; $137,500 W-2 wages X 50% = $68,750; $137,500 W-2 wages X 25% = $34,375 + $187,500 X 2.5% = $4,688 = $39,063. Therefore, Jack's 199A deduction "before reduction" is $68,750, because $68,750 is greater than $39,063, but less than $74,200 and $79,000. Jack's taxable income for 199A purposes is $371,000. $371,00 minus $315,000 = $56,000; Therefore, the $68,750 deduction is reduced by 56% (1% for every $1,000 taxable income exceeds the $315,000 threshold), computed as follows: $68,750 X 56% = $38,500. So, Jack's allowable Section 199A deduction is $30,250 ($68,750 minus $38,500 = $30,250). Jack's $375,000 passthrough share of partnership income is reported on Schedule K-1 (1065) and is subject to self-employment tax.

Section 199A includes certain "anti-abuse" rules which cannot be ignored. One anti-abuse rule is intended to prevent taxpayers from separating parts of what otherwise would be an aggregated SSTB, such as administrative functions, in an attempt to qualify those separated parts as a non-service related business eligible for the Section 199A deduction when its taxable income exceeds the $415,000/$207,500 thresholds. In order to try to skirt the specified service trade or business (SSTB) rules, you can't divide up a partnership into more than one business if there is 50% common ownership and the partnership provides 80% of its property and services to a SSTB. For example, a law firm might try separate a rental building in which the law firm's offices are located into a separate business that would be classified as a non-service trade or business, but this is not allowed under the rules if the 50% and 80% parameters apply. If you were previously an employee of a company and then become an independent contractor, you are still presumed to be an employee of the company. This is another anti-abuse rule that prevents an employee from trying to game the system by becoming an independent contractor. On the other hand, independent contractors who are working for a company can become employees of the company.

Taxable Income of Non-Service Business Over $315,000/$157,500 and up to $415,000/$207,500 – If your passthrough business is a non-service trade or business and your taxable income is over the $315,000/$157,500 threshold, your W-2 wages/property limitation is gradually phased-in until taxable income reaches $415,000/$207,500. The W-2 wages/property limitation is phased in over $100,000 for married filing jointly and $50,000 for non-joint filers. At the top of the income range ($415,000 for married filing jointly and $207,500 for singles), your entire deduction is subject to the W-2 wages/property limitation. The same W-2 wage limitation and qualified property limitation applies for a non-service trade or business as applies for a SSTB: your Section 199A deduction may not exceed the greater of (1) 50% of your share of W-2 wages paid by the business, or (2) 25% of your share of W-2 wages, plus 2.5% of the acquisition cost of qualified depreciable property used in the business. Therefore, if the business has no employees or no qualified depreciable property, no deduction can be taken. However, for a non-service trade or business the phase-in amount is based on 1% for every $1,000 your qualified business income (QBI) exceeds the $315,000 threshold for joint filers, and 2% for every $1,000 your QBI exceeds the $157,500 threshold for non-joint filers. Also, the maximum Section 199A deduction is determined based on the same rules discussed above for taxable income up to $315,000/$157,500. It is a maximum deduction of 20% of QBI and the same limitations and parameters are still in effect as previously discussed.

- **Example** – Jack files a joint return and is a 25% partner in a non-service partnership. The partnership had net taxable income of $1,500,000 for the year of which Jack's allocable passthrough share is $375,000.

The partnership's W-2 wages paid to employees of the partnership are $550,000; so, Jack's allocable share of the W-2 wages is equal to $137,500. The partnership has no qualified property. Jack has no other earned income, but his taxable income includes interest income of $15,000 and qualified REIT dividends of $20,000. Therefore, Jack's taxable income before any Section 199A deduction is $386,000 computed as follows: $375,000 + $15,000 + $20,000 minus $24,000 standard deduction = $386,000. However, his taxable income for Section 199A purposes is $371,000 ($386,000 minus $15,000 interest income = $371,000). Jack's QBI is $395,000 ($375,000 passthrough partnership income + $20,000 REIT dividends = $395,000). Jack's phase-in percentage is 80%, because his $395,000 QBI is $80,000 more than the $315,000 limit for a joint filer. His Section 199A deduction would be $79,000 ($395,000 QBI X 20% = $79,000) if the taxable income limitation did not apply. His full deduction based on W-2 wages is $68,750 ($137,500 W-2 wages X 50% = $68,750). The difference between the two is $10,250 ($79,000 minus $68,750 = $10,250). This amount ($10,250) is multiplied by the 80% phase-in percentage to determine the phase-in amount, which is $8,200 ($10,250 X 80% = $8,200). The phase-in amount is subtracted from the $79,000 deduction based on QBI, which results in a deduction of $70,800 ($79,000 minus $8,200 = $70,800). Jack's allowable Section 199A deduction is $70,800, because 20% of taxable income is $74,200 which is more than $70,800 ($371,000 taxable income X 20% = $74,200). Jack's $375,000 passthrough share of partnership income is reported on Schedule K-1 (1065) and is subject to self-employment tax.

As previously stated, for owners, partners, and shareholders of a qualified trade or business that is not a SSTB (non-service trade or business) there is no limitation on the amount of taxable income, i.e. a non-service trade or business can have an unlimited amount of taxable income and still be eligible for the 20% Section 199A deduction. Also, as previously stated, 20% of any qualified dividends received from: a real estate investment trust (REIT) – other than any portion that is a capital gain dividend; a publicly traded partnership (PTP); and certain cooperatives must be added to QBI. However, qualified payments or dividends from cooperatives that are added to QBI must be reduced by the lesser of 9% of QBI allocable to cooperative sales or 50% of wages allocable to cooperative sales.

- **Example** – Jane files a joint return and is a partner in a successful accounting firm from which she receives passthrough income reported on Schedule K-1 (1065) in the amount of $450,000. She is also a 25% owner in a non-service S-corporation that reports income of $2,000,000 of which she receives 25% reported on a Schedule K-1 (1020S), which is $500,000. She also is an active participant in the S-Corporation and receives a salary reported on Form W-2 in the amount of $200,000. Also, her share of the W-2 wages of employees of the S-corporation is $100,000 and her share of the qualified property of the S-corporation is $250,000. Also, Jane receives dividends from a cooperative in the amount of $20,000. The accounting firm and the S-corporation are unrelated. The accounting firm is a specified service trade or business (SSTB), so Jane doesn't receive a Section 199A deduction for her QBI from the accounting firm, because the taxable income received from the partnership is over the limit of $415,000 for a SSTB. Her taxable income from the S-corporation is $700,000 ($500,000 K-1 distribution + $200,000 W-2 salary), but her QBI is $500,000 because her compensation from the S-corporation reported on Form W-2 is not included in QBI. Jane's $500,000 QBI from the S-corporation is increased by the $20,000 in cooperative dividends, but in turn, QBI is reduced by the lesser of 9% of QBI allocable to cooperative sales or 50% of wages allocable to cooperative sales. Jane's share of QBI allocable to cooperative sales is $10,000 and her share of wages allocable to cooperative sales is $5,000. So, Jane's QBI is $519,100, computed as follows: $500,000 + $20,000 = $520,000 minus (the lesser of $10,000 X 9% = $900, or $5,000 X 50% = $2,500) = $519,100.

Jane's taxable income is $720,000 ($500,000 + $200,000 + $20,000 = $720,000). Therefore, Jane's allowable Section 199A deduction is $50,000, computed as follows: $519,100 QBI X 20% = $103,820; $720,000 taxable income X 20% = $144,000; $100,000 W-2 wages X 50% = $50,000; $100,000 W-2 wages X 25% = $25,000 + $250,000 qualified property X 2.5% = $6,250 + $25,000 = $31,250. Since $50,000 is greater than $31,250, but less than $103,820 and $144,000, Jane's Section 199A deduction is $50,000. NOTE: Jane doesn't have to pay self-employment tax on the $500,000 passed-through to her from the S-corporation reported on Schedule K-1 because the distribution is considered dividends not subject to self-employment tax.

As previously stated, if a qualified business has taxable income in excess of $315,000 (joint filers) or $157,500 (non-joint filers) and has no employees or no qualified depreciable property, no deduction can be taken.

- **Example** – Mary is a single taxpayer who files a Form 1040, and reports her business income on Schedule C. She owns a multi-unit apartment building and several other rental properties. Therefore, this is a non-service business, so she is not constrained by the $207,500 limitation for a specified service trade of business (SSTB). Her taxable income is $300,000. She has no employees. Therefore, her Section 199A deduction is limited to 2.5% of the unadjusted basis of her qualified property, which is the purchase price of the building and the other properties minus the value of the land, and is equal to $600,000. Therefore, her Section 199A deduction is $15,000 ($600,000 X 2.5% = $15,000). Her taxable income in not a factor, because 20% X $300,000 = $60,000. Mary's $300,000 taxable income reported on schedule C is subject to self-employment tax.

As previously stated, a taxpayer's share of "W-2 wages" generally equals the sum of wages subject to withholding, plus elective deferrals and deferred compensation paid by a sole proprietorship, partnership, or S-corporation during a taxable year.

- **Example** – Sam is a 25% partner in a partnership. The partnership's W-2 wages is determined as follows: taxable wages paid to employees of the partnership = $150,000. Non-taxable elective deferrals and deferred compensation of the partnership's employees = $50,000; therefore, the total "W-2 wages" of the partnership = $200,000 ($150,000 + $50,000 = $200,000). Sam's share of the W-2 wages of the partnership for purposes of determining his Section 199A deduction = $50,000 ($$200,000 X 25% = $50,000).

As previously stated, the acquisition cost of qualified property is the "unadjusted basis" of the property which is either the purchase price or other means of determining the initial basis of the property (determined immediately after acquisition of the property and before any depreciation) upon acquisition of the property by the business. Qualified property is all tangible property that is placed in service by the business and is subject to depreciation and: (1) is available for use in the business at the close of the tax year; (2) is used at any point during the tax year in the production of business income; and (3) the depreciable period of the property has not ended before the close of the tax year. The depreciable period is the period beginning on the date the property is placed in service by the taxpayer and ending on the later of either 10 years after the date the property is placed in service or the last day of the last full year of the applicable recovery (depreciable) period for the property.

- **Example** – Sam is a 25% partner in a non-service partnership. The unadjusted basis of the qualified property of the partnership is determined as follows: The purchase price or other initial basis of all qualified property of the partnership that was acquired in years prior to 2018 (no qualified property was acquired in 2018) = $200,000. All of the property of the partnership has been depreciated since its acquisition in accordance with each item of individual property's applicable recovery period, and no item of property has been fully depreciated through 2018. Therefore, Sam's share of the partnership's qualified property for purposes of determining his Section 199A deduction is $50,000 ($200,000 X 25% = $50,000).

The Section 199A deduction is reported on line 9 of the new 1040 postcard form, which is after AGI.

Under proposed regulations, the "New Aggregation Rule" would allow taxpayers to combine businesses that qualify as businesses under Section 162 if the same persons own the businesses being combined, share similar products (cannot be a specified service trade or business (SSTB)), and have the same employees. The owners must be able to demonstrate that the businesses are all a part of an integrated business. The regulations require a "duty of consistency" that requires that once multiple trades or businesses are aggregated, taxpayers must then consistently report the group in following tax years.

In August 2018, the IRS issued proposed regulations concerning the deduction for qualified business income under Section 199A of the Internal Revenue Code. The IRS also issued Notice 2018-64 that provides guidance on methods for calculating W-2 wages for purposes of Section 199A of the Internal Revenue Code. www.irs.gov/pub/irs-drop/reg-107892-18.pdf www.irs.gov/pub/irs-drop/n-18-64.pdf

Real Estate Investment Trusts (REIT)
A Real Estate Investment Trust (REIT) is made up of real estate properties purchased with funds raised from the REIT's shareholders. The properties included in REITs are income-generating properties and REITs attract investors who want the exposure to real estate but don't have the capital or knowledge to invest in properties on their own. REITs are generally pass-through entities that have to "pass through" at least 90% of the profit and losses to their investors. REITs generally don't owe any taxes, leaving more of their earnings to be passed on in the form dividends to investors, who are taxed on that income. Investors receive distributions from REITs either as ordinary dividends (Form 1099-DIV) taxed as ordinary income or as a return of capital. Most REITs focus on a particular property type, such as hotels, retail centers, offices, apartment buildings, and medical facilities. Although some REITs hold diversified types of properties in their portfolios.

The TCJA provides REIT investors with a 20% tax reduction on pass-through income, which reduces the taxes paid by investors in the highest ordinary income tax bracket from 37% down to 29.6% in 2018 (plus the **3.8% surtax on investment income for certain high-income earners)** and shareholders in lower tax brackets have even lower rates on the same dividends. In addition, REIT dividends are excluded from the wage restriction that applies to other pass-through entities under the TCJA, i.e. for REITs, the 20% pass-through deduction is not limited to whichever is greater – 50% of wages paid by the business or 25% of wages, plus 2.5% of the property's original purchase price. Distributions in the form of return of capital are taxed at a rate no higher than the highest capital gain rate of 25%, plus the 3.8% surtax on high-income earners. Under the Foreign Investment in Real Property Tax Act, foreign REIT investors, who were formerly subject to 35% withholding on REIT distributions in 2017 and prior years, are now subject to the 2018 corporate tax rate which is a flat tax of 21%. **(See Chapter 1, "Income Tax"); (See Chapter 2, "0.9% Medicare Surtax"); (See Chapter 6, "Capital Gain Tax Rates")**

The TCJA brings with it other benefits to REITs that were not there before its implementation. First, there is an exception concerning business interest deductions for REITs. Although most corporate taxpayers can no longer deduct net interest expense exceeding 30% of adjusted taxable income of the business, REITs are allowed to elect out of this rule change as long as they do not use regular MACRS depreciation, i.e. they have to use straight line depreciation if they elect out of the rule. However, regular MACRS depreciation is only used by some REITs to meet their 90% distribution requirement. So, almost all of REITs can opt out of the 30% limitation with no consequences. Also, REITs that are formed as partnerships benefit from the elimination of the "technical termination" rule that was in place for partnerships prior to implementation of the TCJA in 2018. The elimination of the technical termination rule by the TCJA provides more flexibility to REITs. **(See Above, "Business Interest Expense")**

Workaround by Businesses to Avoid the $10,000 Limit on Deductions for State and Local Taxes – Businesses that make business-related payments to charitable programs or government entities for which they receive state or local tax credits will be allowed to deduct the full amount of state and local taxes as charitable business expenses if the payments qualify as ordinary and necessary business expenses (not limited to the $10,000 itemized deduction for state and local taxes allowed by the Tax Cuts and Jobs Act for individuals), and such payments which are authorized by some states in lieu of making state and local tax payments to the states are available to any business taxpayer, regardless of whether it is doing business as a sole proprietor, partnership or S-corporation (passthrough entities). This means that the individual owners of the businesses, partners of partnerships, and shareholders of S-corporations could receive the benefit of the full deduction for their state and local taxes that are more than $10,000 on their individual federal tax returns. However, the individual filers will have to reduce the charitable deductions on their federal tax returns by any credits they receive on their state and local taxes for such contributions.

The IRS makes clear that the longstanding rule allowing businesses to deduct payments to charities as business expenses remains unchanged under the Tax Cuts and Jobs Act. The rule concerning the cap on state and local tax deductions has no impact on federal tax benefits for business-related donations to school choice programs and scholarships (mostly contributions to fund private school scholarships). The IRS states that this won't affect corporations, which aren't subject to the $10,000 limit on state and local tax deductions, but it would apply to pass-through entities such as partnerships and S-corporations.

However, the IRS is still not giving individual taxpayers the ability to make charitable contributions to state-run charitable funds as a way to circumvent the $10,000 deduction limit on state and local taxes. In fact, the IRS has issued proposed regulations to block New York, New Jersey, and Connecticut from allowing individuals to make charitable contributions to charitable funds in lieu of paying their state and local taxes, and to stop other high-tax states from considering doing the same thing. But they left open the possibility of allowing business taxpayers to use them. Therefore, business taxpayers who make business-related payments to charities or government entities for which the taxpayers receive state or local tax credits can generally deduct the payments as business expenses, as long as they qualify as ordinary and necessary business expenses. **(See Chapter 12, "Miscellaneous Itemized Deductions Subject to the 2% AGI Floor)**

Businesses That Sell Marijuana
Businesses that sell marijuana are not allowed to write off their business expenses other than the cost of the product and "state excise taxes on marijuana sales." Expenses such as wages, rent, utilities, etc. aren't deductible

against revenue, even for sellers located where it is legal to sell marijuana for medicinal or recreational purposes. The federal government considers marijuana to be an illegally controlled substance and the tax law prohibits deductions for sellers, and there isn't an exception where a state allows the drug to be sold or produced. The result is to effectively make the income tax on a marijuana business as a tax on gross income rather than net income. However, there may be an exception that marijuana businesses can utilize under Code Sec. 280E for cost of goods sold.

The exception allows marijuana businesses to try to allocate as much expense as possible to inventory to preserve more deductions. For example, expenses for producing and storing marijuana can be allocated to inventory, because under the tax code there are relatively few restrictions on voluntarily allocating more expenses to inventory than are required. Direct costs, such as expenses for producing and storing marijuana, are relatively easy to allocate to inventory. But what about indirect costs? Marijuana businesses that cannot otherwise claim deductions and credits, generally can benefit from voluntarily complying with the full absorption rules under Code Sec. 471 and the uniform capitalization rules. But there are still some limits on the ability to allocate indirect costs to the cost of goods sold. There is a general requirement in the regulations that the allocations cannot result in a material distortion of income. Some expenses, such as selling, marketing, and advertising costs, would generally not be allocable to cost of goods sold. The IRS may be taking a strict look at what expenses a marijuana business can properly allocate to cost of goods sold.

Since the enactment of Section 280E, there have been a couple of Court cases where the Court allowed medicinal marijuana and recreational marijuana dispensaries that also offered caregiving services and/or sales of paraphernalia and other items to separate the other parts of their businesses from their marijuana dispensaries. This allowed them to run all of their other expenses, such as payroll and the portion of rent applicable to their caregiving services and sales of paraphernalia and other items through those parts of their businesses (not associated with the marijuana dispensaries). However, companies that deal in sales of marijuana and other services or sales of other paraphernalia must keep impeccable records, because they will most likely be audited and the case could end up in Tax Court. You must be able to show that the expenses cannot be expenses of the dispensary.
http://ustaxcourt.gov/UstcInOp/OpinionViewer.aspx?ID=10586
http://cdn.ca9.uscourts.gov/datastore/opinions/2015/07/09/13-70510.pdf

A legal marijuana business can deposit employment taxes in cash or by money order without penalty, since it isn't allowed to open a bank account under federal banking rules.

Taxpayers that use marijuana for medicinal purposes can't deduct the cost as a medical expense. **(See Chapter 12, "Expenses Generally Not Deductible as Medical Expenses")**

Cash Transactions over $10,000
Businesses and banks are required to file Form 8300 with the IRS to report cash transactions by customers over $10,000 – large cash payments received in one transaction, or two or more related business transactions – including payments with cashier checks, traveler's checks, money orders, and bank drafts. This includes multiple cash payments by the same person or entity within 24 hours that total more than $10,000, whether related or not.
www.irs.gov/pub/irs-pdf/f8300.pdf   www.irs.gov/pub/irs-pdf/i1128.pdf

Changing a Tax Year (Form 1128)

To change a tax year, a company must apply under Rev Proc. 2002-39 and show a business purpose for the change. However, a business can apply for an automatic change if it has not changed its tax year for 48 months. A business can qualify for automatic approval under the 25% gross receipts test i.e. gross receipts in the last 2 months of a requested 12-month period are at least 25% in those two months for the past 3 years. www.irs.gov/pub/irs-access/f1128_accessible.pdf

Business Outside of the USA

If you own a business outside of the U.S. and you are a citizen or a permanent resident (green card holder) or if you have had substantial presence here over the last few years and thus qualify as a resident, you are subject to taxation on your worldwide income and accordingly must file a U.S. tax return related to your overseas business. **(See Chapter 3, "Aliens")**

Federal Excise Taxes for Managed Aircraft – The TCJA clarifies that owner flights on managed aircraft are not subject to the Federal Transportation Excise Tax (FET), but rather such owner flights are subject to the non-commercial fuel tax. This issue has been the subject of controversy for more than 60 years. NBAA has submitted a request for guidance to the IRS to further clarify how this new provision will be implemented.

Taxes Imposed on Beer, Wine, and Distilled Spirits

Under the TCJA, alcohol manufacturers (Breweries, distilleries and wineries) will enjoy a two-year excise tax reduction. The credit against the wine excise tax was expanded, and sparkling wine producers are included. The TCJA includes "Craft Beverage Modernization and Tax Reform" (CBMTR), which is effective until it is scheduled to sunset on December 31, 2019. The TCJA's purpose is to lower federal excise taxes in order to create a more equitable tax structure for brewers, winemakers, distillers and importers of alcoholic beverages by equalizing the federal excise tax on beer, wine and spirits. One provision that affects all three industry segments – beer, wine and spirits – is that all three products are considered finished after the manufacturing process is complete and are no longer subject to interest capitalization. In 2017 and prior years, that threshold was met when alcohol was first put out for sale. Under the new law, the aging process is no longer considered part of the production process for purposes of capitalizing interest into inventory, which allows breweries, wineries and distillers to expense postproduction interest costs.

     Beer – For beer, the federal excise tax is reduced from $7.00 per barrel to $3.50 per barrel on the first 60,000 barrels for domestic brewers producing fewer than two million barrels annually. The federal excise tax is also reduced to $16 per barrel on the first 6 million barrels for large brewers and beer importers while keeping the $18 per barrel excise tax for barrels produced in excess of 6 million ($18 per barrel was applicable to all production in 2017 and prior years). Also, Brewers are allowed to transfer beer between bonded facilities without paying an excise tax. This change likely benefits small and mid-size craft brewers the most, especially with the reduction of the excise tax on the first 60,000 barrels. The ability to transfer beer between bonded facilities without tax liability will likely encourage brewers to collaborate more on new beers by giving them more flexibility to transfer beer between breweries.

     Wine – Wines with alcohol levels from 14% to 16% are taxed at the lower $1.07 per gallon federal excise tax rate that only applied to wines with less than a 14% alcohol level in 2017 and prior years. The old law applied a federal excise tax rate $1.57 per gallon for wines with alcohol levels from 14% to 16%. Wineries are allowed a one dollar per gallon federal excise tax credit for the first 30,000 gallons produced; $0.90 per gallon for the next 100,000 gallons produced; and $0.535 for the next 620,000 gallons produced up to a maximum federal excise tax credit of $451,700 annually, assuming their production is over 750,000 gallons or 315,000 cases of wine. Sparkling wine producers and wine importers also qualify for the new federal excise tax credits.

Distilled Spirits – Under the TCJA, the federal excise tax rates are tiered based on proof gallons – $2.70 per proof gallon on the first 100,000 proof gallons produced, then increased to $13.34 per proof gallon above 100,000 proof gallons up to 22,130,000 proof gallons. The rate increases to $13.50 per proof gallon above 22,130,000. The new law also provides rules that would prevent all members of a controlled group from receiving the lower rate. The TCJA lowers the federal excise tax rate on distilled spirit producers for the first time since the Civil War.

Best Small Business Tax Practices

- Hire a tax accountant who has experience with your kind of business, whether it's a restaurant or a plumbing business.
- Keep good records about which workers are employees and which ones are independent contractors.
- Keep good records on how much you paid for, and the date you placed in service, all business vehicles and equipment.
- Be aware of the places where you may have a physical presence (even unknowingly) to properly comply with state sales tax rules and procedures.
- Invest in good tax and accounting system software that properly tracks your records and regularly provides updates to new IRS rules and regulations.
- Select a tax year for your business that reflects the natural flow of your business's receipts and disbursements. This way, you won't get caught in a cash crunch when tax time comes.
- Pay estimated taxes on time, calculating them correctly.
- Miscalculating any of these steps can be a major problem so talk to someone with knowledge, most likely a tax accountant, who knows the rules inside and out.
- If your spouse, child, or other close relative works in your business, make sure he or she adheres to the same employment rules as your unrelated employees.
- Whatever you do, do not consider using funds you have withheld for employee payroll taxes or any taxes as a short-term loan to tide you over during a shortfall in working capital.
- Keep detailed records on how you use your personal or business-owned vehicle for business.
- You should retain all relevant tax records for at least three years or have your accountant keep them for you. If your records relate to property and depreciation, keep them until the property is disposed of, plus an additional three years.
- Use a reputable third-party administrator to manage your 401(k) plans and other tax-favored employee benefits.
- Make sure that you and your tax accountant are familiar with the tax rules, including the favorable tax credits and deductions that are unique to your business.
- Don't be fooled into thinking that the IRS will have to prove that you have done something that doesn't comply with the tax laws. The burden of proof is always on you, not the IRS.

- If it becomes necessary for your small business to open a foreign bank account in order to pay vendors or others in another country, make sure you and your tax accountant are vigilantly following the new rules in effect on foreign bank accounts as required by FATCA.
- Familiarize yourself with the tax rules surrounding starting, running, selling and shutting down a business. Make a concerted and logical decision about whether you should begin your business operating as a sole proprietorship, a partnership, an S-corporation, or a Limited Liability Company (LLC). Your tax accountant should be closely familiar with these rules.
- If your plan is to have your business continue operating after you die, under the leadership of another family member or designated heir, take steps to protect the business against a forced sale in order to pay inheritance taxes.
- Have a face-to-face conversation with your accountant about the Affordable Care Act (ACA).
- If you can't pay the taxes you owe the IRS, contact you accountant right away. This situation can only get worse by ignoring it.
- If you get paid in cash, it doesn't mean that the payment is not taxable. The IRS can build a case against alleged tax cheats by using state-of-the-art statistical technology and models based on bank accounts and spending habits.

Chapter 15 – Business Travel and Related Expenses

Employee travel and incidental expenses, which were deductible as miscellaneous itemized deductions subject to the 2% AGI floor in 2017 and prior years, are no longer deductible for tax years 2018 – 2025 in accordance with the Tax Cuts and Jobs Act (TCJA). Sole proprietors/self-employed persons, general partners, and shareholders/members of S-corporations can deduct their travel and incidental expenses directly on the applicable form or schedule where their revenues and other expenses are reported (Schedule C, Form 1065, Form 1120, or Form 1120-S). **(See Chapter 12, "Miscellaneous Itemized Deductions Subject to the 2% AGI Floor")**

Claiming Travel Expenses

Work related expenses incurred in traveling away from home to another location can be claimed by business owners. Travel expenses incurred in commuting to work and back are not deductible, no matter how far. The "Sleep and Rest Rule" determines whether or not a trip takes a taxpayer away from his/her "tax home," where it is reasonable that he/she needs sleep and rest during off time, and it is not reasonable to return home. A taxpayer's tax home is where his major post of duty is located. Three factors that define a taxpayer's tax home: (1) taxpayer has living expenses there that are duplicated when work requires him/her to be away from claimed tax home; (2) taxpayer worked in the area of his/her tax home immediately before a job assignment required travel away from his major post of duty and he continues to have work contacts in that area; and (3) taxpayer's spouse and children live at his/her tax home, or taxpayer continues to use that home for lodging. However, your "tax home" isn't always where you live. For example, if you work full-time in one town, but choose to live in another town that is 120 miles away, your tax home is where you work, so you can't claim travel expenses back and forth between where you live and where you work or lodging expenses where you work, which is your real tax home. You can't claim another place other than your real tax home as your tax home. Also, an Itinerant worker is not entitled to deduct travel expenses due to the lack of a regular place of abode. **(See Below, "Deducting Local Travel Expenses")**

You may deduct your transportation expenses, but not the cost of meals on one-day business trips away from your tax home (not an over-night stay). Work assignments of one year or less that take you away from your tax home are generally considered temporary, and thus you can claim travel expenses unless the original assignment was expected to be for more than one year. Work assignments of more than one year are considered indefinite, and thus travel expenses can't be claimed. However, if the assignment is less than two years, a taxpayer can overcome the "one-year presumption" by showing: (1) the job was realistically expected to last less than 2 years; (2) he/she expected to return home after the job ended; and (3) claimed tax home is his/her regular home in a real and substantial sense. If all three factors are met, the assignment may be considered temporary. If two factors are met, there is a strong case for the assignment being considered temporary. If only one factor is met, the assignment would probably not be considered temporary.

Domestic Trips Combining Business and Pleasure – Expenses of traveling to and from a destination in the U.S., i.e. airplane tickets, hotel, meals, etc. can be claimed only if the trip is primarily related to a business purpose. This is determined by the percentage of time spent on business and pleasure, i.e. if 51% or more of a taxpayer's time is spent on business, then the trip is primarily related to a business purpose. Spouses and dependents' travel expenses can't be claimed unless business related. If a traveler spends an extra night in a hotel to visit family, he can't claim that night. If a trip is determined to be primarily for personal reasons or pleasure (51% or more), a taxpayer can claim any expenses he/she has that are directly related to business, but not an airplane ticket, or other travel expenses to get to the destination and back home.

Travel Outside of the U.S. – To be fully deductible, foreign travel must be primarily for business purposes. However, if there are any non-business activities, all of the travel expenses can be claimed if the following tests are met: (1) you spend less than 25% of your time on non-business matters for a trip lasting longer than one week; (2) the trip lasts less than 8 days (don't count the day you leave, but do count the day you return); and (3) a personal vacation or holiday was not a major reason for the trip. You must allocate your expenses between the business portion and the non-business portion of your trip, based on the ratio of business days to total days, if you don't meet these tests.

There are limits on business expenses claimed for trips on cruise ships. The cruise ship must be registered in the U.S., and all ports of call must be located in the U.S. in order to claim any business expenses. Expenses on cruise ships meeting the criteria are limited to twice the per diem rate of the highest per diem rate allowable by the executive branch of the U.S. government. Expenses for trips on cruise ships are limited to $2,000 for an individual in any calendar year.

For foreign conventions, no expenses can be claimed outside of the North America area unless the convention or meeting is directly related to the taxpayer's business, and it is reasonable that the meeting be held outside of the North America area. The North America area includes: the U.S. and its possessions, Canada, Mexico, the Republic of the Marshall Islands, the Federated States of Micronesia, the Republic of Palau, Antigua, Aruba, Barbuda, Bahamas, Barbados, Bermuda, Costa Rica, Dominica, Dominican Republic, Grenada, Guyana, Honduras, Jamaica, Netherlands Antilles, Panama, and Trinidad and Tobago. The term "North America area" also includes a "beneficiary country" if there is an information exchange agreement between that country and the U.S. and there is no finding by the Secretary of the Treasury that the tax laws of the beneficiary country discriminate against conventions held in the U.S. IRS guidance lists all U.S. possessions and all beneficiary countries, along with dates after which conventions held in those countries may generate allowable expenses. Allowable expenses for foreign conventions, seminars, or other meetings are limited to $2,000 for an individual in any calendar year.

Travel Expenses for Investment Purposes – Travel expenses for investment purposes can be claimed only if the expenses are incurred to check out a "specific investment opportunity," but can't be claimed if the expenses are incurred for the sole purpose of seeking general information about making future investments. Travel expenses incurred for conventions, seminars, or similar meetings attended for investment purposes can't be claimed. The Internal Revenue Code forbids investors from claiming costs incurred for attending conventions, seminars or similar meetings at which they obtain information that helps them plot investment strategies. Disallowed expenses include air fares and other travel costs to the meeting site, attendance fees, meals, lodging, and local travel while attending the meetings. However, financial advisors, stock brokers and others who are at the conventions for business reasons can claim travel expenses as business related expenses. Travel expenses incurred by investors when actually acquiring investment property must be capitalized rather than being currently deductible.

Lodging, Meals and Incidental Expenses

Lodging, meals and incidental expenses can be either for actual expenses incurred, or per diem rates established by your business or the federal government. The federal government issues a standard per diem rate for the continental U.S. (CONUS) annually, as well as per diem rates for specific cities and localities that are higher than the standard rate. The standard per diem rate for CONUS for Oct. 1, 2017 through Sept. 30, 2018 is $144 ($93 for lodging and $51 for meals and incidental expenses (M&IE). Expenses for laundry, cleaning and pressing clothes, and business telephone calls are allowed in addition to the M&IE allowance. The standard per diem rate for CONUS for Oct. 1, 2018 through Sept. 30, 2019 is $144 ($93 for lodging and $51 for M&IE). Under the federal governments per diem method (the regular per diem method), you must use the standard per diem rate unless you travel to a specific city or locality that is allowed a higher per diem rate than the standard per diem rate (these rates are available on the GSA website). Per diem rates for specific localities that are higher than the standard per diem rate are listed in the per diem rate table. Per diem rates by specific locality in FY 2018 range from $144 to $498.

www.gsa.gov/travel/plan-book/per-diem-rates

In lieu of using the regular per diem method, businesses are allowed to use the "high-low" per diem method." Under this method, "special" per diem rates are established for a handful of "high-cost areas" with higher costs of living which includes resort areas like Vail and Martha's Vineyard. Certain tourist attraction areas only count as high-cost areas on a seasonal basis. All other locations that aren't listed as "high-cost" automatically fall into the "low-cost" category. Taxpayers can either use the "high-low" method or opt instead to use per diems calculated separately for hundreds of cities when using the regular per diem method (See above). The "high-low" method special per diem rates for CONUS for Oct. 1, 2017 through Sept. 30, 2018 are $284 for travel to any high-cost location ($216 for lodging and $68 for M&IE), and $191 for travel to any low-cost location ($134 for lodging and $57 for M&IE). The special per diem rates for CONUS for Oct.1, 2018 through Sept. 30, 2019 are $284 for travel to high-cost locations ($216 for lodging and $68 for M&IE), and $191 for travel to low-cost locations ($134 for lodging and $57 for M&IE). If you use the high-low per diem method for at any time during the calendar year, you must use the high-low method for all travel during the calendar year, i.e. you cannot switch back and forth between the regular per diem method and the high-low per diem method during the same calendar year. Notices 2017-54 and 2017-54 contain a list of the localities that are designated high-cost localities for fiscal years beginning Oct. 1, 2017 and Oct. 1, 2018. Notice 2017-54 designates localities that have a regular federal per diem rate of $238 or more for all or part of the calendar year as high-cost locations, slightly higher than the year before.
www.irs.gov/pub/irs-drop/n-16-58.pdf   www.irs.gov/pub/irs-drop/n-17-54.pdf

If you rely on the federal per diem rates for the first 9 months of 2018, you may continue to use those rates instead of the new per diem rates, effective Oct 1, 2018, for the last 3 months of 2018. However, you must consistently use one or the other of the two rates for the period 10/1/2018 – 12/31/2018.

Self-employed individuals who do not incur any meal expenses for a calendar day (or partial day) of travel while away from home may claim a per diem rate of $5 a day solely for incidentals. This rate is in lieu of using actual expenses in computing the amount allowable as a deduction for ordinary and necessary incidental expenses. This $5 rate is the same for fiscal years beginning Oct. 1, 2017, and Oct. 1, 2018.

231

The Accountable Plan for Employees – Since employees can't deduct miscellaneous itemized deductions subject to the 2% AGI floor in 2018, employers should establish an "accountable plan" so they can reimburse employees' travel, meals and lodging expenses, and the reimbursements won't be subject to income and payroll taxes. Amounts received by employees under an accountable plan are deductible by the employer without any required inclusion in the employee's income. To have an accountable plan, employers must establish a valid, written plan that sets forth a reimbursement arrangement that complies with the following rules: (1) expenses must have a business connection that are deductible in performing services as an employee of the employer; (2) employees must adequately account to their employer for these expenses within a reasonable period of time; and (3) employees must return any excess reimbursement or allowance within a reasonable period of time. Advances are to be paid back to employers within 30 days of the time the expenses are paid or incurred; expenses are to be adequately accounted for within 60 days after they were paid or incurred; and any excess reimbursements must be returned within 120 days after the expenses are paid or incurred. A log or account book should be used by employees to keep track of lodging, meals, and incidental expenses when traveling away from home. The log book should show time, place, business purpose, and amount of each separate expense. Employees who are under an accountable plan established by their employer are subject to the same travel rules discussed above and below in this chapter.

Expenses accounted for can be either actual expenses that are reimbursed by an employer for lodging, meals and incidental expenses or the annual allowable per diem rates established by the federal government. Accounting for actual expenses generally requires more documentation – employees must keep and present receipts for every meal and other expenses incurred. However, if the federal per diem rates are used, employees don't have to meet the usual recordkeeping rules required when actual expenses are claimed. Instead, the employer pays the specified per diem allowance to employees based on the number of business days, but documentary evidence is still required for any lodging expenses over $75 a day (this also applies to other expenses as well). If an employee is reimbursed for actual expenses or for a per diem rate established by the employer that is more than the federal per diem rate, the employer must include the allowance amount up to the federal per diem rate under Code L in box 12 of the employee's Form W-2. This amount is not taxable. However, the excess allowance must be included in Box 1 of the employee's Form W-2 as taxable wages, even if the employer has established an accountable plan. If employees' actual expenses were more than the federal per diem rates in 2017 and prior years, they could complete Form 2106 and deduct the "excess" expenses as a miscellaneous itemized deduction subject to the 2% AGI floor, but as stated above, employees cannot claim miscellaneous itemized deductions subject to the 2% AGI floor in 2018. **(See Chapter 4, "Wages and Salaries")**

In September 2014, the IRS finalized regulations which explicitly allow local lodging expenses to be treated as working condition fringe benefits for accountable plan reimbursements. In certain circumstances, local lodging expenses to attend business meetings and conferences incurred in carrying on a trade or business can be claimed if: (1) the lodging is necessary for the employee to fully participate in a bona fide business meeting, conference, training activity, or other business function; (2) the lodging must be on a temporary basis not exceeding five calendar days and not occur more than once each calendar quarter; (3) the employer requires the employee to remain at the activity or function overnight; and (4) the lodging is not extravagant or lavish and does not provide a significant element of personal pleasure, recreation or benefit.

Examples of when local lodging expenses are applicable include: employees who are required to stay at a local hotel during a work-related training session; professional athletes who are required to stay at a local hotel before a home game; an employee who is relocating for work and looking for a new home; an employee who has to stay in a hotel near the office while working long hours; and employees who occasionally are on call for a night duty shift and stay at a local hotel.

Businesses and Self-Employed/Independent Contractors – Business meals and incidental expenses are limited to being 50% deductible by businesses, including independent contractors and self-employed persons.

Self-employed persons/independent contractors, and those owning 10% or more of a company cannot use the federal per diem rates to substantiate lodging expenses. However, they may use the federal M&IE rates for meals and incidental expenses instead of keeping records (3/4 of the M&IE rate is allowed for partial days), but they must use actual costs for lodging expenses. However, they can deduct only 50% of business meals and incidental expenses while traveling away from home. This rule also applies when the M&IE allowance is used in lieu of actual meals and incidental expenses, i.e. the 50% limitation is applicable to the M&IE allowance. The only exception to the 50% limit for claiming meals and incidental expenses (including M&IE rates) is if you are a self-employed person/independent contractor who provides adequate records for the expenses to your customer or client, and your customer or client reimburses you or gives you an allowance for the expenses in connection with services you perform, and the amount of the allowance is included on a Form 1099-MISC that you must include in your gross taxable income. If these terms or met, you can deduct 100% of the reimbursements for the expenses. **(See Chapter 14, "Independent Contractors/ Non-Employees")**

Transportation Industry Employees – The federal government M&IE rates for taxpayers subject to the Department of Transportation (DOT) service rules – transportation industry employees (truck drivers, etc.) or self-employed individuals in the transportation industry for Oct. 1, 2017 through Sept. 30, 2018, are: $63 for any locality in CONUS (continental U.S.) and $68 OCONUS (outside of the continental U.S.). The rates for Oct. 1, 2018 through Sept. 30, 2019 are unchanged: $63 for any locality in CONUS and $68 OCONUS. A transportation industry employee is entitled to claim only the lesser of the amount paid to him/her by an employer that qualifies as an allowance paid under a flat rate or stated schedule, or the M&IE rate for the number of days traveled during a month, and of course, he/she can only claim the expenses if under an accountable plan established by the employer, because he/she cannot deduct the expenses as miscellaneous itemized deduction subject to the 2% AGI floor in 2018. For example, a transportation industry employee travels away from home on business for 10 days and based on the number of miles driven by the employee, his/her employer pays an allowance of $500 for the 10 days of business travel. The employee actually drives for 8 days, and does not drive the other 2 days he is away from home. The amount deemed substantiated and paid to the employee is the full $500 because that amount does not exceed $630 (ten days away from home at $63 M&IE rate per day). **(See Below, "Vehicle and Other Transportation Expenses")**

Instead of the 50% limit (see above), and self-employed transportation industry persons subject to the DOT service rules, i.e. truck drivers, etc. who pay their own expenses, can claim 80% of unreimbursed business meals and incidental expenses, including 80% of the special federal M&IE allowance for transportation industry employees. For example, a self-employed truck driver travels away from home for 10 days. Therefore, based on the special

M&IE rates for the transportation industry, he or she can claim $504 in travel expenses ($63 X 10 = $630 X 80% = $504) on Schedule C, Form 1040.

Truck drivers can't claim travel expenses when for weeks or months at a time they are on long trips on the road, if between jobs they stay at different places not considered a permanent home or place of abode, because they are considered to be "itinerant" truck drivers without a permanent home.

Entertainment Expenses

Under the Tax Cuts and Jobs Act (TCJA), any deduction for business entertainment expenses is not allowed for 2018 and subsequent years. The TCJA repeals allowable deductions that a business can take for entertainment and recreation even when directly related to a taxpayer's trade or business. This includes activities considered entertainment, amusement, or recreation; membership dues in business clubs organized for pleasure; and facilities used in connection with entertainment. However, business meals appear to remain 50% deductible under the TCJA, which raises the question of when do business meals become business entertainment?

There is uncertainty as to whether meals provided at a company recreational event, such as a picnic or company party should be included in entertainment expenses or should be deductible by taxpayers. **(See Below, "Company Party")**

Below are the provisions regarding entertainment expenses that were in effect in 2017 and prior years:

There is a 50% cap on deductions and reimbursements for entertainment expenses – a business can deduct only 50% of its entertainment expenses, and if an employee foots the bill personally, he or she can deduct only 50% of the entertainment expenses on his/her tax return. However, it can be a little unclear about what is and is not included in the 50% entertainment category. Expenses subject to the 50% entertainment ceiling include expenses for meals, food, related taxes and tips, cover charges for night club admissions, room rentals for dinners or cocktail parties, parking at sporting events, and casualty losses at entertainment facilities; but not expenses for maintenance of the facilities. In addition, if spouses or significant others are invited along, the costs attributable to them also count toward the 50% limit. Expenses incurred for recreational meetings for highly compensated employees (company executives) are not deductible entertainment expenses. However, expenses for business meetings with stockholders are deductible entertainment expenses.

Only 50% of unreimbursed employee entertainment expenses, including amounts paid for entertainment meals, can be deducted as miscellaneous itemized deductions subject to the 2% of AGI floor. And if you are an employee of a business and are reimbursed by your employer for 50% of your entertainment expenditures under an "accountable plan," you cannot deduct the unreimbursed 50% portion of those outlays as a miscellaneous itemized deduction subject to the 2% of AGI floor on Schedule A, Form 1040. **(See Above, "The Accountable Plan');** **(See Chapter 12, "Miscellaneous Itemized Deductions Subject to the 2% AGI Floor')**

Entertainment expenses must be "directly related" or "associated with" the active conduct of business, and there has to be a substantial and bona fide business discussion directly before, during, or after the dining and entertainment, and in order to claim entertainment expenses, an employee of the organization providing the entertainment must be present when food or beverages are furnished. For instance, meals are "directly related" to your business when they take place in a clear business setting – e.g. lunch served in a hospitality room at a convention where business goodwill is created by displaying or discussing business products. However, entertainment "associated with" your business is more common – in this case, you can deduct meal expenses that follow or precede a "substantial business discussion." A business discussion is not considered substantial unless you can show you actively engaged in the discussion, meeting, or negotiation to get income or some other specific business benefit. The meeting does not have to be for any specified length of time, but you must show that the business discussion was substantial in relation to the meal or entertainment.

A meal or entertainment expense will usually qualify if it takes place on the same day as the substantial business discussion, and when you are hosting business guests from out of town, you can deduct meals and entertainment expenses that take place the day before or after the business discussion. For entertainment tickets, including tickets to sporting events, the cost of a ticket is limited to its face value. In addition, no deduction is allowed when tickets are provided to a client or prospect if an employee or other representative of the company providing the tickets is not present at the event.

- **Example** – A business owner meets in the morning with two clients while they finalize a deal. After the group concludes the business meeting, the business owner invites the clients to his private country club for a round of golf in the afternoon, followed by dinner and drinks that night. Of course, the dues the business owner pays to belong to the club are not partially deductible as entertainment expenses, but expenses that are typically deductible include greens fees, golf club rentals, golf balls and other accessories, travel to and from the club, parking, meals, drinks and similar expenses.

Entertainment expenses must be reasonable in nature. The IRS will disallow deductions for entertaining deemed "extravagant or lavish." Whether or not a meal is considered extravagant or lavish depends on the particular circumstances, but the IRS has conceded that it won't disallow deductions merely because the meals take place at a deluxe restaurant, hotel, nightclub or resort. The IRS tends to view entertainment expense deductions skeptically. Therefore, it's important to document these expenses carefully, including: where the substantial business meeting took place and who attended; the names of the people entertained; the date and place where the entertainment took place; and the business purpose of the entertainment. You should maintain a log of entertainment expenses just like you should do for business travel in a car. This is the best proof you can have if the IRS asks for documentation.

Home entertainment – Like other kinds of meals and entertainment, home entertaining has to satisfy either one of two requirements: it must be directly related or associated with the active conduct of business, and there has to be a substantial bona fide business discussion directly before, during, or after the dining or entertainment. Also, even though the dining or entertainment event takes place in your home, you don't have to limit your expenses to modest home-cooked meals for yourself and your business guests, i.e. you can still have catered events at your home before or after business discussions. However, home entertainment expenses must be reasonable to be deductible.

- **Example** – Suppose you invite some business clients and their spouses to dinner at your home, and you also invite some friends that have no business connection. Because the party directly follows a business discussion with your clients, it passes the test as deductible "associated with" business entertainment. However, you get no deduction for the expenses attributable to your friends who aren't business guests, and you are subject to a cap of 50% on the remaining expenditures. If no business discussion takes place, the mere fact that the guests entertained are "present or potential" customers or clients is not sufficient to allow a deduction.

Company Party – Normally, deductions for home entertainment expenses are limited to 50% of the cost. However, under a special tax law exception, you can write-off 100% of a company party, like a July 4th or Labor Day picnic or barbecue, as long as the entire workforce is invited – you can't restrict the get-together to just the top brass or a select few employees. If you invite business associates to the gathering, their expenses count toward the deductible amount, and at this kind of socializing, business doesn't have to be discussed before, during or after the event. Asking a few friends to the festivities won't negate the tax break, but any cost attributable to them is nondeductible.

Vehicle and Other Transportation Expenses

The establishment of an "accountable plan" by employers for the benefit of employees also applies to business expenses for the use of a personal vehicle and other transportation expenses, such as taxi cabs, buses, and airplanes. **(See Above, "The Accountable Plan")**

A taxpayer may use actual expenses or the standard mileage allowance to substantiate business expenses for the use of a personal vehicle. The standard mileage allowance in 2018 is 54.5 cents per mile (53.5 cents per mile in 2017). Actual expenses include: depreciation or lease payments; gasoline and oil; maintenance and repairs; tires; insurance; license and registration fees; state and local property taxes; and tolls and parking fees. The standard mileage allowance may be used for a vehicle that is either owned or leased by the taxpayer, and you can claim parking fees and tolls in addition to claiming the standard mileage allowance. Also, using the standard mileage allowance won't preclude you from deducting personal property taxes on the vehicle. Claiming either actual expenses or the standard mileage allowance for business use of your vehicle requires you to note the date, destination, purpose, and mileage for each tax-deductible business trip in your vehicle – you have to keep a log of your business trips. Interest paid by an employee on a car loan is not deductible even if the employee uses the vehicle for business purposes. However, a self-employed taxpayer may deduct the interest on a car loan based on the portion of the car used for business purposes. State and local taxes paid in connection with the purchase of a vehicle are considered part of the purchase price of the vehicle. You can't use the standard mileage allowance for more than four vehicles used simultaneously for business purposes (such as fleet operations), i.e. if you are using more than four vehicles for business purposes, you must use the actual expenses method.
www.irs.gov/pub/irs-drop/n-16-79.pdf

The choice to use the standard mileage allowance instead of actual expenses must be made in the first year you place a vehicle into service. You may not use the standard mileage allowance for a vehicle after using any depreciation method under the Modified Accelerated Cost Recovery System (MACRS) or after claiming Section 179 expensing for a vehicle. If the standard mileage allowance is used in the first year a vehicle is placed in service, you can change to using actual expenses in a future year, but then you can't change back to using the standard mileage allowance for any year after that. When actual expenses are used, the amount of actual expenses allocated to business usage in a year is determined based on the percentage of business miles driven during the year compared to total miles driven during the year. **(See Chapter 16, "Modified Accelerated Cost Recovery System (MACRS)"; "Section 179 First-Year Expensing"; & "First-Year Bonus Depreciation")**

Depreciation reduces the basis of a vehicle (but not below zero). If the standard mileage allowance is used, the portion of the business mileage allowance treated as depreciation is 25 cents per mile in 2018 (Also, 25 cents in 2017), which reduces the basis of a vehicle by that amount per business mile driven during the year. Therefore, if you drive your car 10,000 business miles during 2018, the basis of the car is reduced by $2,500 ($.25 X 10,000 miles).

Deducting Local Travel Expenses – Commuting to work, whether in your personal vehicle or by some other means, is not a deductible expense. Local transportation expenses are deductible when: going directly from one job to another, if you have more than one job, or if you're based at one of several job locations and have to travel between them; and going from your residence to a temporary job location when you have a regular work location. However, travel between your residence and a temporary work location that is close to your regular work location (within the same metropolitan area) is considered commuting and is not deductible. Also, if you're taking a course at a local college to improve your job skills, you may go straight to school after work and the cost of the travel between work and the school is deductible (or between school and work if you're taking a morning class).

- **Example** – If your home office is your principal place of business (you are self-employed), your tax home and place of work is the same as your home. In this case, you can deduct the cost of visiting a client or customer across town on Schedule C as long as you keep proper records. But if you stop to buy groceries on your way home, the portion of the trip representing personal travel is nondeductible.

Leasing a Car, Truck, or Van for Business Use – You can use the standard mileage allowance, or actual expenses plus the lease payments (must be allocated based on the percentage of business miles driven compared to total miles driven during the year). If you choose to use actual expenses, you can deduct the part of each lease payment that is for the use of the vehicle in your business. You can't deduct any part of a lease payment that is for personal use of the vehicle, such as commuting. You must spread any advance payments over the entire lease period. Leased vehicles are not depreciated, so if you lease a vehicle for 30 days or more, and you use the actual expenses method, you have to reduce your lease payment deduction by an "inclusion amount" for each tax year you lease the vehicle. The inclusion amount is added to your income in each year of the lease agreement.

The inclusion amount is a percentage of part of the fair market value (FMV) of the leased vehicle in accordance with an amount spelled out in IRS tables multiplied by the percentage of business use of the vehicle for the year. The inclusion amount applies to each tax year that you lease the vehicle and is figured on the fair market value (FMV) of the vehicle on the first day of the lease term. NOTE: Due to the increased depreciation allowances in 2018 in accordance with the Tax Cuts and Jobs Act (TCJA), the inclusion amounts have been substantially changed. There is no inclusion amount if the value of a vehicle first leased in 2018 is $50,000 or less. Inclusion amounts begin when the value of the vehicle first leased in 2018 is more than $50,000. The inclusion amounts for vehicles first leased in 2017 began with passenger automobiles valued at more than $19,000 and trucks and vans valued at over $19,500. **(See Chapter 16, "Passenger Vehicles Used for Transportation")**
www.irs.gov/pub/irs-drop/rp-17-29.pdf

You can't deduct any payments you make to buy a car, truck, or van even if the payments are called lease payments.

Fixed and variable rate (FAVR) Plan – A FAVR plan is an alternative way (in lieu of the standard mileage allowance) for reimbursing employees who use their own or leased vehicles for work related activities. Under a FAVR plan, a standard amount is deemed substantiated for an employer's reimbursement to employees for expenses they incur in driving their vehicle in performing services for the employer. A FAVR allowance includes two types of payments: periodic fixed payments, and periodic variable payments. The fixed payment amount is to cover the cost of owning and operating a vehicle – taxes, insurance, depreciation, etc. The variable payment amount is to cover the cost of operating a vehicle – regular routine maintenance, tires, oil, gasoline, etc. Total fixed and variable costs for operating a vehicle are calculated and then adjusted to reflect the percentage of time the vehicle is used for business purposes. The FAVR allowance depends upon the locality of the employer and must be recomputed quarterly. For purposes of computing the allowance, the maximum standard automobile cost for 2018 is $27,300 ($27,900 in 2017) and $31,000 ($31,300 in 2017) for trucks and vans

These programs are considered a first-rate option to using the standard mileage allowance for reimbursing employees. FAVR programs are flexible and customizable, and can also be tax-free to businesses and employees. Though it offers many of the same benefits as an allowance plan, the expense ratio can be up to 40 percent lower for FAVR programs. FAVR programs consider regional cost differences, which in conjunction with other factors, can save businesses money. Employers must meet a set of IRS requirements in order for their FAVR program to be tax-advantaged. This includes having five or more drivers who drive at least 5,000 miles each annually. www.irs.gov/pub/irs-drop/n-16-79.pdf

Employer Provided Vehicle – An employer provided vehicle is taxable to the employee if the employee uses the vehicle for personal use. An appropriate amount should be included in the employee's wages and reported on his/her Form W-2. **(See Chapter 4, "Employer Provided Vehicle")**

Excise Tax on Heavy Highway Vehicles
The excise tax on heavy highway vehicles is a maximum $550 per vehicle that is due each year on Aug. 31st. Form 2290 has to be filed when paying the tax. The excise tax applies to trucks, tractors, buses, logging vehicles, etc. weighing at least 55,000 pounds. Taxpayers can paper file their return, unless they have 25 or more vehicles, then they must e-file.
www.irs.gov/pub/irs-pdf/f2290.pdf

Chapter 16 – Property Depreciation and Expensing

Generally, a business is entitled to claim depreciation deductions for property, including real estate, beginning in the year the property is "placed in service." Whether or not property is considered to be placed in service for depreciation purposes is based on the property's specific function and when it is in a condition or state of readiness and availability for that function. The determination is made based on the applicable facts and circumstances. For example, a store being open for business is not a requirement for the building being placed in service. An asset may be considered to be placed in service if everything in the taxpayer's power has been done to put the asset to use. In the case of real property, it is important to include land as a separate asset from a building or structure that is on the land, because land is not depreciable. All tangible property that is not inventory must be capitalized and depreciated using the Modified Accelerated Cost Recovery System (MACRS), unless there is an exception.

- **Example** – If you buy equipment to be used in business production, it's generally not enough to merely acquire the equipment and have it delivered to the warehouse. The equipment must be removed from the box and the business must actually start using it for its intended purpose before depreciation can be taken on the equipment.

The tangible property regulations, which were effective for tax years beginning on or after January 1, 2014, addressed a universal issue that needed clarifying regarding repair and maintenance costs – whether payments "to acquire, produce or improve" tangible property must be capitalized and recovered over time (depreciated), or whether they can be deducted immediately. **(See Below, "Modified Accelerated Cost Recovery System (MACRS)")**
www.irs.gov/pub/irs-utl/tangiblepropertyatg9142016.pdf

There are seven classes of assets: (1) real and personal property that can be depreciated, except for land; (2) cash and general deposit accounts other than certificates of deposit; (3) actively traded personal property (stocks and securities); (4) debt instruments; (5) inventory items; (6) all intangibles; and (7) goodwill and going concern values. Tangible property is all real and personal property that can be depreciated. Personal property is generally considered assets that are movable, as opposed to real property or real estate. Reduction in the adjusted basis of real and personal property based on allowable depreciation is mandatory even if not taken. Depreciation and/or cost recovery of tangible assets can be used for both business and investment purposes. Personal vehicles are one kind or personal property that can be used for both business and investment purposes. A taxpayer may use actual expenses, which includes depreciation, or the standard mileage allowance to substantiate business expenses for the use of a personal vehicle. **(See Chapter 15, "Vehicle and Other Transportation Expenses")**

Modified Accelerated Cost Recovery System (MACRS)
All real and personal property placed in service for business use after 1986 must use the Modified Accelerated Cost Recovery System (MACRS) for depreciation. If property is converted to business use, the lesser of the adjusted basis or the fair market value (FMV) of the property on the date it is placed in service must be used as the basis of the property for depreciation purposes. MACRS consists of two depreciation systems – the General Depreciation System (GDS) and the Alternative Depreciation System (ADS). Generally, these two systems provide different methods of depreciation and recovery periods to use in figuring depreciation deductions. Under GDS, there are 3 methods of depreciation: (1) 200% declining balance method; (2) 150% declining balance method; and (3) the

straight-line (SL) method. Under ADS, there is only the SL method of depreciation, and depreciation under ADS is over a longer recovery period than GDS, except for 5-year property.

Taxpayers generally use GDS unless they are specifically required by law to use ADS or they elect to use it. Property for which the use of ADS is required includes: certain "listed" property (see below); any tangible property used predominantly outside the United States during the year; any imported property covered by an executive order of the President of the United States; tax-exempt bond financed property; and tax-exempt use property. There is a test to determine if residential and nonresidential real property is mandatory for ADS: The test is whether there is a disqualified lease – which is a lease whose term is greater than 20 years, including options to renew (ADS applies). The only exception for not including "options to renew" is when the rental is based on the fair market value (FMV) of the property at the time of renewal. A building that is partially financed with tax-exempt bonds will be partially depreciated using ADS and partially with GDS, e.g. a $10 million building financed with $5 million of IDBs would be 50% depreciated using ADS and 50% depreciated using GDS. An office building that is leased to a government agency (tax-exempt use) is depreciated based on the 35% test, which means that if more than 35% of the building (based on square footage) is leased to a tax-exempt entity, the entire building is depreciated using ADS. If ADS is mandatory, then bonus depreciation is not available (See below). Although property may qualify for GDS, taxpayers may elect to use ADS.

Conventions Under MACRS – Property is considered placed in service during the year in accordance with the following conventions:

- Half-year convention – Used for all property, except for real property (residential and nonresidential real property) unless the mid-quarter convention is required. This means that any personal property placed in service during the year will be allowed ½ year of depreciation no matter when the property is placed in service during the year.
- Mid-quarter convention – Used if the aggregate basis of all personal property placed in service during the last 3 months of the year exceeds 40% of the cost of all personal property placed in service during the year. When this happens, personal property purchased in the first quarter of the calendar year will get 10 ½ months of depreciation; personal property purchased in the second quarter will get 7 ½ months of depreciation; personal property purchased in the third quarter will get 4 ½ months of depreciation; and personal property purchased in the fourth quarter will get 1 ½ months of depreciation. Assets expensed under Section 179 are not included in the mid-quarter convention determination. However, if an asset has been partially expensed under Section 179, then the remaining amount that is subject to depreciation will be included in the calculation (See below).
- Mid-month convention – Used for real property, including residential rental property and nonresidential real and rental property. Property is allowed depreciation based on the number of months in the year it has been placed in service.

Property Classifications Under MACRS – There are 9 property classifications:
- 3-Year Classification – Assets are Section 1245 personal property depreciated over a 3-year period using 200% DB/GDS, and includes: tractor units for over-the-road use; race horses; any other horses (other than race horses) over 12 years old when placed in service; and qualified rent-to-own property. If ADS is used, depreciation is over a 4-year period.

- 5-Year Classification – Assets are Section 1245 personal property depreciated over a 5-year period using 200% DB/GDS, and includes: automobiles; light and heavy duty trucks; taxis; buses; computers and peripheral equipment; office machinery and equipment (typewriters, faxes, copiers, calculators, etc.); any property used in research and experimentation; breeding cattle and dairy cattle; appliances, carpet, furniture, etc. used in residential rental properties; and certain geothermal, solar, and wind energy property. If ADS is used, depreciation is also over a 5-year period.
- 5-Year Classification – Original use farm machinery and equipment using 200% DB/GDS, effective for 2018 acquisitions.
- 7-Year Classification – Assets are Section 1245 personal property depreciated over a 7-year period using 200% DB/GDS and includes: office furniture and fixtures such as desks, filing cabinets, safes, and any property that hasn't been assigned a class life. Agricultural machinery and equipment is depreciated using 150% DB/GDS. If ADS is used, depreciation is over a 12-year period.
- 10-Year Classification – Assets are both Section 1245 personal property and Section 1250 real property depreciated over a 10-year period using 200% DB/GDS, and includes: vessels, barges, tugs, and similar water transportation equipment. Agricultural trees or vines bearing fruits or nuts and single purpose agricultural or horticultural structures are depreciated using 150% DB/GDS. If ADS is used, depreciation is over a 15-year period.
- 15-Year Classification – Assets are Section 1250 real property depreciated over a 15-year period using 150% DB/GDS and includes: land improvements such as roads, sidewalks, bridges, fences, landscaping, asphalt parking lots, curbs, decorative walls, and shrubbery and plants.
- 15-Year Classification – Qualified leasehold improvement property; qualified restaurant property; and qualified retail improvement property (consolidated into one category "Qualified Improvement Property" by the TCJA) depreciated using the SL/GDS method. If ADS is used, depreciation is over a 20-year period. **(See Below, "Qualified Leasehold, Restaurant, and Retail Property"; & "Qualified Improvement Property)**
- 20-Year Classification – Assets are Section 1250 real property depreciated over a 20-year period using 150 DB/GDS, and includes: farm buildings (other than single purpose agricultural or horticultural structures); and municipal sewers not classified as 25-year property. If ADS is used, depreciation is also over a 20-year period.
- 25-year Classification – Assets are Section 1250 real property depreciated over a 25-year period using SL/GDS, and includes: water utility property.
- 27 ½ -year Classification – Assets are Section 1250 real property depreciated over a 27 ½ -year period using SL/GDS and includes: residential rental property. If ADS is used, depreciation is over a 30-year period.
- 39-year Classification – Assets are Section 1250 real property depreciated over a 39-year period using SL/GDS, and includes: nonresidential real property. If (ADS) is used, depreciation is over a 40-year period.

Unit of Property

Taxpayers must capitalize and depreciate amounts paid to acquire or produce a "unit of real or personal property," including buildings, land improvements, qualified improvement property, machinery and equipment, and furniture and fixtures. Acquisition costs that must be capitalized include work performed before or after a unit of property is placed in service, such as investigating or pursuing the acquisition; transporting or shipping; appraisals; negotiating the terms; obtaining tax advice; application fees; bidding; preparing sales contracts or purchase agreements;

examining and evaluating the title; obtaining regulatory approval or securing permits; application fees; brokers' commissions or finders fees; architectural, geological engineering, environmental and inspection fees; and services provided by a qualified intermediary or facilitator. Employee compensation and overhead costs are generally not included as acquisition costs. In addition, improvements to a unit of property after acquisition and amounts paid to rehabilitate a unit of property must be capitalized and depreciated.

Whether an expenditure should be capitalized and depreciated or considered a repair expense must be analyzed in the context of each "unit of property." A unit of property consists of all components that are functionally interdependent. Components are functionally interdependent if the placing in service of one component is dependent on the placing in service of other components. However, components are treated as separate units of property when they belong to separate classes of property that are depreciated differently under the Modified Accelerated Cost Recovery System (MACRS) even if they are considered interdependent (e.g. 5, 7, 15-year, etc. properties) – This is often determined by a cost segregation study (see below). Costs that are unrelated to the acquisition, improvement, or rehabilitation of a unit of property may qualify to be expensed as repairs in the current year, and any expenditure can be deducted as an expense if it qualifies under the "materials and supplies rule" or the safe harbors (see below). **(See Above, "Modified Accelerated Cost Recovery System (MACRS"); (See Below, "Cost Segregation Study"; "Safe Harbors"; & "Materials and Supplies Rule")**

Partial Disposition Election – Taxpayers can make a "partial disposition election" to claim losses on components of a unit of property that are retired or replaced, instead of continuing to depreciate them, and in addition, they can deduct the removal costs when they retire or replace a component. If an expenditure replaces a component of a unit of property and is required to be capitalized and depreciated in accordance with the applicable rules and guidelines, then you can take a loss on the old component that is replaced and retired based on the remaining basis of the old component, instead of continuing to depreciate it as well as depreciating the new replacement component. However, if an expenditure is considered a repair cost, then it is deducted as an expense in the current year, and you must continue to depreciate the old component that remains on the books. The partial disposition election applies to both building and non-building properties.

The partial disposition rule is usually elective. However, when a partial disposition results from a casualty, abandonment, like-kind exchange, or in certain other circumstances, the partial disposition rule must be used. A partial disposition election allows taxpayers to treat the retirement of a structural component of a fixed asset, such as the replacement of the roof of a building, as a disposition. Thus, enabling a taxpayer to claim a loss on the remaining cost basis (undepreciated basis) of that component (roof). The partial disposition election reduces the circumstances where there is simultaneous depreciation of a retired component and its replacement component. The partial disposition election is made by simply claiming a gain or loss on the taxpayer's timely filed tax return (including extensions).

- **Example** – A taxpayer replaces a portion of a building's roof with a new component in 2018. The replaced roof component is retired, so the taxpayer can recognize a loss based on the unadjusted basis (undepreciated basis) of the replaced roof component, including the removal cost on the 2018 tax return. The taxpayer capitalizes and depreciates the new replacement roof component.

When claiming partial disposition loss deductions for retired building components that have been replaced or demolished, it is sometimes difficult to determine the basis of each component without a cost segregation study (see below). The IRS not only recognizes a cost segregation study for this purpose, it also allows Producer Price Index (PPI) discounting when doing one of these studies.

- **Example** – In 2018, a taxpayer spends $300,000 on new replacement windows in a building that was purchased in 2012, and because the windows replaced were not new when the taxpayer purchased the building, a cost segregation study can be done and the PPI used to adjust the cost of the old windows to account for the condition they were in when the building was purchased by the taxpayer.

Complying with the Tangible Property Regulations – A taxpayer must have filed Form 3115, "Application for Change in Accounting Method," prior to January 1, 2017, in order to comply with the "Tangible Property Regulations" and to get an automatic change in accounting method. The automatic change in accounting method was beneficial because it allowed taxpayers to take deductions on assets disposed or replaced prior to January 1, 2014, which may have been the largest deductions available to them. The filing of Form 3115 before January 1, 2017, was required by all taxpayers in order to comply with the tangible property regulations, unless they were considered "small business taxpayers." Small business taxpayers were those in existence prior to January 1, 2017, and with total assets of less than $10 million as of the beginning of their first tax year that started on or after January 1, 2014, or with average annual gross receipts of $10 million or less over the three prior tax years. Small business taxpayers were allowed to choose the "simplified option," which in doing so meant that they were in compliance with the tangible property regulations without having to file Form 3115. If small businesses chose the simplified option, they could make accounting method changes prospectively for tax years on or after January 1, 2014, but could not take any deductions available to them for years prior to January 1, 2014. Large businesses (those not considered small businesses under this definition) were required to file Form 3115 in order to be in compliance with the tangible property regulations. It is estimated that 90% of businesses qualified for the simplified option.

Form 3115 was revised on December 15, 2015, so all requests for a change in accounting method should have been filed on the new form if filed after Dec. 15, 2015. However, the IRS gave relief from using the new form until April 19, 2016.

Improvement to a Unit of Property

Whether an expenditure is an improvement to a unit of property is often a matter of degree. The smaller the unit of property the more likely a subsequent cost related to the unit of property must be capitalized: You must analyze each cost in the context of the unit of property, and the IRS suggests that the materiality threshold is plus or minus 30%. So, each subsequent expenditure must be analyzed in relation to the original acquisition cost. Based on this presumption, a $15,000 expenditure on a unit of property with an original acquisition cost of $50,000 would likely be classified as an "Improvement" that is capitalized. On the other hand, the same $15,000 expenditure on a unit of property with an original acquisition cost of $350,000 might, but not necessarily, qualify as a repair expense. However, the materiality threshold is not the only determining factor.

Special rules apply to plant property, leased property, and buildings:
- Plant Property – two pieces of equipment that are functionally interdependent can be considered separate units of property, i.e. components that perform a discrete and major function within functionally interdependent plant equipment should be considered separate units of property. Example: an assembly line has many separate units of property that are interdependent.

- Leased Property – For the lessor, the entire building is the unit of property. For the lessee, the unit of property is the portion of the building being leased. Example: If a lessee in a large building remodels a bathroom in its office, the expenditure is likely a capital improvement because the work was done on a major portion of the plumbing system within their leased office space. Whereas, if the lessor performed the same work, it might be a repair expense because the work only affected a small portion of the building's entire plumbing system. This is a perfect example of how the same expenditure for the same purpose can either be an improvement that must be capitalized, or a repair that is currently expensed based on the materiality threshold.
- Buildings - Commercial buildings are a single unit of property. However, capitalization standards must be applied separately to the building structure and to the defined building systems. The building structure includes exterior walls, roof, windows, doors, etc. Defined building systems include the following: heating, ventilation, and air conditioning systems (HVAC); plumbing systems; electrical systems; escalators; elevators; fire protection and alarm systems; security systems; gas distribution systems; and other structural components identified. Any significant work on any of these systems must be capitalized. Therefore, a taxpayer can recognize a loss on the retirement of a structural component without having to dispose of the entire building, i.e. rather than continue to depreciate the cost of the component replaced while simultaneously starting to depreciate the cost of the new replacement component, you can consider the retirement of a structural component of a building system as a disposition and a loss.

Improvements to a unit of property that must be capitalized include: betterments; adaptations; and restorations. A betterment is a material addition to a unit of property (physical enlargement, expansion, extension or addition), or is reasonably expected to materially increase the strength, productivity, efficiency, or quality of a unit of property.

- **Example** – Replacing asphalt shingles on the roof of a building with new solar shingles is a betterment, so the cost of the new solar shingles must be capitalized. Therefore, the old asphalt shingles can be retired and a loss taken based on the remaining basis of the old asphalt shingles minus any salvage value. Also, the removal costs of the old asphalt shingles can be deducted as an expense.
- **Example** – Replacing wooden shingles that are no longer available with comparable asphalt shingles that are somewhat stronger than the wooden shingles is not a betterment and, therefore, the cost may qualify as a repair expense.
- **Example** – Enhancement due to technological advancements is not necessarily a betterment, i.e. replacing old HVAC equipment with more efficient new HVAC equipment is not necessarily a betterment.

An adaptation is when costs are incurred to adapt a unit of property to a different use than when the property was originally placed in service.

- **Example** – Converting a manufacturing building into a showroom for the business by removing and replacing various structural components to provide a better layout for showroom purposes and its offices is an adaptation and must be capitalized.

A restoration is the replacement of a component of a unit of property; returning a unit of property to its ordinary efficient operating condition if the property has deteriorated to a state of disrepair and is no longer functional for its intended use; rebuilding of a unit of property to a like-new condition after the end of its class life; or replacement of a part or a combination of parts that comprises a major component (or a significant portion of a major component of building property) or a substantial structural part. You must consider all facts and circumstances, both quantitative and qualitative, not just the cost, size, type, function etc. You must first identify the major component of a building system, then see if a significant portion was replaced. The replacement of a minor component of a unit of property will not constitute a major component or material structural part even though it affects the function of the unit of property. If a major component is not replaced, it may be a repair cost, but not necessarily. Again, the IRS suggests that the materiality threshold is 30% – plus or minus.

- **Example** – A taxpayer has a roof leak and discovers that a major portion of the decking and rafters of the roof has rotted and has to be replaced, as well as a significant portion, but not the entire roof – this constitutes a restoration and must be capitalized.
- **Example** – Replacing the roof tiles is not a restoration, nor is replacing a roof membrane with a comparable but new membrane – these are examples that may qualify as repair expenses.
- **Example** – An office building has one HVAC system comprised of 3 furnaces, 3 air conditioning units, and duct work throughout the building. The HVAC system constitutes a major system of the building. If one of the three furnaces breaks down and has to be replaced, it would not be a significant portion of a major component (HVAC system); would not be a restoration of the unit of property (HVAC system); and so, would qualify as a repair expense. This is an example that relates to the 30% +/- materiality threshold.
- **Example** – An office building has one HVAC system comprised of a cooling tower, a boiler, and a chiller. The chiller is replaced with a comparable unit. The chiller functions to cool the water to generate the air conditioning. Since the chiller performs a discrete and critical function of the HVAC system, replacement of the chiller is considered a restoration and must be capitalized.

Casualty Loss Rule – When property is damaged and deducted as a casualty loss, and then restored to its ordinary efficient operating condition, the amount to be capitalized is limited to the cost to restore the damaged property, less the amount claimed as a casualty loss and paid by insurance. The amount of the casualty loss is limited to the adjusted basis of the damaged component. The restoration can even be a repair if the basis of the damaged component is adjusted. **(See Chapter 16, "Business Casualty and Theft Losses")**

Materials and Supplies Rule – The cost of incidental materials and supplies costing $200 or less or with a useful life of 12 months or less and that are not acquired as part of any single unit of property are deductible as expenses in the current year if consumed and used in the operation of the business. This includes amounts paid to acquire, maintain, repair, or improve a unit of property that is owned or leased by a taxpayer, including routine expendable spare parts. It also includes both incidental and non-incidental materials and supplies that fall within the $200 range. Even though this change in accounting method is prospective only, in order to take advantage of the "materials and supplies rule" large taxpayers were required to file Form 3115 by the end of 2016 if the taxpayers had not complied with this accounting method prior to Jan. 1, 2014. However, small business taxpayers who chose the "simplified option" were not required to file Form 3115 (see above). Also, taxpayers that capitalize materials and supplies costing $200 or less for book purposes must make an adjustment for the book/tax difference because the Rule is not elective – any qualified materials and supplies costing $200 or less must be expensed for tax purposes. **(See Above, "Complying with the Tangible Property Regulations")**

Examples of incidental materials and supplies include fuel, lubricants, water, etc. that are expected to be consumed in 12 months or less. Non-incidental materials and supplies for which inventory records are kept are deducted when used or consumed in the taxpayer's operations (removed from inventory and placed in service).

Safe Harbors: The safe harbors available to taxpayers are: (1) the De Minimis safe harbor election; (2) the small taxpayer safe harbor election; and (3) the routine maintenance safe harbor. Using the safe harbors does not require a change in accounting method.

De Minimis Safe Harbor Election – Before using Section 179 expensing and bonus depreciation, taxpayers should consider taking advantage of the De Minimis safe harbor election for expensing amounts. The safe harbor allows businesses to avoid determining whether or not items purchased for a small cost are deductible or must be capitalized, and it eliminates having to depreciate a large number of purchases of small dollar capital assets. The De Minimis safe harbor election allows taxpayers to expense the cost of acquired or produced tangible property that does not exceed a certain dollar amount per invoice or item, including materials and supplies, or items having an economic useful life of 12 months or less. This includes acquisition costs paid for tangible property that make up a unit of property. **(See Below, "Section 179 First-Year Expensing"; & "First-Year Bonus Depreciation")**

Taxpayers with applicable audited financial statements can apply the safe harbor to each invoice or item of property costing $5,000 or less if the taxpayer treats the amounts as expenses on their financial statements. Taxpayers without audited financial statements can apply the safe harbor to each invoice or item of property costing $2,500 or less if they have accounting procedures in place at the beginning of the tax year (the procedures don't have to be written) if the amounts are expensed in the books and records. If the safe harbor is elected, it must be applied to all amounts paid. Amounts properly included under the De Minimis safe harbor election should not be capitalized, but instead must be deducted in the tax year in which they are paid. Also, the thresholds for the De Minimis safe harbor election include expenditures that a taxpayer can include under the "materials and supplies" rule. However, the safe harbor does not apply to materials and supplies acquired for use in manufacturing inventory if capitalization is otherwise required and to amounts paid for inventory and land. Also, the safe harbor applies only to tangible property; intangibles such as computer software are not eligible (see below).

The De Minimis safe harbor threshold is applied at the invoice level or, if multiple items appear on a single invoice, at the item level. Additional costs, such as delivery or installation fees, that appear on the same invoice as the property must be included in the property's cost. If these additional costs are not included on the same invoice as the property, the taxpayer may, but is not required to, include the additional costs in the property's cost. When multiple items of property are purchased on one invoice and additional costs are stated as a single sum, the taxpayer must use a reasonable method to allocate the additional costs among each item of property in computing the per-item cost.

- **Example** – Suppose a taxpayer without an applicable financial statement purchases 10 computers costing $2,500 each and receives an invoice for $25,500, which includes a delivery fee of $500. Pro rata allocation of the delivery fee brings the cost of each computer to $2,550, which exceeds the threshold of $2,500 per computer; therefore, a taxpayer without an audited financial statement may not apply the De Minimis safe harbor election to expense the cost. However, had the delivery fee legitimately appeared on a separate invoice (e.g. an invoice from the freight company instead of the seller), the taxpayer could apply the safe harbor rule and deduct the cost of the 10 computers and the delivery fee as an expense under the De Minimis safe harbor election.

An applicable audited financial statement is a financial statement: (1) filed with the SEC (Form 10-K); a certified audited financial statement used for credit purposes; a financial statement used for reporting to shareholders or partners; or for any other substantial nontax purpose, or (2) a financial statement (other than a tax return) required to be provided to a federal or state government or agency (other than the SEC or IRS). An entity that does not have a separate applicable financial statement, but that is included in a consolidated applicable financial statement is considered to have an applicable financial statement based on its inclusion in the consolidated financial statement.

The De Minimis safe harbor election is an annual, irrevocable election. The election must be a written policy that is included with a taxpayer's timely filed original annual tax return including extensions. Following is an example of wording that can be used for the annual De Minimis safe harbor election:

- "ABC Company elects to adopt for book and Federal income tax purposes the following policy regarding the capitalization of expenses for the year beginning Jan. 1, 2017. In accordance with Internal Revenue Code Sections 167 and 168 and related regulations, ABC company has determined that amounts whose individual cost (including tax, installation and delivery costs) does not exceed $2,500 or has a useful life of 12 months or less will be deducted as an operating expense. Amounts exceeding this dollar amount will be examined individually to determine if their use or purpose requires capitalization under the betterment, adaptation, or restoration rules used by the IRS and will be capitalized or expensed as incurred as a result of the application of those rules." (Companies with audited financial statements should replace $2,500 with $5,000).

Small Taxpayer Safe Harbor Election – Small taxpayers with average annual gross receipts of $10 million or less for the prior three tax years are allowed to deduct all expenditures for a building with an unadjusted basis of $1 million or less. The election is claimed each year by filing an election with their tax returns. If the safe harbor is elected, eligible taxpayers can deduct the total amount paid during the taxable year for improvements, repairs, maintenance, etc. performed on the building that do not exceed the lesser of $10,000 or 2% of the unadjusted basis of the building. The safe harbor is an all-or-nothing provision because, if expenditures exceed the lesser of 2% of the building's unadjusted basis or $10,000, no amount is eligible for the safe harbor. If the safe harbor is elected, it must be applied to all qualified expenditures. Amounts properly included under the safe harbor election should not be capitalized, but instead must be deducted in the tax year in which they are paid provided they otherwise are ordinary and necessary business expenses. For S-corporations or partnerships, the election is made at the entity level and not by the shareholders or partners. The small taxpayer safe harbor election is made by attaching a proper statement every year to a timely filed tax return.

A cost segregation study can be very helpful in some situations in regard to this safe harbor. For example, if a taxpayer purchases a building for $800,000 and later makes $300,000 in capital improvements, the building would not meet the $1,000,000 unadjusted basis rule. However, if the taxpayer performed a cost segregation study in which 30% ($330,000) of the total basis was reclassified as Section 1245 personal property, the building's basis would be reduced to $770,000 and would then qualify for the safe harbor election. **(See Below, "Cost Segregation Study")**

Routine Maintenance Safe Harbor – Under the Routine Maintenance safe harbor, recurring amounts paid to keep a unit of property in ordinary efficient working condition may be treated as repair costs (capitalization and depreciation is not required) for activities that the taxpayer reasonably expects to occur more than once during the class life of a property, or for a building (or structural component of a building system) more than once during the 10-year period beginning at the time the taxpayer places the building in service. The routine maintenance safe harbor applies to amounts that would otherwise be capitalized as improvements. Taxpayers have to consider the recurring nature of the activity, industry practice, manufacturers' recommendations, and the taxpayer's experience with similar property. For example, if a taxpayer expects to resurface a parking lot (15-year property) every 5 years, then under the safe harbor, this expenditure is not an improvement and can be expensed currently.

The Routine Maintenance safe harbor is not elective, but instead it automatically applies when a taxpayer meets the requirements. It is a method of accounting that a taxpayer adopts, and after being adopted must be used every year. However, its adoption is completely voluntary. Taxpayers can adopt the routine maintenance safe harbor by currently deducting allowable expenses on their tax returns.

Cost Segregation Study

For existing buildings (any building placed in service since 1/1/1987), a qualified engineering company accepted by the IRS can perform a cost segregation study to identify building costs and land improvements traditionally depreciated over 27.5 or 39 years that can be reclassified as property that can be depreciated over 5, 7, and 15 years, thus accelerating depreciation of the building cost. Such property is Section 1245 personal property that includes windows, electrical wiring, track and decorative lighting, wall paneling, counters, freezers, flooring, and wall partitions (depreciated over 5 and 7 years) as well as site or land improvements – sidewalks, parking lots, sewers, curbs, etc. (depreciated over 15 years). Cost segregation will allow you to properly identify an asset's cost basis, property class and recovery period. This results in accelerated depreciation deductions, a reduced tax liability, and an increase in cash flow. Cost segregation accelerates depreciation, it does not increase depreciation. Total capitalized costs of a building will fully depreciate over time with or without a cost segregation study. However, the time value of money results in a cost segregation study being valuable, because a dollar today is worth more than a dollar tomorrow. Therefore, an accelerated tax deduction today is worth more than a tax deduction tomorrow. **(See Above, "Modified Accelerated Cost Recovery System (MACRS)")**

Taxpayers should consider taking advantage of a cost segregation study whenever the expenditures for a structure, including leasehold improvements, equal or exceed $750,000. Also, taxpayers that have constructed, acquired or remodeled their real estate assets in the past 10 years should consider the benefit of conducting a cost segregation study. A cost segregation study should be performed: immediately after construction or acquisition of a building; after a change in ownership; following major capital improvements; and during construction of properties. Properties that qualify include: apartment buildings; retail stores; restaurants; office buildings; manufacturing facilities; wineries; grocery stores; hotels, and warehouses. The current bonus depreciation rules allow an immediate deduction of 100% of the total cost of all personal property assets placed in service in 2018. So, there is no better time than right now to maximize the "bang for the buck" of a cost segregation study. **(See Below, "Bonus Depreciation")**

A cost segregation study is not just about accelerated depreciation anymore. A cost segregation study can serve as a supporting document for establishing "unit of property" baseline amounts and determining values of disposed assets for expensing purposes. There is no better time than now to have a cost segregation study performed. In the past, cost segregation studies were used solely to break out the personal property and land improvement costs from the overall building construction or acquisition costs. The unit of property was generally the entire building, including the structural components. But now, due to the favorable tax law changes in the IRS tangible property regulations, improvement analysis requires businesses to segregate their real property building costs into the building structure and eight defined building systems. Cost segregation studies have now become a multi-use tool that can help ensure that taxpayers are complying with the tangible property regulations. A cost segregation study, when performed by qualified engineering professionals, can break out real property assets into various additional categories to allow companies to write-off capitalized repairs and maintenance costs in future years. Cost segregation studies can also be used to minimize a taxpayer's property tax assessments since property tax bills are based on the value of real property. After the breakout of non-value cost items from the real property basis during a cost segregation study, a taxpayer may be able to obtain a lower assessment by subtracting costs that are not real property costs from the reported costs of construction or acquisition. For example, contractor overtime hours, demolition of pre-existing structures, and even some change orders can increase the cost of a construction project, but do not add to the market value of the completed building. These expenditures can be exempted from the building's tax basis in certain states if those costs are correctly identified and documented.

Taxpayers can claim "partial disposition" loss deductions when identifying building components that have been replaced or demolished. However, it is often difficult to determine the tax basis of each component without a cost segregation study. Also, the "Producer Price Index (PPI) discounting approach" can be used. **(See Above, "Partial Disposition Election")**

Section 179 First-Year Expensing

Section 179 first-year expensing was made permanent by the "Protecting Americans from Tax Hikes Act of 2015." Also, the provision that allows a taxpayer to revoke a Section 179 expense election without IRS consent was made permanent. Under the Tax Cuts and Jobs Act (TCJA), the maximum 179 expense deduction is $1 million effective for property placed in service in 2018 and subsequent years, and the allowable amount starts to phase-out when the amount of Section 179 property placed in service during the year exceeds $2.5 million (these amounts are adjusted for inflation beginning in 2019). The maximum 179 expense deduction was $510,000 in 2017, and the level at which the allowable deduction amount started to phase-out was $2,030,000.

The TCJA expands the definition of Section 179 property. Taxpayers can elect to include the following improvements made to nonresidential real property as Section 179 property after the date when the property was first placed in service: (1) Qualified improvement property, which means any improvement to a building's interior. Improvements do not qualify if they are attributable to: **(a)** the enlargement of the building, **(b)** any elevator or escalator, or **(c)** the internal structural framework of the building; and (2) Roofs, HVAC, fire protection systems, alarm systems and security systems. These changes apply to property placed in service in taxable years beginning after Dec. 31, 2017. The changes include depreciable tangible personal property, such as furniture and fixtures used in furnishing buildings, other than residential rental real estate buildings. In 2017 and prior years, air conditioning and heating units placed in service in years beginning after 2015 were considered eligible for Section 179 expensing, as long as the property qualified as Section 1245 property, but the TCJA substantially expands the prior definition of Section 179 property.

- **Example** - If you buy $2,600,000 worth of eligible property in 2018, the maximum 179 expense deduction would be $900,000 ($1,000,000 - $100,000) because $2,600,000 less $2,500,000 = $100,000. Therefore, no Section 179 deduction is available to businesses that place $3,500,000 or more of eligible property into service during the year.

The TCJA also eliminates the separate definitions of qualified leasehold improvement property, qualified restaurant property and qualified retail improvement property, instead providing an expanded definition of qualified real property under Section 179 for all "qualified improvement property." **(See Below, "Qualified Leasehold Improvement Property, Restaurant Property, and Retail Improvement Property (Qualified Improvement Property)" & "Qualified Improvement Property")**

Estates and Trusts are not eligible for 179 expensing. For Partnerships and S-corporations, Section 179 determination is made at that level. However, the maximum dollar limitation and the taxable income limitations apply both at the partnership and S-corporation level, and to the individual partners or shareholders (the basis in Section 179 property is reduced by the allowable amount, even if the partners or shareholders can't deduct the full amount). **(See Chapter 18, "Partnerships"); (See Chapter 19, "Corporations")**

Section 179 expensing can be used when purchasing both new and used Section 1245 personal property if the property is used more than 50% for business purposes, and computer software can be expensed under Section 179, but if not expensed, it must be amortized over a 3-year (36 months) period providing it has a useful life exceeding one year (includes the cost to develop the software). In addition to what is added by the TCJA, Section 1245 property that is eligible for Section 179 expensing includes: equipment (machines, etc.) purchased for business use; tangible personal property used in business; business vehicles; computers and computer software; office furniture; and office equipment. However, Section 179 expensing still cannot be used for the purchase of Section 1245 personal property (appliances, etc.) purchased for use in residential or nonresidential rental properties (investment property). **(See Chapter 6, "Reporting Capital Gains and Losses"; & "Form 1099-B: Proceeds from Broker and Barter Exchange Transactions")**

Unlike first-year bonus depreciation (see below), you can't claim Section 179 expensing that will create a Net Operating Loss (NOL) for a year, i.e. the Section 179 deduction is limited to the business's taxable income from the active conduct of any trade or business during the tax year. However, any amount disallowed by this limitation may be carried forward and deducted in future years. Therefore, you can elect 179 expensing even if there is a lack of income, because it can be carried back and forward to other years – the maximum Section 179 limits are increased by any Section 179 carryovers. However, if Section 179 expensing cannot be used because a business has no income in the current year, bonus depreciation can be used because the use of bonus depreciation can create a NOL. If a person has a Schedule C business, the amount of the Section 179 expensing deduction allowed for a year is always limited to the taxable income of the filer, including both spouses' wages reported on Form W-2 (if married filing jointly). Section 179 expensing must be used before bonus depreciation, unless a business has no income in a year. **(See Chapter 8, "Net Operating Loss (NOL)")**

If a taxpayer's capital expenditures fall within the $1,000,000/$2,500,000 thresholds of Section 179, then the "materials and supplies" rule and the safe harbors that are allowed by the tangible property regulations probably add no incremental tax benefit for a taxpayer. However, the "materials and supplies" allowance and the De Minimis safe harbor election, are simpler and less restrictive to comply with for some taxpayers than the Section 179 deduction. For example, Section 179 expensing imposes an overall deduction ceiling. However, with well thought out planning, businesses can maximize tax savings using provisions set-forth in both the tangible property regulations and Section 179. **(See Above, "Materials and Supplies Rule"; & "De Minimis Safe Harbor Election")**

First-Year Bonus Depreciation

Under the Tax Cuts and Jobs Act (TCJA), first-year bonus depreciation is expanded to include both new and "used" property, and the deduction is increased to 100% for property acquired and placed in service after September 27, 2017 through the 2022 tax year. Property acquired prior to September 28, 2017, but placed in service after September 27, 2017, is subject to the bonus depreciation percentages in effect prior to enactment of the TCJA (50%). After 2022, 80% bonus depreciation will be effective for tax year 2023; 60% for 2024; 40% for 2025; and 20% for 2026, before expiring in 2027. Longer production period property and certain aircraft get an additional year to be placed in service at each rate.

Used qualified property is eligible for bonus depreciation if all the following factors apply:

- The taxpayer didn't use the property at any time before acquiring it.
- The taxpayer didn't acquire the property from a related party.
- The taxpayer didn't acquire the property from a component member of a controlled group of corporations.
- The taxpayer's basis of the used property is not figured in whole or in part by reference to the adjusted basis of the property in the hands of the seller or transferor.
- The taxpayer's basis of the used property is not figured under the provision for deciding basis of property acquired from a decedent.
- The cost of the used qualified property doesn't include any carryover basis of the property.

The TCJA adds qualified film, television and live theatrical productions as types of qualified property that are eligible for 100% bonus depreciation. This provision applies to property acquired and placed in service after Sept. 27, 2017. Also, specified plants planted or grafted after September 27, 2017, and before 2027 are subject to bonus depreciation under the TCJA. Bonus Depreciation is generally allowable **when purchasing Section 1245 personal property, including personal property (appliances, etc.) for use in residential and nonresidential rental properties (investment properties).** Also, bonus depreciation is applicable to specified plants such as trees, vines, and plants bearing fruits or nuts, when planted or grafted. Specified plants include any tree or vine that bears fruits or nuts, or any other plant that will have more than one yield of fruits or nuts and has a pre-productive period of more than two years from the time of planting or grafting to the time when the plant bears fruit or nuts. In addition, bonus depreciation can be used for "Qualified Improvement Property."

Certain types of property are not eligible for bonus depreciation. One such exclusion from qualified property is for property primarily used in the trade or business of the furnishing or sale of:

- Electrical energy, water or sewage disposal services,
- Gas or steam through a local distribution system or
- Transportation of gas or steam by pipeline.

The exclusion from eligibility for bonus depreciation also applies if the rates for the furnishing or sale have to be approved by a federal, state or local government agency, a public service or public utility commission, or an electric cooperative. And the TCJA adds another exclusion from eligibility for bonus depreciation for any property used in a trade or business that has floor-plan financing. Floor-plan financing is secured by motor vehicle inventory that a business sells or leases to retail customers.

Unlike Section 179 expensing, there is no dollar limit for using bonus depreciation, so even the largest businesses are eligible. If your business adds enough depreciable property to generate a net operating loss (NOL) for the year, you can carry the NOL back or forward and recover some or all of the taxes paid in those years. However, Section 179 expensing is generally required to be taken first, followed by bonus depreciation – unless a business has no taxable profit in the tax year. If bonus depreciation is applicable, it is mandatory unless a taxpayer elects out of it. The election out can be by class of asset (e.g. MACRS 5-year property) or for all qualifying assets in a company. Qualified Improvement Property (QIP) that is eligible for Section 179 expensing is also eligible for bonus depreciation. **(See Below, "Qualified Improvement Property"); (See Chapter 8, "Net Operating Loss (NOL)")**

The election to accelerate alternative minimum tax (AMT) credits in lieu of bonus depreciation is repealed by the Tax Cuts and Jobs Act (TCJA) effective as of the 2018 tax year. In 2017 and prior years, taxpayers could elect to accelerate AMT credits in lieu of claiming bonus depreciation and increase the amount of unused AMT credits that could be claimed with the bonus depreciation.

The IRS has issued proposed regulations on 100% bonus depreciation.
https://s3.amazonaws.com/public-inspection.federalregister.gov/2018-16716.pdf

Following Are the Rules That Were in Effect for Bonus Depreciation in 2017 and Prior Years – First-year bonus depreciation is available only when purchasing new property. Used property does not qualify, although current improvements to an old property may qualify. Also, property converted to business use by the original owner qualifies for bonus depreciation. Bonus depreciation is also available for investment property, e.g. when purchasing Section 1245 personal property (appliances, etc.) for use in rental properties. Also, bonus depreciation is expanded in 2016 to cover specified plants such as trees, vines, and plants bearing fruits or nuts, when planted or grafted, rather than when placed in service. Specified plants include any tree or vine that bears fruits or nuts, or any other plant that will have more than one yield of fruits or nuts and has a pre-productive period of more than two years from the time of planting or grafting to the time when the plant bears fruit or nuts.

Qualified Leasehold Improvement Property, Restaurant Property, and Retail Improvement Property (Qualified Improvement Property)
Under the Tax Cuts and Jobs Act (TCJA), qualified leasehold improvement property, qualified restaurant property, and qualified retail improvement property are no longer separately defined. They are consolidated into the "Qualified Improvement Property" category encompassing nonstructural improvements generally placed in service at least three years after the completion of a building and given a special 15-year recovery period using SL/GDS, effective for tax year 2018. These are Section 1250 nonresidential real properties that are eligible for both Section 179 expensing and bonus depreciation. The prior law before implementation of the TCJA described the properties as follows:

- Qualified leasehold improvement Property – This is any improvement, such as remodeling, to the interior portion of a building if made under or pursuant to a lease (not a lease between related parties) but does not include enlargement of a building; elevators and escalators; or improvements to the building structure (structural framework of a building). The improvements must be made more than three years after the date the building opened for business. Either the landlord or the lessee can make the interior improvements. These costs are also eligible for bonus depreciation as they generally meet the criteria for Qualified Improvement Property (QIP).
- Qualified Restaurant Property – This encompasses the entire building structure as well as interior costs if more than 50% of the building's square footage is devoted to the preparation of meals and customer seating. The improvements can be made at any time (not limited to improvements made more than three years after the building opened for business). Improvements that meet the criteria for Qualified Leasehold Improvement (QLI) costs are also eligible for bonus depreciation, but some qualified restaurant property that is eligible for a 15-year recovery period may not be eligible for bonus depreciation, because qualified restaurant property, unlike qualified improvement property (QIP), can consist of an entire building.
- Qualified Retail Improvement Property – This is only for nonresidential building interior costs for a building that is open to the general public and used in the retail business of selling tangible personal property to the general public (excluding enlargement of a building and the interior structural framework of a building), which must be made more than three years after the date the building opened for business. Improvements are eligible for bonus depreciation if they meet the criteria for qualified improvement property (QIP), and most qualified retail improvements would be considered QIP.

(See Below, "Qualified Improvement Property (QIP)")

The IRS has issued proposed regulations on 100% bonus depreciation.
https://s3.amazonaws.com/public-inspection.federalregister.gov/2018-16716.pdf

Qualified Improvement Property (QIP)
Under the Tax Cuts and Jobs Act (TCJA), qualified leasehold improvement property, qualified restaurant property, and qualified retail improvement property are no longer separately defined. They are consolidated into the "Qualified Improvement Property" (QIP) category encompassing nonstructural improvements generally placed in service at least three years after the completion of the building itself and given a special 15-year recovery period using SL/GDS, effective for tax year 2018. These are Section 1250 nonresidential real properties that are eligible for both Section 179 expensing and bonus depreciation. Qualified improvement property means any improvement to a building's interior and roofs, HVAC, fire protection systems, alarm systems and security systems. Improvements do not qualify if they are attributable to: the enlargement of the building; any elevator or escalator; or the internal structural framework of the building.

Following is the Definition of Qualified Improvement Property in 2017, Before the TCJA – The Qualified Improvement Property category was defined as follows in 2017: The "Protecting Americans from Tax Hikes Act of 2015" created a new category of property subject to bonus depreciation called qualified improvement property (QIP) that is depreciated over 39 years. The QIP provisions are effective for property placed in service after Dec. 31, 2015. The qualified improvement property concept is specific to bonus depreciation only. QIP expenses may also be eligible for Sec. 179 expensing and a 15-year recovery period but must be tested under the "qualified real property" (Qualified Leasehold, Restaurant, and Retail Property) definitions discussed above. It appears that most qualified retail improvements would be considered qualified improvement property (QIP). However, some qualified restaurant property that is eligible for a 15-year recovery period may not be eligible for bonus depreciation. For example, qualified restaurant property, unlike QIP, can consist of an entire building. QIP doesn't require that the improvement be subject to a lease, so interior improvements made by the owners of an owner-occupied building that meets the other requirements for qualified improvement property may now qualify for bonus depreciation. The removal of the lease requirement also means that improvements made to property in a situation involving a related-party lease could also qualify for bonus depreciation. **Qualified Improvement Property (QIP) is any improvement to an interior portion of a building (interior common areas) that is nonresidential real property, as long as the improvement is made after the building is "first placed in service."** The IRS clarifies that the term "first placed in service" means the first time the building was placed in service by any taxpayer. Several examples illustrate that so long as an improvement, including a "build out," is placed in service after the building is placed in service (e.g., even one-day later), the improvement can qualify for bonus depreciation. **Although similar to Qualified Leasehold Improvements (QLI), there are subtle but distinct differences: (1) QIP doesn't require that the improvements have to be made more than three years after the building is placed in service; and (2) QIP is not restricted to expenditures pursuant to a lease between non-related parties.** Similar to Qualified Leasehold Improvement (QLI) costs, QIP excludes expenditures for the enlargement of a building; elevators and escalators; and the internal structural framework of a building.

Retailers and Restaurants Remodeling Safe Harbor
A safe harbor allows retailers and restaurants that remodel their premises to deduct 75% of the remodeling costs as repairs, and the other 25% of the costs have to be capitalized and depreciated. This safe harbor is for restaurants and retail stores that remodel every 5 to 10 years.
www.irs.gov/pub/irs-drop/rp-15-56.pdf

Personal Property
Most Section 1245 personal property is classified as either 3-year, 5-Year, 7-Year, or 10-year property. 3-year, 5-year, 7-year, and 10-year properties are depreciated using the 200% declining balance method (GDS), unless an election is made by the taxpayer to use the 150% declining balance method or the straight-line (SL) method, and automatically switches to the SL method when it results in greater depreciation for a year. Taxpayers may elect to use the Alternative Depreciation System (ADS), and if elected, all assets in the same class that are placed in service during the year must be depreciated using ADS. Taxpayers can elect ADS on Form 4562, Line 20 by the extended filing due date for the year the assets are placed in service. **(See Above, "Modified Accelerated Cost Recovery System (MACRS)")**

Residential and Nonresidential Real Property
Section 1250 real property includes both residential and nonresidential real property. Most real property is classified as either 27 ½ -year, 39-year, 20-year, or 15-year property under GDS. Residential rental property (including mobile homes) is depreciated over 27 ½ years using the SL method under the General Depreciation System (GDS), but the Tax Cuts and Jobs Act (TCJA) changes the Alternative Depreciation System (ADS) recovery period for residential rental property from 40 years to 30 years, effective for property placed in service in 2018. Nonresidential real property is depreciated over 39 years using the SL method under GDS. Improvements or additions are depreciated separately from the time the improvements or additions are placed in service.

Under the Tax Cuts and Jobs Act (TCJA), taxpayers engaged in a real property business, including a real estate development, construction, rental, management, or brokerage business, among others, may elect to not have the interest limitation apply to their business, and the election is irrevocable. However, when businesses elect to not have the interest limitation apply, they are required to use the alternative depreciation system for their nonresidential real property, residential rental property, and qualified improvement property. **(See Chapter 14, "Business Expenses")**

15-year and 20-year real properties are depreciated using the 150% DB method under GDS. 15-year real property, which includes land improvements like roads, sidewalks, bridges, fences, landscaping, asphalt parking lots, curbs, decorative walls, shrubbery and plants, are eligible for both Section 179 expensing and bonus depreciation. 20-year real property, which includes farm buildings, is eligible for bonus depreciation but not Section 179 expensing. **(See Above, "Modified Accelerated Cost Recovery System (MACRS)")**

Listed Property

Listed property is 5-year class personal property that has limitations on the amount of depreciation, Section 179 expensing, and bonus depreciation that can be deducted in a year. If listed property is used more than 50% for business purposes, it is eligible for GDS depreciation (200% DB), Section 179 expensing, and bonus depreciation in the year placed in service. However, listed property used 50% or less for business purposes must be depreciated using ADS (SL depreciation), and no Section 179 expensing or bonus depreciation is allowed. **(See Above, "Modified Accelerated Cost Recovery System (MACRS)")**

Personal property that is considered "listed property" includes:
- Passenger vehicles used for transportation and light trucks and vans;
- Other property used for transportation;
- Property used for entertainment, recreation, or amusement purposes – including photographic, phonographic, and video recording equipment – unless the property is used exclusively (100%) in a taxpayer's trade or business;
- Computers and peripheral equipment: Under the tax Cuts and Jobs Act (TCJA), computers and peripheral equipment are removed from the definition of listed property effective with 2018 acquisitions. In 2017 and prior years, computers and related peripheral equipment was considered listed property, unless used only (100%) at a regular business establishment, which includes a home office used regularly and exclusively for business purposes.

Cell phones and other similar telecommunications equipment were removed from being classified as listed property in 2010. Therefore, when employers provide cell phones to their employees or when employers reimburse employees for business use of their cell phones, tax-free treatment is applied without burdensome recordkeeping requirements. **(See Chapter 8, "Employer Provided Tax-Free Benefits")**

When listed property that was formerly used predominately (more than 50%) in a trade or business is converted to personal use (less than 50% business use), any depreciation that exceeds the amount that would have been allowed under the alternative depreciation system (ADS), as well as any 179 expensing and bonus depreciation taken, must be recaptured as ordinary income, reported on Form 4797, and added to the basis of the property. The depreciation that must be recaptured is the difference between 200% declining balance (DB) claimed under

GDS and straight-line depreciation under ADS. When other personal property (not considered listed) that has been used in a trade or business is converted to personal use, the property is treated as disposed of in that year, and no gain, loss, or depreciation recapture is recognized upon conversion, but instead is recognized when the asset is sold.

Vehicles used for transportation – A taxpayer may use actual expenses, including depreciation, or the standard mileage allowance to substantiate business expenses for the use of a personal vehicle. Depreciation is just one component of actual expenses. Passenger automobiles and other vehicles placed in service in 2018 and prior years are listed property that have even further limitations on depreciation than the 50% requirement for business use, i.e. they can only be depreciated each year in accordance with certain parameters. In fact, even though cars and other vehicles are considered 5-year property, you may never fully depreciate a vehicle weighing less than 6,000 pounds. However, a taxpayer may continue to depreciate the vehicle after 6 years if it has not been fully depreciated. **(See Chapter 15, "Vehicle and Other Transportation Expenses")**

The Tax Cuts and Jobs Act (TCJA) greatly increases the limitations on depreciation of vehicles over what the limitations were in 2017 and prior years. The limitations on depreciation of new and used luxury passenger automobiles, and also on new and used light "trucks and vans" acquired by the taxpayer after Sept. 27, 2017 and placed in service in 2018 are: 1st year – $18,000 ($10,000 + $8,000 if 100% bonus depreciation is claimed); 2nd year – $16,000; 3rd year – $9,600; and each succeeding year – $5,760. The limitations on depreciation of new and used luxury passenger automobiles, and also on new and used light "trucks and vans" acquired by the taxpayer before Sept. 28, 2017 and placed in service in 2018 for which bonus depreciation applies are: 1st year – $16,400; 2nd year – $16,000; 3rd year – $9,600; and each succeeding year – $5,760.

- **Example** – A taxpayer who uses a vehicle 60% for business purposes can claim a depreciation deduction in its fourth year of use equal to $3,456 (60% of $5,760 = $3,456).

Luxury passenger automobiles have an "unloaded" weight capacity of less than 6,000 pounds. Light "trucks and vans" (including minivans and SUVs) have a "loaded" weight capacity of 6,000 pounds or less. Please note that the gross "loaded" weight capacity is based on how much the manufacturer says the vehicle weighs when fully loaded and is different from the "unloaded" weight capacity.
www.irs.gov/pub/irs-drop/rp-17-29.pdf

SUVs – SUV's with a gross "loaded" vehicle weight capacity of at least 6,000 pounds, but no more than 14,000 pounds and placed in service in 2018 escape the annual depreciation caps for passenger vehicles and light trucks and vans. First-year Sec. 179 and Bonus depreciation for these vehicles is limited to $25,000 in 2018, but under the TCJA the $25,000 limitation will be indexed for inflation beginning in 2019. Also, they are still used as a means of transportation and are still subject to the definition of listed property, so two restrictions still apply if they are used less than 50% or less for business purposes: (1) depreciation is limited to ADS; and (2) bonus depreciation and Section 179 expensing are not allowed. **(See Chapter 15, "Vehicle and Other Transportation Expenses")**

Certain trucks and vans that have a weight of at least 6,000 pounds, but no more than 14,000 pounds fully loaded are completely exempt from the reduced depreciation rules, including the $25,000 limitation. These are vehicles that are not likely to be used for personal purposes and, therefore, are generally not considered listed property, so they can be totally expensed in the year of purchase. These are vehicles that are: (1) designed to seat more than nine passengers behind the driver's seat. For example, many hotel shuttles and vans qualify for this exemption; (2) equipped with a cargo area that is not readily accessible directly from the passenger compartment and that are at least 6 feet in length. The cargo area can be open or designed to be open, but enclosed by a cap. For example, many pickups with full-size cargo beds (at least 6 feet long) will qualify for this exemption when there is no access to the cargo area from the cab, but some "quad cabs" and "extended cabs" with shorter cargo beds may not qualify for the exemption; or (3) have an integral enclosure that fully encloses the driver's compartment and load carrying device, with no seating behind the driver's seat, and with a body section protruding no more than 30 inches ahead of the leading edge of the windshield (a stub-nosed vehicle). Many delivery vans will qualify for this exemption.

Vehicles "not considered listed property" are considered to be "non-personal use" vehicles and, therefore, are exempt from the listed property restrictions, including: vehicles designed to carry cargo and weighing over 14,000 pounds; moving vans; ambulances and hearses; school buses; dump trucks; fire trucks; tractors and combines; cement mixers; construction vehicles; utility repair trucks; taxis, buses, or vans used to transport people for compensation; trucks and vans specifically modified, such as shelving and painting to display advertising or a company name; boats used for transportation (if a qualified non-personal use vehicle); and planes used for transportation (if a qualified non-personal use vehicle).

Trading in a Vehicle

In 2017 and prior years, trading in a vehicle for another vehicle was considered to be a Section 1031 like-kind exchange, so any gain or loss was deferred (not taxable), and the basis of the new vehicle was the adjusted basis of the old vehicle plus the additional amount paid for the new vehicle, which was used for depreciation purposes. However, since the Tax Cuts and Jobs Act (TCJA) eliminates like-kind exchanges other than for "real property," effective for 2018, any depreciation taken on the old vehicle has to be recaptured, and depreciation on the new vehicle is based on the total purchase price of the new vehicle.

Farm Machinery and Equipment

Under the Tax Cuts and Jobs Act (TCJA), the recovery period (depreciation) is shortened for originally owned farm machinery and equipment from 7 to 5 years in 2018 and subsequent years for 2018 acquisitions, and 200% Declining Balance (DDB/GDS) depreciation is permitted for all property used in the farming business with a recovery period of 10 years of less.

Taxpayers engaged in the farming business may elect out of the interest limitation, and the election is irrevocable. However, an electing farm business is required to use the Alternative Depreciation System (ADS) – with its accompanying restriction on using bonus depreciation and longer depreciation recovery period – for any asset with a useful life of more than 10 years, including land improvements, barns, and other farm buildings in years beginning after 2017. **(See Chapter 14, "Business Expenses")**

A farming business includes the traditional cultivation of land or the raising or harvesting of any agricultural or horticultural commodity. It also includes, but is not limited to, a business of operating a nursery or sod farm,

257

raising or harvesting fruit, nuts, or ornamental trees, or any trade or business of a specified agricultural or horticultural cooperative.

Leased passenger vehicles

You are allowed to use the standard business mileage allowance for leased cars, trucks, and vans. But actual expenses for leasing vehicles are limited – expressed as an income inclusion amount according to tables prescribed by the IRS. However, this only applies if you deduct the cost of leasing a vehicle and other actual expenses for the vehicle as a business expense, instead of using the standard mileage allowance. **(See Chapter 15, "Leasing a Car, Truck, or Van for Business Use")**

Claiming a Recreational Vehicle (RV) As a Business Expense

If you travel away from your tax home to earn income in various locations, you may claim all expenses of a recreational vehicle (RV) used "exclusively" for your business purposes. This usually applies to independent contractors who are not reimbursed for travel expenses. You may claim either the standard mileage allowance for all miles driven, or you may deduct the actual costs involved in the operation of the RV – all expenses associated with its upkeep, maintenance, travel and storage, as well as insurance, interest, taxes, depreciation, and any other associated expenses. Since the standard mileage allowance is based on the average for automobiles, RV owners are much better off taking actual expenses. The deduction requires maintaining very accurate records as to where you are located every day; how many miles driven to get there; and you must keep a log of the nights you sleep in the RV. Also, the RV must be used for travel and lodging only, not entertainment, i.e. no use for parties or business entertainment is allowed. **(See Chapter 15, "Vehicle and Other Transportation Expenses")**

It was ruled by the Tax Court in the Shirely case that an RV used for business purposes is both a transient lodging facility and a means of transportation. The Tax Court didn't have to decide the RV's primary use, because both uses qualified for Section 179 expensing. The court adopted a replacement theory, ruling that the use of a RV or motor home replaced the need to stay in transient hotels. Accordingly, the actual expenses related to upkeep of an RV, including depreciation and Section 179 expensing replaced any temporary lodging expenses that would otherwise be required by a taxpayer. Also, RVs are not considered listed property because, generally, they have a loaded weight capacity of 14,000 pounds or more, and thus are not subject to the $25,000 Section 179 expensing limitation. Therefore, the entire cost of a RV used exclusively for business purposes can be written-off in the year of purchase up to the maximum allowable Section 179 expense deduction for the year, which in 2018 is $1 million. This may result in a net operating loss (NOL) in the year you purchase your RV when it is your first year of business usage (the NOL can be carried back or forward to other years).
www.ustaxcourt.gov/InOpHistoric/shirley.TCM.WPD.pdf

In addition to deducting the actual costs involved in the operation of your RV, you are also allowed a deduction for groceries or restaurant meals for every day you are away from home on business. However, in lieu of actual expenses you may deduct a per-diem allowance for meals and incidental expenses (M&IE). The standard federal M&IE rate for Oct. 1, 2017 through Sept. 30, 2018, is $51 per day (50% of M&IE rates are deductible by independent contractors). However, this rate may be higher for high cost locations. You must maintain accurate documentation of business days you are eligible to claim M&IE in a log book or other record. **(See Chapter 15, "Lodging, Meals and Incidental Expenses")**

If you have no actual permanent home where you reside (an address or an actual place of residence), you are considered a "transient worker" and, therefore, have no home base, so your tax home is wherever you work. In this instance, you cannot deduct any expenses for travel away from home since you are never considered to be away from home. Therefore, you will not be allowed to deduct any of your RV expenses for business purposes.

Can you deduct your RV expenses when it is not used "exclusively" (100%) for business purposes? Well this is a fussy area and is questionable. You may be able to deduct the proportionate share of your RV expenses based on the business miles driven compared to the total miles driven during the year (you must maintain an accurate log of total miles driven and business miles driven). Also, you must keep a log of nights you sleep in the RV and how many of those nights are for personal and business usage. If the RV is used more than 14 days for personal purposes during the year, it is considered a dwelling (e.g. a vacation home), so any RV business expenses are disallowed. Also, if the RV is used less than 100% for business purposes, your business trips may need to be shorter than 30 days for the RV to count as transient lodging. Use of an RV for business purposes is highly likely to be audited by the IRS, especially if the business usage is less than 100% during the year, and the IRS may try to limit your deduction or disallow it altogether. **(See Chapter 7, "Classifying a Vacation Home as a Rental Property")**

- **Example** - In the case of Dellward and Judith Jackson, the Tax Court denied business deductions for the RV because it was used by the taxpayers as a residence, and this ruling was upheld by the Ninth Circuit Court of Appeals. The Jacksons made a really good case that attendance at RV rallies was an integral part of their insurance business which involved the sale of policies tailored to RVs, but any personal use of the RV by them, even watching some TV, counted against them as a personal-use day causing them to break the 14-day limit. Presumably, if they had not exceeded the 14-day limit, they would have been allowed to deduct their business expenses.
  www.ustaxcourt.gov/InOpHistoric/JacksonMemo.Wherry.TCM.WPD.pdf

Deconstruction

Deconstruction is being used by more homeowners who try to avoid the wrecking ball when they remodel or completely tear down an old house and build a new house on the same site. In this process, a crew carefully dismantles an older property by hand instead of using bulldozers. The process costs more than a straightforward demolition, roughly double what would be paid for a wrecking crew. However, you are able to donate home materials such as lumber, roof tiles and even lamps to nonprofit organizations for reuse and get a tax write-off. For example, one family using "deconstruction" donated materials that were "appraised" by an appraisal-and-consulting firm at $159,000, which resulted in a tax savings of $66,000, more than three times the cost of the deconstruction. Spurring the movement is a growing awareness of "green" building, as well as more laws restricting the dumping of building materials into landfills. The growing surge in using deconstruction is currently centered along the West Coast, in areas such as Silicon Valley and cities including San Diego, Los Angeles, Portland, and Seattle.

Depletion

Similar to depreciation, depletion is the cost recovery of a natural resource and in the case of royalty owners includes income from oil and gas royalties. There are two methods of depletion: (1) percentage depletion – allows the taxpayer a deduction based on the gross income from the property; and (2) cost depletion – allows the taxpayer a deduction based on the ratio of units sold to the number of units available at the end of the year plus the units sold during the year. The IRS requires taxpayers to take the higher of cost depletion or percentage depletion. Percentage depletion is limited to royalty owners and independent producers who produce 1,000 barrels of average daily production of domestic crude oil or an equivalent amount of domestic natural gas. Most royalty owners use percentage depletion on royalty income, which normally entitles them to a statutory amount of 15% depletion based on the property's gross income. However, percentage depletion is subject to two limitations: **(See Chapter 5, "Royalty Income")**

1. 100% taxable income limitation – depletion is limited to 100% of taxable income, which is the property's gross income less allowable deductions such as severance taxes and other administrative expenses.

2. 65% taxable income limitation – The taxpayer's taxable income is computed without regard to any depletion on production, any IRC par. 199 deduction, net operating loss carryback to the taxable year or capital loss carryback to the taxable year. The 65% taxable income limitation could come into play if the taxpayer has a loss in another business that is offsetting the royalty income. Any amount that is disallowed may be carried forward and allowed as a deduction in the following year.

Percentage depletion for production from marginal oil and gas wells is not allowable according to the American Taxpayer Relief Act of 2012. Percentage depletion is also not available on lease bonus payments, advance royalty payments or any other amount payable without regard to production from the property. This prevents upfront bonus payments from being eligible for percentage depletion.

- Any gain realized from disposition of royalty property must be treated as ordinary income to the extent deductions for depletion reduced the adjusted basis of the property.

- The amount subject to depletion includes capitalized drilling and development costs, which are added to the basis of the property for the purpose of determining gain on the sale or disposition of the property. Recapture of depletion is treated as ordinary income upon sale of the property.

- For partnerships, the depletion allowance is calculated separately by the partners and not at the partnership level. For S-corporations, the depletion allowance is calculated at the shareholder level. **(See Chapter 18, "Partnerships"); (See Chapter 19, "Corporations")**

- Oil and gas royalty owners benefit by not having percentage depletion considered a tax preference item for Alternative Minimum Tax (AMT) purposes.

- Percentage depletion also applies to mines, timber, and other natural resources, but depletion percentages may be different.

Amortization of Intangible Assets

Generally, you may amortize the capitalized costs of Section 197 intangibles ratably over 15 years (180 months) if you hold the intangible assets in connection with your trade or business or in an activity engaged in for the production of income. Intangibles must have an ascertainable value and a limited life in order to be amortized over a 15-year period. Generally, goodwill, going concern value, etc. must be purchased in order to be amortized. The 15-year period begins with the later of the month the intangible is acquired or the month the trade or business activity engaged in for the production of income begins. You cannot deduct amortization for the month you dispose of the intangible asset. If you pay or incur an amount that increases the basis of an intangible after the 15-year period begins, amortize it over the remainder of the 15-year period beginning with the month the basis increase occurs. The following assets are Section 197 intangibles: goodwill; going concern value; workforce in place; business books and records, operating systems, or any other information base, including lists or other information concerning current or prospective customers; patents, copyrights, formulas, processes, designs, patterns, literary composition, know-how, formats, or similar items; a customer-based intangible; a supplier-based intangible; license, permit, or other right granted by a governmental unit or agency (including issuances and renewals); a covenant not to compete entered into in connection with the acquisition of an interest in a trade or business; and any franchise, trademark, or trade name.

- Corporate goodwill is a separate asset that represents the intangible qualities that bring with them continued patronage. It can be sold, and the gain can be taxed as a capital gain. The buyer can amortize the goodwill on a stepped-up basis. This occurs most often within the context of the sale of a closely held corporation.

- "Personal goodwill" is separate from corporate goodwill and can occur when an individual's personal attributes and relationships constitute a separate asset distinct from corporate goodwill, the sale of which represents compensation to the individual. When a corporation is for sale, a separate sale of a shareholder's personal goodwill associated with the corporation can result in the gain from the sale of the goodwill being taxed to the shareholder at long-term capital gain rates. Personal goodwill can be present when the owner's reputation, expertise, skill, knowledge, and relationships with customers are critical to the business's success and value. A sale of corporate assets and personal goodwill should be planned and executed to establish that personal goodwill exists and is being sold in a separate transaction from the sale of the assets of the corporation.

In 2017 and prior years, a safe-harbor allowed self-created intangibles to be treated as capital assets and the cost of the self-created intangible assets to be amortized over 15 years. However, under the Tax Cuts and Jobs Act (TCJA), self-created intangible assets such as copyrights, literary compositions, musical or artistic compositions, patents, goodwill, etc. are removed from the definition of capital assets effective in 2018. However, transfers of all substantial rights to a patent or an undivided interest in a portion of patent rights by the inventor or a holder of a patent continues to get long-term capital gain treatment under Section 1235 if payments are tied to productivity or are payable periodically over the transferee's use of the patent. A "holder of a patent" means: any individual whose efforts created such property, or any other individual who has acquired an interest in such property in exchange for consideration in money paid to the creator prior to actual reduction to practice of the invention covered by the patent, if such individual is neither: the employer of the creator, or related to such creator. **(See Chapter 6, "Self-Created Intangible Assets")**

Chapter 17 –Self-Employed/Independent Contractors

Sole proprietors who have income reported to them on a Form 1099 (e.g. 1099-MISC), and those who receive payments for goods or services that are not reported to the IRS (e.g. cash payments) are generally considered self-employed or independent contractors and must report their income on Schedule C, Form 1040, and pay self-employment taxes on Schedule SE (see below). A husband and wife who both materially participate in a business, who file a joint return, and who are the sole owners of a business can file a Schedule C instead of filing a partnership return as was required in previous years. Each spouse's share of the net profits is considered their individual earnings for purposes of computing self-employment taxes on Schedule SE, which allows both of them to get credit for Social Security and Medicare benefits. Therefore, they must file separate Schedules SE, reporting their proportionate share of net profit from self-employment. Sole proprietors can also choose to form a limited liability company (LLC) by filing formation documents with the state, and after receiving approval from the state, apply to be taxed as an S-corporation by filing Form 2553 with the IRS. Sole proprietors that become LLCs can also elect to be taxed as a regular C-corporation under the "check-the-box" rules by filing Form 8832 with the IRS. Nevertheless, most sole proprietors are taxed as "disregarded entities" on Schedule C, Form 1040. When individuals receive income reported to them on a Form 1099-MISC, etc. for an activity that is not carried on regularly to make a profit, and they do not carry on a trade or business as a self-employed individual or an independent contractor, the income should be reported as "other income" on Line 21, Form 1040, and in this case they don't have to pay self-employment taxes on the income (see below). **(See Chapter 2, "Payroll Tax (FICA)");** **(See Chapter 4, "Wages and Salaries"); (See Chapter 18, "Limited Liability Company (LLC)")** www.irs.gov/pub/irs-pdf/f1040sc.pdf www.irs.gov/pub/irs-pdf/i1040sc.pdf

Some sole proprietors who are considered self-employed or independent contractors for tax purposes include: newspaper venders (carriers); U.S. citizens who are employees of foreign governments; and some ministers and other members of religious organizations who are not considered to be employees. Earnings of $600 or more paid by a single payer to a sole proprietor in a year is required to be reported to the IRS on Form 1099-MISC. Sole proprietors can deduct expenses on Schedule C that are related to their business operations including: advertising expenses; wages; car and truck expenses; depreciation on assets used in the business; legal and professional fees; office expenses; rent; repairs and maintenance; supplies; taxes and licenses; travel, meals, and entertainment expenses; utilities; and other expenses. A sole proprietor who has employees will have to get an employer identification number (EIN) from the IRS, and will have to withhold income and payroll taxes from their employees' salaries which have to be reported on Forms W-2 and W-3. **(See Chapter 14, "General Business Practices"; "Deductible Business Expenses" & "Independent Contractors/Non-Employees")**

- Uber drivers – Typically, the company will provide a 1099-MISC for low-to-middle-volume drivers, and a 1099-K if they had more than 200 transactions and $20,000 in payments. Uber drivers are treated like any other self-employed individual, which means they usually file a Schedule C, and they shouldn't forget to deduct all those little "extra" expenses they have as a driver, and they are responsible for paying self-employment tax. Frequently, drivers provide snacks and water bottles and other goodies for passengers and use of a cellphone is needed for communication. As with other expenses, their deduction is limited to the costs attributable to business use only. To simplify matters, you might acquire a phone to be used 100 percent for this purpose. **(See Chapter 4, Earned Income"); (See Chapter 14, "Where Payments are Reported on Form 1099-MISC"; & "Form 1099-K, Merchant Card and Third-Party Payments")**

- You don't have to work for UPS or FedEx to be on the road making deliveries. Increasingly, taxpayers are using their own vehicles to deliver goods or food as part of the "sharing economy." For tax purposes, you're generally treated as a self-employed independent contractor. Typically, this means that you must report the income earned from the delivery service as business income on Schedule C taxed at ordinary income tax rates, but you are able to claim deductions for qualified business expenses, subject to the usual rules and regulations. In addition to reporting income from these delivery jobs, you're also responsible for paying self-employment tax.

A sole proprietor's fringe benefits are generally not deductible on Schedule C because a sole proprietor is an owner of the business rather than an employee. However, sole proprietors may set up a retirement plan such as a SIMPLE or SEP IRA to which they may make contributions, which are deductible as an above-the-line deduction on Form 1040. Also, 100% of a sole proprietor's health insurance premiums paid on behalf of himself, spouse, dependents, and any child of the taxpayer under age 27 are deductible as an above-the-line deduction on Form 1040. Therefore, self-employed taxpayers should move their Medicare premiums from being deducted on Schedule A, Form 1040 (where they may be wasted anyway) to being deducted as self-employed health insurance premiums (above-the-line deduction). However, the above-the-line retirement plan contributions and health insurance premium deductions do not reduce the amount of income on which self-employment taxes are paid on Schedule SE. Also, the above-the-line self-employment retirement plan contributions and health insurance premium deductions are limited to the gross earned income from the trade or business. Self-employed persons may not contribute to a Health Savings Account (HSA) on a pre-tax basis and may not take the amount of their HSA contributions as a deduction for self-employment tax purposes. However, they may contribute to an HSA with after-tax dollars and take the above-the-line deduction. **(See Chapter 9, "Contributions to Qualified Employee Retirement Plans"; & "Saving Incentive Match Plans (SIMPLEs)")**

Self-employed persons or independent contractors have the option of using the "nonfarm optional method" to compute net earnings from nonfarm self-employment. This method can be used only if net nonfarm profits were less than $4,894 and also less than 72.189% of gross nonfarm income. To use this method, you must be regularly self-employed. You meet this requirement if your actual net earnings from self-employment were $400 or more in 2 of the 3 years preceding the year that you use the nonfarm optional method. The net earnings of $400 or more could be from either farm or nonfarm earnings or both. The net earnings include your distributive share of partnership income or loss subject to self-employment taxes. Use of the nonfarm optional method is limited to 5 years, which do not have to be consecutive. Under the nonfarm optional method, your net earnings from nonfarm self-employment is either: (1) two-thirds of your gross nonfarm income that is $6,780 or less; or (2) $4,520 if your gross nonfarm income is more than $6,780. **(See Below, "Farm Optional Method")**

In a difficult lending environment, many self-employed small business owners are unable to finance their businesses through normal commercial lending practices. However, taxpayers may refinance their home or obtain a home equity loan, and by using the "interest tracing rules" treat such debt as not secured by their residence and deduct the related interest expense on Schedule C rather than on Schedule A of their tax return. When an individual borrows money, the IRS states that the deduction is based upon the tracing rules, which require that when money is borrowed the deduction for interest paid on that borrowed money is determined by the use of the money or "tracing what the money was used for," rather than what the money was borrowed against. When borrowing against their personal residence for business purposes, taxpayers must make a special "10-T election." This election is made by attaching a statement to your tax return explaining that you are making the 10-T election.

If a sole proprietorship makes a contribution to a local charity, the contribution is deductible, but where? If the payment is viewed as a personal charitable contribution, it is deductible on Schedule A, Form 1040. The payment is only considered a business expense if it is not a charitable contribution and is related to business. For example, if you take-out an ad in a local charity's program booklet costing $50, the primary purpose of the payment is to advertise your business. Thus, the payment is a Schedule C deduction for advertising. However, see "Workaround by Businesses to Avoid the $10,000 Limit on Deductions for State and Local Taxes." **(See Chapter 14, "Workaround by Businesses to Avoid the $10,000 Limit on Deductions for State and Local Taxes")**

A sole proprietor may employ family members, and salaries paid to their children are the children's earned income for purposes of contributing to their own IRAs. In addition, no payroll taxes are due on salaries paid to family members under the age of 18, and no federal unemployment taxes (FUTA) are due for family members younger than age 21. **(See Chapter 2, "Payroll Tax (FICA)")**

Self-Employment Tax (Schedule SE)

The self-employment tax, which is computed on Schedule SE, is equal to 92.35% of net self-employment income, multiplied by 15.3% in 2017 (12.4% OASDI tax and 2.9% Medicare tax). The cap on OASDI (Social Security tax) wages for 2017 is $127,200 ($118,500 in 2016). There is no cap on the Medicare tax. Net earnings from self-employment less than $400 in a year are excluded from self-employment taxes. Employees who have wages of $127,200 on which they pay payroll taxes are not subject to OASDI on any self-employment income. One-half of the amount of self-employment taxes paid in a year is deducted as an above-the-line deduction on Form 1040. The Affordable Care Act (ACA) adds a 0.9% surtax to the 1.45% Medicare tax paid by employees who are high-income earners (wages and self-employment income above the thresholds of $200,000 single; $250,000 joint; and $125,000 married filing separately). For self-employed taxpayers, the 0.9% surtax is added to the 2.9% Medicare tax paid on self-employment income above the thresholds, so the total amount of self-employment Medicare taxes paid on self-employment income above the thresholds is 3.8%. **(See Chapter 2, "Payroll Tax (FICA)"); (See Chapter 4, "Wages and Salaries")**

www.irs.gov/pub/irs-pdf/f1040sse.pdf   www.irs.gov/pub/irs-pdf/i1040sse.pdf

In addition to sole-proprietors, other earnings that generally require payment of self-employment tax are: distributions to general partners in a partnership; distributions to members of LLCs; payments to members of a Board of Directors; payments to executors and trustees of estates (including a business operated by executors); royalties from books; fees for putting on workshops; fees received from speeches; working interests (not royalties) in oil and gas productions; and certain foreign earned income that is excluded from the payment of federal income taxes. Also, certain retirement payments are subject to self-employment tax – this usually applies only to certain payments made to former insurance company salesmen, and even then, only if they meet a number of specific requirements. **(See Chapter 4, "Earned Income")**

- IRS Ruling CONEX-132030-16 stated that the taxpayer's post-retirement payments were subject to self-employment tax because the payments were related to commissions received that resulted from 34 years of services on behalf of the company. The IRS cited another Tax Court case, Newberry v. Commissioner, which states: self-employment tax applies when there is "a nexus (connection) between the retirement income received and a trade or business that is, or was, actually carried on."

264

In Newberry, the Tax Court determined that the income arose from some actual income-producing activity of the taxpayer.

https://www.irs.gov/pub/irs-wd/16-0081.pdf   www.ustaxcourt.gov/InOpHistoric/JACKSON.TC.WPD.pdf

In Hardy v. Commissioner, the Tax Court considered the self-employment tax consequences of a plastic surgeon's share of income earned through his investment in an LLC that owned and operated a surgery center. Whether a professional's share of a pass through's income is subject to self-employment tax is an important issue that affects many taxpayers. In Hardy, the taxpayer successfully argued that his share was more like passive income and was not subject to SE tax. In 2006 Hardy purchased for $163,974 a 12.5 per cent interest in a surgery center run through an LLC. While Hardy performed some of his surgeries at the surgery center, he had no obligation to do so, and Hardy had no meaningful non-surgery related service responsibilities with the surgery center (no management responsibilities). Hardy's share of the LLC income related to the fees patients paid for the use of the centers. In essence, his cut was not explicitly tied to surgeries that he performed. Those fees were due Hardy independent of any services or surgical procedures he chose to perform at the surgery center that generated the income in question. The Tax Court ruled that Hardy was an investor in the surgery center, and therefore, the income he received was passive, and therefore, not subject to self-employment tax. www.ustaxcourt.gov/USTCInOP/OpinionViewer.aspx?ID=11088

Sole proprietors who have a business loss carryforward from a prior year can't offset their income in the current year against a prior year's loss for self-employment tax purposes. Even though the carryforward loss reduces taxable income for income tax purposes in the current year, it does not reduce the amount of self-employment taxes owed in the current year.

Self-Employment or Other Income

Sometimes income reported to a taxpayer on Form 1099 (e.g. 1099-MISC) should be reported as "other income" Form 1040, and not be subject to self-employment tax. In this case, expenses related to the "other income" can only be deducted as a miscellaneous itemized deduction up to the amount of the income, so there can't be loss. A "hobby" falls under this category. There are two primary factors that come into play in making the determination of whether income is subject to self-employment tax or not: **(See Chapter 14, "Business or Hobby")**

- Trade or Business – Is the activity from which the income is derived considered a trade or business? Well, it may be considered a "hobby," which means that it would not be considered a business subject to self-employment tax, but if it is an activity carried on for a livelihood or in good faith to make a profit, then it would be considered a business subject to self-employment tax.

- Regular, Frequent and Continuous Activity – If an activity is carried on frequently and regularly, then it may constitute a trade or business, but if the activity is deemed infrequent enough, then it may not be considered a business, and income from the activity should then be classified as "other income." Income from an occasional act or transaction, absent proof of efforts to continue those acts or transactions on a regular basis, is not income from a trade or business. One example of an income-producing activity that is infrequent enough to escape being classified as a trade or business is acting as an election officer or judge where the income is reported to you on Form 1099-MISC, and the activity is not related to your primary job or business.

Another option available to sole proprietors who are carrying on a trade or business, but have no expenses, is to report their income as "other income" on Form 1040, and pay self-employment taxes on the income on Schedule SE. This option would be applicable when Form 1099-MISC income is related to a taxpayer's primary job, but not considered frequent enough to require filing a Schedule C, and the taxpayer had no expenses related to the income. Also, the amount of income reported on Form 1099-MISC would be another consideration. For example, suppose a police officer provided private security services for three department stores for a total of fifty times during the year and was paid a total of $6,500 on three 1099-MISC's. In this case, the income is related to his primary job, and based on the frequency and amount of the compensation should be reported on Schedule C, and self-employment taxes paid on Schedule SE. However, suppose the same police officer provided private security services to only one store five times during the year and was paid a total of $900 on one Form 1099-MISC, and he/she had no expenses related to the private security services provided. In this case, the private security services were related to his primary job, but the infrequency of the services and the small amount of the compensation would suggest that it could be reported as "other income," and that self-employment taxes should be paid on the income.

Home Office Expenses

Home office expenses can be claimed by sole proprietors/self-employed individuals. Home office expenses are deducted on Schedule C by sole proprietors. If a sole proprietor is taxed as an S-corporation, home office expenses are deducted on Form 1120-S. In order to be allowed to claim home office expenses, sole proprietors who have an office in their homes must be able to meet the "exclusive and regular use of a home test," which is: he or she must have a specific part of a house, mobile home, large boat, or a garage, barn or other structure attached to such – though not necessarily a complete room – set aside and used regularly and exclusively as the principal place of business, or if not the principal place of business, the area may be a separate structure (e.g. garage, studio, or barn) or a place used to "meet or deal" with patients, clients, or customers in the normal course of your business. The area is not limited to a single room – multiple rooms may qualify. However, if a taxpayer uses an area of the home for both business and personal use, no deduction is allowed. If you can deduct the cost of a home office, then any business mileage to and from your home is tax deductible.

Storage of business items qualifies for the home office deduction and does not have to meet the exclusive use test as long as the home is the only fixed location of your trade or business, but the space used must be a space for products sold (inventory) or product samples, and the space must be a separately identifiable space suitable for storage. And Even though a storage space doesn't have to be used exclusively for storage, it must be used on a regular basis.

Regular use of a home office does not imply daily use, but may require more than one use per month and must be a designated area used on a continuing basis, not occasional or incidental. An area designated as a home office will qualify if it is used by an individual to conduct administrative and management activities, even if some administrative or management activities are performed at places other than the home office, i.e. you can do administrative and management activities in the home office and meet with customers, clients, or patients in another location. Meeting and dealing with customers can qualify, even if the home office is not the principal place of business. You can't take the deduction if you use your home for a profit-seeking activity that is not a trade or business. For example, if you use part of your home to manage your personal investments, you can't take a home office deduction.

Employees can't claim a home office unless it is used for the convenience of their employer, i.e. the employer must require an employee to work at home. The fact that an employee voluntarily works at home does not qualify. If the employer provides an office or work space elsewhere, a home office is likely considered a matter of an employee's personal convenience and, therefore, is not deductible. NOTE: The Tax Cuts and Jobs Act (TCJA) eliminates "miscellaneous itemized deductions subject to the 2% floor" as an itemized deduction; thus employees cannot deduct home office expenses beginning in 2018. **(See Chapter 12, "Miscellaneous Itemized Deductions Subject to the 2% AGI Floor")**

In a 2014 decision, the Tax Court ruled that a home office deduction is not precluded by minor personal use. Lauren Miller was employed by BIW, a company headquartered in Los Angeles, while at the time she was hired, Miller was BIW's only employee in New York. Miller used part of her 700-square foot studio apartment in New York as an office in 2009 to conduct business for BIW, working weekdays between 9 a.m. and 7 p.m. but was generally expected to be available for business purposes at all times. Miller's studio apartment was a single room divided into three equal sections, including her office space with a desk, two shelving units, a bookcase, and a sofa. She frequently met with BIW clients in the office space, and she performed work for BIW using a computer on the desk. BIW did not reimburse her for any of the expenses related to her apartment. Although she used the office space primarily for business purposes, she occasionally used the office space for personal purposes. In Summary Opinion 2014-74, the Tax Court concluded that Miller was entitled to the home office deduction. "Although the Petitioner admitted that she used portions of the home office space for nonbusiness purposes, the Court found that her personal use of the space was de minimis and wholly attributable to the practicalities of living in a studio apartment of such modest dimensions."
http://ustaxcourt.gov/InOpHistoric/MillerSummary.Guy.SUM.WPD.pdf

Calculating home office expenses can be done in one of two ways: (1) the actual-expense method, which is computed on Form 8829 by sole proprietors, where the home office deduction is based on actual expenses incurred that are related to the use of the home office, or (2) the safe-harbor method, under which the deduction amount is determined by a formula based on the square footage used as a home office. The optional safe-harbor method was put in place in 2013, when the IRS released Rev. Proc. 2013-13. Taxpayers are allowed to change which method they use to compute home office expenses from year to year; however, the election for any tax year is irrevocable (see below).

Actual Expense Method – The actual-expense method is based on the percentage of a home used as a home office, which is computed by dividing the total square footage of the home office by the total square footage of the home. Allowable expenses are either direct or indirect expenses. Direct expenses – such as painting a room used as a home office – are 100% deductible and are reported separately from indirect expenses on Form 8829. Indirect expenses are either a percentage of expenses that are allowable anyway as an itemized deduction (mortgage interest, property taxes, and casualty losses) or a percentage of operating expenses (home insurance, utilities, repairs and maintenance, miscellaneous deductions, and depreciation of the home). Allowable indirect expenses are determined by multiplying total indirect expenses by the percentage of the home used as a home office. Operating expenses are limited to the net income from the business (not taking into account the operating expenses), and cannot add to a net loss by the business for a year. Also, home office expenses cannot exceed the gross income of the business, but may be carried over to the next year. Allowable depreciation expenses are subject to recapture when the home is sold. www.irs.gov/pub/irs-pdf/f8829.pdf www.irs.gov/pub/irs-pdf/i8829.pdf www.irs.gov/pub/irs-drop/rp-13-13.pdf)

If there is one telephone line in a home (land line), none of the cost is deductible as an operating expense; however, some of the optional services such as call waiting may be proportionally deductible if a business purpose can be established. The cost of internet access is a utility expense that is not subject to strict substantiation rules. So, you can usually say that a certain percentage of your internet access expense is business related without being challenged. Costs of landscaping, lawn care, and repairs to non-business areas have usually been considered not deductible. However, a U.S. Tax Court ruling allowed a sole proprietor who regularly met with clients in his home office to deduct part of the costs of landscaping the property, on the grounds that it was a part of the home being used for business. The Court also allowed a deduction for part of the costs of lawn care and driveway repairs. Depreciation taken as a home office expense is based on the lesser of the adjusted basis or FMV of the home on the date the home becomes eligible – must be depreciated over 39 years. Depreciation on a home office is computed in Part III of Form 8829 and carried to line 28 of that Form. Also, Form 4562 must be filed in years that the home is depreciated as a home office. If the house is sold, any depreciation claimed for a home office must be recaptured as "unrecaptured Section 1250 gain" taxed @ 25%. If you sell your home for a loss, you cannot claim a loss. However, if you took home office depreciation, you may be able to take a portion as a loss: **(See Chapter 16, "Residential and Nonresidential Real Property")**

- **Example** – Suppose the purchase price of your home was $100,000; sale price $85,000; business use 10% ($10,000); depreciation taken $1,000 ($10,000 X 10%); recognized loss = $500 ($8,500 – $9,000).

Safe-Harbor Method – The safe-harbor method is computed by multiplying the allowable square footage of a home used as a home office, not to exceed 300 square feet, by $5. Therefore, the maximum a taxpayer can deduct annually under the safe harbor method is $1,500. The IRS may update the $5 allowance from time to time, but it is not inflation adjusted. Because this is a safe harbor, taxpayers who use the safe harbor method may not deduct any actual expenses related to qualified business use of the home (e.g. no depreciation is allowed for the years in which the safe harbor is elected). Taxpayers who itemize deductions and use the safe harbor for a tax year may deduct, to the extent allowable, any expense related to the home that is deductible anyway as an itemized deduction (mortgage interest, property taxes, and casualty losses). Like the actual expense method, home office expenses can't exceed the gross income of the business. However, unlike the actual expense method, taxpayers can't carry over any excess expenses not used in the current year to another tax year.

Day Care Services in the Home

Special rules apply when computing allowable expenses on Form 8829 for day care services, such as a child care facility or an elderly home care facility in a person's home. The main difference between computing home office expenses and day care service expenses is that it is not necessary to meet the exclusive use test for day care services in the home. Also, the safe-harbor method cannot be used for day care services, i.e. only the actual expense method can be used. The calculation to determine the percentage of total indirect expenses allowable for day care services is computed as follows: (1) the percentage of the home used for day care services is determined by dividing the total square footage of the home available for day care services by the total square footage of the home (including the laundry room and storage area in the garage); (2) the percentage of time the home is used for day care services is determined by dividing the total hours the home is used for day care services during the year by the total number of hours in the year; and (3) the percentage determined by step (1) is then

268

multiplied by the percentage determined by step (2) to get the percentage of total indirect expenses allowed for day care services.

- **Example** – If the total square footage of your home is 2,200 square feet, and 1,100 square feet are available for day care services, then 50% of your home is available for day care services (1,100 divided by 2,200). If there are 8,760 hours in the year (365 X 24), and your home is used 2,500 hours for day care services, then your home is used 29% of the time for day care services during the year (2,500 divided by 8,760). Thus, the percentage of total indirect expenses you are allowed to claim for day care services during the year would be 14.5% (50% X 29%).

Allowable indirect expenses are the same as those allowable for a home office – mortgage interest, property taxes, casualty losses, and operating expenses (home insurance, utilities, repairs and maintenance, miscellaneous deductions, and depreciation of the home). Direct expenses for a day care services facility, such food and toys, are 100% deductible, i.e. only indirect expenses such as mortgage interest, property taxes, home insurance, utility expenses, depreciation, and other indirect miscellaneous expenses are subject to the calculated percentage.

Ministers and Employees of Religious Organizations

Employees of religious organizations have been subject to mandatory payroll tax (FICA) coverage since 1984, but this sometimes does not include ministers. Typically, a minister's compensation includes a salary that is reported on Form W-2, and a home or parsonage that by law is provided to him or her income tax-free and, therefore, is not reported as taxable income on Form W-2. Also, ministers may be provided with a housing allowance rather than a home itself that is part of their pay and is also income tax-free, and the housing allowance can be used to pay for rent, mortgage, utilities, real estate taxes, and repair expenses. Ministers are even allowed to deduct mortgage interest and real estate taxes as itemized deductions, even if paid with a tax-free housing allowance. However, the fair market value (FMV) of a home or a housing allowance provided to ministers as part of their pay is subject to self-employment tax, even though the compensation is income tax-free. In Gaylor v. Mnuchin, a Wisconsin Federal District Court determined that he housing allowance available to ministers and other religious leaders constitutes a violation of the principal of separation of state and church. However, ministers continue to be compensated with tax-free housing allowances. **(See Above, "Self-Employment Tax")**
https://scholar.google.com/scholar_case?case=16712166637391697213&hl=en&as_sdt=6&as_vis=1&oi=scholarr

A minister has to pay self-employment tax on the value of a home provided tax-free, unless he/she has received an exemption from self-employment tax by filing Form 4361 (conscientious objector, which generally applies to Christian Science practitioners) or Form 4029, "Application for Exemption from self-employment tax" on which he states that he is opposed to acceptance of any payments from Social Security or Medicare. Absent an exemption, a minister's wages, the fair rental value of all non-taxable housing or housing allowances, and any other allowances or payments a minister receives but does not pay payroll taxes on, such as fees for performing marriages, funerals, etc., is subject to self-employment tax which is computed on Schedule SE. And of course, if payroll taxes are not withheld from a minister's wages, any such wages are also subject to self-employment taxes on Schedule SE. A box has to be checked at the top of Schedule SE if the minister has an approved copy of Form 4361 or Form 4029. Retired ministers are not subject to self-employment taxes on the rental value of a parsonage or parsonage allowance.

The Tax court held that "a vow of poverty does not insulate a pastor from tax liability when the pastor receives funds directly from his church in exchange for services rendered if the pastor does not remit those funds to the church in accordance with his vow of poverty, has control over the funds, and uses the funds for personal expenditures.

www.irs.gov/pub/irs-pdf/i8829.pdf www.irs.gov/pub/irs-pdf/f4029.pdf

Farmers and Ranchers (Schedule F)

Farming income and expenses are reported on Schedule F. Farmers who are sole proprietors are subject to self-employment taxes, including income earned by sharecroppers. If you earn money managing or working on a farm, you are in the farming business. Farms include plantations, ranches, ranges, and orchards. Farmers may raise livestock, poultry, or fish, or grow fruits or vegetables. Farming does not include commercial freezing and canning. Farmers who claim home office expenses are not required to file Form 8829. Instead, they claim their entire home office deduction directly on one line of Schedule F (see above). Farmers' distributive share from farm partnerships are also subject to self-employment taxes. Taxpayers with income from farming or fishing have until March 1st to file their Form 1040 and pay the tax due to avoid making estimated tax payments. This rule generally applies if farming or fishing income was at least two-thirds of the total gross income in either the current or the preceding tax year. See IRS Publication 225, "Farmer's Tax Guide."

www.irs.gov/pub/irs-pdf/f1040sf.pdf www.irs.gov/pub/irs-pdf/i1040sf.pdf
www.irs.gov/pub/irs-pdf/p225.pdf

Farming Revenues – Farming revenues generally come from: (1) sales of livestock that are purchased and held primarily for resale; (2) sales of livestock, produce, or other farm products raised or grown; (3) livestock held for draft, breeding, or dairy purposes; (4) cooperative distributions received as patronage dividends (Form 1099-PATR); (5) payments from the U.S. Department of Agriculture – Conservation Reserve Program (CRP) payments, Grassland Reserve Program (GRP) payments, etc.; (6) Commodity Credit Corporation (CCC) Loans; (7) crop Insurance proceeds received as the result of crop damage; and (8) pasture income received for taking care of someone else's cattle for a fee.

Livestock that is purchased is either primarily held for sale, or if not, the livestock is held for draft, breeding, or dairy purposes. The basis for determining profit or loss on purchased livestock is cost, plus sales taxes and freight charges for transporting the livestock to the farm. Farmers have two options on how to treat raised livestock. The livestock can either be included in inventory or depreciated. Both options have advantages and disadvantages, so the decision is ultimately based on whether the farmer prefers a current benefit or a future benefit. If farmers opt for a current benefit, they can deduct the costs of raising livestock during the years in which the animals are being raised. If these costs are already deducted in earlier years, the basis of the livestock will be zero when sold. If farmers decide to depreciate their livestock, depreciation will begin when the livestock are mature (i.e. can be worked, milked, or bred). Most farm business assets are depreciated using the MACRS General Depreciation System (GDS). Generally, GDS must be used unless ADS is required by law or is elected. The recovery period for cattle, goats, and sheep is five years (200% DB/GDS), while the recovery period for hogs is three years. Also, all livestock is eligible for Section 179 expensing and 100% bonus depreciation. **(See Chapter 16, "Modified Accelerated Cost Recovery System (MACRS)")**

The U.S. Department of Agriculture (USDA) pays yearly Conservation Reserve Program (CRP) payments to farmers in exchange for removing environmentally sensitive land from agricultural production and planting species that will improve environmental quality. Under the 4-H Act (2009), CRP payments received after 2007 are excluded from self- employment income if the taxpayer is receiving Social Security retirement or disability benefits. Otherwise, payments from the USDA received by both farmers and non-farmers for setting aside land under the CRP and other USDA programs are considered income subject to self-employment taxes. The USDA's other programs include: Grassland Reserve Program (GRP) payments to farmers to prevent them from converting grazing and pasture land to cropland or from being used for urban development; the Conservation Reserve Enhancement Program (CREP), an offshoot of CRP, that pays farmers to remove certain farmland from production for conservation purposes; the Emergency Conservation Program (ECP) that provides funding and technical assistance to farmers and ranchers to restore farmland damaged by natural disasters and for emergency water conservation measures in severe droughts; and the Emergency Forest Restoration Program (EFRP), which is similar to the ECP, in that it provides funding to restore privately owned forests damaged by natural disasters. Farmers who receive USDA payments intended for them as well as another person should show the total amount received on Schedule F, but should not report the amount not belonging to them as taxable income. They should file Form 1099-G to report the identity of the actual recipient.

Farmers can elect to treat loan proceeds from Commodity Credit Corporation (CCC) loans as income in the year received if they choose to pledge part or all of their crop production to secure the CCC loan. Farmers must attach a statement to Schedule F showing details of the loan amount reported as income, which becomes the basis in the crops pledged. If the farmer forfeits the pledged crops to the CCC in full payment of the loan, the forfeiture is treated for tax purposes as a sale of the crops. If farmers don't report the loan proceeds as income in the year received, they must include the loan proceeds as income in the year of forfeiture (reported by CCC on Form 1099A). You can only deduct the interest you paid on a loan on Schedule F if the loan is used for your farming business. You can't deduct interest you paid on a loan that you used for personal purposes.

Farmers may be able to postpone reporting crop insurance proceeds from crop damage to crops as income in the current year to the following year, if they would have normally included income from the damaged crops in the following year (a statement stating this must be attached to Schedule F).

Sales of Livestock – Sales of livestock are reported on Form 4797. Calculation of gain depends on whether the animals were raised by the farmer or purchased. The gain on livestock raised is calculated as the difference between the selling expenses and the gross sales price. If the basis is zero because the costs of raising the livestock were deducted during the years in which they were being raised, then the gain is equal to the selling price. The gain on livestock purchased is calculated by subtracting the adjusted basis and selling expenses from the gross sales price. To be qualified under Section 1231, the animals must be held by the taxpayer for draft, breeding, dairy, or sporting purposes for at least 12 months (24 months for cattle). If the holding period is met, the gain or loss is reported in Part I or Part III of Form 4797, depending on if there is recapture of depreciation. **(See Chapter 6, "Reporting Capital Gains and Losses"); (See Chapter 14, "Sale of Business Property")**

If farmers choose to inventory their livestock, there are two inventory methods available: (1) the simplest method is called the "farm-price method." This method provides for the valuation of inventories at market price less direct cost of disposition; (2) the other inventory method is the "unit-livestock-price method." To determine the valuation under this method, livestock are classified into groups with respect to age and kind. Then, a price for each class is established, taking into account the normal cost of raising those animals. Farmers using this method must reevaluate unit prices each year and adjust either upward or downward to reflect changes in the costs of raising the livestock.

Other Income – Storage fees paid by the CCC under a resale agreement to farmers for storing their own grain is considered other income. Also, the part of the dairy termination program that is not treated as an amount realized on the sale of living cattle is considered other income.

Exclusion of Cost-Sharing Government Payments – Some government payments are excluded from income under certain "cost-sharing conservation programs. Farmers may be able to exclude from income federal or state cost-sharing payments for certain conservation, reclamation, and restoration programs they get for an improvement (capital expenditure), if the USDA certifies that the payment was for conserving soil, water resources, protecting the environment, etc.

Relief to Farmers and Ranchers in Drought Areas – Farmers and ranchers who previously were forced to sell livestock due to drought in an applicable region now have an additional year to replace the livestock and defer tax on any gains from the forced sales, according to the IRS. An applicable region is a county designated as eligible for federal assistance plus counties contiguous to that county. As a result, farmers and ranchers in the applicable region whose drought sale replacement period was scheduled to expire at the end of Dec. 31, 2017, in most cases, will now have until the end of their next tax year (Dec. 31, 2018). Because the normal drought sale replacement period is four years, this extension immediately impacts drought sales that occurred during 2013. But because of previous drought-related extensions affecting some of these localities, the replacement periods for some drought sales before 2013 are also affected. Additional extensions will be granted if severe drought conditions persist.

The IRS provides this extension to farmers and ranchers located in the applicable region that qualified for the four-year replacement period if any county, parish, city, or district, that is included in the applicable region is listed as suffering exceptional, extreme or severe drought conditions by the National Drought Mitigation Center (NDMC), during any weekly period between Sept. 1, 2016, and Aug. 31, 2017. All or part of 42 states, plus the District of Columbia, are listed (See Notice 2017-53)
www.irs.gov/pub/irs-drop/n-17-53.pdf

Rental of Farmland – Rental income received by farm owners for use of their farmland by another person is not farm income, but instead is considered to be rental income that is reported on Form 4835 and is not subject to self-employment tax. This includes leasing a farm to someone else who pays the farmer a share of crop receipts instead of rent. The owner may still receive government payments from the Department of Agriculture when the farmland is rented, and this income is always subject to self-employment tax.
www.irs.gov/pub/irs-access/f4835_accessible.pdf

If the owner materially participates in farming operations on the rented farmland, then he or she should pay self-employment taxes on the rental income. Material participation includes working 100 hours or more over a period of 5 weeks or more in the farming operations, regularly and frequently making management decisions, or paying

272

for at least ½ of the direct cost of producing the crops. Sharecroppers who rent the land from owners and produce the crops must pay self-employment tax.

Farming Expenses – More than 98% of farm and ranches operate as pass-through businesses: sole proprietorships, partnerships and S-corporations. Farmers can deduct ordinary and necessary expenses paid to operate their farm business. An ordinary expense is a common and accepted cost for operating a farm. A necessary expense means a cost that is appropriate for the business. Some expenses must be allocated between personal and business use (rent, electricity, water, telephone, repairs, insurance, interest, taxes, gas, oil, vehicle repairs, etc.). Any reasonable allocation method is acceptable. Other expenses such as feed and fertilizer are 100% farm expenses. Farmers can deduct reasonable wages paid to full and part-time workers, but they must withhold income and payroll taxes from employees' wages. You can deduct the interest paid on a loan only if the loan proceeds are used for your farming business. Farmers can claim the standard mileage allowance for their vehicles used for farm business. Also, farmers may be able to claim a tax credit or refund of federal excise taxes paid on fuel used on their farm for farming purposes.

Under the TCJA, the recovery period for depreciation purposes is shortened for originally owned farm machinery and equipment acquired in 2018 from 7 to 5 years beginning in 2018 and subsequent years, and 150% declining balance (DB) GDS depreciation is repealed for 3, 5, 7 and 10-year property and 200% DB GDS depreciation is permitted for all property used in the farming business with a recovery period of 10 years of less. Following are the depreciation rules in effect for farming and ranching in years before the TCJA, some of which are not affected by the TCJA:

- All farming and ranching equipment with a MACRS life of 20 years or less should be depreciated using 150% DB/GDS with the half-year convention, except for 5-year property which is depreciated using 200% DB/GDS (see below). 15-year farm property includes land improvements such as sidewalks, roads, landscaping, irrigation systems, and drainage systems. 10-year farm property includes single-purpose agricultural structures specifically designed for housing, raising, and feeding a particular type of livestock, and agricultural trees and vines bearing fruit and nuts. 7-year farm property includes machinery and equipment, fencing, and grain bins. 5-year farm property includes general purpose trucks and trailers. Section 1245 personal property, such as machinery and equipment, is also eligible for the Section 179 expensing election, but not real property, such as farm buildings and land improvements. However, all new property with a life of 20 years or less is eligible for Section 179 expensing and 100% bonus depreciation. 20-year farm property includes farm buildings such as barns and equipment sheds, which are eligible for bonus depreciation but not Section 179 expensing. The "Protecting Americans from Tax Hikes Act of 2015" extended the provision allowing 3-year depreciation for race horses two years old and younger that were placed in service in 2015 and 2016. **(See Chapter 16, "Modified Accelerated Cost Recovery System (MACRS)")**

Under the TCJA, the business interest deduction in 2018 is limited to business interest income plus 30 percent of adjusted taxable income. However, taxpayers engaged in the farming business may elect out of the interest limitation, and the election is irrevocable. However, an electing farm business is required to use the Alternative Depreciation System (ADS) – with its accompanying restriction on using bonus depreciation and longer depreciation recovery period – for any asset with a useful life of more than 10 years, including land improvements, barns, and other farm buildings in years beginning after 2017. **(See Below, "Credit for Federal Excise Tax Paid on Fuels"); (See Chapter 4, "Wages and Salaries"); (See Chapter 15, "Vehicle and Other Transportation Expenses")**

Deductible soil and water conservation and prevention of erosion of farmland expenses include: (1) treatment or movement of earth, such as leveling, conditioning, grading, terracing, contour furrowing, and restoration of soil fertility; (2) construction, control, and protection of diversion channels, drainage ditches, irrigation ditches, earthen dams, watercourses, outlets, and ponds; (3) eradication of brush; and (4) planting of windbreaks. You can't deduct expenses to drain or fill wetlands or to prepare land for center pivot irrigation systems – costs must be added to the basis of the land. Endangered species recovery expenditures that achieve site-specific management actions recommended under the Endangered Species Act of 1973 are eligible for a tax deduction of up to 25% of gross farming income for any particular year.

Pass-Through Business Provisions – Under the TCJA, farmers and ranchers are allowed to take a deduction of 20% of their business income in tax years 2018 – 2025. For farms and ranches with joint income beyond $315,000, the deduction is limited by one of two calculations, chosen by the business owner. Those calculations are: (1) 50% of W-2 wages paid to employees; or (2) the sum of 25% of W-2 wages paid plus 2.5% of depreciable business property. The 20% deduction only offsets income tax, not self-employment tax.

Credit for Federal Excise Tax Paid on Fuels – Farmers can claim a tax credit for federal excise taxes paid on fuel used for farming purposes. **(See Chapter 13, "Credit for Federal Excise Tax Paid on Fuels")**

Conservation Easements – The "Protecting Americans from Tax Hikes Act of 2015" makes permanent a provision allowing farmers and ranchers to donate capital gain real property easements for conservation purposes, and to offset up to 100% of the value of the gift from their adjusted gross income in the current year and to carry forward any unused write-off for a full 15 years, potentially zeroing out their tax liability for the next 15 years. Also, non-farmer donors can make a donation of conservation real property and offset up to 50% of the value of the gift from their adjusted gross income in the current year and carry forward any unused write-offs for a full 15 years. How does this work? With a conservation easement, donors give some or all of the development rights on their land to a government agency or not-for-profit charitable organization, and in turn they get a federal income tax deduction for the gift, which is the difference in the value of the land before and after the easement is in place. The donor still owns the land and can enjoy the land, such as farming and fishing on the land. Conservation easements are a powerful tool to protect land from development. **(See Chapter 12, "Non-Cash Contributions")**

Sell of Farmland – Section 1252 property is farmland held more than one year and less than 10 years on which farmers were allowed to take deductions for soil and water conservation expenses. When Section 1252 farmland is sold for a gain, you must treat part of the gain as ordinary income and the rest as Section 1231 gain. If you sell or dispose of the farmland within 5 years, total gain, less total deductions allowed for soil and water conservation expenses, is treated as 100% ordinary income. If you sell or dispose of the farmland within 6 to 9 years, the percentage that is treated as ordinary income is reduced by 20% for each year it is held over 5 years. If you sell or dispose of the farmland held 10 years or more, none of the gain is treated as ordinary income. **(See Chapter 14, "Sale of Business Property")**

Section 1255 property is farmland on which you received cost-sharing payments from the government that were excluded from income. If you sell or dispose of the farmland and it was held less than 10 years, 100% of any gain equal to the cost-sharing payments received is treated as ordinary income. After 10 years, the percentage that is treated as ordinary income is reduced by 10% a year. **(See Above, "Exclusion of Cost-Sharing Government Payments")**

Farm Optional Method – Farmers can use the farm optional method to figure net earnings from farm self-employment if gross farm income is $6,780 or less or net farm profits are less than $4,894. Net farm profits are the total of net farm income and a farmer's distributive share from farm partnerships. There is no limit on how many years you can use this method. Under the optional method, your net earnings from farm self-employment is the smaller of two-thirds of your gross farm income (not less than zero) or $4,520. For a farm partnership, figure your share of gross income based on the partnership agreement. With guaranteed payments, your share of the partnership's gross income is your guaranteed payments plus your share of the gross income after it is reduced by all guaranteed payments made by the partnership. If you are a limited partner, include only guaranteed payments for services you actually rendered to or on behalf of the partnership.

Farm Income Averaging – You may be able to average some or all of the current year's farm income by spreading it out over the past three years (base years). This may lower your taxes if your farm income is high in the current year and low in one or more of the past three years. This method does not change your prior year taxes. It only uses the prior year information to figure your current year taxes. Schedule J is used to make the computation. The Elected Farm Income (EFI) is the amount of income you choose to have taxed at base year rates. www.irs.gov/pub/irs-access/f1040sj_accessible.pdf   www.irs.gov/pub/irs-pdf/i1040sj.pdf

Excess Farm Losses – The law in effect in 2017 and prior years, specifically limited only "excess farm losses." However, the TCJA expanded the law to limit losses from all types of pass-through trades or businesses for taxpayers other than corporations. The provision, which went into effect January 1, 2018 and sunsets on December 31, 2025, limits the excess business losses of all pass-through trades or businesses. Under the 2017 law and the 2014 Farm Bill, farmers that received a Commodity Credit Corporation (CCC) loan were restricted in the deductibility of a farm losses (this rule didn't apply to C corporations). The disallowed portion of the losses were carried to the following year, tested again for limitation purposes and claimed on Schedule F (Form 1040). Under the TCJA, farming losses are now subject to the "excess business loss" limitations that are applicable to all pass-through trades and businesses for tax years 2018 – 2025.

Net Operating Losses (NOLs) – Farmers often end up with a net operating loss (NOL) at the end of any given year when deductible expenses are more than income for the year. Under the Tax Cuts and Jobs Act (TCJA), the 2-year net operating loss carryback is eliminated, except for farmers. Beginning in 2018, a farming NOL may be carried back 2 years instead of 5 years under the rules prior to December 31, 2017, and the 2-year carryback can be waived. Farming NOLs can be carried forward indefinitely but are limited to 80% of taxable income in the carryforward years. In addition, if an NOL consists of both a farming loss and a nonfarming loss, then the two losses are treated separately. The farming NOL is accounted for in carryforward years after the nonfarm loss. That is, the nonfarm NOL, which is subject to the 80% limitation, is first applied to taxable income followed by the application of the farming NOL. **(See Chapter 8, "Net Operating Loss (NOL)")**

Gross Estate – A farmer's gross estate can receive a discount in its valuation via a special-use valuation of farmland, which can reduce the gross estate up to a maximum of $1.12 million. Special-use valuation is a method of valuing farmland by the federal government under Section 2032(a). To qualify, the family must materially participate in the farm's operation for a period of time before the death of the decedent; the farm must stay in the family for a period of time after death; and the family must materially participate in the operation of the farm for a period of time after death.

Chapter 18 – Partnerships

A partnership can either be a general partnership or a limited partnership. A general partnership is an unincorporated organization made up of two or more parties that carries on a trade or business that doesn't have to file formation documents with the state. However, there should be an informal written agreement between partners that addresses such issues as capital contributions, distributions, profit and loss sharing, management responsibilities, dispute resolution, duration and termination of the business, and transferability of the partners' interests. In a general partnership, all owners have unlimited personal liability for all of the partnership's activities. Forming a limited partnership requires filing formation documents with the state (certificate of formation or other documents). A limited partnership must have at least one general partner, and the general partner must run the business. The general partner has unlimited liability for the business's activities, but the limited partners' liability is restricted to their capital investment in the business. The general partner has unlimited liability for company debts and losses, and may lose his home and other personal assets because of losses and obligations that occur as a result of operating the business. Limited partners have personal asset protection against company obligations and debts. The general partner can be either an individual or a corporation. To retain their limited liability status, limited partners cannot be involved in managing the business. All partnerships are required to have an employer identification number (EIN).

Partnership agreements need to reflect the "New Audit Regime." Mandatory implementation of the new audit regime kicks off for audits of partnership tax years starting on or after Jan. 1, 2018. With respect to IRS "Audits of Large Partnerships," the Bipartisan Budget Act (BBA) which applies to partnership tax years beginning after Dec. 31, 2017, makes certain changes to adjustments resulting from IRS audits. The audit can adjust a partnership's income, gain, loss, deduction, or credit, or any partner's distributive share of these items. A key part of the new law is that the tax increases will be paid by the partnership at the highest individual or corporate tax rate for the reviewed year. A partnership will pay an imputed underpayment when the audit adjustment(s) result in an increase to income or decrease to deductions. The payment is born by the current partners. Adjustments that do not result in an underpayment of tax must be taken into account in the adjustment year. This requirement allows the current partners to benefit from audit adjustments that are favorable for the partnership related to the reviewed year. Partners from the reviewed year will not receive a refund for the reviewed year if there is a net partnership-favorable IRS audit adjustment. **(See Below, "Elective Large Partnerships (ELP)")**

A partnership is a pass-through entity that is separate from its owners and is required to file a separate tax return on Form 1065, "U.S. Return of Partnership Income," where partnership revenues and expenses are determined. Since a partnership is a pass-through entity, it doesn't pay any taxes, but instead passes income through to the partners who pay taxes on their individual tax returns. A partnership's annual distributive share of profits or losses are allocable to individual partners based on their ownership percentages and profits are taxable to the partners whether or not actually received by the partners. The loss limitation rule states that partners can't deduct losses in excess of their tax basis in the partnership. Form 1065, Schedule K shows the total income and deductions that will be reported to the partners. These totals are then reported to each partner on Schedule K-1 (Form 1065) based on their ownership percentages. Schedule K-1 is the document used by the partners to include their share of the partnership's income and deductions on their individual 1040 tax returns. Each owner receives a Form K-1 that reports his or her appropriate share of the income (or loss), even if that income is retained by the business and not distributed to the owners. You are obligated to report it on your tax return, regardless of whether you received any payout. In determining partnership income or loss on Form 1065, rental income, interest income, dividends, royalties, capital gains and losses, tax-exempt income, and other portfolio income, as well as Section 179 expensing, must be shown separately from the partnership's ordinary income or loss, because these are items that must be shown separately on the partners' individual tax returns. The IRS matches income shown on Schedules K-1 against individual's tax returns.

www.irs.gov/pub/irs-pdf/f1065.pdf   www.irs.gov/pub/irs-pdf/i1065.pdf

Schedule M-3, Form 1065 "Net Income (Loss) Reconciliation for Certain Partnerships" must be filed by partnerships with total assets of $10 million or more, only if they have a "reportable entity partner" that owns or is deemed to own an interest of 50% or more in the partnership on any day during the partnership's tax year. A "reportable entity" is a partner that owns a corporate interest in a corporation. Schedule M-3 compares tax information the taxpayer disclosed for financial reporting purposes with the partnership's tax position. Schedule M-3 requires the taxpayer to reconcile the differences between their financial statement net income or loss and reported taxable income. If a partnership satisfies all four of the following conditions, then it doesn't have to complete Schedules L, M-1, and M-2:

1. The partnership's total receipts for the year were less than $250,000;
2. The partnership's total assets at the end of the year were less than $1 million;
3. Schedules K-1(s) are filed with the return and furnished to the partners on or before the due date of the partnership return; and
4. The partnership is not filing and is not required to file Schedule M-3.

A partnership's tax year must be the same as the principal partners' tax years, unless there is a business purpose for choosing another tax year. If the principal partners have different tax years, the partnership must adopt a year that results in the least amount of deferral. A principal partner is one that has a 5% or more interest in a partnership. A partner may be an individual, C-corporation, S-corporation, other partnerships, all types of trusts, decedent's estates, and tax-exempt organizations. The due date for partnership tax returns for tax years beginning after Dec. 31, 2015 is March 15th of the following year for calendar year partnerships or the 15th day of the third month following the close of the fiscal year for fiscal year partnerships. Form 7004 can be filed to request a 6-month extension. The partnership must send each partner a Schedule K-1 by April 17, 2018 that reports the partner's share of partnership income and expenses for tax year 2017. A partnership will terminate only if there is no continuity of any business carried on by any of its partners, or if within a 12-month period there is a sale or exchange of 50% or more of the partnership's capital accounts. If a partner sells all or part of his or her partnership interest, the existence of the partnership is not affected unless the transaction terminates the partnership.

www.irs.gov/pub/irs-pdf/f7004.pdf   www.irs.gov/pub/irs-pdf/i7004.pdf

General partners are required to pay self-employment tax on their share of partnership income, but limited partners are not, except on payments for the performance of services. Limited partners' share of partnership income is considered passive income (except for payments for the performance of services) that is not subject to self-employment tax, but a limited partner's share of partnership income may be subject to the 3.8% net investment income (NII) tax if the limited partner is a high-income earner. The 3.8% NII tax is not applicable to general partners. **(See Chapter 2, "Payroll Tax (FICA)")**; **(See Chapter 4, "Wages and Salaries")**; **(See Chapter 10, "3.8% Net Investment Income Tax")**; **(See Chapter 17, "Self-Employment Tax")**

A partnership can elect to be taxed as a corporation without formally becoming a corporation under the "check-the-box" rules by filing Form 8832 with the IRS. A partnership that converts to a corporation may make an immediate S-corporation election by filing Form 2553 with the IRS. A Limited Liability Company (LLC) can elect how to be treated for federal tax purposes, because an LLC is not a federal taxable entity, and there is no provision in the IRS Code that specifically governs the treatment of LLCs for federal tax purposes. Therefore, both a partnership and an LLC can elect to be taxed as a regular C-corporation under the "check-the-box" rules by filing Form 8832. An LLC electing "default status," i.e. to be treated as a disregarded entity and not to be taxed as a separate entity from its owners, should not file Form 8832. The default status for a single owner or husband and wife LLC is to file Schedule C with their individual 1040 tax return, and the default status for an LLC with 2 or more owners is to file a partnership tax return (Form 1065). **(See Chapter 17, "Self-Employed/Independent Contractors")**; **(See Chapter 19, "Limited Liability Company (LLC)")**

A partner can acquire a partnership interest by inheriting it, buying it, contributing services to it, or by receiving it as a gift. A receipt of an interest in a partnership in exchange for services rendered to the partnership is taxable income to that partner. If a partnership interest is inherited, the partner's basis is the fair market value (FMV) of the interest on the date of the decedent's death. If received as a gift, the partner's basis is the same as the donor's basis. If purchased, the new partner's basis is the amount paid for the interest, plus the selling partner's share of total partnership liabilities that the new partner assumes. If non-business personal or real property is contributed to a partnership, the basis is the lesser of FMV or the contributing partner's adjusted basis. If a partner contributes property in exchange for a partnership interest, there is no recognition of gain or loss on the transaction. If a sole proprietor hires someone and agrees to make him a 50% partner after 3 years, the new partner's 50% share of the partnership is taxable income that is taxed to him as ordinary income (See Below).

Loss Limitation Reductions for Charitable Donations and Foreign Taxes

The loss limitation rule states that partners or LLC members that are treated as partners for tax purposes can't deduct losses in excess of the partner's tax basis in the partnership at the end of the partnership year in which such loss occurs. However, for tax years beginning after December 31, 2017, the Tax Cuts and Jobs Act (TCJA) changes the rules for charitable gifts and foreign taxes by stating that a partner's share of a partnership's deductible charitable donations and paid or accrued foreign taxes reduces the partner's tax basis in the partnership for purposes of applying the loss limitation rule. This change can reduce the amount of losses that can be deducted by partners in 2018 and subsequent years compared to the amount that could be deducted in 2017 and prior years. For charitable donations of appreciated property (where the fair market value is higher than the tax basis), the TCJA states that a partner's basis isn't reduced by the excess amount for purposes of applying the loss limitation rule, i.e. the partner's tax basis is reduced only by the partner's share of the basis of the donated appreciated property for purposes of applying the loss limitation rule.

Prior to implementation of the TCJA, the IRS had taken the position in a private letter ruling that a partner's share of the partnership's charitable contributions did not reduce the partner's tax basis in the partnership for purposes of applying the loss limitation rule.

Deduction of Health Insurance Premiums and Retirement Contributions by Partners

Partners are eligible for an above-the-line deduction on their individual tax returns for the cost of health insurance premiums paid during the year if the medical care coverage was established by the partnership, but they can't deduct the health insurance premiums in determining net income for self-employment tax purposes. This also includes the cost of Medicare premiums. Partners are also eligible for an above-the-line deduction for contributions to retirement programs, but again, they can't deduct the contributions to their retirement programs for determining the amount of income subject to self-employment tax. **(See Chapter 11, "Self-Employed Health Insurance Premiums" & "Self-Employed Retirement Contributions")**

Receipt of a Partnership Interest in Exchange for Services

The receipt of a partnership interest in exchange for services performed or to be performed for the partnership is taxable to the recipient. The amount of income is equal to the fair market value (FMV) of the partnership interest, and is taxed as compensation income to the recipient. However, if it is a receipt of a "profits-only" interest in the partnership, it is usually not taxable to the recipient. The receipt of an equity interest in a partnership can give the recipient an interest in the partnership's capital, its profits, or both. Another restriction that qualifies for a different treatment is when the recipient of a capital interest, in exchange for services, is required to continue to perform services. Thus, if a grant of a capital interest will be forfeited due to a violation of this condition then the receipt of the interest will not be taxable until the interest vests in, say, four years, at which time the recipient will have to include the then FMV of his share as compensation income. In this case, the recipient of the interest can make a Section 83(b) election that allows the recipient to override the regular rules of Section 83 and take property as income on the date of the grant rather than the date it vests (4 years later). Therefore, if the grant is likely to be much more valuable by the time it vests, it may make sense to treat the grant as a taxable event on the front end, and thereby avoid having to treat the increase in value at the time of vesting as income.

- **Example** – Betty and John form a partnership by investing $1,000 each. The partnership has a capital balance of $2,000. A week later, the partnership grants a 25% capital interest to Bill in exchange for Bill's promise to perform services for the partnership. If it is a 25% capital interest, Bill is entitled to a capital interest of $500 based on the FMV of the partnership ($2,000 X 25% = $500). Bill will be treated as receiving $500 in compensation as income as a result of the award. The new capital interests and basis in the partnership will be: Betty - $750 (37.5%); John - $750 (37.5%); and Bill - $500 (25%).

- **Example** – Assume the same facts as above, except Bill receives a 25% "profits-only" interest in the partnership. Therefore, the receipt of the profits-only interest is not a taxable event to Bill, because a 25% profits-only interest would entitle Bill to 25% of the profits of the partnership. However, unless the partnership actually earns profits, he is not entitled to anything. The IRS has taken the position that future profits are too speculative to warrant taxing a profits-only interest on the front end. Of course, Bill's receipt of his share of any profits will be taxable to him. The capital interests and basis in the partnership will remain: Betty - $1,000 (50%); John - $1,000 (50%).

- **Example** – Assume the same facts as above. A 25% capital interest is granted to Bill in exchange for his promise to perform services for the partnership. However, the terms of the grant require Bill to forfeit his interest if he doesn't provide certain stated services to the partnership for the next four years. As of the date of the grant, Bill's capital interest is worth $500. Assume that four years from now, Bill's capital interest will be worth $5,000. Absent a Section 83(b) election, Bill will be taxed at the time of vesting in four years on assumed compensation income of $5,000. However, if Bill makes a Section 83(b) election, he is taxed at the time of the grant on compensation income of only $500.

Limited Liability Partnership

Generally, a limited liability partnership (LLP) is a partnership formed by professionals, such as lawyers, accountants, architects, engineers, dentists, and physicians. A LLP is essentially the same as a general partnership in form, with one important difference. Unlike a general partnership, in which individual partners are liable for the partnership debts and obligations, a LLP provides each of its individual partners with protection against personal liability for certain partnership liabilities. A LLP does not have a general partner – all partners of the company are allowed to take part in the management of the company and make management decisions for the company. LLCs and corporations may not be partners in a LLP. LLPs are by default taxed as partnerships and must file Form 1065, and send Schedule K-1s to its partners annually, reporting the partners' share of income and deductions. Every partner in a LLP must pay self-employment taxes on their share of the company's profits and losses. Each partner in a LLP receives profits and losses from the company according to their ownership interest in the company.

In a LLP, all partners generally have limited liability protection against company obligations and debts. In addition, partners in a LLP usually have limited liability protection against malpractice suits that stem from another partner's negligent acts. However, the limit of an individual partner's liability depends on the scope of the state's LLP legislation. Many states provide protection only against tort claims and do not extend protection to a partner's own negligence or incompetence or to the partner's involvement in supervising wrongful conduct. Other states provide broad protection, including protection against contractual claims brought by the partnership's creditors. Starting a LLP requires the filing of formation documents with the state, and in so doing, every partner of a LLP must have the appropriate state-issued occupational license, which is not a requirement in a limited partnership. This requirement prevents a LLP from adding talented partners who are not licensed professionals of the particular LLP.

Limited Liability Company (LLC)

You can form a limited liability company (LLC) with one person, or with two or more persons. A one-member LLC that is a disregarded entity is taxed as a sole proprietorship, and a LLC with two or more members that is a disregarded entity is taxed as a partnership. LLC owners, called "members," can manage their businesses or hire professional managers. In addition, LLCs enjoy a lot of flexibility. For instance, they can have as many members as they like, and corporations are allowed to be members. LLCs enjoy freedom from most state-mandated membership and management reporting requirements that corporations have. Most important, LLCs do not have to pay taxes. Instead, their profits and losses are passed through to their members' individual tax returns. Forming an LLC generally requires filing formation documents with the state (certificate of formation or other document). Small businesses choose to form a LLC more often than a LLP. Some types of businesses such as banks and insurance companies are not allowed to form LLCs. Most states protect the business assets of LLC members from personal creditors. Similarly, the personal assets of members of an LLC are protected from business judgments. This liability protection is one reason the LLC structure has been so popular with small businesses. **(See Chapter 17, "Self-Employed/Independent Contractors"); (See Chapter 19, "Limited Liability Company (LLC)")**

281

Family Limited Partnership (FLP)

A Family Limited Partnership (FLP) is a common device for splitting income among family members. FLPs pool family assets together into one single-owned business partnership that family members own shares in, and the shares can be transferred between generations at lower taxation rates than would be applied to the FLP's holdings. Shares in a FLP can be gifted to family members, thus taking advantage of gift tax exemptions on an annual basis. A FLP is one of the most significant and efficient estate and gift tax planning strategies. The strategy includes freezing the value of the assets owned by a family and transferring the assets at a reduced value and minimizing the taxable portion of the estate or trust in which the assets are placed.

Unless "capital" is a material income producing factor, a family member cannot give an interest in his/her business as a gift to another family member (e.g. mother to daughter) in order to avoid taxes, unless the person receiving the gift participates in performing services for the business, i.e. has actual control over his/her interest. Capital is not a material income producing factor if substantially all partnership income is derived from personal services, such as a law firm or an accounting firm.

Partnership Organizational and Start-Up Costs

A partnership normally incurs both organizational expenses and start-up costs necessary to get it up and running. Organizational expenses are usually formation costs such as legal fees to set-up the partnership agreement and, if necessary, to register with the state. Then after formation, the partnership will usually incur start-up costs before beginning active trade or business, such as marketing costs, costs to train employees, etc. A partnership is permitted to deduct up to $5,000 of organizational costs and up to $5,000 of start-up costs in the year the partnership begins business. However, the allowable deductions are reduced for every dollar the total organizational costs exceed $50,000, and the total start-up costs exceed $50,000. Any costs that aren't immediately deductible are required to be amortized over 15 years. These rules also apply to corporations, including S- corporations. **(See Chapter 14, "Start-Up and Organizational Costs")**

Under final IRS regulations issued in 2014, the balance of any unamortized organizational and start-up costs remaining after a technical termination of a partnership may not be deducted on the original partnership's final tax return. Instead, the new partnership must continue to amortize the costs over the remaining useful life. The final regulations are applicable to any technical partnership terminations that occur after December 9, 2013. **(See Below, "Technical Partnership Terminations")**

- **Example** – Partnership XYZ has an unamortized balance of organizational and start-up costs of $9,000 when it undergoes a technical termination. The costs have been amortized for five of their original 15-year life. Under the final regulations, Partnership XYZ may not deduct the $9,000 of unamortized organizational and start-up costs even though the partnership has terminated under Section 708. Instead, XYZ is treated as having transferred the unamortized balance of $9,000 to the new partnership resulting from the technical termination, and the $9,000 of unamortized organizational and start-up costs must be amortized over the remaining 10 years of their original 15-year life.

Treating Partners as Employees

Employees of a partnership who have received an equity interest in the partnership should be treated as partners and not employees of the partnership. Court case rulings have mostly held that a partner may not be both a partner and an employee of the same partnership. Even a very small partnership interest can cause the employee to be treated as a partner, not an employee, for federal tax purposes, while the partnership often mistakenly continues to treat the partner as an employee. This mistake can have many tax consequences, not the least of which is the mistaken tax treatment of the partner's income as wages reported on Form W-2 subject to payroll tax, FUTA, and income tax withholding, instead of self-employment income subject to self-employment tax, which is not subject to withholding. Also, employees can exclude certain employer-paid benefits from income, but partners may not exclude those benefits – health insurance and fringe benefits paid on behalf of a partner are generally not excluded from the partner's income. And if a partnership decides to treat certain partners as employees for payroll tax purposes, there is a risk that not all of the partner's allocable share of partnership income will be reported on Form W-2, because the partnership tax return may not be completed until after Form W-2s must be filed with the IRS, and the partnership may not have final numbers to use when it prepares the Form W-2. **(See Chapter 2, "Payroll Tax (FICA)"); (See Chapter 4, "Wages and Salaries"); (See Chapter 17, "Self-Employment Tax")**

Taxpayers who are partners in a partnership can somewhat work their way around the prohibition of a partner being treated as an employee by choosing to have an S-corporation hold their interest in a partnership as a means to reduce overall self-employment taxes. Despite the similarities in the tax treatment of S-corporations and partnerships, there are some big differences. If a partner sets up an S- corporation to receive his or her partnership distributions, the S-corporation can pay the partner a reasonable salary that is reported on Form W-2, and then the partner does not have to pay self-employment tax on the remainder of his partnership distributions. Under current law, as long as an S-corporation pays its shareholder(s) reasonable compensation, any S-corporation earnings flowing to the shareholder(s) above and beyond a reasonable compensation are not subject to self- employment tax. **(See Chapter 19, "S-Corporation Status" & "Compensation of S-Corporation Shareholders/Employees")**

Partner's Capital Account and Ownership Percentage

A partner's interest in a partnership is a "capital asset" that must have a "tax basis" so that the amount of any gain or loss realized upon sale, liquidation, or other disposition of a partner's interest can be determined. The tax basis or simply "basis" of a partner's interest in a partnership is determined separately from the partner's capital account and ownership percentage. The ownership percentages of the partners should remain the same after the partnership is formed, unless there are additional contributions of assets made by the partners that change their ownership percentages. The ownership percentages of the partners may not necessarily be the same as their capital accounts, although the ownership percentages should normally be determined by the amount of the partners' capital accounts. The capital accounts and ownership percentages of the partners should be based on the amount of cash and the fair market value (FMV) of property contributed by the partners to the partnership.

After a partner's initial capital account is determined, his or her balance in the capital account is adjusted upward or downward annually to reflect annual profits and distributions to the partners, etc. However, the only way a partner's percentage of ownership in a partnership should normally change is due to additional contributions of cash or property by the partners to the partnership after the partnership is formed. Profits and losses and distributions of those profits and losses and other expenses each year from the partnership to the partners should not change the value of the partners' capital accounts, because the distributions are based on the partners' ownership percentages when the distributions are made to the partners.

- **Example** – Two persons agree to start a 50-50% partnership, and one person contributes $10,000 cash to the partnership, and the other person contributes property worth (FMV) $10,000, but with an adjusted basis of $6,000. Therefore, the 1st partner has a $10,000 capital account and a $10,000 basis in the partnership, but the 2nd partner has a $10,000 capital account and $6,000 basis in the partnership. They each own 50% of the partnership, based on the amount of their capital accounts.

- **Example** – Assume the same facts as above, but during the next year the 1st partner contributes an additional $5,000 in cash to the partnership, and the 2nd partner contributes additional property worth (FMV) $15,000, but with an adjusted basis of $10,000. This increases the total capital account of the partnership from $20,000 to $40,000 ($20,000 + $5,000 additional cash + $15,000 FMV of additional property). Therefore, the 1st partner's ownership in the partnership will change to 37.5% ($10,000 + $5,000 = $15,000/$40,000 = 37.5%), and the 2nd partner's ownership in the partnership will change to 62.5% ($25,000/$40,000 = 62.5%). The 1st partner has a $15,000 basis, which is equal to the $15,000 cash contributed to the partnership, and the 2nd partner has a $16,000 basis, which is equal to the adjusted basis of the properties contributed to the partnership.

Partner and Partnership's Basis

The basis of the partnership is equal to the total bases of the partners and imposes tax accordingly. A partner has a basis in the partnership and the partnership has a basis in the partner's property. A partner's basis in the partnership is equal to the amount of money (cash) contributed, the adjusted basis of property contributed, and the amount of debt assumed by the partner (see below). A partner's basis in the partnership is referred to as the "outside basis" and the partnership's basis, which is a culmination of the partners' bases, is referred to as the "inside basis." When a partnership is started, the partners' collective outside bases are equal to the partnership's inside basis. The partners' bases and the partnership basis are usually the same.

The "basis" of a partner's interest in a partnership is used to determine any gain or loss upon the sale, disposition, or liquidation of the partner's interest in the partnership. A partner's basis in a partnership is increased by: (1) additional contributions; (2) distributive share of partnership income based on ownership percentage; and (3) increase in share of partnership liabilities (debts). A partner's basis in a partnership is decreased by: (1) distributive share of partnership losses based on ownership percentage; (2) share of expenditures not deductible in computing partnership income; (3) share of Section 179 expenses (even if the partner can't deduct the entire amount on his or her individual tax return); (4) liabilities (debts) assumed by the partnership; (5) decrease in share of partnership liabilities; and (6) distributions to the partner based on ownership percentage.

- **Example** – Two persons start a 50-50% partnership. Partner A contributes property worth (FMV) $25,000, with an adjusted basis of $5,000. Partner B contributes property worth (FMV) $25,000, with an adjusted basis of $10,000. Partner's A's basis in the partnership is $5,000 and Partner B's basis in the partnership is $10,000. At this point the total inside basis in the partnership's assets is $15,000, which matches the partners' aggregate outside bases. The annual profit of the partnership is $5,000 and the distribution of the profits to the partners from the partnership is $5,000 – $2,500 to each partner, so the capital account and outside basis of Partner A will remain at $25,000 and $5,000 respectively at the end of the year, and the capital account and outside basis of Partner B will remain at $25,000 and $10,000 respectively at the end of the year. The partnership's capital account and inside basis will remain at $50,000 and $15,000 respectively at the end of the year. The ownership percentages remain the same at 50% for each partner.

Contribution of Assets by Partners to a Partnership

Contributions of assets by partners to a partnership are not taxable (including additional contributions after a partnership is formed). When a partner contributes property to a partnership, no gain or loss is recognized by the partner for tax purposes.

- **Example** – Two persons agree to start a 50-50% partnership, and one person contributes $10,000 cash to the partnership, and the other person contributes property worth (FMV) $10,000, but with an adjusted basis of $6,000. In this scenario, the 1st partner has a $10,000 capital account and a $10,000 basis in the partnership, but the 2nd partner has a $10,000 capital account and $6,000 basis in the partnership. They each own 50% of the partnership, even though one partner has a $10,000 basis and the other partner has a $6,000 basis in the partnership. The partnership's capital account is $20,000 ($10,000 cash contributed by the 1st partner + $10,000 FMV of property contributed by the 2nd partner). The 1st partner's outside basis is $10,000 (cash contributed), and the 2nd partner's outside basis in $6,000 (adjusted basis of property contributed). The partnership's inside basis is $16,000, which matches the cumulative outside bases of the partners.

- **Example** – Betty and John form a 50%/50% partnership with capital accounts of $10,000 each. Betty has an outside basis of $10,000 and John has an outside basis of $6,000. During the next year, Betty contributes additional cash of $50,000 to the partnership, and John contributes additional cash of $30,000 to the partnership. Therefore, their capital accounts and ownership percentages will change to $60,000 (60% ownership percentage) for Betty ($10,000 + $50,000 = $60,000), and to $40,000 (40% ownership percentage) for John ($10,000 + $30,000 = $40,000). Their outside bases, due to the additional contributions by the partners, will increase to $60,000 for Betty ($10,000 + $50,000) and to $36,000 for John ($6,000 +$30,000). If the partnership makes a profit of $20,000 for the year, the profit is distributed 60% to Betty ($12,000) and 40% to John ($8,000). Their capital accounts and bases will remain the same. Their ownership percentages will be 60% for Betty and 40% for John at the end of the year.

An exception to the general rule that contributions to a partnership are not taxable is when the contributions are to an "investment company." An investment company is generally defined as a partnership in which more than 80% of its assets are readily marketable stocks or securities which are held for investment.

- **Example** – Bill forms a company that goes public, in which he holds $2 million in company stock, with a tax basis of $0. Bill then contributes the stock to a pool operated by an investment bank in exchange for a 5% interest. The pool's assets are primarily composed of publicly traded shares in the DJIA and commercial paper. If the pool qualifies as an investment company, Bill must recognize a $2 million taxable gain.

Partner's Assumption of Debt

Partnership liabilities are classified as either: (1) nonrecourse liabilities or debts, which are debts that no partner bears the economic risk of loss, such as a mortgage or loan secured by real property and held by a financial institution; and (2) recourse liabilities or debts, which are debts and obligations for which a partner bears the economic risk of loss. Typically, liabilities are allocated to the partners in the same proportion as their ownership percentages, except for recourse debt, which is allocated based on whoever bears the risk of economic loss. "Bifurcated liabilities" are liabilities that have both recourse and nonrecourse components, i.e. a partnership borrows $500 to acquire an asset; a partner guarantees $200 of the loan. To the extent of the guarantee, the loan is considered a recourse liability, but the rest of the loan is considered a nonrecourse liability.

- **Example** – Betty and John start a 50-50% partnership. Betty contributes $10,000 cash to the partnership, and John contributes property worth $10,000, but the property has an adjusted basis of $6,000. Betty has a $10,000 capital account and a $10,000 basis. John has a $10,000 capital account and a $6,000 basis. After the partnership is started, John loans $6,000 to the partnership which is recourse debt because he bears the economic risk of loss. Thus, John has an adjusted basis in the partnership of $12,000 ($6,000 basis of property contributed + $6,000 recourse debt), and Betty still has a $10,000 basis in the partnership. Their capital accounts stay the same at $10,000 each, and their ownership percentages remain 50-50%. The inside basis of the partnership is $22,000 which matches the cumulative bases of the two partners.

If the property contributed by a partner to the partnership is subject to a loan or mortgage (nonrecourse debt), the partner's capital account and ownership percentage is reduced by the amount of the mortgage or loan. However, the amount of debt assumed by the partners increases their basis in the partnership, and the deemed cash distribution by the contributing partner as a result of the debt assumed by the other partners can result in a capital gain to the contributing partner if it is more than his adjusted basis in the partnership.

- **Example** – Betty and John form a partnership. Betty contributes $300,000 in cash and John contributes land with an adjusted basis of $400,000, but which is worth (FMV) $1.1 million. The land is subject to a mortgage (nonrecourse loan) of $1 million. So, Betty has a 75% ownership percentage in the partnership, and John has a 25% ownership percentage in the partnership – Betty's capital account is $300,000 (cash contribution), and John's capital account is $100,000 ($1.1 million land value less $1 million loan). The $1 million nonrecourse debt is allocated between the two partners based on the ownership percentages – 75% (Betty) - 25% (John). So, John's share of the partnership liability is $250,000 and Betty's share is $750,000 – John is treated as receiving a deemed cash distribution of $750,000. John's basis in the land contributed to the partnership is $400,000, plus his $250,000 share of the partnership debt = $650,000 basis, but the deemed cash distribution to him of $750,000 reduces his basis to $0 and triggers a $100,000 capital gain taxable to John. Betty's basis in the partnership is $1,050,000 ($300,000 + $750,000). In summary, ownership percentages in the partnership are: Betty – 75%; John – 25%. Capital account balances are: Betty - $300,000; John $100,000. Basis in the partnership: Betty – $1,050,000; John – $0, and John has to pay capital gain tax on $100,000. The inside basis of the partnership is $1,050,000, which matches the cumulative outside bases of the partners.

The partnership balance sheet looks like this:

Assets:		Liabilities:
$	300,000 Cash	$1,000,000 Loan
	1,100,000 Land	Equity:
$	1,400,000	$ 300,000 Betty (Capital Account)
		100,000 John (Capital Account)
		$1,400,000

- **Example** – Assume the same facts as in the above example, except Betty contributes only $100,000 in cash, so both partners have a 50% ownership percentage in the partnership. The $1 million nonrecourse debt is allocated $500,000 to Betty and $500,000 to John (50%/50% capital accounts). John is treated as receiving a deemed cash distribution of $500,000 equal to the reduced amount of the liability on the land he contributed ($1 million less $500,000). John's basis in the partnership is $400,000 ($400,000 adjusted basis of land + $500,000 share of partnership liability = $900,000 less the deemed cash distribution of $500,000). Betty's basis in the partnership is $600,000 ($100,000 cash contributed + $500,000 share of the partnership liability). John's capital account is $100,000 (50% ownership interest) – $1.1 million less $1 million, and Betty's capital account in also $100,000 (50% ownership interest) – $100,000 cash contributed. The partnership's liability account is $1 million. The inside basis of the partnership is $1,000,000, which matches the cumulative bases of the partners.

The partnership balance sheet looks like this:

Assets:		Liabilities:
$	100,000 Cash	$1,000,000 Loan
	1,100,000 Land	Equity:
$	1,200,000	100,000 Betty (Capital Account)
		100,000 John (Capital Account)
		$1,200,000

At-Risk Rules – Adequate basis is only one sieve through which a pass-through loss must flow before determining its deductibility. Subsequent to passing the basis test, the next test to be applied is the "at-risk" test. The at-risk rules are applicable at the partner level, rather than the partnership level, and are designed to ensure that a taxpayer deducts losses only to the extent he or she is economically or actually at risk for the investment. A partner may have sufficient basis for taking a loss, but not have a sufficient amount of risk for the loss to be deductible. A partner is considered at risk with respect to an activity for: (1) the amount of money and the adjusted basis of other property contributed to the activity; and (2) amounts borrowed for use in the activity if the partner is personally liable for repayment of the borrowed amount or has pledged property, other than property that is used in the activity as security for the borrowed amount. If property is pledged as security for a borrowed amount, the partner's at-risk amount is limited to the net FMV of the partner's interest in the pledged property. **(See Chapter 14, "At-Risk Rules")**

Nonrecourse debts are relevant for partnership tax purposes, but do not add to partners' "at-risk" amounts, while recourse liabilities or debts add to a partners' at-risk amounts. A partner's share of the nonrecourse liabilities can increase their basis, but not the at-risk limitation. In order to be able to deduct some losses, partners may be tempted to guarantee partnership debt. Depending on the type of partnership, limited liability partnership (LLP) or limited liability company (LLC), the impact on the at-risk limitation can be different than the desired result. The IRS distinguishes a LLC guarantee from a debt guarantee in a limited partnership. Generally, a limited partner in a LLP who guarantees partnership debt is not at risk with respect to the guaranteed debt, because the limited partner has a right to seek reimbursement from the partnership and the general partner for any amounts that the limited partner is called upon to pay under the guarantee. However, in the case of an LLC, all members have unlimited liability with respect to LLC debt. In the absence of any co-guarantors or another similar arrangement, a LLC member who guarantees LLC debt becomes personally liable for the guaranteed debt and is, therefore, at risk in relation to the debt. This is a very complex area, and navigating the rules should be done in coordination with consultations between the taxpayer's attorney and tax advisor. For example, the at-risk rules include an exception for "qualified nonrecourse financing" which can be added to the at-risk amounts.

Distribution of Profits and Losses to Partners

Partnership profits and losses and distributions of such profits and losses to the partners will change the balances in the partners' capital accounts, but not their ownership percentages. Distributions that exceed a partner's adjusted basis are taxed as capital gains, because a partner's basis cannot be reduced below zero. Partnership losses allocated to each partner on Schedule K-1 can be deducted on each partner's individual tax return only to the extent of their basis, but excess losses can be carried forward.

- **Example** – Betty and John are 60%/40% partners. Betty has a capital account with a balance of $90,000 and basis in the partnership of $40,000, and John has a capital account with a balance of $60,000 and a basis of $36,000. The partnership suffers a loss of $80,000 for the year. The loss reduces Betty's capital account to $42,000 ($90,000 – [60% X $80,000 = $48,000]) and John's capital account is reduced to $28,000 ($60,000 – [40% X $80,000 = $32,000]). Betty's basis in the partnership is reduced to $0 and the excess $8,000 loss ($48,000 loss - $40,000 basis) is carried forward (not deductible in the current year). John's basis in the partnership is reduced to $4,000 ($36,000 - $32,000). Their ownership percentages remain the same – 60% Betty and 40% John.

The IRS issued final regulations in 2015 that address how to distribute partnership profits and items among partners whose capital accounts in the partnership change during the tax year. The final regulations set forth an expanded scope which requires that the partners' distributive shares for a tax year must take into account the varying ownership percentages of the partners during the tax year. This adds a certain degree of flexibility in determining a partner's distributive share when ownership percentages change during the year or otherwise.

Sale of Property Contributed by a Partner and Distribution of Property to Partner

A partner who contributes property to a partnership in exchange for a partnership interest does not recognize gain or loss. However, if the partnership subsequently sells the property in a taxable transaction, the gain or loss must be "specially allocated to the original contributing partner." Also, if a partner contributes property to a partnership, and the property is distributed to another partner within 7 years of the contribution, gain or loss must be specially allocated to the original contributing partner. Also, if a partner contributes property to a partnership, and within 7 years receives a distribution of different property, he or she must recognize specially allocated gain or loss. A partner who does not contribute any property to a partnership and who receives a distribution of property from the partnership does not recognize any gain, but instead assumes the carryover inside basis of the distributed property.

- **Example** – Partner B contributed land with a basis of $32,000 and a FMV of $50,000 in exchange for a 50% interest in ABC partnership. If the partnership sells the land three years later for $60,000, the first $18,000 of the gain ($50,000 - $32,000) must be specially allocated to Partner B (contributing partner) as taxable capital gain. The remaining $10,000 gain is distributed equally to the partners (including Partner B) and their bases in the partnership are increased in accordance with their ownership percentages.

- **Example** – Refer to the facts above. Assume the land contributed by Partner B is still owned by the partnership. Partner B receives a distribution of equipment owned by the partnership with a $40,000 FMV and a basis to the partnership of $25,000. B's basis in the partnership is $13,000. Because the distribution of the equipment occurred within 7 years of B's contribution of the land, B must recognize an $18,000 capital gain (the lesser of the $27,000 excess of the FMV of the equipment over B's basis or his $18,000 gain on the land). The partnership increases its $32,000 inside basis in the land by $18,000 to $50,000. B increases his basis in the partnership by $18,000 and decreases it by his $25,000 carryover basis in the equipment, so his new basis will be $6,000.

Disguised Sale Rule – A distribution that occurs within two years of property contribution to a partnership is deemed to result in a disguised sale.

- **Example** – A and B form a partnership by contributing a variety of assets to the partnership. Six months later when the partnership is worth $2 million, C contributes $1 million to the partnership in exchange for a one-third interest in the partnership. However, within a month, the partnership distributes assets to C worth $500,000. This may be treated as a disguised sale, and the partnership is required to recognize capital gain, if any, on the transfer of the assets to C, which would be allocated as capital gain to A and B under the 704(c) rules, because it would be attributable to appreciation prior to the time of C's entry into the partnership.

Substituted Basis Transaction – A partner receives a distribution of property from the partnership and the partner's basis in the partnership is less than the inside basis of the distributed property.

- **Example** – Partner B receives a current distribution of property from ABC partnership. At the date of distribution, the property has a FMV of $15,000 and an inside basis in the partnership of $10,000. Immediately prior to the distribution, Partner B's basis is the partnership is $6,000. After receiving the distribution, Partner B's basis in the partnership would be $0 ($6,000- $6,000) and his basis in the distributed property would be $6,000. This is a tax-fee distribution, but Partner B's basis in the distributed property is $6,000 – this is referred to as a "substituted basis transaction" (the partner's basis in the partnership is less than the inside basis of the distributed property).

Sale of a Partnership Interest

Sale of a partnership interest by a partner is similar to the sale of stock in a corporation (sale of a capital asset). Gain or loss on the sale is capital gain or loss subject to long or short-term capital gain treatment, depending on how long the partner owned the interest in the partnership. A partner recognizes capital gain or loss based on the amount received against his/her outside basis. The amount received in the sale of a partnership interest includes: cash received; FMV of property received; and liabilities of the seller that are assumed or relieved – both formal liabilities and deemed liabilities for tax purposes (i.e. partner's share of all partnership liabilities). A partner's adjusted basis includes: the seller's share of partnership liabilities; and income/loss through the date of sale (as allocated). The holding period requirements for long/short term capital gain or loss are measured by the seller's ownership period of the partnership interest. **(See Chapter 6, "Reporting Capital Gains and Losses" & "Form 1099-B: Proceeds from Broker and Barter Exchange Transactions"); (See Chapter 14, "Sale of Business Property")**

Sale of a Partnership Interest Under the Tax Cuts and Jobs Act (TCJA) – Gain or loss from the sale or exchange of a partnership interest generally is treated as gain or loss from the sale or exchange of a capital asset. However, the amount of money and the fair market value of property received in the exchange that represents the partner's share of certain ordinary income-producing assets of the partnership gives rise to ordinary income rather than capital gain. The Tax Cuts and Jobs Act (TCJA) contains a provision that is important to any person buying or selling an interest in a partnership. The provision makes clear that if a foreign person sells an interest in any U.S. or non-U.S. partnership on or after November 27, 2017, that is engaged in a U.S. trade or business, then any gain that is attributable to the partnership's U.S. trade or business is treated as effectively connected to a U.S. trade or business and subject to U.S. federal income tax. All partners in a partnership are treated as engaged in the conduct of a trade or business within the U.S. if the partnership is so engaged.

As of January 1, 2018, a purchaser (transferee) of a partnership interest is required to withhold 10% of the amount realized on the sale or exchange of a partnership interest, which is usually the purchase price of the interest, and remit the amount to the IRS. This rule applies to sales of both U.S. and non-U.S. partnerships that are engaged in a U.S. trade or business. The withholding is required unless: (1) the purchaser receives an affidavit from the seller to the effect that the seller is a U.S. person and contains the taxpayer identification number of the seller; (2) it is determined that no portion of the gain recognized is attributable to a U.S. trade or business; (3) the IRS agrees to a lower withholding amount (a process which could take months), or (4) pursuant to Notice 2018-08, released on December 29, 2017, interests in the relevant partnership are publicly traded. If the purchaser does not withhold the 10% when required, the partnership is required to withhold from distributions to the purchaser an amount equal to the under-withholding plus interest. Presumably, the partnership will be liable for such amounts if the transferee fails to withhold.

This requirement applies apparently even if only a very small amount of the partnership income is effectively connected with a U.S. trade or business. Thus, a partnership interest that would generate $15 of effectively connected income for a partner and sold for $100,000 could be subject to a 10% withholding tax ($10,000) on sale. Although not expressly stated in the new provision, it appears that the transferor could seek a refund to the extent any withholding exceeds the transferor's U.S. federal income tax liability.

Since it is sometimes difficult to determine whether a partnership is engaged in a U.S. trade or business: (1) a purchaser of U.S. or foreign partnership interests should obtain a U.S. Affidavit from a seller or obtain appropriate assurances from the seller that the partnership is not engaged in a U.S. trade or business. In cases where the risk is large, purchasers should consider a guarantee of any resulting liability; (2) Partnerships should ensure that they are (i) aware of all transfers of their partnership interests and (ii) able to determine whether any transfers that do occur comply with these new rules; and (3) General partners and managers should be especially careful regarding any consent to transfer that they provide to their investors given this new provision. www.irs.gov/pub/irs-drop/n-18-08.pdf

Split Holding Period in a Partnership – If the seller of a partnership interest acquired his/her total partnership interest at different times, split holding periods may come into play. The holding period of a partnership interest is determined by reference to the holder, not the holding period of the underlying partnership assets.

- **Example** – On 1/1/2013, Bill contributed cash and real property to acquire an interest in a partnership. He contributed $1,000 in cash, and real property worth $2,000, but with a basis of $100, that was acquired by Bill on 6/30/2009. On 8/30/2013, Bill sells his entire interest in the partnership for $2,000, resulting in a gain of $900 ($2,000, minus $1,000 basis for the cash, and $100 basis for the real property). However, since Bill has a split holding period, 33% of the gain ($300) is treated as a short-term capital gain because the holding period for the cash contributed began on 1/1/2013, and 67% of the gain ($600) is treated as a long-term capital gain because the holding period for the real property began on 6/30/2009. Bill's capital account was equal to $3,000 ($1,000 cash, or 33%, and $2,000 real property, or 67%).

Hot Asset Rule – Under the "general rule," a sale of a partnership interest gives rise to capital gain or loss. However, there is a significant exception to the general rule, known as the "hot asset rule." This exception can dwarf the general rule depending on the business of the partnership. The hot asset rule applies if a partnership has Section 751 assets ("unrealized receivables" and inventory). If the hot asset rule applies, any sale of a partnership interest that results in a gain/loss attributable to hot assets is re-characterized as ordinary income. Generally, unrealized receivables are for goods delivered (or to be delivered) or for services rendered (or to be rendered). Inventory is: property held for sale to customers in the ordinary course of business (including real estate held by a dealer whether or not included in inventory); and any other property that, upon sale or exchange by the partnership, would be considered property other than a capital asset or Sec. 1231 property. Unrealized receivables are generally valued at present value of net cash expected, reduced by estimated cost of delivery or performance – not face value. Inventory items are valued at market

- **Example** – Dave sells his 25% partnership interest for $1,000; his adjusted basis is $750. Two assets are included in the sale: (1) real estate held for investment (a capital asset, not a Sec. 751 asset) with a tax basis of $750, and a FMV of $500; and (2) inventory items (a Sec. 751 asset) with a $0 tax basis and a FMV of $500. The hot asset rule applies because the partnership has Sec. 751 assets. The total gain on the sale is $250 ($1,000, minus $750 basis), which is re-characterized as follows:

    Total gain/loss = $250
    751 gain/loss = $500 ($500 less $0) ordinary income
    Capital loss   = ($250)

In this case the inherent loss in the capital asset and the large gain in the hot assets are preserved under Sec. 751.

Sale of a Partial Interest in a Partnership – The "ratable allocation approach" should be used in the sale of a partial interest in a partnership. The ratable allocation approach is supported by the regulations and the IRS. The tax regulations require that the tax basis must be "equitably apportioned" between what is sold and what is retained. Also, the IRS's position is that a taxpayer has a single basis, even if he or she owns different types of interests (i.e., owns a limited and general partnership interest or owns Class A and Class B units in a LLC).

- **Example** – In 2010, Bill buys 20 units of a LLC/partnership for $400. In 2011, he buys another 20 units for $2,000. Therefore, Bill has an overall tax basis of $2,400. Bill sells 20 units (retaining the other 20 units) for $4,000. Bill allocates his basis ratably among the units, so the 20 units sold has a tax basis of $1,200 (50% X $2,400). Therefore, Bill's capital gain is $2,800 ($4,000 - $1,200).

Mismatch of Outside Basis and Inside Basis and the Section 754 Election – As a general rule, a current distribution of partnership property to a partner does not cause gain or loss recognition by either the partnership or the partner that receives the property distribution (See " Sale of Property Contributed By a Partner" above). Recipient partners simply assume the carryover basis of the property distributed to them, and in turn reduce their basis in the partnership by the corresponding amount. However, a sale of a partner's interest in a partnership to someone else can create a mismatch between the new partner's outside basis and the partnership's inside basis. This also applies to the transfer of a partnership interest upon the death of a partner. A difference between the outside and inside basis can create tax problems. **(See Above, "Sale of Property Contributed by a Partner and Distribution of Property to Partner")**

If there is a mismatch between the outside and inside basis, a Section 754 election allows partnerships to "step-up" or "step-down" their outside basis of assets in the partnership to the inside basis for tax purposes. Utilizing this election can accelerate deductions into earlier years, which may be beneficial for owners of partnerships and LLCs. This equalization of basis can be beneficial to a partner when the "step-up" is deemed to be related to depreciable or amortizable property. It will allow for depreciation and amortization deductions, starting in the year the election is made, rather than recouping basis when the interest or property is transferred. The Section 754 election is made by filing a written statement with the partnership tax return, which will be in effect for the year filed and all years thereafter. The election must be filed no later than the legal due date of the tax return (including extensions). The election applies to all transactions occurring in the period covered by the tax return. After a 754 election is made, it is binding for all subsequent periods. The election can only be revoked with IRS consent.

- **Example** – If a successful partnership with 2 partners is worth $3,000,000, and Partner A has an outside basis of $500,000 and Partner B has an outside basis of $600,000, there is untaxed appreciation in the business of $1,900,000. If the partnership were to sell all of its assets for $3,000,000, Partner A and Partner B would share the gain based on their ownership percentages which in this example are 50/50%, and accordingly would be taxed on each partner's historic basis. Partner A would have a capital gain of $1,000,000, and Partner B would have a capital gain of $900,000. So, there would be no tax problem.

- **Example** – Referring to the above example, suppose the partners did not sale all of the assets in the partnership, but instead Partner A sells his partnership interest to a third party (Partner C). In this case, Partner A would be taxed accordingly, but Partner C's purchase of A's interest in the partnership could create a problem. If Partner C paid $1,250,000 for the interest acquired from Partner A, Partner C would have an outside basis of $1,250,000, and Partner A would have a capital gain of $750,000. However, the inside basis in the partnership would remain $1,100,000 ($500,000 + $600,000), and the partners' aggregate outside basis would then be $1,850,000 ($600,000 + $1,250,000). If you assume that the entire inside basis of $1,100,000 is concentrated in one asset that is depreciated using the straight-line method, with 5 years remaining, then total depreciation in the year following Partner C's entrance into the partnership would be $220,000. This depreciation expense would be allocated equally to the 2 partners (Partner B and Partner C) – $110,000 each. The results to Partner B would properly reflect the historic basis and adjustments, but the results to Partner C would not reflect C's full purchase price for C's share of the depreciable asset. Therefore, Partner C would not receive the correct proportional share of the tax benefit.

To correct this potential result, Partner C may negotiate into his acquisition agreement a requirement that the partnership make a Section 754 election. A Section 754 election will permit the partnership to adjust the inside basis of its only asset solely with respect to the transferee partner, Partner C. Partner C's share of the basis will be increased to reflect the acquisition price for his interest and will generally operate to put partner C on equal footing with Partner B with respect to basis. With sufficient information, Partner C will be able to quantify the benefit of the election and in the event the other partner refuses to let the partnership make the election, Partner C may be able to negotiate a different purchase price so that the economic results correlate with the tax results. All things being equal, Partner C would not proceed without either the election or an adjustment to the purchase price. If a Section 754 election is made, the inside basis on the partnership's only asset would potentially increase from $1,100,000 to $1,850,000 and the depreciation will increase from $220,000 to $370,000 for the year, and will put the two partners B and C on equal footing by allocating $110,000 of the depreciation to Partner B and $260,000 of the depreciation to partner C.

Substantial Basis Reduction in a Partnership

A partnership generally does not adjust the basis of partnership property following the transfer of a partnership interest unless either the partnership has made a one-time election under Section 754 to make basis adjustments, or the partnership has a substantial built-in loss immediately after the transfer. If an election is in effect, or if the partnership has a substantial built-in loss immediately after the transfer, adjustments are made with respect to the transferee partner. These adjustments are to account for the difference between the transferee partner's proportionate share of the adjusted basis of the partnership property and the transferee's basis in his or her partnership interest.

If a partnership has declined in value so that the outside basis (basis in the partnership) exceeds the partnership's value (capital account), the adjustments permitted when a partnership files a Section 754 election is "required" on the transfer of a partnership interest if there is a "substantial built-in loss" at the time of the transfer, regardless of whether or not the partnership has a Section 754 election in place. A Section 754 election allows a partnership to step-up or step-down the outside basis (basis in the partnership) to the inside basis (capital account) for tax purposes. A substantial basis reduction to partnership property occurs if the basis (outside basis) is $250,000 more than the partnership's value (inside basis or capital account). Therefore, a person that purchases such an interest in a partnership (transferee) will not be able to benefit from a loss that the selling partner (transferor) has already taken into account. This rule also applies when there is a transfer of interest upon the death of a partner. Before these mandatory adjustment provisions were enacted, partnerships were potentially created and used to aid tax-shelter transactions. **(See Above, "Mismatch of Outside Basis and Inside Basis and the Section 754 Election")**

www.irs.gov/pub/irs-wd/201510024.pdf

The TCJA modifies the definition of a "substantial built-in loss" affecting transfers of partnership interests beginning with the 2018 tax year. The substantial built-in loss rule was already in effect for partnership interests prior to 2018. But under the TCJA, the "substantial built-in loss" rule is expanded to apply not only to the partnership but also to the purchaser (transferee) of a partnership interest. Therefore, the Section 754 election is also required when immediately after the transfer of an interest, a recipient of the transferred interest (transferee) would be allocated a net loss in excess of $250,000 upon a hypothetical taxable sale of all of the entity's assets for proceeds equal to the fair market value (outside basis or basis in the partnership), i.e. the 754 election is required when there is a substantial built-in loss in excess of $250,000 for either the partnership as a whole, or for the purchaser (transferee) of a partnership interest.

In July, 2017, the U.S. Tax Court rejected a long-standing Internal Revenue Service ruling and held that when a non-U.S. person sells an interest in a partnership or is completely redeemed from a partnership that is engaged in a trade or business in the United States, the non-U.S. seller is, in general, not subject to U.S. federal income taxes on the gain from the sale (Grecian Magnesite Mining, Industrial and Shipping Co., SA v. Commissioner, 149 T.C. No. 3).

www.ustaxcourt.gov/UstcInOp/OpinionViewer.aspx?ID=11322

Liquidating Distributions to Partners

A liquidating distribution is, generally, the same as a stock redemption. The partner receives a distribution from the partnership in exchange for or liquidation of his or her interest in the partnership. The tax treatment of a liquidating distribution varies depending on what type of property is distributed: cash – gain/loss is recognized; marketable securities – treated the same as cash; all other property – generally no gain/loss recognized – instead partner takes the property with a carryover basis. Cash includes "deemed" cash distributions from relief of liabilities. Marketable securities are "financial instruments" and foreign currencies that are actively traded, which are treated as cash substitutes and with the same tax treatment as cash. Financial instruments are stocks and other equity interests, debt, options, and derivatives. If cash or marketable securities are received, and the total exceeds the partner's adjusted basis, then the difference is recognized as gain. Loss can be recognized, but only if the distribution consists solely of cash or Sec. 751 assets (hot assets). Receipt of other property generally will not result in gain or loss. Instead, the partner's adjusted tax basis will be spread over the received property. **(See Above, "Hot Asset Rule")**

- **Example** – Bill receives a liquidating distribution from the partnership in exchange for his interest in the partnership. He receives a total liquidating distribution of $1,800 in cash and cash equivalents ($1,300 in cash and $500 in marketable securities), and real estate with a FMV of $1,500 and a basis of $900. Also, he relieves $200 in partnership liabilities, so his total deemed cash distribution is $2,000 ($1,800 + $200). Bill's adjusted basis in the partnership is $700. Bill must recognize a $1,300 capital gain (the excess of his cash distribution of $2,000 less his $700 adjusted basis in the partnership). He takes the real estate distributed with a $0 carryover basis because none of the basis in his partnership interest is left over to allocate to the real estate he receives in the distribution.

- **Example** – Bill receives a liquidating distribution of $6,000 in cash and a Section 1231 asset with a FMV of $25,000 and a basis of $14,600. Bill's basis in the partnership is $40,000. In this case, Bill's basis is first reduced by the $6,000 cash distribution, and the remaining $34,000 basis is substituted as the carryover basis for the distributed asset. Neither Bill nor the partnership recognizes gain or loss from the liquidation of Bill's interest in the partnership.

- **Example** – Bill receives a liquidating distribution of $6,000 in cash and an asset with a FMV of $25,000 and a basis of $14,000. Bill's basis in the partnership is only $4,000. In this case, Bill must recognize a $2,000 capital gain (the excess of the $6,000 cash distribution over his $4,000 basis in the partnership). The distributed asset will have a $0 basis to Bill.

- **Example** – Bill receives a liquidating distribution from the partnership. He receives $2,000 in cash and inventory (a Sec. 751 asset – Hot Asset) with a market value of $500. If Bill's adjusted basis in the partnership is $2,400, he has an ordinary loss of $100 ($2,400 less $2,000 cash distribution and less $500 market value of the Sec. 751 asset).

- **Example** – Betty receives a liquidating distribution of $20,000 cash from XYZ partnership, and because she is no longer a partner, Betty is relieved of $13,000 of partnership debt. Therefore, her total cash distribution is $33,000 ($20,000 actual cash + $13,000 constructive cash in the form of debt relief). Betty's basis in the partnership before the distribution is $35,000. Betty must recognize a $2,000 capital loss ($35,000 basis less $33,000 cash distribution).

Retirement Payments to Partners

Sec. 736 governs payments to retiring partners. Payments to retiring partners are separated into two classes: payments for the partner's interest in partnership property (Sec. 736(b) payments); and all other payments (Sec. 736(a) payments). In general, Sec. 736(b) payments are taxed as distributions, therefore, the rules for liquidating distributions generally apply. Sec. 736(a) payments are treated as distributive share payments or guaranteed payments depending on whether they are a function of partnership income. Sec. 736(a) payments are effectively excluded from partnership income and taxed only to the retiring partner.

- **Example** – Dave receives a payment of $2,000 from the partnership as an inducement to retire. At the time, the FMV of his interest in the partnership is $500. Only $500 is treated as a payment for Dave's interest in the partnership, which is a Sec. 736(b) payment and is taxed as a liquidating distribution (see above) – gain is recognized to the extent the $500 exceeds his adjusted basis in the partnership. If Dave's adjusted basis in the partnership is $200, he must recognize a capital gain of $300. The balance of the payment, in the amount of $1,500, is treated as a Sec. 736(a) payment. Because it is a fixed payment, it is treated as a guaranteed payment to Dave, and is taxed to Dave as ordinary income, and the partnership may deduct it as a current expense.

- **Example** – Dave, a 25% general partner in XYZ partnership, retired during the current year. The FMV (capital account balance) of his partnership interest was $30,000 when he retired, but the other partners agreed to pay him $40,000 in cash in complete liquidation of his equity interest – the additional $10,000 payment in grateful recognition of Dave's long years of faithful service. The total liquidating payment to Dave consisted of $42,000 ($40,000 actual cash + $2,000 relief of 25% of the partnership debt). Dave's 25% interest in the value of the partnership assets was $32,000 ($30,000 capital account balance + $2,000 share of partnership debt). Therefore, only $32,000 of the liquidating payment is treated as a distribution. If Dave's adjusted basis in the partnership was $25,000, he must recognize a $7,000 capital gain equal to the excess of the cash distribution over his adjusted basis. The $10,000 payment to Dave was determined without regard to partnership income and is, therefore, classified as a guaranteed payment to Dave that is taxed to Dave as ordinary income, and the partnership may deduct it as a current expense.

Special Rule Applied to Payment By a Service Partnership To a Retiring Partner – A service partnership is one in which capital is not a material income producing factor. Sec. 736(a) payments include payments for a partner's share of unrealized receivables, and a partner's share of unstated goodwill. Also, Sec. 736(a) treatment is expanded to include some payments that are for the partner's interest in certain types of partnership property. Effectively, a partnership can convert part of a liquidating distribution into an income exclusion that is taxed only to the retiring partner.

- **Example** – Bill, a 25% general partner in a law firm (service partnership), retired during the current year. The FMV (capital account balance) of his partnership interest was $10,000 when he retired, but the other partners paid him $20,000 in complete liquidation of his interest in the partnership, which included payment for Bill's share of unrealized receivables, goodwill, and for certain partnership property. The $10,000 difference between the $20,000 payment and the FMV of Bill's partnership interest is treated as a Sec. 736(a) payment classified as a guaranteed payment to Bill that is taxed to him as ordinary income, and the partnership may deduct it as a current expense.

Technical Partnership Terminations

Generally, a partnership continues indefinitely unless the partners agree upon a termination date. A partnership terminates in one of two ways, either: (1) when no part of any business of the partnership continues to be carried on by any of its partners, or (2) when there is a sale or exchange of 50% or more of the total interest in the partnership capital and profits within a 12- month period. The second of the two ways of terminating a partnership is referred to as a "technical termination." This is referred to as a technical termination because the partnership isn't actually terminated for legal purposes, but instead it ends the tax life of one partnership and immediately begins the life of a second partnership. When the new or second partnership is created, the old or terminated partnership contributes all of its assets and liabilities to the new partnership in exchange for an interest in the new partnership in a Section 721 transaction, and immediately thereafter, the terminated partnership distributes interests in the new partnership to the partners of the old partnership in a Section 731 transaction.

The Tax Cuts and Jobs Act (TCJA) repealed the technical partnership termination provision for tax years beginning after December 31, 2017. Therefore, technical terminations of partnerships can no longer happen in 2018 and subsequent years. The repeal didn't change the rule that a partnership is considered terminated if no part of any business, financial operation, or venture of the partnership continues to be carried on by any of its partners. A technical termination of a partnership had four major tax consequences in 2017 and prior years: (1) the tax attributes of the old partnership were terminated; (2) the old partnership's taxable year closed; (3) any elections previously made by the old partnership ceased to apply; and (4) depreciation recovery periods restarted for the new partnership's assets.

Implementation of the 3.8% Net Investment Income Tax

In implementation of the 3.8% net investment income (NII) tax for partnerships, net investment income (NII) includes: traditional pass-through investment income items (interest, dividends, rents, royalties, annuities – less allocable deductions) to partners (whether passive or non-passive); gains or losses allocable to partners from dispositions of marketable securities held in partnerships (whether passive or non-passive); all business income or losses related to limited partners in partnership activities (passive activities); gains or losses from the disposition of property (equipment) held by limited partners in passive partnership activities; and gains or losses on the sale or disposition of passive interests in partnerships by limited partners. NII does not include: income or losses derived in the ordinary course of a general partnership trade or business; gains or losses from the disposition of property (equipment) held by general partners in a partnership (non-passive); and gains or losses on the sale or disposition of an interest in a partnership by a general partner (non-passive trade or business). A general (non-passive) partnership is one in which a taxpayer "materially" participates in the management and/or operation of the entity. (See Chapter 10, "3.8% Net Investment Income Tax")

- **Example** – For tax year 2014: Disposition of a partnership interest in activity X results in a $20,000 loss for limited partner A; passive activity partnership Y has a gain of $32,000 for limited partner A; non-passive activity partnership Z has a gain of $60,000 for general partner A; and the sale of marketable securities results in a gain of $8,000 for A. Limited partner/general partner A's gain applicable to the 3.8% NIIT is $20,000 ($32,000 - $20,000 = $8,000). $20,000 of A's overall gain of $80,000 in 2014 is NII.

Suspended passive losses from a former passive activity (after the activity becomes active or non- passive) are allowed in the calculation of NII, but only to the extent of the non-passive income from the former passive activity.

Deferred Partnership income from 2009 and 2010 Cancelled Debts

Some partnerships were able to defer income from cancelled or forgiven debts in 2009 and 2010 and allowed to start paying taxes on the cancelation of debt (COD) income over 5 years beginning in 2014. The deferrals helped the partnerships get through the recession because usual procedures would have forced the affected partners to report a higher on-paper income in 2009 and 2010 and then to pay taxes on that income when they didn't have the cash or assets to pay the taxes. Beginning in 2014, the taxable amounts will remain the same as they were in 2009 and 2010, and will be spread over 5 years through 2018.

Elective Large Partnerships (ELP)

A partnership chooses "electing large partnership" (ELP) status by filing Form 1065-B, "U.S. Return of Income for Electing Large Partnerships," instead of Form 1065. The election applies to the tax year for which it was made and all later tax years. This election cannot be revoked without IRS consent. To make the election, the partnership must have had 100 or more partners during the preceding tax year. Thus, a partnership cannot make the election for its first tax year of existence. Once a partnership has made the election by filing Form 1065-B, this treatment on the return will bind the partnership and all of its partners. The IRS, however, is not bound by the treatment on the return. To the extent provided in future regulations, a partnership may cease to be treated as an electing large partnership for a tax year in which the number of its partners falls below 100.

www.irs.gov/pub/irs-pdf/f1065b.pdf www.irs.gov/pub/irs-pdf/i1065b.pdf

The number of partners is determined by counting only persons directly holding partnership interests, including persons holding partnership interests through nominees. Service partners are not counted as partners for this purpose. Service partners are those partners who perform substantially all services in connection with the partnership's activities or who have performed such services in the past. This includes: individuals performing substantial services in connection with the partnership's activities; personal service corporations with the owner-employees performing the services; retired partners who had performed the services; and spouses of partners performing or who had performed the services. However, partnership interests held by children, grandchildren, and trusts for the benefit of children and grandchildren are not treated as held by service providers for purposes of the "substantially all" test. In addition, commodity partnerships are not eligible to make the election. Commodity partnerships have as their principal activity the buying and selling of commodities (other than inventory described in section 1221(a)(1)) or options, futures, or forwards relating to commodities.

ELP rules depart significantly from the historical pass-through tax treatment of partnerships; therefore, partnerships that qualify to elect ELP status should carefully consider whether, and under what circumstances, they would actually benefit from choosing to be subject to the ELP rules. Partners in ELPs take into account only eleven items on a flow-through basis, which significantly limits the items an ELP must separately report to its partners. These flow-through items are: (1) taxable income or loss from passive loss limitation activities; (2) taxable income or loss from other activities; (3) net capital gain or loss, separately computed to the extent allocable to passive loss limitation activities and other activities; (4) tax-exempt interest; (5) net alternative minimum tax adjustment, separately computed for passive loss limitation activities and other activities; (6) general credits; (7) low-income housing credits; (8) rehabilitation credits; (9) foreign income taxes; (10) credit for producing fuel from a nonconventional source; and (11) dividends received that constitute qualified dividend income. The IRS also has the authority to specify additional items that must be separately reported. Income or loss from passive loss limitation activities is defined as income or loss from any activity involving the conduct of a trade or business, or any rental activity. Income or loss from "other activities" is always treated as investment income or loss. As is generally the case with partnerships, the ELP partner's characterization of separately reported items is generally determined as if realized or incurred directly from the same source as the partnership.

Services Performed by Fund Managers for an Investment Partnership – The TCJA imposes a three-year holding period instead of a one-year holding period to qualify for long-term capital gain treatment with respect to profits received in connection with the performance of services by a fund manager (hedge fund manager) for an investment partnership or LLC. **This is referred to as "carried interest."** Under the new holding period for "carried interest," gains from profits interests held for three years or less are short-term capital gains subject to tax at ordinary income tax rates, which could be as high as 37%.

The new tax statute applies to both gain from the sale of profits interests (for example, if the holder of the profits interest sells his or her profits interest to a third party for cash) and gain allocated to a partner with respect to his or her profits interest to the extent the gain relates to the sale of assets held by the partnership or LLC (for example, if the holder of the profits interest does not sell his or her profits interest, but instead the underlying entity sells an asset for a capital gain and allocates some of that capital gain to the profits interest holder).

Accordingly, under the new tax law, both of the following would be subject to tax at the taxpayer's ordinary income rate (and not eligible for capital gains):

1. A profits interest holder's share of gain from the sale by the underlying entity of any assets (even a capital asset) disposed of by the underlying entity within the first three years of someone receiving his or her profits interest grant, or
2. A profits interest holder directly selling his or her profits interest to someone before having held such interest for three years.

As the new statute does not grandfather partnership interests issued prior to the enactment of the TCJA, partners, partnerships and LLCs should be aware that this new provision may impact partnership interests issued in 2015, 2016 or 2017. **(See Chapter 6, "Carried Interest")**

Chapter 19 – Corporations

The only difference between an S-corporation and a C-corporation is how they are treated by the IRS. Unlike a C-corporation, and like a partnership, an S-corporation is a pass-through entity that does not pay income tax. Thus, the primary advantage of an S-corporation is that it is not taxed as a separate entity like a C-corporation, but rather income and losses are reported by its shareholders on their individual tax returns, thus avoiding double taxation.

A C-corporation is subject to the double taxation regime. If a C-corporation earns income, the income is taxed first at the corporation level. Then, if the corporation distributes the income, the recipient shareholders pay tax on the income a second time as a dividend. If instead, the corporation retains the income and the value of the shareholders' stock increases, the shareholders will effectively pay tax on the income a second time in the form of capital gains upon selling the stock. Tax returns for C-corporations are due by April 15th beginning with the 2016 tax year. For 2015 and prior years, C-corporation tax returns were due by March 15th. A C-corporation files its tax return every year on Form 1120.

www.irs.gov/pub/irs-pdf/f1120.pdf   www.irs.gov/pub/irs-pdf/i1120.pdf

The following business entities are automatically classified as corporations: organizations formed under a federal or state law (or under a statute of a federally recognized Indian tribe) that refers to the entity as incorporated or as a corporation, body corporate, or body politic; associations such as Sec. 501(a) tax-exempt organizations; organizations formed under a state law that refers to them as joint-stock companies or joint-stock associations; insurance companies; certain state-chartered banks; organizations wholly owned by a state or local government or by foreign governments or entities; organizations specifically required to be taxed as corporations (e.g., certain publicly traded partnerships); foreign organizations and business entities formed under the laws of U.S. territories and possessions; real estate investment trusts (REITs); entities created or organized under more than one jurisdiction (i.e., business entities with multiple charters), if the entity is treated as a corporation by any one of these jurisdictions; and other organizations electing to be classified as corporations by filing Form 8832, Entity Classification Election.

In 2017 and prior years, the United States taxed the worldwide income of resident multinational C-corporations. This meant that so long as a corporation was considered a resident in the United States, all of the earnings of a corporation, both foreign and domestic, were subject to the U.S. top corporate tax rate of 35% regardless of the location of those earnings. The Tax Cuts and Jobs Act (TCJA) eliminates the progressive C-corporation tax structure (maximum tax rate of 35%) and replaces it with a flat tax rate of 21%, effective for 2018 and subsequent years. The TCJA also eliminates the special corporate tax rate on personal service corporations (PSCs). In addition, the TCJA repeals the corporate alternative minimum tax for tax years beginning after Dec. 31, 2017. Any AMT credit carryovers may be used against regular tax liability, and in 2018, 2019, and 2020, 50% of any AMT credit carryovers that exceed regular tax liability are refundable. Any remaining AMT credits will be fully refundable in 2021.

Following are the C-corporation tax rates that were in effect for 2017: Taxable Income below $50,000 (15%); $50,000 - $75,000 ($7,500 + 25% of amount over $50,000); $75,000 - $100,000 ($13,750 + 34% of amount over

$75,000); $100,000 - $335,000 ($22,250 + 39% of amount over $100,000); $335,000 - $10,000,000 ($113,900 + 34% of amount over $335,000); $10,000,000 - $15,000,000 ($3,400,000 +35% of amount over $10,000,000); $15,000,000 - $18,333,333 ($5,150,000 + 38% of amount over $15,000,000); Over $18,333,333 (35%). **(See Chapter 6, "Reporting Capital Gains and Losses")**

S-corporations are subject to only a single level of taxation. Thus, when an S-corporation generates income, the corporation generally does not pay tax on that income at the corporate level. Instead, the income is divvied up among and allocated to the corporation's shareholders (members), who report the income and pay the corresponding tax on their individual tax returns. If the S-corporation then distributes the income, or the corporation retains the income, thus increasing the value of the shareholders' stock, neither the distribution nor the sale of the shareholder's stock will result in the income of the S-corporation being taxed a second time. An S-corporation must have an employer identification number (EIN) and must file a tax return every year on Form 1120S that reports its income, distributions, and deductions and each shareholder's pro rata share of income on Schedule K-1. Shareholders/members pay taxes on their individual tax returns (Form 1040) based on what is shown on the Schedule K-1s issued to them by the S-corporation. An S-corporation's tax return is due by March 15th, but Form 7004 can be filed to get a 6-month extension. S-corporations must use the calendar year unless there is an established business purpose for using a fiscal year.
www.irs.gov/pub/irs-pdf/f1120s.pdf   www.irs.gov/pub/irs-pdf/i1120s.pdf   www.irs.gov/pub/irs-pdf/f1120ssk.pdf   www.irs.gov/pub/irs-pdf/f7004.pdf   www.irs.gov/pub/irs-pdf/i7004.pdf

The basis adjustment rules act as the mechanism by which the extremely vital preservation of the single level of taxation specific to S-corporations is accomplished by ensuring that a distribution of S-corporation income or sale of shareholder stock does not result in a second level of taxation. However, it is the stockholder's responsibility to track his or her stock basis or loan basis in an S-corporation, i.e. the S-corporation does not have a responsibility to keep track of shareholders' stock and loan bases.

- **Example** – If you invest $1,000 in cash in an S-corporation, your initial basis is $1,000. If the S-Corporation then earns $500 in the first year, the income is not taxed at the corporate level; rather it is allocated to the shareholders/members on Schedule K-1, and if your share is $100, you pay tax on the $100 on your individual tax return (Form 1040). However, if the S-corporation retains the $500 of income instead of distributing it, the value of your stock presumably increases from $1,000 to $1,100 ($1,000 + $100). If someone then comes along and offers you $1,100 for the stock, and you haven't adjusted your original $1,000 basis, the sale will give rise to a $100 gain that you have to pay taxes on. If this happens, you will have paid tax on the same $100 earned by the corporation twice – once when it was earned and allocated to you, and again upon the sale of the stock. To prevent this from happening, the S-corporation statute requires that when the S-corporation allocates $100 of income to you (whether you receive it or not), you must increase your stock basis from $1,000 to $1,100. Then, if you sell the stock for $1,100, no further gain arises. By increasing your stock basis to account for your share of the S-corporation's income, you have preserved the single level of taxation that is required by the subchapter S statute.

Also, unlike a partnership, S-corporation shareholders do not have to pay self-employment tax on their pro-rata share of S-corporation income, because distributed income is considered equivalent to dividends and, therefore not subject to self-employment tax. However, just like employees, shareholders' salaries paid to them by S-corporations for services provided are reported on Form W-2 and are subject to income tax and payroll tax withholding and are deducted in determining an S-corporation's income. **(See Below, "Compensation of S-Corporation Shareholders/Employees"); (See Chapter 4, "Wages and Salaries'); (See Chapter 17, "Self-Employment Tax")**

Repatriation Tax

The Tax Cuts and Jobs Act (TCJA) imposes a one-time mandatory repatriation tax under Section 965 applicable to the "2017 tax year." The Section 965 tax is a forerunner to the U.S. version of a territorial taxation system commencing beginning with the 2018 tax year (see below). As part of the transition to a territorial taxation system, a U.S. entity owning directly or indirectly 10% or more of a deferred foreign income corporation (DFIC) is subject to a one-time Section 965 tax on the U.S. entity's share of the DFIC's "accumulated post-1986 deferred foreign income" (E&P) that is greater than zero as of November 2, 2017 or December 31, 2017 (whichever is greater). The Repatriation tax applies to U.S. entities (including individuals, corporations, and domestic investors of pass-through entities.) who own 10% or more of the shares of a DFIC, which include: controlled foreign corporations (CFCs); and foreign corporations that have a U.S. corporate shareholder that owns 10% or more of the shares in the foreign corporation. U.S. entities who are shareholders of "passive foreign investment companies" are not subject to the repatriation tax so long as they are not also controlled foreign corporations. Affected U.S. entities are required to include in income their share of a DFIC's undistributed earnings and profits. This rule works "as if" the DFIC had not already repatriated all of its earnings and profits as of December 31, 2017 through dividend distributions. Deficits are permitted to offset deferred foreign income in accordance with the allocation rules under Section 965. A controlled foreign corporation (CFC) is any foreign corporation where 50% of the total combined voting power of all classes of stock of the corporation is owned directly or indirectly by U.S. shareholders. **(See Below "Implementation of a Territorial Tax System by the TCJA Beginning in 2018")**

Under the repatriation tax provisions, the "Subpart F income" of a DFIC's **last taxable year that begins before January 1, 2018** is increased by the greater of the DFIC's accumulated post-1986 ("E&P") determined as of November 2, 2017 or December 31, 2017 (Measurement Dates). The increased Subpart F income (inclusion amount) must be recognized and taxed in the 2017 tax year. Therefore, a U.S. entity that owns 10% of a DFIC must pick-up additional taxable income on its pro rata share of the "E&P" on its 2017 tax return. E&P is excluded to the extent such earnings were treated as income effectively connected with a U.S. trade or business or is considered previously taxed income, and when determining E&P for purposes of the income inclusion, adjustments may be required to the extent that there were intercompany distributions during 2017. **Dividends paid during the inclusion year generally are not taken into account as a reduction in the determination of post-1986 earnings and profits (E&P), unless the recipient is another specified foreign corporation.** The determination of E&P involves an annual analysis of the DFIC's income, which is then converted to U.S. generally accepted accounting principles (GAAP), and adjustments are made to convert U.S. GAAP income to E&P using U.S. tax principles. Also, E&P deficits are allowed to offset positive earnings, however this is not necessarily an equal offset. In addition, adjustments may be required for deductible payments between specified foreign corporations occurring between November 2, 2017 and December 31, 2017.

- **Example** – ABC a U.S. domestic corporation and DEF a foreign corporation unrelated to ABC own 70% and 30% respectively of all of FC, a foreign corporation. ABC and FC are both calendar year corporations. FC had no income until its taxable year ending Dec. 31, 2016, is which year it had earned income equivalent to $200, all of which was Subpart F income. Therefore, ABC included $140 (70% X $200) in income that was taxed in accordance "Subpart F." FC had no income in 2017. So, FC's accumulated post-1986 deferred foreign income (E&P) was $200 of which $140 was attributable to ABC and would be ABC's "inclusion amount" on which the Repatriation Tax would be calculated, because none of the $140 had been distributed to ABC's shareholders, even though it had been taxed in accordance with Subpart F taxation rules (Subpart F income does not include dividends paid to U.S. shareholders).

Under Section 965, a U.S. shareholder pays the repatriation tax at reduced rates on the "inclusion amount." The tax rate reduction is accomplished via a participation exemption whereby Section 965 permits a deduction against a U.S. shareholder's subpart F inclusion amount that is necessary to result in a 15.5% tax rate on cash or cash equivalents, and an 8% tax rate on non-cash equivalents. However, the actual tax calculation looks at the foreign corporation's cash position on multiple dates.

Subpart F Income – Subpart F operates by treating the shareholders of a controlled foreign corporation (CFC) as if they have actually received the income from the CFC even if they haven't yet received it. The income of a CFC that is currently taxable to its U.S. shareholders under the Subpart F rules is referred to as "Subpart F income." Subpart F income does not include dividends paid to U.S. shareholders. In general, it consists of moveable income such as Foreign Base Company Income (FBCI), which includes foreign personal holding company income, which consists of investment income such as dividends, interest, rents and royalties received. It also may consist of income received by a CFC from the purchase or sale of personal property involving related persons and from the performance of services by or on behalf of a related person (foreign base company services income). But what if a DFIC is not a CFC?

The Repatriation tax is applicable to 10% owners of DFICs whether or not the DFIC is a CFC. A specified foreign corporation that is not a CFC does not generally track E&P under U.S. tax principles. So, are taxpayers who are 10% owners of non-CFCs allowed to use an alternative measurement method for determining its post-1986 E&P and cash position, such as audited financial statements? The IRS has not determined that it would be appropriate to use alternative measurement methods, but that generally, audited financial statements may serve as a starting point in the determination of a specified non-CFC's E&P. The IRS appreciates that obtaining accurate information for U.S. federal income tax purposes may present administrative challenges, particularly in the case of U.S. shareholders that do not have a majority interest in a specified foreign corporation.

Calculation of the Repatriation Tax – The calculation of the tax is complicated, but the ultimate goal is to tax accumulated E&P attributable to liquid assets such as cash at the rate of 15.5% and accumulated E&P attributable to illiquid assets at 8%. A calendar year DFIC's foreign cash position must be measured as of the following three dates: The cash position measurement dates are the following: (1) the final cash measurement date is the close of the last taxable year that begins before January 1, 2018, and ends on or after November 2, 2017; (2) the second cash measurement date is the close of the last taxable year that ends after November 1, 2016, and before November 2, 2017; and (3) the first cash measurement date is the close of the last taxable year that ends after November 1, 2015, and before November 2, 2016. A U.S. shareholder takes into account its pro rata share of the cash position on any cash measurement date, regardless of whether the shareholder is a shareholder on any other cash measurement date, including the final cash measurement date. A shareholder's cash position is the greater of its cash position on the final cash measurement date or 50% of the sum of its cash positions on the second cash measurement date and the first cash measurement date.

Instead of 15.5% and 8% for corporate shareholders, individuals in the highest 2017 tax bracket (39.6%), are subject to a repatriation tax on E&P of 17.5% on cash assets and 9% on noncash assets. Individuals can elect to be treated as corporate shareholders for purposes of the repatriation tax. However, the overall effects of this election should be evaluated as there may be other ancillary effects. An individual is considered to own all the foreign stock owned by his or her spouse, children; and the family attribution rules extend to all grandparents and any number of great-grandparents or grand-children and their spouses.

- **Example** – Assume U.S. shareholder "A" owns 100% of two DFICs. DFIC-1 is a calendar year corporation that has the following cash positions: $400 on 12/31/2015; $400 on 12/31/2016; and $600 on 12/31/2017. Therefore, taking into account only DFIC-1's cash position, A's cash position would be $600, because 50% of $400 + $400 = $400, which is less than DFIC-1's $600 cash position on 12/31/2017. However, DFIC-2 is not a calendar year corporation – its tax years for cash measurement purposes end on 10/31/2016; 10/31/2017; and 10/31/2018 and DFIC-2 has the following cash positions: $600 on 10/31/2016; $600 on 10/31/2017; and $800 on 10/31/2018. So, taking into account both DFIC-1's and DFIC-2's cash positions, A's cash position for purposes of determining the repatriation tax would be $1,200 ($600 for DFIC-1 and $600 for DFIC-2), because since DFIC-2's final cash measurement date ends after 12/31/2017, DFIC-2's final cash position is considered to be zero, and 50% of $600 + $600 = $600. And $600 + $600 = $1,200.

The aggregate foreign cash position is the sum of: cash held by the corporation; the net accounts receivable of the corporation (reduced by accounts payable); and the fair market value (FMV) of the following "cash equivalent" assets held by the corporation: (a) personal property which is of a type that is actively traded and for which there is an established financial market ("actively traded property"); (b) commercial paper, certificates of deposit, the securities of the Federal government and of any State or foreign government; (c) any foreign currency; (d) any obligation with a term of less than one year ("short-term obligation"); and (e) any other cash equivalent asset.

- **Example** – Assume that a U.S. shareholder is a calendar year "individual shareholder" who owns 100% of a foreign corporation (DFIC) that is a controlled foreign corporation (CFC) with the follow assets:

Liquid Assets (12/31/2017):

Cash	$2,000
Accounts Receivable (less Accounts Payable)	5,000
Marketable Securities	3,000
Total Liquid Assets	$10,000

Illiquid Assets

Inventories	$1,000

Plant, Property & Equipment (net of Accumulated Depreciation)	2,000
Other Assets	$ 500
Total Assets	$13,500

Assume the DFIC had post-1986 non-previously taxed E&P of $11,000 on Nov. 2, 2017 and $12,000 on Dec. 31, 2017. E&P determined as of Dec. 31, 2017 is used for this calculation because it is more than the E&P on Nov. 2, 2017

Calculation of Repatriation Tax on Liquid Assets: Total Liquid Assets = $10,000 X 17.5% = $1,750

Calculation of Repatriation Tax on Illiquid Assets: $12,000 (E&P) minus $10,000 (Liquid Assets) = $2,000 X 9% = $180 (Illiquid assets are determined based on total E&P (Mandatory Inclusion Amount) less the foreign cash position)

Calculation of Total Repatriation Tax: $1,750 + $180 = $1,930

The above calculation is applicable to an individual shareholder of a DFIC. However, due to the deemed-paid foreign tax credit, the calculation is much more complex for a C-corporation shareholder. The 15.5% tax rate on cash assets and 8% tax rate on non-cash assets assumes that all of the foreign tax credits are allowable. However, foreign tax credits are disallowed to the extent they are attributable to the portion of the mandatory inclusion amount excluded from taxable income. Therefore, C-corporation shareholders are subject to a "participation deduction" or a "haircut" of 55.7% attributable to the cash portion of the inclusion amount taxed at 15.5% and a haircut of 77.1% attributable to the non-cash portion of the inclusion amount taxed at 8%. These percentages are equal to the amount of a shareholder's mandatory inclusion that is offset by the participation exemption using a corporate tax rate of 35%. This requires a "gross-up" of a C-corporation's tax, which is an additional tax on the "Net Income Inclusion Amount."

Example – Refer to the above example, except that the shareholder is a C-corporation instead of an individual shareholder. As in the example above, assume the DFIC had post-1986 non-previously taxed E&P of $11,000 on Nov. 2, 2017 and $12,000 on Dec. 31, 2017. E&P determined as of Dec. 31, 2017 is used for this calculation because it is more than the E&P on Nov. 2, 2017

Calculation of Repatriation Tax on Liquid Assets: Total Liquid Assets = $10,000 X 15.5% = $1,550

Calculation of Repatriation Tax on Illiquid Assets: $12,000 (E&P) minus $10,000 (Liquid Assets) = $2,000 X 8% = $160 (Illiquid assets are determined based on total E&P (Mandatory Inclusion Amount) less the foreign cash position)

Calculation of Total Repatriation Tax: $1,550 + $160 = $1,710

Total Liquid Assets of $10,000 X 44.3% (100% minus 55.7%) = $4,430; Illiquid Assets of $2,000 X 22.9% (100% minus 77.1%) = $458; $4,430 + $458 = $4,888 (Net Income Inclusion Amount)

Computation of additional tax on the Net Income Inclusion Amount: $4,888 X 35% (maximum corporate tax rate in 2017) = $1,711 (Tax at Marginal Rate – Subpart F Inclusion Amount)

In order to calculate the Section 965 Repatriation Tax correctly, taxpayers should refer to IRS Publication 5292

(2017), How to Calculate Section 965 Amounts and Elections Available to Taxpayers. www.irs.gov/publications/p5292

A taxpayer may need to report Section 965 amounts on its 2016 tax return. For example, a DFIC and its sole U.S. shareholder are both fiscal year taxpayers with a November 30th tax year end, and the DFIC dissolved on November 29, 2017. So, the last tax year of the DFIC beginning before Jan. 1, 2018, would be its tax year beginning Dec. 1, 2016, and ending Nov. 29, 2017. An inclusion amount with respect to the DFIC would be properly included on the U.S. shareholder's 2016 tax return for its tax year beginning on Dec. 1, 2016, and ending on Nov. 30, 2017.

Paying the Repatriation Tax – U.S. corporations may offset the tax with a deemed foreign tax credit. But, all U.S. shareholders, including individuals and corporations, can pay the tax in lump sum or elect to pay the net tax liability in unequal installments over eight years, beginning with the due date of the 2017 tax return. However, the first installment payment must be made by the original due date of the 2017 tax return (without extensions). In order to make a payment for the Section 965 Repatriation Tax, a taxpayer needs to make two separate payments with their tax return and include two separate payment vouchers. One payment needs to reflect the tax owed on the tax return without regard to the Repatriation Tax. The second payment needs to reflect tax owed for the Repatriation Tax. Both payments must be paid by the due date of the applicable return without extension. Also, A U.S. shareholder that has to pay the repatriation tax is required to include with its return a Section 965 Transition Tax Statement. It can be attached as a PDF to an electronically filed return. At a minimum the Transition Tax Statement must include: the taxpayer's total amount of income required to be included by Code Section 965(a); the taxpayer's aggregate foreign cash position; the taxpayer's total deduction available under Code Section 965(c); the taxpayer's deemed paid foreign taxes with respect to the income being included (for C corporations only); the taxpayer's disallowed deemed paid foreign taxes with respect to the income being included (C corporation only); the total net tax liability for the repatriation tax; the amount of net tax liability to be paid in eight installments; and a listing of elections under Code Section 965 provided for in Notice 2018-13.

www.irs.gov/pub/irs-drop/n-18-13.pdf

When a taxpayer elects to pay the tax over eight years, 8% of the tax must be paid in each of the first five years, 15% in the sixth year, 20% in the seventh year, and 25% in the eighth year. The payment of the tax must be accelerated upon the occurrence of certain "triggering events," such as failure to timely pay any installment due, or a liquidation or sale of substantially all of a shareholder's interest in the foreign corporation.

S-corporations – Shareholders of S-corporations may elect to defer paying its net repatriation tax liability until the tax year that a "triggering event" occurs. A "triggering event" includes the corporation ceasing to be an S-corporation, a liquidation or sale of substantially all of the assets of such S- corporation, a cessation of business by such S-corporation, the S-corporation ceases to exist, and a transfer of any share of stock of the S-corporation (including by death or otherwise). An S-corporation shareholder that elects to defer paying its net tax liability may also elect to pay the liability in equal installments over an 8-year period after a triggering event has occurred. However, this election is available only with consent if the triggering event is a liquidation, sale of substantially all of the S-corporation's assets, termination of the S-corporation or cessation of its business, or a

306

similar event. The first installment must be paid by the due date (without extensions) of the shareholder's federal income tax return for the year that includes the triggering event. If any S-corporation shareholder elects to defer paying its net tax liability, the S-corporation is jointly and severally liable for the payment of the deferred tax and any penalty, additions to tax, or additional amounts attributable thereto, and the limitation on collection is not treated as beginning before the triggering event.

Section 965 Tax Provisions – Important provisions regarding the Repatriation Tax:

- It is significant to note that the Section 965 tax is imposed on deferred foreign income whether or not it is actually repatriated. If the income is repatriated post December 31, 2017, then it is treated as previously taxed income under Section 951 and not subject to double taxation.

- For purposes of determining the fair market value of a cash-equivalent asset, the value of the cash-equivalent asset must be adjusted by the fair market value of any cash equivalent asset hedging transaction with respect to the cash-equivalent asset, but only to the extent that the cash-equivalent asset hedging transaction does not reduce the fair market value of the cash-equivalent asset below zero.

- The term "accumulated post-1986 deferred foreign income" means the post-1986 E&P of the specified foreign corporation except to the extent that such E&P: (1) is attributable to income of the specified foreign corporation that is effectively connected with the conduct of a trade or business within the United States; or (2) in the case of a controlled foreign corporation (CFC), is distributed and, therefore, excluded from the gross income of a U.S. shareholder ("previously taxed E&P").

- The term "E&P deficit foreign corporation" means that as of November 2, 2017: (1) such specified foreign corporation has a deficit in post-1986 earnings and profits (E&P); and (2) such corporation is a specified foreign corporation. The term "specified E&P deficit" means that an E&P deficit foreign corporation has a deficit in post-1986 earnings and profits as of November 2, 2017.

- If a specified foreign corporation satisfies the definition of a deferred foreign income corporation (DFIC) under Section 965, it is classified solely as a deferred foreign income corporation (DFIC) and not also as an E&P deficit foreign corporation even if it otherwise satisfies the requirements for being an E&P deficit foreign corporation.

- The amount by which the post-1986 E&P of a specified foreign corporation is reduced as a result of a distribution made to a specified foreign corporation in the last taxable year of the foreign corporation that begins before January 1, 2018, may not exceed the amount of the the post-1986 E&P.

- Solely for purposes of determining whether a foreign corporation is a specified foreign corporation within the meaning of Section 965, stock owned, directly or indirectly, by or for a partner ("tested partner") will not be considered as being owned by a partnership if the tested partner owns less than 5% of the interests in the partnership's capital and profits. However, an interest in the partnership owned by another partner will be considered as owned by the tested partner.

- If a domestic pass-through entity (partnership and S-corporation) is a U.S. shareholder of a DFIC, the Section 965 inclusion amount and deduction amount are each determined at the level of the passthrough entity. However, the owners of the domestic pass-through entity are subject to federal income tax on their share of the aggregate Section 965 inclusion amount of the pass-through entity.

- The E&P of a DFIC is reduced by previously taxed earnings and profits of the corporation. In certain cases, the Section 965 inclusion amount, and therefore previously taxed earnings and profits of the DFIC with respect to a U.S. shareholder, may exceed the E&P. For example, this will be the case when a DFIC incurs a loss after the E&P measurement date on which it determines its Section 965 earnings amount and before the end of its inclusion year. In such a case, a deficit in E&P will be created or increased.

- In computing post-1986 E&P on November 2, 2017, in certain cases, a reduction is allowed for a portion of foreign income taxes that accrue after November 2, 2017, and on or before December 31, 2017. In particular, post-1986 E&P on November 2, 2017, is reduced by the portion of the applicable taxes that are attributable to the portion of the taxable income (as determined under foreign law) that accrues on or before November 2, 2017, and during the specified foreign corporation's U.S. taxable year that includes November 2, 2017.

- For purposes of determining a shareholder's pro rata share of a specified E&P deficit, the value of the common stock is determined as of the last day of the last taxable year of the E&P deficit foreign corporation that begins before January 1, 2018.

- Each shareholder of an S-corporation may elect to defer payment of their net tax liability under Section 965 until the shareholder's taxable year which includes the triggering event with respect to such tax liability.

- In determining the accumulated post-1986 deferred foreign income of a specified foreign corporation as of an E&P measurement date, the earnings and profits of the specified foreign corporation that are or would be included in subpart F income is excluded from the E&P income on the measurement date to the extent that such income has been accrued by the specified foreign corporation and included in subpart F income as of the E&P measurement date.

- Partners own their share of any foreign corporations owned by their partnerships, and corporations own their share of any foreign subsidiaries no matter how far down the chain.

- Beneficiaries own their share of foreign corporations inside a trust.

- There have been significant changes to the attribution rules and now certain corporations which were not previously considered CFCs will be CFCs. The attribution rules are very complex and need to be evaluated on a case-by-case basis.

To date, The IRS has issued Notices 2018-07 and 2018-13 that provide guidance on the calculation of the Repatriation Tax. The IRS has also issued Publication 5292 "How to Calculate Section 965 Amounts and Elections Available to Taxpayers" for use in preparing 2017 Returns. Publication 5292 provides a workbook to help taxpayers calculate the Section 965 Repatriation Tax. The IRS has also issued a 249-page document that sets-forth proposed regulations in regard to the Repatriation Tax.
www.irs.gov/pub/irs-drop/n-18-07.pdf www.irs.gov/pub/irs-drop/n-18-13.pdf
www.irs.gov/pub/irs-pdf/p5292.pdf www.irs.gov/pub/irs-drop/reg-104226-18.pdf

Implementation of a Territorial Tax System by the TCJA Beginning in 2018

The Tax Cuts and Jobs Act (TCJA) made several changes to the taxation of subpart F income of U.S. shareholders of controlled foreign corporations (CFCs). Among other things, the TCJA expands the definition of a U.S. shareholder to include U.S. persons who own 10% or more of the total value (not just vote) of shares of all classes of stock of the CFCs. In addition, the requirement that a corporation must be controlled for 30 days before Subpart F inclusions apply has been eliminated. The TCJA introduces four new major corporate tax provisions: (1) the "participation exemption," which exempts all foreign profits paid back to the United States from domestic taxation. This is what changed the U.S. corporate tax system from a "worldwide" tax system closer to a "territorial" tax system; (2) the second and third provisions, "Global Intangible Low Tax Income" (GILTI) and "Foreign Derived Intangible Income" (FDII), are two new categories of foreign income subject to taxation at reduced rates after the exemption of all foreign profits from taxation that are paid back to the U.S. in the form of dividends. **GILTI and FDII taken together are in effect a worldwide tax on intangible income of controlled foreign corporations (CFC) that is taxed at a lower rate than the new designated 21% corporate tax rate. They** create a worldwide minimum tax on intangible income and **are meant as "supplement taxes" after the exemption of all foreign profits by the new participation exemption;** and (3) Lastly, "The Base Erosion and Anti-Abuse Tax" (BEAT) is in effect a new minimum tax, aimed at preventing multinationals from stripping income from the U.S. tax base with excess payments to foreign-affiliated corporations. **(See Above, "Subpart F Income")**

The Participation Exemption – Beginning in 2018 (tax years beginning after December 31, 2017), the TCJA eliminates the additional U.S. tax on foreign profits through what is called the "participation exemption." The participation exemption allows a 100% deduction for dividends received from foreign corporations by U.S. domestic parent corporations in determining their taxable income. The 100% dividend received deduction (DRD) is available to domestic C-corporations that own at least 10% of a controlled foreign corporation (CFC). The result is that these foreign profits paid to U.S. domestic corporations in the form of dividends do not face additional U.S. taxation as they did under the previous law that was in effect in 2017 and prior years. Eligible C-corporations for the participation exemption cannot be real estate investment trusts (REITs) or regulated investment companies. Also, domestic partnerships and individuals are not considered eligible U.S. shareholders for the participation exemption. In addition, dividends received from passive foreign investment companies (PFICs) do not qualify for the participation exemption. However, a **domestic S-corporation that owns 10% or more of the stock of a foreign corporation is eligible for the participation exemption. Therefore, large individual shareholders should benefit from transferring their stock in a foreign corporation they own into an S-corporation.** A U.S. domestic corporation must qualify as a 10% shareholder of the specified foreign corporation at all times during the period the participation exemption applies to distributions of dividends. U.S. corporations are not allowed to receive a foreign tax credit for the dividends getting the participation exemption and, therefore, excluded from taxable income.

To qualify for the participation exemption, U.S. corporations have to satisfy three requirements: (1) they must own 10% of the controlled foreign corporation's (CFC) stock; (2) they must hold the CFC's stock for at least 366 days; and (3) they cannot deduct a dividend against U.S. taxable income if that dividend received a tax benefit in a foreign country. This is to prevent "hybrid dividends" that receive a deduction in the foreign country before being paid to the U.S. parent corporation from being excluded from the taxable income of the U.S. corporation, resulting effectively in no tax on that income. The TCJA changes the definition of a "10% U.S. Shareholder." Before the enactment of the TCJA, a "10% U.S. Shareholder" was defined as a U.S. person who owned (directly, indirectly or constructively) 10% or more of the total combined voting power of a corporation. The TCJA expands the definition to include a U.S. person who owns 10% or more of the stock of the corporation by vote or value. The participation exemption excludes ordinary foreign profits paid to U.S. parent corporations in the form of dividends, but it does not exclude capital gains from being taxed. U.S. corporations that sell, or otherwise dispose of shares in CFCs, do not get an income exclusion on gains from selling those shares.

U.S. corporations that have received dividends that are allowed the participation exemption and then sell the CFC stock at a loss must reduce its basis (but not below zero) in the stock of the foreign corporation by the amount of the dividends allowed the 100% participation exemption. When a U.S. corporation transfers substantially all of the assets of a foreign branch to a foreign subsidiary, the U.S. corporation must include in income the amount of any post-2017 losses realized by the branch.

Global Intangible Low Tax Income (GILTI) – In 2017 and prior years, U.S. shareholders (whether corporations or individuals) that owned 10% or more of the voting stock in a controlled foreign corporation (CFC) generally were taxed on the CFC's earnings only when they received a dividend, with an exception referred to as the "Subpart F rules," which require the inclusion of certain types of income earned by a CFC on a current basis, regardless of whether distributions in the form of a dividends were received. Thus, a U.S. taxpayer that structured its operations in a manner that was mindful of the Subpart F rules generally was able to defer U.S. tax on income earned by a CFC until the U.S. taxpayer received a dividend. **(See Above "Subpart F Income")**

Under the TCJA, Global Intangible Low Tax Income (GILTI) was implemented as a new anti-deferral tax on certain earnings of a CFC, effective starting with the first tax year of the CFC beginning after Dec. 31, 2017. Similar to the taxation of Subpart F income, a 10% U.S. shareholder of one or more CFCs is required to include its GILTI currently as taxable income (in addition to any Subpart F income), regardless of whether any amount is distributed to the U.S. shareholder. The tax on GILTI essentially serves to tax a U.S. shareholder currently on the shareholder's allocable share of CFC earnings for a tax year to the extent such earnings exceed a 10% return on the shareholder's allocable share of tangible assets held by CFCs. The tax on GILTI applies equally to U.S. shareholders that are corporations or flow-through taxpayers. A U.S. shareholder's GILTI is calculated as the shareholder's "net CFC tested income" less "net deemed tangible income return" determined for the tax year. Net CFC tested income is calculated by determining the U.S. shareholder's pro rata share of tested income or tested loss of each CFC held by the U.S. shareholder, and aggregating those amounts. Tested income or loss is calculated as a CFC's gross income after excluding high-taxed foreign base company income, Subpart F income, related-party dividends, certain foreign oil and gas extraction income, and income of the CFC taxable in the United States as effectively connected income, less deductions allocable to tested income. High-taxed income that is not foreign base company income is included as tested income. Thus, in the simple case where a single shareholder owns 100% of a CFC with none of the categories of excluded income as stated above, net CFC tested income will equal the CFC's net income. For pass-through taxpayers that do not benefit from foreign tax credits on GILTI, high-taxed income included in Subpart F income is excluded, but high-taxed income that is not included in Subpart F income is not.

After the net CFC tested income is determined, it is reduced by the shareholder's "net deemed tangible income return" to arrive at the shareholder's GILTI. This amount is the excess of a U.S. shareholder's allocable share of the basis of a CFC's depreciable tangible assets used in the production of tested income, multiplied by 10% (subject to certain adjustments). "Net deemed tangible income return" is also referred to as "Qualified Business Asset Investment" (QBAI). So, net tested income minus 10% of QBAI, less the amount of interest expense taken into account in determining the shareholder's net CFC tested income for the tax year to the extent the interest income attributable to such expense is not taken into account in determining the shareholder's net CFC tested income, is equal to GILTI. For this purpose, the basis of a CFC's depreciable assets is determined by applying

310

depreciation on a straight-line basis.

- **Example** – As of Dec. 31, 2018, a U.S. shareholder owns 100% of CFC-1 and 50% of CFC-2. CFC-1 has $160,000 of tested income and a tax basis in tangible assets or QBAI of $400,000. CFC-2 has $100,000 of tested income and QBAI of $1 million. The U.S. shareholder has net tested income of $210,000 (100% X $160,000 + 50% X $100,000 = **$210,000**.

  GILTI = **$120,000**: (10% X $400,000 = $40,000) + (10% X [50% X $1 million = $500,000] = $50,000; $210,000 less ($40,000 + $50,000 = $90,00) = $120,000

Once the GILTI amount is determined, a U.S. corporate taxpayer can deduct 50% of its GILTI (reduced to 37.5% for tax years starting after 2025). This results in a 10.5% minimum tax on a corporate U.S. shareholder's GILTI (50% × 21% corporate tax rate). In addition to this "GILTI deduction," a foreign tax credit may be claimed by a U.S. corporate taxpayer equal to 80% of the foreign income taxes paid by a CFC on a U.S. shareholder's tested income. Application of the deduction and the tax credit eliminates any U.S. taxes owed above 13.125% on the U.S. corporate shareholder's GILTI because the maximum tax on GILTI is 13.125% for tax years before 2026, and 16.406% thereafter.

- **Example** – From the example above, the GILTI amount is equal to $120,000; Foreign Tax Liability on the GILTI = $6,000; $6,000 X 80% = $4,800 (Foreign Tax Credit); $120,000 X 10.5% = $12,600 (Initial Tax on GILTI); $12,600 minus $4,800 (Foreign Tax Credit) = $7,800 (Final U.S. Tax on GILTI).

  $7,800 + $6,000 (Foreign Tax Liability on GILTI) = $13,800 (Total Tax on GILTI); $13,800 divided by $120,00 (GILTI) = **11.5% TOTAL EFFECTIVE TAX RATE ON GILTI**.

Flow-through and Individual Taxpayers – Though the amount of a U.S. shareholder's GILTI is calculated the same for corporate, individual and flowthrough (Partnership and S-corporation) taxpayers, only corporate taxpayers are entitled to the 50% GILTI deduction and related 80% foreign tax credit. Therefore, individual and flow-through taxpayers subject to tax on GILTI are taxed on the entire amount of GILTI. In addition, because the tax on GILTI arises from foreign business operations, flow-through taxpayers that would otherwise potentially qualify for the new Sec. 199A deduction cannot include the amount of the GILTI in the base for determining the 20% deduction. Accordingly, under most circumstances, noncorporate U.S. taxpayers will pay a current tax on GILTI at a rate up to 37% (the newly enacted highest marginal rate for individuals). A noncorporate taxpayer may make the election under Sec. 962(a) to be taxed as a C-corporation and generally obtain the benefits of the lower tax rate applicable to C-corporations and the foreign tax credit (but not the 50% GILTI deduction). However, making such an election generally requires future distributions of what would otherwise be a return of previously taxed profits to be taxable.

Foreign Derived Intangible Income (FDII) – Foreign Derived Intangible Income (FDII) is a second new category of foreign income that is added to U.S. corporate taxable income each year beginning in 2018 (tax years beginning after December 31, 2017). Generally, FDII is income from the use of intellectual property in the United States in creating an export. Unlike GILTI, FDII and BEAT (See below) somewhat resemble a destination-based tax. FDII effectively creates a new preferential tax rate for income derived by U.S. domestic corporations serving foreign markets. A U.S. domestic C-corporation pays an effective tax rate of 13.125% (rather than 21%) on its income arising from foreign markets. This new deduction is described as a deduction for foreign-derived intangible income, or FDII. The FDII deduction is available to domestic corporations that are taxed as C-corporations. This includes U.S. corporate subsidiaries of foreign-based multinationals. However, foreign corporations with income effectively connected with a U.S. trade or business, S-corporations, regulated investment companies, real estate investment trusts, partnerships and individuals are not eligible to claim a FDII deduction.

In general, FDII is equal to foreign-derived income minus 10% of "Qualified Business Asset Investment" (QBAI). Foreign-derived income is the share of a corporation's U.S. income related to the export of goods or services. QBAI for purposes of the FDII is equal to the value of tangible assets used by a U.S. corporation in earning foreign-derived income. U.S. corporations are allowed to deduct 37.5% of their FDII against their taxable income. This results in a special lower effective tax rate of 13.125% (rather than 21%) on income generated from export sales or services.

The FDII benefit is determined based on a multi-step calculation:

1. A domestic corporation's gross income is determined and then reduced by certain items of income, including amounts included in income under Subpart F, dividends received from controlled foreign corporations and income earned in foreign branches. This amount is reduced by deductions (including taxes) properly allocable to such income, yielding deduction eligible income.

2. The foreign portion of such income is determined. This amount includes any income derived from the sale of property to any foreign person for foreign use. The term "sale" is defined for this purpose to include any lease, license, exchange or other disposition. The term "foreign use" is defined as any use, consumption, or disposition which is not within the United States. Qualifying foreign income also includes income derived in connection with services provided to any person not located within the United States, or with respect to property that is not located in the United States. The services may be performed within or outside the United States (but not in a foreign branch of the domestic corporation, which limits the extent of permissible qualifying activity outside the United States). The gross foreign sales and services income is reduced by expenses properly allocated to such income. The sum of these two amounts yields foreign derived deductible eligible income.

3. A domestic corporation's foreign derived intangible income (FDII) is determined. This is the excess (if any) of the corporation's deduction eligible income minus 10% of its qualified business asset investment (QBAI). A domestic corporation's QBAI is the average of its adjusted bases (using a quarterly measuring convention) in depreciable tangible property used in the corporation's trade or business to generate the deduction eligible income. The adjusted bases are determined using straight line depreciation. A domestic corporation's QBAI does not include land, intangible property or any assets that do not produce the deductible eligible income. U.S. corporations are allowed to deduct 37.5% of their FDII against their taxable income.

- **Example** – ABC company, a U.S. corporation, earned $1,900 in total income in the United States of which 10% ($190) was earned from exporting goods overseas. The company has $800 in QBAI (value of its tangible assets used in earning foreign derived income). Therefore, the company's FDII is $110 ($190 in foreign derived income minus 10% of QBAI [$800 X 10% = $80]). The company is allowed to deduct 37.5% of its FDII, which is $41.25 ($110 X 37.5%) from its FDII. Taxable income is $68.75 ($110 minus

$41.25 = $68.75) X 21% corporate tax rate = **$14.44 tax on FDII which is an effective tax rate of 13.125%** ($14.44 divided by $110 FDII)

Together GILTI and FDII are a backstop to the Participation Exemption and are meant to prevent companies from moving intellectual property and shifting corporate profits out of the U.S. On 9/13/2018, the IRS issued proposed regulations meant to clarify the computation of GILTI and FDII. www.irs.gov/pub/irs-drop/reg-104390-18.pdf

The Base Erosion and Anti-Abuse Tax (BEAT) – The "Base Erosion and Anti-Abuse Tax," or BEAT is effective for tax years beginning after December 31, 2017. The BEAT is essentially a 10% minimum tax (5 percent in 2018) that is meant to prevent foreign and domestic corporations operating in the United States from avoiding domestic tax liability by shifting profits out of the U.S. The BEAT only applies to multinational domestic corporations and to foreign corporations with income connected with a U.S. trade or business whose annual gross receipts for the 3-year-taxable period ending with the preceding tax year that is $500 million or more. The BEAT does not apply to individuals, S-corporations, regulated investment companies or real estate investment trusts.

The BEAT is 10% of "modified taxable income" less a corporation's regular tax liability, generally reduced by certain tax credits. However, the tax rate is 5% instead of 10% for 2018, and increases to 12.5% beginning in 2025. These rates are increased by one percent for certain banks and securities dealers. The BEAT calculations are made on a group basis, i.e. the related-party payments, deductions, and income of affiliated domestic corporations are aggregated for BEAT purposes. A corporation's modified taxable income is determined by adding back to taxable income current year deductions involving payments to related foreign corporations owning at least 25% of the stock of the taxpayer. Add-backs include payments for services, interest, rents and royalties. The 50% deduction for amounts included in income as global intangible low-taxed income (GILTI) is not added back. The add backs are what are considered "base erosion" payments that corporations based in the U.S. make to related foreign corporations.

The BEAT does not apply unless current year deductions involving payments to related foreign corporations exceed 3% (2% for certain financial firms such as banks and securities dealers) of total deductions taken by the corporations.

- **Example** – Assume a U.S. multinational corporation has gross receipts for the 3-year-taxable period of $1 million. The corporation's regular taxable income is $210,000. The corporation's modified taxable income after adding back current year deductions involving payments to 25% related foreign corporations is equal to $215,000. Total deductions taken by the corporation equal $250,000. The BEAT does not apply, because the deductions involving payments to related foreign corporations is less than 3% of the total deductions taken by the corporation ($215,000 minus $210,000 = $5,000; however 3% X $250,000 = $7,500.

- **Example** – A U.S. multinational corporation's regular taxable income is $210,000, and its modified taxable income is $250,000. Its deductions involving payments to related foreign corporations are more than 3% of the total deductions taken by the corporation. Therefore, the corporation's BEAT is $2,000 in 2018 and $4,000 in 2019 ($250,000 modified taxable income, minus $210,000 regular taxable income = $40,000 X 5% = $2,000 BEAT in 2018; $40,000 X 10% = $4,000 BEAT in 2019.

313

Deduction of Compensation of Public Company Executives

There is a $1 million limit on the deduction of compensation paid by a public corporation to a "covered employee" in determining taxable income. A covered employee includes the CEO or one of the top 4 other executives whose compensation must be reported on a public company's proxy statement. However, prior to 2018, the following exemptions and exceptions were allowed to avoid the $1 million limit, which means these exemptions and exceptions were allowed to be deducted as compensation in computing taxable income:

- Bonuses and other compensation meeting the requirements to be considered "qualified performance-based compensation" was fully deductible.

- Commissions were fully deductible.

- Compensation paid to former employees and current employees who were formerly top-five executives was fully deductible.

- Compensation paid to the CFO was fully deductible.

The Tax Cuts and Jobs Act (TCJA) eliminates all of the exemptions and exceptions, effective for 2018 and subsequent years. Therefore, for 2018 all compensation in excess of $1 million paid to any employee or former employee who is or was the CEO, the CFO, or one of the other top three executives whose compensation is required to be reported on the proxy statement is not deductible by the company in computing its taxable income. However, compensation payable pursuant to a legally binding agreement that was in place prior to November 2, 2017, is not affected by the TCJA (Grandfather Clause). IRS guidance seems to imply that the "Grandfather Clause" applies only if any amount of remuneration to a covered employee does not exceed the amount of remuneration that applicable law obligates the corporation to pay under a written binding contract that was in effect on November 2, 2017, or if the terms of the contract state that it will be automatically renewed after November 2, 2017, and neither the corporation nor the employee provides at least a 30-day notice of termination of the contract prior to the scheduled renewal date.

Once an employee is treated as a covered employee, the individual remains a covered employee for all future years, including payments made after retirement, death, etc. Also, the definition of a "public corporation" is expanded to include all domestic publicly traded corporations and all foreign public companies and may include some corporations that are not publicly traded, such as large private C or S corporations. But the TCJA does not appear to extend beyond SEC filers.

On August 21, 2018, the IRS issued Notice 2018-68 which offers early guidance on the meaning of this provision of the TCJA. The Guidance seems to imply that the "Grandfather Clause" applies only if any amount of remuneration to a covered employee does not exceed the amount of remuneration that applicable law obligates the corporation to pay under a written binding contract that was in effect on November 2, 2017, or if the terms of the contract state that it will be automatically renewed after November 2, 2017, and neither the corporation nor the employee provides at least a 30-day notice of termination of the contract prior to the scheduled renewal date.

www.irs.gov/pub/irs-drop/n-18-68.pdf

Contributions to Capital of Corporations by Governmental Entities

Under the Tax Cuts and Jobs Act (TCJA), contributions to a corporation's capital by governmental entities after December 22, 2017, are generally reportable as income. Before then, such contributions were generally excluded from income by corporations. This means that property contributed to a corporation after December 22, 2017, by a governmental unit or by a civic group for the purpose of inducing the corporation to locate its business in a particular town, city, community etc. or to enable the corporation to expand its facilities in those areas is taxable to the corporation. States, cities and utilities can continue to contribute undeveloped land, improved land and other assets to corporations to entice them to locate in a community, but the value of such incentives has been diminished by the TCJA. This change does not apply to any contributions by a governmental entity under a development plan that was approved before December 22, 2017.

Dividends Received Deduction

Prior to January 1, 2018, dividends received by a C-corporation from a less than 20% owned domestic corporation were 70% excluded from income by the C-corporation, and dividends received by a C-corporation from a more than 20% owned domestic corporation were 80% excluded from income by a C-corporation. Under the Tax Cuts and Jobs Act (TCJA), effective for 2018 and subsequent years, the percentages of dividends excluded by a C-corporation are decreased from 70% to 50% for a less than 20% owned corporation, and from 80% to 65% for a more than 20% owned corporation.

Deduction of Charitable Contributions by Corporations

Businesses are allowed a deduction for donations to qualified Sec. 501(c)(3) organizations, which are the only tax-exempt organizations to which contributions are deductible as charitable contributions. If contributions are made to organizations that are not qualified Sec. 501(c)(3) organizations, businesses should consider whether the contributions can be classified as either an advertising and marketing expense or an entertainment expense depending on the specific goods or services donated. To determine the amount of the charitable contribution deduction, charitable contributions must be reduced by the FMV of goods or services received in return for the charitable contributions. The excess amount contributed over the FMV is fully deductible as a charitable contribution. The FMV of the goods or services received in return for the contributions may be included in meals and entertainment, if requirements are met, of which the business can deduct 50%. To claim the meals and entertainment deduction, a taxpayer must keep adequate records about the expense, including the amount, time and place, business purpose, and business relationship of the attendees.

Regulations require taxpayers to substantiate charitable contributions of $250 or more by obtaining an acknowledgment letter from the qualified Sec. 501(c)(3) charitable organization. The acknowledgment letter must contain the following information: (1) the amount of cash and a description of any property other than cash contributed; (2) a statement whether the donee organization provided any goods or services in consideration for the contribution; and (3) a description and good-faith estimate of the value of any goods or services provided in consideration for the contribution. **(See Chapter 12, "Charitable Contribution Deduction")**

S-Corporation Status

An S-corporation cannot have more than 100 shareholders, which includes individuals, estates, and some trusts, but none can be C-corporations, partnerships, or nonresident aliens. A husband and wife (and all family members) may be treated as one shareholder. To attain S-corporation status, a small business entity only needs to incorporate under state law, and then elect to be treated as an S-corporation by filing Form 2553 with the IRS. Form 2553 cannot be filed before the corporation has been approved and is in existence under state law. S-corporation status is an IRS designation. States do not grant S-corporation status to taxpayers. If your business is already incorporated, you generally have until March 15th of a particular year to elect to be taxed as an S-corporation by filing Form 2553 with the IRS. Electing S-corporation status by this date lets you be treated as an S-corporation for the entire year. If you are already incorporated, you have two months and 15 days from the start of the corporation to make the election. For example, if you incorporate on Jan. 7th, you have until March 21st to file the election with the IRS to become an S-corporation. Otherwise, it will not be effective until the next year (with some exceptions). S-corporation status is lost if it has passive investment income in excess of 25% of its gross income for each of 3 consecutive years or it has accumulated earnings and profits at the end of 3 consecutive years. And if this happens, S-corporation status cannot be elected again for 3 years.

www.irs.gov/pub/irs-pdf/f2553.pdf www.irs.gov/pub/irs-pdf/i2553.pdf

Limited Liability Company (LLC) – One entity that can be formed by filing formation documents with a state is a "Limited Liability Company" (LLC), which is not a corporation that issues stock but instead is an association that has percentages of ownership by individual members. An LLC is not a partnership or a corporation but rather a distinct type of entity that has powers of both a corporation and a partnership. Unlike a partnership, where the element is the individual, the essence of the LLC is the entity in which the owners are called members. LLCs are qualified to apply for S-corporation status with the IRS; otherwise they are taxed as a "disregarded entity." A disregarded entity with one owner is a sole proprietorship and files a Schedule C on Form 1040. A disregarded entity with two or more owners is a partnership and files Form 1065. The deemed election to be classified as an S-corporation will apply upon approval by the IRS within 60 days of submission of Form 2553. Following are details of how a corporation and an LLC can become an S-corporation: **(See Chapter 18, "Limited Liability Company (LLC)")**

- An entity must first attain corporation or LLC status with the state. The entity must have two or more owners and file articles of incorporation with the state, where state law provides that corporate existence begins and stock subscribers become shareholders or members upon approval by the state.
- The corporation or LLC must timely file Form 2553 with the IRS to make the S-corporation election. All shareholders or members must consent to the election in writing.
- The question of whether a person is a LLC member is decided under the IRS code rather than state law; thus, a person who is not a member of record under state law may still be considered a member for IRS purposes. Therefore, an LLC may in reality have only one owner, but a spouse who consents to the election by signing Form 2553 as a 50% owner of the LLC qualifies as a member, so the LLC will have 2 members for IRS purposes.
- LLC's can elect how to be treated for federal tax purposes because an LLC is not a federal tax entity, and there is no provision in the IRS Code that specifically governs the treatment of LLCs for federal tax purposes. Therefore, both a partnership and an LLC can elect to be taxed as a C-corporation under the "check-the-box" rules by filing Form 8832, "Entity Classification Election."
- An LLC electing the "default status", i.e. to be treated as a disregarded entity and not to be taxed as a separate entity from its owners, should not file Form 2553 or Form 8832. The default status for a single owner or husband and wife LLC is to file Schedule C with their individual 1040 tax return; and the default status for an LLC with 2 or more owners is to file a Partnership tax return (Form 1065). **(See**

316

Chapter 17, "Self-Employed/Independent Contractors")
- LLCs only need to file Form 2553 "Election by a Small Business Corporation" with the IRS, which is the Form requesting to be treated as an S-corporation. The deemed election to be classified as an S-corporation will apply upon approval by the IRS. Approval or disapproval should be received within 60 days of submission of Form 2553. **(See Chapter 18, "Limited Liability Company (LLC)")**

www.irs.gov/pub/irs-pdf/f8832.pdf

Conversion of a C-Corporation to an S-Corporation

A C-corporation can convert to an S-corporation if it meets all of the requirements. However, certain C-corporations are ineligible to convert to an S-corporation, which are: (1) any corporation that is a financial institution and that uses a certain reserve method of accounting for bad debts; (2) an insurance company; (3) an electing (possessions) corporation; and (4) a Dynamic Information Systems Corporation (DISC) or former DISC.

When an eligible C-corporation converts to S-corporation status, and assets are acquired from the C-corporation in a tax-free carryover basis transaction, the acquired assets are subject to "built-in gains tax" on the appreciation of the assets at the highest corporate tax rate (35% prior to 2018 and 21% in 2018 and subsequent years) if the acquired assets are sold or disposed of within a 5-year recognition period that begins on the date of the conversion (this was made permanent on 12/18/2015 by the "Protecting Americans from Tax Hikes Act of 2015"). In other words, the S-corporation must hold the assets for 5 years following the conversion in order to avoid paying the built-in gains tax on the appreciation of the acquired assets from the C-corporation. The original 10-year recognition period was reduced to 7 years for sales in 2009 and 2010, and to 5 years for sales in 2011, 2012, and 2013, reverting back to 10-years in 2014, before the 5-year recognition period was made permanent in 2015.
- **Example** – A calendar year C-corporation converted to an S-corporation effective Jan. 1, 2008. The S-corporation acquired assets in a tax-free carryover basis transaction from the C-corporation. The S-corporation would be subject to the built-in gains tax if the acquired assets were sold in 2009 through 2012; would not be subject to the built-in gains tax if the acquired assets were sold in 2013 or 2015 (5-year recognition period); but would be subject to the built-in gains tax if the acquired assets were sold in 2014 (10-year recognition period).

If an S-corporation has to pay the built-in gains tax, the tax is in addition to – and not in lieu of – the tax that may be imposed on its shareholders under the rules applicable to S-corporations. To replicate the effects of C-corporation taxation, the shareholders or members are subject to tax on the corporate-level gain, net of the corporate-level tax. This result is achieved by permitting the shareholders or members to treat the corporate-level tax as a loss that has the same character as the gain that gives rise to the tax.
- **Example** – Suppose an S-corporation sells an asset, carried over from when it converted from a C-corporation, during the 5-year recognition period, and realizes a $100 long-term capital gain on the sale. If the S-corporation recognizes a $100 long-term capital gain on the sale, it would also incur and have to pay a $35 built-in gains tax. After the S-corporation pays the built-in gains tax, the shareholders (members) would recognize a $100 long-term capital gain and a $35 capital loss, resulting in a net long-term capital gain of $65 that is recognized by the shareholders or members.

Conversion of an S-Corporation Back to a C-Corporation – The Tax Cuts and Jobs Act (TCJA) contains two generally favorable provisions that allows applicable "eligible S- corporations" to revoke their S-corporation status after enactment of the TCJA. For purposes of both provisions, an eligible S-corporation is one that had previously been a C-corporation (before enactment of the TCJA) and elected to convert back to a C-corporation following the enactment of the TCJA and: (1) revokes its S-corporation election during the two-year period beginning on the date of enactment of the TCJA; and (2) the owners of the stock on the date of revocation of S-corporation status are the same as, and such owners hold the stock in the same proportions as, on the date of enactment of the TCJA. The first provision relates to accounting method changes required as a result of an S-corporation's conversion back to a C-corporation. Specifically, the TCJA provides that, in the case of an eligible terminated S-corporation, any section 481 adjustment arising from an accounting method change attributable to the corporation's revocation of its S-corporation election will be taken into account ratably during the six-tax year period beginning with the year of the accounting method change. Thus, a corporation that must change a method of accounting (e.g. from the cash method to the accrual method) as a result of the revocation of its S-corporation election would include any income resulting from that change over six tax years (as opposed to four-years under the old law).

The second provision revises the treatment of distributions made by corporations following their conversion back to C-corporation status. Under the law in effect in 2017 and prior years, distributions by an S-corporation that revokes its S-corporation status are generally treated as coming first from the earnings and profits (E&P) of the corporation during the post-transition termination period, which means the distributions are treated as dividends received by the shareholders and taxable at ordinary income tax rates. Whereas, under the TCJA, distributions by an S-corporation that revokes its S-corporation status are generally treated as coming pro-rata from E&P and the "accumulated adjustments account" (AAA) of the corporation during the post-transition termination period. This means that only the distributions received by the shareholders coming from E&P are taxable as ordinary income but the distributions coming from AAA are considered already taxed and will be only subject to capital gains treatment upon disposition. Therefore, the treatment of distributions is favorable to the shareholders under the TCJA.

In August 2018, the IRS issued Revenue Procedure 2018-44 which provides guidance on switching back from an S-corporation to C-corporation status.
www.irs.gov/pub/irs-drop/rp-18-44.pdf

Compensation of S-Corporation Shareholders/Employees

Most S-corporations have shareholders or members performing substantial services for the corporation as officers and otherwise. The term "employee" includes an officer of a corporation or any individual who has the status of an employee. Corporate officers are clearly employees, and any payments to them for performance of services should be considered wages subject to payroll taxes and federal income tax withholding. Reasonable salaries paid to S-corporation shareholders/members have not been determined, but such salaries should usually follow industry standards. Sources of information on comparable compensation for services include the U.S. Department of Labor's Bureau of Labor Statistics, employment agencies, and a market analysis. One key in defending a claimed compensation amount is to document all research to support the amount. **(See Chapter 14, "Independent Contractors/Non-Employees")**

318

Some factors considered by the courts in determining reasonable compensation are: training and experience; duties and responsibilities; time and effort devoted to the business; dividend history; payments to non-shareholder employees; timing and manner of paying bonuses to key people; what comparable businesses pay for similar services; compensation agreements; and the use of a formula to determine compensation.

Compensation that is disguised as S-corporation distributions to avoid self-employment taxes is subject to being (and often is) reclassified by the IRS. If the business is primarily a service business with the services performed by the principal shareholder(s), the IRS will tend to expect that the majority of the earnings of the business should be treated as compensation (salary). A service S-corporation with large dividend payouts compared to the amount treated as compensation could be a potential candidate for an IRS audit. Beginning in 2013, the additional 0.9% Medicare surtax imposed by the Affordable Care Act (ACA) on high-income earners (but not on employers) provides an even greater incentive for shareholders to take less salary and more cash as a distribution from the corporation. **(See Chapter 2, "0.9% Medicare Surtax"); (See Chapter 14, "Voluntary Classification Settlement Program (VCSP)")**

Determining a shareholder-employee's reasonable compensation is dependent upon a number of factors and is far from an exact science – there is no right answer for reasonable compensation, but there are wrong ones, such as guessing at what your salary should be. Any reasonable compensation figure can be challenged by the IRS. Surviving a challenge requires backup data to support your figure. The IRS and tax courts have made it clear that S-corporation shareholder-employees should both research and document how their reasonable compensation figure was reached. As with any other wage determination, you should consider all the available information, and make a rational determination. You should be aware that: (1) the IRS is now looking much more closely at reasonable compensation for S-corporation shareholder-employees; (2) IRS audits of S-corporations are up 33% and are expected to continue increasing; and (3) the cost of an IRS reclassification is high – typically more than double the original tax that would have been due.

In addition to low compensation/salaries, loans made by S-corporations to employee/shareholders have also been attacked successfully by the IRS and reclassified as compensation, as has paying personal expenses out of corporate accounts, and distribution of assets to employee/shareholders rather than cash. If the IRS is successful in making such reclassifications, they can not only collect back employment taxes but can also assert significant penalties exceeding 100% of the employment taxes due to failure to timely deposit the taxes, failure to timely file employment tax returns, failure to withhold income taxes on compensation, and even negligence. However, if you do not take any funds out of an S-corporation in a year, you are not required to pay yourself a reasonable salary in that year. Also, if the S-corporation is not profitable in a year, you are not required to pay yourself and other shareholders a reasonable salary.

Watson Case – Revenue Ruling 59-221 was the IRS's incentive to start taking aim at taxpayers who abuse the employment tax advantage of S-corporations by minimizing salaries. In February 2012, the Eighth Circuit affirmed the district court's decision in the Watson Case. Watson, in many respects, was a precedent-setting case in the S-corporation reasonable compensation arena as it shed much needed light on the methodology the IRS and the courts will employ to determine an amount of reasonable compensation. David Watson – like many of the subjects of reasonable compensation scrutiny who are in a service oriented business – was a CPA. He was also the sole shareholder and employee of the S-corporation that in turn was a 25% shareholder in a very successful accounting firm. Watson's share of the revenue generated by the accounting firm was allocated to his S-corporation, which would then pay Watson a salary and distribute earnings to him from the accounting firm. Any amounts not paid out in salary by the corporation were reported by Watson as his share of the S-corporation's income on his personal tax return, where it was not subject to payroll tax. In Watson, the court held that an S-corporation shareholder-employee (Watson) who paid himself $24,000 in salary per year in 2002 and 2003 while receiving $203,651 and $175,470, respectively in distributions, in those years was not reasonably compensated for his services. The court further upheld the district court's determination of an annual reasonable compensation amount of $93,000, requiring Watson to re-characterize $69,000 of distributions in each year as salary. As a result, the S-corporation and Watson were held liable for over $23,000 in payroll taxes, penalties, and interest. The result was that Watson was required to pay himself about 50% of the S-corporation's profits in salary.

http://media.ca8.uscourts.gov/opndir/12/02/111589P.pdf www.irs.gov/pub/irs-wd/03-0026.pdf

Fleischer Case – Service providers who wish to have income from the services they provide be treated as income of their S-corporations should draft or revise their independent contractor agreements so that payments are made to their S-corporations, not to them as individuals (See T.C. Memo. 2016-238)

www.ustaxcourt.gov/UstcInOp/OpinionViewer.aspx?ID=11057

If you get audited, you may have to compromise with the IRS examiner. No matter what Reasonable Compensation figure you present to the examiner, it will be suspect, because the examiner knows that you probably pulled the figure out of thin air. Usually the Reasonable Compensation figure you come up with is somewhere between the figure you submitted to the IRS examiner and the figure being proposed by the examiner. Negotiation with the examiner is the key. You can use the Watson case to support your Reasonable Compensation figure, and if you get lucky, maybe it will be accepted by the auditor.

Deduction of Health Insurance Premiums by 2% Shareholders – 2-percent shareholder-employees of an S-corporation are eligible for an above-the-line deduction on their individual tax returns of the cost of health insurance premiums paid during the year if the medical care coverage was established by the S-corporation and the shareholder meets the other self-employed medical insurance deduction requirements. If, however, the shareholder or the shareholder's spouse was eligible to participate in any subsidized health care plan, then the shareholder is not entitled to the above-the-line deduction. In accordance with IRS Notice 2008-1, a shareholder may claim an above-the-line deduction for health insurance premiums that are ultimately paid by the S-corporation and reported as taxable compensation on the shareholder's W-2. This also includes premiums that 2% shareholders pay for Medicare premiums. **(See Chapter 11, "Self-Employed Health Insurance Premiums")**

Shareholder's Stock Basis in an S-Corporation

A shareholder/member's initial stock basis in a newly formed S-corporation is equal to cash contributed and the lesser of the adjusted basis or the fair market value (FMV) of any property contributed to start the business. Generally, transfers of money and property to a corporation in exchange for stock can be made on a tax-free basis (the rules are the same for both C and S-corporations). Where the stock (ownership) is actually purchased, its basis is equal to its purchase price. If a shareholder holds stock in a C-corporation that elects S-corporation status, the shareholder/member's initial basis in the S-corporation is his/her basis in the C-corporation stock at the time of conversion. It is irrelevant whether the C-corporation possessed earnings and profits, retained earnings, or a net operating loss, as those are corporate level attributes. Stock or ownership in an S-corporation acquired by gift is generally the donor's basis, and stock or ownership acquired by inheritance is generally the FMV of the stock at the date of death of the decedent. **(See Chapter 22, "Basis of Property Inherited or Gifted")**

A shareholder (member) must increase the basis of his S-corporation stock (ownership percentage) for the following items:

- Capital contributions;
- Non-separately stated income shown on Schedule K-1, 1120S;
- Separately stated income (capital gain, Section 1231 gain, interest, dividends,etc.) shown on Schedule K-1, 1120-S;
- Tax-exempt income; and
- The excess of the deductions for depletion over the basis of property subject todepletion.

A shareholder (member) must decrease the basis of his S-corporation stock (ownership percentage) for the following items:

- Distributions to shareholders;
- Non-separately stated loss shown on Schedule K-1, 1120-S;
- Separately stated items of loss and deduction shown on Schedule K-1, 1120-S;
- Non-deductible expenses that are not properly chargeable to a capital account; and
- The amount of the shareholder deduction for depletion to the extent such deduction does not exceed the shareholder's share of the adjusted basis of any oil and gas property held by the S-corporation.
- Charitable donations reduce the shareholders basis by the cost of an asset donated instead of by the value of the asset on the date of donation.

A shareholder's or member's basis in S-corporation stock is adjusted in thefollowing order:

- First, basis is adjusted for the required increases in basis. This takes basis to its highest possible point;
- Next, stock basis is reduced by distributions prior to any reduction for losses or nondeductible expenses;
- Next, basis is reduced for nondeductible expenses;and
- Finally, after reduction for distributions and non-deductible expenses, basis is reduced by any items of loss (but not below zero).

A stockholder/member's basis in an S-corporation received in exchange for property transferred to a corporation is equal to the lower of the adjusted basis or the fair market value (FMV) of the property transferred, but the stockholder's "capital account" (ownership percentage) is based on the transferred property's FMV. Transferring assets subject to liabilities in exchange for S-corporation stock does not result in boot to the transferor unless the corporation assumes liabilities that exceed the transferor's adjusted basis in the transferred assets. The capital accounts (ownership percentage) of the shareholders generally will remain the same after an S-corporation is formed, unless there are additional contributions made by the shareholders that change the ownership percentages.

- **Example** – Betty and John form an LLC that is treated as an S-corporation for tax purposes. Betty contributes $300,000 in cash and John contributes land with an adjusted basis of $400,000, but which is worth $1.1 million. The land is subject to a nonrecourse loan of $1 million. Unlike treatment as a partnership, John's basis in the S-corporation would be $0, and he would have to recognize a gain of $600,000 ($1,000,000 nonrecourse loan, less $400,000 adjusted basis of land). Betty's basis would be $300,000. Betty's capital account would be $300,000 and John's capital account would be $100,000

($1.1 million FMV of contributed land, less $1 million nonrecourse loan). So, their ownership interests would be: Betty – 75% ($300,000); and John – 25% ($100,000). (See the example of the same situation when establishing a partnership).

- **Example** – You contribute a personal computer in exchange for stock (ownership) in an S-corporation. The computer has an adjusted basis of $2,000 (purchase price) and a FMV of $1,500. So, both your basis and the capital account in the S-corporation would be $1,500. However, if the computer had already been used in a business and Section 179 expensing had already been taken, your basis would be $0 and your capital account would be $1,500

A shareholder (not the S-corporation) must keep track of his or her basis in the corporation for three reasons: (1) to determine gain or loss upon sale of the stock; (2) If the corporation allocates a loss to a shareholder, to determine the amount of the loss the shareholder may currently utilize and how much must be suspended and carried forward; and (3) to determine the taxability of distributions received by the shareholder from the corporation.

There are two distinct types of basis in an S-corporation – the shareholder (member) holds a basis in the stock (ownership) of the corporation, but also in any debt that is owed directly from the corporation back to the shareholder. However, a shareholder's debt basis has but one specific purpose – to utilize losses allocated to the shareholder in excess of his or her stock basis – and has no bearing on determining the gain or loss on the sale of stock (ownership in the S-corporation), nor does it impact the taxability of an S-corporation's distributions.

Basis of S-Corporation Stock Received in Exchange for Services – An individual who receives stock in exchange for services to a corporation must recognize income equal to the value of the stock received.

Basis Adjustment for Charitable Contributions – The rule that a shareholder's basis in the stock of an S-corporation is reduced by the shareholder's pro rata share of the adjusted basis of the property contributed by the S-corporation for charitable purposes was made permanent by the "Protecting Americans from Tax Hikes Act of 2015." **(See Chapter 12, "Charitable Contribution Deduction")**

- **Example** – The only shareholder in an S-corporation has a basis of $50,000 in his S-corporation stock at the beginning of the year. The S-corporation contributes property with an adjusted basis of $30,000 and a FMV of $60,000 to a charitable organization. The shareholder may take a full $60,000 charitable deduction on his tax return, and the basis of his S-corporation stock is reduced to $20,000 ($50,000 - $30,000).

Shareholder's Debt Basis in an S-Corporation

Debt basis in an S-Corporation is only relevant in utilizing losses, and debt basis is only utilized to absorb losses after stock basis has been reduced to zero. Under the partnership rules, a partner gets basis in his share of all the partnership's debts, even those owed to third parties. However, a shareholder in an S-corporation gets basis only for debts made directly from the shareholder to the S-corporation. Amounts owed by the S-corporation to anyone but the shareholder do nothing to increase the shareholder's debt basis. One thing a shareholder can do who needs debt basis in order to use anticipated losses, is to borrow money from the bank, loan it to the corporation, have the corporation give him a security interest in the assets of the S-corporation, and then give the bank a security interest in his/her S-corporation stock. That will generate the necessary debt basis increase.

(See Chapter 18, "Partner's Assumption of Debt")

In July 2014, the IRS issued final regulations that clarify when a shareholder of an S-corporation can increase basis in the S-corporation because of the S-corporation's indebtedness to the shareholder. As a result, new opportunities may exist for S-corporation shareholders to deduct losses. For many years, shareholders have tried to argue that by merely giving a personal guarantee to amounts borrowed by the S-corporation from a third party, the shareholder should be given debt basis, but time after time, the courts have shot this argument down. The new regulations support what the courts have concluded in the past. The final regulations provide two different standards.

- For a shareholder's loan to an S-corporation, the debt must be "bonafide."
- For a guarantee of S-corporation debt, there must be an "actual outlay" by the shareholder.

A shareholder does not increase basis in an S-corporation merely by guaranteeing a loan or acting as a surety, accommodation party, or in any similar capacity. In the past, efforts of shareholders to increase debt basis in an S-corporation by having another related party (S-corporation 2) make a loan to the first S-corporation has always been thwarted by the requirement that in order for a shareholder to obtain debt basis, the shareholder had to make an "economic outlay" that leaves him "poorer in a material sense." But the new regulations largely do away with the economic outlay requirement that has been responsible for preventing shareholders from increasing their debt basis in the past. Instead the economic outlay requirement has been replaced by the "bona fide indebtedness" requirement which appears much more permissive than the economic outlay requirement. The bona fide indebtedness requirement provides that regardless of how debt between a shareholder and an S-corporation is created, the shareholder will be given debt basis if the end result is that the debt between the S-corporation and the shareholder is bona fide indebtedness.

By substituting "bona fide indebtedness" for "economic outlay" the final regulations provide one nearly full-proof method for fixing the related party mess. How? The IRS provides the following example:

- ***Example*** – *Loan restructuring through distributions – Shareholder A is the sole shareholder of two S corporations, S1 and S2. In March 2013, S1 made a loan to S2. In December 2013, S1 assigned its creditor position in the note to shareholder A by making a distribution of the note to shareholder A. Under local law, after S1 distributed the note to shareholder A, S2 was relieved of its liability to S1 and was directly liable to shareholder A. Whether S2 is indebted to shareholder A rather than to S1 is determined under general federal tax principles and depends upon all of the facts and circumstances. See paragraph (a)(2)(i) of this section. If the note constitutes bona fide indebtedness from S2 to shareholder A, the note increases shareholder A's basis of indebtedness in S2 under paragraph (a)(2)(i) of this section.*

The settlement of a debt is seldom a taxable event. However, for S-corporation purposes, when a shareholder uses losses to reduce debt basis, his basis in the debt will drop below the face amount. As a result, if the debt is repaid prior to the basis in the debt being restored to face value, the shareholder will have to recognize a gain – generally taxable – for the excess amount (the difference between the amount repaid and the shareholder's basis in the debt). Of course, the shareholder's basis is usually identical to the face amount of the debt, which is precisely why there is rarely a taxable amount upon repayment of the debt.

- **Example** – Bill owns 100% of an S-corporation. At the beginning of the year, Bill had a stock basis of $50,000 and a debt basis of $100,000. During the year, the S-corporation allocated to Bill a non-separately stated loss of $82,000, long-term capital gain of $10,000, and a Section 1231 loss of $12,000. The basis in Bill's stock at the end of the year is computed as follows: $50,000+ $10,000 long-term capital gain - $60,000 loss = $0 ending basis. Carried-over loss = $22,000 excess non-separately stated loss + $12,000 Section 1231 loss = $34,000. Therefore, Bill must recognize a $34,000 capital gain if the S-corporation repays the $100,000 debt before the debt basis is restored – the excess of the $100,000 repayment over Bill's $66,000 basis in the debt ($100,000 - $34,000) = $66,000). To restore the debt basis, Bill must realize a net increase (other than capital contributions) in the basis of his S-corporation stock of at least $34,000 in a subsequent year. When this happens, the S-corporation can repay the $100,000 debt without Bill having to recognize a $34,000 capital gain. If he realizes a net increase sufficient to cover the difference in a subsequent year, and a repayment of the debt is made, the increase is deemed to occur immediately before the repayment, sparing Bill from having to recognize a capital gain upon repayment of the debt.

Computation of S-Corporation Income

Taxable income of an S-corporation is generally computed on Form 1120S in the same manner as for an individual, except deductions are not allowed for personal exemptions, foreign taxes, and standard or itemized deductions. Although the tax rules for S-corporations are similar to those for partnerships, there are some differences: An S-corporation shareholder's basis does not include his/her portion of all of the S-corporation's debt, and a shareholder's direct loans to the S-corporation result in a separate "debt basis" in the S-corporation. The passive activity rules can apply to some S-corporation shareholders, but they do not apply to general partners in a partnership. Fringe benefits (health Insurance, etc.) of a 2% or more shareholder are included in the shareholder's income and are deductible by the S-corporation as a business expense. But "retirement plans" are not considered fringe benefits. **(See Chapter 9, "Contributions to Qualified Employee Retirement Plans")**

S-corporation income must be allocated among its shareholders (members in the case of LLCs) based on the number of shares owned or the percentage of ownership. Distributions of S-corporation income is taxed under a two-tier approach. First the distribution is a tax-free reduction of the shareholder's basis in the corporation's stock. Then, any distribution in excess of the shareholder's stock basis is treated as gain from the sale or exchange of the underlying stock. Because S-corporation income first increases a shareholder's basis, the subsequent reduction in basis for the distribution of the income usually will not create a taxable event. However, if the distribution is in excess of the shareholder's stock basis, the shareholder will have a taxable capital gain for the difference. It is completely irrelevant whether the shareholder has basis in the debt of the S-corporation, because the excess distribution may not be applied to reduce the debt basis. Gain or loss is recognized by shareholders upon the sale of S-corporation stock. A passive S-corporation shareholder is subject to the passive-activity loss limitations. **(See Above, "Shareholder's Stock Basis in an S-Corporation"; & "Shareholder's Debt Basis in an S-Corporation")**

In determining S-corporation income on Form 1120S – rental income, interest income, dividends, royalties, capital gains and losses, tax-exempt income, and other portfolio income, as well as Section 179 expensing, passive activity items, etc. must be shown separately from the S-corporation's ordinary income on the S-corporation's Schedule K and each shareholder's Schedule K-1, because these are items that must be shown separately on the shareholders' individual tax returns (similar to a Partnership tax return). **(See Chapter 5, "Portfolio Income"); (See Chapter 7, "Rental Income"); (See Chapter 16, "Section 179 First-Year Expensing")**

Schedule M-3, Form 1120S, "Net Income (Loss) Reconciliation for S-Corporations with Total Assets of $10 Million or More" does not have to be completed unless the S-corporation has assets of $10 million or more. Question 10 on Form 1120S is "Does the corporation satisfy both of the following conditions." If the answer is "Yes," then the corporation is not required to complete Schedules L and M-1. The two conditions are:

- The corporation's total receipts for the tax year were less than $250,000; and
- The corporation's total assets at the end of the year were less than $250,000.

Distribution to Shareholder Exceeds Shareholder's Basis – When a distribution to a shareholder exceeds the shareholder's basis in his stock, the excess generates a capital gain. By requiring distributions to reduce basis before losses, it is more likely that a distribution will be a nontaxable return of basis, while losses will be suspended and carried forward. This is typically a more desirous result than if the order rules were switched, which would generate useable losses but also current capital gain on the excess distribution. To the extent losses exceed the remaining stock basis after reductions for distributions and nondeductible expenses, the excess losses are applied to reduce any basis the shareholder has in indebtedness of the S-corporation to the shareholder. To the extent the losses exceed the shareholder's basis in both stock and debt, the losses are suspended and may be carried forward indefinitely. **(See Above, "Shareholder's Debt Basis in an S-Corporation")**

- **Example** – Bill begins the year with a basis of $10,000 in his S-corporation stock. During the year, the S-corporation accumulates $4,000 of ordinary income and has a $14,000 long-term capital loss, and makes a $10,000 distribution to Bill. In adjusting his basis at the end of the year, Bill begins by increasing his beginning basis to its highest point by the $4,000 of ordinary income. The adjusted basis of $14,000 is then decreased first by the $10,000 distribution to him, reducing Bill's basis to $4,000. Bill then reduces his basis to zero with $4,000 of the $14,000 long-term capital loss. Assuming Bill has no basis in the indebtedness of the S-corp., the remaining $10,000 of long-term capital loss must be carried forward, where it will be treated as a newly incurred $10,000 loss at the beginning of the next year.

A shareholder can make an irrevocable election to reduce his basis for losses prior to reducing it for nondeductible expenses. Under the default order rules (see example above), if a shareholder's nondeductible expenses exceed his stock basis, they do not carry forward to reduce basis in a succeeding year. If, however, a shareholder makes the irrevocable election to reverse the order rules, any nondeductible expenses that don't currently reduce basis will carry forward and eventually be available, reducing basis in a subsequent year.

- **Example** – At the beginning of the year, Bill has a $10,000 basis. During the year, the S-corporation allocates $5,000 of income to Bill, $17,000 of nondeductible expenses, and $10,000 of losses. If Bill doesn't make an election to reverse the order rules, his basis will be adjusted as follows: Beginning basis = $10,000 + $5,000 income = $15,000 - $15,000 of nondeductible expenses = $0 ending basis; carry-over losses = $10,000; carry-over nondeductible expenses = $0 ending basis. However, if Bill makes the election, his basis will be adjusted as follows: Beginning basis $10,000 + $5,000 income = $15,000 - $10,000 carry-over losses, and - $5,000 nondeductible expenses = $0 ending basis; carry-over losses = $0; carry-over nondeductible expenses = $12,000.

Liquidation of an S-Corporation

The liquidation of an S-corporation is a complex area of tax law. Part of the complexity arises from the two different aspects of liquidation, one at the corporation level and one at the shareholder level. Complete corporate liquidation rules are set-forth in the Code – Gain or Loss to Shareholders in Corporate Liquidations (shareholder level), and – Gain or Loss Recognized on Property Distributed in Complete Liquidation (corporation level). A corporation is considered liquidated when it has distributed all of its assets and made provisions for all of its liabilities. When an S-corporation has been liquidated, the final corporate return can be timely filed and the final payments to the shareholders can be made.

An S-corporation is required to file Form 966 with the IRS within 30 days after adopting a plan of dissolution or liquidation. An additional Form 966 must be filed within 30 days after adopting an amendment or supplement to the original plan. A certified copy of the dissolution must be attached to the Form 966. The form must be filed whether or not the shareholders recognize gain or loss from the liquidation. A formal plan of liquidation is not required (Kennermer v. Comm.). However, a formal adoption is evidently necessary to satisfy the reporting requirements. The existence of a plan of liquidation is often overlooked, but it is important because it establishes that the corporation is undergoing a complete liquidation. This is necessary to qualify liquidating distributions from the corporation for sale or exchange treatment by the shareholders.
www.irs.gov/pub/irs-pdf/f966.pdf   www.ustaxcourt.gov/InOpHistoric/RENDINA.TCM.WPD.pdf

After a plan of dissolution or liquidation is adopted, liquidating distributions made to shareholders are reported to shareholders on Form 1099-DIV, "Dividends and Distributions," instead of on Schedule K-1 of Form 1120S. The amount reported on Form 1099-DIV flows to Schedule D of the shareholder's Form 1040 as the amount realized on the stock redemptions. The shareholder's stock basis is deducted to arrive at the shareholder's gain or loss. The S-corporation must file its final Form 1120S by the 15th day of the third month following the end of the month in which it liquidates. Box H(1) on Form 1120S and the "Final K-1" Box on Schedule K-1 should be checked to indicate these are the final forms that will be filed for the liquidating corporation. A corporation is considered liquidated when it has distributed all of its assets and made provisions for all of its liabilities. **(See Chapter 5, "Dividends"); (See Chapter 6, "Qualified Dividends")**

S-Corporation Level – In a liquidation, an S-corporation recognizes gain or loss as if its property is sold at fair market value (FMV). This treatment applies when the assets are either distributed to the shareholders and/or sold and the proceeds distributed to the shareholders. The character of the gain or loss as capital or ordinary income depends on the character of the asset distributed or sold. Also, the depreciation recapture rules apply to distributions or sales that are done in liquidation. The taxable gain flows through to the shareholders under the normal S-corporation pass-through rules. The liquidating S-corporation will not recognize corporate-level tax unless the built-in gains tax applies as a result of the corporation being a former C-corporation.

- **Example** – John is the 100% shareholder of an S-corporation that is liquidating. The corporation has assets with a current FMV of $100,000 and a basis of $75,000. The assets are distributed to John in the liquidation. When the assets are distributed, the S-corporation will recognize a $25,000 gain. Since the corporation was never a C-corporation, there is no built-in tax at the corporate level.

When a shareholder assumes a liability of the liquidating corporation or takes property subject to a liability, the FMV of the distributed property is not less than the liability. Therefore, if the liability exceeds the FMV of the distributed property, the amount of the liability will be the FMV of the property.

- **Example** – An S-corporation owns a machine with an adjusted basis of $15,000 and a FMV of $17,000, but with a loan on it with a balance of $20,000. Therefore, the machine's FMV is deemed to be $20,000 for determining gain or loss. Therefore, when the machine is distributed to a shareholder in a liquidation transaction, the shareholder's stock basis will increase by $5,000 ($20,000 - $15,000 adjusted basis of machine).

When loss assets are distributed to related persons, "anti-abuse rules" prevent loss recognition on distributions to related persons. The definition of related persons are shareholders who own, directly or indirectly, more than 50% of the outstanding stock of the corporation. Losses cannot be recognized when the S-corporation liquidates if the distribution to related persons are not pro rata.

- **Example** – An S-corporation is liquidating and is owned 75% by Betty and 25% by John. The corporation has two assets – X and Y. X has a FMV of $10,000 and an adjusted basis of $15,000; Y has a FMV of $20,000 and an adjusted basis of $17,000. A loss can be recognized from the distribution of asset X if the corporation distributes 75% interest in each of the two assets to Betty and 25% to John. However, if the corporation distributes asset X (the loss asset) to Betty and the Y asset (the gain asset) to John, it cannot recognize the loss because the loss asset was distributed on a non-pro rata basis to a related person (Betty who owns more than 50% of the stock). However, if the Y asset is distributed to Betty and the X asset is distributed to John, it can recognize the loss because the loss asset was not distributed to a related person (John who owns less than 50% of the stock). If the last situation occurs, Betty's stock basis will increase by $3,000 ($20,000 - $17,000 basis of asset Y); and John's stock basis will decrease by $5,000 ($10,000 - $15,000 basis of asset X).

Also, losses cannot be recognized when an S-corporation liquidates if the property distributed to a related person (50% or more owner) is "disqualified property," even if the property is distributed on a pro rata basis. Disqualified property is property acquired by the liquidating corporation in a Par. 351 transfer or as a contribution to capital during the five-year period ending on the distribution date. It also includes property whose adjusted basis is determined in whole or in part by reference to the adjusted basis of other disqualifying property. Any losses disallowed are permanently lost. In addition, loses cannot be recognized if the distribution has a "tax avoidance purpose." A property has a tax avoidance purpose if it had a built-in loss in either a Par. 351 transaction or as a contribution to the capital acquired by the corporation within two years of adopting the plan of liquidation by the corporation. If this anti-abuse rule is applicable, the basis of the distributed property for computing the loss is reduced by the built-in loss that existed on the date the property was contributed to the corporation. This rule applies even if the distribution is to a shareholder owning 50% or less of the corporation's stock.

Shareholder Level – Pass-through items in the year of liquidation are allocated in the normal way – by the shareholders' percentage of ownership. Liquidation distributions received by shareholders are treated as full payment for the exchange of stock. A shareholder's stock basis is determined at the end of the S-corporation's tax year. The adjusted basis of stock held in a liquidating corporation is adjusted for the year's pass-through items prior to determination of gain or loss from the liquidating distributions. If a shareholder has different bases in different blocks of stock, the computation of gain or loss depends on whether there is a single distribution or a series of liquidating distributions. The shareholder recognizes gain when the adjusted basis of each block of stock has been recovered. Loss is not recognized until the S-corporation has made its final distribution.

- **Example** – Jack holds two blocks of stock in an S-corporation. One block has 10 shares with a basis of $10,000; the second block has 20 shares with a basis of $30,000. The corporation distributes $40,000 cash in a single payment to Jack in return for all of his stock. The $40,000 is allocated pro rata to the two blocks of stock. $13,333 is allocated to block one (10/30X $40,000), and $26,667 is allocated to block two (20/30 X $40,000). Jack recognizes a $3,333 gain on block one ($13,333 - $10,000 basis) and a $3,333 loss on block two ($26,667 - $30,000 basis). A $3,333 liquidating distribution payment is made to Jack for his stock in block one and reported to him on Form 1099-DIV. A $3,333 loss for Jack's stock in block two is reported to him on another Form 1099-DIV.

- **Example** – Assume the same facts as in the previous example. If Jack receives $40,000 in 2013 and an additional $100,000 in 2014, each distribution is allocated ratably among the blocks in proportion to the number of shares in each block to the total number of shares held. The 2013 distribution is allocated the same as in the previous example. Jack recognizes a $3,333 gain on block 1. The basis of block 1 is reduced to zero after the distribution. Jack recognizes no gain or loss on block 2, and the basis in block 2 is $3,333. The 2014 distribution is allocated $33,333 to block 1 (10/30 X $100,000) and $66,667 is allocated to block 2 (20/30 X $100,000). Jack recognizes a $33,333 gain on block 1 ($33,333 - $0 basis) and a $63,334 gain on block 2 ($66,667 - $3,333 basis). Jack's gains on the liquidation of his stock are reported to him on Forms 1099-DIV.

Long-term or short-term classification of a liquidation that qualifies for capital gain treatment depends on the shareholder's holding period. **(See Chapter 6, "Reporting Capital Gains and Losses")**

If the S-corporation stock qualifies for Section 1244 treatment, the loss on the stock up to the limitation is reported on Form 4797. **(See Chapter 6, "Section 1244 Small Business Stock")**

- **Example** – XYZ S-corporation liquidated. It qualified as a small business corporation when it was created. Its assets were sold to pay off its debts. Therefore, nothing was left to distribute to the shareholders. Betty, a single taxpayer and the only shareholder of the S-corporation, has a $125,000 basis in her stock. Betty claims a $50,000 loss on Form 4797, Part II. The remaining $75,000 loss is reported on Schedule D as a capital loss taking into account her holding period.

A shareholder's basis in the assets received in an S-corporation liquidation is the FMV at the time of the distribution of the assets to the shareholder. Basis is not affected by the shareholder assuming corporate liabilities or receiving corporate property that is subject to a liability.

- **Example** – XYZ S-corporation incorporated in 2007 and is liquidating in 2013. Jack is the only shareholder of XYZ with an adjusted stock basis of $2,000. He receives a car as a liquidating distribution that has a FMV of $15,000 and an attached liability (loan) of $10,000. XYZ has an adjusted basis of $13,000 in the car, so XYZ recognizes a $2,000 gain ($15,000 - $13,000 basis) by treating the car as if it were sold for FMV. The $2,000 gain will increase Jack's basis in his corporation stock to $4,000 ($2,000 +$2,000). Jack receives a $5,000 liquidating distribution ($15,000 - $10,000 liability assumed), which will be reported to him as a $1,000 capital gain on Form 1099-DIV ($5,000 - $4,000 adjusted stock basis). He will have a $15,000 basis in the car and a $10,000 liability.

A bad debt deduction may be available to an S-corporation shareholder under certain circumstances upon liquidation of the corporation. This occurs when a shareholder is unable to receive what is owed to him, or if a shareholder takes on responsibility for the payment of corporate debts to the extent the debts exceed the FMV of the assets received in the liquidation. The shareholder takes a deduction for the excess assumed debts as the debt is paid off. When a shareholder is allowed a bad debt deduction, the debt is reported as a short-term capital loss on Schedule D. **(See Chapter 6, "Non-Business Bad Debt")**

- **Example** – John received property from his solely owned S-corporation upon its liquidation. The property has a FMV of $30,000 and an attached debt (loan) of $35,000. John is treated as receiving $0 for his S-corporation stock. The first $30,000 of the debt repayment is considered his basis in the property he received in the distribution, and the remaining $5,000 of debt gives him a bad debt deduction as the payments are made by John.

In a complete liquidation, losses due to basis limitations that remain after the basis of the redeemed stock has been reduced to zero are lost (but assumed debt may result in a bad debt deduction). Because these losses are lost, shareholders in that situation might consider making additional capital contributions or loans prior to liquidation in order to create additional basis. Passive losses (resulting before liquidation proceedings) which are limited by the passive activity rules are suspended at the shareholder level and are carried forward indefinitely to offset future passive losses. Also, losses limited by the at-risk rules are eligible for indefinite carryover.

S-Corporation Becomes Totally Worthless

When an S-corporation's stock becomes totally worthless, shareholders who are considered passive owners are treated as having disposed of their entire interest in the S-corporation for passive activity loss purposes, allowing the shareholders to deduct all of their suspended passive losses from the S-corporation without regard to the passive activity loss rules – in other words the suspended passive losses can be deducted from active (non-passive) income. **(See Chapter 7, "Suspended Passive Losses")**

Rental Losses Against S-Corporation Income

You cannot write off rental losses against S-corporation income, if you "materially" participate in the S-corporation, i.e. if you work more than 100 hours per year, etc. in the S-corporation you cannot write off rental losses (passive losses) against the income (non-passive) generated from the S-corporation. But if you work less than 100 hours per year, etc. in the S-corporation, you can, because the income from the S-corporation would then be considered passive income. Material participation S-corporation income is "not" considered passive, even though it is considered passive for other purposes of the tax code. **(See Chapter 7, "Rental Income")**

Implementation of the 3.8% Net Investment Income Tax

In implementation of the 3.8% net investment income tax (NIIT) for S-corporations, net investment income (NII) includes: traditional pass-through investment income items (interest, dividends, rents, royalties, annuities – less allocable deductions) to owners/shareholders of S-corporations (whether passive or non-passive); gains or losses allocable to owners/shareholders of S-corporations from dispositions of marketable securities held in S-corporations (whether passive or non-passive); all business income or losses related to interests in passive S-corporation activities; gains or losses from the disposition of property (equipment) held in passive S-corporations; and gains or losses on the sale or disposition of passive interests in S-corporations. **(See Chapter 10, "3.8% Net Investment Income Tax")**

NII does not include: income or losses derived in the ordinary course of a non-passive S-corporation trade or business; gains or losses from the disposition of property (equipment) held in a non-passive S- corporation; and gains or losses on the sale or disposition of an interest in a non-passive S-corporation trade or business. A non-passive S-corporation is one in which a taxpayer "materially" participates in the management and/or operation of the entity.

- **Example** – For tax year 2014: Disposition of S-corporation stock in passive activity X results in a $20,000 loss for shareholder A; passive activity S-corporation Y has a gain of $32,000 for shareholder A; non-passive activity S-corporation Z has a gain of $60,000 for shareholder A; and the sale of marketable securities results in a gain of $8,000 for shareholder A. ShareholderA's gain applicable to the 3.8% NIIT is $20,000 (- $20,000 + $32,000 + $8,000). $20,000 of A's overall gain of $80,000 in 2014 is NII.

Suspended passive losses from a former passive activity (after the activity becomes active or non- passive) are allowed in the calculation of NII, but only to the extent of the non-passive income from the former passive activity.

Insurance Companies

New Rules for Life Settlements – Life settlements allow owners of life insurance policies that would otherwise be cancelled, resulting in little or no return, to instead recoup part of their losses by finding an institutional buyer willing to pay a percentage of the face amount of the policy, particularly if the life expectancy of the insured party is less than normal (i.e., 10 years or less). Although some tax may be owed on that amount, the net is generally more than if there was no life settlement market.

Under the TCJA, beginning in 2018, when determining the basis of a life insurance or annuity contract for a potential life settlement, no adjustment is required for mortality, expense, or other reasonable charges incurred under the contract. This change reverses the position taken by the IRS in Revenue Ruling 2009-13 that, upon the sale of the cash value of a life insurance contract, the insured's (seller's) basis was reduced by the cost of insurance for mortality, expense, or other reasonable charges incurred. This change also applies retroactively to transactions entered into after August 25, 2009, which coincides with the effective date of Revenue Ruling 2009-13. Therefore, taxpayers who paid additional taxes as a result of that Revenue Ruling and have returns from open tax years could potentially apply for a refund.
www.irs.gov/pub/irs-drop/rr-09-13.pdf

The TCJA also added some new reporting requirements that apply to life settlements and the payment of reportable death benefits occurring after December 31, 2017. The language of the TCJA refers to a "reportable policy sale," which means the acquisition of an interest in a life insurance contract, directly or indirectly, if the purchaser has no substantial family, business, or financial relationship with the insured apart from the purchaser's interest in the life insurance contract. This includes acquisition of an interest in a partnership, trust, or other entity that holds an interest in the life insurance contract. Any person who purchases a life insurance contract or any interest in a life insurance contract in a reportable policy sale during a tax year must report the following: (1) name, address, and taxpayer identification number (TIN) of the person; (2) name, address, and TIN of each recipient of payment in the reportable policy sale; (3) date of the sale; (4) name of the issuer of the life insurance contract sold and the policy number of the contract; and (5) the amount of each payment. Anyone required to report the above information must furnish to each person named a written statement showing: (1) name, address, and phone number of the person required to submit the report; and (2) information required to be shown on the return (see above), except that in the case of an issuer of a life insurance contract, the transfer-for-value statement is not required to include the amount of each payment. Also, the TCJA sets-forth that for transfers made after December 31, 2017, the exception to the transfer-for-value rules do not apply to a transfer of a life insurance contract, or any interest in a life insurance contract, that is a reportable policy sale (life settlement). As for the impact of this provision, in the typical life settlement, the acquirer is a hedge fund or a bank, which will likely know that it does not fall under the exception to the transfer-for-value rule. Thus, this provision is presumably intended to cut off the possibility of creating some mechanism to avoid the transfer-for-value rule, because it is going to apply to any reportable policy sale as that term is now defined.

Insurance Company Reserves – Under the TCJA, the rules for computation of insurance company reserves for both life and property and casualty (P&C) insurance companies are changed. Beginning in 2018, the TCJA provides that life insurance reserves for any contract are to be determined based on the greater of the net surrender value or 92.81% of the amount determined using the applicable tax reserve method. However, the tax reserves may not exceed the statutory reserve applicable to the contract as calculated for statutory reporting. Under a transition rule, life insurance companies are required to recalculate their 2017 reserves as if the 2018 TCJA rules were in effect then, compare it to their actual 2017 reserves and account for the difference over eight years beginning in 2018.

Prior to implementation of the TCJA, P&C loss reserves were discounted using a discount rate based on the applicable federal midterm rate. The TCJA changes the basis of the discount rate to the corporate bond yield curve, i.e. yields on investment grade corporate bonds with varying maturities. In addition to effectively increasing the discount rate, the TCJA extends the periods for determining loss payment patterns and repeals the election, allowing taxpayers to use their own historical loss payment pattern rather than the industrywide loss payment pattern for certain businesses. Similar to the transition rules applicable to life insurance companies, P&C insurance companies have to restate their reserves as of the end of 2017 and take the resulting reduction into account over eight years.

Adjustment for Change in Computing Reserves – Under the TCJA, the special 10-year adjustment period for taking into account changes in a life insurance company's basis for computing reserves is repealed. Beginning in 2018, the TCJA requires aligning reserve strengthening and weakening with the general rules under Section 481 for accounting method changes, which means that the strengthening or weakening of reserves is changed from a 10-year period of inclusion to a four-year period of inclusion for unfavorable changes and to a one-year period of inclusion for favorable changes.

Capitalization of Certain Policy Acquisition Expenses – The TCJA changes the rules that require insurance companies to capitalize and amortize a portion of policy acquisition expenses on certain specified insurance contracts. The TCJA extends the amortization period for such expenses from 120 months to 180 months and increases the percentage of expenses subject to the capitalization rule from: 1.75% to 2.1% for annuity contracts; 2.05% to 2.46% for group life insurance contracts; and 7.7% to 9.24% for all other specified insurance contracts.

Net Operating Loss Utilization – Under the TCJA, life insurance companies are subject to the new limits on net operating losses (NOLs) that are applicable to all noninsurance companies. As it is for noninsurance companies, NOLs arising for life insurance companies arising in tax years before December 31, 2017, will remain subject to the two-year carryback and 20-year carryforward rule until their expiration and also will continue to be available to offset 100% of taxable income. However, the new rules for NOLs that are applicable to noninsurance companies and life insurance companies do not apply to P&C insurance companies. The NOLs of P&C insurance companies are still subject to the old rules, i.e. can be carried back two years and carried forward 20 years and continue to be available to offset 100% of taxable income in subsequent years instead of 80% under the new rules. Therefore, consolidated insurance groups that include both life and P&C companies will have to separately track the different NOL limitations for each of their companies. **(See Chapter 8, "Net Operating Loss (NOL)")**

Proration Rules for P&C Insurance Companies – The TCJA modifies the proration rules for P&C insurance companies with respect to tax-exempt interest and the dividends-received deduction by replacing the 15% reduction under the law in effect in 2017 and prior years with a reduction equal to 5.25% divided by the top corporate tax rate. Since the corporate tax rate is a flat 21% rate beginning in 2018, the current proration percentage is 25%, resulting in the same after-tax yield for tax-exempt bonds as under prior law.

Base Erosion and Anti-Abuse Tax – The specific language of the TCJA indicates that the Base Erosion and Anti-Abuse Tax (BEAT) is imposed on the gross amount of reinsurance premiums, instead of net reinsurance payments, as some have argued. For example, for quota share arrangements the gross amount of reinsurance premiums would be subject to the BEAT without taking into account any inbound payments such as reserve adjustments, ceding commissions and claims payments. Also, in the case of modified coinsurance or funds withheld coinsurance, the BEAT would apply to the whole outbound gross premium as well as to the interest on the funds withheld paid over to the assuming company. In addition, the TCJA did not repeal the excise tax payable on outbound insurance and reinsurance premiums. Thus, in addition to potentially attracting a BEAT liability, insurance and reinsurance premiums paid to foreign insurers and reinsurers with respect to risks located in the U.S. continue to be subject to an excise tax at the rate of 1% or 4%. **(See Above, "The Base Erosion and Anti-Abuse Tax (BEAT)")**

PFIC Rules - The TCJA changed the passive foreign investment company (PFIC) statutory provision that in 2017 and prior years excluded income derived from the active conduct of an insurance business from the definition of passive income. Under the TCJA, beginning in 2018 the exclusion is available only to "qualified insurance companies." A qualified insurance company must have applicable insurance liabilities that exceed 25% of its total assets. Applicable insurance liabilities generally include loss and loss adjustment expenses and reserves other than deficiency, contingency or unearned premium reserves. However, due to vagueness in the definition of applicable insurance liabilities, uncertainty exists as to how the liability reserves of P&C insurance companies are taken into account to determine applicable insurance liabilities. The TCJA provides potential relief for a foreign corporation that fails to meet the 25% test by allowing a U.S. shareholder to elect to treat a foreign corporation as a qualifying insurance company if: its applicable insurance liabilities constitute at least 10% of its total assets; and the corporation is predominantly engaged in the insurance business, and its failure to qualify under the 25% threshold is due solely to runoff-related or rating-related circumstances involving such insurance business.

Banks – Phased-Out Deduction for FDIC Premiums

Beginning in 2018, the Tax Cuts and Jobs Act (TCJA) phases out the FDIC premium deduction for banks with total consolidated assets between $10 billion and $50 billion, and eliminates the deduction for banks with assets of $50 billion or more. Banks with less than $10 billion in assets may continue to fully deduct FDIC premiums. In 2017, and prior years, banks could deduct 100% of their FDIC premiums no matter the amount of their assets.

Chapter 20 – Tax-Exempt Organizations

Tax-exempt entities are classified as Section 501(c) organizations, and there are more than 50 different Section 501(c) classifications that organizations can be, depending on their purpose and activities. Charitable entities are 501(c)(3) organizations, and the major difference between charitable organizations and other tax-exempt organizations is that contributions made by individuals and corporations to 501(c)(3) organizations are tax deductible, whereas contributions made to other kinds of tax-exempt entities are not tax deductible. There are more than a million 501(c)(3) charitable organizations recognized by the IRS. Other tax-exempt classifications include: 501(c)(4), which are social welfare/political organizations; 501(c)(6), which are business leagues; and 501(c)(7), which are social clubs. Sports booster organizations are not tax exempt, because they provide no public benefit. In addition to being exempt from federal income tax, 501(c)(3) charitable organizations may not be subject to some state and local sales taxes. The "gift tax" does not apply to contributions made to 501(c)(3), 501(c)(4), 501(c)(5), and 501(c)(6) tax-exempt organizations.

Requirement to File Annual Returns

Tax-exempt organizations are required to file annual returns using either Form 990, Form 990-EZ, or Form 990-N (See below), depending on their status. However, certain religious organizations are not required to file an annual return. These include a church, an interchurch organization of local units of a church, a convention or association of churches, or an integrated auxiliary of a church as described in Regulations section 1.6033-2(h) – such as a men's or women's organization, religious school, mission society, or youth group. Also, not required to file is a church-affiliated organization that is exclusively engaged in managing funds or maintaining retirement programs, and a school below college level affiliated with a church or operated by a religious order.

Failure to file annual returns by tax-exempt organizations, that are required to file, may revoke an organization's tax-exempt status. The law automatically revokes organizations' tax exemption if they fail to file their annual return for three consecutive years. Annual returns are due on the 15th day of the fifth month after an organization's tax year ends. Many organizations use the calendar year as their tax year, making May 15, 2018, the deadline for filing their 2017 annual return. However, filing Form 8868, "Application for Extension of Time to File an Exempt Organization Return," provides an automatic three-month extension to file the return. Organizations can request a second three-month extension, but it is not automatic and requires IRS approval. However, tax-exempt organizations filing for the 2017 tax year will be able to get an automatic six-month extension to Nov. 15, 2018, for calendar year filers. The IRS urges tax-exempt organizations to file their annual returns electronically in order to reduce the risk of including unneeded personal information, including Social Security numbers on the forms. Social Security numbers should not be put on the forms because tax-exempt forms must be made public by the IRS, and inadvertently including Social Security numbers and other personal information could give rise to identity theft. Significant penalties are imposed when an organization does not timely file its annual return. Generally, if an organization has gross receipts of $1 million or less, the penalty is $20 per day (maximum of $10,000). If gross receipts are greater than $1 million, then the penalty is $100 per day (to a maximum of $50,000). The ultimate penalty is the revocation of tax-exempt status.

An amended return can be filed if needed, and it must provide all the information called for by the form and instructions, not just the new or corrected information – check the Amended Return box in the heading of the return. Also, state in Schedule O of the form which parts and schedules of the Form 990 were amended and describe the amendments. If the return is a final return, you must follow the specific instructions for Schedule N, "Liquidation, Termination, Dissolution or Significant Disposition of Assets."
www.irs.gov/pub/irs-pdf/f8868.pdf

Application for Tax-Exempt Status

501(c)(3) charitable organizations applying for the first time to be recognized as tax-exempt organizations by the IRS have to file either Form 1023, "Application for Recognition of Exemption," or Form 1023-EZ, "Streamlined Application for Recognition of Exemption Under Section 501(c)(3) of the Internal Revenue Code. The IRS has also released a new easier-to-use Form 1023-EZ, "Streamlined Application for Recognition of Exemption Under Section 501(c)(3) of the Internal Revenue Code." The new Form 1023-EZ is only three pages long. Forms 1023 and 1023-EZ can only be used by 501(c)(3) charitable organizations to apply for tax-exempt status. All other classifications requesting tax exempt status must use Form 1024. The IRS said that most small charitable organizations, including as many as 70% of applicants qualify to use the new streamlined form. Most 501(c)(3) organizations with gross receipts of $50,000 or less and assets of $250,000 or less are eligible. The change will allow the IRS to speed the approval process for smaller 501(c)(3) charitable organization groups and free up resources to review applications from larger, more complex organizations. Also, beginning July 1, 2016 the fee for filing by using Form 1023-EZ dropped from $400 to $275.

www.irs.gov/pub/irs-pdf/f1023.pdf) www.irs.gov/pub/irs-pdf/i1023.pdf www.irs.gov/pub/irs-pdf/f1023ez.pdf
www.pay.gov/public/form/start/62759871 www.irs.gov/pub/irs-pdf/i1023ez.pdf
www.irs.gov/pub/irs-pdf/p557.pdf www.irs.gov/pub/irs-pdf/f1024.pdf www.irs.gov/pub/irs-pdf/i1024.pdf

The new 1023-EZ form must be filed online using pay.gov, and a $275 user fee is due at the time the form is submitted. The instructions include an interactive 26-question eligibility worksheet that organizations must complete before filing the form. If an organization answers "yes" to any of the questions, it is not eligible to apply using Form 1023-EZ but can still apply for tax-exempt status using Form 1023. Various entities are ineligible for the streamlined application process, even if they meet the gross receipts and assets tests. These ineligible organizations include foreign entities, entities that are not corporations, unincorporated associations, schools, hospitals, credit counseling groups, and some others, such as nonprofits organized as LLCs (they must file using Form 1023). Eligible charitable organizations that have a pending Form 1023 can instead submit a Form 1023-EZ as long as the IRS has not yet assigned the organization's Form 1023 for review. However, the organization's fee paid for the Form 1023 will not be refunded.

The IRS has introduced a new Interactive Form 1023 that features pop-up information boxes for most lines of the form. These boxes contain explanations and links to related information on IRS.gov and StayExempt.irs.gov. Once the application has been completed, applicants will be able to print and mail the form and its attachments, just like the standard Form 1023. Some of the benefits of the new interactive form will be that applicants will be able to submit a more complete form, while IRS processing time will be reduced. In addition, applicants will receive a tax-exempt determination more quickly.

The use of Form 1023-EZ by applicants has reduced processing to as little as one month from the traditional nine to 15 months to process applications when using Form 1023. Previously, all nonprofits went through a lengthy application process, and accounting fees associated with compiling required documents for submission were almost the same for most of them, regardless of the size of the organization. Therefore, the new form 1023-EZ is helping to reduce higher costs for smaller nonprofit organizations. The change has not only allowed the IRS to speed up the approval process for smaller organizations, but it will also free up resources to review applications from larger more complex organizations. Rather than using large amounts of IRS resources up front reviewing complex applications, the streamlined Form 1023-EZ will allow the IRS to devote more compliance activity on the back end to ensure organizations are actually doing the charitable work that they are supposed to be doing.

The IRS is also changing some of the forms and procedures that organizations other than 501(c)(3) organizations can use to apply for tax-exempt status as it emerges from a high-profile scandal over how it handled applications from 501(c)(4) political groups.

Social Welfare Organizations – Section 501(c)(4) of the Tax Code, which applies to social welfare organizations has also been used by many political groups that want to avoid disclosing the names of their donors. A number of conservative organizations complained that the IRS was taking a long time to approve their applications for tax-exempt status under Section 501(c)(4) and subjecting them to extra scrutiny. The IRS released documents indicating that it had not only given extra scrutiny to some conservative groups, but also to some liberal groups filing for tax-exempt status. As a result of the scandal, the IRS has released guidance on new application requirements for 501(c)(4) groups.

A new provision provides for a streamlined recognition process for organizations established after July 8, 2016, that are seeking tax exemption under Section 501(c)(4). Newly formed organizations are required to notify the IRS of their formation and intention to operate as a 501(c)(4) social welfare organizations within 60 days of formation. The current, voluntary 501(c)(4) application process will be eliminated. The process requires 501(c)(4) organizations to file a simple one-page notice of registration with the IRS, which is Form 8976 that must be filled electronically along with a $50 user fee. The form asks for basic information about the organization, such as its statement of purpose and when its accounting period ends (calendar year or fiscal year). Within 60 days after an application is submitted, the IRS is required to provide a letter of acknowledgement of the registration, which the organization can use to demonstrate its exempt status with entities such as state and local tax authorities. However, the acknowledgment by the IRS isn't a determination that the organization meets the requirements to qualify for tax-exempt status as a 501(c)(4) social welfare organization. Organizations that want additional certainty about their status can seek an IRS determination by filing Form 1024 for this purpose. Also, they must provide more information about their qualifications to be a 501(c)(4) organization when they file their first Form 990 return. Organizations that were in existence before July 9, 2016, that had not already filed an exemption application or a Form 990 return had until Sept. 6, 2016, to comply with the application requirements. Non-filers must pay a $20 per day penalty unless their failure to file is due to a reasonable cause.

https://services.irs.gov/datamart/mainMenu.do;jsessionid=z7opdQSODb33KilF6bbh4elo

www.reginfo.gov/public/do/PRAViewIC?ref_nbr=201605-1545-011&icID=221672

file:///C:/Users/timel/Downloads/Draft%20Form%208976.pdf

www.irs.gov/charities-non-profits/electronically-submit-your-form-8976-notice-of-intent-to-operate-under-section-501c4   www.irs.gov/pub/irs-pdf/f1024.pdf   www.irs.gov/pub/irs-pdf/i1024.pdf)

501(c)(4) organizations and other tax-exempt organizations can seek declaratory judgment reviews in Federal court of any revocation of tax-exempt status by the IRS.

Compensation of Executives of Tax-Exempt Organizations

Tax-exempt organizations should plan and document their executive compensation packages to ensure they are not over-compensating their executives. IRC Section 4958 defines excess compensation or benefit as an exchange that occurs between a "disqualified person" and a tax-exempt organization where the value received is less compared to the consideration given. In other words, more compensation is paid to a person than it is worth to the organization. The definition of a disqualified person is not limited to individuals who hold influential positions in a tax-exempt organization. It also extends to the members of their families or any companies where they control more than 35% of the entity. To ensure that tax-exempt organizations are being good stewards of their donors, or taxpayers' contributions, the IRS wields significant power to impose onerous penalties on over-compensated executives.

Beginning in 2018, the Tax Cuts and Jobs Act (TCJA) imposes a 21% excise tax on tax-exempt organizations that provide their executives with annual compensation in excess of $1 million. And this also applies to severance payments (parachute payments) paid to their executives in excess of $1 million. This excise tax is meant to put tax-exempt organizations, which are generally exempt from income taxation, in about the same position as for-profit companies which cannot deduct excess compensation payments made to their covered employees. However, unlike the changes made by the TCJA to the excess compensation rules for profit companies, there is no transition relief for existing tax-exempt organization compensation arrangements.

The new excise tax imposed by the TCJA applies to most tax-exempt organizations including: any organization that is exempt under Code Section 501(a); any state and local governmental entity with tax exempt income; any tax-exempt political organization; and any tax-exempt farmers' cooperative. However, it isn't certain whether the excise tax applies to colleges and universities. Employees covered by the excise tax includes the five highest paid employees of a tax-exempt organization in any year after 2016. Therefore, the excise tax applies to any person who is currently or was formerly one of the five highest paid employees of the organization for the current tax year or for any preceding tax year beginning after Dec. 31, 2016. Compensation that is subject to federal income tax withholding is counted for purposes of the excise tax, but Roth contributions made by a covered employee under an organization's 401(k) or 403(b) Plan are not included. **(See Chapter 19, "Deduction of Compensation of Public Company Executives")**

Entertainment Expenses

The TCJA provides that expenditures for entertainment, amusement, or recreation, including club dues paid on behalf of employees, are no longer deductible by the employer, even if the club is used for business purposes. Because tax-exempt organizations do not generally receive a tax deduction for salary expense, coupled with the elimination of the deduction for social club dues and other entertainment expenses, tax-exempt organizations must include such benefits in the employee's taxable compensation beginning in the 2018 tax year. **(See Chapter 15, "Entertainment Expenses")**

Excise Tax on Investment Income of Private Colleges and Universities

Effective for tax years beginning in 2018, the Tax Cuts and Jobs Act (TCJA) imposes a 1.4% excise tax on the net investment income of private tax-exempt colleges and universities that have at least 500 tuition-paying students (50% of which are located in the U.S.). Also, the applicable college or university must have had an aggregate fair market value of assets (other than those used directly in carrying out the college or university's tax-exempt purpose) at the end of the preceding tax year of at least $500,000 per student. Generally, such assets include assets held by related organizations, including supporting organizations controlled by the school and the applicable net investment income on which the excise tax is imposed is derived from those assets. The number of students is based on the daily average number of full-time equivalent students (full-time students and part-time students on an equivalent basis). Net investment income is gross investment income minus expenses to produce the investment (but disallowing the use of accelerated depreciation methods or percentage depletion).

Filing Annual Returns
An organization is required to file Form 990 if the organization claims tax-exempt status under Section 501(c) but has not yet established such exempt status by filing Form 1023 or Form 1024 and has not received an IRS letter recognizing tax-exempt status. In such case, the organization must check the "application pending" checkbox in Item B of the Form 990 header.

It is important to identify the type of tax-exempt organization you are and which forms have to be filed since the requirements differ for each type of organization. Although any tax-exempt organization may file its annual return to the IRS using Form 990, it is only required to file Form 990 if gross receipts exceed $200,000 or assets exceed $500,000. Otherwise, 501(c) organizations can file Form 990-EZ, or if gross receipts normally do not exceed $50,000 Form 990-N (which is a postcard-size form) can be filed. Private foundations should file Form 990-PF. There are significant differences in the compliance burden, so the decision as to which form to file should be made carefully, because some rating organizations will evaluate only charities that file the full-length Form 990. www.irs.gov/charities-non-profits/annual-electronic-filing-requirement-for-small-exempt-organizations-form-990-n-e-postcard   www.irs.gov/pub/irs-pdf/p5248.pdf

https://taxmap.ntis.gov/taxmap/ts0/form990nepostcard_o_32a0e616.htm

www.irs.gov/pub/irs-pdf/f990pf.pdf   www.irs.gov/pub/irs-pdf/i990pf.pdf

Form 990 – A tax-exempt organization has a significant exposure due to the vast public disclosure of Form 990. A tax-exempt organization needs to be sure that it files an accurate and complete annual return. As most exempt organizations know, preparing a Form 990 can be a time consuming and complicated process. The IRS has to determine whether an organization meets the legal requirements for tax-exempt status. The IRS's goals for Form 990 are increased transparency, good governance and increased accountability for filing organizations. One requirement relates to the amount of political campaign intervention ("political activity") that the organizations may engage in. Section 501(c)(3) organizations are prohibited from engaging in any political activity. Other organizations, including Sec. 501(c)(4) organizations, may only engage in a limited amount of political activity. The IRS has introduced a greatly expanded Form 990, "Return of Organization Exempt from Income Tax" (see above). Other than ensuring that its filing is completely accurate, the organization should use every part of the Form 990 to include all relevant information. Every possible space on Form 990 should be completed.

Form 990 and related forms, schedules, and attachments can be filed electronically. If an organization files at least 250 returns of any type, including quarterly Forms 941 and excise tax returns, during the calendar year and has assets of $10 million or more at the end of the year, it must file electronically. If an organization is required to file returns electronically but doesn't, the organization is considered to have not filed the returns, even if paper returns are submitted.

Organizations seeking an exemption must be organized and operated so that no part of their net earnings benefit any stakeholder or individual. Therefore, any such benefit (regardless of amount) could endanger an organization's exempt status. Organizations have lost their exempt status because of unreasonable compensation. Unreasonable compensation is one of the IRS's most active areas of inquiry and enforcement. The detailed compensation reporting requirements in Form 990 facilitate accurate and more complete compensation reporting. To avoid loss of tax-exempt status and/or intermediate sanctions, the organization should use a process for determining compensation. The process should include the following: review and approval by a governing body or compensation committee; use of data as to comparable compensation for similarly qualified persons in functionally comparable positions at situated organizations; and contemporaneous documentation and record keeping for the deliberations and decisions regarding the compensation arrangements for senior management as well as staff.

It is very important to have a competent professional who understands the complexities of Form 990 to prepare it. Some significant errors that occur when completing Form 990 include: not properly identifying the executive director as a top management official who is a person that is treated as an officer for Part VII purposes; reporting no conflict-of-interest policy or indicating that the organization has one but it is not enforced; failing to properly identify key employees; including Social Security numbers and personal information such as a person's mailing address that is not needed on the form; and not adequately describing the organization's charitable activities in Part III per the instructions.

Preparers of Form 990 have to include historical financial information, as well as a number of narrative descriptions of the organization's status and accomplishments in the prior year. This is totally different from other kinds of tax returns that generally do not require narrative descriptions. The preparer of a Form 990 should have a planning meeting with the organization's directors and staff, and designate the persons who will be responsible for writing required narrative descriptions. The organization should generally use the same accounting method on the return to report revenue and expenses that it regularly uses to keep its books and records in order to be acceptable for Form 990 reporting purposes.

Form 990, Schedule A is used to provide required information regarding an organization's public charity status and financial support. Part I, Schedule A, requires an organization to indicate why it is not a private foundation by checking the box for one of 11 categories of public charities. Many publicly supported organizations must describe their revenue in either Part II or III. This information allows the IRS to determine whether an entity meets the applicable public support test. An organization is not required to use the same public support test specified in its determination letter from the IRS. It can annually use the support test that best reflects its sources of support and that enables it to retain public charity status. For those organizations whose exemption category requires performing the support tests in parts II or III of Schedule A, failure to pass both of these tests may result in their loss of public charity status and being characterized as a private foundation.

Form 990, Schedule C provides the IRS with information concerning political campaign activities and/or lobbying activities of Section 501(c)(3) organizations. Given the many crucial issues facing nonprofit organizations and the people they serve, it is more important than ever when those charities become involved in the public policy debate. Many nonprofit organizations mistakenly assume that it is illegal for nonprofits to lobby. To the contrary, federal laws actually exist to encourage charities to lobby within certain specified limits. Knowing what constitutes lobbying under the law, and what the limits are, is the key to being able to lobby legally and safely. Unlike lobbying, Section 501(c)(3) organizations are prohibited from participating in political campaigns.

Schedule O, Supplemental Information to Form 990, and Part III, "Statement of Program Service Accomplishments," are both important to complete. Form 990, Part III asks the organization to describe its charitable mission and the programs or activities it undertook during the year for the three largest programs, measured by expenses. Part III should contain specific information, such as the number of events held, number of clients served, and anything else that describes that particular program. Another way to use this part is to explain that the financial measurements, standing alone, do not fully describe the success of the programs. Schedule O is a continuation sheet which is used to answer specific questions on Form 990 as well as to provide additional important information. Thus, organizations can use this schedule as an addendum to provide detailed descriptions of their accomplishments in the previous year. Schedule O can also be used to explain any area of the core form or schedules that may not be clearly understood from reading the main part of the form. For example, one organization whose CEO left in the middle of the year used Schedule O to explain why the CFO's salary was more than the CEO's salary.

Part VI, "Governance, Management and Disclosure," should be used to prompt the organization to make governance changes. In preparing Part VI, the organization should be made aware of the need to implement changes to its governance policies. One way is for the organization to adopt a conflict-of-interest policy so the organization can check "yes" to Question 12 in Part VI. This is a chance to improve the organization and show perspective donors and other stakeholders that proper governance is an absolute priority.

Form 990 Part IX allocates expenses for the organization into three functional categories: program service; management and general; and fund raising. Some costs incurred by an organization clearly relate to a specific function and should be charged directly to that function. The function of other costs may not be readily identifiable (e.g. rent or telephone). An organization is allowed to use any reasonable method to allocate these expenses. Proper allocation of expenses between these functions is very important. The amount of funds spent on program services, when compared to total expenses, is a measurement of the organization's effective stewardship of its assets. Donors want to know the extent to which their contributions are used primarily for charitable purposes. Likewise, the IRS and watchdog agencies examine expense classifications to verify that the organization is operating within certain guidelines.
www.irs.gov/pub/irs-pdf/f990.pdf   www.irs.gov/pub/irs-pdf/i990.pdf

Form 990-EZ – The IRS has issued an updated Form 990-EZ, "Short Form Return of Organization Exempt from Income Tax," that will help tax-exempt organizations avoid common mistakes when filing their annual return. The updated Form 990-EZ includes 29 "help" icons describing key information needed to complete many of the fields within the form. The icons also provide links to additional helpful information available on IRS.gov. These "pop-up" boxes share information to help small and mid-size exempt organizations avoid common mistakes when filling out the form and filing their return. Although many large exempt organizations are required to file Form 990-series information returns electronically, the IRS encourages all exempt organizations to consider filing electronically. Forms 990-EZ are filed by smaller exempt organizations with gross receipts of less than $200,000 and assets of less than $500,000 at the end of the year. On the new form, the help icons are marked in boxes with a blue question mark. The icons and underlying links work on any device with Adobe Acrobat Reader and internet access. Once completed, filers can print Form 990-EZ and mail it to the IRS. In 2016, the error rate for electronically-filed 990-EZ returns was only 1 percent, compared to a 33 percent error rate for paper-filed returns. In 2016, the IRS processed over 263,000 Forms 990-EZ, with the majority of the filings submitted on paper.

www.irs.gov/pub/irs-pdf/f990ez.pdf   www.irs.gov/pub/irs-pdf/i990ez.pdf

www.irs.gov/charities-non-profits/new-form-990-n-submission-website-now-open

www.expresstaxexempt.com/e-file-form-990-ez/?utm_source=google&utm_medium=cpc&utm_campaign=990ez&gclid=CL_fnbjojNYCFQ6qaQodKg8CfQ

Unrelated Business Income Tax (UBIT)

Even though an organization is recognized as a tax-exempt organization, it still may be liable for taxes in accordance with the unrelated business income tax (UBIT) rules, because some Income earned by nonprofits may not be tax-exempt. A tax-exempt organization may be subject to UBIT if it has income from a trade or business that is regularly carried on and unrelated to its exempt purpose, and if this is the case, the organization must annually file Form 990-T, "Exempt Organization Business Income Tax Return." Tax-exempt organizations should not fear having unrelated business income (UBI), but it is important to recognize when it might arise so the appropriate IRS (and state, if applicable) filings are made. By planning for UBI, and recognizing under which circumstances it might appear, organizations can effectively manage it in accordance with regulations. Income usually does not threaten an organization's tax-exempt status, and in many cases provides a more stable and predictable source of funding than contributions, grants or other forms of exempt income. However, there might be consequences if the income from the activity is significant and it is determined that the organization is no longer organized and operated exclusively for an exempt purpose.

www.irs.gov/pub/irs-pdf/f990t.pdf

Any activity that is carried on for production of income and possesses the characteristics required to constitute a trade or business will generally be considered a trade or business under the UBTI rules, even if it generates a loss. An activity is "regularly carried on" for business if it has frequency and continuity. To avoid classification as UBTI, the conduct of the trade or business that produces the income must be substantially related (other than the production of funds) to the purposes for which the exemption is granted. An activity is related to the organization's exempt purpose if it contributes importantly and bears a substantial causal relationship to the achievement of the exempt purpose. The primary purpose of UBIT is to put tax-exempt entities and "for profit" enterprises on equal footing with respect to their trade or business activities. The intention of the UBIT rules is not to curb the occasional fundraiser but rather to focus on activities that are carried on regularly and frequently, such as a commercial parking lot.

Beginning in 2018, the Tax Cuts and Jobs Act (TCJA) requires tax-exempt organizations to determine the net unrelated business income tax (UBIT) "separately" for each unrelated trade or business, i.e. gains and losses have to be calculated separately for each unrelated trade or business. A loss by an unrelated trade or business can't be used to offset income from a tax-exempt organization's other unrelated trades or businesses. In addition, net operating loss (NOL) deductions are only allowable to offset income from the same unrelated trade or business from which the loss occurred. This TCJA change does not apply to any NOLs arising in a tax year beginning before January 1, 2018. So, such NOLs can be used to reduce aggregate UBTI for all unrelated trades or businesses of tax-exempt organizations.

In 2017 and prior years, A tax-exempt organization determined its UBTI by subtracting, from its gross unrelated business income, deductions directly connected with all of its unrelated trades or businesses. A tax-exempt organization that operated multiple unrelated trades or businesses aggregated income from all such activities and subtracted from the aggregate gross income the aggregate of deductions. Therefore, an organization could use a deduction from one unrelated trade or business to offset income from another, thereby reducing total unrelated business taxable income.

There are three ways to define unrelated business Income (UBI) in nonprofit organizations:

- Trade or business — Any activity for the production of income from the sale of goods or performance of services.
- Regularly carried on for production of income — Frequently and consistently pursued in a manner similar to commercial activities.
- Unrelated to the organization's exempt purpose — The purpose on which the organization's exempt status is based.

In order to assist tax-exempt organizations to monitor their activities and determine whether Form 990T must be filed, following are some common revenue sources that might be classified as unrelated to their exempt purpose:

- Regular and online advertising – Since advertisements promote the business of the advertiser and not the tax-exempt entity, the sale of advertising in an exempt publication, such as a trade journal or newsletter, or on an organization's website is typically considered UBI. It is often argued that this activity is not UBI because it is not "regularly carried on" or lacks a profit motive. Even so, advertising contracts should be analyzed to make sure the income is properly classified.
- Services provided to other entities – It is not uncommon for exempt organizations to enter into arrangements to provide services to other entities. For example, a nonprofit entity might provide marketing services for a strategic partner that is looking to expand service offerings to its members. While some services might fall within the mission of the organization or be rendered in a manner in which the entity lacks a profit motive, many organizations cannot rely on these exceptions. When an organization receives revenue from the rendering of services, and the performance of those services does not further the tax-exempt mission of the organization, the income might be classified as UBI.
- Tax-free corporate sponsorship or advertising – Nonprofit organizations that receive corporate sponsorship payments need to determine whether the revenue is a tax-free sponsorship (charitable contribution) or if it should be classified differently when other benefits are provided to the sponsor. Although not all benefits provided to a sponsor would be deemed to generate UBI, a benefit such as advertising might be classified as such. And while it might be the intent that a sponsorship payment be treated as tax free, advertising could be an unintended consequence to the nonprofit. A best practice when developing and implementing a sponsorship program is to craft the agreement language to ensure that the intended outcome is obtained.
- Income from controlled organizations – Certain payments from controlled organizations are subject to

342

regulations under IRC Section 512(b)(13). This generally includes interest, rent, royalty, or annuity payments from the controlled entity. An arrangement where a nonprofit owns a building and rents space to a for-profit subsidiary would generate payments that might be considered UBI from a controlled organization. That income could create a tax liability. While the definition of control, for this purpose, is dependent on the structure of the organization, these payments should still be reviewed to determine how they should be classified.

- Passive royalties from licensing agreements – The licensing of an organization's intangible property, such as its name or logo, is deemed to be a passive royalty and is excluded from UBI. However, it is not uncommon for royalty agreements to contain provisions that require the exempt organization to perform services for or promote the organization licensing the intangible asset. When this type of structure occurs, the income might be considered unrelated. Any organization choosing to enter into a royalty agreement should address the specifics of the arrangement to ensure a complete understanding of potential consequences.

- Debt-financed income – IRC Section 514 requires certain items of income to be included in the computation of UBI when the income is derived from debt financed property. To be classified as debt financed property, the property must be held for the production of income and subject to acquisition or improvement indebtedness. Acquisition indebtedness is any debt that would not have been incurred were it not for the acquisition — so the debt does not have to be secured on the property to be treated as acquisition indebtedness. Most commonly, the debt financed property rules apply to rental real estate. However, the rules might apply to royalties or other investment income that has outstanding acquisition indebtedness.

- Income from partnerships – Investment portfolios of exempt organizations continue to become more diversified and complex, and UBI might be generated when an exempt organization is in a partnership that undertakes activities unrelated to its exempt purpose. The flow through nature of a partnership requires that the parties characterize income the same as the underlying entity. Therefore, even the tax-exempt partner must include the income or loss from unrelated trade or business activities conducted within a partnership in its computation of UBI.

- Income from S-corporations – With the transfer of wealth that is occurring in today's society, many exempt organizations are receiving interests in S-corporations through donations or bequests. Sometimes an organization will accept this type of contribution without realizing the full tax implications. All items of income, deductions and other amounts reported on a shareholder's Schedule K-1 are subject to UBIT. **While investment income items are generally excluded from UBTI for partnerships, all investment income and related deductions reported by S-corporations on Schedule K-1 are subject to UBTI.** In addition, the gain or loss from the sale of S-corporation stock is also considered UBI. Commonly, a donor will make a contribution of S-corporation stock with unrealized gain. However, the transfer results in the tax liability being paid by the tax-exempt organization. Again, the tax-exempt organization must be aware of the potential tax consequences before accepting such contribution.

Chapter 21 – Estates and Trusts

Estates and trusts are recognized as separate taxable entities for tax purposes. Both estates and trusts must file a tax return on Form 1041, "U.S. Income Tax Return for Estates and Trusts," on or before the 15th day of the fourth month following the close of the tax year if it has gross income of $600 or more in the year (April 15th for calendar year taxpayers in 2018). However, executors or administrators of estates can obtain an automatic 6-month extension by filing Form 7004, but trusts can only get a maximum 5 ½ month extension by filing Form 7004. Estates may have a fiscal year, which is a taxable year other than the calendar year, but a trust is generally required to have a calendar tax year. Estates and trusts are conduits of income to beneficiaries, and as such are allowed a deduction for income that is currently distributed to beneficiaries. Form 1041, Schedule K-1 is used to report distributions to beneficiaries, which must be reported and taxed as income to the beneficiaries on their individual tax returns.

www.irs.gov/pub/irs-pdf/f1041.pdf www.irs.gov/pub/irs-pdf/i1041.pdf www.irs.gov/pub/irs-pdf/i7004.pdf
www.irs.gov/pub/irs-access/f1041sk1_accessible.pdf www.irs.gov/pub/irs-pdf/f7004.pdf

Income distributed to beneficiaries retains the same character that it had in the hands of the estate or trust. In determining the income of an estate or trust, gross income is reduced by: (1) deductions for expenses paid or incurred in connection with the administration of the estate or trust that would not have been incurred if the assets were not held in an estate or trust; (2) deductions for income distributions to beneficiaries; and (3) allowable exemptions. **(See Chapter 5, "Distributable Net Income from Estates and Trusts"**

Under the Tax Cuts and Jobs Act, the number of income tax brackets for estates and trusts is cut from 5 in 2017 and prior years, to 4 under the Tax Cuts and Jobs Act (TCJA) for tax years 2018 – 2025, with the 37% tax bracket commencing at over $12,500.

2018 Tax Brackets for Estates and Trusts:

0 - $2,550 (10%); $2,551 - $9,150 ($255.00 + 24% of the amount over $2,550); $9,151 - $12,500 ($1,839.00 + 35% of the amount over $9,150); Over $12,500 ($3,011.50 + 37% of the amount over $12,500).

The Affordable Care Act (ACA) adds a 3.8% surtax on the "net investment income" (NII) of estates and trusts. The threshold for the surtax is the dollar amount at which the highest tax bracket for estates and trusts begins for the tax year, which in 2018 is $12,500. Thus, the primary planning objective for estate and trust administrators should be to avoid the condensed estate and trust tax brackets, and to avoid the 3.8% surtax. By making distributions to beneficiaries, estates and trusts may be able not only to avoid the 3.8% surtax, but also take advantage of the beneficiaries' lower income tax brackets. The key to achieving these results is to effectively use the special deduction from income available to estates and trusts for distributions to beneficiaries. Because estates and trusts operate as conduit entities, substantial tax savings may result from distributing the income, including net investment income, to a beneficiary who is in a lower tax bracket. Administrators should first take the opportunity to distribute income that would be included in net investment income, which consists of passive activity income, interest, dividends, and capital gain income. **(See Chapter 10, "3.8% Net Investment Income Tax"); (See Chapter 5, "Portfolio Income"); (See Chapter 6, "Capital Gains and Losses')**

344

<u>**Deductions Allowable in Determining Income of Estates and Trusts**</u>

The gross and taxable income of estates and trusts are computed as they are for individuals – deductions and credits allowed to individuals are also allowed to estates and trusts. In addition:

- Estates and trusts are allowed to deduct distributions to beneficiaries in determining adjusted gross income.
- A $600 exemption is allowed in determining adjusted gross income (but not on the final return filed by an estate or trust).
- Expenses incurred in connection with the administration of an estate or trust are allowable in arriving at adjusted gross income. However, certain costs incurred by Estates and Non-Grantor Trusts are subject to the 2% floor on miscellaneous deductions as set-forth in the "Final Rules on Fiduciary Fees." **(See Below, "Final Rules on Bundled Fiduciary Fees for Estates and Trusts")**

<u>**Final Rules on Bundled Fiduciary Fees for Estates and Trusts**</u>

In May 2014, the IRS issued final regulations on the controversial question of which costs incurred by estates and trusts are subject to the 2% floor for miscellaneous deductions. The final regulations apply to tax years beginning after December 31, 2014. The regulations stem from the Supreme Court's decision in Knight 552 U.S. 181 (2008), on the income tax deductibility by estates and non-grantor trusts of investment advisory and other fees. The final regulations are:

www.irs.gov/pub/irs-drop/n-10-32.pdf

- Investment advisory and other fees paid to an investment advisor by an estate or a non-grantor trust are generally miscellaneous itemized deductions subject to the 2% of adjusted gross income (AGI) floor, rather than fully deductible as an expense of administering an estate or trust under Sec. 67(3)(1). Such fees are fully deductible to the extent the fees exceed the fees generally charged to an individual investor.
- Appraisal fees are fully deductible by estates and non-grantor trusts if they are needed to determine the value of property as of the decedent's date of death (or the alternate valuation date) for purposes of making distributions or to properly prepare the estate and trust's tax returns. **(See Chapter 22, "Basis of Property Inherited or Gifted")**
- Fiduciary fees that are not commonly or customarily incurred by individuals and are, therefore, fully deductible by estates and trusts include: probate court fees and costs; fiduciary bond premiums; legal publication costs of notices to creditors or heirs; the cost of certified copies of the decedent's death certificate; and costs related to fiduciary accounts.
- Bundled fees – fees that are billed together, where a portion is fully deductible and another is subject to the 2% of AGI floor – must be "unbundled," i.e. the costs have to be allocated between costs that are subject to the 2% floor and those that are not. Generally, under the final regulations, the portion of a bundled fiduciary fee attributable to investment advice (including any related services that would be provided to any individual investor as part of an investment advisory fee) will be subject to the 2% floor. Any fiduciary fee not allocated to investment advice and not calculated on an hourly basis may be fully deductible, except for: (1) payments made to a third party out of the bundled fee that would have been subject to the 2% floor if paid directly by the estate or trust; and (2) separately assessed expenses (in addition to usual or basic fees or commissions) that are commonly or customarily incurred by an

individual. If amounts are allocable to investment advice but are not traceable to separate payments, the final regulations allow the use of "any reasonable method" to make the allocation between costs that are subject to the 2% floor and those that are not.

www.supremecourt.gov/opinions/07pdf/06-1286.pdf

Net Investment Income Tax Applicable to Estates and Trusts

An estate or trust is subject to the 3.8% Net Investment Income (NII) tax to the extent of the lesser of: the estate's or trust's undistributed net investment income; or the excess (if any) of the estate's or trust's AGI over the dollar amount at which the highest tax bracket begins for the year ($12,500 for 2018). Unlike the thresholds for individuals, the thresholds for estates and trusts is adjusted for inflation each year. Grantor trust income flows-through to the grantor; therefore, only non-grantor trusts are required to pay the NII tax. Non-grantor trusts should consider paying distributions to beneficiaries to avoid the 3.8% NII tax, which kicks in for trusts at $12,500 in 2018. The 65-day rule can be used to defer distributions to as late as March 6th of the following year and still have them apply to the current year. Trusts that are subject to the NII tax include: non-grantor trusts; electing small business trusts; non-grantor charitable lead trusts; pooled income funds; cemetery perpetual care funds; qualified funeral trusts; Alaska Native Settlement Trusts; and foreign trusts with U.S. beneficiaries. The NII tax does not apply to common trust funds, real estate investment trusts, designated settlement funds, wholly charitable trusts, other trusts exempt from tax and foreign trusts without U.S. beneficiaries. **(See Chapter 10, "Net Investment Income Tax Applicable to Estates and Trusts")**

Final Return of Decedent

When a person dies, a "final return" through the date of death must be filed if required according to the gross income test. However, a surviving spouse may file a joint return that includes the income of the decedent up to the date of death and the income of the surviving spouse for the entire year. Also, if the surviving spouse is the decedent's beneficiary, all of the income that the decedent would have received for the entire year may be included on the joint return filed by the surviving spouse. If a surviving spouse remarries before the end of the year in which the decedent died, the filing status of the decedent is "married filing separately." If a joint return is filed, the surviving spouse should sign the return and write in the signature space for the deceased "Filing as surviving spouse." The word "DECEASED," name of decedent, and the date of death should be written across the top of the return when either a joint return is filed or when a joint return is not filed. If a Joint return is not filed, either a court-appointed personal representative or another person can sign the return as the personal representative. A court-appointed personal representative will have a certificate from the court. The personal representative – including a court-appointed representative – who is signing the return has to submit Form 1310 with the decedent's final tax return. The personal representative does not have to be a court-appointed representative.

www.irs.gov/pub/irs-pdf/f1310.pdf

The final return of a decedent is due by the regular filing due date (April 17th for the 2017 tax year). All income that the decedent would have received had death not occurred is "income in respect of the decedent" (IRD) and must be included in the income and tax return of one of the following: (1) the joint return of the deceased and the surviving spouse; (2) the beneficiary (other than the surviving spouse), if the right to the income is passed directly to the beneficiary and the beneficiary receives it; or (2) The decedent's estate, if the estate receives it. When a decedent's estate receives "income in respect of a decedent" (IRD) instead of the surviving spouse or another beneficiary, an Estate Income Tax Return (Form 1041) must be filed. In a community property state , when one spouse dies, the IRS's position is that income from community property should be included ½ in the surviving spouse's income and ½ in the decedent's estate. This does not apply to income from joint accounts where the spouse has the right to the income. It also does not apply if all income and the underlying assets are passed directly to a beneficiary (including the surviving spouse) and the beneficiary receives it. Income and deductions of the decedent should be identified through the date of death of the decedent and included in the final return of the decedent. **(See Below, "Estates"); (See Chapter 3, "Married Filing Separately and Community Property")**

- Forms 1099 that report dividends, interest etc. – interest and dividends earned and included on Forms 1099 should be allocated between dividends and interest paid to the deceased prior to death; and interest, dividends, etc. paid to beneficiaries or to the Estate after the date of death. **(See Chapter 5, "Portfolio Income")**

- All deductions for medical expenses should be taken on the decedent's final return, as long as they are paid within one year of the decedent's death and the decedent has no Estate Tax liability. However, if the decedent has an Estate tax liability, any unpaid medical expenses that are not deducted on the decedent's final return should be deducted on Form 706 - Estate Tax return (not to be confused with the Estate income tax return - Form 1041). **(See chapter 12, "Medical Expenses")**

- When annuity payments end because of a taxpayer's death and there is an unrecovered non-taxable investment, that amount is deducted on the taxpayer's final return as a "miscellaneous itemized deduction not subject to the 2% AGI floor." **(See Chapter 12, "Miscellaneous Itemized Deductions Not Subject to the 2% AGI Floor")**

Carryovers

Generally, carryovers can be used on the decedent's final income tax return, but are lost forever thereafter. For a single taxpayer, this is fairly straightforward. It is more complicated when the decedent is married and files jointly. When the surviving spouse files a joint return with the decedent for the year of his or her death, the full amount of carryovers can still be used in the year of death, even if they are used to offset income of the surviving spouse that was generated after death. However, after the year of death, the carryovers must be examined carefully to determine which carryover amounts, if any, belonged to the decedent, because any amounts attributable to the decedent are lost and cannot be transferred to the surviving spouse.

- Net Operating Loss (NOL) Carryovers – The decedent's NOLs that are not used in the year of death are lost forever. NOL carryovers are deductible only by the taxpayer who sustained the losses, and they cannot be transferred to or used by another taxpayer, including the surviving spouse. Where losses are passed through to business owners, any NOLs on a couple's joint tax return can be attributed to each spouse based on his or her ownership in the business. If NOLs cannot be attributed to the surviving spouse, the surviving spouse can generate additional income during the remainder of the tax year after the decedent dies, and any income generated by the surviving spouse after the decedent's death but before the end of the year can be used to offset the decedent's NOLs. A surviving spouse can generate additional income by accelerating IRA or pension distributions; electing out of bonus depreciation; and delaying payment of state, local, and property taxes to the next year when itemizing deductions. If the taxpayer's death is imminent, he or she can withdraw additional IRA funds to offset the NOLs. The IRA distribution will not be subject to taxation because the NOLs will offset it.

- Capital Loss Carryovers – The capital losses of a decedent spouse can be used on the final joint return, but cannot be carried over to the decedent's Estate income tax return. Also, the surviving spouse cannot carry the excess capital losses of the decedent forward for use by the surviving spouse in future years, which means the excess capital losses are lost, unless the capital losses were generated by a joint account in the names of both the deceased spouse and the surviving spouse; in which case, half of the capital losses are allocated to the surviving spouse and can be carried over. After one spouse dies during a year, the surviving spouse can continue to generate capital gain income during the remainder of the tax year to offset the decedent's capital loss carryovers. Any remaining capital losses are lost, and the estate or the heirs cannot deduct them. If a taxpayer in failing health is holding property that would generate a capital loss if sold, he or she should consider gifting the property to the spouse before death. This will preserve any capital loss that would have been lost had the taxpayer died holding the asset. The basis of property gifted to a spouse is its original cost even when the FMV of the gifted property has dropped below its original cost. Also, taxpayers in failing health who are holding a capital asset with an FMV less than its cost basis should consider selling the property before death if the capital loss can offset capital gains on the final tax return. If the taxpayer dies holding the property, the cost basis will be stepped down at death, and the unrealized loss will disappear and cannot be deducted in the future. **(See Chapter 6, "Reporting Capital Gains and Losses")**
- Charitable Contribution Carryovers – A couple's original contributions must be recomputed as if separate returns had been filed for the contribution years. The portion of the carryovers allocated to the surviving spouse is the amount that bears the same ratio to the total carryover as the spouse's carryover on a separate basis bears to the total contribution carryovers of both spouses on a separate basis. Any carryover allocated to the deceased spouse is lost if not used in the year of death. However, in the year of death, the decedent's excess charitable contributions can be used against the income of the surviving spouse. **(See Chapter 12, "Charitable Contribution Deduction")**
- Passive Activity Loss Carryovers – Suspended passive activity losses must be traced to the owner of the activity. the amount of loss equal to the step-up (difference between the stepped-up basis and the decedent's adjusted basis) in basis at death is not allowed to the decedent or to anyone else on the final return because the heirs receive that tax benefit from the step-up in basis. Example: A taxpayer owns a rental property, which is a building that has an adjusted basis of $700,000; a FMV of $750,000; and passive suspended losses of $100,000. The taxpayer does not have any other passive income. If the taxpayer dies during the tax year, the deductible suspended passive loss on the taxpayer's final income tax return will be limited to $50,000 ($100,000 – $50,000 step-up in basis). The deductible loss can offset other income such as interest, dividends, and earned income. The remaining $50,000 of passive loss will be permanently lost as a tax deduction.
- Other carryovers – Other carryovers, such as investment interest expense, foreign tax credits, and alternative minimum tax (AMT) credit carryovers, must also be allocated between the decedent and the surviving spouse, based on which spouse generated the tax credit.

Estates

All income of a decedent in the year of death that is not included in the "final return" of the decedent or in the income of beneficiaries must be included in the decedent's estate. An estate for tax purposes is treated as a separate entity and must have a separate tax identification number (TIN), and a tax return (Form 1041) must be filed each year for a domestic estate that has taxable income of more than $600, which is the exemption amount.

However, the $600 exemption is not allowed in the final year of the estate when all items have to pass through to the beneficiaries. An estate only pays income tax on income generated by its underlying assets that are not distributed to beneficiaries. If "income in respect of a decedent" (IRD) is received by a decedent's estate, the estate must get a tax identification number (TIN) and a final estate income tax return (Form 1041) must be filed to close-out the estate, even if there is no income to report. The estate consists of all assets held in the decedent's name after the following exclusions: one-half of assets held jointly with the right of survivorship; all assets received by a surviving spouse as the decedent's sole beneficiary; retirement assets that are passed automatically or directly to designated beneficiaries, such as traditional and Roth IRAs, annuities, etc.; assets with specific payable at death directions; and certain property held in trust, such as property held in a revocable trust created by the decedent. The exclusion of these assets is important because it means that they do not have to go through probate. Probate is generally required only when the value of the assets exceed a threshold dollar amount, depending on the particular state of residence. For estates under the threshold, an "affidavit of heirship" or similar document or procedure can usually be used or followed, so the "will" would not have to be probated and no separate entity will have to be established for the estate (no separate TIN required).

An estate of a deceased person is a taxable entity separate from the decedent, and it continues to exist until the final distribution of all assets held in the estate is made to heirs and other beneficiaries. The income earned from the property of the estate during the period of administration or settlement must be accounted for and reported by the estate. However, the estate only pays tax on income that is not distributed to beneficiaries. If a fiscal year begins in 2016 and ends in 2017, the information reported on the Form 1041 and Schedule K-1 is reported on the beneficiary's 2017 tax return. An Estate that has been established by obtaining a tax identification number (TIN) from the IRS must file a final return in order to properly close-out the estate, even if there is no income to report.

Distinctions Between Individual and Estate Tax Returns

There are distinctions between individual tax returns and estate income tax returns, including the following:

- There is no standard deduction for estates.
- No deductions are allowed for medical expenses, because all deductions for medical expenses must be taken on the decedent's final return as long as they are paid within one year of the decedent's death. However, if the decedent has an estate tax liability, any unpaid medical expenses that are not deducted on the decedent's final return can be deducted on Form 706 – Estate Tax return. **(See Chapter 12, "Medical Expenses")**
- No deduction is allowed for funeral expenses. Funeral expenses can only be taken as a deduction from the decedent's gross estate when there is an estate tax liability – Form 706 is filed. NOTE: Funeral expenses are not deductible on individual tax returns.
- If a decedent engaged in business had a net operating loss (NOL) prior to death, it cannot be carried forward to the estate income tax return, but instead must be taken on the decedent's final tax return or carried back to prior years. **(See Chapter 8, "Net Operating Loss (NOL)")**
- Estates cannot take the Sec. 179 expense deduction on depreciable assets. **(See Chapter 16, "Section 179 First-Year Expensing")**
- Any left-over capital losses from before the death of the decedent cannot be deducted on the decedent's estate income tax return.

An Estate may have a net operating loss (NOL) on the final Estate income tax return if Line 22 on Form 1041 is a loss due to excess deductions. To determine if there is a NOL, do not include any deductions claimed on Line 13 (charitable deductions), Line 18 (income distributions to beneficiaries) or Line 20 (the $600 exemption – remember you can't take the $600 exemption on the final return). If there is a NOL, enter the beneficiary's share of the excess deductions in Box 11 of Form 1041 Schedule K-1 using Code A. Figure the deductions on a separate sheet of paper and attach it to the return. The NOL can include net capital losses.

Beneficiaries of Estates

Beneficiaries who receive distributions from decedents' estates or who obtain income and assets passed directly to them are required to file tax returns that include the inherited assets and all income that the decedent would have received had death not occurred. In accordance with certain laws and regulations, beneficiaries are required to report assets and income on their individual tax returns in the following manner:

- Capital gains are not recognized by beneficiaries on appreciated assets distributed to them by the estate because the beneficiaries are allowed to take the stepped-up basis, which is the fair market value (FMV) of the inherited assets at the decedent's death. **(See Chapter 22, "Basis of Property Inherited or Gifted")**
- Any gain on the sale of inherited property subsequent to distribution to beneficiaries is always long-term capital gain regardless of how long the decedent or heirs held it. The tax law gives an automatic long-term holding period to inherited property. It is a capital gain and not ordinary income, unless the asset inherited is excluded from the definition of capital gain property. **(See Chapter 6, "Reporting Capital Gains and Losses")**
- For property acquired from a decedent, a new provision requires that the basis in inherited property reported by the heir not exceed the basis in the property reported by the estate. The executor of the estate is also required, along with filing an estate tax return, to file an information return reporting basis information to the IRS and those inheriting property. A penalty is provided for inconsistent basis reporting. These changes apply to property with respect to which an estate tax return is filed after July 31, 2015.

Upon termination of the decedent's estate, beneficiaries are allowed to deduct their share of any net operating losses (NOLs), which are excess deductions reported on their 1041 Schedule K-1s, on Schedule A, Line 23 of their individual tax returns. The NOLs can also be carried back to beneficiaries' prior 2 tax years. Beneficiaries can only deduct $3,000 of net capital losses reported on Schedule K-1 on their current year tax return, but any excess losses can be carried over to the next year. Any excess deductions that are not capital losses such as tax preparation and legal fees, fiduciary bond fees, out-of-pocket expenses for the administrator of the estate, etc. that may be a portion of the NOL are shown in Box 11, Code C "final deductions" on Schedule K-1 and a separate written list is attached detailing the excess deductions. These excess deductions are then shown on Schedule A (itemized deductions) of the beneficiary's 1040 tax return.

You may deduct a capital loss on the sale of a house acquired by inheritance or as a gift if you personally did not use it and offered it for sale or rent immediately or within a few weeks after acquisition. The basis of the property is the stepped-up basis when inherited, which would be the appraised value in the year inherited. If there is a gain on the inherited house, it is always long-term capital gain. The basis of a house acquired as a gift for determining gain is the donor's adjusted basis on the date of the gift, but the basis of a house acquired as a gift for determining loss is the lower of FMV or the donor's adjusted basis. If gifted property is sold for an amount between the FMV and the adjusted basis, then no gain or loss is recognized. The beneficiary of gifted

350

property assumes the same holding period as the donor for determining gain or loss.

Trusts

A trust is a separate taxable entity that can be created pursuant to a trust agreement executed during a person's lifetime or upon a person's death pursuant to his or her written "will." Therefore, a separate tax identification number (TIN) has to be obtained for a trust either during the lifetime of the person establishing a trust or upon the death of that person. The grantor of the trust is the person who creates the trust, the trustee is the person or entity that controls the assets, and the beneficiary is the person or entity that ultimately benefits from the assets. In an irrevocable trust, in order for the assets to be removed from the estate, the grantor cannot be associated with the trust. What that means is that he or she can't be the trustee of the trust. Usually the lawyer or accountant would be the best choice for the trustee. an irrevocable trust is a taxable entity. The trust needs to have a fiduciary tax return filed, and the beneficiaries of the trust will receive K-1 forms. This usually isn't a big issue, as the trust simply invests the corpus of the trust. A trustee, who must be an unrelated person, takes title to property for the benefit of another person in order to protect or conserve the property of that person (grantor) or a beneficiary as expressed in the trust agreement or will. Two or more trusts are treated as one trust for tax purposes if they have substantially the same grantor/grantors and substantially the same primary beneficiaries.

You can classify trusts in different ways. If a grantor has powers over the trust, it is deemed a grantor or revocable trust. If a grantor does not have powers over the trust and all the assets in it, then it is an irrevocable trust or non-grantor trust. When the grantor renounces powers, then it becomes a non- grantor trust. The gross and taxable income of trusts is essentially determined like it is for an estate.

Grantor/Revocable Trust

As a separate taxable entity, a trust reports all income received on assets owned by it and deducts all expenses paid by it that are otherwise deductible. However, if the grantor has sufficient control of trust income or principal, the income is taxed directly to the grantor. This is a so-called a "grantor trust" that becomes a separate entity for tax purposes "upon the grantor's death," and at that point has to obtain a separate TIN. A grantor trust may have more than one grantor which are each treated separately as the owner of their portion of the trust. Chances are that if you have significant assets that will be subject to estate tax on Form 706, you will want to use a grantor trust, with the intention of eventually transferring the assets to children and other beneficiaries. The grantor retains substantial control over the trust, or power to revoke the trust and, therefore, a grantor trust does not have to file tax returns because everything still belongs to the grantor who must report all income, deductions, and credits on his or her own income tax return (example: a living trust, which is a revocable trust). The grantor's spouse also has the same powers.

Following the death of the grantor, the trustee must obtain a separate TIN for the trust and treat it as a separate entity for tax purposes. However, a qualified revocable trust, upon the grantor's death, can elect to be treated as part of the estate for income tax purposes. Making this election qualifies the trust for favorable tax treatment, including the ability to report on a fiscal-year basis. The election is made by filing Form 8855 and, once made, the election cannot be revoked. This election must be filed on time, as there is no provision to cure a delinquent or incomplete election. Form 56, "Notice Concerning Fiduciary Relationship," should be prepared and filed if needed. This form is used to notify the IRS of any change, e.g., creation or termination, of a fiduciary relationship and provide the qualification for the new relationship. The election allows the revocable trust to be

treated and taxed as part of the estate during the election period, which begins at the decedent's death and lasts for a minimum of two years. But the executor of the Estate must agree to the election or it will terminate. If an election isn't made, the trustee has to file tax returns for the trust on Form 1041, and start distributing income and assets to the beneficiaries. The trust is entitled to an annual exemption of $300 if it is required under its terms to distribute all income currently, which is a "simple trust."
www.irs.gov/pub/irs-pdf/f8855.pdf   www.irs.gov/pub/irs-pdf/f56.pdf
www.irs.gov/pub/irs-pdf/i56.pdf

Living Trust – A living trust is created to hold title to an individual's assets. The benefits of a living trust include: avoidance of probate; continuity of management of assets if the individual becomes incapacitated and unable to take care of his/her financial affairs; privacy as to one's assets upon his/her death; and possible reduced cost, time, and aggravation in settling one's estate. Houses, cars, life insurance, bank accounts, and investments should be put into a "revocable living trust," but not tax deferred annuities and IRAs, because they are passed directly to designated beneficiaries. Taxpayers with substantial estates should generally create a "Revocable Living Trust" in order to avoid the hassle and cost of probate.

Benefits of a Revocable Trust – Revocable trusts are powerful estate planning tools. Here are several situations in which having a revocable trust might be helpful:

1. Probate Avoidance – One of the main uses of a revocable trust is to help avoid probate, because upon death, the trust will dictate how assets will pass to heirs. This can be very beneficial, because in many states the probate process can be extremely time consuming and expensive. Although a trust is not the only way to avoid probate, a revocable trust is the only way to avoid probate and provide other benefits. Other ways to avoid probate are joint accounts, beneficiary designations and transfer-on-death accounts. However, a revocable trust is important for individuals who own real estate in more than one state – a situation that can result in a second (or ancillary) probate in another jurisdiction. Without a revocable trust, ancillary probate processes usually require retaining estate lawyers licensed in the second jurisdiction, potentially costing thousands of dollars in legal and probate court costs that would not be necessary if you had a revocable trust. Ordinarily, the cost of creating a revocable trust, and having a deed prepared to transfer the ownership of the real estate to the trust is less expensive.

2. Privacy – A revocable trust can provide privacy that isn't possible without one. You may not want either friends and neighbors or any relatives who are not provided for in the estate, to learn about the extent or disposition of your assets. When wills are filed with the court upon death, they become public record. However, revocable trusts are not public – they remain private.

3. Blended Families – A revocable trust can remedy the problems that can arise when married persons have children from previous marriages or relationships, and both parties leave all their assets to each other. Without a revocable trust, a surviving spouse can disinherit the stepchildren.

4. Incapacity – A revocable trust allows a co-trustee or a successor trustee to have unrestricted access to assets in the event of incapacity of the grantor. The trust holds all of the assets during the individual's life, but allows seamless access to the assets by adult children of sick or elderly individuals. In addition to the trust, a durable power of attorney may still be needed for dealing with the hospital or nursing home and with insurance companies.

5. Special Needs Loved Ones – A revocable trust may be beneficial for persons seeking a careful approach to providing for loved ones with special needs.

6. Naming a Trust as an IRA Beneficiary – Among married couples, naming the spouse as the IRA beneficiary is often the default choice. However, naming a trust as an IRA beneficiary with the surviving

spouse as the primary beneficiary of the trust may be a logical move for some people for several reasons. The surviving spouse might be inexperienced in financial matters or have health issues that require protection from bad decisions. Also, married couples who have children from previous marriages may create doubts as to how an inherited IRA will be handled. An IRA owner can arrange for a trust to be the beneficiary, and naming a reliable relative as the trustee responsible for seeing that the surviving spouse has necessary but not excessive cash flow from the trust. In some situations, a financial advisor could be a co-trustee to see that the IRA's investments are managed appropriately for the trust's beneficiaries.

7. Using Trusts for Vacation Homes – Trusts can be very helpful when it comes to vacation homes. A trustee can be appointed to make decisions about the house. A trust names the beneficiaries who will have use of the house, and can also describe the terms of use by the beneficiaries, and can even create a usage schedule. Trusts can also create a fund to pay the expenses for maintaining the house. A certain amount of funds from the estate can be designated to cover the annual costs associated with the house for a certain number of years, and doing so can help the heirs avoid conflict over paying the house expenses. Also, a trust can be used to dictate how, when, and to whom the house will be sold, including which party or parties have the right of first refusal, and how to establish the value of the sale to a family member. For example, the trust can provide that a sale will be triggered if all the heirs decide to sell, or if a majority of all competent beneficiaries would like to sell.

Discharge of Indebtedness – In June 2016, the IRS issued final regulations regarding how discharge of indebtedness affects grantor trusts, disregarded entities and their owners. Basically, the rules state that the responsibility for any discharge of indebtedness by these entities lies with their owners. For example, if a partnership holds an interest in a grantor trust or a disregarded entity, any discharge of indebtedness is the responsibility of each individual partner to whom the income is allocable. Also, the insolvency and bankruptcy exclusions applicable to discharge of indebtedness are available only to any individual owners that qualify for the exclusions. **(See Chapter 5, "Cancellation of Debt"); (See Chapter 9, "Cancellation of Debt Excluded from Income")**

Intentionally Defective Grantor Trust (IDGT) – An IDGT is a very complex instrument and is one way to work around the downside of a Grantor Retained Annuity Trust (GRAT). An IDGT is a term used for a trust that is purposely drafted to invoke the grantor trust rules. It can be created in one or more of the following ways: (1) The grantor or his or her spouse retains the power to recover the trust assets (e.g., the grantor retains the right to reacquire property out of the trust in exchange for property of equal value); (2) The grantor or his or her spouse can or does benefit from the trust income (e.g., the grantor and/or a nonadverse trustee can sprinkle income for the benefit of the grantor's spouse); (3) The grantor or his or her spouse possesses a reversionary interest worth more than 5 percent of the value of the trust upon its creation; or (4) The grantor or his or her spouse controls to whom and when trust income and principal is to be distributed, or possesses certain administrative powers that may benefit the grantor or his or her spouse (e.g., a nonadverse trustee may add beneficiaries of the trust income and/or principal). **(See Below, "Grantor Retained Annuity Trust (GRAT")**

- **Example** – A revocable living trust that avoids probate and allows for full use of the applicable exclusion amount for estate tax is the most common form of an IDGT. **(See Above, "Living Trust")**

Irrevocable trusts, held for the benefit of the grantor's beneficiaries, can also be an IDGT. Because the grantor pays the income taxes incurred by the IDGT, and the assets held in the IDGT can grow unreduced by such income taxes. This, in turn, increases the value of the assets available for the trust beneficiaries. In essence, the payment of taxes by a grantor is a gift to the trust beneficiaries that is not subject to transfer tax.

Electing Small Business Trust (ESBT)

As a general rule, trusts cannot be S-corporation shareholders. However, an exception allows electing small business trusts (ESBTs) to be S-corporation shareholders. An electing small business trust (ESBT) is treated as two separate trusts. The portion of an ESBT that consists of stock in one or more S-corporations is treated as one trust. The portion of an ESBT that consists of all the other assets in the trust is treated as a separate trust. The grantor or another person may be treated as the owner of all or a portion of either or both such trusts under subpart E, part I, subchapter J, chapter 1 of the Internal Revenue Code. The ESBT is treated as a single trust for administrative purposes, such as having one taxpayer identification number and filing one tax return. The grantor portion of an ESBT is the portion of the trust that is treated as owned by the grantor or another person under subpart E. The S-corporation portion of an ESBT is the portion of the trust that consists of S-corporation stock and is not treated as owned by the grantor or another person under Subpart E. The non-S-corporation portion of an ESBT is the portion of the trust that consists of all assets other than S-corporation stock that is not treated as owned by the grantor or another person under subpart E.

Qualifying Beneficiaries of an ESBT – Generally, eligible beneficiaries of an ESBT include individuals, estates, and certain charitable organizations eligible to hold S-corporation stock directly. Prior to the enactment of the Tax Cuts and Jobs Act (TCJA), a nonresident alien individual could not be a shareholder of an S-corporation and could not be a potential current beneficiary of an ESBT. However, effective as of January 1, 2018, the TCJA allows a nonresident alien individual to be a potential current beneficiary of an ESBT. In 2017 and prior years, an ESBT couldn't have a current beneficiary who was a nonresident alien individual. But in accordance with the TCJA, such individuals can now be ESBT beneficiaries. This change is effective for 2018 and subsequent years.

Charitable Contribution Deduction for ESBTs – Generally, a trust is allowed a charitable contribution deduction for amounts of gross income, without limitation, which pursuant to the terms of the governing instrument are paid for a charitable purpose. No carryover of excess contributions is allowed. An individual is allowed a charitable contribution deduction limited to certain percentages of adjusted gross income, generally with a 5-year carryforward of amounts in excess of this limitation. For tax years beginning after Dec. 31, 2017, the TCJA provides that the charitable contribution deduction of an ESBT is not determined by the rules generally applicable to trusts but rather by the rules applicable to individuals. Thus, the percentage limitations and carryforward provisions applicable to individuals apply to charitable contributions made by the portion of an ESBT holding S-corporation stock. However, in 2017 and prior years the deduction for charitable contributions was determined by the rules applicable to trusts rather than to the rules applicable to individuals.

Non-Grantor/Irrevocable Trust

A non-grantor trust is treated as a separate entity for tax purposes, and must immediately obtain a separate TIN. When you put assets into an irrevocable trust, you no longer own the assets – the trust does. Thus, an irrevocable trust establishes control over the use of assets and money in the trust. A non-grantor or irrevocable trust is taxed on its income only to the extent it is not distributed. Form 1041 must be filed on a calendar year basis by the trustee or fiduciary of the trust, and Form 1041 Schedule K-1 is used to report distributions to the beneficiaries, which must be reported on their individual tax returns. All distributions retain the same character – passive income, etc. as they were in the hands of the person who establishes the trust. Non-grantor trusts are treated somewhat like a partnership as to distributed income, and like a corporation as to undistributed income. Essentially, there are two kinds of non-grantor trusts: (1) Simple Trust; and (2) Complex Trust.

A "simple" trust is one that's not a grantor trust and requires that all trust income must be distributed to its beneficiaries annually. In addition, the trust is prohibited from making any distributions of trust assets (corpus) or charitable contributions. Whereas, a complex trust may retain current income within the trust and it can also distribute trust assets and make charitable contributions. Generally, the taxable income of a trust as reported on Form 1041 is calculated similarly to an individual taxpayer: Taxable income received by the trust is reported; trusts are allowed a personal exemption; and various ordinary and necessary expenses are allowed as a deduction against taxable income. Complex trusts are allowed a deduction for charitable contributions if permitted by the trust agreement, and of course, a deduction is allowed for income that the trust distributes to its beneficiaries. Since a simple trust is required to distribute all of its income annually, its potential taxable income is generally reduced to zero by the income distribution deduction taken (discussed below) and it will have no tax liability. A revocable trust that had been treated as a grantor trust would become irrevocable upon the death of the grantor. When this occurs, the trust is then required to begin filing its own separate Form 1041 (See above).

In an irrevocable trust, you can put any provisions or restrictions that you want on the assets or corpus of the trust. For example, you can add a provision that says the beneficiaries (e.g. children) can have access to 25 percent of the corpus (trust assets) at age 20 if they are full-time students, maintain an A average, and are drug and alcohol free. The rest of the assets can be doled out in any manner you choose – you can specify that the beneficiaries get another 25 percent of the money when they are 25, and the remainder when they are 35. Also, assets in an irrevocable trust are protected from creditors. However, the assets inside the trust (corpus) are usually invested in something, and any money that is made on the investments (annual earnings) are taxable to the beneficiaries, but they are usually in a lower tax bracket than the person who established the trust. Except that any earnings generally exclude capital gains generated by the trust assets, so capital gains are excluded from distributable net income and, therefore, are not taxed at the trust level. The capital gains may never be taxed to the beneficiaries because the basis of the assets inside the trust get the "stepped-up" valuation in the Estate, which means the capital gains are never taxed.

An irrevocable trust is another way to save for college for your children. You can put, for example, $14,000 into the trust per year. If you are married and you and your spouse agree to gift splitting, your spouse can also put $14,000 into the trust per year, for a total of $28,000. The only problem with putting money into the trust is that any money that the trust earns is taxable to the beneficiary each year. However, if your children decide not to go to college, this would be the best way to give your children money, while at the same time putting restrictions on how they can use it. This is just another of several ways to give money to your kids and still control the use of the money. Whether it be through college savings plans or an irrevocable trust, you are in control of your money. **(See Chapter 8, "Gifts and Inheritances"); (See Chapter 22, "Exemption for Lifetime Taxable Gifts and Estates ")**

Grantor Retained Annuity Trust (GRAT) – A GRAT is used to remove a family business from a taxable estate. Typically, the grantor is still working in the business and creates a GRAT, which is an irrevocable trust in which the grantor retains a right to receive fixed amounts payable at least annually for life or for a term of years. In essence, a GRAT is a fixed annuity. At the end of the term or life of interest, the remaining trust principal is distributed to the designated beneficiaries free of any additional gift tax, even if the property has appreciated while held in the trust. The purpose of the GRAT is to freeze the value of the asset(s).

- **Example** – Jane owns a pet store that is taxed as an S-corporation. She wants to pass the family business on to her daughter, Alice. The store has traditionally had a very steady cash flow and earnings are expected to rise. Jane decided to use a GRAT to assist in the business succession plan after her tax planner told her that a GRAT could be used to transfer the stock at a substantially reduced gift tax cost while providing a steady cash flow. Assuming the GRAT qualifies as a grantor trust (in which all of the income and principal is treated as if it is owned by the grantor), the S-corporation status will be preserved, and cash generated from the business could be used to make the required annuity payment. As the S-corporation's earnings increase, as expected, it will be easier for the S-corporation to meet the cash requirements of the fixed annuity payments. Any appreciation in the stock's value will be removed from Jane's estate and distributed to Alice. The big downside to a GRAT is that if the grantor (Jane) dies before the term of the GRAT is over, it remains in the taxable estate.

Alaskan Native Corporation Payments and Contributions to Settlement Trusts

The TCJA created new possibilities for Alaska Native Settlement Trusts and Alaska Native Corporations. Congress first authorized Native Corporations to establish Settlement Trusts in 1988 "to promote the health, education, and welfare of its beneficiaries and preserve the heritage and culture of Natives." But the Trusts have been relatively underutilized thus far by Native Corporations. Among the changes made by the TCJA was the addition of section 247 to the Internal Revenue Code (I.R.C.), which permits a Native Corporation to make contributions to Settlement TrustS on a tax-deductible basis rather than an after-tax basis. This should make the use of Settlement Trusts more attractive to Native Corporations.

Chapter 22 – Estate and Gift Tax

The purpose of the Estate and Gift tax is to impose a wealth transfer tax on benefactors' estates that are transferred from one generation to the next generation on amounts over a certain threshold. An Estate tax return is filed on Form 706, and a Gift tax return is filed on Form 709. The exemption amount is the same for both Estate and Gift tax purposes, hence making the wealth transfer tax truly a "unified tax." However, beginning in 2012, any unified credit allocated to gifts in prior periods must be re-determined using the current unified tax rate, not the rates in effect for the years when prior gifts were made (the instructions provide a worksheet for making this calculation, and the result is reported on Form 709, Schedule B, Gifts from Prior Periods). The Estate tax is not an issue for most people. In fact, in the past only about 3,000 individuals per year have had to pay the Estate tax. The main issue is to maximize and maintain the basis of assets passed on to heirs. Most estate tax returns are filed to secure portability of the Estate tax exemption. **(See Below, "Portability of the Estate Tax Exemption")**
www.irs.gov/pub/irs-pdf/f706.pdf www.irs.gov/pub/irs-pdf/i706.pdf www.irs.gov/pub/irs-pdf/f709.pdf
www.irs.gov/pub/irs-pdf/i709.pdf

Under the Tax Cuts and Jobs Act (TCJA), the exemption amount for Estates and Gifts and Generation-Skipping Tax is doubled for tax years 2018 – 2025 to $11.2 million (indexed for inflation beginning in 2019). The exemption is scheduled to revert back to half of the 2025 adjusted amount in 2026, which would be approximately the exemption amount in 2017 before being doubled. The exemption amount in 2017 is $5.49 million. The top tax rate remains at 40%. With the availability of the "Portability of the Estate Tax Exemption" (See below), the Estate and Gift Tax for married couples should only apply to estates in excess of $22.4 million in 2018.

An alternative regime applies to certain individuals who are non-resident non-citizens by virtue of having relinquished their U.S. citizenship or long-term residency. Special rules for income, gift, and estate tax purposes apply for 10 years following their expatriation to alleviate avoidance of taxation.

Following are the unified Estate and Gift tax lifetime exemptions and tax rates for 2018 and prior years:

Exemption for Lifetime Taxable Gifts and Estates:
- 2005: $1,500,000
- 2006 – 2008: $2,000,000
- 2009: $3,500,000
- 2010: SEE BELOW
- 2011: $5,000,000
- 2012: $5,120,000
- 2013: $5,250,000
- 2014: $5,340,000
- 2015: $5,430,000
- 2016: $5,450,000
- 2017: $5,490,000
- 2018: $11,200,000

Graduated Tax Rates for Computation of Estate and Gift Taxes in 2018:

$0 - $10,000 (18%); $10,001 - $20,000 ($1,800 + 20% of the amount over $10,000); $20,001 - $40,000 ($3,800 + 22% of the amount over $20,000); $40,001 - $60,000 ($8,200 + 24% of the amount over $40,000); $60,001 - $80,000 ($13,000 + 26% of the amount over $60,000); $80,001 - $100,000 ($18,200 + 28% of the amount over $80,000); $100,000 - $150,000 ($23,800 + 30% of the amount over $100,000); $150,001 - $250,000 ($38,800 + 32% of the amount over $150,000); $250,001 - $500,000 ($70,800 + 34% of the amount over $250,000); $500,001 - $750,000 ($155,800 + 37% of the amount over $500,000); $750,001 - $1,000,000 ($248,300 + 39% of the amount over $750,000); Over $1,000,000 ($345,800 + 40% of the amount over $1,000,000).

States That Impose Estate or Inheritance Taxes

Nineteen states and the District of Columbia impose estate or inheritance taxes, or both, in addition to the federal estate tax. These state taxing authorities generally reach nonresident estates owning real estate or tangible property within their borders. Florida, Texas, and Nevada don't have income taxes or estate taxes. Some of the states that have an estate or inheritance tax use the federal exemption amounts. Other states have exemption amounts less than the federal amounts.

For estate tax purposes, you should be aware that you can be considered a resident of more than one state, even though you are domiciled in only one state. Domicile is defined as a person's fixed or permanent abode that a person intends to return to. Residency is a much more flexible term and may be defined differently depending on the state. For example, some states determine residency by looking at whether a person has a permanent place of abode in the state and lives in it a certain number of days in the year. Often, just owning a vacant lot or even tangible personal property located in another state can require a nonresident estate tax return to be filed. The filing requirement for a nonresident estate tax return in some states generally is triggered when the value of the decedent's worldwide assets exceeds the state's exemption amount, not when the value of the nonresident's assets located in the state exceeds the exemption amount. For example, the estate of a widow living in Florida with $2.4 million in cash and a vacant lot in Connecticut worth $100,000 will have to file a Connecticut estate tax return and pay estate taxes on all of her assets.

Basis of Property Inherited or Gifted

The basis of property inherited by beneficiaries is generally the fair market value (FMV) at the decedent's date of death, which is known as the "stepped-up basis." In community property states, a surviving spouse is entitled to the stepped-up basis in the entire property; in contrast to the allowable ½ stepped-up basis for property in non-community property states. The stepped-up basis is not allowed for appreciated property acquired by the decedent as a gift within one year before the date of death. If a Form 706 is required to be filed, executors can elect to value the estate on an "alternate valuation date" that is six months after the date of death. Any property distributed, sold, exchanged or otherwise disposed of during the six months is valued as of the date of disposition. However, any property whose value changed by merely the lapse of time is valued as of the date of death, with an adjustment allowed for any difference in value due to any factor other than the lapse of time. The alternate valuation date can only be used if it will decrease both the value of the gross estate and the taxes payable as well as any generation skipping transfer tax (GST) payable as a result of the taxpayer's death.

The stepped-up basis rule does not apply to "Gifts" made during the decedent's lifetime. The basis of property acquired as a gift is generally the donor's adjusted basis in the property (carryover basis). However, the recipient's basis for computing a loss is the lesser of the donor's adjusted basis or fair market value (FMV). The recipient's basis is increased by any Gift tax and Generation-Skipping Transfer Tax (GST) attributable to the gift, but not more than the FMV of the property at the time of the gift. When the donee sales the gift (such as marketable securities), the basis of property received as a gift in the hands of the beneficiary (donee) depends on whether the selling price of the property is more or less than the basis for gain or loss. If the property is sold at a gain, the beneficiary's basis is the same as it would have been in the hands of the donor (gifter). If the property is sold at a loss, the beneficiary's basis is the same as it would have been in the hands of the donor or the fair market value (FMV) of the property on the date of the gift, whichever is lower. If the gifted property is sold for an amount between the donor's adjusted basis and the FMV on the date of the gift, then no gain or loss is reported.

- **Example** – Bill's mother gifted him 100 shares of stock. His mother's basis in the stock was $4,000 and the market value on the date of the gift was $3,000. Bill sold the stock for $3,500. Bill reports no gain or loss on the sale (Bill's mother paid no gift tax).

For property acquired from a decedent, a new law enacted on July 31, 2015, requires that the basis of inherited assets reported by heirs not exceed the basis in the property reported by the estate. Executors of taxable estates are required, along with filing Estate tax returns (Form 706), to report to heirs and to the IRS the basis of inherited assets on Form 8971 within 30 days of filing Form 706, and heirs are required to use the basis reported by executors for the assets. The reason is to prevent heirs from using an inflated basis when the assets are eventually sold. Heirs who use a higher basis can be hit with a 20% substantial understatement penalty. An overstatement of the basis of inherited assets by beneficiaries of estates upon sale of those assets is an omission from gross income and, therefore, will engage the six-year statute of limitations as opposed to the usual three-year statute of limitations.

www.irs.gov/pub/irs-pdf/f8971.pdf   www.irs.gov/pub/irs-pdf/i8971.pdf

When a gift tax return is required to be filed, the donor must fully describe the gift or gifts and the methodology used to value the gifts on Form 709. If not, the usual three years that the IRS has to assess additional gift taxes will not apply, i.e. the statute of limitations for the IRS to assess additional gift taxes will remain open indefinitely.

Gift Tax Return (Form 709)
The Gift tax is a cumulative lifetime tax, which is equal to the tax imposed for each calendar year at the graduated unified rates, which is a maximum of 40% in 2018, on the sum of all taxable gifts for the current year and for all prior years, reduced by the total gift taxes previously owed for all prior years. Taxable gifts made in any one year include all gifts made, reduced by the applicable exclusions (See below), i.e. no gift tax return has to be filed if gifts made by a donor to a donee in a year are less than the gift tax exclusion. However, there is an unlimited gift tax exclusion for: (1) gifts made to 501(c)(3) tax-exempt charitable organizations, as well as 501(c)(4), 501(c)(5), and 501(c)(6) tax-exempt organizations; (2) transfers made between spouses, unless a non-citizen spouse is involved; and (3) transfers to pay for tuition and medical expenses made directly to educational institutions and providers of medical care regardless of the amount.**(See Chapter 12, "Charitable Contribution Deduction"); (See Chapter 20, "Tax-Exempt Organizations")**

 Gift Tax Exclusion – A gift tax return has to be filed on Form 709 by April 15, 2019 (unless an extension is filed) if a gift is made to any one person, other than your spouse, that exceeds $15,000, which is the annual exclusion amount in 2018. Therefore, to avoid filing a Gift tax return (Form 709), as well as to avoid owing gift tax in any one year, you should generally limit the amount of gifts made to any one person to the gift tax exclusion amount, which is $15,000 per person in 2018 (but see exceptions below). However, even if a gift tax is owed, no gift tax is actually payable until the total amount of accumulated gifts exceeds the "unified exemption for lifetime taxable gifts and estates," which is $11.2 million in 2018. Any amount of the lifetime exemption that is used in any one year reduces the amount of the life time exemption that you can use in later years. If "gift splitting" is used with your spouse you must file a gift tax return, but no gift tax is actually due if the amount of the gifts to any one person is $30,000 or less. If you don't use up the full $15,000 per recipient exclusion in any one year, the shortfall is lost forever, because you can't give a recipient an extra amount next year to make up for the shortfall. The exemption from gift tax on gifts made to a spouse who is not a U.S. citizen is $152,000 in 2018.

When a Gift tax return has to be filed to report gifts of over $15,000 to any one person, then all gifts made to charities also have to be reported on the return, even though no gift tax is owed on the gifts to charities. Each spouse must file a separate gift tax return for their own individual gifts, unless the married couple consents to split gifts. Then, only the donor spouse is required to file a return if a gift of over $15,000 is made to any one person. However, no gift tax is owed if the "split" gift to any one person is $30,000 or less. If you pay off your son's mortgage of $30,000 and he is not your dependent, it is a gift to him, and you must file a gift tax return. This also applies to giving your house to your son or daughter or giving them another property or asset worth over $15,000. If a parent pays student loan interest for a child not claimed as a dependent, the IRS treats the payment as a Gift to the child, who can then deduct the interest on his/her own tax return. The annual Gift Tax exclusion ($15,000; $30,000 if a married couple) can be used to fund a 529 Plan (QTP). And according to the 5-year averaging rule a donor can contribute up to $75,000; $150,000 if a married couple and average it over 5 years with no gift tax consequences. However, a Gift tax return must be filed, and the election for 5-year averaging must be made on the donor's Gift tax return. If you guarantee a loan as a personal favor to a family member, relative or friend, with no profit motive and without consideration, it will likely be characterized as a Gift by the IRS. **(See Chapter 8, "Distributions from Qualified Tuition Programs – 529 Plans")**

- **Example** – If you make gifts in the amount of $115,000 to each of your two children in 2018 ("gift-splitting" is not applicable in this example), then the taxable amount of the gifts is $200,000 ($230,000 minus $15,000 X 2 = $30,000 = $200,000 taxable amount of gifts). You have to file Form 709 reporting $200,000 in taxable gifts, but you don't actually have to pay any gift tax, because the $200,000 is deducted from the unified exemption for lifetime taxable gifts and estates of $11.2 million. Therefore, the remaining lifetime exemption for use in future years after the offset is $11,000,000 ($11,200,000 - $200,000 = $11,000,000).
- **Example** – If you and your spouse use "gift-splitting" to make gifts in the amount of $30,000 to each of your two children in 2018, you have to file Form 709, but the amount of the gifts are not taxable because the gifts are not more than the exclusion amount of $30,000 for each child when gift-splitting is used.

A Gift tax return (Form 709) must be filed if you make a gift of a future interest in a property – regardless of the value. Although an interest in property may vest immediately in the recipient, it is a future interest if the recipient cannot immediately use or enjoy the property. Transfers to "trusts" fail to qualify as a gift of a present interest if the recipient does not have an unrestricted right to the immediate use, possession, or enjoyment of the property, or the income from the property. In order to have transfers to a trust qualify as a gift of a present interest, a provision must be included giving the beneficiary notice of "withdrawal rights" with respect to transfers to the trust. It is advisable that such a notice must be given if the annual gift tax exclusion is being claimed.

Payments by parents or grandparents for a dependent child's tuition and medical costs that are made directly to the providers (e.g. university, school, hospital or doctor) are excluded from the child's income, and the direct payments don't reduce the annual gift tax exclusion allowable to the parents or grandparents for the benefit of the children, i.e. such direct payments are not considered "gifts."

When making year-end gifts by check, you should be sure that the recipient deposits the check before the end of the year if you want it to count as a 2018 gift for gift tax purposes. If the check is deposited after the end of the year, it will be considered a 2019 gift for gift tax purposes. However, if you make the gift with a certified check it will count as a 2018 gift, even if the recipient doesn't deposit the check until after the end of the year. If you give securities as a gift, you should endorse them to the donee and deliver them by the end of the year.

Estate Tax Return (Form 706)

A graduated tax rate (See above) is applied to a taxable estate to obtain the amount of the estate tax. An Estate tax return (Form 706) is due nine months after the date of death, but an Estate tax return has to be filed only if a taxpayer's gross estate plus adjusted taxable gifts – after specific exclusions for gifts made in prior years – exceeds the exemption amount, which is $11.2 million in 2018, which doesn't take into account the portability provision. A decedent's gross estate is not the same as the probate estate used to compute estate income tax on Form 1041. The gross estate for Estate tax purposes includes property, such as life insurance and retirement accounts, that are not part of the decedent's gross estate for probate purposes. A decedent's gross estate for Estate tax purposes includes interests he or she holds in all property (real, personal, tangible or intangible). Included in the decedent's gross estate for Estate tax purposes are: life insurance proceeds received by a beneficiary; retirement assets that pass directly to designated beneficiaries (traditional and Roth IRAs, annuities, etc.); and those assets held in revocable trusts created by the decedent. **(See Below, "Portability of the Estate Tax Exemption"); (See Chapter 21, "Estates")**

In the case of jointly owned property held by a husband and wife, only ½ of the property is included in the decedent's gross estate. A married person's estate is allowed a deduction for property passing directly to the surviving spouse (reported on Schedule M of Form 706). Property that generally passes tax-free to a spouse includes: jointly owned property; life insurance; retirement accounts; property passing in trust, such as a "Revocable Living Trust," and bequests (inheritances) included in the will; although bequests included in the will are generally subject to probate.

If a decedent makes a taxable gift to someone other than a spouse within three years before the date of death, then the taxable gift is included in the gross estate. In order for this rule to apply, the property given away must have been property that would have been included in the estate and subject to estate tax. Thus, if you make a gift within three years of death that is excluded from the estate tax because it does not exceed the annual gift tax exclusion amount ($15,000 for 2018), then the gift will not be included in the calculation of estate taxes.

- **Example** – Ben makes a gift of $10,000 to Adam on June 1, 2017. Ben died on May 31, 2018. Since the gift was excluded from tax when it was made (less than the $14,000 annual gift tax exclusion amount in 2017), that $10,000 will not be included in the amount of assets included in Ben's gross estate.

Certain expenses are deductible from a gross estate for determining the taxable amount of the estate: medical expenses of the decedent that could not be deducted on the decedent's final tax return; unreimbursed funeral expenses; administration expenses not deducted from Estate income tax returns (Form 1041), including executor expenses; attorney and accountant fees; fees for maintaining and storing estate property; selling expenses if necessary to pay estate tax liabilities and expenses; claims against the estate; unpaid mortgages on any indebtedness on property included in the gross estate; and other claims and expenses against the estate, which may not be known at the time of filing Form 706.

Exclusion for Qualified Small Business Property or Qualified Farm Property – A gross estate can receive a discount in its valuation based on a special-use valuation for business real estate and farm land, which can reduce the gross estate up to a maximum of $1,140,000 in 2018. Qualified small business and farm property must meet the following requirements:

- The value of the property was included in the decedent's federal adjusted taxable estate, which is after deductions, including debts, expenses and bequests to a surviving spouse (both small business and farm property).
- The property consists of trade or business property or shares of stock or other ownership interests that are not publicly traded (small business property).
- The decedent or decedent's spouse materially participated in the trade or business during the taxable year that ended before the decedent's death (small business property).
- The trade or business had gross annual sales of $10 million or less during the last taxable year that ended before the decedent's death (small business property).
- The property does not consist of cash or cash equivalents (small business property).
- The decedent continuously owned the property for the three-year period ending at the decedent's death (both small business and farm property).
- A family member continuously uses the property in the operation of the trade or business for three years following the decedent's death (both small business and farm property).
- The estate and qualified heir agree to pay the recapture tax, if applicable (both small business and farm property).
- The property was classified for property tax purposes as the homestead of the decedent and/or decedent's spouse (farm property)

Portability of the Estate Tax Exemption

The Tax Relief, Unemployment Insurance Reauthorization, and Job Creation Act of 2010 introduced the concept of portability of the estate tax exemption for the first time. In June 2015, the IRS issued final rules governing the requirements for electing portability of a deceased spouse's unused exemption. The final rules apply to estates of decedents dying on or after June 12, 2015. Portability allows a surviving spouse's estate to use the portion of the estate tax exemption that was not used upon the death of the first spouse. However, executors of estates who want to make the portability election have to file an Estate tax return (Form 706) for individuals who die even if the deceased person does not owe any estate tax. Estates that file an estate tax return solely to make the portability election do not have to file Form 8971. **(See Above, "Basis of Property Inherited or Gifted")**

To ease the filing burden, executors can estimate the value of assets included in the estate that are passing to surviving spouses. Also, small estates that failed to make the portability election on time can request a ruling from the IRS for extra time to make the election. But, to ease the burden of requesting a ruling, the IRS released a revenue procedure that offers an easier way to get an extension of time to file a return to opt for portability of the deceased spousal unused exclusion amount. Revenue Procedure 2017-34 applies to estates that aren't typically required to file an estate tax return because the value of the gross estate and adjusted taxable gifts is under the filing threshold. To qualify for the simplified late election, the executor must file a complete and properly prepared Form 706 on or before the second annual anniversary of the decedent's date of death. The executor must state at the top that the return: "FILED PURSUANT TO REV. PROC. 2017-34 TO ELECT PORTABILITY UNDER § 2010(c)(5)(A)."

www.irs.gov/pub/irs-drop/rp-17-34.pdf

The provision allows both spouses' exemptions to be utilized without having to set-up trusts or engage in other tax planning maneuvers that were previously necessary.

- **Example** – Bill and Jane are married – Jane dies in 2018 and has $1 million in her estate. An Estate tax return (Form 706) should be filed for Jane, even though she owes no Estate tax, so that the $10.2 million of her remaining exemption is transferred to Bill, who will then have a total exemption of $21.4 million in 2019 (adjusted for inflation). After Jane dies, Bill marries Mary. If Bill then dies in 2019 with a $4 million estate and leaves the remaining $17.4 million to Mary, a Form 706 should be filed for Bill even though he owes no Estate Tax. Mary will then have a $28.6 million total exemption amount available.

There are several reasons in favor of filing a Form 706, even if not needed. It is possible that the surviving spouse will get remarried to a wealthy person and the unused exemption will be needed. In addition, the exemption has economic value. A single person with a very large estate may see a financial benefit in marrying someone with little or no assets and two available exemptions. If the situation arises where you have a taxable estate and are required to file Form 706 but do not want to make the portability election, you will have to attach a statement to the Form 706 indicating that the estate is not making the election under I.R.C. section 2010(c)(5) or write "No Election Under Section 2010(c)(5)" on the top of the first page of the Form 706. The portability provision was made "permanent" as of Jan. 1, 2013.

Generation-Skipping Transfer Tax (Form709, Form 706-GS(D), and Form 706-GS(T)

The purpose of the Generation-Skipping Transfer Tax (GST) is to prevent families from avoiding estate tax in younger generations by skipping a generation and transferring property to the next generation. A GST tax return must be filed only in any year in which a GST tax is owed. This is a tax imposed in addition to the Estate and Gift tax on certain transfers from a grandparent generation to a grandchild's generation. The GST tax is part of the unified Estate and Gift tax: the same exemption amount of $11.2 million applies, and the same annual exclusion as the Gift tax of $15,000 applies. However, for gifts to trusts, the annual exclusion may not be available unless the trust provides the beneficiaries the right to withdraw an amount that does not exceed the gift tax annual exclusion amount. The tax return is due on April 15th following the year of transfer. The donor's cost basis and holding period generally carry over to the recipient. The portability provisions do not apply to the GST tax. There are three types of transfers subject to the GST tax:

- A direct skip is a gift from a grandparent to a grandchild. In a direct skip during the life of the transferor, the transferor is responsible for filing Form 709 and paying the GST tax.
- A taxable distribution is when the trust of a grandparent makes a distribution of principal to the grandchild. In this case, the transferee (grandchild) is required to pay the GST tax. For example, suppose Sam dies with a $15 million estate and leaves all of his property in trust with income payable to his child, Mark, and upon Mark's death the trust assets go to the grandchild, George. Upon his death, Sam's estate is subject to the estate tax. On the subsequent death of Mark, none of the trust property is taxable to Mark's estate. The family would have "skipped" a generation of estate taxes. George is required to file Form 706-GS(D) and pay the GST tax.
- See the same example above, but instead the assets in the trust would go to the grandchild upon

the termination of the trust, which would be a "taxable termination." This would require the trustee of the estate to file Form 706-GS(T) and pay the GST tax.

Alternatives to Making Gifts to Family Members

Gifts by grandparents to grandchildren reduce taxable estates, but there are other alternatives that can make sense also. For example, payments for college tuition and medical costs made directly to the provider (e.g. school, hospital or doctor) are tax free in any amount, and they don't reduce the annual gift tax exclusion for the benefit of the grandchildren being helped, plus they reduce the size of the grandparents' estate.

Loans– Grandparents can lend money to a grandchild to buy a home, start a business, or for any other purpose. If there is no interest charged, or the interest is below the applicable federal rate for the term of the loan, the lender must report "imputed" interest even though no funds are received. However, there are two conditions where imputed interest does not have to be reported on the lender's tax return: (1) the amount of the loan does not exceed $10,000, and (2) the amount of the loan does not exceed $100,000 and the borrower's total "investment income" for the year does not exceed $1,000. It is important to put any loan of this kind in writing and include important loan terms – interest rate if any, repayment schedule, and what happens if there is a default on the loan. If the loan terms are formalized in writing, the lender can write-off the loan if the grandchild fails to repay it, and without a valid promissory note, the IRS may try to claim that the grandparents merely made a "gift" of the money which may be taxable to the grandparents, and which is not potentially deductible.

Taxation of Gifts and Bequests Received from Covered Expatriates

In September 2015, the IRS issued proposed regulations to tax gifts and bequests received by U.S. persons from certain expatriates. The tax would be reported and paid by U.S. citizens who receive covered gifts and bequests on new Form 708.

U.S. citizens or residents who receive covered gifts or bequests (inheritances) from certain individuals who gave up their U.S. citizenship or residency will be subject to the tax, at the highest applicable gift or estate tax rate, on the gifts or bequests received from covered expatriates. An individual is defined as a covered expatriate at all times after the expatriation date, except during any period beginning after that date during which he or she is subject to U.S. estate or gift tax as a U.S. citizen or resident. A covered gift is defined as a direct or indirect gift from an expatriate regardless of whether the property transferred was acquired by the donor or decedent before or after expatriation. A covered bequest is defined as any property acquired directly or indirectly because of the death of an expatriate, which is generally property that would have been includible in the expatriate's gross estate had he or she been a U.S. citizen or resident at death.

The tax is calculated on the value of the covered gifts and bequests received, reduced by the amount of the gift tax exclusion ($15,000 in 2018), and the property's value is determined on the date of receipt. The net amount is then multiplied by the highest gift or estate tax rate in effect for the calendar year. A gift is considered received on the date it would be considered received for gift tax purposes. A bequest is considered received on the date the bequest is distributed from the estate, or in some cases upon the date of death of the decedent.

Exceptions – Taxable gifts reported on a covered expatriate's timely filed gift tax return, and properly included in the covered expatriate's gross estate and reported on the expatriate's timely filed estate tax return are exempt from the tax, if the gift or estate tax is timely paid. Also, gifts or bequests to a covered expatriate's

U.S. citizen spouse are exempt if they qualify for the gift or estate tax marital deduction. For a gift or bequest in trust, this means that, to the extent the gift or bequest to the trust would qualify for the estate or gift tax marital deduction, the gift or bequest is not a covered gift or bequest.

Transfer Taxes Applicable to Aliens Domiciled in the United States

If foreign persons (aliens) are domiciled in the U.S., they may be subject to U.S. transfer taxes on their estates (Estate and Gift taxes). The test to determine if an alien individual is considered a U.S. resident for transfer tax purposes is different from the test to determine if an individual is considered a U.S. resident for income tax purposes. An individual can simultaneously be "domiciled" in the United States and be subject to U.S. transfer taxes while also being a U.S. non-resident who is not subject to U.S. income taxes. A foreign alien is a resident alien for U.S. income tax purposes if he or she meets one of three tests: the "green card" test; substantial presence test; or the first-year election test. However, for transfer tax purposes, the residency test is a facts-and-circumstances test based on the concept of domicile. A foreign alien individual is subject to U.S. transfer taxes if he or she "acquires a domicile in the U.S." by living there, for even a brief period of time with no definite present intention of moving from the U.S. Therefore, one of the primary considerations is the individual's intention to remain in the United States, as well as other facts that suggest domicile in the U.S., such as the individual's employment history, real property owned, and his or her extended family's country of residence.

An alien domiciled in the United States who is subject to transfer taxes has the same exemption amount as U.S. citizens. So, considering the size of the exemption, many aliens need not concern themselves with the U.S. gift or estate tax. However, foreigners are at a disadvantage under the U.S. gift and estate tax system, because unlike U.S. citizens, gifts or bequests to foreign spouses are not eligible for the unlimited U.S. marital deduction. For example, a U.S. citizen can give a $10 million gift to a U.S. citizen spouse without any concern of using up some of their exemption amount or paying any gift tax. However, if a U.S. citizen or foreign person makes a gift to a non-citizen spouse, those gifts will be taxable gifts to the extent they exceed the annual gift tax exclusion. Although unavailable for gift tax purposes, bequests to a non-U.S. citizen spouse can qualify for the U.S. unlimited marital deduction for estate tax purposes if the bequest is to a qualified domestic trust (QDOT). Therefore, if a deceased spouse's assets are placed in a QDOT, the U.S. estate tax will be deferred generally until the death of the surviving spouse, or sooner if the surviving spouse receives distributions of principal from the QDOT. The QDOT must have a U.S. citizen serving as the trustee, be solely for the benefit of the surviving spouse, and require the distribution of income to the surviving spouse on at least an annual basis. Also, the executor of the deceased person's estate must make an election to qualify the trust as a QDOT trust.

Chapter 23 – Alternative Minimum Tax

The alternative minimum tax (AMT) is another tax system that runs parallel to the ordinary income tax system, based on an alternative set of tax calculation rules that limits or excludes many common deductions and credits allowed in the ordinary tax system. All taxpayers are subject to the ordinary income tax, and can be subject to the AMT, including individuals, estates, and trusts. Partnerships and S-corporations are not subject to the AMT. The AMT is computed on Form 6251 – the tax rates are 26% and 28%. To determine how much income is subject to AMT, alternative minimum taxable income (AMTI) is calculated by adding back "preference" items to ordinary taxable income that are allowed to reduce ordinary taxable income but not AMTI, and also by adding or subtracting certain "adjustments" allowed in determining ordinary taxable income but not AMTI. Once the initial AMTI is determined, an exemption amount further reduces AMTI, but the exemption amounts are phased-out when the initial AMTI exceeds certain thresholds.

The Tax Cuts and Jobs Act (TCJA) sets forth much higher thresholds for phasing out exemption amounts applicable to alternative minimum taxable income (AMTI) in 2018 than were effective in 2017 and prior years. The thresholds for phaseout of AMTI exemption amounts in 2018 are: $1 million for married filing jointly; $500,000 for single, head of household and married filing separately; and $75,000 for estates and trusts. The exemption amounts for 2018 and subsequent years are also more in 2018 than in 2017 and prior years. The exemption amounts are reduced by 25% of the amount by which the initial AMTI exceeds the thresholds (See the exemption amounts below).

- **Example** – If a married couple has an initial AMTI of $1,200,000, the exemption amount $109,400 is reduced to $59,400 computed as follows: $1,200,000 minus $1,000,000 = $200,000 X 25% = $50,000; $109,400 minus $50,000 = $59,400. So, $59,400 is the reduced exemption amount that is deducted from the married couples initial AMTI to get a final taxable AMTI of $1,140,600.
- **Example** – If a married couple has an initial AMTI of $900,000, the exemption amount of $109,400 is not reduced because the initial AMTI is not over $1 million. So, the married couple's final taxable AMTI is $790,600 ($900,000 - $109,400 = $790,600.
- **Example** – If an estate has a taxable income $100,000, the exemption amount of $22,500 is reduced to $16,250 computed as follows: $100,000 minus $75,000 = $25,000 X 25% = $6,250; $22,500 minus $6,250 = $16,250. So, $16,250 is the reduced exemption amount that is deducted from the estate's final AMTI to get a final taxable AMTI of $83,750.

If your ordinary income tax is greater than the "Tentative Minimum Tax," you are not subject to AMT. However, if your "Tentative Minimum Tax" is higher, the excess is reported as an additional tax on Form 1040. In the example above, the married couples' Tentative Minimum Tax would be $315,538 ($191,500 X 26% = $49,790; $1,140,600 – $191,500 = $949,100 X 28% = $265,748; $49,790 + $265,748 = $315,538).
www.irs.gov/pub/irs-pdf/f6251.pdf   www.irs.gov/pub/irs-pdf/i6251.pdf

Prior to the 2018 tax year, the characteristics most likely to give rise to an AMT liability for ordinary taxpayers are a large number of personal exemptions, high deductions for state and local taxes, a large amount of miscellaneous itemized deductions, and incentive stock options. The most likely victims of the AMT were upper-middle income individuals who pay high state and local income taxes and property taxes and are married with children. The truly rich have been rarely hit with the AMT.

With the higher exemption amounts and the higher phaseouts of the AMT exemptions and fewer itemized deductions figuring into the calculation for tax years 2018 – 2025, the number of taxpayers hit with the AMT should be significantly reduced in 2018.

Form 6251 must be attached to any tax return if the deductions taken on the return for ordinary tax purposes are greater than adjusted gross income (AGI), or alternative minimum taxable income (AMTI) is more than the exemption amounts applicable to AMT for the taxpayer's filing status.

2018 – 2025 AMT Tax Rates and Exemption Amounts (Set by the Tax Cuts and Jobs Act):

Rates: All Except Married	Up to $191,500	X	26%	
Filing Separately	Above	X	28%	
Married Filing Separately	Up to $ 95,750	X	26%	
	Above	X	28%	

Exemptions:

Married Filing Jointly & Surviving Spouses	$109,400
Single & Head-of-Household	$70,300
Married Filing Separately	$54,700
Estates & Trusts	$22,500

*All of the AMT amounts shown will be adjusted for inflation after 2018

Starting in 2012 all non-refundable tax credits are "permanently" available to offset AMT, including all general business tax credits generated (including the R&D tax credit). However, tax credits carried back cannot offset AMT. Bonus depreciation and Section 179 expensing are not tax preference items and do not have to be added back to ordinary taxable income in determining AMTI. The taxation of net capital gains and qualified dividends is the same for ordinary income tax and AMT purposes. However, the capital gain or loss amounts may differ because of adjustments that affect the basis of capital assets in computing AMTI. **(See Chapter 13, "Non-Refundable Tax Credits"; & "Non-Refundable Business Tax Credits"); (See Chapter 16, "Section 179 First-Year Expensing"; & "First-Year Bonus Depreciation")**

Tax Preferences (Must Be Added Back to Ordinary Taxable Income in Determining AMTI):

Personal exemptions. **(No longer a deduction for tax years 2018 – 2025)**

The standard deduction. If you use the standard deduction for computing your ordinary tax, you can't recalculate using itemized deductions for AMT purposes. **(See Chapter 1, "Standard Deduction")**

Itemized Deductions. If you itemize deductions instead of taking the standard deduction, the following items have to be added back to ordinary taxable income in determining AMTI:

- State and local income taxes, real estate taxes, sales taxes, and personal property taxes have to be added back. However, taxes are deductible for AMT if they are reported on a business schedule (Schedule C), rental schedule (Schedule E), or Farm schedule (Schedule F or Form 4835) and, thus, do not have to be added back. **(See Chapter 12, "State and Local Tax Deductions")**
  www.irs.gov/pub/irs-access/f4835_accessible.pdf)
    - If your business qualifies for a home office, you are allowed to deduct part of your home's real estate taxes on Schedule C for both ordinary tax and AMT purposes. **(See Chapter 17, "Home Office Expenses")**
    - If you have vacant land on which you are paying real estate taxes, you can turn it into a farm rental and deduct the taxes on Form 4835 for both ordinary tax and AMT purposes. **(See Chapter 17, "Rental of Farmland")**
    - If you have a farm operation and use your car in your work, you might be able to deduct the personal property tax on the car on Schedule F for AMT purposes.
- Mortgage Interest – Any mortgage interest claimed as an itemized deduction is only deductible for AMT if the loan was used to buy, build or improve your home. A boat with cooking and bathroom facilities is not considered an acceptable second home for AMT purposes, so any interest on a loan for a boat must be added back. In addition, points deducted for ordinary tax purposes allowed when refinancing a home loan must be added back.
- Miscellaneous Itemized Deductions – Miscellaneous itemized deductions subject to the 2% AGI floor are not deductible in determining ordinary taxable income beginning in 2018, but in 2017 and prior years they were. So, for 2017 and prior years, miscellaneous itemized deductions subject to the 2% AGI floor must be added back to ordinary taxable income in determining AMTI. Miscellaneous itemized deductions not subject to the 2% AGI floor do not have to be added back in 2018, and also in 2017 and prior years. **(See Chapter 12, "Miscellaneous Itemized Deductions Subject to the 2% AGI Floor"; & "Miscellaneous Itemized Deductions Not Subject to the 2% AGI Floor")**

Section 1202 Small Business Stock Exclusion – 42% of the gain excluded from the sale of small-business stock acquired before 1/1/2001 for ordinary tax purposes must be added back; 7% of the gain excluded from the sale of small-business stock acquired after 1/1/2001 must be added back; and 28% of the gain from the sale of small-business stock sold after 12/31/2012 must be added back. In order for the gain to be excluded for ordinary tax purposes, small business stock must be held more than 5 years. 100% of the gain from the sale of small business stock is excluded for ordinary tax purposes on stock acquired after 9/27/2010 and before 1/1/2014. The 100% exclusion is unique in allowing it to apply for both ordinary tax and AMT purposes. **(See Chapter 6, "Gain on the Sale of Section 1202 Small Business Stock")**

Net Operating Loss – If you claimed a net operating loss, you have to add it back in determining AMTI. **(See Chapter 8, "Net Operating Loss")**

Tax Adjustment Items:

Tax adjustment items can either increase or decrease AMT. The portion of the AMT that arises from tax preferences and some adjustments are permanent, but some AMT adjustments are deferred items which reflect a difference in the timing of an item of income or deduction between the ordinary tax and the AMT, thus having an impact not only on the current year's taxes but on future years' taxes. An AMT tax liability stemming from adjustments resulting from "timing differences" can be carried forward and eventually recovered through "AMT credits" in years in which the AMT tax is not applicable.

State tax refunds – Recoveries of state income taxes paid in a prior year that are included in ordinary taxable income in the current year requires a deduction of the amount from ordinary taxable income in determining AMTI, because you did not receive a corresponding deduction for state income taxes for AMT purposes. **(See Chapter 12, "State and Local Tax Deductions")**

Investment Interest Deduction – The investment interest deduction, which is an itemized deduction, may be different for AMT purposes when you have tax-exempt bond interest not included in income for ordinary tax purposes that is added back for AMT purposes. Investment interest expense related to tax-exempt bonds for ordinary tax purposes is not deductible for ordinary tax purposes but should be deducted for AMT purposes. **(See Chapter 12, "Investment Interest Deduction")**

Depletion – You can calculate depletion from oil and gas, mining and other similar activities for ordinary tax purposes using either the percentage depletion method or the cost depletion method. However, for AMT purposes, only the cost depletion method is allowed, so you have to make a necessary adjustment for any difference. **(See Chapter 16, "Depletion")**

Incentive stock options – This is an adjustment for timing differences allowed for ordinary tax and AMT purposes. If you exercise an Incentive Stock Option (ISO) but do not sell the stock in the year of exercise, the transaction is not taxable that year for ordinary tax purposes. However, the difference between the exercise price and the fair market value (FMV) of the stock on the day of exercise is income for AMT purposes, and is added to ordinary taxable income in determining AMTI. Essentially, for AMT purposes you are being taxed on a hypothetical profit (what you might have made if you had sold the stock on the day you bought it). **(See Chapter 6, "Incentive Stock Options")**

- **Example requiring an adjustment** – An ISO is granted on 1/1/2013 for 100 shares of stock, and is exercised on 1/31/2013 when the exercise price is $10 per share and the market price is $15 per share. The stock is not sold until 2/1/2015 (more than 2 years after the ISO grant date). Therefore, in 2013 no income is recognized for ordinary tax purposes. For AMT purposes, $500 of ordinary income would be recognized ($1,500 minus $1,000). So, in 2013, $500 is added to ordinary taxable income in determining AMTI. For ordinary tax purposes a disqualifying disposition occurs if you sell the stock within one year of the exercise date or within two years from the date the ISO is granted, which would trigger ordinary income for ordinary tax purposes equal to the difference between the exercise price and the market price on the date of exercise. In this case, the basis of the stock would be the market price, and any difference between the selling price and the market price would be a capital gain or loss. If this happens, no adjustment would be required in determining AMTI.

Alternative tax net operating loss deduction – Net operating loss (NOL) deductions for ordinary tax purposes must be recomputed in calculating AMTI. The alternative tax NOL (ATNOL) is generally computed in the same manner as an ordinary NOL, except that all AMT adjustments are taken into account first, and tax preference items reduce ATNOL to the extent they increased the amount of the NOL for the tax year. The ATNOL may not offset more than 90% of AMTI, determined without regard to the ATNOL deduction and the domestic production activities deduction. Unused ATNOLs are carried forward or back to the earliest year in which they can be used, according to the same rules as NOLs for ordinary taxes. The amount of ATNOLs carried forward or back is reduced by 90% of the AMTI for any year in which they are carried, whether or not the taxpayer is liable for the AMT in that year. **(See Chapter 8, "Net Operating Loss")**

Disposition of Property Difference – The tax basis in assets you sold may be different for ordinary tax and AMT purposes depending on the depreciation method used, or on your incentive stock options. **(See Chapter 16, "Modified Accelerated Cost Recovery System (MACRS)")**

- **Example requiring an adjustment** – A Section 1245 asset is sold for $2,000, with a basis of $1,000 for ordinary tax purposes after being depreciated using the 200% declining balance (DB) method. The same asset would have a basis of $1,500 for AMT purposes, because the 150% DB method is the maximum allowable depreciation for the AMT. Therefore, an adjustment of $500 has to be deducted from ordinary taxable income in determining AMTI ($1,000 gain for ordinary tax purposes, minus $500 gain for AMT purposes).

Depreciation on Assets Placed in Service after 1986 – This is an adjustment for timing differences between depreciation allowed for ordinary tax and AMT purposes. For AMT purposes you generally must depreciate business assets over a longer period of time than you can for ordinary tax purposes. MACRS (GDS) depreciation is allowed on Sec. 1245 assets at a maximum 200% declining balance (DB) rate for ordinary tax purposes and at a maximum 150% DB rate for AMT purposes. No adjustment is required if 150% declining balance or straight-line depreciation is used for ordinary tax purposes. However, if 200% DB is used for ordinary tax purposes, an adjustment is required. In the case of residential real property, MACRS (GDS) straight-line depreciation over 27 ½ years is used for ordinary tax purposes but must be depreciated using MACRS (ADS) straight-line depreciation over 40 years for AMT purposes. **(See Chapter 16, "Modified Accelerated Cost Recovery System (MACRS)")**

- **Example requiring an adjustment** – In 2015, you have depreciable Sec. 1245 capital assets with a basis of $100,000 and you use MACRS (GDS) 200% DB to claim $15,000 in depreciation expenses for ordinary tax purposes. However, for AMT purposes MACRS (GDS) 150% DB is the maximum allowable for computing depreciation, which would be $10,000 in depreciation expenses allowed for AMT purposes. So, in 2015, $5,000 must be added to ordinary taxable income in determining AMTI ($15,000 minus $10,000).

Passive Activities – You have to complete separate Forms 8582 "Passive Activity Loss Limitations" for ordinary tax and AMT purposes in order to determine differences between AMT and ordinary tax deductions for passive activities, such as depreciation differences for rental properties. **(See Chapter 7, "Passive Income and Losses"); (See Chapter 14, "Passive Activities")**

- **Example requiring an adjustment** – In 2015, you own a rental house on which you take these deductions on Schedule E: mortgage interest -$5,000; property tax - $7,000, and straight-line GDS depreciation over 27 ½ years - $8,000. The mortgage interest and property taxes are allowed for AMT purposes. However, only straight-line ADS depreciation over 40 years is allowable for AMT purposes, reducing allowable depreciation to $6,000 for AMT purposes. So, in 2015, $2,000 must be added to ordinary taxable income in determining AMTI ($8,000 minus $6,000).

Mining Costs – This adjustment is related to a timing difference between deducting mining exploration and development costs for ordinary tax and AMT purposes. Mining exploration and development costs are deductible in the current year for ordinary tax purposes but must be amortized over a 10-year period for AMT purposes. You can avoid making an adjustment if you elect to amortize mining exploration and development costs over ten years for ordinary tax purposes. Also, if a taxpayer materially participates in the activity, he/she is exempt from an AMT adjustment when mining exploration and development costs are deducted in the current year.

Research and Experimental Expenditures – A taxpayer who materially participates in an activity does not have to make an adjustment for R&D expenditures that are deducted in the current year. However, for taxpayers who do not materially participate in the activity, an adjustment is for the timing difference between deducting R&D expenditures for ordinary tax and AMT purposes may be required – In this case, R&D expenditures are deductible in the current year for ordinary tax purposes, but must be amortized over a 10-year period for AMT purposes. You can avoid making an adjustment if you elect to amortize R&D expenditures over ten years for ordinary tax purposes. **(See Chapter 13, "Research and Development (R&D) Tax Credit")**

Intangible Drilling Costs – if you write off intangible drilling costs in the current year for ordinary tax purposes, you must add the amount back to ordinary taxable income in determining AMTI, because intangible drilling costs must be amortized over 60 months for AMT purposes. You can make an election to write off intangible drilling costs over 60 months for ordinary tax purposes in order to avoid this adjustment.

Other Adjustments
- The limitation on itemized deductions for ordinary tax purposes in 2017 does not apply for AMT tax purposes. This could result in an adjustment requiring a deduction from ordinary taxable income in determining AMTI. **(See Chapter 12, "Itemized Deductions")**
- A domestic production activities deduction (above-the-line deduction) is allowed for both ordinary tax and AMT purposes but is computed separately for each, so an adjustment would probably be required. **(See Chapter 11, "Domestic Production Activities Deduction")**
- The additional tax (10% penalty) on early distributions from retirement plans is not applicable to the AMT and, therefore, is deducted from ordinary tax in determining AMTI. **(See Chapter 5, "Distributions from Retirement Plans: Traditional IRAs and Qualified Retirement Plans")**
- The additional tax imposed on distributions from Health Savings Accounts (HSAs) that are not used for qualified medical expenses is not applicable to the AMT and, therefore, is deducted from ordinary tax in determining AMTI. **(See Chapter 9, "Health Savings Account (HSA)"); (See Chapter 11, "Contributions to a Health Savings Account (HSA)")**
- The recapture of the first-time homebuyer credit included in income for ordinary tax purposes is deducted from ordinary tax in determining AMTI. **(See Chapter 13, "Repayment of the First-Time Homebuyer Credit")**

Tentative Minimum Tax is computed by multiplying AMTI (less the AMT exemption amount) by the AMT tax rate and then subtracting the AMT foreign tax credit (if any), which is limited to the foreign tax on foreign source AMTI instead of foreign tax on ordinary taxable income (a separate Form 1116 must be prepared for AMT purposes). If Tentative Minimum Tax is more than your ordinary tax on Line 44 of Form 1040, add the difference on Line 45 of Form 1040 – this is your Alternative Minimum Tax (AMT).

Example Computation of the Tentative Minimum Tax:

Alternative Minimum Taxable Income (AMTI)	- $ 200,000	
Exemption amount (married filing jointly)	- (109,400)	
	$ 90,600	
AMT tax rate	X 26%	
Tentative Minimum Tax	= $ 23,556	

If the calculation on Form 6251 shows that your Tentative Minimum Tax is less than your ordinary income tax, you don't owe any AMT, but you may still be affected by the AMT in other ways. Because of the AMT, you may not be receiving all of your tax credits such as the Work Opportunity Credit. Your Tentative Minimum Tax limits this credit and most other general business credits, other than the energy credits, because these credits cannot reduce the tax you pay below the Tentative Minimum Tax. However, any general business credits not allowed may be carried back 2 years and carried forward 20 years.

AMT Credit

AMT credits can only be used in years when the ordinary tax liability exceeds the "Tentative Minimum Tax" for the year. You might get an "AMT credit" for Alternative Minimum Tax (AMT) paid in a prior year. This credit, calculated on Form 8801, determines how much of the AMT was related to "timing differences," which generate credits for future years, as opposed to exclusion items which are not deductible for AMT, and consequently are lost forever in the AMT tax system – such as taxes, certain equity mortgage interest, and miscellaneous itemized deductions. Examples of items creating timing differences are depreciation differences between the two tax systems and the phantom income from exercising incentive stock options (ISOs). To calculate and report your AMT credit, you need to fill out Form 8801 "Credit for Prior Year Minimum Tax." www.irs.gov/pub/irs-pdf/f8801.pdf www.irs.gov/pub/irs-pdf/i8801.pdf

There are two ways to claim an AMT credit: the "regular credit," and the "refundable credit." The first step in determining the amount of your regular AMT credit is to find out how much of your AMT liability from a prior year is eligible for the credit. In order to do this, you have to find out how much of your AMT liability came from timing items, which are the only ones that can give rise to an AMT credit. Timing items are those accounted for in different tax years in the ordinary tax system and the AMT tax system. For example, the exercising of incentive stock options (ISOs), and the difference between 200% declining balance depreciation allowed in the ordinary tax system and 150% declining balance depreciation allowed in the AMT tax system.

Under the regular credit rules, you can begin claiming the credit in the first year after you paid AMT if you are not subject to and are not paying the AMT in the next year. Also, the amount of the credit you can use is limited to the difference between your ordinary tax liability and the tax calculated under the AMT rules. For example: you have a $10,000 AMT credit available from 2013; your ordinary 2014 tax is $39,000; your tax calculated under the AMT rules would be $33,000; you don't have to pay AMT in 2014 because your ordinary tax is higher than the tax calculated under the AMT rules. Thus, you can claim a $6,000 AMT credit in 2014, reducing your ordinary tax to $33,000 (credit limited to the tax calculated under the AMT rules). And you still have $4,000 of AMT credit you haven't used and is carried over to the next year. Unused AMT credit can be carried over for an unlimited number of years. If you only had a $4,000 AMT credit available from 2013, your ordinary tax would be reduced to $35,000 in 2014, and you would have no AMT credit available to carry over.

372

AMT Refundable Credit – Beginning in 2007, taxpayers with old unused AMT credits were allowed to start using the "refundable credit" rules. This allowed a taxpayer to claim the credit without regard to the limitation of the "regular" rules described above, but only if the taxpayer had unused AMT credits from four or more years earlier. The refundable AMT credit was enacted to give relief to individuals who exercised incentive stock options (ISO) that generated AMT credits that lost all or a significant portion of their value in later years due to the loss in value of the stocks. Since the difference between the fair market value (FMV) and the option price is an adjustment item for AMT purposes, these taxpayers paid an increased amount in tax and generated an AMT credit for use in later years when the stock was sold for a profit. The loss in value of the stocks resulted in these individuals being unable to use any of the sizable amount of AMT credit to offset their tax liability, and they kept carrying the amount forward to the next year with the same results. Unfortunately for these taxpayers, this meant the AMT credit was of limited benefit if the stock was sold at a loss, i.e. at a lower price than the market price on the day the options were exercised. However, as a result of 2006 legislation, a taxpayer was eligible to receive a refundable AMT credit beginning in 2007 if the following conditions were met:

- AGI was below the threshold amounts of $234,600 for married individuals filing jointly; $156,400 for unmarried individuals; and $195,500 for heads-of-households (adjusted for inflation). The AMT refundable credit was gradually phased out if income was above the threshold amounts.
- The AMT credit arose from an incentive stock option (ISO) that was exercised before the third immediately preceding tax year. In other words, the AMT refundable credit for tax year 2007 was available for AMT credits generated during 2003 or earlier.

If a taxpayer satisfied these criteria for 2007 and later years, he or she was generally eligible to receive the "AMT refundable credit amount" which is the greater of (1) the lesser of $5,000 or the long-term unused minimum tax credit, or (2) 20% of the long-term unused minimum tax credit. Also, taxpayers could use their first-year refundable credit amount for the succeeding four years, and theoretically get the entire refundable credit over a five-year period. The long-term unused minimum tax credit for any taxable year means the portion of the minimum tax credit attributable to the adjusted net minimum tax for taxable years before the third taxable year immediately preceding the taxable year. In the case of an individual whose AGI for a taxable year exceeds the threshold amounts (see above), the "AMT refundable credit amount" is reduced by an applicable percentage.

- **Example** – In 2013, John has an AGI that does not exceed the applicable threshold amount. He has an ordinary tax payable of $50,000, and a tentative minimum tax of $40,000, so his ordinary tax exceeds his tentative minimum tax by $10,000; therefore, he is eligible for an AMT tax credit (no other credits are available). John has a long-term unused minimum tax credit available of $500,000, so the minimum tax credit allowable for the 2013 taxable year is $100,000 (20% X $500,000, which is greater than $10,000). $10,000 of the credit – without regard to this provision – is nonrefundable under the regular AMT rules ($50,000 ordinary taxable income, less the tentative minimum tax of $40,000 computed under the AMT tax system), which reduces John's taxable income to $40,000. Therefore, the additional $90,000 of the credit – allowable by reason of this provision – is treated as a "refundable credit." Thus, John has an overpayment of $50,000 ($90,000 less $40,000) in 2013. The $50,000 overpayment of taxes is allowed as a refund or credit to John. The remaining $400,000 minimum tax credit is carried forward to future taxable years.

To claim the AMT credit, including the refundable portion, taxpayers must complete Form 8801, "Credit for Prior Year Minimum Tax – Individuals, Estates, and Trusts." The additional (refundable) credit is limited to the lesser of

$30 million or 6% of the AMT credit carry forwards generated in tax years beginning before 1/1/2006 that were not used in tax years ending before April 1, 2008. The minimum AMT credit allowed in a year is not less than the greater of the amount of the AMT refundable credit amount determined for the preceding year or 50% of the unused credit.

The PATH Act provides an election that allows taxpayers to claim accelerated AMT credit in lieu of first-year bonus depreciation. If taxpayers decide to do this, they must agree to forgo the use of bonus depreciation on qualified property placed in service and depreciate it using the straight-line method. **(See Chapter 16, "First-Year Bonus Depreciation")**

Chapter 24 – Affordable Care Act (ACA)

The Patient Protection and Affordable Care Act (ACA), also known as Obamacare, requires all health insurance plans offered by employers to offer essential health benefits which overall are equal to the scope of benefits typically offered by insurance plans offered through the government insurance "Exchanges" (Marketplace). All Medicaid and Medicare plans began offering essential health benefits starting in 2014. Since then, most employers that offer health insurance to their employees have complied with the requirements, and all new large group and private insurance plans offered by health insurance carriers have offered the required or equivalent coverage. Grandfathered plans still in effect from before the ACA was enacted don't have to offer essential benefits. The ACA incorporates four main instruments to fund and implement the law: (1) Government Insurance "Exchanges" (Marketplaces); (2) Mandates; (3) Federal Subsidies (Tax Credits); and (4) Taxes on High-Income earners, Insurance Providers, and Other Entities. In addition, the ACA has reporting requirements that were effective starting with the 2015 tax year.

All aspects of the ACA remain in effect in 2018, including the 0.9% Medicare Surtax and the 3.8% Net Investment Income Tax, in spite of extensive efforts to repeal and replace the ACA by President Trump and the Republican-majority Congress. However, the individual shared responsibility provision or "Individual Mandate" requiring taxpayers to pay a penalty if they don't have health insurance coverage has been repealed by the Tax Cuts and Jobs Act (TCJA), effective beginning with the 2019 tax year. Nevertheless, the IRS has informed taxpayers and tax practitioners that it will not accept electronically filed individual income tax returns for 2018 unless taxpayers indicate on their tax returns that they and everyone on their return (spouse and all dependents) have health insurance coverage; qualify for an exemption; or are making a shared-responsibility payment (penalty). The 2017 tax year was the first year that the IRS had enforced this requirement and the requirement will be enforced in 2018. But of course, this requirement (individual mandate) will go away beginning with the 2019 tax year. **(See Below, "Individual Mandate"); (See Chapter 2, "0.9% Medicare Surtax"); (See Chapter 10, "3.8% Net Investment Income Tax")**

In 2016, the Trump administration issued an executive order directing the government to limit any burdens imposed by the Patient Protection and Affordable Care Act, P.L. 111-148, pending repeal. In response, the IRS did not enforce the health care reporting requirement on 2016 returns filed in 2017, although taxpayers were still required to pay the shared-responsibility payment if they didn't have coverage or qualify for an exemption. However, for 2017 and 2018, the IRS has determined that enforcing the ACA requirements will make return filing easier on taxpayers and also reduce refund delays. Therefore, for the 2018 tax year, the individual mandate will require most taxpayers and their families to have some form of health coverage or qualify for a special health coverage exemption. Form 1040 has a "box" that taxpayers can check indicating that they have "full-year coverage" or their return will not be accepted unless they have an exemption.

Government Insurance "Exchanges" (Marketplace)

The Department of Health and Human Services (HHS) is the overall administrator of the Health Insurance Marketplace (HealthCare.gov). Health insurance Exchanges in the Marketplace may be established either by a state or by the Secretary of HHS as a "federally-facilitated Exchange." The Marketplace offers government health insurance through the "Exchanges" that are operated by both the federal government in those states that don't have their own Exchanges and by states that do have their own Exchanges; offers government regulated and standardized healthcare plans offered by insurance providers; and provides the only mechanism available to individuals to purchase insurance eligible for federal subsidies (premium tax credits). Health insurance premiums are based on the level of coverage provided – Medical expenses are covered: 60% (bronze plan); 70% (silver plan); 80% (gold plan); and 90% (platinum plan). The ACA requires that all plans offered in the government Exchanges cap the maximum out-of-pocket costs that individuals have to pay annually. Individuals can apply online for insurance plans offered by the federal Exchange at HealthCare.gov during the open enrollment periods. **(See Below, "Federal Subsidies")**

www.healthcare.gov

Insurance plans offered in the federal government and state "Exchanges" are required to cover "Essential Health Benefits." Some essential health benefits are provided to enrollees for free (no out-of-pocket costs) – annual wellness visits and many types of preventive services and immunizations. Wellness services include: many types of screenings and counseling. Some of these benefits haven't been previously covered by any health insurance plans. There are no dollar limits on essential benefits, and there is a cap on out-of-pocket costs on all plans that cover essential benefits. Plans offering essential benefits must cover at least 60% of covered out-of-pocket expenses and must have reasonable out-of-pocket maximums (including co-pays, coinsurance and deductibles). The out-of-pocket maximum (limit) is the most someone has to pay during the policy period (usually a year) before the health insurance plan begins to pay 100% of the allowed amount. The maximum out-of-pocket expenses for any Exchange (Marketplace) plan for 2018 are $7,350 ($7,150 in 2017) for an individual plan and $14,700 ($14,300 in 2017) for a family plan.

The Department of Health and Human Services (HHS) has established a program to determine whether individuals are eligible to enroll in qualified health plans offered by the government Exchanges and are eligible for other benefits, including Medicaid and the Children's Health Insurance Program (CHIP). In order to carry out this requirement, the IRS discloses to HHS certain tax return information to help the government Exchanges determine taxpayer eligibility where income verification is required. NOTE: In October 2017, Congress did not renew the CHIP Program.

> **Open Enrollment Period** – The open enrollment period for individual health insurance coverage through the government "Exchanges" (Marketplace) typically runs from November 1st to December 15th. During the open enrollment period, individuals can choose to enroll in a new policy, switch to a policy with a higher deductible and a lower premium, or switch to a higher premium with more comprehensive coverage. Individuals who are already enrolled, and do not indicate otherwise, will be re-enrolled in their same plan on December 31st. The delay in re-enrollment allows consumers time to explore their health insurance options.

Some people may qualify for a "special enrollment period" while the Marketplace is closed if they experience a "qualifying life event" outside of the open enrollment period, which allows them to purchase a new individual health insurance policy, or switch their existing policy. But only persons who have a specific "qualifying life event" will qualify for a special enrollment period. Examples of special enrollment events include marriage or divorce, birth or adoption of a child, moving between states, gaining citizenship, returning from active military duty, being released from incarceration, changing dependent status after turning age 26, losing full-time employment status, losing employer-sponsored insurance, and becoming newly eligible or ineligible for premium tax credits. The special enrollment period is 60 days following a qualifying life event. If you experience a specific event that you think may qualify you for special enrollment outside of the open enrollment period, contact the Marketplace call center at 800-318-2596.

Penalty on Employers That Don't Notify Employees about the Exchanges – Qualifying employers are required to notify their employees by October 1st of each year informing them about the open enrollment period for obtaining health insurance through the government insurance "Exchanges" (Marketplace). The employer notification requirement can be enforced by imposing a penalty on employers that don't comply, and the penalty can be as much as $100 per worker per day. The penalty applies to qualifying employers that have at least $500,000 of annual gross revenue and at least one employee. The requirement also applies to government agencies, hospitals, and facilities for care of the elderly, ill, etc.

Mandates

Mandates impose penalties on individuals, employers, and insurance providers when provisions required by the ACA are violated or not implemented in accordance with the law. The two mandates that affect individuals and employers the most are the "Individual Mandate" and the "Employer Mandate." The IRS has stated that it will not accept electronically filed 2017 and 2018 individual income tax returns unless taxpayers indicate on their tax returns that they and everyone on their return (spouse and all dependents) had health insurance coverage; qualified for an exemption; or are making a shared-responsibility payment. The IRS also said that any returns filed on paper that do not address the health coverage requirements will be suspended until the IRS receives additional information, and any refund due may be delayed.

Individual Mandate

NOTE: The individual mandate is still in effect in 2018 but has been repealed effective for the 2019 tax year.

All individuals who can afford health insurance must carry health insurance that provides minimum essential coverage, unless they are covered by a grandfathered plan, or they are exempt from having to have health insurance coverage. If they don't, they have to pay a Shared Responsibility Payment (penalty). The responsibility to get health insurance coverage falls upon individuals themselves if they are not employed by large employers with 50 or more full-time or full-time equivalent (FTE) employees or their employers don't offer coverage. Minimum essential coverage (MEC) must be maintained each month of the year for the taxpayer and all of the taxpayer's dependents. A taxpayer is liable for the Shared Responsibility Payment for a person without minimum essential coverage if that person is eligible to be the taxpayer's dependent, regardless of whether the taxpayer actually claims the dependent. MEC does not include coverage consisting solely of excepted benefits, such as stand-alone dental or vision care, workers' compensation, or accident and disability policies.

The requirement to have health insurance is satisfied and the Shared Responsibility Payment is not assessed if individuals are insured for the whole year through a combination of any of the following sources: Health insurance coverage provided by employers including retiree coverage; Medicare Part A coverage and Medicare Advantage plans; Medicaid or the Children's Health Insurance Program (CHIP); TRICARE (for service members, retirees, and their families); The veteran's health program; Defense Department's Non-appropriated Fund Health Benefits Program; Student health plans offered by universities; Coverage provided to Peace Corps volunteers; COBRA coverage; Other coverage offered in the private insurance market that is recognized by the Department of Health and Human Services (HHS) as minimum essential coverage (MEC); or a grandfathered health plan in existence before the ACA was enacted.

Individuals not covered by any of the above are eligible to purchase insurance in the government Exchanges and receive premium tax credits based on their "household income." If individuals are eligible for insurance offered by their employers that meets the minimum essential coverage (MEC) requirements, then they are prohibited from buying insurance in the government Exchanges and receiving premium tax credits, unless the insurance offered by their employers doesn't meet the minimum value and affordability requirements. If you are offered insurance through your employer and you apply for insurance in the government Exchanges, the Health Insurance Marketplace will determine if the health plan provided by your employer is affordable, of value, and provides minimum essential coverage, i.e. if you are paying more than 9.56% of your household income in 2018, based on your family size, toward insurance premiums, or the insurance offered to you by your employer doesn't meet minimum requirements, you will generally be eligible to purchase insurance through the government Exchanges and get a premium tax credit, even though you have health insurance available through your employer. **(See Below, "Employer Mandate"; & "Premium Tax Credits")**

Employers offering a grandfathered health plan may still keep the plan, as long as there are no significant plan changes, and individuals and their family members can continue to enroll in the plan. Also, new employees can enroll in a grandfathered plan. Health insurance plans purchased before March 23, 2010 that still exist without major plan changes are considered to have grandfathered status and do not have to follow certain ACA rules. To maintain grandfathered status, the health insurance plan must not: (1) eliminate or substantially eliminate benefits for a particular condition; (2) increase cost-sharing percentages (e.g. deductibles), regardless of the amount; (3) increase co-pays by more than $5 or a percentage equal to medical inflation (9.56% in 2018), plus 15%, whichever is greater; (4) raise fixed amount cost-sharing other than co-pays by more than medical inflation (9.56% in 2018), plus 15%; (5) lower the employer contribution rate by more than 5% for any group of covered persons; and (6) add or reduce an annual limit. Additionally, to maintain grandfathered status the plan also must: maintain records of its plan design and contribution levels as of March 23, 2010 and any changes since that date; and include a notice about the plan's grandfathered status in significant participant communications, such as enrollment materials and summary plan descriptions.

Taxpayers who have minimum essential coverage (MEC) for the entire year are supposed to simply check a box on Form 1040, certifying they had "full-year coverage" for themselves and their dependents. Most taxpayers have full-year coverage and will just have to check the box.
www.irs.gov/pub/irs-pdf/f1040.pdf

    IRS Notice – the ACA requires that, each year by June 30th, the IRS must send out a notice to taxpayers who have filed a tax return but have not enrolled in "minimal essential health coverage," giving them information about the health insurance marketplace in their state. However, the IRS has not always sent out the required notifications to taxpayers who did not have health insurance coverage, and the notices it did send out underreported the cost of coverage. The Treasury Inspector General for Tax Administration (TIGTA) found that the average cost for health coverage for those who enrolled through an exchange was $168 a month after financial assistance – not $75, as cited in the letters sent to taxpayers by the IRS. Also, the IRS didn't send the notices at all in 2015, deciding instead to analyze tax return information to learn more about the taxpayer response to the individual mandate in its first year. In 2016, the IRS coordinated with the Centers for Medicare and Medicaid Services to create the notification letters and identify the taxpayers to whom the notices would be sent. It mailed more than 7 million letters between November 2016 and January 2017. TIGTA found, however, that the IRS did not send notifications to approximately 3.3 million taxpayers who did not report that they were covered by health insurance, exempt from coverage, or was claimed as an exemption on someone else's tax return. According to the TIGTA, the Centers for Medicare and Medicaid Services told the IRS not to send letters to taxpayers who filed so-called "silent returns" (returns that did not indicate whether or not they had health insurance coverage).

Employee Shared Responsibility Payment – The individual mandate penalty (Shared Responsibility Payment) is applicable to individuals who can afford health insurance coverage, but choose to forgo it. The flat penalty amount in 2018 is $695 per adult and $347.50 per dependent child under 18, but the penalty amount is capped at a family maximum of $2,085. However, the applicable penalty amount is the greater of the flat penalty amount or 2.5% of "household income" over the filing thresholds ($12,000 for singles; $24,000 for married filing jointly; $18,000 for head-of-household), whichever is greater. Penalties are prorated based on the number of months without coverage or without an exemption, and the maximum penalty cannot exceed the national average premium for the lowest cost "Bronze level" health plan available through the government Marketplace, or $3,211 per year ($268 per month) for an individual and $16,056 per year ($1,338 per month) for a family with five or more members. The penalty is not deductible on individuals' tax returns. A taxpayer is liable for the Shared Responsibility Payment for a person without minimum essential coverage if that person is eligible to be the taxpayer's dependent, regardless of whether the taxpayer actually claims the dependent. Form 8965, "Health Coverage Exemptions" must be filed with your tax return when the Shared Responsibility Payment is assessed, and the amount of the penalty must be shown on Form 1040.

www.irs.gov/pub/irs-pdf/f8965.pdf www.irs.gov/pub/irs-pdf/i8965.pdf
www.healthcare.gov/taxes/tools/#bronzeplan

Household Income for purposes of the Shared Responsibility Payment includes the Modified Adjusted Gross Income (MAGI) of the taxpayer and the taxpayer's spouse, plus the MAGI of all the dependents in the household who are required to file a tax return because their income is more than the filing threshold – if a dependent files a return just to get a refund, then his/her income should not be included in household income. MAGI is Adjusted Gross Income (AGI) increased by the Foreign Earned Income Exclusion and tax-exempt interest received or accrued during the taxable year. **(See Chapter 12, "Itemized Deductions")**

You are considered to have minimum essential coverage (MEC) for the entire month as long as you have MEC for at least one day during the month. For example, if you start a new job on August 29th and are covered under your employer's health coverage plan starting on that day, you are treated as having coverage for the entire month of August. Similarly, if you're eligible for an exemption for any one day of a month, you're treated as exempt for the entire month (See below). Coverage gaps are allowed one time per year up to 3 consecutive months. The penalty is calculated as one-twelfth of the yearly penalty times the number of months you are uninsured (if you are uninsured for three consecutive months or less in a year, then there is no penalty).

Exemptions from Having to Have Health Insurance Coverage – Individuals do not have to pay a Shared Responsibility Payment if they are exempt from having to have health insurance coverage. How you get an exemption depends upon the type of exemption for which you are eligible. Some exemptions are available when you file your tax return, other exemptions are available only through the Marketplace. Form 8965, "Health

Coverage Exemptions" must be filed with your tax return in order to claim the exemptions. Only one Form 8965 should be filed for each tax household.
www.irs.gov/pub/irs-pdf/f8965.pdf

Exemptions available when you file your tax return:

- No filing requirement – Either your household income is below the income tax filing threshold, or your gross income is below the filing threshold. The filing thresholds for 2018 are $12,000 for singles, $24,000 for married couples, and $18,000 for heads-of-household and surviving spouses. This exemption is applicable even if you only file a return in order to get a refund for taxes withheld. **(See Chapter 1, "Filing Requirements")**

- Short coverage gap – You didn't have coverage for 3 consecutive months or less, including CHIP coverage. A gap in coverage that lasts 3 months or less qualifies as a short coverage gap. If an individual has more than one short coverage gap during the year, the short coverage gap exemption only applies to the first gap.

- Income below the poverty level – Individuals with incomes below the federal poverty levels are exempt from having to have health insurance. In 2018, the federal poverty levels are: $12,140 for one individual; $16,460 for a 2-person household; $20,780 for a 3-person household; $25,100 for a 4-person household; $29,420 for a 5-person household; $33,740 for a 6-person household; $38,060 for a 7-person household; and $42,380 for an 8-person household.

- Coverage is considered unaffordable – The lowest priced coverage available to you would cost more than 8.05% of your household income in 2018 (8.16% in 2017), after taking into account any employer contributions, if any. This is applicable if the lowest self-only coverage available in the government Marketplace exceeds 8.05% of household income, as does the cost of any available employer-sponsored coverage for the entire family. Also, see coverage considered unaffordable based on "projected income" which provides a prospective exemption that can be granted only by the Marketplace if the minimum amount you would have paid for coverage is more than 8.05% of your projected household income for the year. **(See Below, "Exemptions Available Only Through the "Marketplace")**

- Citizens living abroad and certain noncitizens:
  - Citizens living abroad: You are a U.S. citizen that lived abroad for at least 330 full days during the year, or you are a U.S. citizen who was a bona fide resident of a foreign country or a U.S. territory, including dependents of U.S. citizens who are living in the United States. This exemption applies regardless of whether you actually had health insurance in the country or U.S. territory where you lived. However, you have to have health insurance if you return to the U.S. during the year from the time you returned. **(See Chapter 3, "U.S. Citizens Living Abroad")**
  - Certain noncitizens: You were not lawfully present in the U.S., or you were a resident alien who was a citizen of a foreign country with which the U.S. has an income tax treaty with a nondiscrimination clause (you qualify for this exemption even if you have a social security number). This exemption applies to all foreign nationals who live in the U.S. for a short enough period that they do not become resident aliens for federal income tax purposes. This exemption is not available to aliens who are permanent residents of the U.S. and foreign nationals who are in the U.S. long enough during a calendar year to qualify as resident aliens for tax purposes. You are considered a resident alien if you meet one of the following tests for the calendar year: (1) The green card test – you have a green card; (2) The substantial presence test – you have been physically present in the U.S. for at least: 31 days during the current year, and

183 days during the 3 year period that includes the current year and the 2 years immediately before. **(See Chapter 3, "Aliens")**

- You would have been eligible for Medicaid but your state did not expand Medicaid (Texas, Pennsylvania, Wisconsin, etc.). In this case, you will get an exemption from the IRS based on your residence, or from the Exchange based on your unsuccessful application for Medicaid.
- You are a member of a federally recognized Indian tribe (including an Alaska Native Claims Act Corporation Shareholder), or you are otherwise eligible for services through an Indian health care provider or the Indian Health Service.
- You are a member of a recognized health care sharing ministry (an organization described in Section 501(c)(3)), which is an organization whose members share a common set of ethical or religious beliefs and have shared medical expenses in accordance with those beliefs continuously since at least December 31, 1999. **(See Chapter 20, "Tax-Exempt Organizations")**
- You are incarcerated – in jail, prison, or a similar penal institution or correctional facility.

Exemptions available only through the Marketplace:
- You are a member of a recognized religious sect in existence since December 31, 1950, that is recognized by the Social Security Administration as conscientiously opposed to accepting any insurance benefits, including Medicare and Social Security.
- You were determined ineligible for Medicaid coverage solely because the state in which you live does not participate in Medicaid expansion under the Affordable Care Act (hardship exemption). NOTE: a similar exemption is available when you apply for Medicaid and are found ineligible due to the lack of Medicaid expansion in your state.
- Your health insurance plan was not renewed or was cancelled and you consider the other plans available to be unaffordable (hardship exemption).
- You do not have access to coverage that is considered affordable based on your projected household income.
- You are engaged in service in the AmeriCorps State and National, VISTA, or NCCC programs and are covered by short-term duration coverage or self-funded coverage provided by these programs.
- You have another hardship (defined by HHS) which includes the following circumstances that affects your ability to purchase health insurance coverage: You recently experienced domestic violence; You were evicted from your home in the past 6 months or are facing eviction or foreclosure; You filed for bankruptcy in the last 6 months; You are homeless; You have received a shut-off notice from a utility company; You experienced the death of a close family member within the past three years; You have experienced a disaster such as a fire, flood, or other natural or human-caused disaster that caused substantial damage to your property; You are being forced to pay high medical bills for yourself or a close family member; You have had to pay unexpected medical expenses due to having to care for an ill, disabled, or aging family member; You have filed for Medicaid for a dependent child and have been denied coverage; or You are suffering from another reasonable hardship.

You have to file an "exemption application" with the Marketplace to claim exemptions that are only available through the Marketplace. The Marketplace will review your exemption application and mail you a notice of exemption eligibility. If you are granted an exemption, the Marketplace notice will provide you with a unique

Exemption Certificate Number (ECN) that must be included on Form 8965 when you file your tax return. Exemptions from the Marketplace need to be applied for at the earliest opportunity, because it may take time for the Marketplace to review your application. Hardship exemptions are usually provided for several months and up to a full calendar year. Individuals ineligible for Medicaid because their state refused to expand Medicaid will be granted an exemption for the entire year. Exemption application forms are supplied by the Health Insurance Marketplace administered by HHS. The various applications approved by HHS (Form OMB No. 0938-1190) are available online at HealthCare.gov, and completed applications have to be mailed to: Health Insurance Marketplace – Exemption Processing, 465 Industrial Blvd., London, KY 40741; or to the applicable state Marketplace if your state has its own health insurance Exchange.

www.healthcare.gov www.treasury.gov/press-center/press-releases/Documents/3-17-16%20ACA%20Exemptions%20One%20Pager%20-%20Unaffordable%20Coverage.pdf

If you are not required to file a tax return because either your household income or your gross income is below the income tax filing threshold, you don't have to do anything to claim the exemption ("No filing requirement" exemption). However, if you are not required to file a tax return, but choose to file one anyway, e.g. to get a refund of taxes withheld, you are required to file Form 8965 with your tax return, and claim the exemption in Part II of Form 8965. Form 8965 must be submitted with your tax return to claim any of the other exemptions (See above). The Form contains separate parts for claiming the different exemptions available:

- Part I has to be completed if you have a Marketplace granted coverage exemption for yourself or other members of your household (the exemption may be for only one or more members of your household). You can check a box if an exemption is granted for the full year or check boxes for the individual months to claim a partial year exemption granted to you, your spouse (if married), or dependents. Part I requires you to include the "Exemption Certificate Number (ECN)" provided to you by the Marketplace to verify that you or other household members were granted an exemption. If you have applied for an exemption, but the Marketplace has not processed it before you file your tax return, you can substitute "Pending" on the Form for the ECN, which subjects the exemption to "hold" status until you receive a determination from the Marketplace.
- Part II requires all filers of Form 8965 to simply check either "yes" or "no" in reply to the only two questions asked in Part II – (1) Are you claiming an exemption because your household income is below the filing threshold; and (2) Are you claiming an exemption because your gross income is below the filing threshold.
- Part III has to be completed if you are claiming an exemption for yourself, or other members of your household, that is only available when you file your tax return. Part III has a box that allows you to select the type of exemption you are claiming: Exemption Type A – Unaffordable Coverage; B – Short Coverage Gap; C – Citizens living abroad and certain noncitizens; D – Members of a health care sharing ministry; E – Members of Federally-recognized Indian tribes; F – Incarceration; G – Resident of a state that did not expand Medicaid. You can check a box to claim the exemption for the full year or check boxes for the individual months to claim a partial year exemption (exemption for only those months when you did not have MEC) for yourself, your spouse (if married), or dependents.

The Shared Responsibility Payment is computed on the Shared Responsibility Payment worksheet (Form 8965). The Shared Responsibility Payment worksheet does not have to be submitted with Form 8965, when you file your tax return. However, the amount of the penalty computed on the worksheet must be shown on Form 1040 and if you have to pay the penalty you should not check the box certifying that you had "full-year coverage." The Shared

Responsibility Payment worksheet computes the penalty just as shown in the examples below. You don't owe a Shared Responsibility Payment if you can be claimed as a dependent by another taxpayer, and you don't need to file Form 8965 or check the box certifying that you had full-year coverage.

The IRS cannot collect the Shared Responsibility Payment penalty using traditional enforcement methods, such as liens and levies. Therefore, the IRS will have to separate the Shared Responsibility Payment penalty from regular income tax assessments. To collect the penalty, the IRS can collect the penalty using refund offsets, but if this is not possible it will send a new series of assessment and collection notices ("H" Notices). The first notice sent will probably be the CP 15H, Shared Responsibility Payment (SRP) Civil Penalties Notice, or the CP 21H/22H, Shared Responsibility Payment (SRP) Adjustment Notice. If the taxpayer does not pay the penalty, the IRS will continue to issue a series of H Notices requesting payment.

- **Example** – You are an unmarried person with no dependents, you didn't have minimum essential coverage for any month in 2017, and you didn't qualify for an exemption. Your household income is $50,000 (filing threshold is $10,400). Under the income formula, your penalty would be equal to $991.25 ($50,000 - $10,400 = $39,600 X 2.5% = $990). Suppose, the national average premium for a Bronze level plan in 2017 is $2,500 (not an actual figure). Therefore, because $990 is greater than $695 and less than $2,085 (maximum penalty per household) and $2,500 (national average premium for a Bronze level plan), your Shared Responsibility Payment for 2018 is $990, or $82.50 for each month you are uninsured. You will make your Shared Responsibility Payment for the months you are uninsured when you file your 2018 tax return on Form 8965 attached to the return.

- **Example** – You are a married person with 2 dependents under 18. You and one of your dependents had minimum essential coverage for January through September, but didn't have any insurance for October through December. Your spouse and the other dependent had minimum essential coverage for January through August, but didn't have any insurance for September through December. Since you and one of your dependents had insurance coverage for 9 months during the year, no penalty is assessed because you both qualify for the short coverage gap exemption. However, since your spouse and the other dependent had insurance for only 8 months during the year, they are assessed a penalty for the 4 months they were without coverage. Your household income is $85,000, which includes your MAGI of $65,000 (your spouse had no income) and the MAGI of one dependent of $20,000 who is required to file a tax return. The other dependent had earned income of $2,500 during the year, so he/she was not required to file a tax return, so the income is not included in the household income. Under the income formula, your penalty would be equal to $1,071.68 ($85,000 - $20,800 = $64,200 X 2.5% = $1,605 or $133.75 for each month uninsured X 4 months = $535 X 2 persons uninsured = $1,070). Suppose, the national average premium for a Bronze level plan in 2018 for a 4-person household is $4,000 (not an actual figure). Therefore, because $1,070 is greater than $1,042.50 ($695 + $347.50) and less than $2,085 (maximum penalty per household) and $4,000 (national average premium for a Bronze level plan), your Shared Responsibility Payment for 2018 is $1,070, which you will pay when you file your 2018 tax return with Form 8965 attached to the return.

Employer Mandate

No employer is required to provide healthcare coverage to its employees, but in 2018, the Employer Mandate requires an "applicable large employer (ALE)" to offer health care coverage to its full-time employees and their dependents that is affordable, of minimum value, and provides minimum essential coverage (MEC). An ALE is an employer that has 50 or more full-time or full-time equivalent (FTE) employees. Dependents are children under age 26; a spouse is not considered a dependent. The law requires ALEs to provide healthcare coverage that is affordable, of minimum value, and provides MEC to at least 95% of their full-time employees. An ALE that doesn't comply with these requirements has to pay a penalty referred to as the Employer Shared Responsibility Payment (ESRP), which is also referred to as the "Pay-or-Play" penalty. Part-time employees and seasonal employees are included in calculating whether an employer has 50 or more full-time or FTE employees, but they are not included in calculating the ESRP. The definition of an ALE and the employer mandate also applies to non-profit and governmental entities. ALEs include related entities which must be considered together as one employer. Related entities include companies with a common owner or controlled groups and affiliated service groups. Controlled groups are (1) parent-subsidiary groups which are owned 80% together up and down the chain, and (2) brother-sister companies which are owned by the same 5 or fewer people. Therefore, creating new companies in the same controlled group will not allow you to get below the ALE threshold. An affiliated service group has direct or indirect ownership interests. These types of entities are treated as a single employer for determining ALE status. Each separate employer or member in a group is part of the "large employer" and is subject to the employer shared responsibility provisions, even if separately a member would not be considered an ALE. However, although employers with a common owner or that are otherwise related generally are combined and treated as a single employer for determining whether an employer is an ALE, potential liability for the ESRP is determined separately for each of the ALE members.

Affordability, Minimum Value, and Minimum Essential Coverage Requirements – The affordability, minimum value, and minimum essential coverage (MEC) requirements for purposes of the employer mandate are:

- Affordability – For the 2018 tax year, insurance premiums have to cost an employee no more than 9.56% of household income (9.5% adjusted for inflation) based on the cost of the premium for a self-only Bronze Level plan available in the government Marketplace – the plan cannot exceed 9.56% of the lowest hourly rate paid by the employer, multiplied by 130 hours per month, and cannot exceed 9.56% of the federal poverty rate. Three safe harbors allow employers to apply the 9.56% standard to: income as reported on an employee's Form W-2; the hourly rate of pay for hourly employees multiplied by 130 hours per month; or the federal poverty rate which is $13,960 per year for an individual in 2018 (See Individual Mandate above).
- Minimum Value – The plan must pay a least 60% of the cost of medical claims. For example, someone who goes to the hospital should not have to pay more than 40% of the total cost.
- Minimum Essential Coverage (MEC) – Insurance plans offered by ALEs must cover "Essential Health Benefits" that are included in health insurance plans offered by the government insurance "Exchanges" (Marketplaces). This includes substantial coverage for inpatient hospital and physician services. **(See Above, "Government Insurance Exchanges (Marketplaces)"); & "Individual Mandate")**

Also, if you are offered insurance through your employer and you apply for insurance in the government Exchanges, the Health Insurance Marketplace will determine if the health plan provided by your employer is affordable, of value, and provides minimum essential coverage, i.e. if you are paying more than 9.56% of your household income in 2018, based on your family size, toward insurance premiums, or the insurance offered to you by your employer doesn't meet minimum requirements, you will generally be eligible to purchase insurance through the government Exchanges and get a premium tax credit, even though you have health insurance available through your employer. **(See Below, "Premium Tax Credits")**

Employer Shared Responsibility Payment (ESRP) – There are three ways that an ALE with 50 or more full-time or FTE employees can be penalized in 2018:

1. If the ALE doesn't offer any health insurance coverage to its full-time employees, then the annual ESRP payment is $2,320 in 2018 ($2,000 adjusted for inflation) per full-time employee, computed on a monthly basis, excluding the first 30 full-time employees from the computation. Example: for an employer with 120 full-time employees in 2018, the penalty is calculated as follows: 120 – 30 = 90 X $193.33 ($2,320 divided by 12) = $17,399.70 per month X 12 = $208,796 annually.

2. If an ALE offers otherwise qualified health insurance coverage to its full-time employees, but only one qualifies to purchase insurance through the government Exchanges and receives a premium tax credit because the insurance offered by the employer is unaffordable, does not provide minimum value, or is not offered to that particular employee, then the employer will have to pay an annual ESRP payment of $3,480 in 2018 ($3,000 adjusted for inflation) per full-time employee, computed on a monthly basis, excluding the first 30 full-time employees from the computation. The penalty is calculated just like the penalty for an employer that doesn't offer any insurance coverage to its employees, except the annual penalty is $3,480 per full-time employee who goes to the government Exchanges and receives a premium tax credit and $2,320 for the rest of its full-time employees.

3. The test to determine the 95% requirement is month to month. If an ALE offers otherwise qualified health insurance coverage to less than 95% of its full-time employees, then the ALE will have to pay an annual ESRP payment of $2,320 per full- time employee if only one of its employees goes to the government Exchanges and receives a premium tax credit for buying insurance in the Exchanges (computed on a monthly basis, excluding the first 30 full-time employees from the computation).

The ACA also prohibits employers from requiring new employees or dependents who are eligible to enroll under the terms of an employer group health plan to wait longer than 90 calendar days before being allowed to enroll in the plan. The penalty is $100 per day per employee if this requirement is violated.

Payment of ESRP by Employers – The IRS will determine the amount of the ESRP, if any, based on required year-end reporting by the employer, and then notify the employer of the amount due. The employer will have a chance to respond to the IRS with documentation explaining why it doesn't owe a penalty. However, if this is not acceptable, the IRS will send a notice of assessment to the employer and a demand for payment. **(See Below, "Affordable Care Act Reporting Requirements")**

Full-Time-Equivalent (FTE) Employees – FTE employees are only used for purposes of determining whether the ESRP provisions apply to a particular employer. The calculation of an employer's number of full-time and full-time equivalent (FTE) employees includes full-time, part-time, and seasonal employees. The hours worked by an employee in determining his/her status should include not only hours worked but also hours for which an employee is paid or entitled to payment even when no work is performed including: vacations, holidays, illness, incapacity, layoffs, jury duty, military duty or leave of absence. Service outside of the U.S. is generally not counted. For tax-exempt entities, time spent by volunteers – such as firefighters and emergency first responders – won't cause them to be treated as full-time employees.

The ACA's definition of a full-time employee is a worker who averages 30 hours or more per week, or 130 hours per month. The definition of a part-time employee is a worker who is reasonably expected to be employed on average less than 30 hours per week. The definition of a "seasonal worker" is someone who customarily works less than 120 days a year. Employers that have 50 or more full-time or full-time equivalent (FTE) employees are considered ALEs in 2018. However, if the "Seasonal Worker Exemption" applies, an employer that has 50 or more full-time or FTE employees due to having seasonal workers will not be considered an ALE. The IRS has determined that if seasonal workers are required to be counted as FTE workers, they might unfairly push an employer past the large employer threshold. In determining whether or not an employer is an ALE, employees who are recipients of Tricare or Veterans Administration (VA) health benefits should not be counted in determining whether an employer has 50 or more full-time or FTE employees in any month.

Whether or not an employer is an ALE is generally determined each calendar year based on the average size of the employer's workforce during the prior year (Measurement Period). Therefore, the "Measurement Period" for 2018 is calendar year 2017 (1/1/2017 – 12/31/2017). The calculation of an employer's number of full-time and FTE employees for 2018 is as follows:

1. Determine how many full-time employees it had for each of the 12 months in 2017 (Measurement period) – workers that worked an average of 30 hours or more per week or 130 hours per month.
2. Determine how many FTE employees it had in 2017 – add up the hours worked by part-time and seasonal workers for each of the 12 months during the Measurement Period and divide their total hours worked by 120.
3. Add the two numbers determined in steps 1 and 2 for each of the 12 months.
4. Add up the 12 monthly numbers in step 3 and divide by 12.
5. If less than 50, the employer is not an ALE in 2018.
6. If equal to or greater than 50 during the Measurement period, the employer is an ALE in 2018, unless the "Seasonal Worker Exemption" applies, and the Seasonal Worker Exemption applies only if the employer had seasonal workers.
7. To determine if the Seasonal Worker Exemption applies, first determine if the employer had any seasonal workers in 2017 (includes workers employed during holiday periods). If the employer had seasonal workers, look at how many full-time or FTE employees it had in each of the 12 months during the Measurement Period. If it had 50 or more full-time or FTE employees for 120 days (4 months) or less during the Measurement Period, then the Seasonal Worker exemption applies, and the employer is not considered an ALE. The 120 days (4 months) don't even have to be consecutive if the employer had seasonal workers in those months.

Failure of employers to correctly apply ACA methodologies in determining whether workers are full-time employees, inevitably leads to problems with proper reporting to the IRS. For example, ALEs with workforces that have a number of variable-hour, part-time or multi-position employees find it especially difficult to make accurate full-time determinations under the ACA. Tax advisors might want to ask their clients how they are faring in determining these classifications.

- **Example** – An employer has 52 full-time and FTE employees during the 12-month measurement period: 42 full-time employees + 10 FTE employees (average for the 12-month period). The FTE employees, include both part-time and seasonal workers. When looking at each of the individual months during the measurement period, the employer has 50 or more full-time or FTE employees in only 4 months or 120 days when the seasonal workers were working. Therefore, the employer is not considered an ALE.

Employers don't need to immediately offer insurance to an employee if it isn't certain whether the employee will work full or part-time. For such workers, the employer can use measurement periods ranging for 3 -12 months in determining whether an employee is full or part-time. However, these measurement periods need to be consistent within certain groups of workers but can change from year to year.

The employer-employee relationship is determined under the common law standard, i.e. an employer is one for whom services are performed by the employee and who has the right to control the result of the services and the details and means by which they are performed. An employee is subject to the employer's will and control not only as to what is done but how it is done. The requirement that part-time employees be part of the calculation to determine the number of FTE employees could be a problem due to businesses misclassifying employees as independent contractors. Therefore, the ACA provides employers with yet another reason to misclassify workers as independent contractors. This suggests that the status of part-time workers could see increased scrutiny by the IRS. **(See Chapter 14, "Independent Contractors/Non-Employees"); (See Chapter 17, "Self-Employment Tax")**

Excise Tax on Employers That Reimburse Employees for Health Insurance

In order for applicable large employers (ALE) to be in compliance with the Affordable Care Act (ACA), the IRS has determined that they can't use stand-alone tax-advantaged spending accounts to assist their employees with health insurance premiums, but instead, such plans have to be "integrated" with group health insurance plans offered to their employees. So, in 2018, ALEs have to pay an excise tax (penalty) if they reimburse employees for health insurance premiums using stand-alone Health Reimbursement Arrangements (HRAs) or directly pay the premiums for health insurance coverage that employees purchase on their own (other than insurance for excepted benefits, e.g. dental, vision, disability, long-term care, accident-only coverage, etc.). The penalty ALEs have to pay is an excise tax of $100 per affected employee per day ($36,500 per affected employee per year). **(See Chapter 9, "Health Reimbursement Arrangement (HRA)")**

www.irs.gov/pub/irs-access/f8928_accessible.pdf   www.irs.gov/pub/irs-pdf/i8928.pdf

The 21st Century Cures Act allows small employers (fewer than 50 FTE employees) to use stand-alone Qualified Small Employer Health Reimbursement Arrangements (QSEHRAs) to assist their employees with out-of-pocket health insurance premiums and medical costs and not be subject to the excise tax (penalty).

Qualified Small Employer Health Reimbursement Arrangement (QSEHRA) – A qualified small employer health reimbursement arrangement (QSEHRA), or small business HRA, is an employer funded tax-free health benefit that allows small businesses with fewer than 50 full-time or full-time-equivalent (FTE) employees to reimburse their employees for individual health care expenses. QSEHRAs were signed into law by the "21st Century Cures Act" in December 2017. Most stand-alone health reimbursement arrangements (HRAs), which is an HRA that is not offered in conjunction with a group health plan, have been prohibited since 2014 by the Affordable Care Act (ACA). However, the 21st Century Cures Act (Act) allows small employers that do not maintain group health plans to establish stand-alone HRAs that are called QSEHRAs, effective for plan years beginning on or after Jan. 1, 2017. Like all HRAs, a QSEHRA must be funded solely by the employer. Employees cannot make their own contributions to an HRA, either directly or indirectly through salary reduction contributions. Specific requirements apply, including a maximum benefit limit and a notice requirement. For 2018, the maximum reimbursements cannot exceed $5,050 for those with self-only coverage and $10,250 for those with family coverage. In 2017, the QSEHRA contribution limits were $4,950 annually for self-only employees and $10,000 annually for family coverage. For employees who become eligible for the QSEHRA midyear, the limits must be prorated to reflect the total amount of time the employee is eligible. For example, an employee who is eligible for the QSEHRA for 6 months in 2018 can receive up to $2,524.98 through the benefit that year. **(See Chapter 9, "Qualified Small Employer Health Reimbursement Arrangement (QSEHRA)")**

Calculating whether a QSEHRA provides affordable coverage: First – an employee determines whether their QSEHRA qualifies as affordable coverage. In 2018, the federal definition of "affordable coverage" is an insurance policy that costs 9.56% or less of a person's household income, which means that for a Small Business HRA to be considered affordable coverage for the month, the employee's premium for self-only coverage through the second-lowest-cost silver plan offered on their local exchange, after subtracting the employee's monthly HRA allowance, is less than 9.56% of the employee's household income for the month. If these conditions are met, the employee has affordable coverage and doesn't qualify for a premium tax credit. If the conditions are not met, the employee may be eligible for a credit, depending on a second set of calculations as demonstrated by the following example: Alice, an employee at ABC Company, is granted $5,000 a year through her employer's QSEHRA. This is equal to a monthly allowance of $417 a month. If Alice's premium for self-only coverage through the second-lowest cost silver plan on her exchange is $417 or less, she doesn't qualify for a tax credit. If the premium cost is more than that, however, she must subtract the amount of her HRA monthly allowance from that cost. Let's say the exchange premium is $500, and $500 –$417 = $83. If $83 is equal to or less than 9.56 percent of Alice's income for the month, the QSEHRA is affordable and she doesn't qualify for a premium tax credit for that month. In this example, Alice would not qualify for premium tax credits if she were earning $868 per month or more. However, if $83 is greater than 9.56 percent of Alice's monthly income (i.e., Alice is earning $868 per month or less), she "does" qualify for a premium tax credit (Note: to do this calculation for yourself, take the amount of the second-lowest-cost silver plan in your area minus your monthly HRA allowance, and divide by 0.0956. If that number is bigger than what you earn every month, you will qualify for a premium tax credit).

After determining that you qualify for a premium tax credit, you have to calculate the amount of the premium tax credit: First, you must make sure the amount of the tax credit is adjusted to reflect the monthly HRA allowance. The law requires any premium tax credit to be reduced by the amount of the monthly HRA allowance. For example, let's assume Alice of ABC Company is eligible for a $600 premium tax credit per month. Because she receives a $417 HRA allowance from her company, she must subtract $417 from $600, leaving her with a tax credit of $183 for the month. It's possible that an employee's tax credit will be reduced entirely by the HRA allowance; however, it cannot be reduced below zero. As a small business owner, you may be concerned about the affordability of your HRA offering. However, small business employers are never involved with making premium tax credit calculations for their employees. Not only would that violate the employee's privacy, but it's also nearly impossible to do. An employer cannot know whether an employee has additional sources of income, whether from a spouse, a second job, or property ownership. As for their employees, they must disclose their HRA monthly allowance to the exchange, which will help calculate the employees' eligibility.

Small employers that want to establish a group health insurance plan for their employees can use the government's "SHOP" Marketplace to get cost assistance to buy fairly priced group health insurance plans. **(See Below, "Small Business Healthcare Tax Credit")**

Group Health Insurance and Tax-Advantaged Health Spending Accounts for ALEs – Large employers (50 or more FTE employees) can avoid payment of the excise tax by offering group health insurance plans to their employees. Large employers that offer tax-advantaged health spending accounts (HRAs, HSAs, and FSAs) to their employees (other than for excepted benefits) as part of their benefit package must be in compliance with the ACA by integrating the tax-advantaged health spending accounts with qualified group health insurance plans, and employees must participate in the group health insurance plans to be eligible to participate in tax-advantaged health spending accounts. The group health insurance plans offered by ALEs to their employees must be structured to provide minimum essential health care coverage in accordance with the ACA. **(See Chapter 9, "Health Reimbursement Arrangement (HRA)")**

Charitable Hospitals

The ACA requires charitable (tax-exempt) hospitals to conduct community health needs assessments at least once every three years and adopt an implementation strategy to meet the needs identified through the assessments. These assessments must be widely available to the public and should take into account input from a broad cross section of the community. After the needs are identified, an implementation strategy must be approved indicating which needs will be addressed and why other needs will not be addressed. Also, charitable hospitals are expected to establish a written financial assistance policy (FAP) and a written policy relating to emergency medical care; not use gross charges and to limit the amounts charged for emergency or other medically necessary care provided to individuals eligible for financial assistance to not more than the amounts generally billed to individuals who have insurance; and to make reasonable efforts to determine whether an individual is eligible for financial assistance before engaging in aggressive collection actions. Complying with the regulations means that certain information is supposed to be put on the hospital's website, including an application for financial assistance, a plain language summary of the hospital's financial assistance policies, and a community health needs assessment, which identifies local health issues and how the hospital plans to address them. The ACA requirements are in addition to meeting the general requirements of Sec. 501(c)(3) as a tax-exempt entity. **(See Chapter 20, "Tax-Exempt Organizations")**

The only consequence of a hospital's noncompliance with the requirements after being allowed to correct its failures will be revocation of the hospital's tax-exempt status and taxing of all its income as unrelated business income (UBI), which can be disastrous for a tax-exempt hospital.

The ACA requirements apply to organizations that operate licensed hospitals in any of the 50 states and the District of Columbia, including government hospitals that have Sec. 501(c)(3) tax-exempt status. Where a hospital has ownership in a pass-through entity, such as a partnership or LLC treated as a partnership or a disregarded entity, activities of the entity are treated as activities of the hospital and must comply with the ACA requirements, or the income from the activity will be treated as UBI and taxed as ordinary income.

Federal Subsidies

Federal subsidies (tax credits) are available to individual taxpayers and small employers if they meet the necessary requirements in accordance with the ACA.

Premium Tax Credits

The Health Insurance Marketplace, operated by HHS, administers payments of premium tax credits (subsidies) to qualified individuals. Premium tax credits are "refundable" tax credits that are only available to individuals eligible to purchase health insurance through the government "Exchanges" (Marketplace). If married, individuals have to file their tax return jointly to qualify for a premium tax credit, except for certain victims of domestic abuse and spousal abandonment (See below). Individuals are generally eligible if they are ineligible for coverage through an employer or government insurance plan, such as Medicare Part A, and they are within certain income limits. Premium tax credits are only available for plans purchased through an ACA exchange. The government uses the term "Marketplace," which has been confusing to some people and has caused them to think that their health insurance, which was not purchased through the exchanges, qualified them for a premium tax credit. In the case of Nelson v. Commissioner, the Nelsons petitioned the Tax Court claiming they qualified for a premium tax credit for their health insurance which was not purchased through the ACA exchanges; claiming they were confused by the term "Marketplace." **(See Chapter 13, "Affordable Care Act Premium Tax Credits")**

www.ustaxcourt.gov/UstcDockInq/DocumentViewer.aspx?IndexID=7093214

When individuals apply for coverage in the government Exchanges, they have to provide estimated income and other information, and they must declare if they are tobacco users, which could increase their premiums up to an additional 50% (surcharge for tobacco use), because the premium tax credits they receive will not apply to the tobacco surcharge. The information provided will be cross-checked with information provided by the IRS which will help determine whether individuals applying for health insurance in the government Exchanges are eligible for premium tax credits and how much advance credit they are eligible to receive. The IRS will disclose to the Marketplace certain tax return information, including the taxpayer's identity and filing status, the number of personal exemptions claimed, the taxpayer's adjusted gross income (AGI), the amount of the taxpayer's Social Security benefits included in income, tax-exempt interest, and the fact that a taxpayer did not have a filing requirement. **(See Above, "Government Insurance Exchanges (Marketplace)")**

Also, if you are offered insurance through your employer and you apply for insurance in the government Exchanges, the Health Insurance Marketplace will determine if the health plan provided by your employer is affordable, of value, and provides minimum essential coverage, i.e. if you are paying more than 9.56% of your household income in 2018, based on your family size, toward insurance premiums, or the insurance offered to you by your employer doesn't meet minimum requirements, you will generally be eligible to purchase insurance through the government Exchanges and get a premium tax credit, even though you have health insurance available through your employer. **(See Above, "Individual Mandate")**

Individuals who qualify for premium tax credits when they enroll for coverage through the government Exchanges have two choices: (1) they can choose to have some or all of the estimated tax credit paid in advance directly to the insurance company to lower their monthly premiums, or (2) they can wait to get all of the credit when they file their tax return. When you apply for government Marketplace coverage, the Marketplace will estimate the amount of the premium tax credit that you may be able to claim for the year by using information you provide about your family composition, projected household income, and other factors, such as whether the family members you are enrolling are eligible for other, non-Marketplace coverage. Based on the estimate, you can decide if you want all, some, or none of the estimated credit paid in advance directly to your insurance provider to lower your monthly premiums. If you choose to have advance payments made on your behalf, you will be required to file Form 8962, "Premium Tax Credit (PTC)" with your income tax return to reconcile the amount of advance payments with the actual amount of premium tax credit you are allowed based on your actual household income and family size that is shown on your tax return. If you wait to get the credit, it will either increase your refund or lower the balance due on your tax return. If you choose to receive an "advanced premium tax credit," changes in your actual income compared to the estimated income on which the credit is based, and changes in family size will affect the actual credit you're ultimately eligible to receive when you file your tax return.

www.irs.gov/pub/irs-pdf/f8962.pdf   www.irs.gov/pub/irs-pdf/i8962.pdf

If you decide to get the credit in advance, it's important to report any changes to the Marketplace (either HealthCare.gov or the applicable state Marketplace website) such as: birth or adoption, marriage or divorce, increases or decreases in number of dependents, increase or decrease in household income, gaining or losing employer health care coverage or eligibility, and changes in filing status. Reporting these changes will help you get the proper amount of advanced premium tax credit you are entitled to, so you can avoid getting too much or too little in advance. If you get divorced or legally separated during the year and both you and your former spouse are enrolled in the same government Exchange health plan, you must allocate policy amounts on your separate tax returns in order to reconcile any advance premium tax credit payments made on your behalf. There is no penalty for miscalculation of your advance premium tax credit, but if the actual credit you are eligible to receive on your tax return doesn't match the amount you received in advance, which is likely, you will have to repay any excess advanced payments, or you may get a larger refund if you are entitled to more credit than you received in advance. Either way, Individuals who qualify to receive premium tax credits have to file Form 8962 with their tax return to reconcile advanced premium tax credits with actual credits they are entitled to. A tax return with Form 8962 must be filed to reconcile advanced premium tax credit payments regardless of any other filing requirement.

Calculating Premium Tax Credits – In 2018, individuals with estimated household (HH) incomes between 100% and 400% of the 2018 federal poverty levels ($12,140 to $48,560 for singles; $16,460 to $65,840 for a family of 2; $20,780 to $83,120 for a family of 3; $25,100 to $100,400 for a family of 4, etc.) are eligible to receive premium tax credits. Premium tax credits, which are on a sliding scale, are based on a percentage of estimated household income, ranging from 2.01% at 133% of the federal poverty level to 9.56% at 300% to 400% of the federal poverty level. Household income for purposes of the premium tax credit is the Modified Adjusted Gross Income (MAGI) of the taxpayer, the taxpayer's spouse, and all dependents who are required to file a tax return because their income meets the tax return filing threshold. MAGI is an individual's adjusted gross income (AGI) from the federal tax return, plus any excluded foreign income, non-taxable Social Security benefits (including tier 1 railroad benefits), and tax-exempt interest received or accrued during the taxable year. MAGI does not include Supplemental Social Security Income (SSI). For most people, MAGI will be the same as AGI.

An individual's allowable Premium Tax Credit is equal to the lesser of the premium for the plan purchased by the taxpayer on the government Exchanges less the individual's contribution amount (See below), or the national average premium for the second lowest Silver plan less the taxpayer's contribution amount (second lowest Silver plan can be found at: https://www.healthcare.gov/taxes/tools/#silverplan).

You can use the "Premium Tax Credit Calculator," on HealthCare.gov to calculate your estimated premium tax credit for the upcoming year based on your estimated household income. The Calculator uses your household's MAGI and household size to determine if you are eligible for a tax credit. A taxpayer's 2018 "contribution amount" is equal to the taxpayer's household income in accordance with the Federal poverty guidelines for 2018 based on family size, times the applicable percentages as set forth in the following table:

Household income % of Federal poverty line	Min Premium Cap	Max Premium Cap
Less than 133%	2.01%	2.01%
At least 133% but less than 150%	3.02%	4.03%
At least 150% but less than 200%	4.03%	6.34%
At least 200% but less than 250%	6.34%	8.10%
At least 250% but less than 300%	8.10%	9.56%
At least 300% but not more than 400%	9.56%	9.56%

The percentage amounts are adjusted to reflect the excess of the rate of premium growth over the rate of income growth for the preceding calendar year.

- **Example** – A taxpayer with a family of 4 has a household income of $37,650 which is exactly 150% of the federal poverty level in 2018. Therefore, the taxpayer's contribution amount in 2018 is $1,517.30 ($37,650 X 4.03% = $1,517.30). If the taxpayer purchases a Bronze level plan on the Exchange that costs $6,500 a year, the taxpayer's "Premium Tax Credit" would be $4,982.70 ($6,500 – $1,517.30 = $4,982.70)
- **Example** – A taxpayer with a family of 4 has a household income of $95,400, which is at least 300% but not more than 400% of the federal poverty level in 2018. Therefore, the taxpayer's contribution amount is $9,120.24 ($95,400 X 9.56% = $9,120.24). If the taxpayer purchases a Platinum level plan on the Exchange that costs $16,000 a year, and the premium for the second lowest Silver plan (benchmark) would cost the taxpayer $11,500 a year, the taxpayer's "Premium Tax Credit" would be $2,379.76 ($11,500 – $9,120.24 = $2,379.76).

For taxpayers who divorce during a plan year, the rules allow them to allocate the premium tax credit as they agree (e.g. 40%/60%). If they don't agree, the rules require a 50/50 split. **(See Chapter 3, "Marital Status and Divorce")**

Individuals making less than 133% of the poverty level – for example, $32,000 for a family of four (133% of the federal poverty level in 2018 is $33,383) – are eligible to receive Medicaid unless they live in states that opted out of the Expanded Medicaid Program (Texas, Pennsylvania, Wisconsin, etc.). If individuals live in a state that did not expand Medicaid, one of two situations will apply: if household income is more than 100% of the federal poverty level or $12,140 a year in 2018 for a single person ($25,100 for a family of 4, etc.), individuals will be able to purchase insurance in the government Exchanges and receive a premium tax credit; but If household income is less than 100% of the poverty level for the applicable family size, individuals won't be eligible for the premium tax credit. Persons who fall into this insurance coverage gap, because the state they live in did not accept federal funds for expanding Medicaid, might be able to go to a community health center, which provides primary care for millions of Americans. The health care law has expanded funding to these community health centers that provide services either for free or on a sliding scale based on income. Children and adults under 30 are eligible to purchase "catastrophic" coverage in 2018 and pay out-of-pocket expenses of no more than $7,350 for an individual plan and $14,700 for a family plan, but their preventive care services are 100% covered. Individuals that fall into this category will not have to pay a penalty if they don't have health insurance coverage.

A general exception to the requirement that married taxpayers have to file jointly to be able to claim a premium tax credit under the ACA includes the following provisions: files as married filing separately, lives apart from his or her spouse for the last six months of the year, and maintains a household that is also the principal place of abode of a dependent child for more than half of the year and furnishes over half the cost of the household during the tax year. However, as the IRS points out, many abused spouses may not meet some or all of these requirements. Therefore, the final regulations maintain the exception for the limited and unique situations when the taxpayer is unable to file a joint return either because the taxpayer fears for his or her safety or, through no fault of the victim, can neither file a joint return because the nonfiling spouse cannot be located nor obtain a divorce or legal separation because sufficient time has not lapsed under state law. The relief is limited to three consecutive years. Thus, a "married individual who is living apart from his or her spouse, and who is unable to file a joint return as a result of domestic abuse, will be permitted to claim a premium tax credit when filing a tax return with a filing status of married filing separately." **(See Chapter 3, "Head of Household"; & "Married Filing Separately")**

Specifically, a married taxpayer will satisfy the joint filing requirement by filing as married filing separately if the taxpayer (1) is living apart from his or her spouse when the taxpayer files the tax return; (2) is unable to file jointly because he or she is a victim of domestic violence; and (3) indicates on the tax return in accordance with the return instructions that he or she meets the criteria of (1) and (2). The IRS guidance allows survivors of domestic violence and spousal abandonment to claim the tax credits in future enrollment periods. Victims of domestic abuse and spousal abandonment now have protection for up to three consecutive years to assure access to continuous, discrimination-free health coverage.

Self-employed taxpayers are eligible for the premium tax credit but no double dipping is allowed, i.e. they must reduce their health insurance premiums claimed as an above-the-line deduction by the amount of tax credit received for purchasing insurance coverage in the government Exchange. Under the rules, self-employed taxpayers are allowed an above-the-line deduction for health insurance premiums not to exceed the lesser of (1) the premiums less the premium tax credits, or (2) the sum of the specified premiums not paid through premium advance credit payments and the additional tax imposed (if any) for excess advanced credit payments on the premiums (which are limited to the amount of advance credit payments taxpayers have to repay depending on their income level). **(See Chapter 11, "Self-Employed Health Insurance Premiums")**

Reconciliation of Premium Tax Credits – If you purchase health insurance through the government Exchanges, Form 1095-A, "Health Insurance Marketplace Statement" will be provided to you at the end of the year by the Marketplace as proof of health insurance coverage. Form 1095-A lists everyone in your household who has coverage; monthly premium amounts you paid during the year; monthly premium amounts of the Second Lowest Cost Silver Plan; and monthly advanced premium tax credits. Form 8962 is filed with your tax return to reconcile the monthly advanced premium tax credits you received with the actual credit you are entitled to receive on your tax return. If the premium tax credit advanced to you by the Marketplace is more than the amount you are entitled to, the excess should be reported as an additional tax due on Form 1040. If the premium tax credit advanced to you by the Marketplace is less than the amount you are entitled to, the difference should be reported as an additional tax payment on Form 1040. **(See Above, "Government Insurance Exchanges (Marketplace)")**

www.irs.gov/pub/irs-prior/f1095a--2015.pdf); https://marketplace.cms.gov/technical-assistance-resources/training-materials/1095a-cover-page.pdf

On July 6, 2016, the IRS issued proposed rules stating that a taxpayer will not lose premium tax credit eligibility and will not have to pay back advanced premium tax credits if the Marketplace determines at enrollment that a taxpayer's household income will be at least 100% of the federal poverty level or that the taxpayer is not eligible for Medicaid, CHIP, or a similar government-sponsored program, and unexpectedly the taxpayer's income turns out to be below 100% of the federal poverty level or the taxpayer is indeed eligible for Medicaid, CHIP, etc. This will be true unless the taxpayer provided incorrect information intentionally or with reckless disregard of the facts. The Proposed rules will generally take effect for tax years beginning after Dec. 31, 2016, although taxpayers may rely on the rules if the proposed rules are in their favor for years ending after Dec. 31, 2013.

Cost Sharing Reduction Subsidies (CSR)

NOTE: In October 2017, President Trump signed an Executive Order to stop the payment of CSR reduction subsidies (federal subsidies) to insurance companies. This would be an apparent violation of the Affordable Care Act law, which has yet to be repealed, and California along with about 15 other states are suing the Trump administration. The subsidies that are supposed to be paid to the insurance companies under the law are then paid directly by the insurance companies to eligible lower-income families to reduce their health insurance premiums. Therefore, the President's Executive Order will increase the premiums that eligible lower-income families will have to pay if it is allowed to stand. Cost sharing reduction subsidies that reduce the health insurance premiums paid by eligible families are explained below:

The only eligibility requirement to get Cost Sharing Reduction (CSR) subsidies is to be a lower-income family who purchases a "Silver" health plan in the government Exchanges. CSR subsidies only affect individuals' covered costs and, therefore, do not take effect until individuals actually use their covered health care services. CSR subsidies are in addition to premium tax credits. CSR subsidies reduce the out-of-pocket costs of lower-income individuals and families, which means they reduce the amount families pay-out for deductibles, coinsurance, and copayments. The subsidies don't lower individuals' premiums like advanced premium tax credits, as they only apply to cost sharing amounts. CSR subsidies only apply to covered benefits, meaning they won't reduce the costs of services not covered by the health plan. Unlike premium tax credits, CSR subsidies are not refundable. The subsidies are received directly from the insurance providers, and families won't ever owe back any cost assistance they get for out-of-pocket costs if their income changes from the projected amounts at the beginning of the year. Therefore, one of the best deals anyone who meets the income requirements can get under the ACA is to purchase a Silver plan in the government Exchanges, because unlike advanced premium tax credits, CSR subsidies don't have to be reconciled at the end of the year. Members of federally recognized Indian tribes or an Alaska Native Claims Settlement Act (ANCSA) Corporation shareholder may also qualify for additional cost-sharing reductions. **(See Above, "Exemptions from Having to Have Health Insurance Coverage")**

CSR subsidies are available to lower-income families who are those with incomes between 100% and 250% of the federal poverty level (FPL), which is equivalent to an individual earning between $12,140 and $30,350, or a family of four earning between $25,100 and $62,750. There are three levels of CSR subsidies: CSR 94; CSR 87, and CSR 73. CSR 94 applies to individuals and families with incomes between 100% and 150% of the FPL – this means that they have to pay 6% of covered out-of-pocket expenses instead of 30% without cost sharing subsidies. CSR 87 applies to individuals and families with incomes between 150% and 200% of the FPL – this means that they have to pay 13% of covered out-of-pocket expenses instead of 30% without cost sharing subsidies. CSR 73 applies to individuals and families with incomes between 200% and 250% of the FPL – this means that they have to pay 27% of covered out-of- pocket expenses instead of 30% without cost sharing subsidies.

The maximum out-of-pocket limit for most ACA plans in 2018 is $7,350 for single coverage and $14,700 for family coverage. However, for those purchasing Silver plans with incomes between 100 and 200 percent of the federal poverty level and, therefore, receiving CSR subsidies (subsidized Silver plans), the maximum out-of-pocket limit is $2,450 ($4,900 for a family). Those with incomes between 200 and 250 percent of the federal poverty level can select a Silver plan with a maximum out-of-pocket limit of $5,850 ($11,700 for a family). These plans only appear on the exchange websites for applicants who qualify for them.

Small Business Healthcare Tax Credit (Form 8941)

Small businesses with 25 or fewer full-time or FTE employees are eligible for the Small Business Healthcare Tax Credit only if they offer health insurance coverage to all of their full-time employees; pay at least 50% of their full-time employees' health insurance premiums; purchase their insurance through the government's Small Business Health Options Program (SHOP) (See below); and their employees have average annual wages of approximately $52,000 or less. The Small Business Healthcare Tax Credit is 50% of all health insurance premiums paid on behalf of employees (35% for small tax-exempt organizations). In 2018, small employers with up to 10 full-time or FTE employees can receive the maximum credit. The credit is reduced on a sliding scale for small employers with from 11 to 25 FTE employees, and is phased-out completely for businesses with more than 25 FTE employees or average annual wages in excess of approximately $52,000. The Small Business Healthcare Tax Credit is calculated on Form 8941, "Credit for Small Employer Health Insurance Premiums," and then claimed as a general business credit on Form 3800, which is reflected on Form 1040. Tax-exempt organizations should include the amount of the credit on line 44f of Form 990-T, "Exempt Organization Business Income Tax Return." **(See Chapter 13, "Affordable Care Act – Small Business Healthcare Tax Credit"); (See Chapter 20, "Tax-Exempt Organizations")**
www.irs.gov/pub/irs-pdf/f8941.pdf   www.irs.gov/pub/irs-pdf/i8941.pdf

Wages, for purposes of the credit, are wages paid that are subject to payroll tax (FICA), determined without considering the Social Security wage limitation. The credit amount is based on a percentage of the lesser of: (1) the amount of contributions for health insurance premiums paid by the eligible small employer on behalf of employees under a qualifying arrangement during the tax year, or (2) the amount of contributions for health insurance premiums the employer would have paid under the arrangement if each employee were enrolled in a plan that had a premium equal to the average premium for the small group market in the rating area in which the employee enrolls for coverage. A "qualifying arrangement" is an arrangement under which an eligible small employer pays a uniform percentage (no less than 50%) of the premium cost of the health insurance coverage for each employee enrolled in the employer's health insurance plan. Premiums paid on behalf of a former employee may be treated as paid on behalf of an employee provided the former employee is also treated as an employee for purposes of the uniform percentage requirement. The credit can be applied against both regular tax and the Alternative Minimum Tax (AMT). The tax credit is available only for plans purchased through SHOP (See below).

There is a two-year limit for taking the credit, which means that if you took the credit in 2016 and 2017, you can't take the credit in 2018. A small business employer that is eligible for the credit but doesn't owe any tax for the year, can carry the credit back or forward to other tax years. Also, since the amount of the health insurance premium payments is more than the allowable credit, eligible small businesses can still claim a business expense deduction for the premiums in excess of the credit. For tax-exempt organizations, the credit is refundable, so even if they have no taxable income, they are eligible to receive the credit as a refund as long as it does not exceed their income tax withholding and Medicare tax liability.

- For purposes of the Small Business Healthcare Tax Credit, self-employed individuals, partners, 2% shareholders of an S-corporation, 5% owners of an employer, and family members and dependents are not counted as employees in determining the number of full-time or FTE employees.
- If you're self-employed with no employees, you can get coverage through the government Exchange, not through SHOP.
- S-corporation shareholders and partners in service provider entities are considered self-employed, so they can get coverage through the government Exchange(s), not through SHOP.

Small Business Health Options Program (SHOP) – SHOP is the program set-up to simplify buying health insurance for small businesses. A business's employees must be enrolled in a SHOP plan for small employers to qualify for the Small Business Health Care Tax Credit. SHOP is the government Marketplace open to employers with 50 or fewer full-time or FTE employees (employers that have exactly 50 employees can purchase coverage for their employees through SHOP). SHOP is open year-round, so small employers can enroll at any time during the year. If employee enrollments are submitted between the 1st and 15th day of the month, group coverage begins the first day of the next month. For enrollments submitted after the 15th of the month, coverage begins on the first day of the second following month. Employers with fewer than 50 full-time or FTE employees are not subject to the Employer Shared Responsibility Payment (ESRP) provisions. However, these small employers may still offer health insurance coverage that they purchase on their own, or through SHOP. There are four categories of plans in the SHOP Marketplace: Bronze; Silver; Gold; and Platinum. The plan that employers choose affects how much employees will pay for things like deductibles and copayments, and the total amount they spend out-of-pocket for the year.

If a small employer decides to offer insurance coverage to their employees through SHOP, they select a plan; notify their employees; and employees either enroll or decline coverage. In many states, 70% of employees offered coverage must enroll in order for the employer to be able to buy insurance through SHOP. Employees with coverage through other avenues (spouses plan, Medicare, etc.) are not included in the calculation of the 70% threshold. However, employees with individual non-group private coverage are included in the calculation. Agents and brokers enrolling small employers in SHOP must be identity proofed on the Centers for Medicare and Medicaid Services (CMS) Enterprise Portal in order to gain access to the online SHOP Marketplace portal. Employers can change the broker authorized to act on their behalf no more than two times within the same plan year, which advisors should be aware of when advising clients. Employers can make these changes through the SHOP online portal or by calling the SHOP call center.

Taxes on High-Income Earners, Insurance Providers and Other Entities

The "0.9 Medicare Surtax" and the "3.8% Net Investment Income Tax" on high income earners are the taxes imposed on individuals to help fund provisions of the Affordable Care Act (ACA). The following are other taxes imposed by the ACA to help fund provisions of the law. **(See Chapter 2, "Payroll Tax (FICA)"); (See Chapter 10, "3.8% Net Investment Income Tax")**

Tax on Covered Insurance Entities

One of the main ways that the ACA pays for the benefits provided by the law is with a tax on insurers and reinsurers ("Covered Insurance Entities"). In this regard, the ACA generally imposes an annual fee that began in 2014 on covered entities engaged in providing health insurance coverage. The aggregate fee imposed on all covered entities was $8 billion in 2014 and $11.3 billion in 2015. The fee is $11.3 billion in 2016, $13.9 billion in 2017, and $14.3 billion in 2018. For 2019 and following years, the aggregate fee is indexed to the rate of premium growth. Each covered insurance entity must file Form 8963, "Report of Health Insurance Provider Information" by April 15th of each year (April 17, 2018). The fee applies to covered entities providing health insurance for any U.S. health risk during the calendar year in which the fee is due. The fee does not apply to subject entities whose net premiums written are $25 million or less in a year. For entities with more than $25 million in net premiums, but not more than $50 million, the fee is computed on 50% of the net premiums written. For subject entities whose net premiums written or more than $50 million in a year, the fee is computed on 100% of the net premiums written. The IRS will notify each covered entity of the preliminary fee calculation by June 15th of each fee year, and the final fee calculation on or before August 31st. The fee must be paid by September 30th of each fee year.

www.zillionforms.com/2016/F507726266.PDF   www.irs.gov/pub/irs-pdf/i8963.pdf

Covered insurance entities include any entity that provides health insurance for any U.S. health risk during the calendar year in which the fee is due. Generally, excluded from the definition of covered entities are: (1) self-insured employers; (2) governmental entities; (3) certain nonprofit corporations; and (4) certain voluntary employees' beneficiary associations. A controlled group does not have to include a "controlled group member" who would not qualify to be covered if it were a single entity. "Controlled groups" include: parent-subsidiary chains; brother-sister controlled groups; and combined groups that include both parent-subsidiary chains and brother-sister controlled groups.

For purposes of the fee, health insurance does not include: coverage only for a specified disease or illness; hospital indemnity or other fixed indemnity insurance; insurance for long-term care; or any Medicare supplemental health insurance. A fully-insured multiple employer welfare arrangement (MEWA) is not a covered entity because, even though the MEWA receives premiums, it applies the premiums to pay an insurance company to provide the coverage it purchases. If the MEWA is not fully insured, it is a covered entity to the extent it uses premiums it receives to provide the health coverage rather than pay an insurance company to provide the coverage.

10% Excise Tax on Indoor Tanning Services

A 10% excise tax is assessed on amounts paid for indoor tanning services (tanning salons). Providers of indoor tanning services collect the tax at the time the purchaser pays for the tanning service. The provider then pays quarterly with IRS Form 720 (Quarterly Federal Excise Tax Return). Form 720 must be filed using the name and employer identification number of a disregarded entity providing the services and not the entity's owner. Amounts paid for indoor tanning services includes any amount paid by insurance. Tanning providers do not have to collect the tax on other goods and services if the charges are separable. The tax does not apply to spray-on tanning services, topical creams and lotions or to phototherapy services performed by a licensed medical professional on his or her premises. In addition, there is an exemption for qualified physical fitness facilities that include access to indoor tanning facilities as part of a membership fee without a separately identifiable fee for the tanning services.   www.irs.gov/pub/irs-pdf/f720.pdf   www.irs.gov/pub/irs-pdf/i720.pdf

2.3% Excise Tax on Medical Devices

The Federal Register Printing Savings Act of 2017 delays until 2020 the 2.3% excise tax on certain medical devices. The new law replaces the previous law – The "Protecting Americans from Tax Hikes Act of 2015" which imposed a 2-year moratorium on the 2.3% excise tax on medical devices (the excise tax was not imposed in tax years 2016 and 2017).

The tax is imposed on manufacturers, producers, or importers of medical devices based on gross sales to wholesale distributors. Like other manufacturer excise taxes, the medical device excise tax is reported on Form 720, which is filed quarterly. The excise tax is on the use and lease of medical devices, and applies to most devices used by health care professionals, ranging from X-ray and MRI machines and experimental cancer treatment devices all the way down to tongue depressors. Certain items such as biologics, devices intended solely for use by animals, software updates or sales of software, and most home medical equipment devices aren't subject to the tax. Retail products consumed by the general public such as eyeglasses, contact lenses, and hearing aids are also exempt from the tax, as are prosthetic or orthotic devices. Consumers who use the internet or telephone to buy a firm's medical equipment fall under the retail category, so the tax is not imposed on the manufacturers, producers, or importers for their purchases. A wholesale distributor is defined as a firm involved in the business of selling products to people or firms who resell such products. Retailers are considered to be those who sell to end users. A device is treated as an exempt retail item if it is regularly available for purchase and use by individual consumers who aren't medical professionals.
www.congress.gov/115/plaws/publ120/PLAW-115publ120.pdf

Branded Prescription Drug Fee

An annual fee is imposed on pharmaceutical manufacturers and importers (covered entities) based on branded prescription drug sales of over $5 million made to specified government programs – Medicare Part B program, the Medicare Part D program, the Medicaid program, Department of Veterans Affairs, Department of Defense, and the Tricare retail pharmacy program. The fees are to be paid by the covered entities no later than September 30th of each year. Sales data for the fee is generally provided by the Centers for Medicare and Medicaid Programs of the Department of Health and Human Services (CMS), VA and DOD. In addition, each covered entity may volunteer relevant information regarding the determination of the fee by annually submitting Form 8947, "Report of Branded Prescription Drug Information." The fee for each covered entity is calculated by determining the ratio of each covered entity's branded prescription drug sales to the total sales for all covered entities during the year, and applying the ratios to the applicable amount to be collected each year. The applicable amounts to be collected were/are: 2011 - $2.5 billion; 2012 - $2.8 billion; 2013 - $2.8 billion; 2014 through 2016 - $3 billion each year; 2017 - $4 billion; 2018 - $4.1 billion; and 2019 and thereafter - $2.8 billion.

The fees collected under the branded prescription drug fee program are transferred to the Medicare Part B Trust Fund, which is used to subsidize a portion of the Medicare Part B program. By accurately assessing and promptly collecting the branded prescription drug fees, the IRS ensures timely availability of these funds to the Medicare Part B program. Each year the IRS makes a preliminary fee calculation for each covered entity and notifies them. The IRS has developed procedures and a database to process covered entities' sales data and to accurately calculate the annual fees. Data on branded prescription drug sales are reported to the IRS from both the government agencies and the covered entities, creating a dual reporting process. The IRS merges and compares the data from each source to identify any inconsistencies and promptly follows up to resolve them.

Patient-Centered Outcomes Research Trust Fund Fee

The Patient-Centered Outcomes Research Trust Fund fee helps to fund the Patient-Centered Outcomes Research Institute (PCORI). The Institute assists in making informed health decisions by advancing the quality and relevance of evidence-based medicine, i.e. reviews pharmaceutical medicines to determine if they are of sufficient quality and are relevant to patients' needs. Funding for PCORI comes from a fee imposed on health insurance policies and self-insured plans whose plan year ended after Sept. 30, 2012 and before Oct. 1, 2019. Therefore, insurance issuers (providers) and employers that have self- insured plans, including small employers (fewer than 50 full-time or FTE employees) have to pay the fee. The fee for policy or plan years ending after September 30, 2015 and before October 1, 2016 is $2.17 multiplied by the average number of participants covered by each policy or plan. For policy or plan years ending after September 30, 2016, and before October 1, 2019, the fee per participant will be further adjusted to reflect inflation. The fee is paid annually using Form 720, "Quarterly Federal Excise Tax Return." Companies can write-off the fee as a business expense.

40% Excise Tax on High-Cost Employer-Provided Health Plans ("Cadillac" Health Plans)

The Federal Register Printing Savings Act of 2017 delays until 2022 the "Cadillac" tax on employers for excess employer-sponsored health insurance coverage. The excise tax which has never been imposed in any tax year so far was to be paid by the coverage provider or person who administered the plan benefits. The idea is to give employers that much more reason to avoid expensive insurance policies and thus give insurers that much more reason to hold costs down.

The tax was supposed to be imposed on the cost of health plans in excess of $10,200 for single coverage and $27,500 for family coverage, subject to cost-of-living and other adjustments. But the tax has, of yet, never been implemented in any tax year. The limit on the cost of premiums was to be increased to $11,850 for single coverage and $30,950 for family coverage for retired individuals age 55 and older and for plans that cover employees engaged in high risk professions (e.g. public safety, construction, mining, etc.).
www.congress.gov/115/plaws/publ120/PLAW-115publ120.pdf

Affordable Care Act Reporting Requirements

All taxpayers who have health insurance coverage in 2018 should receive one of the following forms as proof of health insurance coverage for themselves and their dependents: Form 1095-A, "Health Insurance Marketplace Statement;" Form 1095-C, "Employer-Provided Health Coverage Insurance Offer and Coverage;" or Form 1095-B, "Health Coverage." Depending on the circumstances, a taxpayer could get a Form 1095-A, Form 1095-B, and Form 1095-C, or any combination of these in the same year.

2015 was the first year that information reporting was required by each applicable large employer (ALE) and each insurance provider. ALEs with 50 or more full-time or full time equivalent employees (FTEs) are required to issue reports to both the IRS and their full-time employees for two purposes: (1) to assist the IRS with enforcing the employer ESRP provisions (pay-or-play penalty); and (2) to help employees determine their eligibility for the premium tax credit. Also, insurance issuers (providers) are required to report information to the IRS about the type of health insurance and the number of employees covered. For insurance providers, there are two unique reporting requirements. The first is the individual mandate reporting requirement, and the second is the employer mandate or "pay-or-play" reporting requirement. For pay-or-play reporting, insurance providers have to demonstrate that they have satisfied the obligation to offer coverage to employees and their dependents that is affordable, of minimum value, and provides minimum essential coverage (MEC). **(See Above, "Individual Mandate"; & "Employer Mandate")**

ACA Penalty Notices

Businesses that have not complied with the ACA's filing requirements are subject to penalties and the penalty notices will be coming soon. Large employers were told by the IRS that assessments were coming in 2015, 2016 and 2017, but the IRS has been behind on assessing those fees, and some companies ignored the filing requirements. Also, with the possibility of an ACA repeal, some employers thought they'd never be affected. But now, employers may receive three years of catch up tax assessments within a short period of time. Employers that have not filed correctly or that have misclassified employees will be subject to substantial penalties, with a $3,193,000 maximum. And companies that have intentionally disregarded ACA compliance requirements will be subject to substantial penalties, with no maximum limit.

Government Marketplace (Exchanges)

Form 1095-A, "Health Insurance Marketplace Statement.," is provided by the government Marketplace to individuals who purchased health insurance through the government Exchanges (Marketplace) as proof of coverage for 2017. The form lists everyone in the household who had coverage during the year, and lists by each month during the year the monthly premium amounts; the premium amount of the second lowest cost Silver Plan; and the monthly advanced payments of premium tax credits (subsidies). Form 1095-A is used by taxpayers to compute the premium tax credits they are eligible to receive, and to reconcile with advanced premium tax credits they received during the year with actual allowable premium tax credits. Form 8962 has to be filed with individuals' tax returns to reconcile the monthly advanced premium tax credits they received (if any) with the actual premium tax credit they are entitled to receive based on their actual household income. Any excess premium tax credit received should be reported as an additional tax due on Form 1040, Line 46. If the premium tax credit advanced by the Marketplace is less than the amount they are entitled to, the difference should be reported as a tax payment on Form 1040, Line 69. A tax return with Form 8962 attached must be filed to reconcile advanced premium tax credit payments regardless of any other filing requirement. **(See Above, "Government Insurance Exchanges (Marketplace)")**

www.irs.gov/pub/irs-pdf/f1095a.pdf   www.healthreformbeyondthebasics.org/wp-content/uploads/2016/03/Premium-Tax-Credit_Tips-and-Tricks.pdf

Fully Insured and Self-Insured Large Employers (50 or More Full-Time or FTE Employees)

Individuals acquiring health insurance through a company-sponsored (employer) health insurance provider or a self-insured large employer (50 or more full-time or full-time equivalent (FTE) employees), including government employers, should receive Form 1095-C as proof of coverage for 2017. Form 1095-C identifies whether insurance was offered to the employee and their dependents and the actual coverage provided. Individual taxpayers who had multiple employers during the year should receive a Form 1095-C from each of their employers, and if they had coverage through the government Exchanges (Marketplace) for part of the year, they should also receive Form 1095-A. Individuals acquiring health insurance through a company-sponsored (employer) health insurance provider should also receive Form 1095-B.

Form 1095-C, "Employer-Provided Health Insurance Offer and Coverage" must be filed and furnished by ALEs to each employee who is a full-time employee for one or more months of the calendar year. Form 1095-C reports insurance coverage information for all 12 months of the calendar year for each of their full-time employees whether or not insurance coverage was provided to them in 2017. Also, ALEs must furnish the IRS with copies of all Forms 1095-C sent to their employees. ALEs must use Form 1094-C "Transmittal of Employer-Provided Health Insurance Offer and Coverage Information Returns" to transmit Forms 1095-C to the IRS. The transmittal Form 1094-C provides information about the employers, while Form 1095-C provides information about the employees. The reporting requirements are applicable to all ALEs, including for-profit, government agencies, and nonprofit employers.

ALEs that file more than 250 Forms 1095-C must e-file the information returns to the IRS. Form 1095-C provides specific information on a monthly basis about each full-time employee, spouse, and their dependents that were offered insurance coverage, the cost of self-only coverage, and why insurance wasn't provided to an employee (if applicable). Reporting is required for any employee who was a full-time employee for at least one month during the calendar year. Parts I and II of Form 1095-C are to be completed by all fully insured (insured through a health insurance provider) ALEs, while Parts I, II, and III are to be completed by all self-insured ALEs. Self-insured employers are those that would rather pay employees' health expenses themselves rather than get coverage for employees through a health insurance provider. Employees of fully insured ALEs will also receive a Form 1095-B from the insurance issuers (providers).

Form 1095-C provides information to the IRS that helps determine whether or not the individual and employer mandates have been satisfied by the employees and the employer. For employer mandate reporting, large fully-insured and self-insured employers have to demonstrate that they have satisfied the obligation to offer coverage to employees and their dependents that is affordable, of minimum value, and provides minimum essential coverage (MEC). Reporting by self-insured employers shows that employees were covered and, therefore, not liable for the individual shared responsibility payment (penalty) for the months they were covered under the plan.

Small employers (fewer than 50 full-time or FTE employees) are not required to provide any reports to their employees or the IRS. However, small self-insured employers are required to send Form 1095-B to their full-time employees and to the IRS, which is the same form that Health Insurance providers are required to send to their policy holders and the IRS (See Below).
www.irs.gov/pub/irs-pdf/f1094c.pdf   www.irs.gov/pub/irs-prior/f1095c--2015.pdf

<u>Summary of the Information Required to Be Reported on the Forms</u>:
- <u>Form 1094-C</u>, "Transmittal of Employer-Provided Health Insurance Offer and Coverage Information Returns:"
  - Part I – Applicable Large Employer (ALE) Member: Employer's name; EIN; address; name and telephone number of employer's contact person; and total number of Forms 1095-C submitted.
  - Part II – ALE Member Information: Total number of Forms 1095-C filed on behalf of the employer, including those filed for individuals enrolled in an employer self-insured plan; whether or not the employer is a member of an Aggregated ALE Group; and whether the employer is using one of the "Qualifying Offer Methods"/ Simplified Reporting Options. **(See Below, "Simplified Reporting Options")**

401

- Part III – ALE Member Information: Monthly Minimum Essential Coverage (MEC) Offer Indicator – must check the applicable box (offered MEC to 95% of full-time employees and dependents for entire year; offered MEC to 95% of full-time employees and dependents for only certain months; did not offer MEC to 95% of full-time employees and dependents for any of the 12 months; and report the number of full-time employees and all employees for each month during the year.
- Part IV – Other ALE Members of an Aggregated ALE Group.

- Form 1095-C, "Employer-Provided Health Insurance Offer and Coverage:"
  - Part I – Employee: Employee's name; Social Security Number; address; and telephone number of the person to contact.
  - Part II – Employee Offer and Coverage: Enter offer code for each calendar month – employer offered MEC for all 12 months; or offered MEC for only certain months: indicate the months where MEC was offered and the type of insurance coverage offered – only to employee; employee and dependents; employee and spouse (not dependents); employee, spouse, and dependents; employee was not offered MEC; or employee was not a full-time employee. The names and Social Security numbers of all individuals covered should be provided.
  - Part III – Covered Individuals: Names and Social Security numbers of individuals covered. This part should only be completed when the employer offered employer-sponsored self-insured health insurance coverage in which the employee was enrolled.

Insurance Issuers (providers)

Individuals acquiring health insurance directly from an insurance company; through a company-sponsored (employer) health insurance provider; or from small self-insured employers (fewer than 50 FTE employees) should receive Form 1095-B as proof of coverage for 2017. Form 1095-B should be sent to individuals by the health insurance issuers (providers). Small self-insured employers should provide Form 1095-B to their employees. Individuals acquiring health insurance through a company-sponsored (employer) health insurance provider should also receive Form 1095-C.

Form 1095-B, "Health Coverage" has to be provided by insurance providers to all policyholders (insured employees) as proof of coverage for 2017. Insurance providers must file Form 1094-B, "Transmittal of Health Coverage Information Returns," and individual Forms 1095-B for each policyholder to the IRS and provide a copy of Form 1095-B to each of their policyholders whether they are employees of large employers or small employers (fewer than 50 FTE employees). The transmittal Form 1094-B provides information about the insurance issuers (providers), while Form 1095-B provides information about the insured (policyholders). Filers of more than 250 Forms 1095-B must e-file the information returns to the IRS. Policyholders that are employed by large employers will also receive Form 1095-C from their employers.

www.irs.gov/pub/irs-pdf/f1094b.pdf   www.irs.gov/pub/irs-prior/f1095b--2015.pdf
www.irs.gov/pub/irs-pdf/i109495b.pdf

Summary of the Information Required to Be Reported on the Forms:
- Form 1094-B, "Transmittal of Health Coverage Information Returns" – Insurance company's (provider's) name; EIN; name and telephone number of person to contact who is responsible for answering any questions; provider's address; and total number of Forms 1095-B submitted.
- Form 1095-B, "Health Coverage:"

- Part I – Employee/Policyholder: Name; Social Security No.; date of birth; and address. Also, indicate the type of policy – employer-sponsored plan; SHOP; government-sponsored plan; individual market insurance; multiemployer plan; self-insured small employer; or other designated MEC.
- Part II – Employer-Sponsored Coverage: Name, EIN, and address of the employer sponsoring the coverage.
- Part III – Issuer or Other Coverage Provider: Name; EIN; and address of the insurance company (provider). The issuer/provider of the coverage is the carrier of the insurance, sponsor of a self-insured employer plan, governmental agency providing government-sponsored coverage, or other coverage sponsor.
- Part IV – Covered Individuals: Names, Social Security Numbers; and dates of birth of all individuals covered by the plan and also indicate whether: each individual was covered for at least one day per month for all 12 months; if not covered for all 12 months; and which months the individuals were covered for at least one day.

Simplified Reporting Options

Simplified Reporting Options are available to ALEs that provide a "qualifying offer" to any of their full-time employees for all 12 months. A qualifying offer is an offer that is affordable, of minimum value, and provides minimum essential coverage to employees:

- An ALE employer that certifies it made a "qualifying offer" to any of its full-time employees for all 12 months does not have to report the monthly details required by the regular reporting method (See above). Instead, the employer is permitted to simply report each applicable employee's name, address, and Social Security number for those employees on Form 1095-C (simplified reporting). For all of its other employees that did not receive a qualifying offer for all 12 months, the employer must file Forms 1095-C under the regular reporting method. The employer must still provide Forms 1095-C to the IRS and to all of its full-time employees, including those who received a qualifying offer for all 12 months and those that did not receive an offer. Transmittal Form 1094-C, Line 22 is where the employer can check Box A, certifying it made a "qualifying offer" to any of its full-time employees.

- An ALE that certifies it made a "qualifying offer" to at least 98% of its full-time employees and their dependents for all 12 months does not have to identify or specify the total number of full-time employees per month, and the employer can use "simplified reporting" on Forms 1095-C which goes to each of its employees. The employer's only required reporting to the IRS is on Transmittal Form 1094-C, Line 22 where the employer can check Box D, certifying it satisfies the 98% Offer Method. However, if any of the employer's employees claim a premium tax credit for Exchange (Marketplace) coverage, the employer may be contacted by the IRS to determine whether the employee was a full-time employee for the months in question.

Forms 1095-C and Forms 1095-B have to be furnished to individual taxpayers by Jan. 31, 2018. The due dates for submitting Forms 1095-C and 1095-B to the IRS are Feb. 28, 2018 for paper forms and March 31, 2018 for e-filed forms, and if employers and insurance providers have to file forms for 250 or more employees, the forms must be e-filed to the IRS. Also, ALEs that have more than 250 workers have to report the cost of healthcare benefits provided on employees' behalf, which should appear on Form W-2 in Box 12, using code DD. Employers and insurance providers must use the Affordable Care Act Information Returns (AIR) Program when filing their statements to the IRS. Employee statements must be furnished to individuals in paper format by mail, unless the individual affirmatively consents to receiving the statement electronically. The employee statements can be mailed along with their W-2 Forms. Employers may want to provide a cover memo with an explanation. Small employers with less than 50 full-time or FTE employees are not subject to any reporting requirements, unless they have self-funded group health plans that are subject to individual mandate reporting (See above). For small employers that provide a health plan through an insurance company, the insurance company is responsible for the individual mandate reporting. **(See Chapter 4, "Wages and Salaries")**

www.irs.gov/pub/irs-pdf/fw2.pdf www.irs.gov/pub/irs-pdf/iw2w3.pdf

An applicable large employer (ALE) that fails to comply with the reporting requirements may be subject to penalties for failure to file correct information forms to the IRS and failure to file correct taxpayer statements. The penalty for failure to file correct information forms to the IRS ranges from $50 a return if a mistake is corrected within 30 days to $500 per return for intentional errors. And the same penalty parameters apply to failure to provide correct taxpayer statements.

For purposes of the individual mandate, if any taxpayer owes the Shared Responsibility payment for not having adequate health insurance coverage, Form 8965 "Health Coverage Exemptions" must be filed with their tax return, and the amount of the penalty must be shown on Form 1040, Line 61. For purposes of the employer mandate (pay-or-play), if an ALE employer with 50 or more full-time or FTE employees doesn't offer any health insurance coverage or offers inadequate insurance to its full-time employees in 2017, the employer will owe a ESRP payment for each full-time employee, if only one of its employees goes to the government Exchanges (Marketplace) and qualifies for a premium tax credit. **(See Above, "Individual Mandate"; & "Employer Mandate")**

Tax Cuts and Jobs Act

This 92-Page Section was updated as of October 30, 2018. The Tax Cuts and Jobs Act (TCJA) is the most significant and far reaching tax law change since 1986. It is a $1.4 trillion tax cut with the majority of the corporate tax changes being permanent and the majority of the individual tax changes being temporary in that they generally expire on December 31, 2025, unless they are extended or made permanent. Overall, the goal of simplifying taxes was not accomplished – some rules were simplified such as eliminating personal and dependent exemptions; essentially doubling the standard deduction; and increasing the estate tax exemption. But the new law creates new complexity and compliance issues. So overall, taxes are now more complicated under the TCJA than before the new law was implemented. Also, the new law weakens the Affordable Care Act (ACA) by eliminating the requirement that everyone has to obtain adequate health insurance coverage or pay a penalty beginning in 2019. Therefore, it will raise health insurance premiums and reduce health insurance coverage which is an undesirable change caused by the TCJA. In addition, the new law adds $1.4 trillion to the national deficit.

In general, the TCJA is more of a tax cut for the wealthy than it is for lower- and middle-income Americans. Higher income households receive larger average tax cuts as a percentage of after-tax income, with the largest cuts as a share of income going to taxpayers in the upper 5% of the population. By 2027, taxes on average will change little for lower- and middle-income Americans and will decrease for higher-income Americans. In comparison to the former tax law in effect in 2017 and prior years, 5% of taxpayers will pay more taxes in 2018, 9% in 2025, and 53% in 2027. The new higher estate tax exclusion under the TCJA benefits wealthy individuals and families, not lower- and middle-income Americans. Also, the effect on charitable giving could be devastating due to the new tax law doubling the standard deduction. 26% of taxpayers itemized their deductions in 2017 and those taxpayers were responsible for 82% of charitable giving. Assuming taxpayers have a tax motive for making donations to charity, the impact on charitable giving may be significant. Also, the doubling of the estate tax exclusion from $5.6 million to $11.18 million, may make charitable giving of decreased importance in estate tax planning for the wealthy.

The TCJA will cause U.S. revenues to be significantly less than what is required to address long-term fiscal shortfalls. Therefore, over the next several years reconsideration of the new law's tax policy choices and changes may be necessary. Reconsideration of those choices and changes may be necessary, because the new law will reduce federal revenues by a significant amount, even after allowing for the impact on economic growth. The TCJA will make distribution of after-tax income more unequal. If it is not financed with spending cuts or other tax increases, the TCJA will raise the federal deficit and create an undue burden on future generations. And spending cuts or other tax increases, under most scenarios, will end up making most households worse off than if the Tax Cuts and Jobs Act had never been passed and signed into law by President Donald Trump on December 22, 2017. www.congress.gov/115/bills/hr1/BILLS-115hr1enr.pdf

TABLE OF CONTENTS

411

Income Tax

Personal Exemptions – The Tax Cuts and Jobs Act (TCJA) eliminates personal exemptions as a deduction in determining taxable income in 2018. Personal exemptions have been suspended for tax years 2018 – 2025 but are scheduled to return in 2026. In 2017 and prior years, taxpayers and their dependents were each entitled to a personal exemption in determining taxable income. The personal exemption in 2017 was $4,050 for each eligible individual, but the personal exemption was subject to phase-out when a taxpayer's adjusted gross income (AGI) reached certain high income thresholds.

Standard Deduction – Under the TCJA, the standard deduction is almost doubled in 2018 compared to what it was in 2017. The standard deduction in 2018 is $24,000, $18,000, and $12,000 for married filing jointly, head of household and single taxpayers, and is adjusted for inflation for tax years 2019 – 2025, before returning to the previous lower rates in 2026. Taxpayers can deduct either the standard deduction or itemized deductions from AGI in determining taxable income in 2018. The applicable standard deduction in 2018 for each filing status is the following:

- Single under 65 - $12,000; age 65 or over, blind or disabled - $13,600
- Married filing jointly under 65 - $24,000; one age 65 or over, blind or disabled - $25,300; both age 65 or over, blind or disabled - $26,600
- Surviving spouse under 65 - $24,000; age 65 or over, blind or disabled - $25,300
- Head-of-household under 65 - $18,000; age 65 or over, blind or disabled - $19,60
- Married filing separately - $12,000; age 65 or over, blind or disabled - $13,300
    * Amount included in the above for each person age 65 or over, blind or disabled
    - $1,600 (Single and Head-of-household)
    * Amount included in the above for each person age 65 or over, blind or disabled
    - $1,300 (Married filing jointly, Surviving Spouse and Married filing separately)

- A dependent child's standard deduction is total earned income plus $350, up to a maximum of $12,000
- The standard deduction for a dependent who is age 65 or over, blind or disabled is total earned income plus $350, up to a maximum of $13,600

2018 Ordinary Income Tax Brackets
Under the TCJA, reduced tax rates are effective for tax years 2018 – 2025, before expiring on January 1, 2026. Indexing for cost of living begins in 2019. There are still 7 tax brackets, but the tax rates are reduced to: 10%; 12%; 22%; 24%; 32%; 35%; and a top rate of 37%.

Married Filing Jointly or Qualified Surviving Spouse

If Taxable Income Is:	The Tax Is:
$0 - $19,050	10%
$19.051 - $77,400	$1,905 + 12% of the amount over $19,050
$77,401 - $165,000	$8,907 + 22% of the amount over $77,400
$165,001 - $315,000	$28,179 + 24% of the amount over $165,000

$315,001 - $400,000	$64,179 + 32% of the amount over $315,000
$400,001 - $600,000	$91,379 + 35% of the amount over $400,000
$600,001 +	$161,379 + 37% of the amount over $600,000

Head of Household

If Taxable Income Is:	The Tax Is:
$0 - $13,600	10%
$13,601 - $51,800	$1,360 + 12% of the amount over $13,600
$51,801 - $82,500	$5,944 + 22% of the amount over $51,800
$82,501 - $157,500	$12,698 + 24% of the amount over $82,500
$157,501 - $200,00	$30,698 + 32% of the amount over $157,500
$200,001 - $500,000	$44,298 + 35% of the amount over $200,000
$500,001 +	$149,298 + 37% of the amount over $500,000

Single Taxpayers

If Taxable Income Is:	The Tax Is:
$0 - $9,525	10%
$9,526 - $38,700	$952.50 + 12% of the amount over $9,525
$38,701 - $82,500	$4,453.50 + 22% of the amount over $38,700
$82,501 - $157,500	$14,089.50 + 24% of the amount over $82,500
$157,501 - $200,000	$32,089.50 + 32% of the amount over $157,500
$200,001 - $500,000	$45,689.50 + 35% of the amount over $200,000
$500,001 +	$150,689.50 + 37% of the amount over $500,000

Married Filing Separately

If Taxable Income Is:	The Tax Is:
$0 - $9,525	10%
$9,526 - $38,700	$952.50 + 12% of the amount over $9,525
$38,701 - $82,500	$4,453.50 + 22% of the amount over $38,700
$82,501 - $157,500	$14,089.50 + 24% of the amount over $82,500
$157,501 - $200,000	$32,089.50 + 32% of the amount over $157,500
$200,001 - $300,000	$45,689.50 + 35% of the amount over $200,000
$300,001 +	$80,689.50 + 37% of the amount over $300,000

New Indexing Method for Cost of Living Adjustments (COLAs) – Effective for 2018 and subsequent years, the TCJA reduces all cost of living adjustments (COLAs) that are applicable throughout the Internal Revenue Code. COLAs for tax rate thresholds, standard deduction amounts, and other amounts for inflation are reduced by converting indexing to chained CPI-U (C-CPI-U) rather than using the consumer price index (CPI) in effect in 2017 and prior years. The new method uses "chained CPI," which assumes consumers look for substitute items rather than absorbing rising prices during periods of inflation. Chained CPI will generally result in smaller annual increases. The difference between the old and new method is quite small in a single year but will get quite large over time due to the effect of compounding. The change to chained CPI for inflation indexing is effective for tax years beginning after 2017 and will remain in effect after 2025 – it is not subject to the sunsetting provisions that apply to most of the other individual tax provisions under the TCJA.

<u>**Extended Time to File Administrative Claim or Bring Suit for wrongful Levy**</u> – The TCJA extends the time for individuals and businesses to file an administrative claim with the IRS or bring a civil action suit for wrongful levy by the IRS from 9 months to 2 years. Additionally, if an administrative claim for the return of property is made within the 2-year period, the 2-year period for bringing suit is then extended for 12 months from the date of filing the claim or for 6 months from the disallowance of the claim by the IRS, whichever is shorter. The change applies to levies made after Dec. 22, 2017, and on or before that date, if the previous nine- month period hadn't yet expired.

Payroll Tax

0.9% Medicare Surtax

Under the Tax Cuts and Jobs Act (TCJA), the 0.9% Medicare surtax added by the Affordable Care Act is still in effect. The 0.9% surtax is added to the 1.45% Medicare tax paid by certain high- income earners. High income earners are those with wages and self-employment income above $200,000 single; $250,000 married filing jointly; and $125,000 married filing separately (not indexed for inflation). There is no employer match for this tax. Therefore, high income employees have to pay a 2.35% Medicare tax on any income earned above the applicable thresholds. For self-employed taxpayers, the surtax is added to the 2.9% Medicare tax paid on self-employment income of high-income earners, so they have to pay a 3.8% Medicare tax on any income above the applicable thresholds. **(See "Affordable Care Act")**

Determining Filing Status and Dependency Exemptions

Head of Household – Under the Tax Cuts and Jobs Act (TCJA), the due diligence requirement for claiming the Earned Income Tax Credit, the Child Tax Credit, the Additional Child Tax Credit, and the American Opportunity Education Tax Credit is expanded to include "Claiming Head of Household." Effective for tax years beginning after December 31, 2017, the TCJA expands the due diligence requirements to paid tax preparers to cover determining eligibility for a taxpayer to file as head of household. A penalty of $500 (adjusted for inflation) will be imposed if a paid tax preparer fails to answer required due diligence questions regarding a taxpayer's eligibility to claim head of household status in 2018. **(See Tax Credits, "Earned Income Tax Credit (EITC)"; Additional Child Tax Credit"; "Child Tax Credit")**

To claim "head-of-household" status, you must either be unmarried (not a surviving spouse), or not live with your spouse during the last 6 months of the year while still considered married, and you must pay more than ½ of the cost of maintaining a home as a household, which is the principal place of abode of a "qualifying child" or another person that can be claimed as a dependent. If you can claim head-of-household while still married, the other spouse must file as "married filing separately."

Dependents – In the TCJA, the deduction of a personal exemption for taxpayers and their dependents in determining taxable income is eliminated in 2018. Personal exemptions are suspended for tax years 2018 –

414

2025. However, determining who are qualified dependents and who can claim them is important for other purposes, including who is eligible for the Earned income Tax Credit (EITC), the Affordable Care Tax Credit, head-of-household filing status, liability for individual mandate penalties, and repayment of advance premium tax credits. The deemed personal exemption for other purposes in 2018 is $4,150 (adjusted for inflation in subsequent years), even though there is no personal exemption in 2018. **(See Income Tax, "Personal Exemptions")**

Other Persons Qualifying as Dependents – Other persons besides a "qualifying child" may qualify as a taxpayer's dependent if they satisfy all of the following : (1) the taxpayer provides more than ½ of their support, i.e. food, shelter, clothing, medical, dental, education, etc. (see definition of ½ support for a qualifying child) – Social Security benefits used for support count toward the ½ support test only if the Social Security benefits are taxable; (2) the taxpayer has a specified relationship with the person (mother, father, etc.) or if not a relative, the person was a member of the taxpayer's household for the entire year; (3) the person is a U.S. citizen; (4) the person meets the gross income test; and (5) the person meets the joint return test – does not file a joint return with his or her spouse unless the return is filed only to collect a tax refund and neither spouse would have owed tax if they had filed separate returns. Also, a person cannot be a dependent of another person who is not required to file a return for the year or files solely to claim a refund of taxes withheld.

In accordance with the TCJA, the gross income test for the 2018 tax year is the following: the person has gross income of less than $4,150 (adjusted for inflation in subsequent years). **(See Above, "Dependents")**

Kiddie Tax – The kiddie tax applies to unearned income of qualified dependent children under the age of 19, and to unearned income of qualified dependent children under the age of 24 who are full-time students (at least 5 months in a year). Unearned income is income from sources other than wages and salary, such as dividends, interest and capital gains. Under the TCJA, for tax years 2018 – 2025, all of the income (both earned and unearned) of a dependent child is added together; the child's standard deduction (if any) is then subtracted from the child's total income (the standard deduction is the child's earned income + $350 up to a maximum of $12,000); if any earned income is left after subtracting the standard deduction, it is taxed at the ordinary income tax rates for a single individual; and the remaining unearned income that exceeds $2,100 is then taxed at the kiddie tax rates. A child's kiddie tax rates for his/her unearned income are the rates applicable to estates and trusts for interest and ordinary dividends, which are the following in 2018: $0 - $2,550 (10%); $2,551 - $9150 ($255 + 24% of the amount over $2,550); $9,151 - $12,500 ($1,839 + 35% of the amount over $9,150); and $12,501 + ($3,011.50 + 37% of the amount over $12,500).

A child's kiddie tax rates for capital gains and qualified dividends are the following: $0 - $2,600 (0%); $2,601 - $12,700 (15%); $12,701 + (20%), which are the long-term capital gain rates for estates and trusts.

- **Example** – Jim (age 17) who is a dependent child, has $2,000 of earned income from delivering newspapers and $8,000 of interest and ordinary dividends in 2018. His standard deduction is $2,350 ($2,000 of earned income + $350), so he has no taxable earned income left over. After subtracting the standard deduction, he has $7,650 of unearned income ($2,000 + $8,000 = $10,000 – $2,350 = $7,650). Therefore, Jim has to pay a kiddie tax of $975 on $5,550 of unearned income at the applicable kiddie tax rates. The tax is computed as follows: $7,650 – $2,100 = $5,550 taxable unearned income; the tax is $255

+ 24% of the amount over $2,550 = $975 ($255 + $720 = $975).

In 2017 and prior years, the first $1,050 of a child's unearned income was tax free; the next $1,050 of unearned income was taxed at 10%; and any unearned income over $2,100 was taxed at the "parents' highest tax rate." Any earned income of a child, after the allowable standard deduction, was taxed at the child's tax rate (ordinary income tax rate for a single individual). **(See Estates and Trusts, "Income Tax Rates for Estates and Trusts"**

Disaster Tax Relief and Airport and Airway Extension Act of 2017 – On Sept. 29, 2017, the "Disaster Tax Relief and Airport and Airway Extension Act of 2017" (Act) was passed, which provides temporary tax relief to victims impacted by 2016 and 2017 qualified disasters. 2016 qualified disasters are major disasters declared by the President of the United States under Section 401 of the Robert T. Stafford Disaster Relief and Emergency Assistance Act in calendar year 2016. 2017 qualified disasters include Hurricanes Harvey, Irma, and Maria and the California wildfires. These disasters were declared by the President of the United States under Section 401 of the Robert T. Stafford Disaster Relief and Emergency Assistance Act in calendar year 2017. Following are details of relief under the Act:

https://www.congress.gov/bill/115th-congress/house-bill/3823

Early Withdrawals from Qualified Retirement Plans – The Act eliminates the 10% penalty on earlyywithdrawals of up to $100,000 from qualified retirement plans, including 401(k)s, 403(b) governmental plans, IRAs and tax-sheltered annuities for victims of presidentially declared disasters. These "qualified disaster distributions" are defined as distributions from an eligible retirement plan made on or after Jan. 1, 2016, and before Jan. 1, 2018, to an individual whose principal place of abode at any time during the calendar year 2016 or who resided in the affected areas in 2017 and sustained an economic loss by reason of the events that gave rise to the Presidential disasters. Such withdrawals are normally included in income in the year in which they are distributed. The Act allows the withdrawals to be re- contributed back to retirement plans at any time over a 3-year period without any tax consequences and allows taxpayers to spread out any income inclusion amounts resulting from the withdrawals ratably over a 3-year period. Also, qualified withdrawals aren't treated as rollover distributions, which are generally subject to 20% withholding. The Act also allows the re-contribution of certain retirement plan withdrawals made for home purchases or construction, which were received after Feb. 28, 2017 and before Sept. 21, 2017, where the home purchase or construction was cancelled on account of Hurricanes Harvey, Irma, or Maria (without tax consequences). With respect to retirement plan loans, the Act: increased the maximum amount that a victim can borrow from a qualified employer plan from $50,000 to $100,000.

Employee Retention Tax Credit for Employers – The Act provides a new "employee retention credit" for "eligible employers" affected by Hurricanes Harvey, Irma, and Maria. Eligible employers are generally defined as employers that conducted an active trade or business in a disaster zone as of a specified date (for Hurricane Harvey, Aug. 23, 2017; Irma, Sept. 4, 2017; and Maria, Sept. 16, 2017), and the active trade or business on any day between the specified dates and Jan. 1, 2018, were rendered inoperable as a result of damage sustained by the hurricanes. In general, the credit is equals to 40% of up to $6,000 of "qualified wages" with respect to each "eligible employee" of such employer for the tax year. Therefore, the maximum credit per employee is $2,400 ($6,000 × 40%).

416

- **Example** – Employer Y is an eligible employer in the Hurricane Harvey disaster zone. Y has two eligible employees, A and B, to whom Y pays qualified wages of $4,000 and $7,000 respectively. Y is entitled to a total credit of $4,000; $1,600 for the wages paid to A ($4,000 × 40%) and $2,400 for $6,000 the wages paid to B ($6,000 × 40%).

An eligible employee with respect to an eligible employer is one whose principal place of employment with the employer was in the Hurricane Harvey, Irma, or Maria disaster zones. Qualified wages are wages paid or incurred by an eligible employer to an eligible employee on any day after the specified dates (See above) and before Jan. 1, 2018. An employee cannot be taken into account more than one time for purposes of the employee retention tax credit. So, for instance, if an employee is an eligible employee of an employer with respect to Hurricane Harvey for purposes of the credit, the employee cannot also be an eligible employee with respect to Hurricane Irma or Hurricane Maria. An eligible employee cannot be "related" to an employer. **(See Tax Credits, "Employee Retention Tax Credit for Employers")**

Eased Casualty Loss Rules for Disaster Loss Victims – The Act eliminated the requirement that personal casualty losses must exceed 10% of AGI to qualify for a deduction, and eliminated the requirement that taxpayers must itemize deductions in order to claim casualty losses—it does so by increasing an individual taxpayer's standard deduction by the amount of the taxpayer's net disaster loss. However, the Act increased the $100 per-casualty loss floor from $100 to $500 for qualified disaster-related personal casualty losses. The Act provides that Code Sec. 56(b)(1)(E), which generally disallows the standard deduction for alternative minimum tax (AMT) purposes, does not apply for the portion of the standard deduction attributable to the amount of the net disaster loss.

Under the Act, individual disaster loss victims in the hurricane affected areas may elect to claim a casualty loss in the tax year immediately preceding the tax year in which the disaster occurred. Victims have six months after the due date for filing their tax return for the year in which the disaster occurred to make the election, and they have 90 days after that to revoke the election. Taxpayers make the election by deducting the disaster loss on either an original or an amended tax return for the prior year, and by including an election statement on the return indicating they are making a Section 165(i) election and the name or description of the disaster and the date or dates of the disaster that caused the claimed loss. **(See Itemized Deductions, "Casualty, Disaster, and Theft Losses")**

Revenue Procedure 2018-08 sets forth seven safe harbors that taxpayers can use for determining the amount of their personal casualty losses. The seven safe harbors provide tax relief for those who suffered casualty losses in 2017 as a result of Hurricanes Harvey, Irma, and Maria, as well as those who suffer losses in 2018 – Hurricanes Michael and Florence. Individuals can use the seven safe harbors to determine decreases in the fair market value of their properties and the IRS will not challenge these safe harbor methods if they are properly applied. To qualify for the five safe harbor methods applicable to personal residences, an individual must have at least one personal residence that suffered a casualty loss. The residence cannot be a rental property or contain a home office used for business purposes. Also, it cannot be a condominium, cooperative unit, or a mobile home or trailer. The cost of any repair estimates to a personal residence that increases the value of the property beyond its pre-casualty value must be excluded from the estimate. Losses to personal belongings must be tangible personal property owned by individuals and not used in a trade or business (this does not include a boat, aircraft, mobile home, trailer, or vehicle

417

nor an antique or other asset that maintains or increases its value over time). Casualty losses must be reduced by any insurance or other amounts received, including the value of repairs provided by another party, such as volunteers, at no cost to the individual (no-cost repairs). The seven safe harbors are:

Personal-Use Residence Safe Harbors:
- Estimated Repair Cost Method – To determine the decrease in the fair market value (FMV), an individual may use the lesser of two repair estimates prepared by two separate licensed or registered independent contractors. The individual cannot have insurance that pays for any of the repairs, and this method is only available for casualty losses of $20,000 or less.
- De Minimis Method – Individuals may estimate the cost of repairs required to restore their personal-use residence to the condition existing immediately prior to the casualty. The estimate must be a good-faith estimate and records must be kept detailing the methodology used to determine the loss. This method is only available for casualty losses of $5,000 or less.
- Insurance Method – Individuals may use the estimated loss detailed in his homeowner's or flood insurance company's report setting for the estimated loss to the personal-use residence. This method has no dollar amount limit.
- Contractor Method – Individuals may use the estimate of the repairs specified in a contract prepared by a licensed or registered independent contractor. A binding contract must be signed by the contractor and the individual. This method has no dollar amount limit.
- Disaster Loan Appraisal Method – Individuals may use an appraisal prepared for the purpose of obtaining a loan of federal funds or loan guarantee from the federal government setting forth the estimated loss the individual sustained as a result of damage to or destruction of the individual's personal-use residence. This method has no dollar amount limit.

Personal Belongings Safe Harbors:
- De Minimis Method – Individuals make a good faith estimate of the decrease in the FMV of their personal belongings and they must have records describing the affected personal belongings, detailing the methodology used for the estimate. This method is available for any casualty or theft loss of $5,000 or less.
- Replacement Cost Method – Individuals must determine the current cost to replace a personal belonging with a new one and then determine the pre-disaster market value of the item by reducing the replacement cost by 10% for each year the individual has owned the item (if the item has been owned by the individual for 9 or more years, the pre-disaster market value is 10% of the current replacement cost). The estimated decrease in value of an item is the difference between the current cost to replace the item and the pre-disaster market value of the item. If a personal belonging is destroyed or stolen as a result of the disaster, its after-disaster value is deemed to be zero. Any insurance reimbursement received or expected to be received must then be subtracted from this amount.

www.irs.gov/pub/irs-drop/rp-18-08.pdf

IRS Publication 584, "Casualty, Disaster, and Theft Loss Workbook (Personal-Use-Property)" is designed to help individuals figure their loss on personal-use property in the event of a disaster, casualty, or theft. www.irs.gov/pub/irs-pdf/p584.pdf

Charitable Deduction Limitations Suspended for Disaster Loss Victims – For qualifying charitable contributions, the Act: Provides an exception from the overall limitation on itemized deductions for certain qualified contributions; Temporarily suspends the majority of the limitations on charitable contributions in Code Sec. 170(b); and Provides for eased rules governing the treatment of excess contributions. "Qualified contributions" must have been paid during the period beginning on Aug. 23, 2017, and ending on Dec. 31, 2017, in cash to an organization described in Code Sec. 170(b)(1)(A), for relief efforts in the Hurricane Harvey, Irma, or Maria disaster areas. Qualified contributions must have been substantiated, with a contemporaneous written acknowledgement that the contribution was or is to be used for hurricane relief efforts, and the taxpayer must make an election for the Act to apply. For partnerships and S-corporations, the election is made separately by each partner or shareholder. **(See Itemized Deductions, "Charitable Contribution Deduction")**

Special Rule on "Earned Income" for Earned Income Tax Credit (EITC) and Child Tax Credit Purposes – The Act provides that, in case a "qualified taxpayer's" earned income, which includes the applicable dates shown below, is less than the taxpayer's earned income for the preceding tax year, then the taxpayer may elect, for purposes of the EITC and the Child Tax Credit, to substitute the earned income for the preceding year for the earned income for the current tax year in computing the EITC and the Child Tax Credit for the current year. For Hurricane Harvey, a "qualified taxpayer" is one whose principal place of abode on Aug. 23, 2017 was located either in the Hurricane Harvey disaster zone, or in the Hurricane Harvey disaster area and the individual was displaced from their principal place of abode by reason of Hurricane Harvey. Similar definitions apply for Hurricanes Irma (using a Sept. 4, 2017 date) and Hurricane Maria (using a Sept. 16, 2017 date). In the case of joint filers, the above election may apply if either spouse is a qualified individual. **(See Tax Credits, "Earned Income Tax Credit" & "Child Tax Credit")**

Other Relief Provided by the IRS in Federally Declared Disaster Areas

The IRS provides relief by giving extensions of time to file tax returns and make payments to businesses and individuals in parts of Texas and Florida, as well as Puerto Rico and the U.S. Virgin Islands affected by Hurricanes Harvey, Irma and Maria; and to victims of the California wildfires. The relief applied to, among other situations, individuals who had returns on valid extensions due Oct. 16, 2017, and businesses whose returns were on valid extensions and were due Sept. 15, 2017. Both had until Jan. 31, 2018, to file. Also, tax-exempt organizations in the affected disaster areas that had a filing due date before Jan. 31, 2018, were allowed more time to file their returns. The IRS gave tax-exempt organizations until Jan. 31, 2018 to file, and it said the relief applied to both the original and extended due dates in this period. (www.irs.gov/pub/irs-drop/rp-16-53.pdf); (www.irs.gov/pub/irs-pdf/f4684.pdf); (www.irs.gov/pub/irs-pdf/i4684.pdf); (www.irs.gov/pub/irs-pdf/f1040x.pdf); (www.irs.gov/pub/irs-pdf/i1040x.pdf)

Employees were allowed to forgo their vacation, sick or personal leave in exchange for cash payments the employer makes, before Jan. 1, 2019, to charitable organizations providing relief for the victims of Hurricanes Harvey, Irma, and Maria. Under this special relief, the donated leave will not be included in the income or wages of the employees, and employers will be permitted to deduct the cash payments as business expenses.

Owners and operators of low-income housing projects in the affected hurricane areas were allowed to offer temporary housing to qualified disaster victims, but they were not required to do so. For those who did this, special rules are applied as spelled out in Revenue Procedure 2014-49 and Revenue Procedure 2014-50.

Notice 2017-56 offers relief to residents of Puerto Rico and the U.S. Virgin Islands who evacuated or couldn't return because of Hurricanes Irma or Maria. Most individuals can otherwise lose their status as "bona fide residents" of Puerto Rico or the U.S. Virgin Islands for tax filing and reporting purposes. Notice 2017-56 extended the usual 14-day absence period to 117 days, beginning Sept. 6, 2017 and ending Dec. 31, 2017, for the presence test for residency under the tax rules. An individual who was absent from either U.S. territory on any day during the 117-day period were treated as leaving or being unable to return to the relevant U.S. territory as a result of Hurricane Irma and Maria on that day. There were some exceptions to the general 183-day presence test that requires individuals to be in the location where they claim residence for 183 days during the tax year. Generally, residents can include up to 14 days within the 183-day period because of a declared disaster. Nevertheless, because of the catastrophic damage caused by the monster storms to Puerto Rico and the U.S. Virgin Islands, the Federal Emergency Management Agency issued Notices of a Presidential declaration of a major disaster for both territories, and 117 days of absence were allowed. (www.irs.gov/pub/irs-drop/n-17-56.pdf)

The IRS is offering regulatory relief and assistance for victims of Hurricane Michael, as well as extending tax-filing deadlines and making it easier to provide low-income housing for people affected by the hurricane. the IRS announced that it was extending the Oct. 15, 2018, tax extension deadline until Feb. 28, 2019, for Hurricane Michael victims. The IRS also offered temporary relief from some requirements of the Tax Code to make it easier for owners and operators of low-income housing projects in the U.S. and U.S. territories to provide temporary emergency housing to people who were displaced from their main residences, regardless of income, by Hurricane Michael as well as the earlier Hurricane Florence that struck in September 2018. Relief also includes the waiver of late penalties for quarterly estimated tax payments normally due on January 15, 2019, as well as quarterly federal payroll and excise tax returns normally due on October 31, 2018, and January 31, 2019. The IRS automatically provides filing and penalty relief to any taxpayer located in the disaster area. Revenue Procedures 2014-49 and 2014-50 provide details of the relief provided by the IRS to victims of Hurricanes Michael and Florence.
www.irs.gov/pub/irs-drop/rp-14-49.pdf   www.irs.gov/pub/irs-drop/rp-14-50.pdf

IRS Publication 2194, "Disaster Resource Guide for Individuals and Businesses" provides information to individuals and businesses affected by a federally declared disaster and the assistance available to disaster victims.
www.irs.gov/pub/irs-pdf/p2194.pdf

Expensing Certain Citrus Replanting Costs – The Tax Cuts and Jobs Act (TCJA) includes a special rule for replanting costs paid or incurred after December 22, 2017, but not more than 10 years later – until December 22, 2027, for citrus plants lost or damaged due to a casualty such as freezing temperatures, disease, drought, or pests. Such replanting costs may be deducted by a person other than the affected taxpayer, but the affected taxpayer must have at least a 50% equity interest in the replanted citrus plants and the other person must own the remaining equity interest in the replanted citrus plants, or the other person must have acquired all of the affected taxpayer's equity interest in the land on which the citrus plants are located when damaged and replanted on that land. Any accounting method change must follow the automatic change procedures in Rev. Proc. 2018-32 as modified.

420

Unearned Income

Gambling Winnings – Gambling winnings of casual gamblers are taxable unearned income and are reported as "other income" on Form 1040. Gambling losses can be taken to the extent of gambling winnings as "miscellaneous itemized deduction not subject to the 2% floor" (casual gamblers cannot have an overall loss in a year). "Expenses" of gamblers are allowed to be included as an addition to their losses that can offset their winnings in tax years 2018 – 2025 by the Tax Cuts and Jobs Act (TCJA). For instance, an individual's expenses in traveling to and from a casino are expenses that can offset gambling winnings beginning in 2018. The expenses of casual gamblers were not allowed to be included as part of their losses in 2017 and prior years. Also, gambling winnings for the casual gambler will not necessarily be brought to zero by equal gambling losses, because the losses are only deductible as an itemized deduction.

Gambling losses can offset all gains from wagering transactions, not merely gambling winnings, i.e. raffle, lottery, and horse race winnings are treated as gambling winnings that can be offset by gambling losses, and the cost of a losing raffle ticket paid to a charity is a gambling loss, not a charitable contribution.

A professional gambler's winnings and losses are shown on Schedule C, and therefore, any profit is subject to ordinary income tax and self-employment tax. In a 2011 Tax Court decision (Mayo vs. Commissioner), the court held that while gambling losses are limited to the extent of gambling winnings, any non-loss expenses of a professional gambler – items like meals, lodging, travel expenses, admission fees and handicapping data – are not subject to the limitation. Therefore, in 2017 and prior years, professional gamblers could incur a net loss on Schedule C related to their non-loss expenses. However, the TCJA reversed the Tax Court decision in Mayo vs. Commissioner and, therefore, for tax years 2018 – 2025 professional gamblers are not allowed to incur a loss on Schedule C due to their non-loss expenses such as meals, lodging, travel expenses, etc. (professional gamblers can't have an overall loss in a year, beginning with the 2018 tax year). Professional gambler status is hard to achieve. Casual gamblers cannot become professional gamblers in the eyes of the IRS simply by gambling frequently. Strict requirements include the ability of the gambler to show activities being treated in a business-like manner using plans, strategies, and schedules. **(See Itemized Deductions, "Miscellaneous Itemized Deductions Not Subject to the 2% Adjusted Gross Income (AGI) Floor")**
www.irs.gov/pub/irs-aod/aod201106.pdf
www.irs.gov/pub/irs-aod/aod201106.pdf

Alimony and Separate Maintenance – The TCJA does not require any change in the treatment of alimony payments under divorce or separation agreements executed before December 31, 2018. However, the TCJA eliminates the deduction of alimony payments as an above-the-line deduction by payers and the inclusion of alimony payments in income by recipients under divorce or separation instruments that are: (1) executed after December 31, 2018, or (2) executed before December 31, 2018 that are modified after that date if the modification specifically states that the TCJA treatment of alimony payments now applies. Also, this change is a permanent part of the tax code and doesn't sunset at the end of 2025, as do many of the individual income tax provisions of the TCJA.

Social Security Benefits – The TCJA provides Social Security recipients with a 2% cost-of-living adjustment in their monthly benefit starting in January 2018.

The full retirement age for Social Security (SS) benefits has been 66 years of age for a long time, but under the TCJA, the full retirement age gradually increases to 67 years of age in 2018 for Americans born after 1954. If you were born in 1955, your full retirement age is 66 years and 2 months; 1956 – 66 years and 4 months; 1957 – 66 years and 6 months; 1958 – 66 years and 8 months; 1959 – 66 years and 10 months; and 1960 or later – your full retirement age is 67 years of age. Your SS benefits will be reduced if you decide to start taking SS benefits before your full retirement age. For example, if your full retirement age is 66 in 2018, and you decide to start taking Social Security (SS) benefits at age 62, you will receive 75% of your full benefit payments. If your full retirement age is 66 years and 4 months, and you decide to start taking SS benefits at age 62, you will receive 74.2% of your full benefit payments.

If you work and are at full retirement age, you can earn any amount without your SS benefits being reduced. If you are younger than full retirement age when you start receiving SS benefits, $1.00 is deducted from your benefits for each $2.00 of earned income above $17,040 in 2018 ($16,920 in 2017). If you reach full retirement age during 2018, $1.00 is deducted for each $3.00 earned above $45,360 in 2018 ($44,880 in 2017) until the month you reach full retirement age, so you won't lose any benefits if you make $45,360 or less before you reach full retirement age in 2018. If you work for more than one employer in 2018, and Social Security taxes of more than $7,979 ($128,700 x 6.2%) are withheld from your wages in the tax year, the excess may be claimed as a credit on Form 1040.

The Social Security wage base is $128,700 in 2018 ($127,200 in 2017). The maximum Social Security benefit an individual can receive per month in 2018 is $2,788 or $33,456 for the year. You have to have $1,320 of earned income in order to earn one Social Security quarter of credit in 2018, so earning $5,280 anytime during 2018 will net you the maximum four quarters of credits for the year. You need 40 quarters of coverage to qualify for Social Security retirement benefits (10 years).
www.irs.gov/pub/irs-pdf/p915.pdf#page=20

Conversion of Traditional IRAs to Roth IRAs – For tax years beginning after Dec. 31, 2017, you cannot undo your decision to rollover a traditional IRA to a Roth IRA and re-characterize the Roth IRA back into a traditional IRA and recoup the taxes paid on the conversion. For 2017 and prior years, if you converted a traditional IRA to a Roth IRA, you had until October 15th to undo your decision and recoup the taxes paid. And, if you had already filed your 2017 tax return, you could amend it. For example, if you converted to a Roth and owed 25% tax on the amount converted and the Roth lost value in the meantime, you could save the taxes paid by re- characterizing the Roth IRA back into a traditional IRA by 10/15/2018 (due date of the 2017 tax return including the allowed 6-month extension). But no more under the TCJA beginning with the 2018 tax year.
www.irs.gov/pub/irs-pdf/f1099r.pdf   www.irs.gov/pub/irs-pdf/i1099r.pdf

Taxpayers with MAGIs of more than $100,000 who are eligible to convert a traditional IRA to a Roth in 2018 may not be eligible to contribute to the Roth annually because the MAGI thresholds for contributing to a Roth in 2018 are between $120,000 - $135,0000 (single and head-of-household), and between $189,000 - $199,000 (married filing jointly).

Capital Gains and Losses

Capital Gain Tax Rates – Capital gains are taxable on all capital assets, which includes tangible property, stocks, bonds, and other securities. A taxpayer must hold a capital asset for one year and a day in order to get long-term capital gain treatment (taxed at capital gain tax rates). If not, it will be a short-term capital gain subject to ordinary income tax rates. Under the Tax Cuts and Jobs Act (TCJA), the long-term capital gain rates for 2018 are 0%, 15%, and 20%, and the tax brackets are as follows:

Married Filing Jointly or Qualified Surviving Spouse

If Taxable Income Is:	The Tax Is:
$0 - $77,200	0%
$77,201 - $479,000	15%
$479,000 and above	20%

Head of Household

If Taxable Income Is:	The Tax Is:
$0 - $51,700	0%
$51,701 - $452,400	15%
$452,401 and above	20%

Single Taxpayers

If Taxable Income Is:	The Tax Is:
$0 - $38,600	0%
$38,601 - $425,800	15%
$425,801 and above	20%

Married Filing Separately

If Taxable Income Is:	The Tax Is:
$0 - $38,600	0%
$38,601 - $239,500	15%
$239,501 and above	20%

Trusts and Estates

If Taxable Income Is:	The Tax Is:
$0 - $2,600	0%
$2,601 - $12,700	15%
$12,701 and above	20%

Capital Gain Rollover to Specialized Small Business Investment Companies – The TCJA repeals the provision that allowed a taxpayer to defer capital gains from the sale of publicly traded securities by rolling over the proceeds of the sale to purchase interests in a "specialized small business investment corporation" (SSBIC), effective for sales after December 31, 2017. An SSBIC is an investment fund licensed by the U.S. Small Business Administration. And even though the SSBIC program was repealed in 1996, certain grandfathered SSBIC's still exist.

Carried Interest – Receipt of a capital interest for services provided to a partnership or LLC results in taxable compensation to fund managers. Typically, hedge fund managers guide the investment strategy and act as general partners to an "investment partnership," while their client investors act as limited partners. Fund managers are compensated in two ways. First, to the extent they invest their own capital in the funds, they share in the appreciation of fund assets. Second, they charge their client investors two kinds of annual fees: a management fee which is typically 2%, and a percentage of the fund's earnings and profits, typically 20%, which is usually carried over from year to year until a cash payment is made, usually following the closing out of an investment. This is called "carried interest."

Prior to enactment of the TCJA, "carried interest" was taxed in the hands of hedge fund managers at favorable long-term capital gain rates, provided it was held for at least one year. However, in 2018 and subsequent years, the TCJA states that "carried interest" held by hedge fund managers for less than three years (3-year holding period) will be taxed at short-term capital gain rates instead of at long-term capital gain rates. (Code Sec. 1061, Partnership Interests Held in Connection with Performance of Services, added by Act Sec. 13309(a)). If the 3-year holding period is not met with respect to an applicable partnership interest held by fund managers, their gains will be treated as short-term gains taxed at ordinary income tax rates. Also, the new TCJA statute does not grandfather partnership interests issued prior to the enactment of the TCJA; therefore, fund managers should be aware that this new provision may impact investment partnerships initiated in 2015, 2016 or 2017, i.e. the 3-year holding period requirement will be applicable in the 2018 tax year to "carried interest" on partnership investments going back to 2015. **(See Partnerships, "Services Performed by Fund Managers for an Investment Partnership")**

Self-Created Intangible Assets – Under the TCJA, self-created intangible assets such as copyrights, literary compositions, musical or artistic compositions, patents, etc. are removed from the definition of capital assets effective beginning in 2018. However, transfers of all substantial rights to a patent or an undivided interest in a portion of patent rights by the inventor or a holder of a patent continues to get long-term capital gain treatment under Section 1235 if payments are tied to productivity or are payable periodically over the transferee's use of the patent. A "holder of a patent" means: any individual whose efforts created such property, or any other individual who has acquired an interest in such property in exchange for consideration in money paid to the creator prior to actual reduction to practice of the invention covered by the patent, if such individual is neither: the employer of the creator, or related to such creator. In 2017 and prior years, a safe-harbor allowed self-created intangibles to be treated as capital assets and the cost of the self-created intangible assets could be amortized over 15 years. **(See Property Depreciation and Expensing, "Amortization of Intangible Assets")**

Qualified Opportunity Zones – As of December 22, 2017, the chief executive officer (probably the Governor) of each U.S. state or possession (including the District of Columbia) is allowed to designate a limited number of low-income communities as "qualified opportunity zones." A qualified opportunity zone is the same as the community development entity (CDE) designation for the New Markets Tax Credit. The TCJA provides that investments made in qualified opportunity zones will result in the temporary deferral of capital gains from inclusion in gross income when the capital gains are reinvested in a qualified opportunity fund, and the permanent exclusion of capital gains from inclusion in gross income on sales of such investments when the investments are held for at least 10 years. A qualified opportunity fund is an investment vehicle organized as a corporation or a partnership for the purpose of investing in and holding at least 90% of its assets in qualified opportunity zone property, which includes any qualified opportunity zone stock, any qualified opportunity zone partnership interests, and any qualified opportunity zone business property. The certification of a qualified opportunity fund is done by the Secretary of the Community Development Financial Institutions (CDFI) Fund, effective on the date of enactment. The TCJA states that there is no exclusion from income for investments in qualified opportunity zones made after December 31, 2026.

On October 19, 2018, the IRS issued proposed regulations providing investors with guidelines on how they can qualify for the special tax breaks available for investments in Qualified Opportunity Zones. Investors have 180 days from the sale of their stock or business to put the proceeds into a "qualified opportunity fund" to qualify for the available tax breaks. IRS rules provide that qualified opportunity funds have 30 months from when investors' money is received to do the renovations. The proposed regulations specify that investments made in qualified opportunity zones don't have to include the value of land when calculating how much the law requires investors to spend renovating or refurbishing property. For example, if a qualified opportunity fund were to pay $900,000 for a building and land, with the building valued at $500,000, the fund would have to pay for renovations in the amount of $500,000, not the total purchase price. This allows investors to spend less to meet the rules for what would constitute substantially improving a building under the law.

www.irs.gov/pub/irs-drop/rr-18-29.pdf

Deferral Election for Qualified Equity Grants – Code Sec. 83 governs the amount and timing of income inclusion for property, including employer stock, transferred to an eligible employee (excluding most shareholders and officers) in connection with the performance of services. The TCJA provides that an eligible employee can "elect" to defer for income tax purposes the recognition of income attributable to qualified stock (settled restricted stock units or exercised options) transferred to the employee by a qualified employer after December 31, 2017. A qualified employer is one which offers the benefit to at least 80% of employees working at least 30 hours per week. The employee election applies only to the recognition of income for income tax purposes and not to the recognition of income for FICA and FUTA purposes. An employee's election must be made within 30 days of the earlier of when the stock is substantially vested or first transferable, whichever occurs first. If an employee makes the election, the election defers the recognition of income for income tax purposes for a period up to 5 years (with forced recognition earlier if the corporation goes public or the employee becomes an "excluded employee" (see below). The employee must recognize income for income tax purposes before the end of 5 years if any of the following occurs:

1. The stock becomes readily tradable on an established securities market (public stock offering).
2. The employee becomes an "excluded employee," which is an individual: (a) who is a one-percent owner of the corporation; (b) who is the chief executive officer or chief financial officer of the corporation, including acting as such; or (c) who is one of the four highest compensated officers of the corporation.

3. The employee revokes his or her election (Code Sec. 83(i)(1)(B), as amended by the Act Sec. 13603(a)). **www.irs.gov/pub/irs-drop/rr-04-37.pdf**

Passive Income and Losses

Rental Income – The Tax Cuts and Jobs Act (TCJA) brings several important changes that owners of rental properties can take advantage of, because a real property business includes any real property rental, development, redevelopment, construction, reconstruction, acquisition, conversion, operation, management, leasing or brokerage business. In general, rental property owners enjoy lower ordinary income tax rates for tax years 2018 through 2025, and the TCJA retains the existing tax rates for long-term capital gains. And, in accordance with the law that was in effect in 2017 and prior years, you can still deduct mortgage interest and state and local real estate taxes on rental properties. While the TCJA imposes new limitations on deducting personal residence mortgage interest and state and local taxes (including property taxes on personal residences), those limitations do not apply to rental properties, unless you also use the property for personal purposes. In that case, the new limitations only apply to mortgage interest and real estate taxes that are allocable to your personal use and deducted as an itemized deduction. In addition, you can still deduct all of the other standard operating expenses for rental properties, including depreciation, utilities, insurance, repairs and maintenance, yard care and association fees. **(See Income Tax, "2018 Ordinary Income Tax Brackets"); (See Capital Gains and Losses, "Capital Gain Tax Rates"); (See Itemized Deductions, "State and Local Tax Deductions" & "Home Mortgage Interest Deduction")**

The TCJA also changes the way rental income is taxed beginning in 2018. Starting in 2018, taxpayers with qualified business income (including rental income), are eligible to take a tax deduction up to 20% of their "qualified business income" (QBI). Determining whether or not you will be eligible to capture the full 20% deduction on your rental income is based on your "total taxable income" for the year. If your total taxable income is below the thresholds of $315,000 (Married filing jointly) or $157,000 (Single), you can simply take a deduction of 20% of your net rental income. For example, if you are married filing jointly and your total taxable income is $250,000 and your net rental income is $20,000, you get a deduction of $4,000 ($20,000 X 20% = $4,000). "Total taxable income" is not your AGI (adjusted gross income) and it's not just income from your rental property or self-employment activities. **(See Business Structures and Provisions, "20% Deduction Allowed on Passed-Through QBI (Section 199A)")**

Rental Losses – As stated above, rental activities are considered passive (unless you are a real estate professional), and this is still the case under the TCJA. And only real estate professionals are generally eligible for the 20% deduction because they are considered actively participating in the real estate business. Generally, passive losses can only be offset against passive income in a year, but there is an exception for owners who "significantly" participate in managing a rental property. Significant participation is a lower standard than material participation, which means the owner of a residential rental property always meets the significant participation standard (not the active participation standard), even if the owner hires a property manager to manage the property. The exception is that individuals who own and "significantly" participate in the management of residential rental property can offset up to $25,000 of passive losses against non-passive income in any year. If rental expenses are more than rental revenues, then you have a loss.

426

However, the $25,000 loss allowance is phased-out if the taxpayer's modified adjusted gross income (MAGI) is between $100,000 –$150,000 (Married filing jointly) or $50,000 – $75,000 (Single). Also, married persons must file jointly to take advantage of the entire $25,000 rental loss allowance (the allowance is reduced to $12,500 if filing status is "married filing separately.") Rental real estate losses in excess of $25,000 are allowed just like other passive losses, i.e. to the extent of income from other passive activities.

www.irs.gov/pub/irs-pdf/f1040se.pdf

- **Example** – Suppose your filing status is married filing jointly, and your MAGI is $125,000. Then your rental loss allowance is reduced by 50% to $12,500.

Non-Taxable Income

Combat Pay Earned by Military Personnel
The Tax Cuts and Jobs Act (TCJA) grants combat zone benefits to military personnel performing services in the Sinai Peninsula of Egypt, retroactively effective to June 9, 2015. Benefits include tax-free income, excise tax exclusions, and surviving spouse benefits. This provision is scheduled to sunset at the end of the 2025 tax year.

Combat pay of enlisted military personnel, including non-commissioned officers, is tax-free. Part of military officers' combat pay is tax-free – limited to the maximum salary of a non- commissioned officer. This covers all compensation for any month the individual served in a combat zone or was hospitalized as result of wounds, disease, or injury in a combat zone.

Combat pay is shown in Box 14, Form W-2 and is not included in Box 1, Form W-2. See Publication 3, "Armed Forces' Tax Guide" for details.

www.irs.gov/pub/irs-pdf/p3.pdf

Employee Achievement Awards – Employee achievement awards provided by employers to employees are tax-free. However, the TCJA limits tax free employee achievement awards and other employee awards such as length of service awards to tangible personal property effective for tax year 2018 and subsequent years. This includes watches, golf clubs, and other tangible personal property. Normally, the value of such items cannot exceed $1,600 in a year. The purpose of this change is intended to eliminate disguised compensation to employees. In 2017 and prior years, such awards to employees could include certain intangible items, such as vacations, meals, lodging, tickets to events, and gift certificates. But no more beginning in 2018.

Distributions from ABLE Accounts – The Achieving a Better Life Experience Act (ABLE) creates tax-favored savings accounts for individuals with disabilities and their families for tax years beginning January 1, 2015. Contributions to the accounts are not deductible and can be made by the person with the disability (the "designated beneficiary"), parents, family members or others. In 2017, the annual contribution was limited to the amount of the annual gift-tax exclusion ($15,000 in 2018; $14,000 in 2017).

The TCJA increases the annual ABLE contribution limit for tax years 2018 – 2025 to more than $15,000 in 2018, by allowing the disabled beneficiary or others to contribute an additional amount equal to the lesser of the beneficiary's compensation for the current year or the poverty level for a one-person household for the preceding year ($12,060 in 2017). Therefore, a designated beneficiary with no compensation in 2018 could have $27,060 ($15,000 + $12,060) contributed to his/her ABLE account (indexed for inflation beginning in 2019). The TCJA also allows the designated beneficiary of the ABLE account to claim the Savers Tax Credit in an amount equal to 10% to 50% of the annual contributions to his/her account based on the filing status and adjusted gross income (AGI) of the designated beneficiary, limited to a maximum credit of $1,000. In addition, tax-free rollovers are allowed from 529 Plans to ABLE accounts, either for the benefit of the disabled transferee or for a disabled family member, effective as of December 22, 2017 through December 31, 2025, and the rollovers count toward the annual ABLE contribution limit. **(See Below, "Distributions from Qualified Tuition Programs (QTPs) – 529 Plans"); (See Tax Credits, "Savers Credit")**

www.irs.gov/pub/irs-prior/f1099qa--2015.pdf   www.irs.gov/pub/irs-prior/f1099qa--2015.pdf

Distributions from ABLE accounts that are used for a disabled person's expenses are tax-free. Allowable expenses are for basic living expenses to help a beneficiary improve his/her quality of life, including expenses for housing, transportation, job training, and even for such items as smartphones that can help, for example, autistic people navigate and communicate better. The expenses don't have to be medically necessary. Distributions (earnings only) for nonqualified purposes are subject to income tax, but not payroll tax, and a 10% penalty is payable. The ABLE Act allows families to set aside money in accounts to be used for a disabled person's expenses without risking the loss of government benefits. The beneficiary must have become blind or disabled before age 26 to qualify for an ABLE account. ABLE accounts are administered by the states, and the "Protecting Americans from Tax Hikes Act of 2015" allows individuals to set-up ABLE accounts in any state, not just in the state of their residence. However, the law allows families to open just one account per beneficiary (individuals can choose the state program that best fits their needs). Distributions from ABLE accounts are reported on Form 1099-QA. www.irs.gov/pub/irs-pdf/f1099qa.pdf www.irs.gov/pub/irs-prior/i1099qa--2018.pdf

Generally, a disabled person with more than $2,000 in personal assets is ineligible for Medicaid and Supplemental Social Security benefits. However, money held in an ABLE account is generally exempt from the $2,000 limit on personal assets for individuals who wish to qualify for government benefits such as Medicaid and other federal means-tested programs, or in determining the amount of any benefit or assistance provided under those programs, although special rules and limits apply for Supplemental Security Income (SSI) purposes. With an ABLE account, a disabled person can have up to $100,000 in assets before their savings affect their ability to qualify for most federal benefit programs. Rollovers to another ABLE account for the individual or a disabled sibling are limited. When the disabled person dies, amounts left over in an ABLE account goes to the state to recover its Medicaid costs and any other costs paid-out for the benefit of the deceased. However, any money left after the state takes its share goes to a designated beneficiary, who would owe income tax on the amount received, but with no penalty. See ABLE Accounts – Tax Benefit for People with Disabilities and Publication 907, "Tax Highlights for Persons with Disabilities."

www.irs.gov/pub/irs-pdf/p907.pdf   www.irs.gov/government-entities/federal-state-local-governments/able-accounts-tax-benefit-for-people-with-disabilities

Distributions from Qualified Tuition Programs (QTPs) – 529 Plans – A 529 Plan (QTP) is an education savings plan operated by a state or educational institution designed to help families set aside funds for future education costs.

Distributions from the plans are tax-free if used for qualified education expenses. Beginning in 2018, the TCJA allows distributions of up to $10,000 per year from a 529 Plan for a child to attend public or private (secular or religious) elementary or secondary schools. For 2017 and prior years, distributions from 529 plans could only be used for qualified higher education expenses. Distributions from 529 Plans are not allowed for home schooling expenses. Tax-free rollovers are allowed from 529 Plans to ABLE accounts, either for the benefit of the disabled transferee or for a disabled family member, effective as of December 22, 2017 through December 31, 2025, and the rollovers count toward the annual ABLE contribution limit. 529 plan distributions are reported on Form 1099-Q, which should show the tax-free earnings portion of each distribution. **(See Above, "Distributions from ABLE Accounts")**

www.irs.gov/pub/irs-pdf/f1099q.pdf   www.irs.gov/pub/irs-pdf/f1099q.pdf

Anyone can be a 529 account owner and anyone can be named a beneficiary. The only requirements for being a beneficiary are that the person must be a U.S. citizen and have a Social Security number. There are absolutely no age restrictions for a participant. For example, if a beneficiary decides to go back to school later in life, the assets are there for them because there is no time limit for keeping funds in a 529 plan. However, if you realize you won't be able to use all of the funds in a 529 account and decide to close it, the income earned on the contributions will be taxable unearned income, in addition, there is a 10% penalty on the income withdrawn.

Contributions to Qualified Tuition Programs (QTPs, or 529 Plans) are not deductible. Many states don't cap annual contributions to 529 plans. However, you should consider limiting your annual contributions to the annual allowable Gift Tax exclusion for a single beneficiary ($15,000 or $30,000 in 2018, if married and gift-splitting is used) in order to avoid Gift taxes. Also, according to the 5-year averaging rule a donor can contribute up to $75,000 in a year to a beneficiary; $150,000 if a married couple, and average it over 5 years with no gift tax consequences (however, a gift tax return must be filed, and the election for 5-year averaging must be made on the donor's Gift tax return). A 529 plan is the only investment vehicle allowing five years of tax-free gifts in a single year. One person can be the beneficiary of numerous accounts, and if a beneficiary chooses not to go to college, plan assets can be transferred to another close relative without penalty. You can transfer assets among family members with no tax repercussions. Grandparents can also take their required minimum distributions (RMDs) from their IRA accounts and transfer those funds to a 529 plan, where the funds can continue to grow tax deferred. Multiple family members and friends can give to the same 529 plan account to help create larger education funds.

Employer Provided Tax-Fee Benefits:

Transit Benefits – The TCJA discontinued the bicycle commuter benefit for tax years 2018 – 2025. Before 2018, businesses were able to offer employees up to a $20 tax-free subsidy per month for biking to work. However, beginning in 2018, businesses can continue to provide the $20 benefit to employees, but it will be considered taxable income to employees for tax years 2018 – 2025.

The TCJA disallows any employer deduction for qualified transportation benefits provided to employees after 2017, including employee buses, van pools, subway or transit cards, and parking fees (unless the expenses are necessary for ensuring the safety of employees). Employees are still able to take advantage of pre-tax transit benefits. However, for tax years 2018 – 2025, employers will no longer be able to directly subsidize their employees for the transportation benefits without the subsidies being considered taxable income to employees.

Employer Furnished Meals and Lodging – Meals provided to employees by an employer during working hours, including meals provided at on-premises dining facilities and for the convenience of the employer, that were tax-free to employees and 100% deductible by employers in 2017 and prior years, including de minimis food and beverages, have been reduced to being 50% deductible by employers for tax years 2018 – 2025, and will be nondeductible starting in 2026 per the TCJA. (The TCJA doesn't mention anything about lodging expenses). However, an employer has the choice of including the cost of employee provided meals and de minimis food and beverages in employees' taxable income and then taking a tax deduction for the meals and de minimis items in 2018 – 2025.

Net Operating Loss (NOL) – Under the TCJA, the 2-year net operating loss carryback that was available in 2017 and prior years is eliminated, except for farmers, effective for 2018 and subsequent years. However, the TCJA allows an indefinite carryforward of a NOL, but a NOL carryforward can be used only against 80% of a subsequent year's taxable income. The rules for pre-2018 NOLs remain the same – they can be carried back 2 years and forward 20 years. There is no taxable income limit for usage of pre-2018 NOLs. **(See Self-Employed/Independent Contractors, "Net Operating Losses")**

Exclusions from Taxable Income

Combat-Zone Contract Workers Qualify for Foreign Earned Income Exclusion – Certain U.S. citizens or resident aliens, specifically contractors or employees of contractors supporting the U.S. Armed Forces in designated combat zones, now qualify for the foreign earned income exclusion. The Bipartisan Budget Act of 2018, changed the tax home requirement for eligible taxpayers, enabling them to claim the foreign earned income exclusion even if their "abode" is in the United States. The new law applies for tax year 2018 and subsequent years. Therefore, these taxpayers, if eligible, will be able to claim the foreign earned income exclusion on their income tax return for 2018. Under prior law, many otherwise eligible taxpayers who lived and worked in designated combat zones failed to qualify because they had an abode in the United States. Publication 54, "Guide for U.S. Citizens and Resident Aliens Abroad," will be revised later this year to reflect this clarification. www.irs.gov/pub/irs-pdf/p54.pdf

The maximum foreign earned income exclusion includes the "housing exclusion." You must claim the housing exclusion before claiming the rest as the "foreign earned income exclusion," and both are considered foreign earned taxable income paid by your employer. However, even if you can exclude foreign earned income from U.S. income taxes, you still must pay payroll taxes on the income if you work for an American employer, which includes the U.S. government, a U.S. corporation, or a foreign affiliate of an American employer (10% or more American ownership), and they are required to withhold payroll taxes (FICA) based on the amount of the foreign earned income exclusion. However, if you are a consultant or contractor (compensation reported on Form 1099-MISC), you must pay self-employment tax.

Forgiveness of Mortgage Debt on a Principal Residence – Forgiveness of Mortgage debt on a principal residence was originally not available in 2017, because the "Debt Forgiveness Relief Act" was only extended through 2016 by the "Protecting Americans from Tax Hikes Act of 2015." But in February 2018, the Bipartisan Budget Act of 2018 retroactively extended it to cover tax year 2017, and it was also made available in 2018.

In accordance with the Debt Forgiveness Relief Act, up to $2 million, or $1 million (married filing separately) in mortgage debt is forgiven and excluded from taxable income. However, even if you are entitled to mortgage debt forgiveness, you may still receive a Form 1099-C (Cancellation of Debt) from the mortgage company. If this happens, in order to claim mortgage debt forgiveness, you will need to complete Form 982 and check the appropriate box to tell the IRS that you're entitled to an exclusion from taxable income for the cancelled debt. Foreclosure on a home can result in income to the owner that is forgiven, if at the time of foreclosure the fair market value (FMV) of the encumbered property is less than the outstanding debt. Also, a "short sale" can result in forgiven income to the owner. A short sale in real estate occurs when the outstanding loans against a property are greater than what the property is worth and the lender agrees to accept less than what is owed to permit a sale of the property (home) that secures the note. This benefit also covers an agreement or "work-out" with the lender to make payments lower.
www.irs.gov/pub/irs-pdf/f1099c.pdf www.irs.gov/pub/irs-pdf/i1099ac.pdf
www.irs.gov/pub/irs-pdf/f982.pdf

A lender who acquires a taxpayer's property through foreclosure, repossession or abandonment should send the taxpayer Form 1099-A, which is the form used by the taxpayer to calculate gain or loss and any ordinary income from disposition of the property. www.irs.gov/pub/irs-pdf/f1099a.pdf

Forgiveness of Student Loans – Under the TCJA, federal and private student loan forgiveness due to death or permanent disability is excluded from taxable income for tax years 2018 – 2025 (this includes forgiveness in the event of death if there is a cosigner on the loan). In 2017 and prior years, forgiveness of student loans due to death or disability was considered taxable unearned income, and a Form 1099-C was issued to the benefactor.

Section 1031 Like-Kind Exchange – The TCJA eliminates like-kind exchanges other than for "real property" effective beginning in tax year 2018. However, like-kind exchanges for other than real property that were in progress as of December 31, 2017, are protected, i.e. they can proceed until finalized. Section 1031 like-kind exchanges of other than real property that were allowed through 2017, included exchanges of vehicles, equipment, livestock, other business property, and even Intangibles (trademarks, trade names, etc.) – except for goodwill. You can't apply Section 1031 to any personal use real property such as your residence. No gain or loss is recognized in a Section 1031 like-kind exchange except to the extent of "boot" received – money, other property, or a transferred liability (mortgage). If you receive any cash or other property in addition to the like-kind property, then gain, but not loss, is recognized equal to the lesser of the boot received or the gain realized, and the gain is subject to long-term capital gain treatment. No loss is ever recognized to any extent.

Form 8824 must be filed when there is a Section 1031 like-kind exchange. Like-kind or Section 1031 exchanges are used by owners who would otherwise have a large gain on the sale of investment or business real property they have held for years. The exchange of like-kind real property means the exchanged properties must be of the same nature or character – the grade or quality of the properties is not relevant. For example, in a real estate for real

estate exchange, it can be an apartment building for raw land. Like-kind real estate can be: vacant land; commercial rental property; commercial property; industrial property; 30-year or more leasehold interest property; farm property; or residential rental property. The replacement property must be identified within 45 days from the sale of the relinquished property, and the exchange must be completed within 180 days. Also, the replacement property must be of equivalent or higher in value, the cash invested in the replacement property must be equal to or greater than the cash received from the sale of the relinquished property, and the debt placed or assumed on the replacement property must be equal to or greater than the debt on the relinquished property. After the transfer, the business nature of the transaction must remain intact.
www.irs.gov/pub/irs-access/f8824accessible.pdf   www.irs.gov/pub/irs-pdf/i8824.pdf

Retirement Plan Loans – If an employee stops making payments on a retirement plan loan before the loan is repaid, a deemed distribution of the outstanding loan balance generally occurs. Such a distribution is generally taxed as though an actual distribution occurred, including being subject to a 10% early distribution penalty and the deemed distribution isn't eligible for rollover to another eligible retirement plan. However, in certain circumstances (for example, if an employee terminates employment), an employee's obligation to repay a retirement plan loan is accelerated and, if the loan is not repaid, the loan is cancelled and the amount in the employee's account balance is offset by the amount of the unpaid loan balance, referred to as a loan offset.

For retirement plan loan offset amounts which are treated as distributed in tax years beginning after Dec. 31, 2017, the TCJA provides that the period during which a qualified plan loan offset amount may be contributed to another eligible retirement plan as a rollover contribution is extended from 60 days (in 2017 and prior years) to the due date (including extensions) for filing the tax return for the tax year in which the plan loan offset occurs. For this purpose, a qualified plan loan offset amount is a plan loan offset amount that is treated as distributed from a qualified 403(b) or 457(b) retirement plan solely by reason of termination of the plan or the failure to meet the repayment terms of the loan because of an employee's separation from service, whether due to layoff, cessation of business, termination of employment, or otherwise.

Length of Service Award Programs for Public Safety Volunteers – For 2018 and subsequent years, the TCJA increases the amount of "length of service awards" that may accrue under 457 retirement plans for bona fide volunteers (volunteer firefighters and prevention services, emergency medical services, and ambulance services, including services performed by dispatchers, mechanics, ambulance drivers, and certified instructors) from $3,000 in 2017 and prior years to $6,000 with respect to any year of service, with cost of living adjustments beginning in 2019. If the volunteers are under a defined benefit retirement plan, the limit applies to the actuarial present value of the aggregate amount of length of service awards accruing with respect to any year of service. Actuarial present value is calculated using reasonable actuarial assumptions and methods, assuming payment will be made under the most valuable form of payment under the plan, with payments commencing at the later of the earliest age at which unreduced benefits are payable under the plan or the participant's age at the time of the calculation. For 2017 and prior years, any 457 plan that soley provided length of service awards to bona fide volunteers or their beneficiaries, on account of qualified services performed by the volunteers, was not treated as a plan of deferred compensation.

Health Reimbursement Arrangement (HRA) – On October 23, 2018, the Departments of the Treasury, Labor and Human Services issued proposed regulations on HRAs that would increase the usability of HRAs (primarily for large employers) by expanding employers' ability to offer HRAs to their employees and allow HRAs to be used in conjunction with nongroup health insurance coverage (generally coverage on the individual market). The proposed regulations would remove the prohibition on integrating HRAs with individual health insurance coverage if certain conditions are met, but would prevent plan sponsors from intentionally or unintentionally directing any participants with certain adverse health conditions away from the plan sponsor's traditional group health plan into the individual market place. Also, the proposed regulations require all HRAs to be offered on the same terms to all employees, subject to certain exceptions. HRA participants have always been ineligible for the premium tax credit; however, the proposed regulations provide a path where employees whose employers have HRAs that may or may not be integrated with individual health insurance coverage may qualify for the premium tax credit. If the amount an employee must pay in premiums is more than the product of the required contribution percentage and the employee's household income, the premium tax credit would be allowable. **(See Tax Credits, "Affordable Care Act (ACA) Premium Tax Credits"); (See "Affordable Care Act")**
https://s3.amazonaws.com/public-inspection.federalregister.gov/2018-23183.pdf

Qualified Small Employer Health Reimbursement Arrangement (QSEHRA) – A qualified small employer health reimbursement arrangement (QSEHRA), or small business HRA, is an employer funded tax-free health benefit that allows small businesses with fewer than 50 full-time or full-time-equivalent (FTE) employees to reimburse their employees for individual health care expenses. QSEHRAs were signed into law by the "21st Century Cures Act" in December 2017.

In order to calculate whether a QSEHRA provides affordable coverage in accordance with the Affordable Care Act (ACA), employees have to determine whether the premium for the QSEHRA offered by their employer costs 9.56% or less of their household income in 2018. If the QSEHRA's premium meets that cost standard, the employee has affordable coverage and doesn't qualify for a premium tax credit. However, if the premium costs more than 9.56% of their household income, employees may be eligible for a premium tax credit.

Most stand-alone health reimbursement arrangements (HRAs), which is an HRA that is not offered in conjunction with a group health plan, have been prohibited since 2014 by the Affordable Care Act (ACA). However, the 21st Century Cures Act (Act) allows small employers that do not maintain group health plans to establish stand-alone HRAs that are called QSEHRAs, effective for plan years beginning on or after Jan. 1, 2017. Like all HRAs, a QSEHRA must be funded solely by the employer. Employees cannot make their own contributions to an HRA, either directly or indirectly through salary reduction contributions. Specific requirements apply, including a maximum benefit limit and a notice requirement. For 2018, the maximum reimbursements cannot exceed $5,050 for those with self-only coverage and $10,250 for those with family coverage. In 2017, the QSEHRA contribution limits were $4,950 annually for self-only employees and $10,000 annually for family coverage. For employees who become eligible for the QSEHRA midyear, the limits must be prorated to reflect the total amount of time the employee is eligible. For example, an employee who is eligible for the QSEHRA for 6 months in 2018 can receive up to $2,524.98 through the benefit that year. **(See Tax Credits, "Affordable Care Act (ACA) Premium Tax Credits"); (See Affordable Care Act, "Qualified Small Employer Health Reimbursement Arrangement (QSEHRA)")**

Advance Refunding Bonds

The exclusion from gross income of interest earned on State and local bonds was applicable to "refunding bonds" with some limitations on advance refunding bonds in 2017 and prior years. However, the TCJA repealed the exclusion from gross income of interest earned on advance refunding bonds for bonds issued after December 31, 2017. A refunding bond is defined as any bond used to pay principal, interest, or redemption price on a prior bond issue (the refunded bond). A current refunding occurs when the refunded bond is redeemed within 90 days of issuance of the refunding bonds. Conversely, a bond is classified as an advance refunding if it is issued more than 90 days before the redemption of the refunded bond. In general, governmental bonds and qualified 501(c)(3) bonds may be advance refunded only one time, while private activity bonds (other than qualified 501(c)(3) bonds) may not be advance refunded at all. Proceeds of advance refunding bonds are generally invested in an escrow account and held until a future date when the refunded bond may be redeemed.

The IRS plans to issue proposed regulations clarifying that the market discount on a bond is not includible in income. A market discount is the difference between a bond's purchase price and the stated redemption price when it matures. Notice 2018-80 provides some important information.
www.irs.gov/pub/irs-drop/n-18-80.pdf

3.8% Net Investment Income Tax

Under the Tax Cuts and Jobs Act (TCJA), the 3.8% Net Investment Income (NII) Tax added by the Affordable Care Act is still in effect. It was implemented to provide additional revenue for Medicare. The tax is also referred to as the "unearned income contribution tax," because it is imposed on the unearned income of high-income individuals and it also applies to estates and trusts. High-income individuals are those with adjusted gross income (AGI) above $200,000 single; $250,000 married filing jointly and surviving spouse; $125,000 married filing separately; and $200,000 head-of-household, and the thresholds are not adjusted for inflation. The 3.8% NII tax is in addition to the ordinary income taxes and capital gain taxes already paid by high- income individuals. The tax imposed on individuals is on the lesser of their "net investment income" or the amount by which their modified adjusted gross income (MAGI) exceeds the above stated thresholds for high-income earners. **(See "Affordable Care Act")**

Deductions in Determining Adjusted Gross Income

Tuition and Fees for Higher Education – The tuition and fees for higher education deduction was originally unavailable in 2017, because it was only extended through 2016 by the "Protecting Americans from Tax Hikes Act of 2015." But in February 2018, the Bipartisan Budget Act of 2018 retroactively extended it to the 2017 tax year and it is also available in 2018. A tuition and fees deduction of up to $4,000 per student is available for single taxpayers with modified adjusted gross incomes (MAGI) up to $65,000 (up to $130,000 for joint filers), and a deduction of up to $2,000 per student is available for single taxpayers with MAGIs over $65,000 and up to $80,000 (over $130,000 and up to $160,000 for joint filers) in 2018. No deduction is available for taxpayers with MAGIs over $80,000 for single filers ($160,000 for joint filers). The deduction is not available to married taxpayers filing separately. The deduction cannot be taken if one of the available Education Credits is taken. Also, the deduction is reduced by the tax-free earnings portion of any distributions from Coverdell savings accounts and 529 plans that pay for the same expenses. **(See Non-Taxable Income, "Distributions from Qualified Tuition Programs (QTPs) – 529 Plans")**

Tuition and fees must be required for enrollment in an accredited post-secondary institution for the taxpayer, spouse or dependents. Allowable expenses do not include expenditures for room and board or books, supplies and equipment. You must attach Form 8917 to your tax return to claim the deduction.
www.irs.gov/pub/irs-pdf/f8917.pdf www.congress.gov/115/bills/hr1892/BILLS- 115hr1892enr.pdf

Taxpayers cannot claim the deduction unless they receive a Form 1098-T from the college or university containing information showing the actual expenses paid by the student during the calendar year, which are to be reported on form 8917. Colleges and universities are supposed to report actual tuition fees and other qualified payments received from students during the calendar year on Form 1098-T.
www.irs.gov/pub/irs-pdf/f1098t.pdf

Moving Expenses – Under the Tax Cuts and Jobs Act (TCJA), the deduction for moving expenses is suspended for tax years 2018 – 2025, except for members of the Armed Forces on active duty, including spouses and dependents, who move under official military orders to a permanent change of station. In 2017 and prior years, all taxpayers could claim a deduction for moving expenses incurred in connection with starting a job if the new workplace was at least 50 miles farther from the taxpayer's former residence than the former place of work.

Also, under the TCJA, the exclusion from taxable income by taxpayers (except for members of the Armed Forces) of qualified moving expense reimbursements by employers is suspended for tax years 2018 – 2025. In 2017 and prior years, all taxpayers could exclude qualified moving expense reimbursements from their gross income and from their wages when the moving expenses were in connection with their employment. Moving expenses that were reimbursed by employers and included in taxable income were deductible by all taxpayers by filing Form 3903. However, it was not necessary to file Form 3903 when moving expenses were reimbursed by employers, and not included in taxable income, because the non-taxable reimbursements offset allowable moving expenses, and therefore were not deductible by the taxpayer. www.irs.gov/pub/irs-pdf/f3903.pdf
http://taxmap.ntis.gov/taxmap/pubs/p521-004.htm   www.irs.gov/pub/irs-pdf/fw2.pdf

The IRS announced that employer payments or reimbursements for moving expenses in 2018 for all employees' legitimate moving expenses that occurred in 2017 and any prior years could still be deducted or excluded from their taxable income in 2018.

Allowable moving expenses (by members of the Armed Forces on active duty in 2018) include the following if authorized: cost of packing and moving household goods; storage of household goods for 30 days; cost of transporting a vehicle(s); cost of transporting family members to new location including airfare and by car at a mileage rate of 18 cents per mile in 2018 (17 cents in 2017); the cost to disconnect utilities at your old residence and connect them at your new residence; and one night's lodging at both old and new locations. Meals are not deductible. You can write-off the cost of hiring movers or renting a moving truck plus the cost of one-way travel to your new home for everyone in your household – whether it's by airfare, train, or by car.

Also, you can deduct lodging expenses while traveling to your new home. In addition, because your dog is considered property, you can deduct expenses to move your dog.

Domestic Production Activities Deduction – Under the TCJA, the 9% deduction attributable to domestic production activities (Section 199) is repealed for tax years starting in 2018. In 2017 and prior years, qualified taxpayers were allowed an above the line deduction equal to 9% of the smaller of: (1) adjusted gross income for an individual, estate, or trust, or (2) qualified production activities income (QPAI), defined as the gross receipts from the sale of qualified production property (QPP) minus the cost of the QPP sold and minus any expenses allocable to the QPP. The deduction couldn't exceed 50% of Form W-2 wages of the taxpayer's employees for the year. Generally, QPP was tangible personal property manufactured, produced, grown, or extracted substantially within the United States. QPP was property in which the form or function of the property had been changed. Only one taxpayer could take the deduction. When a taxpayer had a contract with an unrelated third party to manufacture the product, the taxpayer had to possess the benefits and burdens of ownership during the production process to take the deduction. However, determining which party had the "benefits and burdens" of ownership was often a complex process. The deduction was calculated on Form 8903. www.irs.gov/pub/irs-pdf/f8903.pdf www.irs.gov/pub/irs-pdf/i8903.pdf

Eligible activities centered around manufacturing products in the United States, but many other businesses could qualify. In addition to manufacturing, the parameters for qualifying for the deduction were broad but generally had to go beyond mere repackaging to qualify. For example, such activities as software development, producing electricity, producing films, assembling gift baskets, assembling and selling single doses of medicine, making hamburgers, or roasting coffee qualified for the deduction. In past years, about one-third of corporate activities in the U.S. qualified for the deduction.

In a technical advice memorandum (TAM 201638022), the IRS National Office of the Chief Counsel determined a taxpayer's substantial renovation, construction, and erection of certain property qualified as the construction of real property under Sec. 199 such that the gross receipts derived from those activities qualified as domestic production gross receipts (DPGR). In reaching its decision, the Chief Counsel determined that the property was "inherently permanent structures." https://www.irs.gov/pub/irs-wd/201638022.pdf

Deduction of Living Expenses by Members of Congress – Members of Congress were able to deduct up to $3,000 per year in living expenses while away from their home states or Congressional districts. However, the TCJA repealed their ability to deduct these expenses beginning with the 2018 tax year.

www.senate.gov/CRSpubs/9c14ec69-c4e4-4bd8-8953-f73daa1640e4.pdf

Itemized Deductions

Itemized Deduction Phase-Outs – Under the Tax Cuts and Jobs Act (TCJA), allowable itemized deductions are not phased-out, i.e. the "Pease limitations" are suspended for tax years 2018 – 2025 but are scheduled to return in 2026. In 2017, itemized deductions were phased-out at adjusted gross income (AGI) thresholds of: $261,500 – $384,000 (singles); $313,800 –$436,300 (married filing jointly and surviving spouse); $287,650 – $410,150 (head-of- household); and $156,900 – $218,150 (married filing separately). www.irs.gov/pub/irs-pdf/f1040sa.pdf

Medical Expenses – Expenditures incurred as a medical necessity and that are not reimbursed by insurance are fully deductible as itemized deductions if they are more than 7 ½ % of adjusted gross income (AGI) in 2018. In 2017, the floor was originally 10% of AGI, until it was retroactively changed by the TCJA to 7 ½ % of AGI for the 2017 tax year, and the 7 ½ % floor also applies to 2018. However, the TCJA returns the floor for deducting medical expenses to 10% for all individuals in 2019.

Medical expenses of a qualifying child can be claimed, even if you can't claim the child as a dependent. Also, medical expenses of a qualifying relative who is not your child can be claimed, even if you can't claim the relative as a dependent due to the gross income test ($4,150 in 2018), but you must furnish more than ½ of the support of the relative, e.g. your mother. You can claim the medical expenses of a supported person who doesn't meet the relationship test if you live in the same household and the other tests are met. **(Determining Filing Status and Dependency Exemptions, "Dependents" & "Other Persons Qualifying as Dependents")**

Medical expenses that are paid with funds from Health Reimbursement Arrangements (HRAs), Health Savings Accounts (HSAs), and Flexible Spending Accounts (FSAs) are generally not deductible, because they are usually funded with pre-tax dollars, or contributions to HSAs are deductible in determining AGI. Also, medical expenses paid with money from a withdrawal of the cash surrender value of a life insurance contract are not deductible – instead, the amount is not included in income and the investment in the contract is reduced by that amount. Reimbursements received in excess of medical expenses are not taxable, unless your employer paid all or part of your health insurance premiums, then part must be included in gross income. Reimbursements for medical expenses, received in the next year, are taxable if beneficial to the taxpayer in the prior year.

State and Local Tax Deductions – Expenditures incurred for state and local taxes that are deductible as itemized deductions are capped at $10,000 ($5,000 for married filing separately) in 2018, because the TCJA suspends the full deduction of state and local taxes as an itemized deduction for tax years 2018 – 2025. The definition of state and local taxes includes: property taxes; personal property taxes; state, local and foreign income taxes; and sales taxes. State and local taxes were fully deductible as itemized deductions in 2017. Prepayments of 2018 state and local taxes in 2017 were prohibited by statute, and the IRS used tax case precedent to prevent the deduction of prepayments of 2018 taxes on 2017 tax returns. Taxes paid on unimproved land that is considered investment property were included in miscellaneous itemized deductions subject to the 2% AGI floor in 2017 but the TCJA repealed "miscellaneous itemized deductions subject to the 2% AGI floor" as an itemized deduction for tax years 2018 – 2025. **(See Business Structures and Provisions, "Workaround by Businesses to Avoid $10,000 Limit on SALT Deductions")**

Home Mortgage Interest Deduction – Home mortgage interest is deductible as an itemized deduction in 2018. However, the TCJA suspends the deduction of interest on "home equity loans" for tax years 2018 – 2025, unless the loan is used to buy, build or substantially improve the home that secures the loan. Therefore, if you take out an equity loan to pay for things like an addition to the home, a new roof or a kitchen renovation, you can still deduct the interest on a so-called home equity loan.

437

In 2018, mortgage interest is deductible on qualifying mortgage loans up to a maximum of $750,000 ($375,000 for married filing separately) on a principal residence, and a maximum of $750,000 on a second residence ($375,000 for married filing separately). The TCJA reduced the maximum loan amount from $1 million to $750,000 effective December 16, 2017 (except in the case of binding contracts scheduled to close in 2017 that actually closed by March 31, 2018), and this change is in effect through the 2025 tax year. Existing mortgage loans before the effective date of the TCJA, including refinancing, are still subject to the prior $1 million maximum that was in effect in 2017 and prior years.

Mortgage Insurance Premiums – The mortgage insurance premium deduction was originally unavailable in 2017, because the "Protecting Americans from Tax Hikes Act of 2015" extended the deduction only through 2016. But in February 2018, the Bipartisan Budget Act of 2018 retroactively extended the deduction through the 2017 tax year. However, it is unsure whether the deduction will be available in 2018, because the bill that extended the deduction through 2017 is silent about future deductions, including for 2018.

Charitable Contribution Deduction – Charitable contributions are generally fully deductible as itemized deductions for most people. However, the TCJA increased the maximum deduction for cash donations from 50% to 60% of AGI in 2018. But the maximum deduction for any property contributions remains at 50% of AGI and is applied before determining allowable cash contributions. Any excess contributions over 60%/50% of AGI can be carried forward for 5 years in the same category.

The TCJA repealed a provision that exempted donors from having to substantiate charitable contributions of $250 or more with a contemporaneous written acknowledgment from the donee organization if the donee organization filed a return with the required information. This applies retroactively to contributions made starting in 2017.

Beginning in 2018, deductions for donations coupled with preferred seating at college sports events are disallowed as a charitable contribution. But in 2017 and prior years, persons who purchased season tickets to college football games or other college sporting events were allowed to claim a charitable contribution deduction. Here's how it worked – if they paid $1,640 to buy tickets to 8 games, and in addition they were required to donate an additional $3,700 to the college or university to be able to buy the tickets, they were allowed to deduct 80% of the $3,700, or $2,960 as a charitable contribution. But no more beginning in 2018.

On Sept. 29, 2017, the "Disaster Tax Relief and Airport and Airway Extension Act of 2017" was passed, which provides temporary tax relief to victims of Hurricanes Harvey, Irma, and Maria. For qualifying charitable contributions, the Act provides an exception from the overall limitation on itemized deductions for certain qualified contributions, temporarily suspends the majority of the limitations on charitable contributions in Code Sec. 170(b), and provides for eased rules governing the treatment of excess contributions. "Qualified contributions" must have been paid during the period beginning on Aug. 23, 2017, and ending on Dec. 31, 2017, in cash to an organization described in Code Sec. 170(b)(1)(A), for relief efforts in the Hurricane Harvey, Irma, or Maria disaster areas. Qualified contributions must have been substantiated, with a contemporaneous written acknowledgement that the contribution was or is to be used for hurricane relief efforts, and the taxpayer must make an election for the Act to apply. For partnerships and S-corporations, the election is made separately by each partner or shareholder. **(See Determining Filing Status and Dependency Exemptions, Disaster Tax Relief & Airport**

438

Casualty, Disaster, and Theft Losses – The TCJA eliminates personal theft and casualty losses as an itemized deduction for tax years 2018 – 2025, except for losses in federal disaster areas declared by the President of the United States. However, non-disaster personal casualty and theft losses may be used to reduce personal casualty and theft gains in the same year. Business theft and casualty losses are still deductible in 2018.

On Sept. 29, 2017, the "Disaster Tax Relief and Airport and Airway Extension Act of 2017" was passed, which provides temporary tax relief to victims of Hurricanes Harvey, Irma, and Maria. The Act eliminates the requirement that personal casualty losses must exceed 10% of AGI to qualify for a deduction and eliminates the requirement that disaster victims must itemize deductions in order to claim casualty losses—it does so by increasing their standard deduction by the amount of the victim's net disaster casualty loss. However, the TCJA also increases the $100 per-casualty loss floor from $100 to $500 for qualified disaster-related personal casualty losses. The TCJA provides that Code Sec. 56(b)(1)(E), which generally disallows the standard deduction for alternative minimum tax (AMT) purposes, does not apply for the portion of the standard deduction attributable to the amount of the net disaster loss.

Under the TCJA, individual disaster loss victims in the hurricane affected areas may elect to claim a casualty loss in the tax year immediately preceding the tax year in which the disaster occurred or in the current year, whichever saves them more money. Victims have six months after the due date for filing their tax return for the year in which the disaster occurred to make the election, and they have 90 days after that to revoke the election. Taxpayers make the election by deducting the disaster loss on either an original or an amended tax return for the prior year, and by including an election statement on the return indicating they are making a Section 165(i) election and the name or description of the disaster and the date or dates of the disaster that caused the claimed loss. **(See Determining Filing Status and Dependency Exemptions, Disaster Tax Relief & Airport & Airway Extension Act of 2017, "Eased Casualty Loss Rules for Disaster Loss Victims")**

Miscellaneous Itemized Deductions Subject to the 2% Adjusted Gross Income (AGI) Floor – The TCJA) suspends the deduction for "miscellaneous itemized deductions subject to the 2% of adjusted gross income (AGI) floor" for tax years 2018 – 2025. Therefore, a deduction for miscellaneous itemized deductions subject to the 2% AGI floor is no longer allowed in 2018. The unallowed deductions includes the following and more:

- **Employee Business Expenses** – Unreimbursed employee travel and entertainment expenses, and other employee business expenses are no longer deductible. Travel and entertainment expenses were reported on Form 2106 in 2017 and prior years, while other employee business expenses could be reported directly as miscellaneous itemized deductions subject to the 2% AGI floor on Form 1040, Schedule A. The TCJA has in effect eliminated the use of Form 2106 for tax years 2018 – 2025 by employees. **(See Business Travel and Related Expenses, "Employee Travel and Incidental Expenses" & "Entertainment Expenses")**

- **Employee Home Office Expenses** – Employee home office expenses, even if necessary and for the convenience of the employer, are no longer deductible.

- **Hobby Expenses** – A hobby is an activity that is deemed not to be a profit-motivated activity or business. Hobby expenses are no longer deductible as a miscellaneous itemized deduction. In 2017 and prior years, hobby expenses were deductible as a miscellaneous itemized deduction subject to the 2% AGI floor, but only to the extent of income from the activity (a loss was not allowed). Hobby Income still has to be reported as "other income," on Form 1040. **(See Business Structures and Provisions, "Hobby Expenses are Not Deductible")**

- **Expenses to Look for a New Job in the Same Line of Work** – Expenses to look for a new job in the same line of work are no longer deductible – travel and entertainment expenses, including meals, lodging, and transportation expenses were reported on Form 2106. Other expenses such as the cost of resumes, employment agency fees, and costs of printing resumes, business cards, postage, and advertising were reported directly as miscellaneous itemized deductions subject to the 2% AGI floor.

- **Work Related Education Costs** – Work related education costs, but not education costs that qualified a person for a new profession, are no longer deductible. The costs of education expenses were generally deductible if the courses taken were to maintain or improve skills required by the individual's employment or trade or business or to meet the express requirements of the individual's employer or the requirements of applicable law.

- **Special Work Clothes** – Special work clothes not suitable to wear off the job and that were "ordinary and necessary" in relation to business, such as special protective clothing and safety boots worn by police officers and firemen are no longer deductible. Work clothes, uniforms and costumes qualified if they satisfied a two-step test: (1) required as a condition of employment, and (2) unsuitable for everyday use.

- **Investment Expenses** – Safe deposit boxes, IRA custodial fees, brokers' commissions, fees for investment advice, trust administration fees, subscriptions to investment and financial planning journals, and clerical help and office rent in caring for investments are no longer deductible.

- **Legal Expenses** – Some legal expenses that were deductible as miscellaneous itemized deductions subject to the 2% AGI floor are no longer deductible including: (1) Legal fees and other fees paid in connection with the preparation of tax returns or in connection with any proceedings involved in determining the extent of your tax liability or in contesting a tax liability; (2) Legal fees for preparing wills and estate planning; (3) tax planning advice, including investment advice by attorneys, CPAs, etc.; (4) Legal fees paid in connection with a claim for disputed Social Security benefits due to a disability; (5) Some legal fees related to divorce, such as legal fees related to collecting child support and alimony; and (6) Legal expenses that were deductible tied to or related to keeping your job, including fees paid to defend yourself against criminal charges arising out of your trade or business.

- **Fiduciary Bundled Fees** – Fiduciary bundled fees are allocated between costs that are subject to the 2% AGI floor and those that are fully deductible elsewhere. The fees that are subject to the 2% AGI floor are no longer deductible, including: fees attributable to investment advice (including any related services that would be provided to any individual investor as part of an investment advisory fee); and payments made to a third party if paid directly by an estate or trust. If amounts are allocable to investment advice but are not traceable to separate payments, the final regulations allow the use of "any reasonable method" to make the allocation between costs that are subject to the 2% AGI floor and those that are fully deductible.

- **Other Miscellaneous Itemized Deductions Subject to the 2% AGI Floor That are No Longer Deductible** – Personal income tax preparation fees and counsel; dues and subscriptions to professional journals; professional and trade association dues; appraisal fees for charitable contributions or casualty losses; union dues and costs; professional liability insurance; small tools necessary for employment; gifts to business associates or clients; depreciation of a computer used to manage investments.

The elimination of miscellaneous itemized deductions subject to the 2% AGI floor will result in some legal fees that were allowable miscellaneous itemized deductions in prior years being non-deductible beginning in 2018, which may be construed as unfair to individuals seeking taxable damages (other than damages for discrimination where the legal fees are deducted as an above-the-line deduction). For example, assume a plaintiff in a law suit related to his employment (other than job discrimination) is awarded a $600,000 settlement; the attorney gets one-third of the award on a contingency ($200,000); and the plaintiff has to pay taxes on the full $600,000 settlement without getting any offsetting deduction for the legal fees in 2018, like he or she would have gotten in 2017 and prior years. Another example that may be construed as unfair is when a taxpayer has income from a hobby but can no longer deduct expenses related to the hobby as a miscellaneous itemized deduction in 2018, like he or she could in 2017 and prior years. And there are many other examples where the elimination of miscellaneous itemized deductions subject to the 2% AGI floor can be construed as unfair.

Miscellaneous Itemized Deductions Not Subject to the 2% Adjusted Gross Income (AGI) Floor – Under the TCJA, miscellaneous itemized deduction "not" subject to the 2% AGI floor are still deductible as an itemized deduction, and that includes gambling losses. However, the TCJA made some changes to the law that was in effect in 2017 and prior years. First, for casual gamblers, expenses are allowed to be included as an addition to their losses that can offset their gambling winnings in tax years 2018 – 2025. For instance, an individual's expenses in traveling to and from a casino are expenses that can offset gambling winnings beginning in 2018. The expenses of casual gamblers were not allowed to be included as part of their losses in 2017 and prior years. However, gambling losses can be taken only to the extent of gambling winnings in 2018 and subsequent years (casual gamblers cannot have an overall loss in a year).

Second, the TCJA reversed the Tax Court decision in Mayo vs. Commissioner that allowed professional gamblers to incur an overall loss on Schedule C. Beginning in 2018, professional gamblers are no longer allowed to incur a loss on Schedule C due to their non-loss expenses such as meals, lodging, travel expenses, admission fees and handicapping data, i.e. professional gamblers can take gambling losses (including non-loss expenses) only to the extent of gambling winnings in 2018 and subsequent years (professional gamblers cannot have an overall loss). In 2017 and prior years, professional gamblers could incur a net loss on Schedule C due to their non-loss expenses. **(See Unearned Income, "Gambling Winnings")**
www.irs.gov/pub/irs-aod/aod201106.pdf

Tax Credits

Refundable Tax Credits:

Earned Income Tax Credit (EITC) – On Sept. 29, 2017, the "Disaster Tax Relief and Airport and Airway Extension Act of 2017" was passed, which provides temporary tax relief to victims of Hurricanes Harvey, Irma, and Maria. The Act provides that, in case a "qualified taxpayer's" earned income, which includes the applicable dates shown below, is less than the taxpayer's earned income for the preceding tax year, then the taxpayer may elect, for purposes of the EITC and the Child Tax Credit, to substitute the earned income for the preceding year for the earned income for the current tax year in computing the EITC and the Child Tax Credit for the current year. For Hurricane Harvey, a "qualified taxpayer" is one whose principal place of abode on Aug. 23, 2017 was located either in the Hurricane Harvey disaster zone, or in the Hurricane Harvey disaster area and the individual was displaced from their principal place of abode by reason of Hurricane Harvey. Similar definitions apply for Hurricanes Irma (using a Sept. 4, 2017 date) and Hurricane Maria (using a Sept. 16, 2017 date). In the case of joint filers, the above election may apply if either spouse is a qualified individual. **(See Determining Filing Status and Dependency Exemptions, Disaster Tax Relief & Airport & Airway Extension Act of 2017, "Special Rule on Earned Income for Earned Income Tax Credit (EITC) and Child Tax Credit Purposes")**

The earned income tax credit (EITC) was made permanent by the "Protecting Americans from Tax Hikes Act of 2015," and is claimed on Schedule EIC, Form 1040. A taxpayer must be over age 24 and below age 65 to claim the EITC. Also, the taxpayer (and spouse, if married) must have a valid Social Security number and be a U.S. citizen or resident alien for the entire year in order to claim the EITC. A taxpayer (or spouse) who is a nonresident alien for any part of the year cannot claim the EITC unless the taxpayer files jointly with his or her spouse who is a U.S. citizen or resident. If they make this election, the couple will be subject to U.S. taxes on their worldwide income. A taxpayer who has an "individual tax identification number" (ITIN) cannot claim the credit even if he or she has dependent children with valid Social Security numbers who would otherwise qualify for the EITC. An ITIN always begins with the number 9, and will have a 7, 8, or 9 in the fourth digit of the number. Also, an individual cannot retroactively claim the EITC by amending a return (or filing an original return if he failed to file) for any prior year in which he did not have a valid Social Security number.

www.irs.gov/pub/irs-pdf/f1040sei.pdf) http://f1040.com/-%20IRS/Worksheets/EIC%20Worksheet%20B%20-%20Lines%2064a%20and%2064b%20.pdf

Tax preparers must answer due diligence questions on Form 8867, "Paid Preparer's Due Diligence Checklist," regarding the EITC, and beginning with the 2018 tax year, Form 8867 also applies to the Child Tax Credit/Additional Child Tax Credit, the American Opportunity Credit, and qualification for Head of Household status. **(See Determining Filing Status and Dependency Exemptions, "Head of Household"); See Below, "Additional Child Tax Credit" & "Child Tax Credit")**
www.irs.gov/pub/irs-pdf/f8867.pdf www.irs.gov/pub/irs-pdf/i8867.pdf

Additional Child Tax Credit – The additional child tax credit was made permanent by the "Protecting Americans from Tax Hikes Act of 2015 (PATH)." The Tax Cuts and Jobs Act (TCJA) doubles the Child Tax Credit to $2,000 for each "qualifying child" for tax years 2018 – 2025. The Additional Child Tax Credit is the refundable portion of the child tax credit available to taxpayers who can't take advantage of the full amount of the credit due to a limited amount of income tax liability. The additional child tax credit is 15% of earned income greater than $2,500, up to a maximum of $1,400 per child in 2018. **(See Determining Filing Status and Dependency Exemptions, Disaster Tax Relief & Airport & Airway Extension Act of 2017,"Special Rule on Earned Income for Earned Income Tax Credit (EITC) and Child Tax Credit Purposes")**

Affordable Care Act (ACA) Premium Tax Credits – On October 18, 2018, the IRS issued Notice 2018-84 that provides guidance on how the suspension of the personal exemption deduction for determining taxable income by the TCJA will affect some of the rules under the ACA for claiming the premium tax credit for health insurance. This guidance can be relied on until the IRS issues regulations to clarify how the rules should apply. The guidance states that (1) taxpayers are considered to have claimed a personal exemption for themselves if they file a return in 2018 and don't

qualify as a dependent of another taxpayer, and (2) taxpayers are considered to have claimed a personal exemption for individuals they list on Form 1040 or on Form 1040NR for the year. **(See Income Tax, "Personal Exemptions");** **(See Determining Filing Status and Dependency Exemptions, "Dependents"); (See "Affordable Care Act")**
https://www.irs.gov/pub/irs-drop/n-18-84.pdf

Non-Refundable Tax Credits:

Savers Credit – The TCJA allows the designated beneficiary of an ABLE account to claim the Savers Tax Credit in an amount equal to 10% to 50% of the annual contributions to his/her ABLE account based on the filing status and adjusted gross income (AGI) of the designated beneficiary, limited to a maximum savers credit of $1,000. This change is applicable for tax years 2018 – 2025. **(See Non-Taxable Income, "Distributions from ABLE Accounts")**

The Savers Credit is for low-income taxpayers who have made elective contributions to tax deferred employee 401(k), 403(b), 457, SIMPLE IRA, and SEP IRA retirement plans, as well as to both traditional and Roth IRAs. You can take the credit regardless of the deductibility of the contributions, i.e. if your traditional IRA contributions are deductible, you can still take the Savers Credit if you qualify. The maximum Savers Credit you can claim is 50%, 20%, or 10% of the first $2,000 you contribute to a retirement account, and any unused credit can be carried forward. To be eligible for the credit a taxpayer must be at least age 18, not a full-time student, and not claimed as a dependent by someone else. The savers credit is reported on Form 8880, "Credit for Qualified Retirement Savings Contributions."
www.irs.gov/pub/irs-pdf/f8880.pdf

Child Tax Credit – The TCJA doubles the Child Tax Credit to $2,000 for each "qualifying child" for tax years 2018 – 2025, with the refundable portion (Additional Child Tax Credit) equal to 15% of earned income greater than $2,500, up to a maximum of $1,400 per child in 2018. The credit is $2,000 per qualifying child in 2018, but the credit is subject to cost of living increases in 2019 and subsequent years. In 2018, the credit is phased-out at $50 per $1,000 or fraction thereof on incomes over the following thresholds: $400,000 for married couples filing jointly and $200,000 for all others. Also, for tax years 2018 – 2025, the TCJA establishes a new $500 nonrefundable tax credit applicable to qualifying dependents, other than qualifying children, who are U.S. citizens or residents. To be eligible for the maximum $2,000 credit, a child must be issued a Social Security number by the due date of the tax return. In addition to other qualifying dependents, the $500 nonrefundable tax credit applies to a qualifying child under 17 who doesn't have a Social Security number by the due date of the tax return, e.g. a child who has an Individual Tax Identification number (ITIN) instead of a Social Security number is only eligible for the $500 nonrefundable tax credit. Unused credits in a year can be carried forward to future years if not refundable in the current year. The child tax credit is allowed against the Alternative Minimum Tax (AMT), and the refundable portion is not reduced by the AMT. **(See Above, "Additional Child Tax Credit"); (See "Alternative Minimum Tax")**

On Sept. 29, 2017, the "Disaster Tax Relief and Airport and Airway Extension Act of 2017" was passed, which provides temporary tax relief to victims of Hurricanes Harvey, Irma, and Maria. The Act provides that, in case a "qualified taxpayer's" earned income, which includes the applicable dates shown below, is less than the taxpayer's earned income for the preceding tax year, then the taxpayer may elect, for purposes of the EITC and the Child Tax Credit, to substitute the earned income for the preceding year for the earned income for the current tax year in computing the EITC and the Child Tax Credit for the current year. For Hurricane Harvey, a "qualified taxpayer" is one whose principal place of abode on Aug. 23, 2017 was located either in the Hurricane Harvey disaster zone, or in the Hurricane Harvey disaster area and the individual was displaced from their principal place of abode by reason of Hurricane Harvey.

Similar definitions apply for Hurricanes Irma (using a Sept. 4, 2017 date) and Hurricane Maria (using a Sept. 16, 2017 date). In the case of joint filers, the above election may apply if either spouse is a qualified individual. **(See Determining Filing Status and Dependency Exemptions, Disaster Tax Relief & Airport & Airway Extension Act of 2017, "Special Rule on Earned Income for Earned Income Tax Credit (EITC) and Child Tax Credit Purposes")**

Due diligence applies to tax preparers regarding the Child Tax Credit. A $500 penalty (adjusted for inflation) will apply to tax preparers who fail to comply with the due diligence requirements, including filing Form 8867. **(See Above, "Earned Income Tax Credit (EITC)"**

Nonbusiness Energy Property Credit – The nonbusiness energy property credit was originally unavailable in 2017. But in February 2018, it was retroactively extended to the 2017 tax year by the Bipartisan Budget Act of 2018. However, it is not available in 2018. The credit is worth up to 10% of the amount paid for allowable energy-efficient home improvements to your principal residence (not a new home) up to a lifetime maximum of $500. The credit is from $50 to $500, but you can take advantage of the credit only if you didn't take advantage of at least $500 of the $1,500 aggregate credit offered in 2009 and 2010, or you had not already taken advantage of credits in prior years (since 2005) of $500 or more. The credit is available for: home insulation; exterior doors; exterior windows and skylights; metal and certain asphalt roofs designed to reduce heat loss or gain; electric heat pumps; electric heat pump water heaters; central air conditioning systems; natural gas, propane or oil hot water heaters; stoves that use biomass fuel; natural gas, propane or oil furnaces; natural gas, propane or oil hot water boilers; and advanced main air-circulating fans for natural gas, propane or oil furnaces. Of the combined $500 lifetime allowable credit, there are limits on certain items: for example, a maximum credit of $200 can be claimed for windows and skylights; a maximum credit of $150 can be claimed for water heaters and furnaces; a maximum credit of $300 can be claimed for biomass fuel stoves; and a maximum credit of $50 can be claimed for an advanced main air circulating fan. The credit is claimed on Form 5695.
www.irs.gov/pub/irs-pdf/f5695.pdf) www.irs.gov/pub/irs-pdf/i5695.pdf
www.congress.gov/115/bills/hr1892/BILLS-115hr1892enr.pdf
www.congress.gov/bill/115th-congress/house-bill/1892/text#toc-H514FC9B8F1BC41E3B61ED883360ECDA1

Residential Energy Property Credit – The credit for solar panels and solar energy systems installed in your residence is available in 2017 through the 2019 tax year and then phases out and ends after 2021. But the rest of the credit was originally unavailable in 2017. But in February 2018, the credit for wind turbines, geothermal heat pumps, and fuel cell equipment was retroactively extended to match the availability of the credit for solar panels and solar energy systems (2017 through the 2019 tax year and phasing out through 2021). The credit is worth up to 30% of the total cost of installing certain renewable energy sources in your home and is not restricted to your primary residence (except for fuel cell equipment) and can be claimed for newly constructed homes. However, the home must be located in the United States. You can claim a credit of 30% of the total cost of solar panels and solar energy systems installed in your residence in 2018, and there is no upper limit on the amount of this credit. You can claim the credit for geothermal heat pumps, small wind turbines up to $4,000, and fuel cells in 2017 and 2018. The maximum credit that can be claimed for fuel cells is $500 for each 0.5 kilowatt of power capacity.

If your credit is more than the tax you owe, you can carry forward the unused portion of the credit to next year's tax return. Following is the phaseout schedule for the credits available for solar panels and solar energy systems, geothermal heat pumps, wind turbines, and fuel cells: 2017 (30% credit); 2018 (30% credit); 2019 (30% credit); 2020 (26% credit); and 2021 (22% credit). The credit is claimed on Form 5695. **(See Above, "Nonbusiness Energy Property Credit")**

Non-Refundable Business Tax Credits:

Rehabilitation Credit – Beginning in 2018, the TCJA eliminates the 10% credit for qualified expenditures on buildings placed in service before 1936. The TCJA retains the 20% credit for qualified expenditures on certified historic structures but specifies that the credit has to be taken ratably over 5 years starting with the date the rehabilitated structure is placed in service. Before 2018, the entire credit could be taken in the year the structure was placed in service. A transition rule is also provided for certain buildings owned or leased at all times on and after January 1, 2018. The rehabilitation credit applies to costs incurred for rehabilitation and reconstruction of certain buildings. Rehabilitation includes renovation, restoration, and reconstruction. It does not include enlargement or new construction. Also, the credit is not allowed for expenditures with respect to property that is considered to be tax-exempt use property. The credit is claimed on Form 3468.

www.irs.gov/pub/irs-pdf/f3468.pdf   www.irs.gov/pub/irs-pdf/i3468.pdf

Orphan Drug Credit – Prior to 2018, the Orphan Drug Tax Credit provided a credit of 50% of clinical drug testing costs for drugs being tested under Section 505(i) of the Federal Food, Drug and Cosmetic Act. However, the TCJA cuts the credit in half from 50% to 25% beginning in 2018. Taxpayers that claim the full 25% credit have to reduce the amount of any otherwise allowable deduction for the expenses regardless of limitations under the general business credit.

Similarly, taxpayers that capitalize, rather than deduct their expenses have to reduce the amount charged to their capital account. However, the TCJA gives taxpayers the option of taking a reduced credit that if elected allows them to avoid reducing otherwise allowable deductions or charges to their capital account. The election for the reduced credit for any tax year must be made no later than the time for filing the tax return for that year (including extensions). Once the reduced credit election is made, it is irrevocable. The credit is claimed on Form 8820.

The orphan drug credit provides an incentive for pharmaceutical companies to seek treatments and cures for rare diseases affecting Americans. Normally, companies may not be motivated to make a drug for a small population because sales may be insufficient to justify the research and development costs of creating the drug.

www.irs.gov/pub/irs-access/f8820_accessible.pdf

Energy Efficient Homebuilder Credit – The Energy Efficient Homebuilder credit was originally unavailable in 2017, but in February 2018 the Bipartisan Budget Act of 2018 reinstated this credit for homes constructed in 2017. Any

445

qualified homes constructed prior to January 1, 2018 are eligible for this credit. Homes constructed on or after January 1, 2018 are not eligible for the credit. Tax credits of up to $2,000 are provided to builders of all new energy-efficient homes, including manufactured homes constructed in accordance with the Federal Manufactured Homes Construction and Safety Standards. Initially scheduled to expire at the end of 2007, the tax credit was extended several times, and expired at the end of 2017.

Newly constructed homes qualify for a $2,000 credit if they are certified to reduce heating and cooling energy consumption by 50% relative to the International Energy Conservation Code (IECC) of 2006 and meet minimum efficiency standards established by the Department of Energy. Building envelope component improvements must account for at least one-fifth of the reduction in energy consumption. Manufactured homes qualify for a $2,000 credit if they conform to Federal Manufactured Home Construction and Safety Standards and meet the energy savings requirements of site-built homes described above. Manufactured homes qualify for a $1,000 credit if they conform to Federal Manufactured Home Construction and Safety Standards and reduce energy consumption by 30% relative to IECC of 2006. In this case, building envelope component improvements must account for at least one-third of the reduction in energy consumption. Alternatively, manufactured homes can also qualify for a $1,000 credit if they meet ENERGY STAR Labeled Home requirements. The credit is claimed on Form 8908. www.irs.gov/pub/irs-pdf/f8908.pdf

Alternative Fuel Vehicle Refueling Property Credit – The Alternative Fuel Vehicle Refueling Property Credit was originally unavailable in 2017, because it was only extended through 2016 by the "Protecting Americans from Tax Hikes Act of 2015." But in February 2018, the Bipartisan Budget Act of 2018 extended the credit through December 31, 2017. However, unless it is extended again, it is not available in 2018. Taxpayers are allowed a 30% credit for the cost of installation of qualified alternative fuel vehicle refueling property, which includes commercial and retail refueling stations placed in service in 2017 – any fuel at least 85% of which consists of one or more of the following: ethanol, natural gas, compressed natural gas, liquified natural gas, liquefied petroleum gas, or hydrogen; any mixture which consists of two or more of the following: biodiesel, diesel fuel, or kerosene and at least 20% of the volume of which consists of biodiesel determined without regard to any kerosene in such mixture; or electricity. The credit is claimed on Form 8911. www.irs.gov/pub/irs-pdf/f8911.pdf   www.irs.gov/pub/irs-pdf/i8911.pdf

Employee Retention Tax Credit for Employers Affected by Hurricanes Harvey, Irma and Maria On Sept. 29, 2017, the "Disaster Tax Relief and Airport and Airway Extension Act of 2017" was passed, which provides temporary tax relief to victims of Hurricanes Harvey, Irma, and Maria. The Act provides a new "employee retention credit" for "eligible employers" affected by Hurricanes Harvey, Irma, and Maria. Eligible employers are generally defined as employers that conducted an active trade or business in a disaster zone as of a specified date (for Hurricane Harvey, Aug. 23, 2017; Irma, Sept. 4, 2017; and Maria, Sept. 16, 2017), and the active trade or business on any day between the specified dates and Jan. 1, 2018, were rendered inoperable as a result of damage sustained by the hurricanes. In general, the credit is equals to 40% of up to $6,000 of "qualified wages" with respect to each "eligible employee" of such employer for the tax year. Therefore, the maximum credit per employee is $2,400 ($6,000 × 40%).

- **Example** – Employer Y is an eligible employer in the Hurricane Harvey disaster zone. Y has two eligible employees, A and B, to whom Y pays qualified wages of $4,000 and $6,000 respectively. Y is entitled to

446

a total credit of $4,000; $1,600 for the wages paid to A ($4,000 × 40%) and $2,400 for the wages paid to B ($6,000 × 40%).

An eligible employee with respect to an eligible employer is one whose principal place of employment with the employer was in the Hurricane Harvey, Irma, or Maria disaster zones. Qualified wages are wages paid or incurred by an eligible employer to an eligible employee on any day after the specified dates (See above) and before Jan. 1, 2018. An employee cannot be taken into account more than one time for purposes of the employee retention tax credit. So, for instance, if an employee is an eligible employee of an employer with respect to Hurricane Harvey for purposes of the credit, the employee cannot also be an eligible employee with respect to Hurricane Irma or Hurricane Maria. An eligible employee cannot be "related" to an employer. The credit is claimed on Form 5884a. **(See Determining Filing Status and Dependency Exemptions, Disaster Tax Relief & Airport & Airway Extension Act of 2917, "Employee Retention Tax Credit for Employers")** www.irs.gov/pub/irs-pdf/f5884a.pdf   www.irs.gov/pub/irs-dft/i5884a--dft.pdf

Paid Family and Medical Leave Credit – The TCJA adds a new credit to the general business credit that is available to employers with a written family and medical leave policy for full and part time employees who are on family and medical leave. The credit is temporary – available only for employer years beginning in 2018 and 2019 and won't be available for employer tax years beginning in 2020 or later, unless extended by Congress. The credit is available to employers as long as the amount paid to employees on family and medical leave is at least 50% of their normal wages, and the payments are made in 2018 and 2019. Paid leave provided as vacation leave, personal leave, or other medical or sick leave is not considered family and medical leave. For payments of 50% of normal wages, the credit is 12.5% of wages paid to employees while they are on leave. If the leave payment is more than 50% of normal wages, the credit is raised by .25% for each 1% by which the leave payment is more than 50% of normal wages. So, if the leave payment is 100% of normal wages, the credit is 25% of an employee's normal wages. The maximum leave payment allowed for any employee for any tax year is 12 weeks.

Employers must have a written policy in place allowing: (1) qualifying full-time employees at least 2 weeks of paid family and medical leave a year, and (2) less than full-time employees a pro-rated amount of family and medical leave. Qualifying employees are those who (1) have been employed by the employer for one year or more, and (2) in the preceding year, had compensation not above 60% of the compensation threshold for highly compensated employees under the qualified retirement plan rules.

On October 3, 2018, the IRS issued Notice 2018-71 which answers 34 questions about the Paid Family and Medical Leave Credit. For purposes of the credit, the reasons an employee may take a family or medical leave are the same as those for which an employee may take leave under Title I of the Family and Medical Leave Act of 1993 (FMLA), P.L. 103-3. If an employer employs qualifying employees who are not covered by Title I of the FMLA, the employer's written policy must include language providing "non-interference" protections, as described in Section A of Notice 2018-71. Thus, the written policy must incorporate the substantive rules that must be met for an employer to be eligible for the credit. Any leave paid by a state or local government or required by state or local law is not taken into account for any purpose in determining the amount of paid family and medical leave provided by the employer, meaning those amounts do not qualify for the credit. For purposes of the credit, an employer is any person for whom an individual performs services as an employee under the usual common law rules applicable in determining the employer-employee relationship. Wages qualifying for the credit are determined under the Federal

447

Unemployment Tax Act (FUTA) rules but disregarding the $7,000 FUTA wage limit.
www.irs.gov/pub/irs-drop/n-18-71.pdf   www.gpo.gov/fdsys/pkg/STATUTE-107/pdf/STATUTE-107-Pg6.pdf

Tax-Credit Bonds – Tax-credit bonds provide tax credits to investors to replace part of the portion of the interest they have to pay on the bonds. The subsidy or credits are generally determined by reference to the credit rate set by the Department of the Treasury. Qualified tax credit bonds have certain common general requirements, and include clean renewable energy bonds, new clean renewable energy bonds, qualified energy conservation bonds, qualified zone academy bonds, qualified school construction bonds, qualified forestry conservation bonds, and Build America Bonds. The TCJA repeals the authority to issue tax-credit bonds and direct-pay bonds after December 31, 2017, but the repeal does not affect the tax treatment of existing obligations.

The TCJA also repeals the election that allows an issuer of tax credit bonds to receive a payment in lieu of the holder receiving a credit and a provision that permits an eligible taxpayer that holds a qualified zone academy bond to claim a credit against taxable income. **(See Exclusions from Taxable Income, "Advance Refunding Bonds")**

Business Structures and Provisions

Hobby Expenses Are Not Deductible – Hobby income is reported as "Other Income," on Form 1040, and is not subject to self-employment tax. In 2017 and prior years, hobby expenses were deductible as a miscellaneous itemized deduction subject to the 2% AGI floor, but only to the extent of income from the activity. Therefore, a loss was not allowed. In accordance with the Tax Cuts and Jobs Act (TCJA), the deduction for miscellaneous itemized deductions subject to the 2% of adjusted gross income (AGI) floor is eliminated for tax years 2018 – 2025. Therefore, a deduction for hobby expenses is no longer allowed in 2018. Some expenses that may be related to a hobby may be deductible anyway, such as mortgage interest and property taxes that are still deductible as itemized deductions. For entities such as limited partnerships, the hobby loss rule applies to tax shelters, which are investments structured to provide favorable tax treatment, and may be used to deny deductions to the partners or shareholders if the entity was set-up primarily to generate large tax losses and not to make a profit. **(See Itemized Deductions, "Hobby Expenses")**

Accounting Method Changes Under the Tax Cuts and Jobs Act (TCJA) – The TCJA includes several accounting method changes that are effective beginning in 2018 that involve the overall method of accounting for a business, and several changes that affect certain types of businesses. Most of the changes are favorable for businesses, and unlike most of the changes involving personal income taxes, the accounting method changes for businesses are permanent. Revenue Procedure 2018-40 outlines how eligible existing small business taxpayers can obtain automatic consent to change accounting methods that are now permitted under the Tax Cuts and Jobs Act (TCJA). New businesses can simply start using the appropriate method under the TCJA in 2018. A 4-year adjustment period will be allowed if a change in accounting method increases taxable income.
www.irs.gov/pub/irs-pdf/f3115.pdf   www.irs.gov/pub/irs-pdf/i3115.pdf
www.irs.gov/pub/irs-drop/rp-18-40.pdf

Cash Method of Accounting – Effective for the 2018 tax year, the TCJA allows cash basis accounting for all businesses including C-corporations (except for "tax shelters") when their average gross receipts (revenues) for the three preceding years are less than $25 million (indexed for inflation beginning in 2019). This is more

448

favorable for businesses than the $5 million threshold that was in effect in 2017 and prior years. The same $25 million threshold also applies to partnerships with C-corporation partners. Under cash basis accounting, transactions are recorded when the corresponding cash is received or payments are made. Revenue is recognized when payments are received and expenses are recognized when they are paid. Thus, you record revenue only when a customer pays for a billed product or service, and you record a payable only when it is actually paid by the company.

Accrual Method of Accounting – Under the accrual basis of accounting, the "matching principle" governs the recognizing of income in the books for financial accounting purposes. The tax law is largely unconcerned with the matching principle. Therefore, for tax purposes, an accrual basis taxpayer is required to recognize income when "all events" have occurred to fix the taxpayer's right to the income and the amount can be determined with reasonable accuracy, which would be the earlier of three dates: the date on which the income is earned, due, or received. Expenses are recognized when it is established that the company owes the bill regardless of when it is actually paid. Under the TCJA, effective for the 2018 tax year, accrual basis businesses are permitted to defer the reporting of advance payments to the next year, but income deferrals are prohibited beyond the year when the income is recognized on the applicable financial statements.

Inventory Accounting – Beginning in 2018, businesses with inventories that satisfy the $25 million revenue test can now use cash basis accounting and account for their inventories as non-incidental materials and supplies or use their financial accounting treatment for inventories (See above – cash method of accounting). In 2017 and prior years there were two exceptions to the accrual basis accounting requirement: (1) certain small business's average annual gross receipts (based on the prior 3 years) did not exceed $1 million; and (2) businesses in certain industries had annual gross receipts (based on the prior 3 tax years) did not exceed $10 million.

Under the TCJA, producers or resellers with average annual gross receipts of $25 million or less are exempt from the UNICAP rules (Revenue Code Section 263A) with respect to personal property acquired for resale. This exemption applies to both resellers and manufacturers. In 2017 and prior years, a business with $10 million or less in average annual gross receipts were exempt from the UNICAP rule with respect to property acquired for resale. **(See Above, "Cash Method of Accounting")**
www.irs.gov/pub/irs-drop/rr-05-53.pdf

Long-Term Contract Accounting – The $25 million revenue test applies when defining what a "small contractor" is for purposes of Internal Revenue Code 460 and the long-term contract accounting rules. Businesses that fall under the $25 million average are allowed to use the completed contract method for contracts entered into during tax years beginning after December 31, 2017. The threshold before 2018 was $10 million. In Shea Homes v. Commissioner, the Ninth Circuit Court of Appeals ruled that developers using the completed contract method should report net income only on completion of the development and not for each home. However, the IRS will not follow that ruling outside of the Ninth Circuit. www.gpo.gov/fdsys/granule/USCODE-2013-title26/USCODE-2013-title26-subtitleA-chap1- subchapE-partII-subpartB-sec460 www.irs.gov/pub/irs-utl/Construction_ATG.pdf

For accrual basis businesses, the completed contract method is used to recognize all of the revenue and profits associated with a project only after the project has been completed. This method is used when there is uncertainty about the collection of funds due from a customer under the terms of a contract. This method yields the same results as the percentage of completion method but only after a project has been completed. Prior to completion, this method does not yield any useful information for the reader of a company's financial statements. However, the delay in income recognition allows a business to defer the recognition of related income taxes.

Deferred Revenue/Advance payments – Generally revenue can only be deferred if it is deferred for financial statement purposes. This affects both one-year and two-year deferral items. Essentially, this codifies the IRS position taken in Revenue Procedure 2004-34 on the issue, meaning that for accrual basis businesses, advance payments can only be deferred to the next year but, in any case, are prohibited from being deferred beyond the year when the income is shown on the applicable financial statements. Not all financial statements are applicable financial statements, so you will need to review that definition, which has changed from the definition in Revenue Procedure 2004-34. This deferral change doesn't apply to long- term contract accounting or installment sale reporting.
www.irs.gov/pub/irs-drop/rp-04-34.pdf

Research and Experimental Expense Accounting – The TCJA specifies that research and experimental (R&E) expenditures and software development costs paid or incurred in tax years beginning after December 31, 2021, should be capitalized and amortized ratably over a 5-year period, beginning with the midpoint of the tax year in which the R&E expenditures are paid or incurred. Also, R&E expenditures paid or incurred outside of the United States should be capitalized and amortized ratably over a 15-year period after December 31, 2021. The "United States" includes Puerto Rico and other U.S. possessions. In the event of abandonment, retirement or disposal of property included in R&E expenditures, no immediate write off of the unamortized portion is allowed, but instead such property must continue to be amortized over the remaining amortization period. Currently, in 2018, R&E expenditures and software development costs can be expensed in the year in which the expenses are incurred, or a company may elect to defer the expenses and deduct them ratably over a period of not less than 60 months. And, of course, the R&D tax credit is still available in 2018 and subsequent years.

Business Interest Expense Limitation – Under the TCJA, businesses are not allowed to deduct business interest expenses exceeding the sum of: (1) business interest income; (2) 30% of the adjusted taxable income of the business; and (3) the floor-plan financing interest of the business. Business interest expense is considered any interest paid or accrued on indebtedness properly allocable to a trade or business. Indexing for inflation begins in 2019. Any disallowed business interest deduction can be carried forward indefinitely. For S-corporations, partnerships and limited liability corporations that are treated as partnerships for tax purposes, this limit is applied at the entity level rather than at the owner level. The new limitation is effective for tax years beginning after December 31, 2017, so it is effective for the 2018 tax year. The limitation applies to all businesses with average annual gross receipts greater than $25 million for the prior three tax years. Floor plan financing is a type of short-term loan used by retailers to purchase high-cost inventory such as automobiles. These loans are generally secured by the inventory purchased as collateral and is commonly used in new and used car dealerships.

Businesses, such as utility companies, are not subject to the business interest limitation if they furnish or sell any of the following: electrical energy, water, or sewage disposal services; gas or steam through a local distribution system; or transportation of gas or steam by pipeline.

Taxpayers engaged in a real property business, including real estate development, construction, rental, management, or brokerage business, among others, may elect to not have the interest limitation apply to their business, and the election is irrevocable. However, when businesses elect not to have the limitation apply, they are required to use the alternative depreciation system (ADS) for their nonresidential real property, residential rental property, and qualified improvement property.

Taxpayers engaged in the farming business may elect out of the interest limitation, and the election is irrevocable. However, an electing farm business is required to use the alternative depreciation system (ADS) – with its accompanying restriction on using bonus depreciation and longer depreciation recovery period – for any asset with a useful life of more than 10 years, including land improvements, barns, and other farm buildings in years beginning after 2017. **(See Self-Employed/Independent Contractors, Farmers and Ranchers, "Business Interest Deduction")**

- **Computing the Business Interest Limitation** – a taxpayer's deduction for net business interest is limited to 30% of adjusted taxable income, which is taxable income without taking into account: (1) Non-business income, like gains from the sale of assets held for investment; (2) Business interest expense or business interest income; (3) Net operating loss deductions; (4) The 20% qualified business income deduction (the TCJA includes new Code 199A which allows a deduction of 20% for certain pass-through income); and (5) Depreciation, amortization, or depletion.

The limitation does not apply to investment interest. The adjustment for depreciation, amortization, or depletion applies only through 2021, so the limitation will be much more restrictive for capital-intensive businesses for tax years starting in 2022.

The deduction for floor plan interest — which is interest on debt incurred to finance a dealer's purchase of motor vehicle inventory for sale or lease — is not limited. However, most businesses that have floor plan financing will not be able to claim the new 100% bonus depreciation deduction (beginning in 2018) with respect to any of their asset purchases.

- **Example** – Ace Company is a C-corporation that has the following items of income and expense during the 2018 tax year:

Gross receipts	$ 150
Interest income	5
Cost of goods sold	(100)
Interest expense	(30)
Depreciation	(10)
Taxable income before Interest expense limitation	$ 15

451

Ace Company's interest expense deduction is computed as follows:

Taxable income before interest limitation		$15
Add back: net interest expense		30
Add back: depreciation		10
Adjusted taxable income		$55
Multiply by 30%	X	30%
Equals: business interest expense limitation		$17

Therefore, Ace Company's deduction for net interest expense is limited to $17 in 2018, resulting in disallowance of $13 of interest expense ($30 – $17 = $13)

Lobbying Expenses – The TCJA disallows the deduction for lobbying expenses at the local level after December 22, 2017 – lobbying for legislation before local government bodies (including Indian tribal governments). This exclusion conforms to what were already nondeductible lobbying and political expenditures at all other levels of government in 2017 and prior years. However, expenses associated with other common local government affairs, such as monitoring legislation, attempts to influence rules and regulations, and relationship building at the local government level, are considered deductible as ordinary and necessary business expenses. Deduction for Penalties – The TCJA disallows the deduction for fines and penalties related to a violation of law paid to or at the direction of a government or governmental entity on or after December 22, 2017, except for the following 3 exceptions: amounts constituting restitution; certain court-ordered amounts; and penalties on taxes due.

Sexual Harassment – The TCJA disallows deductions related to any settlement, payout, or attorney fees related to sexual harassment or sexual abuse if such payments are subject to a nondisclosure agreement, effective on or after December 22, 2017.

Excess Business Losses Under the Tax Cuts and Jobs Act (TCJA) – Beginning in 2018, and for tax years 2018 – 2025, the TCJA restricts the use of excess business losses by individuals if the taxpayer's losses from all pass-through trades or businesses exceeds the taxpayer's income from all pass-through trades or businesses by more than $250,000 ($500,000 for taxpayers who file joint returns). The $250,000/$500,000 amount is adjusted for inflation in years after 2018. The excess business loss limitation is applied after the passive loss rules. This means that if a loss is disallowed under the passive activity loss rules, income and deductions from that activity would not be included in the excess business loss calculation. Excess business losses aren't allowed for the current tax year but are instead carried forward and treated as part of the taxpayer's net operating loss (NOL) carryforward to subsequent tax years where they can be used to offset 80% of subsequent years' taxable income (starting in 2018, net operating losses can't be carried back to prior years). In 2017 and prior years, all business losses recognized by individuals could reduce non-business income after the passive loss rules were applied. **(See Non-Taxable Income, "Net Operating Loss (NOL)")**

Several questions exist in regard to this new provision, including how "excess business losses" carried over will be synchronized with the "qualified business income deduction" (Code 199A which allows a deduction of 20% for certain pass-through income). **(See Below, "20% Deduction Allowed on Passed-Through QBI (Section 199A)")**

<u>20% Deduction Allowed on Passed-Through Qualified Business Income (Section 199A)</u> – Under the Tax Cuts and Jobs Act (TCJA), a deduction of up to 20% is allowed on qualified business income (QBI) passed-through to taxpayers for tax years beginning after December 31, 2017 and ending on December 31, 2025 (eight years). A qualified trade or business for this purpose is the same as the definition of a qualified business under Section 162, i.e. the primary purpose of the business must be for income or profit and the owner(s) must be actively engaged in the operation of the business. This includes passthrough entities such as sole proprietorships, partnerships, S-corporations, limited liability companies (LLC), and limited liability partnerships (LLP). These types of businesses pay no taxes themselves, but instead profits (or losses) are passed through to the individual owners, partners or shareholders (individual taxpayers) who are active participants in the businesses and pay taxes on their individual tax returns, and in the case of these passthrough entities, the 20% deduction is determined at the owner, partner or shareholder level. **And for purposes of this provision individual taxpayers include trusts and estates.** Of course, this means that income from passthrough entities that are passive trades or businesses are not eligible for the 20% deduction.

There is one special exception to the qualified trade or business rule – the 20% deduction is available for rental or licensing of tangible or intangible property to a commonly controlled business (self-rental rule) which will benefit those who are in the business of renting property or providing services to a commonly controlled business. This is a special case where direct real estate investment automatically counts as a trade or business and qualifies for the 20% deduction – when someone rents property to another trade or business they own at least 50% of. For example, if you rent an office building to a corporation or partnership that qualifies as a trade or business and you own at least 50% of that business, your rental property by law counts as a qualified trade or business.

So, what about rental real estate, is it considered a qualified trade or business? Well it depends – if you are in the business of renting or leasing rental property it may be a qualified trade or business depending on what kind and how many properties are being rented or leased, how actively involved you are in the business, the types of rentals, terms of the leases, etc. Therefore, rental real estate businesses may be eligible for the 20% Section 199A deduction if they rise to the level a qualified trade or business which is considered regular, continuous, and with a profit motive.

When taxpayers have passthrough income from a sole proprietorship, partnership, S- corporation or other passthrough entity, their maximum Section 199A deduction is 20% of their qualified business income (QBI) from each of their non-passive, for-profit trades or businesses. An individual taxpayer's qualified business income (QBI) for the tax year is the net amount of domestic qualified items of income, gain, deduction, and loss (determined by taking-into- account only items included in the determination of taxable income) with respect to the taxpayer's business. If the amount of qualified business income for a tax year is less than zero (i.e., a loss), the loss is treated as a loss from qualified businesses in the next tax year. Under the "abrogation rule," profitable trades or businesses can be offset against those with losses.

The QBI of each qualified trade or business must be determined separately, i.e. the 20% deduction has to be figured separately for each business. And when a taxpayer's annual taxable income is $315,000 or less for married individuals filing jointly or $157,500 for non-joint filers, the only limitation is that the allowable 20% deduction is either 20% of QBI or 20% of taxable income, whichever is less. The deduction is available to taxpayers that itemize deductions, as well as those that do not.

A taxpayer's taxable income for Section 199A purposes is taxable income on which federal income tax is owed (not taking-into-account any Section 199A deduction that may be available), i.e. all deductions available must be deducted in determining adjusted gross income (AGI), and either the standard deduction or itemized deductions must be deducted in determining taxable income. The 20% deduction is not allowed in computing AGI; instead, it is allowed as a deduction in reducing final taxable income (but not for Section 199A purposes). Also, any interest income, qualified dividends (non-REIT dividends), and capital gains included in taxable income must be deducted in determining taxable income for purposes of computing the Section 199A deduction.

The QBI for each trade or business is the "net amount" of income, gains, deductions, and losses for each business, but excluding reasonable compensation paid by the business to the owner, guaranteed payments to partners of a partnership under Section 707(c), and other allowable payments in accordance with Section 707(a). Specifically, QBI does not include an amount paid to a shareholder/owner of an S-corporation as reasonable compensation (generally included on a Form W-2). Further, it does not include a payment by a partnership to a partner in exchange for services, regardless of whether that payment is characterized as a guaranteed payment or one made to a partner acting outside his or her partner capacity. The Section 199A deduction has no effect on the adjusted basis of a partner's interest in a partnership or a shareholder's basis in S-corporation stock. 20% of any qualified dividends received from: a real estate investment trust (REIT) – other than any portion that is a capital gain dividend; a publicly traded partnership (PTP); and certain cooperatives must be added to QBI for purposes of computing the Section 199A deduction. No QBI deduction is attributable to REIT losses. Qualified publicly traded partnership (PTP) income includes any gain recognized on the sale of an interest in a publicly traded partnership to the extent that gain is characterized as ordinary income under section 751.

W-2 wages reported by a third party that are applicable to more than one trade or business should be allocated to those businesses in the same proportion that total W-2 wages are associated with those businesses.

- **Example** – Ben is a sole proprietor consultant to oil companies who earned net income of $150,000 from his consulting business that is reported on Schedule C, Form 1040. He had no other earned income during the year, but he received $1,000 in qualified dividends and $2,000 in REIT dividends. Ben is single and, therefore, a non-joint filer. His taxable income for filing purposes is $141,000 computed as follows ($150,000 +$1,000 + $2,000 = $153,000 minus $12,000 standard deduction = $141,000). But for purposes of computing his Section 199A deduction his taxable income is $140,000 ($141,000 minus $1,000 in qualified dividends = $140,000). So, Ben's annual taxable income is below the $157,500 cap for a single filer. Ben's qualified business income (QBI) is $150,000. His Section 199A deduction based on his QBI would $30,400 computed as follows: $150,000 X 20% = $30,000 + (20% X $2,000 REIT dividends = $400) = $30,400. His Section 199A deduction based on this taxable income is $28,000 ($140,000 X 20% = $28,000). So,

454

Ben's allowable Section 199A deduction for the year is $28,000, because it is less than the $30,400 based on his QBI. Ben's $150,000 taxable income reported on Schedule C is subject to self-employment tax.

- **Example** – Charles is a 25% partner in a law firm that had net earnings of $800,000; therefore, his share of the annual net passthrough earnings from the partnership is $200,000. Charles' wife also works as an employee for a manufacturing company and she earned a salary of $100,000 for the year. Charles and his wife had no other income. Therefore, their taxable income for both filing and Section 199A deduction purposes is $276,000 computed as follows: ($200,000 + $100,000 = $300,000 minus $24,000 standard deduction = $276,000), which is below the $315,000 cap for joint filers. Charles' QBI is $200,000, so his allowable Section 199A deduction based on QBI is $40,000 ($200,000 X 20% = $40,000), which is less than what it would be based on taxable income, which would be $55,200 ($276,000 X 20% = $55,200). Charles' $200,000 passthrough share of partnership income is reported on Schedule K-1 (1065) and is subject to self-employment tax.

When your taxable income is more than $315,000 (married filing jointly), or $157,500 (non-joint filers), calculating your Section 199A deduction becomes much more complicated. The first thing you need to do is determine if the business from which you receive passthrough income is a "specified service trade of business." A specified service trade or business (SSTB) is any trade or business activity involving the performance of services in the fields of health, law, accounting, actuarial science, performing arts, consulting, athletics, financial services, brokerage services, any business that involves the performance of services that consist of investment and investment managing, trading, or dealing in securities, partnership interests, or commodities, or any trade or business where the principal asset is the reputation or skill of one or more of its owners or employees (excluding engineering and architecture). In determining whether a business is a SSTB, the meaning of the phrase: "the principal asset is the reputation or skill of an owner or an employee" has raised many questions, but it has generally been determined that under the "Kardashian Rule" a truck driver or similar profession would not be considered a SSTB. Also, under the De minimis rule, a business is not a SSTB if it has gross receipts of $25 million or less in a tax year and less than 10% of its gross receipts are attributable to services, or if the business's gross receipts are greater than $25 million in a tax year, and less than 5% of its gross receipts are attributable to services. Pass-through entities must determine whether it is a specified service trade or business (SSTB) and disclose it to the owners, partners or shareholders of the business.

Passthrough owners, partners, and shareholders of a SSTB are "ineligible" for the 20% Section 199A deduction when their taxable income is above the thresholds of $415,000 (joint filers) and $207,500 (non-joint filers). However, for owners, partners, and shareholders of a qualified trade or business that is not a SSTB (non-service trade or business) there is no such limitation, i.e. a non-service trade or business can have an unlimited amount of taxable income and still be eligible for the 20% Section 199A deduction.

<u>Taxable Income of a SSTB Over $315,000/$157,500 and up to $415,000/$207,500</u> – If your passthrough business is a specified service trade or business (SSTB) and your taxable income is over the $315,000/$157,500 threshold, your pass-through deduction is gradually phased-out until taxable income reaches $415,000/$207,500, i.e. it is phased out over the next $100,000 of taxable income for married individuals filing jointly ($50,000 for other individuals). Your maximum Section 199A deduction is determined based on the same rules discussed

455

above for taxable income up to $315,000/$157,500. It is a maximum deduction of 20% of QBI and the same limitations and parameters are still in effect as previously discussed, but in addition your deduction may not exceed the greater of (1) 50% of your share of W-2 wages paid by the business, or (2) 25% of your share of W-2 wages, plus 2.5% of the acquisition cost of qualified depreciable property used in the business. Therefore, if the business has no employees or no qualified depreciable property, no deduction can be taken. However, if the SSTB has employees, your deduction is phased-out by 1% for every $1,000 your taxable income exceeds the $315,000 threshold for joint filers, and by 2% for every $1,000 your taxable income exceeds the $157,500 threshold for non-joint filers and your allowable deduction is completely phased- out when your taxable income reaches $415,000 (joint filers) and $207,500 (non-joint filers).

A taxpayer's share of "W-2 wages" generally equals the sum of wages subject to withholding, plus elective deferrals and deferred compensation paid by a sole proprietorship, partnership, or S-corporation during a taxable year. The acquisition cost of qualified property is the "unadjusted basis" of the property which is either the purchase price or other means of determining the initial basis of the property (determined immediately after acquisition of the property and before any depreciation) upon acquisition of the property by the business.

Qualified property is all tangible property that is placed in service by the business and is subject to depreciation and: (1) is available for use in the business at the close of the tax year; (2) is used at any point during the tax year in the production of business income; and (3) the depreciable period of the property has not ended before the close of the particular tax year. The depreciable period is the period beginning on the date the property is placed in service by the taxpayer and ending on the later of either 10 years after the date the property is placed in service or the last day of the last full year of the applicable recovery (depreciable) period for the property. In the case of a trust or estate, rules similar to Code section 199 (as in effect on December 1, 2017) would apply for purposes of apportioning between fiduciaries and beneficiaries any W-2 wages and the unadjusted basis of qualified property.

- **Example** – Jack files a joint return and is a 25% partner in a law firm partnership that is a SSTB. The partnership had net taxable income of $1,500,000 for the year of which Jack's allocable passthrough share is $375,000. The partnership's W-2 wages paid to employees of the partnership are $550,000; so, Jack's allocable share of the W-2 wages is equal to $137,500. The partnership's qualified property is equal to $750,000; so, Jack's allocable share of the partnership's qualified property is $187,500. Jack has no other earned income, but his taxable income includes interest income of $15,000 and qualified REIT dividends of $20,000. Therefore, Jack's taxable income before any Section 199A deduction is $386,000, computed as follows: $375,000 + $15,000 + $20,000 minus $24,000 standard deduction = $386,000. However, his taxable income for Section 199A purposes is $371,000 ($386,000 minus $15,000 interest income = $371,000). Jack's QBI is $395,000 ($375,000 passthrough partnership income + $20,000 REIT dividends = $395,000). Jack's 199A deduction is computed as follows: $371,000 taxable income X 20% = $74,200; $395,000 QBI X 20% = $79,000; $137,500 W-2 wages X 50% = $68,750; $137,500 W-2 wages X 25% = $34,375 + $187,500 X 2.5% = $4,688 = $39,063. Therefore, Jack's 199A deduction "before reduction" is $68,750, because $68,750 is greater than $39,063, but less than $74,200 and $79,000. Jack's taxable income for 199A purposes is $371,000. $371,00 minus $315,000 = $56,000; Therefore, the $68,750 deduction is reduced by 56% (1% for every $1,000 taxable income exceeds the $315,000 threshold), computed as follows: $68,750 X 56% = $38,500. So, Jack's allowable Section 199A deduction is $30,250 ($68,750 minus $38,500 = $30,250). Jack's $375,000 passthrough share of partnership income is reported on Schedule K-1 (1065) and is subject to self- employment tax.

Section 199A includes certain "anti-abuse" rules which cannot be ignored. One anti-abuse rule is intended to prevent taxpayers from separating parts of what otherwise would be an aggregated SSTB, such as administrative functions, in an attempt to qualify those separated parts as a non-service related business eligible for the Section 199A deduction when its taxable income exceeds the $415,000/$207,500 thresholds. In order to try to skirt the specified service trade or business (SSTB) rules, you can't divide up a partnership into more than one business if there is 50% common ownership and the partnership provides 80% of its property and services to a SSTB. For example, a law firm might try separate a rental building in which the law firm's offices are located into a separate business that would be classified as a non-service trade or business, but this is not allowed under the rules if the 50% and 80% parameters apply. If you were previously an employee of a company and then become an independent contractor, you are still presumed to be an employee of the company. This is another anti-abuse rule that prevents an employee from trying to game the system by becoming an independent contractor. On the other hand, independent contractors who are working for a company can become employees of the company.

Taxable Income of Non-Service Business Over $315,000/$157,500 and up to
$415,000/$207,500 – If your passthrough business is a non-service trade or business and your taxable income is over the $315,000/$157,500 threshold, your W-2 wages/property limitation is gradually phased-in until taxable income reaches $415,000/$207,500. The W-2 wages/property limitation is phased in over $100,000 for married filing jointly and $50,000 for non-joint filers. At the top of the income range ($415,000 for married filing jointly and $207,500 for singles), your entire deduction is subject to the W-2 wages/property limitation. The same W-2 wage limitation and qualified property limitation applies for a non-service trade or business as applies for a SSTB: your Section 199A deduction may not exceed the greater of (1) 50% of your share of W-2 wages paid by the business, or (2) 25% of your share of W-2 wages, plus 2.5% of the acquisition cost of qualified depreciable property used in the business. Therefore, if the business has no employees or no qualified depreciable property, no deduction can be taken.

For a non-service trade or business the phase-in amount is based on 1% for every $1,000 your qualified business income (QBI) exceeds the $315,000 threshold for joint filers, and 2% for every $1,000 your QBI exceeds the $157,500 threshold for non-joint filers.

Also, the maximum Section 199A deduction is determined based on the same rules discussed above for taxable income up to $315,000/$157,500. It is a maximum deduction of 20% of QBI and the same limitations and parameters are still in effect as previously discussed.

- **Example** – Jack files a joint return and is a 25% partner in a non-service partnership. The partnership had net taxable income of $1,500,000 for the year of which Jack's allocable passthrough share is $375,000. The partnership's W-2 wages paid to employees of the partnership are $550,000; so, Jack's allocable share of the W-2 wages is equal to $137,500. The partnership has no qualified property. Jack has no other earned income, but his taxable income includes interest income of $15,000 and qualified REIT dividends of $20,000. Therefore, Jack's taxable income before any Section 199A deduction is $386,000 computed as follows: $375,000 + $15,000 + $20,000 minus $24,000 standard deduction = $386,000. However, his taxable income for Section 199A purposes is $371,000 ($386,000 minus $15,000 interest income = $371,000). Jack's QBI is $395,000 ($375,000 passthrough partnership income + $20,000 REIT dividends = $395,000). Jack's phase-in percentage is 80%, because his $395,000 QBI is $80,000 more than the $315,000 limit for a joint filer. His Section 199A deduction would be $79,000 ($395,000 QBI X 20% = $79,000) if the taxable income limitation did not apply. His full deduction based on W-2 wages is $68,750 ($137,500 W-2 wages X 50% = $68,750). The difference between the two is $10,250 ($79,000 minus $68,750 = $10,250). This amount ($10,250) is multiplied by the 80% phase-in percentage to determine the phase-in amount, which is $8,200 ($10,250 X 80% = $8,200). The phase-in amount is subtracted from the $79,000 deduction based on QBI, which results in a deduction of $70,800 ($79,000 minus $8,200 = $70,800). Jack's allowable Section 199A deduction is $70,800, because 20% of taxable income is $74,200 which is more than $70,800 ($371,000 taxable income X 20% = $74,200). Jack's $375,000 passthrough share of partnership income is reported on Schedule K-1 (1065) and is subject to self-employment tax.

As previously stated, for owners, partners, and shareholders of a qualified trade or business that is not a SSTB (non-service trade or business) there is no limitation on the amount of taxable income, i.e. a non-service trade or business can have an unlimited amount of taxable income and still be eligible for the 20% Section 199A deduction. Also, as previously stated, 20% of any qualified dividends received from: a real estate investment trust (REIT) – other than any portion that is a capital gain dividend; a publicly traded partnership (PTP); and certain cooperatives must be added to QBI. However, qualified payments or dividends from cooperatives that are added to QBI must be reduced by the lesser of 9% of QBI allocable to cooperative sales or 50% of wages allocable to cooperative sales.

- **Example** – Jane is a partner in a successful accounting firm from which she receives passthrough income reported on Schedule K-1 (1065) in the amount of $450,000. She is also a 25% owner in a non-service S-corporation that reports income of $2,000,000 of which she receives 25% reported on a Schedule K-1 (1020S), which is $500,000. She also is an active participant in the S-Corporation and receives a salary reported on Form W-2 in the amount of $200,000. Also, her share of the W-2 wages of employees of the S-corporation is $100,000 and her share of the qualified property of the S-corporation is $250,000. Also, Jane receives dividends from a cooperative in the amount of $20,000. The accounting firm and the S-corporation are unrelated. The accounting firm is a specified service trade or business (SSTB), so Jane doesn't receive a Section 199A deduction for her QBI from the accounting firm, because the taxable income received from the partnership is over the limit of $415,000 for a SSTB. Her taxable income from the S-corporation is $700,000 ($500,000 K-1 distribution + $200,000 W-2 salary), but her QBI is $500,000 because her compensation from the S-corporation reported on Form W-2 is not included in QBI. Jane's $500,000 QBI from the S-corporation is increased by the $20,000 in cooperative dividends, but in turn, QBI is reduced by the lesser of 9% of QBI allocable to cooperative sales or 50% of wages allocable to cooperative sales. Jane's share of QBI allocable to cooperative sales is $10,000 and her share of wages allocable to cooperative sales is $5,000. So, Jane's QBI is $519,100, computed as follows: $500,000 + $20,000 = $520,000 minus (the lesser of $10,000 X 9% = $900, or $5,000 X 50% = $2,500) = $519,100. Jane's taxable income is $720,000 ($500,000 + $200,000 + $20,000 = $720,000). Therefore, Jane's allowable Section 199A deduction is $50,000, computed as follows: $519,100 QBI X 20% = $103,820; $720,000 taxable income X 20% = $144,000; $100,000 W-2 wages X 50% = $50,000; $100,000 W-2 wages X 25% = $25,000 + $250,000 qualified property X 2.5% = $6,250 + $25,000 = $31,250. Since $50,000 is greater than $31,250, but less than $103,820 and $144,000, Jane's Section 199A deduction is $50,000. NOTE: Jane doesn't have to pay self-employment tax on the $500,000 passed-through to her from the S-corporation reported on Schedule K-1 because the distribution is considered dividends not subject to self-employment tax.

As previously stated, if a qualified business has taxable income in excess of $315,000 (joint filers) or $157,500 (non-joint filers) and has no employees or no qualified depreciable property, no deduction can be taken.

- **Example** – Mary is a single taxpayer who files a Form 1040, and reports her business income on Schedule C. She owns a multi-unit apartment building and several other rental properties. Therefore, this is a non-service business, so she is not constrained by the $207,500 limitation for a specified service trade of business (SSTB). Her taxable income is $300,000. She has no employees. Therefore, her Section 199A deduction is limited to 2.5% of the unadjusted basis of her qualified property, which is the purchase price of the building and the other properties minus the value of the land, and is equal to $600,000. Therefore, her Section 199A deduction is $15,000 ($600,000 X 2.5%= $15,000). Her taxable income in not a factor, because 20% X $300,000 = $60,000. Mary's $300,000 taxable income reported on schedule C is subject to self-employment tax.

As previously stated, a taxpayer's share of "W-2 wages" generally equals the sum of wages subject to withholding, plus elective deferrals and deferred compensation paid by a sole proprietorship, partnership, or S-corporation during a taxable year.

- **Example** – Sam is a 25% partner in a partnership. The partnership's W-2 wages is determined as follows: taxable wages paid to employees of the partnership = $150,000. Non-taxable elective deferrals and deferred compensation of the partnership's employees = $50,000; therefore, the total "W-2 wages" of the partnership = $200,000 ($150,000 + $50,000 = $200,000). Sam's share of the W-2 wages of the partnership for purposes of determining his Section 199A deduction = $50,000 ($$200,000 X 25%= $50,000).

As previously stated, the acquisition cost of qualified property is the "unadjusted basis" of the property which is either the purchase price or other means of determining the initial basis of the property (determined immediately after acquisition of the property and before any depreciation) upon acquisition of the property by the business. Qualified property is all tangible property that is placed in service by the business and is subject to depreciation and: (1) is available for use in the business at the close of the tax year; (2) is used at any point during the tax year in the production of business income; and (3) the depreciable period of the property has not ended before the close of the tax year. The depreciable period is the period beginning on the date the property is placed in service by the taxpayer and ending on the later of either 10 years after the date the property is placed in service or the last day of the last full year of the applicable recovery (depreciable) period for the property.

- **Example** – Sam is a 25% partner in a non-service partnership. The unadjusted basis of the qualified property of the partnership is determined as follows: The purchase price or other initial basis of all qualified property of the partnership that was acquired in years prior to 2018 (no qualified property was acquired in 2018) = $200,000. All of the property of the partnership has been depreciated since its acquisition in accordance with each item of individual property's applicable recovery period, and no item of property has been fully depreciated through 2018. Therefore, Sam's share of the partnership's qualified property for purposes of determining his Section 199A deduction is $50,000 ($200,000 X 25% = $50,000).

The Section 199A deduction is reported on line 9 of the new 1040 postcard form, which is after AGI.

Under proposed regulations, the "New Aggregation Rule" would allow taxpayers to combine businesses that qualify as businesses under Section 162 if the same persons own the businesses being combined, share similar products (cannot be a specified service trade or business (SSTB)), and have the same employees. The owners must be able to demonstrate that the businesses are all a part of an integrated business. The regulations require a "duty of consistency" that requires that once multiple trades or businesses are aggregated, taxpayers must then consistently report the group in following tax years.

In August 2018, the IRS issued proposed regulations concerning the deduction for qualified business income under Section 199A of the Internal Revenue Code. The IRS also issued Notice 2018-64 that provides guidance on methods for calculating W-2 wages for purposes of Section 199A of the Internal Revenue Code.
www.irs.gov/pub/irs-drop/reg-107892-18.pdf   www.irs.gov/pub/irs-drop/n-18-64.pdf

Real Estate Investment Trusts (REIT) – The TCJA provides REIT investors with a 20% tax reduction on pass-through income, which reduces the taxes paid by investors in the highest ordinary income tax bracket from 37% down to 29.6% in 2018 (plus the 3.8% surtax on investment income for certain high-income earners) and shareholders in lower tax brackets have even lower rates on the same dividends. In addition, REIT dividends are excluded from the wage restriction that applies to other pass- through entities under the TCJA, i.e. for REITs, the 20% pass-through deduction is not limited to whichever is greater – 50% of wages paid by the business or 25% of wages, plus 2.5% of the property's original purchase price. Distributions in the form of return of capital are taxed at a rate no higher than the highest capital gain rate of 25%, plus the 3.8% surtax on high-income earners. Under the Foreign Investment in Real Property Tax Act, foreign REIT investors, who were formerly subject to 35% withholding on REIT distributions in 2017 and prior years, are now subject to the 2018 corporate tax rate which is a flat tax of 21%. **(See Above, "20% Deduction Allowed on Passed-Through QBI (Section 199A"); (See Payroll Tax, "0.9% Medicare Surtax"); (See "3.8% Net Investment Income Tax")**

The TCJA brings with it other benefits to REITs that were not there before its implementation. First, there is an exception concerning business interest deductions for REITs. Although most corporate taxpayers can no longer deduct net interest expense exceeding 30% of adjusted taxable income of the business, REITs are allowed to elect out of this rule change as long as they do not use regular MACRS depreciation, i.e. they have to use straight line depreciation if they elect out of the rule. However, regular MACRS depreciation is only used by some REITs to meet their 90% distribution requirement. So, almost all REITs can opt out of the 30% limitation with no consequences. Also, REITs that are formed as partnerships benefit from the elimination of the "technical termination" rule that was in place for partnerships prior to implementation of the TCJA in 2018. The elimination of the technical termination rule by the TCJA provides more flexibility to REITs. **(See Above, "Business Interest Expense Limitation"); (See Partnerships, "Technical Partnership Terminations")**

Workaround by Businesses to Avoid the $10,000 Limit on Deductions for State and Local Taxes (SALT) – Businesses that make business-related payments to charitable programs or government entities for which they receive state or local tax credits will be allowed to deduct the full amount of state and local taxes as charitable business expenses if the payments qualify as ordinary and necessary business expenses (not limited to the $10,000 itemized deduction for state and local taxes allowed by the Tax Cuts and Jobs Act for individuals), and such payments which are authorized by some states in lieu of making state and local tax payments to the states are available to any business taxpayer, regardless of whether it is doing business as a sole proprietor, partnership or S-corporation (passthrough entities). This means that the individual owners of the businesses, partners of partnerships, and shareholders of S-corporations could receive the benefit of the full deduction for their state and local taxes that are more than $10,000 on their individual federal tax returns. However, the individual filers will have to reduce the charitable deductions on their federal tax returns by any credits they receive on their state and local taxes for such contributions.

The IRS makes clear that the longstanding rule allowing businesses to deduct payments to charities as business expenses remains unchanged under the Tax Cuts and Jobs Act. The rule concerning the cap on state and local tax deductions has no impact on federal tax benefits for business-related donations to school choice programs and scholarships (mostly contributions to fund private school scholarships). The IRS states that this won't affect corporations, which aren't subject to the $10,000 limit on state and local tax deductions, but it would apply to pass-through entities such as partnerships and S-corporations.

However, the IRS is still not giving individual taxpayers the ability to make charitable contributions to state-run charitable funds as a way to circumvent the $10,000 deduction limit on state and local taxes. In fact, the IRS has issued proposed regulations to block New York, New Jersey, and Connecticut from allowing individuals to make charitable contributions to charitable funds in lieu of paying their state and local taxes, and to stop other high-tax states from considering doing the same thing. But they left open the possibility of allowing business taxpayers to use them. Therefore, business taxpayers who make business-related payments to charities or government entities for which the taxpayers receive state or local tax credits can generally deduct the payments as business expenses, as long as they qualify as an ordinary and necessary business expenses. **(See Itemized Deductions, "State and Local Tax Deductions")**

Federal Excise Taxes for Managed Aircraft – The TCJA clarifies that owner flights on managed aircraft are not subject to the Federal Transportation Excise Tax (FET), but rather such owner flights are subject to the non-commercial fuel tax. This issue has been the subject of controversy for more than 60 years. NBAA has submitted a request for guidance to the IRS to further clarify how this new provision will be implemented.

Taxes Imposed on Beer, Wine, and Distilled Spirits
Under the TCJA, alcohol manufacturers (Breweries, distilleries and wineries) will enjoy a two- year excise tax reduction. The TCJA includes "Craft Beverage Modernization and Tax Reform" (CBMTR), which is effective until it is scheduled to sunset on December 31, 2019. The TCJA's purpose is to lower federal excise taxes in order to create a more equitable tax structure for brewers, winemakers, distillers and importers of alcoholic beverages by equalizing the federal excise tax on beer, wine and spirits. One provision that affects all three industry segments – beer, wine and spirits – is that all three products are considered finished after the manufacturing process is complete and are no longer subject to interest capitalization. In 2017 and prior years, that threshold was met

when alcohol was first put out for sale. Under the new law, the aging process is no longer considered part of the production process for purposes of capitalizing interest into inventory, which allows breweries, wineries and distillers to expense postproduction interest costs.

Beer – For beer, the federal excise tax is reduced from $7.00 per barrel to $3.50 per barrel on the first 60,000 barrels for domestic brewers producing fewer than two million barrels annually. The federal excise tax is also reduced to $16 per barrel on the first 6 million barrels for large brewers and beer importers while keeping the $18 per barrel excise tax for barrels produced in excess of 6 million ($18 per barrel was applicable to all production in 2017 and prior years). Also, Brewers are allowed to transfer beer between bonded facilities without paying an excise tax. This change likely benefits small and mid-size craft brewers the most, especially with the reduction of the excise tax on the first 60,000 barrels. The ability to transfer beer between bonded facilities without tax liability will likely encourage brewers to collaborate more on new beers by giving them more flexibility to transfer beer between breweries.

Wine – Wines with alcohol levels from 14% to 16% are taxed at the lower $1.07 per gallon federal excise tax rate that only applied to wines with less than a 14% alcohol level in 2017 and prior years. The old law applied a federal excise tax rate $1.57 per gallon for wines with alcohol levels from 14% to 16%. Wineries are allowed a one dollar per gallon federal excise tax credit for the first 30,000 gallons produced; $0.90 per gallon for the next 100,000 gallons produced; and $0.535 for the next 620,000 gallons produced up to a maximum federal excise tax credit of $451,700 annually, assuming their production is over 750,000 gallons or 315,000 cases of wine. Sparkling wine producers and wine importers also qualify for the new federal excise tax credits.

Distilled Spirits – Under the TCJA, the federal excise tax rates are tiered based on proof gallons– $2.70 per proof gallon on the first 100,000 proof gallons produced, then increased to$13.34 per proof gallon above 100,000 proof gallons up to 22,130,00 proof gallons. The rate increases to $13.50 per proof gallon above 22,130,000. The new law also provides rules that would prevent members of a controlled group from all receiving the lower rate. The TCJA lowers the federal excise tax rate on distilled spirit producers for the first time since the Civil War.

Business Travel and Related Expenses

Employee Travel and Incidental Expenses – Employee travel and incidental expenses, which were deductible as miscellaneous itemized deductions subject to the 2% AGI floor in 2017 and prior years, are no longer deductible for tax years 2018 – 2025 in accordance with the Tax Cuts and Jobs Act (TCJA). Sole proprietors/self-employed persons, general partners, and shareholders/members of S-corporations can deduct their travel and incidental expenses directly on the applicable form or schedule where their revenues and other expenses are reported (Schedule C, Form 1065, Form 1120, or Form 1120-S). **(See Itemized Deductions, "Miscellaneous Itemized Deductions Subject to the 2% AGI Floor")**

Entertainment Expenses – Under the Tax Cuts and Jobs Act (TCJA), any deductions for "business entertainment expenses" are not allowed in 2018 and subsequent years. The TCJA repeals allowable deductions that a business can take for entertainment and recreation even when directly related to a taxpayer's trade or business. This includes activities considered entertainment, amusement, or recreation; membership dues in business clubs organized for pleasure; and facilities used in connection with entertainment. However, business meals are still 50% deductible under the TCJA, which raises the question – when do business meals become business entertainment?

The TCJA doesn't specifically address the deductibility of expenses for business meals. However, according to guidance released by the IRS, taxpayers can still deduct 50% of the cost of business meals if the taxpayer (or an employee of the business) is present at the meal, and food or beverages aren't considered to be "lavish or extravagant." The meals can involve a current or potential business customer, client, consultant or similar business contact. Food and beverages provided during entertainment events won't be considered entertainment if they are bought separately from the entertainment events.

But there is uncertainty as to whether meals provided at a company recreational event, such as a picnic or company party, should be classified as entertainment expenses or should be considered allowable expenses by businesses.

The IRS plans to publish proposed regulations that will clarify exactly when business meal expenses are deductible and what constitutes entertainment. But until those regulations are issued, taxpayers can rely on guidance in Notice 2018-76, which was issued on October 3, 2018.
www.irs.gov/pub/irs-drop/n-18-76.pdf

Leasing a Car, Truck, or Van for Business Use – You can use the standard mileage allowance, or actual expenses plus the lease payments (must be allocated based on the percentage of business miles driven compared to total miles driven during the year). If you choose to use actual expenses, you can deduct the part of each lease payment that is for the use of the vehicle in your business. You can't deduct any part of a lease payment that is for personal use of the vehicle, such as commuting. You must spread any advance payments over the entire lease period. Leased vehicles are not depreciated, so if you lease a vehicle for 30 days or more, and you use the actual expenses method, you have to reduce your lease payment deduction by an "inclusion amount" for each tax year you lease the vehicle. The "inclusion amount" is added to your income in each year of the lease agreement.

Due to the increased depreciation allowances in 2018 in accordance with the TCJA, the inclusion amounts for leasing a car, truck or van for business use have been substantially changed. There is no inclusion amount if the value of a vehicle (cars, trucks or vans) first leased in 2018 is $50,000 or less. Inclusion amounts begin when the value of the vehicle first leased in 2018 is more than $50,000. The inclusion amounts for vehicles first leased in 2017 began with passenger automobiles valued at more than $19,000 and trucks and vans valued at over $19,500. The inclusion amount is a percentage of the fair market value (FMV) of the leased vehicle in accordance with an amount spelled out in the IRS Tables multiplied by the percentage of business use of the vehicle for the year. The inclusion amount applies to each tax year that you lease the vehicle and is figured on the fair market value (FMV) of the vehicle on the first day of the lease term. **(See Property Depreciation and Expensing, "Vehicles Used for Transportation")**
www.irs.gov/pub/irs-drop/rp-17-29.pdf

Property Depreciation and Expensing

Section 179 First-Year Expensing – Under the Tax Cuts and Jobs Act (TCJA), the maximum 179 expense deduction is $1 million effective for property placed in service in 2018 and subsequent years, and the allowable amount starts to phase-out when the amount of Section 179 property placed in service during the year exceeds $2.5 million (these amounts are adjusted for inflation beginning in 2019). The maximum 179 expense deduction was $510,000 in 2017, and the level at which the allowable deduction amount started to phase-out was $2,030,000.

- **Example** – If you buy $2,600,000 worth of eligible property in 2018, the maximum 179 expense deduction would be $900,000 ($1,000,000 - $100,000) because $2,600,000 less $2,500,000 = $100,000. Therefore, no Section 179 deduction is available to businesses that place $3,500,000 or more of eligible property into service during the year (2018).

The TCJA expands the definition of Section 179 property. Taxpayers can elect to include the following improvements made to nonresidential real property as Section 179 property after the date when the property was first placed in service: any improvement to a building's interior and roofs, HVAC, fire protection systems, alarm systems and security systems. Improvements do not qualify if they are attributable to: the enlargement of the building; any elevator or escalator; or the internal structural framework of the building. These changes apply to property placed in service in taxable years beginning after Dec. 31, 2017. The changes also include depreciable tangible personal property, such as furniture and fixtures used in furnishing buildings, other than residential and nonresidential rental real estate buildings. In 2017 and prior years, air conditioning and heating units placed in service in years beginning after 2015 were considered eligible for Section 179 expensing, as long as the property qualified as Section 1245 property, but the TCJA substantially expands the prior definition of Section 179 property.

Section 179 expensing can be used when purchasing both new and used Section 1245 personal property if the property is used more than 50% for business purposes. In addition to what is added by the TCJA, Section 1245 property that is eligible for Section 179 expensing includes: equipment (machines, etc.) purchased for business use; tangible personal property used in business; business vehicles; computers and computer software; office furniture; and office equipment. However, Section 179 expensing still cannot be used for the purchase of Section 1245 personal property (appliances, etc.) purchased for use in residential or nonresidential rental properties.

Unlike first-year bonus depreciation, you can't claim Section 179 expensing that will create a Net Operating Loss (NOL) for a year, i.e. the Section 179 deduction is limited to the business's taxable income from the active conduct of any trade or business during the tax year. However, any amount disallowed by this limitation may be carried forward and deducted in future years. Therefore, you can elect 179 expensing even if there is a lack of income, because it can be carried back and forward to other years – the maximum Section 179 limits are increased by any Section 179 carryovers. However, if Section 179 expensing cannot be used because a business has no income in the current year, bonus depreciation can be used because the use of bonus depreciation can create a NOL. Section 179 expensing must be used before bonus depreciation, unless a business has no income in a year. **(See Below, "First-Year Bonus Depreciation")**

The TCJA eliminates the separate definitions of qualified leasehold improvement property, qualified restaurant property and qualified retail improvement property, instead providing an expanded definition of qualified real

464

property under Section 179 to all "qualified improvement property." **(See Below, "Qualified Improvement Property")**

First-Year Bonus Depreciation – Under the TCJA, first-year bonus depreciation is expanded to include both new and "used" property, and the deduction is increased to 100% for property acquired and placed in service after September 27, 2017 through the 2022 tax year. Property acquired prior to September 28, 2017, but placed in service after September 27, 2017, is subject to the bonus depreciation percentages in effect prior to enactment of the TCJA. After 2022, 80% bonus depreciation will be effective for tax year 2023; 60% for 2024; 40% for 2025; and 20% for 2026, before expiring in 2027. Longer production period property and certain aircraft get an additional year to be placed in service at each rate.

Used qualified property is eligible for bonus depreciation if all the following factors apply:

- The taxpayer didn't use the property at any time before acquiring it.
- The taxpayer didn't acquire the property from a related party.
- The taxpayer didn't acquire the property from a component member of a controlled group of corporations.
- The taxpayer's basis of the used property is not figured in whole or in part by reference to the adjusted basis of the property in the hands of the seller or transferor.
- The taxpayer's basis of the used property is not figured under the provision for deciding basis of property acquired from a decedent.
- The cost of the used qualified property doesn't include any carryover basis of the property.

The TCJA adds qualified film, television and live theatrical productions as types of qualified property that are eligible for 100% bonus depreciation. This provision applies to property acquired and placed in service after Sept. 27, 2017. Also, specified plants planted or grafted after September 27, 2017, and before 2027 are subject to the bonus depreciation under the TCJA. Bonus Depreciation is generally allowable when purchasing Section 1245 personal property, including personal property (appliances, etc.) for use in residential and nonresidential rental properties. Also, bonus depreciation is applicable to specified plants such as trees, vines, and plants bearing fruits or nuts, when planted or grafted. Specified plants include any tree or vine that bears fruits or nuts, or any other plant that will have more than one yield of fruits or nuts and has a pre-productive period of more than two years from the time of planting or grafting to the time when the plant bears fruit or nuts.

Unlike Section 179 expensing, there is no dollar limit for using bonus depreciation, so even the largest businesses are eligible. If your business adds enough depreciable property to generate a net operating loss (NOL) for the year, you can carry the NOL forward and recover some or all of the taxes paid in those years. However, Section 179 expensing is generally required to be taken first, followed by bonus depreciation – unless a business has no taxable profit in the tax year, because Section 179 expensing is limited to taxable income from all of a taxpayer's active trades or businesses. If bonus depreciation is applicable, it is mandatory unless a taxpayer elects out of it. Taxpayers may elect out of bonus depreciation but only for one or more full classes of property, such as all 5-year MACRS property (taxpayers are not allowed to pick and choose which properties they want to apply 100% bonus depreciation to).

Certain types of property are not eligible for bonus depreciation. One such exclusion from qualified property is for property primarily used in the trade or business of the furnishing or sale of:

- Electrical energy, water or sewage disposal services,
- Gas or steam through a local distribution system or
- Transportation of gas or steam by pipeline.

The exclusion from eligibility for bonus depreciation also applies if the rates for the furnishing or sale have to be approved by a federal, state or local government agency, a public service or public utility commission, or an electric cooperative. And the TCJA adds another exclusion from eligibility for bonus depreciation for any property used in a trade or business that has floor-plan financing. Floor-plan financing is secured by motor vehicle inventory that a business sells or leases to retail customers.

The election to accelerate alternative minimum tax (AMT) credits in lieu of bonus depreciation is repealed by the Tax Cuts and Jobs Act (TCJA) effective as of the 2018 tax year. In 2017 and prior years, taxpayers could elect to accelerate AMT credits in lieu of claiming bonus depreciation and increase the amount of unused AMT credits that could be claimed with the bonus depreciation. **(See "Alternative Minimum Tax")**

The IRS has issued proposed regulations on 100% bonus depreciation.
https://s3.amazonaws.com/public-inspection.federalregister.gov/2018-16716.pdf

Qualified Improvement Property – Under the Tax Cuts and Jobs Act (TCJA), qualified leasehold improvement property, qualified restaurant property, and qualified retail improvement property are no longer separately defined. They are consolidated into the "Qualified Improvement Property" (QIP) category encompassing nonstructural improvements generally placed in service at least three years after the completion of a building and given a special 15-year recovery period using SL/GDS, effective for tax year 2018. These are Section 1250 nonresidential real properties that are eligible for both Section 179 expensing and bonus depreciation. Qualified improvement property means any improvement to a building's interior and roofs, HVAC, fire protection systems, alarm systems and security systems.

Improvements do not qualify if they are attributable to: the enlargement of the building; any elevator or escalator; or the internal structural framework of the building. **(See Above, "Section 179 First-Year Expensing" & "First-Year Bonus Depreciation")**

Residential Rental Property – Residential rental property (including mobile homes) is depreciated over 27 ½ years using the SL method under the General Depreciation System (GDS), but the TCJA changes the Alternative Depreciation System (ADS) recovery period for residential rental property from 40 years to 30 years, effective for property placed in service in 2018.

Residential and Nonresidential Real Property –Under the TCJA, taxpayers engaged in a real property business, including a real estate development, construction, rental, management, or brokerage business, among others, may elect to not have the interest limitation apply to their business, and the election is irrevocable. However, when businesses elect to not have the interest limitation apply, they are required to use the alternative depreciation system (ADS) for their nonresidential real property, residential rental property, and qualified improvement property. **(See Business Structures and Enterprises, "Business Interest Expense Limitation")**

Listed Property – Under the TCJA, computers and peripheral equipment are removed from the definition of listed property effective for 2018 acquisitions. In 2017 and prior years, computers and related peripheral equipment were considered listed property, unless they were used only (100%) at a regular business establishment, which included a home office used regularly and exclusively for business purposes.

Listed property is 5-year class personal property that has limitations on the amount of depreciation, Section 179 expensing, and bonus depreciation that can be deducted in a year. If listed property is used more than 50% for business purposes, it is eligible for General Depreciation System/200% declining balance (GDS/200% DB) depreciation, Section 179 expensing, and bonus depreciation in the year placed in service. However, listed property used 50% or less for business purposes must be depreciated using the Alternative Depreciation System/straight-line (ADS/SL) depreciation, and no Section 179 expensing or bonus depreciation is allowed. **(See Above, "Section 179 First-Year Expensing;" & "First-Year Bonus Depreciation")**

Personal property that is considered "listed property" includes:

- Passenger vehicles used for transportation and light trucks and vans;
- Other property used for transportation;
- Property used for entertainment, recreation, or amusement purposes – including photographic, phonographic, and video recording equipment – unless the property is used exclusively (100%) in a taxpayer's trade or business.

When listed property that was formerly used predominately (more than 50%) in a trade or business is converted to personal use (less than 50% business use), any depreciation that exceeds the amount that would have been allowed under the alternative depreciation system (ADS), as well as any 179 expensing and bonus depreciation taken, must be recaptured as ordinary income, reported on Form 4797, and added to the basis of the property. The depreciation that must be recaptured is the difference between 200% declining balance (DB) depreciation claimed under GDS and straight-line depreciation under ADS.
www.irs.gov/pub/irs-pdf/f4797.pdf   www.irs.gov/pub/irs-pdf/i4797.pdf

Vehicles Used for Transportation – The TCJA greatly increases the limitations on depreciation for vehicles (listed property) over what the limitations were in 2017 and prior years. The limitations on depreciation for new and used luxury passenger automobiles, and also on new and used light "trucks and vans" acquired after Sept. 27, 2017 and placed in service in 2018 are: first year – $18,000 ($10,000 + $8,000 if 100% bonus depreciation is claimed); second year – $16,000; third year – $9,600; and each succeeding year – $5,760. For vehicles acquired before Sept. 28, 2017 and placed in service in 2018, the limitations on depreciation are: first year – $16,400; second year – $16,000; third year – $9,600; and each succeeding year – $5,760.

- **Example** – A taxpayer who uses a vehicle 60% for business purposes can claim a depreciation deduction in its fourth year of use equal to $3,456 (60% of $5,760 = $3,456).

SUVs – SUV's with a gross "loaded" vehicle weight capacity of at least 6,000 pounds, but no more than 14,000 pounds and placed in service in 2018 escape the annual depreciation caps for passenger vehicles and light trucks and vans. First-year Sec. 179 and Bonus depreciation for these vehicles is limited to $25,000 in 2018, but under the TCJA the $25,000 limitation will be indexed for inflation beginning in 2019. Also, they are still used as a means of transportation and are still subject to the definition of listed property, so two restrictions still apply if they are used less than 50% for business purposes: (1) depreciation is limited to ADS; and (2) bonus depreciation and Section 179 expensing are not allowed. **(See Above, "Section 179 First-Year Expensing" & "First-Year Bonus Depreciation")**

Certain trucks and vans that have a weight of at least 6,000 pounds, but no more than 14,000 pounds fully loaded are completely exempt from the reduced depreciation rules, including the $25,000 limitation. These are vehicles that are not likely to be used for personal purposes and, therefore, are generally not considered listed property, so they can be totally expensed in the year of purchase. These are vehicles that are: (1) designed to seat more than nine passengers behind the driver's seat; (2) equipped with a cargo area that is not readily accessible directly from the passenger compartment and that are at least 6 feet in length (the cargo area can be open or designed to be open, but enclosed by a cap); or (3) have an integral enclosure that fully encloses the driver's compartment and load carrying device, with no seating behind the driver's seat, and with a body section protruding no more than 30 inches ahead of the leading edge of the windshield (a stub-nosed vehicle).

Other vehicles "not considered listed property" are considered to be "non-personal use" vehicles and, therefore, are exempt from the listed property restrictions, including: vehicles designed to carry cargo and weighing over 14,000 pounds; moving vans; ambulances and hearses; school buses; dump trucks; fire trucks; tractors and combines; cement mixers; construction vehicles; utility repair trucks; taxis, buses, or vans used to transport people for compensation; trucks and vans specifically modified, such as shelving and painting to display advertising or a company name; boats used for transportation (if a qualified non-personal use vehicle); and planes used for transportation (if a qualified non-personal use vehicle).

Trading in a Vehicle – In 2017 and prior years, trading in a vehicle for another vehicle was considered to be a Section 1031 like-kind exchange, so any gain or loss was deferred (not taxable), and the basis of the new vehicle was the adjusted basis of the old vehicle plus the additional amount paid for the new vehicle, which was used for depreciation purposes for the new vehicle. However, since the Tax Cuts and Jobs Act (TCJA) eliminates like-kind exchanges other than for "real property," effective for 2018, any depreciation taken on the old vehicle has to be recaptured, and depreciation on the new vehicle is based on the total purchase price of the new vehicle. **(See Exclusions from Taxable Income, "Section 1031 Like-Kind Exchange")**

Farm Machinery and Equipment – Under the TCJA, the recovery period for depreciation purposes is shortened for originally owned farm machinery and equipment acquired in 2018 from 7 to 5 years beginning in 2018 and subsequent years. And 200% declining balance GDS depreciation is permitted for all property used in the farming business with a recovery period of 10 years of less. Farmers that elect out of business interest deduction limitation, must use the Alternative Depreciation System (ADS) – with its accompanying restriction on using bonus depreciation and longer depreciation recovery period – for any asset with a useful life of more than 10 years, including land improvements, barns, and other farm buildings in years beginning after 2017. **(See Self-Employed/Independent Contractors, Farmers and Ranchers, "Depreciation")**

Amortization of Intangible Assets – In 2017 and prior years, a safe-harbor allowed self-created intangibles to be treated as capital assets and the cost of the self-created intangible assets to be amortized over 15 years. However, under the Tax Cuts and Jobs Act (TCJA), self-created intangible assets such as copyrights, literary compositions, musical or artistic compositions, patents, goodwill, etc. are removed from the definition of capital assets effective in 2018. However, transfers of all substantial rights to a patent or an undivided interest in a portion of patent rights by the inventor or a holder of a patent continues to get long-term capital gain treatment under Section 1235 if payments are tied to productivity or are payable periodically over the transferee's use of the patent. A "holder of a patent" means: any individual whose efforts created such property, or any other individual who has acquired an interest in such property in exchange for consideration in money paid to the creator prior to actual reduction to practice of the invention covered by the patent, if such individual is neither: the employer of the creator, or related to such creator. **(See Capital Gains and Losses, "Self-Created Intangible Assets")**

Generally, you can amortize the capitalized costs of Section 197 intangible assets ratably over 15 years (180 months) if you hold the intangible assets in connection with your trade or business or in an activity engaged in for the production of income. Intangibles must have an ascertainable value and a limited life in order to be amortized over a 15-year period. Generally, goodwill, going concern value, etc. must be purchased in order to be amortized. The 15-year period begins with the later of the month the intangible is acquired or the month the trade or business activity engaged in for the production of income begins.

Self-Employed/Independent Contractors

Farmers and Ranchers – Farming income and expenses are reported on Schedule F. Farmers who are sole proprietors are subject to self-employment taxes, including income earned by sharecroppers. If you earn money managing or working on a farm, you are in the farming business. Farms include plantations, ranches, ranges, and orchards. Farmers may raise livestock, poultry, or fish, or grow fruits or vegetables. Farming does not include commercial freezing and canning. See IRS Publication 225, "Farmer's Tax Guide."
www.irs.gov/pub/irs-pdf/f1040sf.pdf   www.irs.gov/pub/irs-pdf/i1040sf.pdf
www.irs.gov/pub/irs-pdf/p225.pdf

> **Depreciation** – Under the TCJA, the recovery period for depreciation purposes is shortened for originally owned farm machinery and equipment acquired in 2018 from 7 to 5 years beginning in 2018 and subsequent years, and 150% declining balance (DB) GDS depreciation is repealed for 3, 5, 7 and 10-year property and 200% DB/GDS depreciation is permitted for all property used in the farming business with a recovery period of 10 years or less. **(See Property Depreciation and Expensing, "Farm Machinery and Equipment")**

> **Business Interest Deduction** – Under the TCJA, the business interest deduction in 2018 is limited to business interest income plus 30 percent of adjusted taxable income. However, taxpayers engaged in the farming business may elect out of the interest limitation, and the election is irrevocable. However, an electing farm business is required to use the Alternative Depreciation System (ADS) – with its accompanying restriction on using bonus depreciation and longer depreciation recovery period – for any asset with a useful life of more than 10 years, including land improvements, barns, and other farm buildings in years beginning after 2017. **(See Business Structures and Provisions, "Business Interest Expense Limitation")**

Pass-Through Business Provisions – Under the TCJA, farmers and ranchers are allowed to take a deduction of 20% of their business income in tax years 2018 – 2025. For farms and ranches with joint income beyond $315,000, the deduction is limited to: (1) 50% of W-2 wages paid to employees; or (2) the sum of 25% of W-2 wages paid plus 2.5% of depreciable business property. The 20% deduction only offsets income tax, not self-employment tax. **(See Business Structures and Provisions, "20% Deduction Allowed on Passed-Through QBI (Section 199A)")**

Excess Farm Losses – The law in effect in 2017 and prior years, specifically limited only "excess farm losses." However, the TCJA expanded the law to limit losses from all types of pass-through trades or businesses for taxpayers other than corporations. The provision, which went into effect January 1, 2018 and sunsets on December 31, 2025, limits the excess business losses of all pass-through trades or businesses. Under the 2017 law and the 2014 Farm Bill, farmers that received a Commodity Credit Corporation (CCC) loan were restricted in the deductibility of farm losses (this rule didn't apply to C-corporations). The disallowed portion of the losses were carried to the following year, tested again for limitation purposes and claimed on Schedule F (Form 1040). Under the TCJA, farming losses are now subject to the "excess business loss" limitations that are applicable to all pass-through trades and businesses for tax years 2018 – 2025. **(See Business Structures and Enterprises, "Excess Business Losses Under the Tax Cuts and Jobs Act (TCJA)")**

Net Operating Losses (NOLs) – Farmers often end up with a net operating loss (NOL) at the end of any given year when deductible expenses are more than income for the year. Under the Tax Cuts and Jobs Act (TCJA), the 2-year net operating loss carryback is eliminated, except for farmers. Beginning in 2018, a farming NOL may be carried back 2 years instead of 5 years under the rules prior to December 31, 2017, and the 2-year carryback can be waived. Farming NOLs can be carried forward indefinitely but are limited to 80% of taxable income in the carryforward years. In addition, if an NOL consists of both a farming loss and a nonfarming loss, then the two losses are treated separately. The farming NOL is accounted for in carryforward years after the nonfarm loss. That is, the nonfarm NOL, which is subject to the 80% limitation, is first applied to taxable income followed by the application of the farming NOL. **(See Non- Taxable Income, "Net Operating Loss (NOL)")**

Partnerships

New Audit Regime – Partnership agreements need to reflect the "New Audit Regime." Mandatory implementation of the new audit regime kicks off for audits of partnership tax years starting on or after Jan. 1, 2018. With respect to IRS "Audits of Large Partnerships," the Bipartisan Budget Act (BBA) which applies to partnership tax years beginning after Dec. 31, 2017, makes certain changes to adjustments resulting from IRS audits. The audit can adjust a partnership's income, gain, loss, deduction, or credit, or any partner's distributive share of these items. A key part of the new law is that the tax increases will be paid by the partnership at the highest individual or corporate tax rate for the reviewed year. A partnership will pay an imputed underpayment when the audit adjustment(s) result in an increase to income or decrease to deductions. The payment is born by the current partners. Adjustments that do not result in an underpayment of tax must be taken into account in the adjustment year. This requirement allows the current partners to benefit from audit adjustments that are favorable for the partnership related to the reviewed year. Partners from the reviewed year will not receive a refund for the reviewed year if there is a net partnership-favorable IRS audit adjustment.

Loss Limitation Reductions for Charitable Donations and Foreign Taxes – The loss limitation rule states that partners or LLC members that are treated as partners for tax purposes can't deduct losses in excess of the partner's tax basis in the partnership. However, for tax years beginning after December 31, 2017, the Tax Cuts and Jobs Act (TCJA) changes the rules for charitable gifts and foreign taxes by stating that a partner's share of a partnership's deductible charitable donations and paid or accrued foreign taxes reduces the partner's tax basis in the partnership for purposes of applying the loss limitation rule. This change can reduce the amount of losses that can be deducted by partners in 2018 and subsequent years compared to the amount that could be deducted in 2017 and prior years. For charitable donations of appreciated property (where the fair market value is higher than the tax basis), the TCJA states that a partner's basis isn't reduced by the excess amount for purposes of applying the loss limitation rule, i.e. the partner's tax basis is reduced only by the partner's share of the basis of the donated appreciated property for purposes of applying the loss limitation rule. **(See Itemized Deductions, "State and Local Tax Deductions" & "Charitable Contribution Deduction"); (See Business Structures and Provisions, "Excess Business Losses Under the Tax Cuts and Jobs Act (TCJA)")**

Sale of a Partnership Interest Under the Tax Cuts and Jobs Act (TCJA) – Gain or loss from the sale or exchange of a partnership interest generally is treated as gain or loss from the sale or exchange of a capital asset. However, the amount of money and the fair market value of property received in the exchange that represents the partner's share of certain ordinary income-producing assets of the partnership gives rise to ordinary income rather than capital gain.

The Tax Cuts and Jobs Act (TCJA) contains a provision that is important to any person buying or selling an interest in a partnership. The provision makes clear that if a foreign person sells an interest in any U.S. or non-U.S. partnership on or after November 27, 2017, that is engaged in a U.S. trade or business, then any gain that is attributable to the partnership's U.S. trade or business is treated as effectively connected to a U.S. trade or business and subject to U.S. federal income tax. All partners in a partnership are treated as engaged in the conduct of a trade or business within the U.S. if the partnership is so engaged.

As of January 1, 2018, a purchaser (transferee) of a partnership interest is required to withhold 10% of the amount realized on the sale or exchange of a partnership interest, which is usually the purchase price of the interest, and remit the amount to the IRS. This rule applies to sales of both U.S. and non-U.S. partnerships that are engaged in a U.S. trade or business. The withholding is required unless: (1) the purchaser receives an affidavit from the seller to the effect that the seller is a U.S. person and contains the taxpayer identification number of the seller; (2) it is determined that no portion of the gain recognized is attributable to a U.S. trade or business; (3) the IRS agrees to a lower withholding amount (a process which could take months), or (4) pursuant to Notice 2018-08, released on December 29, 2017, interests in the relevant partnership are publicly traded. If the purchaser does not withhold the 10% when required, the partnership is required to withhold from distributions to the purchaser an amount equal to the under-withholding plus interest. Presumably, the partnership will be liable for such amounts if the transferee fails to withhold. www.irs.gov/pub/irs-drop/n-18-08.pdf

Since it is sometimes difficult to determine whether a partnership is engaged in a U.S. trade or business: (1) a purchaser of U.S. or foreign partnership interests should obtain a U.S. Affidavit from a seller or obtain appropriate assurances from the seller that the partnership is not engaged in a U.S. trade or business. In cases where the risk is large, purchasers should consider a guarantee of any resulting liability; (2) Partnerships should ensure that they are (i) aware of all transfers of their partnership interests and (ii) able to determine whether any transfers that do occur comply with these new rules; and (3) General partners and managers should be especially careful regarding any consent to transfer that they provide to their investors given this new provision.

Substantial Built-In Loss – A partnership generally does not adjust the basis of partnership property following the transfer of a partnership interest unless either the partnership has made a one-time election under Section 754 to make basis adjustments, or the partnership has a substantial built-in loss immediately after the transfer. If an election is in effect, or if the partnership has a substantial built-in loss immediately after the transfer, adjustments are made with respect to the transferee partner. These adjustments are to account for the difference between the transferee partner's proportionate share of the adjusted basis of the partnership property and the transferee's basis in his or her partnership interest.

If a partnership has declined in value so that the outside basis (basis in the partnership) exceeds the partnership's value (capital account), the adjustments permitted when a partnership files a Section 754 election is "required" on the transfer of a partnership interest if there is a "substantial built-in loss" at the time of the transfer, regardless of whether or not the partnership has a Section 754 election in place. A Section 754 election allows a partnership to step-up or step-down the outside basis (basis in the partnership) to the inside basis (capital account) for tax purposes. A substantial basis reduction to partnership property occurs if the basis (outside basis) is $250,000 more than the partnership's value (inside basis or capital account). Therefore, a person that purchases such an interest in a partnership (transferee) will not be able to benefit from a loss that the selling partner (transferor) has already taken into account. This rule also applies when there is a transfer of interest upon the death of a partner. Before these mandatory adjustment provisions were enacted, partnerships were potentially created and used to aid tax-shelter transactions.

www.irs.gov/pub/irs-wd/201510024.pdf

The TCJA modifies the definition of a "substantial built-in loss" affecting transfers of partnership interests beginning with the 2018 tax year. The substantial built-in loss rule was already in effect for partnership interests prior to 2018. But under the TCJA, the "substantial built-in loss" rule is expanded to apply not only to the partnership but also to the purchaser (transferee) of a partnership interest. Therefore, the Section 754 election is also required when immediately after the transfer of an interest, a recipient of the transferred interest (transferee) would be allocated a net loss in excess of $250,000 upon a hypothetical taxable sale of all of the entity's assets for proceeds equal to the fair market value (outside basis or basis in the partnership), i.e. the 754 election is required when there is a substantial built-in loss in excess of $250,000 for either the partnership as a whole, or for the purchaser (transferee) of a partnership interest.

In July, 2017, the U.S. Tax Court rejected a long-standing Internal Revenue Service ruling and held that when a non-U.S. person sells an interest in a partnership or is completely redeemed from a partnership that is engaged in a trade or business in the United States, the non-U.S. seller is, in general, not subject to U.S. federal income taxes on the gain from the sale (Grecian Magnesite Mining, Industrial and Shipping Co., SA v. Commissioner, 149 T.C. No. 3).

472

Technical Partnership Terminations – The TCJA repeals the technical partnership termination provision for tax years beginning after December 31, 2017. Therefore, technical terminations of partnerships can no longer happen in 2018 and subsequent years. In 2017 and prior years, a technical termination of a partnership occurred when there was a sale or exchange of 50% or more of the total interest in the partnership's capital and profits within a 12-month period. The repeal didn't change the rule that a partnership is considered terminated if no part of any business, financial operation, or venture of the partnership continues to be carried on by any of its partners.

A technical termination resulted in a deemed contribution of all the partnership's assets and liabilities to a new partnership in exchange for an interest in the new partnership, followed by a deemed distribution of interests in the new partnership to the purchasing partners and the other remaining partners. A technical termination of a partnership had four major tax consequences in 2017 and prior years: (1) the tax attributes of the old partnership were terminated; (2) the old partnership's taxable year closed; (3) any elections previously made by the old partnership ceased to apply; and (4) depreciation recovery periods restarted for the new partnership's assets.

Before the TCJA repealed the technical partnership termination provision, a partnership was terminated in one of two ways, either: (1) when no part of any business of the partnership continued to be carried on by any of its partners, or (2) when there was a sale or exchange of 50% or more of the total interest in the partnership capital and profits within a 12- month period (technical partnership termination).

Services Performed by Fund Managers for an Investment Partnership – The TCJA imposes a three-year holding period instead of a one-year holding period to qualify for long-term capital gain treatment with respect to profits received in connection with the performance of services by a fund manager (hedge fund manager) for an investment partnership or LLC. **This is referred to as "carried interest."** Under the new holding period for "carried interest," gains from profits interests held for three years or less are short-term capital gains subject to tax at ordinary income tax rates, which could be as high as 37%.

The new tax statute applies to both gain from the sale of profits interests (for example, if the holder of the profits interest sells his or her profits interest to a third party for cash) and gain allocated to a partner with respect to his or her profits interest to the extent the gain relates to the sale of assets held by the partnership or LLC (for example, if the holder of the profits interest does not sell his or her profits interest, but instead the underlying entity sells an asset for a capital gain and allocates some of that capital gain to the profits interest holder).

Accordingly, under the new tax law, both of the following would be subject to tax at the taxpayer's ordinary income tax rate and not eligible for capital gains:

1. A profits interest holder's share of gain from the sale by the underlying entity of any assets (even a capital asset) disposed of by the underlying entity within the first three years of someone receiving his or her profits interest grant, or
2. A profits interest holder directly selling his or her profits interest to someone before having held such

473

interest for three years.

As the new statute does not grandfather partnership interests issued prior to the enactment of the TCJA, partners, partnerships and LLCs should be aware that this new provision may impact partnership interests issued in 2015, 2016 or 2017. **(See Capital Gains and Losses, "Carried Interest")**

Corporations

C-Corporation Tax Rates – In 2017 and prior years, the United States taxed the worldwide income of resident multinational C-corporations. This meant that so long as a corporation was considered a resident in the United States, all of the earnings of a corporation, both foreign and domestic, were subject to the U.S. top corporate tax rate of 35% regardless of the location of those earnings. The Tax Cuts and Jobs Act (TCJA) eliminates the progressive C- corporation tax structure (maximum tax rate of 35%) and replaces it with a flat tax rate of 21%, effective for 2018 and subsequent years. The TCJA also eliminates the special corporate tax rate on personal service corporations (PSCs). In addition, the TCJA repeals the corporate alternative minimum tax for tax years beginning after Dec. 31, 2017. Any AMT credit carryovers may be used against regular tax liability, and in 2018, 2019, and 2020, 50% of any AMT credit carryovers that exceed regular tax liability are refundable. Any remaining AMT credits will be fully refundable in 2021.

A C-corporation is subject to the double taxation regime. If a C-corporation earns income, the income is taxed first at the corporation level. Then, if the corporation distributes the income, the recipient shareholders pay tax on the income a second time as a dividend. If instead, the corporation retains the income and the value of the shareholders' stock increases, the shareholders will effectively pay tax on the income a second time in the form of capital gains upon selling the stock. Tax returns for C-corporations are due by April 15 beginning with the 2016 tax year. For 2015 and prior years, C-corporation tax returns were due by March 15. A C-corporation files its tax return every year on Form 1120.

www.irs.gov/pub/irs-pdf/f1120.pdf   www.irs.gov/pub/irs-pdf/i1120.pdf

Repatriation Tax

The Tax Cuts and Jobs Act (TCJA) imposes a one-time mandatory repatriation tax under Section 965 applicable to the "2017 tax year." The Section 965 tax is a forerunner to the U.S. version of a territorial taxation system commencing beginning with the 2018 tax year. As part of the transition to a territorial taxation system, a U.S. entity owning directly or indirectly 10% or more of a deferred foreign income corporation (DFIC) is subject to a one-time Section 965 tax on the U.S. entity's share of the DFIC's **"accumulated post-1986 deferred foreign income"** (E&P) that is greater than zero as of November 2, 2017 or December 31, 2017 (whichever is greater). The Repatriation tax applies to U.S. entities (including individuals, corporations, and domestic investors of pass-through entities.) who own 10% or more of the shares of a DFIC, which include: controlled foreign corporations (CFCs); and foreign corporations that have a U.S. corporate shareholder that owns 10% or more of the shares in the foreign corporation.

474

U.S. entities who are shareholders of "passive foreign investment companies" are not subject to the repatriation tax so long as they are not also controlled foreign corporations. Affected U.S. entities are required to include in income their share of a DFIC's undistributed earnings and profits. This rule works "as if" the DFIC had not already repatriated all of its earnings and profits as of December 31, 2017 through dividend distributions. Deficits are permitted to offset deferred foreign income in accordance with the allocation rules under Section 965. A controlled foreign corporation (CFC) is any foreign corporation where 50% of the total combined voting power of all classes of stock of the corporation is owned directly or indirectly by U.S. shareholders. **(See Below, "Implementation of a Territorial Tax System by the TCJA Beginning in 2018")**

Under the repatriation tax provisions, the "Subpart F income" of a DFIC's **last taxable year that begins before January 1, 2018** is increased by the greater of the DFIC's accumulated post-1986 earnings and profits ("E&P") determined as of November 2, 2017 or December 31, 2017 (Measurement Dates). The increased Subpart F income (inclusion amount) must be recognized and taxed in the 2017 tax year. Therefore, a U.S. entity that owns 10% of a DFIC must pick-up additional taxable income on its pro rata share of the "E&P" on its 2017 tax return. E&P is excluded to the extent such earnings were treated as income effectively connected with a U.S. trade or business or is considered previously taxed income, and when determining E&P for purposes of the income inclusion, adjustments may be required to the extent that there were intercompany distributions during 2017. **Dividends paid during the inclusion year generally are not taken into account as a reduction in the determination of post-1986 earnings and profits (E&P), unless the recipient is another specified foreign corporation.** The determination of E&P involves an annual analysis of the DFIC's income, which is then converted to U.S. generally accepted accounting principles (GAAP), and adjustments are made to convert U.S. GAAP income to E&P using U.S. tax principles. Also, E&P deficits are allowed to offset positive earnings, however this is not necessarily an equal offset. In addition, adjustments may be required for deductible payments between specified foreign corporations occurring between November 2, 2017 and December 31, 2017.

- **Example** – ABC a U.S. domestic corporation and DEF a foreign corporation unrelated to ABC own 70% and 30% respectively of all of FC, a foreign corporation. ABC and FC are both calendar year corporations. FC had no income until its taxable year ending Dec. 31, 2016, is which year it had earned income equivalent to $200, all of which was Subpart F income. Therefore, ABC included $140 (70% X $200) in income that was taxed in accordance "Subpart F." FC had no income in 2017. So, FC's **accumulated post-1986 deferred foreign income (E&P) was $200 of which $140 was attributable to ABC and would be ABC's "inclusion amount" on which the Repatriation Tax would be calculated, because none of the $140 had been distributed to ABC's shareholders,** even though it had been taxed in accordance with Subpart F taxation rules (**Subpart F income does not include dividends paid to U.S. shareholders**).

Under Section 965, a U.S. shareholder pays the repatriation tax at reduced rates on the "inclusion amount." The tax rate reduction is accomplished via a participation exemption whereby Section 965 permits a deduction against a U.S. shareholder's subpart F inclusion amount that is necessary to result in a 15.5% tax rate on cash or cash equivalents, and an 8% tax rate on non-cash equivalents. However, the actual tax calculation looks at the foreign corporation's cash position on multiple dates.

Subpart F Income – Subpart F operates by treating the shareholders of a controlled foreign corporation (CFC) as if they have actually received the income from the CFC even if they haven't yet received it. The income of a CFC that is currently taxable to its U.S. shareholders under the Subpart F rules is referred to as "Subpart F income." Subpart F income does not include dividends paid to U.S. shareholders. In general, it consists of moveable income such as Foreign Base Company Income (FBCI), which includes foreign personal holding company income, which consists of investment income such as dividends, interest, rents and royalties received. It also may consist of income received by a CFC from the purchase or sale of personal property involving related persons and from the performance of services by or on behalf of a related person (foreign base company services income). But what if a DFIC is not a CFC?

The Repatriation tax is applicable to 10% owners of DFICs whether or not the DFIC is a CFC. A specified foreign corporation that is not a CFC does not generally track E&P under U.S. tax principles. So, are taxpayers who are 10% owners of non-CFCs allowed to use an alternative measurement method for determining its post-1986 E&P and cash position, such as audited financial statements? The IRS has not determined that it would be appropriate to use alternative measurement methods, but that generally, audited financial statements may serve as a starting point in the determination of a specified non-CFC's E&P. The IRS appreciates that obtaining accurate information for U.S. federal income tax purposes may present administrative challenges, particularly in the case of U.S. shareholders that do not have a majority interest in a specified foreign corporation.

Calculation of the Repatriation Tax – The calculation of the tax is complicated, but the ultimate goal is to tax accumulated E&P attributable to liquid assets such as cash at the rate of 15.5% and accumulated E&P attributable to illiquid assets at 8%. A calendar year DFIC's foreign cash position must be measured as of the following three dates: The cash position measurement dates are the following: (1) the final cash measurement date is the close of the last taxable year that begins before January 1, 2018, and ends on or after November 2, 2017; (2) the second cash measurement date is the close of the last taxable year that ends after November 1, 2016, and before November 2, 2017; and (3) the first cash measurement date is the close of the last taxable year that ends after November 1, 2015, and before November 2, 2016. A U.S. shareholder takes into account its pro rata share of the cash position on any cash measurement date, regardless of whether the shareholder is a shareholder on any other cash measurement date, including the final cash measurement date. A shareholder's cash position is the greater of its cash position on the final cash measurement date or 50% of the sum of its cash positions on the second cash measurement date and the first cash measurement date.

Instead of 15.5% and 8% for corporate shareholders, "individuals" in the highest 2017 tax bracket (39.6%), are subject to a repatriation tax on E&P of 17.5% on cash assets and 9% on noncash assets. Individuals can elect to be treated as corporate shareholders for purposes of the repatriation tax. However, the overall effects of this election should be evaluated as there may be other ancillary effects. An individual is considered to own all the foreign stock owned by his or her spouse, children; and the family attribution rules extend to all grandparents and any number of great-grandparents or grand-children and their spouses.

- **Example** – Assume U.S. shareholder "A" owns 100% of two DFICs. DFIC-1 is a calendar year corporation that has the following cash positions: $400 on 12/31/2015; $400 on 12/31/2016; and $600 on 12/31/2017. Therefore, taking into account only DFIC-1's cash position, A's cash position would be

476

$600, because 50% of $400 + $400 = $400, which is less than DFIC-1's $600 cash position on 12/31/2017. However, DFIC-2 is not a calendar year corporation – its tax years for cash measurement purposes end on 10/31/2016; 10/31/2017; and 10/31/2018 and DFIC-2 has the following cash positions: $600 on 10/31/2016; $600 on 10/31/2017; and $800 on 10/31/2018. So, taking into account both DFIC-1's and DFIC-2's cash positions, A's cash position for purposes of determining the repatriation tax would be $1,200 ($600 for DFIC-1 and $600 for DFIC- 2), because since DFIC-2's final cash measurement date ends after 12/31/2017, DFIC- 2's final cash position is considered to be zero, and 50% of $600 + $600 = $600. And $600 + $600 = $1,200.

The aggregate foreign cash position is the sum of: cash held by the corporation; the net accounts receivable of the corporation (reduced by accounts payable); and the fair market value (FMV) of the following "cash equivalent" assets held by the corporation: (a) personal property which is of a type that is actively traded and for which there is an established financial market ("actively traded property"); (b) commercial paper, certificates of deposit, the securities of the Federal government and of any State or foreign government; (c) any foreign currency; (d) any obligation with a term of less than one year ("short-term obligation"); and (e) any other cash equivalent asset.

- **Example** – Assume that a U.S. shareholder is a calendar year "individual shareholder" who owns 100% of a foreign corporation (DFIC) that is a controlled foreign corporation (CFC) with the following assets:

Liquid Assets (12/31/2017):

Cash	$2,000
Accounts Receivable (less Accounts Payable)	5,000
Marketable Securities	3,000
Total Liquid Assets	$10,000

Illiquid Assets

Inventories	$1,000
Plant, Property & Equipment (net of Accumulated Depreciation)	2,000
Other Assets	500
Total Assets	$13,500

Assume the DFIC had post-1986 non-previously taxed E&P of $11,000 on Nov. 2, 2017 and $12,000 on Dec. 31, 2017. E&P determined as of Dec. 31, 2017 is used for this calculation because it is more than the E&P on Nov. 2, 2017. Calculation of Repatriation Tax on Liquid Assets: Total Liquid Assets = $10,000 X 17.5% = $1,750. Calculation of Repatriation Tax on Illiquid Assets: $12,000 (E&P) minus $10,000 (Liquid Assets) = $2,000 X 9% = $180 **(Illiquid assets are determined based on total E&P (Mandatory Inclusion Amount) less the foreign cash position) Calculation of Total Repatriation Tax: $1,750 + $180 = $1,930**

The above calculation is applicable to an individual shareholder of a DFIC. However, due to the deemed-paid foreign tax credit, the calculation is much more complex for a C-corporation shareholder. The 15.5% tax rate on cash assets and 8% tax rate on non-cash assets assumes that all of the foreign tax credits are allowable. However, foreign tax credits are disallowed to the extent they are attributable to the portion of the mandatory inclusion amount excluded from taxable income. Therefore, C-corporation shareholders are subject to a "participation deduction" or a "haircut" of 55.7% attributable to the cash portion of the inclusion amount taxed at 15.5% and a haircut of 77.1% attributable to the non-cash portion of the inclusion amount taxed at 8%. These percentages are equal to the amount of a shareholder's mandatory inclusion that is offset by the participation exemption using a corporate tax rate of 35%. This requires a "gross-up" of a C-corporation's tax, which is an additional tax on the "Net Income Inclusion Amount."

- **Example** – Refer to the above example, except that the shareholder is a C-corporation instead of an individual shareholder. As in the example above, assume the DFIC had post-1986 non-previously taxed E&P of $11,000 on Nov. 2, 2017 and $12,000 on Dec. 31, 2017. E&P determined as of Dec. 31, 2017 is used for this calculation because it is more than the E&P on Nov. 2, 2017. Calculation of Repatriation Tax on Liquid Assets: Total Liquid Assets = $10,000 X 15.5% = $1,550. Calculation of Repatriation Tax on Illiquid Assets: $12,000 (E&P) minus $10,000 (Liquid Assets) = $2,000 X 8% = $160 **(Illiquid assets are determined based on total E&P (Mandatory Inclusion Amount) less the foreign cash position).** Calculation of Repatriation Tax: $1,550 + $160 = **$1,710**

  Total Liquid Assets of $10,000 X 44.3% (100% minus 55.7%) = $4,430; Illiquid Assets of $2,000 X 22.9% (100% minus 77.1%) = $458; $4,430 + $458 = $4,888 (Net Income Inclusion Amount). Computation of additional tax on the Net Income Inclusion Amount: $4,888 X 35% (maximum corporate tax rate in 2017) = **$1,711 (Tax at Marginal Rate: Subpart F Inclusion Amount). Total Repatriation Tax for C-corporation: $3,421 ($1,710 + $1,711 = $3,421)**

A taxpayer may need to report Section 965 amounts on its 2016 tax return. For example, a DFIC and its sole U.S. shareholder are both fiscal year taxpayers with a November 30 tax year end, and the DFIC dissolved on November 29, 2017. So, the last tax year of the DFIC beginning before Jan. 1, 2018, would be its tax year beginning Dec. 1, 2016, and ending Nov. 29, 2017. An inclusion amount with respect to the DFIC would be properly included on the U.S. shareholder's 2016 tax return for its tax year beginning on Dec. 1, 2016, and ending on Nov. 30, 2017.

To date, The IRS has issued Notices 2018-07 and 2018-13 that provide guidance on the calculation of the Repatriation Tax. The IRS has also issued Publication 5292 "How to Calculate Section 965 Amounts and Elections Available to Taxpayers" for use in preparing 2017 Returns. Publication 5292 provides a workbook to help taxpayers calculate the Section 965 Repatriation Tax. The IRS has also issued a 249-page document that sets-forth proposed regulations in regard to the Repatriation Tax.

www.irs.gov/pub/irs-drop/n-18-07.pdf   www.irs.gov/pub/irs-drop/n-18-13.pdf
www.irs.gov/pub/irs-pdf/p5292.pdf   www.irs.gov/pub/irs-drop/reg-104226-18.pdf

Paying the Repatriation Tax – U.S. corporations may offset the tax with a deemed foreign tax credit. But, all U.S. shareholders, including individuals and corporations, can pay the tax in lump sum or elect to pay the net tax liability in unequal installments over eight years, beginning with the due date of the 2017 tax return. However, the first installment payment must be made by the original due date of the 2017 tax return (without extensions).

In order to make a payment for the Section 965 Repatriation Tax, a taxpayer needs to make two separate payments with their tax return and include two separate payment vouchers. One payment needs to reflect the tax owed on the tax return without regard to the Repatriation Tax. The second payment needs to reflect tax owed for the Repatriation Tax. Both payments must be paid by the due date of the applicable return without extension. Also, A U.S. shareholder that has to pay the repatriation tax is required to include with its return a Section 965 Transition Tax Statement. It can be attached as a PDF to an electronically filed return. At a minimum the Transition Tax Statement must include: the taxpayer's total amount of income required to be included by Code Section 965(a); the taxpayer's aggregate foreign cash position; the taxpayer's total deduction available under Code Section 965(c); the taxpayer's deemed paid foreign taxes with respect to the income being included (for C corporations only); the taxpayer's disallowed deemed paid foreign taxes with respect to the income being included (C corporation only); the total net tax liability for the repatriation tax; the amount of net tax liability to be paid in eight installments; and a listing of elections under Code Section 965 provided for in Notice 2018-13.

www.irs.gov/pub/irs-drop/n-18-13.pdf

When a taxpayer elects to pay the tax over eight years, 8% of the tax must be paid in each of the first five years, 15% in the sixth year, 20% in the seventh year, and 25% in the eighth year. The payment of the tax must be accelerated upon the occurrence of certain "triggering events," such as failure to timely pay any installment due, or a liquidation or sale of substantially all of a shareholder's interest in the foreign corporation.

S-corporations – Shareholders of S-corporations may elect to defer paying its net repatriation tax liability until the tax year that a "triggering event" occurs. A "triggering event" includes the corporation ceasing to be an S-corporation, a liquidation or sale of substantially all of the assets of such S- corporation, a cessation of business by such S-corporation, the S- corporation ceases to exist, and a transfer of any share of stock of the S-corporation (including by death or otherwise). An S-corporation shareholder that elects to defer paying its net tax liability may also elect to pay the liability in equal installments over an 8-year period after a triggering event has occurred. However, this election is available only with consent if the triggering event is a liquidation, sale of substantially all of the S-corporation's assets, termination of the S-corporation or cessation of its business, or a similar event. The first installment must be paid by the due date (without extensions) of the shareholder's federal income tax return for the year that includes the triggering event. If any S-corporation shareholder elects to defer paying its net tax liability, the S-corporation is jointly and severally liable for the payment of the deferred tax and any penalty, additions to tax, or additional amounts attributable thereto, and the limitation on collection is not treated as beginning before the triggering event.

Implementation of a Territorial Tax System by the TCJA Beginning in 2018 –The TCJA made several changes to the taxation of subpart F income of U.S. shareholders of controlled foreign corporations (CFCs). Among other things, the TCJA expands the definition of a U.S. shareholder to include U.S. persons who own 10% or more of the total value (not just the vote) of shares of all classes of stock of the CFC. In addition, the requirement that a corporation must be controlled for 30 days before Subpart F inclusions apply has been eliminated. The TCJA introduces four new major corporate tax provisions: (1) the "participation exemption," which exempts all foreign profits paid back to the United States from domestic taxation. This is what changed the U.S. corporate tax system from a "worldwide" tax system closer to a "territorial" tax system; (2) the second and third provisions, "Global Intangible Low Tax Income" (GILTI) and "Foreign Derived Intangible Income" (FDII), are two new categories of foreign income subject to taxation at reduced rates after the exemption of all foreign profits from taxation that are paid back to the U.S. in the form of dividends. **GILTI and FDII taken together are in effect a worldwide tax on intangible income of controlled foreign corporations (CFC) that is taxed at a lower rate than the new designated 21% corporate tax rate. They** create a worldwide minimum tax on intangible income and are meant as "supplement taxes" after the exemption of all foreign profits by the new participation exemption; and (3) Lastly, "The Base Erosion and Anti-Abuse Tax" (BEAT) is in effect a new minimum tax, aimed at preventing multinationals from stripping income from the U.S. tax base with excess payments to foreign-affiliated corporations. **(See Above, "Subpart F Income")**

U.S. companies have been anxiously waiting for guidance on how to implement and calculate these provisions, because they don't want to underestimate their GILTI liability or they could have to pay penalties if they don't pay enough on their quarterly tax installments to the IRS. IRS guidance has been a piecemeal process, and the complexity of these provisions has made understanding of how to calculate these taxes somewhat arbitrary. Clarification of these provisions has been needed. But finally, on September 13, 2018, the IRS issued proposed regulations (157 pages) that provide some details on which assets are subject to the tax on GILTI, and how to calculate it. Another measure would allow large multinational corporations to consolidate, or calculate the tax one time for all of their entities, rather than requiring them to do potentially dozens of calculations for individual subsidiaries. However, many questions remain unanswered. And according to the IRS, additional guidance will not be forthcoming for about another 60 days.

www.irs.gov/pub/irs-drop/reg-104390-18.pdf

The Participation Exemption – Beginning in 2018 (tax years beginning after December 31, 2017), the TCJA eliminates the additional U.S. tax on foreign profits through what is called the "participation exemption." The participation exemption allows a 100% deduction for dividends received from foreign corporations by U.S. domestic parent corporations in determining their taxable income. The 100% dividend received deduction (DRD) is available to domestic C-corporations that own at least 10% of a controlled foreign corporation (CFC). The result is that these foreign profits paid to U.S. domestic corporations in the form of dividends do not face additional U.S. taxation as they did under the previous law that was in effect in 2017 and prior years. Eligible C-corporations for the participation exemption cannot be real estate investment trusts (REITs) or regulated investment companies. Also, domestic partnerships and individuals are not considered eligible U.S. shareholders for the participation exemption. In addition, dividends received from passive foreign investment companies (PFICs) do not qualify for the participation exemption. However, a **domestic S-corporation that owns 10% or more of the stock of a foreign corporation is eligible for the participation exemption.**

Therefore, large individual shareholders should benefit from transferring their stock in a foreign corporation they own into an S-corporation. A U.S. domestic corporation must qualify as a 10% shareholder of the specified foreign corporation at all times during the period the participation exemption applies to distributions of dividends. U.S. corporations are not allowed to receive a foreign tax credit for the dividends getting the participation exemption and, therefore, excluded from taxable income.

To qualify for the participation exemption, U.S. corporations have to satisfy three requirements: (1) they must own 10% of the controlled foreign corporation's (CFC) stock; (2) they must hold the CFC's stock for at least 366 days; and (3) they cannot deduct a dividend against U.S. taxable income if that dividend received a tax benefit in a foreign country. This is to prevent "hybrid dividends" that receive a deduction in the foreign country before being paid to the U.S. parent corporation from being excluded from the taxable income of the U.S. corporation, resulting effectively in no tax on that income. **The TCJA changes the definition of a "10% U.S. Shareholder."**

Before the enactment of the TCJA, a "10% U.S. Shareholder" was defined as a U.S. person who owned (directly, indirectly or constructively) 10% or more of the total combined voting power of a corporation. The TCJA expands the definition to include a U.S. person who owns 10% or more of the stock of the corporation by vote or value. The participation exemption excludes ordinary foreign profits paid to U.S. parent corporations in the form of dividends, but it does not exclude capital gains from being taxed. U.S. corporations that sell, or otherwise dispose of shares in CFCs, do not get an income exclusion on gains from selling those shares.

U.S. corporations that have received dividends that are allowed the participation exemption and then sell the CFC stock at a loss must reduce its basis (but not below zero) in the stock of the foreign corporation by the amount of the dividends allowed the 100% participation exemption. When a U.S. corporation transfers substantially all of the assets of a foreign branch to a foreign subsidiary, the U.S. corporation must include in income the amount of any post-2017 losses realized by the branch.

Global Intangible Low Tax Income (GILTI) – In 2017 and prior years, U.S. shareholders (whether corporations or individuals) that owned 10% or more of the voting stock in a controlled foreign corporation (CFC) generally were taxed on the CFC's earnings only when they received a dividend, with an exception referred to as the "Subpart F rules," which require the inclusion of certain types of income earned by a CFC on a current basis, regardless of whether distributions in the form of a dividends were received. Thus, a U.S. taxpayer that structured its operations in a manner that was mindful of the Subpart F rules generally was able to defer U.S. tax on income earned by a CFC until the U.S. taxpayer received a dividend. **(See Above "Subpart F Income")**

Under the TCJA, Global Intangible Low Tax Income (GILTI) was implemented as a new anti- deferral tax on certain earnings of a CFC, effective starting with the first tax year of the CFC beginning after Dec. 31, 2017. Similar to the taxation of Subpart F income, a 10% U.S. shareholder of one or more CFCs is required to include its GILTI currently as taxable income (in addition to any Subpart F income), regardless of whether any amount is distributed to the U.S. shareholder. The tax on GILTI essentially serves to tax a U.S. shareholder currently on the shareholder's allocable share of CFC earnings for a tax year to the extent such earnings exceed a 10% return on the shareholder's allocable share of tangible assets held by CFCs. The tax on GILTI applies equally to U.S. shareholders that are corporations or flow-through taxpayers.

A U.S. shareholder's GILTI is calculated as the shareholder's "net CFC tested income" less "net deemed tangible income return" determined for the tax year. Net CFC tested income is calculated by determining the U.S. shareholder's pro rata share of tested income or tested loss of each CFC held by the U.S. shareholder, and aggregating those amounts. Tested income or loss is calculated as a CFC's gross income after excluding high- taxed foreign base company income, Subpart F income, related-party dividends, certain foreign oil and gas extraction income, and income of the CFC taxable in the United States as effectively connected income, less deductions allocable to tested income. High-taxed income that is not foreign base company income is included as tested income. Thus, in the simple case where a single shareholder owns 100% of a CFC with none of the categories of excluded income as stated above, net CFC tested income will equal the CFC's net income. For passthrough taxpayers that do not benefit from foreign tax credits on GILTI, high-taxed income included in Subpart F income is excluded, but high-taxed income that is not included in Subpart F income is not.

After the net CFC tested income is determined, it is reduced by the shareholder's "net deemed tangible income return" to arrive at the shareholder's GILTI. This amount is the excess of a U.S. shareholder's allocable share of the basis of a CFC's depreciable tangible assets used in the production of tested income, multiplied by 10% (subject to certain adjustments). "Net deemed tangible income return" is also referred to as "Qualified Business Asset Investment" (QBAI). So, net tested income minus 10% of QBAI, less the amount of interest expense taken into account in determining the shareholder's net CFC tested income for the tax year to the extent the interest income attributable to such expense is not taken into account in determining the shareholder's net CFC tested income, is equal to GILTI. For this purpose, the basis of a CFC's depreciable assets is determined by applying depreciation on a straight-line basis.

- **Example** – As of Dec. 31, 2018, a U.S. shareholder owns 100% of CFC-1 and 50% of CFC-2. CFC-1 has $160,000 of tested income and a tax basis in tangible assets or QBAI of $400,000. CFC-2 has $100,000 of tested income and QBAI of $1 million. The U.S. shareholder has net tested income of $210,000 (100% X $160,000 + 50% X $100,000= **$210,000**. GILTI = **$120,000**: (10% X $400,000 = $40,000) + (10% X [50% X $1 million = $500,000] = $50,000; $210,000 less ($40,000 + $50,000 = $90,000) = $120,000

Once the GILTI amount is determined, a U.S. corporate taxpayer can deduct 50% of its GILTI (reduced to 37.5% for tax years starting after 2025). This results in a 10.5% minimum tax on a corporate U.S. shareholder's GILTI (50% × 21% corporate tax rate). In addition to this "GILTI deduction," a foreign tax credit may be claimed by a U.S. corporate taxpayer equal to 80% of the foreign income taxes paid by a CFC on a U.S. shareholder's tested income. Application of the deduction and the tax credit eliminates any U.S. taxes owed above 13.125% on the U.S. corporate shareholder's GILTI because the maximum tax on GILTI is 13.125% for tax years before 2026, and

482

16.406% thereafter.

- **Example** – From the example above, the GILTI amount is equal to $120,000; Foreign Tax Liability on the GILTI = $6,000; $6,000 X 80% = $4,800 (Foreign Tax Credit); $120,000 X 10.5% = $12,600 (Initial Tax on GILTI); $12,600 minus $4,800 (Foreign Tax Credit) = $7,800 (Final U.S. Tax on GILTI). $7,800 + $6,000 (Foreign Tax Liability on GILTI) = $13,800 (Total Tax on GILTI); $13,800 divided by $120,00 (GILTI) = **11.5% TOTAL EFFECTIVE TAX RATE ON GILTI.**

Flow-Through and Individual Taxpayers – Though the amount of a U.S. shareholder's GILTI is calculated the same for corporate, individual and flow-through (Partnership and S- corporation) taxpayers, only corporate taxpayers are entitled to the 50% GILTI deduction and related 80% foreign tax credit. Therefore, individual and flow-through taxpayers subject to tax on GILTI are taxed on the entire amount of GILTI. In addition, because the tax on GILTI arises from foreign business operations, flow-through taxpayers that would otherwise potentially qualify for the new Sec. 199A deduction cannot include the amount of the GILTI in the base for determining the 20% deduction. Accordingly, under most circumstances, noncorporate U.S. taxpayers will pay a current tax on GILTI at a rate up to 37% (the newly enacted highest marginal rate for individuals). A noncorporate taxpayer may make the election under Sec. 962(a) to be taxed as a C-corporation and generally obtain the benefits of the lower tax rate applicable to C-corporations and the foreign tax credit (but not the 50% GILTI deduction). However, making such an election generally requires future distributions of what would otherwise be a return of previously taxed profits to be taxable.

Foreign Derived Intangible Income (FDII) – Foreign Derived Intangible Income (FDII) is a second new category of foreign income that is added to U.S. corporate taxable income each year beginning in 2018 (tax years beginning after December 31, 2017). Generally, FDII is income from the use of intellectual property in the United States in creating an export. Unlike GILTI, FDII and BEAT (See below) somewhat resemble a destination-based tax. FDII effectively creates a new preferential tax rate for income derived by U.S. domestic corporations serving foreign markets. A U.S. domestic C-corporation pays an effective tax rate of 13.125% (rather than 21%) on its income arising from foreign markets. This new deduction is described as a deduction for foreign-derived intangible income, or FDII. The FDII deduction is available to domestic corporations that are taxed as C-corporations. This includes U.S. corporate subsidiaries of foreign-based multinationals. However, foreign corporations with income effectively connected with a U.S. trade or business, S-corporations, regulated investment companies, real estate investment trusts, partnerships and individuals are not eligible to claim a FDII deduction.

In general, FDII is equal to foreign-derived income minus 10% of "Qualified Business Asset Investment" (QBAI). Foreign-derived income is the share of a corporation's U.S. income related to the export of goods or services. QBAI for purposes of the FDII is equal to the value of tangible assets used by a U.S. corporation in earning foreign-derived income. U.S. corporations are allowed to deduct 37.5% of their FDII against their taxable income. This results in a special lower effective tax rate of 13.125% (rather than 21%) on income generated from export sales or services.

The FDII benefit is determined based on a multi-step calculation:

1. A domestic corporation's gross income is determined and then reduced by certain items of income, including amounts included in income under Subpart F, dividends received from controlled foreign corporations and income earned in foreign branches. This amount is reduced by deductions (including taxes) properly allocable to such income, yielding deduction eligible income.

2. The foreign portion of such income is determined. This amount includes any income derived from the sale of property to any foreign person for foreign use. The term "sale" is defined for this purpose to include any lease, license, exchange or other disposition. The term "foreign use" is defined as any use, consumption, or disposition which is not within the United States. Qualifying foreign income also includes income derived in connection with services provided to any person not located within the United States, or with respect to property that is not located in the United States. The services may be performed within or outside the United States (but not in a foreign branch of the domestic corporation, which limits the extent of permissible qualifying activity outside the United States).

3. The gross foreign sales and services income is reduced by expenses properly allocated to such income. The sum of these two amounts yields foreign derived deductible eligible income.

A domestic corporation's foreign derived intangible income (FDII) is determined. This is the excess (if any) of the corporation's deduction eligible income minus 10% of its qualified business asset investment (QBAI). A domestic corporation's QBAI is the average of its adjusted bases (using a quarterly measuring convention) in depreciable tangible property used in the corporation's trade or business to generate the deduction eligible income. The adjusted bases are determined using straight line depreciation. A domestic corporation's QBAI does not include land, intangible property or any assets that do not produce the deductible eligible income. U.S. corporations are allowed to deduct 37.5% of their FDII against their taxable income.

- **Example** – ABC company, a U.S. corporation, earned $1,900 in total income in the United States of which 10% ($190) was earned from exporting goods overseas. The company has $800 in QBAI (value of its tangible assets used in earning foreign derived income). Therefore, the company's FDII is $110 ($190 in foreign derived income minus 10% of QBAI [$800 X 10% = $80]). The company is allowed to deduct 37.5% of its FDII, which is $41.25 ($110 X 37.5%) from its FDII. Taxable income is $68.75 ($110 minus $41.25 = $68.75) X 21% corporate tax rate = **$14.44 tax on FDII which is an effective tax rate of 13.125%** ($14.44 divided by $110 FDII)

GILTI and FDII combined is in effect a worldwide tax on deemed intangible income. Together, GILTI and FDII are a backstop to the Participation Exemption and are meant to prevent companies from moving their intellectual property in order to shift corporate profits out of the United States. On Sept. 13, 2018, the IRS issued proposed regulations meant to clarify aspects of GILTI and FDII, including how the taxes are computed.

www.irs.gov/pub/irs-drop/reg-104390-18.pdf

The Base Erosion and Anti-Abuse Tax (BEAT) – The "Base Erosion and Anti-Abuse Tax," or BEAT is effective for tax years beginning after December 31, 2017. The BEAT is essentially a 10% minimum tax (5 percent in 2018) that is meant to prevent foreign and domestic corporations operating in the United States from avoiding domestic tax liability by shifting profits out of the U.S. The BEAT only applies to multinational domestic corporations and to foreign corporations with income connected with a U.S. trade or business whose annual gross receipts for the 3-year-taxable period ending with the preceding tax year that is $500 million or more. The BEAT does not apply to individuals, S-corporations, regulated investment companies or real estate investment trusts.

The BEAT is 10% of "modified taxable income" less a corporation's regular tax liability, generally reduced by certain tax credits. However, the tax rate is 5% instead of 10% for 2018, and increases to 12.5% beginning in 2025. These rates are increased by one percent for certain banks and securities dealers. The BEAT calculations are made on a group basis, i.e. the related-party payments, deductions, and income of affiliated domestic corporations are aggregated for BEAT purposes. A corporation's modified taxable income is determined by adding back to taxable income current year deductions involving payments to related foreign corporations owning at least 25% of the stock of the taxpayer. Add-backs include payments for services, interest, rents and royalties. The 50% deduction for amounts included in income as global intangible low-taxed income (GILTI) is not added back. The add backs are what are considered "base erosion" payments that corporations based in the U.S. make to related foreign corporations.

The BEAT does not apply unless current year deductions involving payments to related foreign corporations exceed 3% (2% for certain financial firms such as banks and securities dealers) of total deductions taken by the corporations.

- **Example** – Assume a U.S. multinational corporation has gross receipts for the 3-year- taxable period of $1 million. The corporation's regular taxable income is $210,000. The corporation's modified taxable income after adding back current year deductions involving payments to 25% related foreign corporations is equal to $215,000. Total deductions taken by the corporation equal $250,000. The BEAT does not apply, because the deductions involving payments to related foreign corporations is less than 3% of the total deductions taken by the corporation ($215,000 minus $210,000 = $5,000; However 3% X $250,000 = $7,500.

- **Example** – A U.S. multinational corporation's regular taxable income is $210,000, and its modified taxable income is $250,000. Its deductions involving payments to related foreign corporations are more than 3% of the total deductions taken by the corporation. Therefore, the corporation's BEAT is $2,000 in 2018 and $4,000 in 2019 ($250,000 modified taxable income, minus $210,000 regular taxable income = $40,000 X 5% = $2,000 BEAT in 2018; $40,000 X 10% = $4,000 BEAT in 2019.

Deduction of Compensation of Public Company Executives – There is a $1 million limit on the deduction of compensation paid by a public corporation to a "covered employee" in determining taxable income. A covered employee includes the CEO or one of the top 4 other executives whose compensation must be reported on a public company's proxy statement. However, prior to 2018, the following exemptions and exceptions were allowed to avoid the $1 million limit, which means these exemptions and exceptions were allowed to be deducted as compensation in computing taxable income:

- Bonuses and other compensation meeting the requirements to be considered "qualified

performance-based compensation" was fully deductible.
- Commissions were fully deductible.
- Compensation paid to former employees and current employees who were formerly top-five executives was fully deductible. Compensation paid to the CFO was fully deductible.

The TCJA eliminates all of the exemptions and exceptions, effective for 2018 and subsequent years. Therefore, for 2018 all compensation in excess of $1 million paid to any employee or former employee who is or was the CEO, the CFO, or one of the other top three executives whose compensation is required to be reported on the proxy statement is not deductible by the company in computing its taxable income. However, compensation payable pursuant to a legally binding agreement that was in place prior to November 2, 2017, is not affected by the TCJA (Grandfather Clause). IRS guidance seems to imply that the "Grandfather Clause" applies only if any amount of remuneration to a covered employee does not exceed the amount of remuneration that applicable law obligates the corporation to pay under a written binding contract that was in effect on November 2, 2017, or if the terms of the contract state that it will be automatically renewed after November 2, 2017, and neither the corporation nor the employee provides at least a 30-day notice of termination of the contract prior to the scheduled renewal date.

Once an employee is treated as a covered employee, the individual remains a covered employee for all future years, including payments made after retirement, death, etc. Also, the definition of a "public corporation" is expanded to include all domestic publicly traded corporations and all foreign public companies and may include some corporations that are not publicly traded, such as large private C or S corporations. But the TCJA does not appear to extend beyond SEC filers.

On August 21, 2018, the IRS issued Notice 2018-68 which offers early guidance on the meaning of this provision of the TCJA. The Guidance seems to imply that the "Grandfather Clause" applies only if any amount of remuneration to a covered employee does not exceed the amount of remuneration that applicable law obligates the corporation to pay under a written binding contract that was in effect on November 2, 2017, or if the terms of the contract state that it will be automatically renewed after November 2, 2017, and neither the corporation nor the employee provides at least a 30-day notice of termination of the contract prior to the scheduled renewal date.

www.irs.gov/pub/irs-drop/n-18-68.pdf

Contributions to Capital of Corporations by Governmental Entities – Under the TCJA, contributions to a corporation's capital by governmental entities after December 22, 2017, are generally reportable as income. Before then, such contributions were generally excluded from income by corporations. This means that property contributed to a corporation after December 22, 2017, by a governmental unit or by a civic group for the purpose of inducing the corporation to locate its business in a particular town, city, community etc. or to enable the corporation to expand its facilities in those areas is taxable to the corporation. States, cities and utilities can continue to contribute undeveloped land, improved land and other assets to corporations to entice them to locate in a community, but the value of such incentives has been diminished by the TCJA. This change does not apply to any contributions by a governmental entity under a development plan that was approved before December 22, 2017.

Dividends Received Deduction

Prior to January 1, 2018, dividends received by a C-corporation from a less than 20% owned domestic corporation were 70% excluded from income by the C-corporation, and dividends received by a C-corporation from a more than 20% owned domestic corporation were 80% excluded from income by a C-corporation. Under the TCJA, effective for 2018 and subsequent years, the percentages of dividends excluded by a C-corporation are decreased from 70% to 50% for a less than 20% owned corporation, and from 80% to 65% for a more than 20% owned corporation.

Conversion of an S-Corporation Back to a C-Corporation – The TCJA contains two generally favorable provisions that allows applicable "eligible S- corporations" to revoke their S- corporation status after enactment of the TCJA. For purposes of both provisions, an eligible S- corporation is one that had previously been a C-corporation (before enactment of the TCJA) and elected to convert back to a C-corporation following the enactment of the TCJA and: (1) revokes its S-corporation election during the two-year period beginning on the date of enactment of the TCJA; and (2) the owners of the stock on the date of revocation of S- corporation status are the same as, and such owners hold the stock in the same proportions as, on the date of enactment of the TCJA. The first provision relates to accounting method changes required as a result of an S-corporation's conversion back to a C-corporation.

Specifically, the TCJA provides that, in the case of an eligible terminated S-corporation, any section 481 adjustment arising from an accounting method change attributable to the corporation's revocation of its S-corporation election will be taken into account ratably during the six-tax year period beginning with the year of the accounting method change. Thus, a corporation that must change a method of accounting (e.g. from the cash method to the accrual method) as a result of the revocation of its S-corporation election would include any income resulting from that change over six tax years (as opposed to four-years under the old law).

The second provision revises the treatment of distributions made by corporations following their conversion back to C-corporation status. Under the law in effect in 2017 and prior years, distributions by an S-corporation that revokes its S-corporation status are generally treated as coming first from the earnings and profits (E&P) of the corporation during the post-transition termination period, which means the distributions are treated as dividends received by the shareholders and taxable at ordinary income tax rates. Whereas, under the TCJA, distributions by an S-corporation that revokes its S-corporation status are generally treated as coming pro- rata from E&P and the "accumulated adjustments account" (AAA) of the corporation during the post-transition termination period. This means that only the distributions received by the shareholders coming from E&P are taxable as ordinary income but the distributions coming from AAA are considered already taxed and will be only subject to capital gains treatment upon disposition. Therefore, the treatment of distributions is favorable to the shareholders under the TCJA.

In August 2018, the IRS issued Revenue Procedure 2018-44 which provides guidance on switching back from an S-corporation to C-corporation status.
www.irs.gov/pub/irs-drop/rp-18-44.pdf

Insurance Companies:

      New Rules for Life Settlements – Life settlements allow owners of life insurance policies that would otherwise be cancelled, resulting in little or no return, to instead recoup part of their losses by finding an institutional buyer willing to pay a percentage of the face amount of the policy, particularly if the life expectancy of the insured party is less than normal (i.e., 10 years or less). Although some tax may be owed on that amount, the net is generally more than if there was no life settlement market.

Under the TCJA, beginning in 2018, when determining the basis of a life insurance or annuity contract for a potential life settlement, no adjustment is required for mortality, expense, or other reasonable charges incurred under the contract. This change reverses the position taken by the IRS in Revenue Ruling 2009-13 that, upon the sale of the cash value of a life insurance contract, the insured's (seller's) basis was reduced by the cost of insurance for mortality, expense, or other reasonable charges incurred. This change also applies retroactively to transactions entered into after August 25, 2009, which coincides with the effective date of Revenue Ruling 2009-13. Therefore, taxpayers who paid additional taxes as a result of that Revenue Ruling and have returns from open tax years could potentially apply for a refund.
www.irs.gov/pub/irs-drop/rr-09-13.pdf

The TCJA also added some new reporting requirements that apply to life settlements and the payment of reportable death benefits occurring after December 31, 2017. The language of the TCJA refers to a "reportable policy sale," which means the acquisition of an interest in a life insurance contract, directly or indirectly, if the purchaser has no substantial family, business, or financial relationship with the insured apart from the purchaser's interest in the life insurance contract. This includes acquisition of an interest in a partnership, trust, or other entity that holds an interest in the life insurance contract. Any person who purchases a life insurance contract or any interest in a life insurance contract in a reportable policy sale during a tax year must report the following: (1) name, address, and taxpayer identification number (TIN) of the person; (2) name, address, and TIN of each recipient of payment in the reportable policy sale; (3) date of the sale; (4) name of the issuer of the life insurance contract sold and the policy number of the contract; and (5) the amount of each payment.

Anyone required to report the above information must furnish to each person named a written statement showing: (1) name, address, and phone number of the contact of person required to submit the report; and (2) information required to be shown on the return (see above), except that in the case of an issuer of a life insurance contract, the transfer-for-value statement is not required to include the amount of each payment. Also, the TCJA sets-forth that for transfers made after December 31, 2017, the exception to the transfer-for-value rules do not apply to a transfer of a life insurance contract, or any interest in a life insurance contract, that is a reportable policy sale (life settlement). As for the impact of this provision, in the typical life settlement, the acquirer is a hedge fund or a bank, which will likely know that it does not fall under the exception to the transfer-for-value rule. Thus, this provision is presumably intended to cut off the possibility of creating some mechanism to avoid the transfer-for-value rule, because it is going to apply to any reportable policy sale as that term is now defined.

      Insurance Company Reserves – Under the TCJA, the rules for computation of insurance company reserves for both life and property and casualty (P&C) insurance companies are changed. Beginning in 2018, the

TCJA provides that life insurance reserves for any contract are to be determined based on the greater of the net surrender value or 92.81% of the amount determined using the applicable tax reserve method. However, the tax reserves may not exceed the statutory reserve applicable to the contract as calculated for statutory reporting. Under a transition rule, life insurance companies are required to recalculate their 2017 reserves as if the 2018 TCJA rules were in effect then, compare it to their actual 2017 reserves and account for the difference over eight years beginning in 2018.

Prior to implementation of the TCJA, P&C loss reserves were discounted using a discount rate based on the applicable federal midterm rate. The TCJA changes the basis of the discount rate to the corporate bond yield curve, i.e. yields on investment grade corporate bonds with varying maturities. In addition to effectively increasing the discount rate, the TCJA extends the periods for determining loss payment patterns and repeals the election, allowing taxpayers to use their own historical loss payment pattern rather than the industrywide loss payment pattern for certain businesses. Similar to the transition rules applicable to life insurance companies, P&C insurance companies have to restate their reserves as of the end of 2017 and take the resulting reduction into account over eight years.

Adjustment for Change in Computing Reserves – Under the TCJA, the special 10-year adjustment period for taking-into-account changes in a life insurance company's basis for computing reserves is repealed. Beginning in 2018, the TCJA requires aligning reserve strengthening and weakening with the general rules under Section 481 for accounting method changes, which means that the strengthening or weakening of reserves is changed from a 10- year period of inclusion to a four-year period of inclusion for unfavorable changes and to a one- year period of inclusion for favorable changes.

Capitalization of Certain Policy Acquisition Expenses – The TCJA changes the rules that require insurance companies to capitalize and amortize a portion of policy acquisition expenses on certain specified insurance contracts. The TCJA extends the amortization period for such expenses from 120 months to 180 months and increases the percentage of expenses subject to the capitalization rule from: 1.75% to 2.1% for annuity contracts; 2.05% to 2.46% for group life insurance contracts; and 7.7% to 9.24% for all other specified insurance contracts.

Net Operating Loss Utilization – Under the TCJA, life insurance companies are subject to the new limits on net operating losses (NOLs) that are applicable to all noninsurance companies. As it is for noninsurance companies, NOLs arising for life insurance companies arising in tax years before December 31, 2017, will remain subject to the two-year carryback and 20-year carryforward rule until their expiration and also will continue to be available to offset 100% of taxable income. However, the new rules for NOLs that are applicable to noninsurance companies and life insurance companies do not apply to property and casualty (P&C) insurance companies. The NOLs of P&C insurance companies are still subject to the old rules, i.e. can be carried back two years and carried forward 20 years and continue to be available to offset 100% of taxable income in subsequent years instead of 80% under the new rules. Therefore, consolidated insurance groups that include both life and P&C companies will have to separately track the different NOL limitations for each of their companies. **(See Non- Taxable Income, "Net Operating Loss (NOL)")**

Proration Rules for P&C Insurance Companies – The TCJA modifies the proration rules for P&C insurance companies with respect to tax-exempt interest and the dividends-received deduction by replacing the 15%

reduction under the law in effect in 2017 and prior years with a reduction equal to 5.25% divided by the top corporate tax rate. Since the corporate tax rate is a flat 21% rate beginning in 2018, the current proration percentage is 25%, resulting in the same after-tax yield for tax-exempt bonds as under prior law.

Base Erosion and Anti-Abuse Tax – The specific language of the TCJA indicates that the Base Erosion and Anti-Abuse Tax (BEAT) is imposed on the gross amount of reinsurance premiums, instead of net reinsurance payments, as some have argued. For example, for quota share arrangements the gross amount of reinsurance premiums would be subject to the BEAT without taking into account any inbound payments such as reserve adjustments, ceding commissions and claims payments. Also, in the case of modified coinsurance or funds withheld coinsurance, the BEAT would apply to the whole outbound gross premium as well as to the interest on the funds withheld paid over to the assuming company. In addition, the TCJA did not repeal the excise tax payable on outbound insurance and reinsurance premiums. Thus, in addition to potentially attracting a BEAT liability, insurance and reinsurance premiums paid to foreign insurers and reinsurers with respect to risks located in the U.S. continue to be subject to an excise tax at the rate of 1% or 4%. **(See Above, "The Base Erosion and Anti-Abuse Tax (BEAT)")**

PFIC Rules - The TCJA changed the passive foreign investment company (PFIC) statutory provision that in 2017 and prior years excluded income derived from the active conduct of an insurance business from the definition of passive income. Under the TCJA, beginning in 2018 the exclusion is available only to "qualified insurance companies." A qualified insurance company must have applicable insurance liabilities that exceed 25% of its total assets.

Applicable insurance liabilities generally include loss and loss adjustment expenses and reserves other than deficiency, contingency or unearned premium reserves. However, due to vagueness in the definition of applicable insurance liabilities, uncertainty exists as to how the liability reserves of P&C insurance companies are taken-into-account to determine applicable insurance liabilities. The TCJA provides potential relief for a foreign corporation that fails to meet the 25% test by allowing a U.S. shareholder to elect to treat a foreign corporation as a qualifying insurance company if: its applicable insurance liabilities constitute at least 10% of its total assets; and the corporation is predominantly engaged in the insurance business, and its failure to qualify under the 25% threshold is due solely to runoff-related or rating-related circumstances involving such insurance business.

Banks – Phased-Out Deduction for FDIC Premiums – Beginning in 2018, the Tax Cuts and Jobs Act (TCJA) phases out the FDIC premium deduction for banks with total consolidated assets between $10 billion and $50 billion, and eliminates the deduction for banks with assets of $50 billion or more. Banks with less than $10 billion in assets may continue to fully deduct FDIC premiums. In 2017, and prior years, banks could deduct 100% of their FDIC premiums no matter the amount of their assets.

Tax-Exempt Organizations

Compensation of Executives of Tax-Exempt Organizations – Beginning in 2018, the Tax Cuts and Jobs Act (TCJA) imposes a 21% excise tax on tax-exempt organizations that provide their executives with annual

490

compensation in excess of $1 million. And this also applies to severance payments (parachute payments) paid to their executives in excess of $1 million. This excise tax is meant to put tax-exempt organizations, which are generally exempt from income taxation, in about the same position as for-profit companies which cannot deduct excess compensation payments made to their covered employees. However, unlike the changes made by the TCJA to the excess compensation rules for profit companies, there is no transition relief for existing tax-exempt organization compensation arrangements.

The new excise tax imposed by the TCJA applies to most tax-exempt organizations including: any organization that is exempt under Code Section 501(a); any state and local governmental entity with tax exempt income; any tax-exempt political organization; and any tax-exempt farmers' cooperative. However, it isn't certain whether the excise tax applies to colleges and universities. Employees covered by the excise tax includes the five highest paid employees of a tax-exempt organization in any year after 2016. Therefore, the excise tax applies to any person who is currently or was formerly one of the five highest paid employees of the organization for the current tax year or for any preceding tax year beginning after Dec. 31, 2016. Compensation that is subject to federal income tax withholding is counted for purposes of the excise tax, but Roth contributions made by a covered employee under an organization's 401(k) or 403(b) Plan are not included. **(See Corporations, "Deduction of Compensation of Public Company Executives")**

Entertainment Expenses

The TCJA provides that expenditures for entertainment, amusement, or recreation, including club dues paid on behalf of employees, are no longer deductible by the employer, even if the club is used for business purposes. Because tax-exempt organizations do not generally receive a tax deduction for salary expense, coupled with the elimination of the deduction for social club dues and other entertainment expenses, tax-exempt organizations must include such benefits in the employee's taxable compensation beginning in the 2018 tax year. **(See Travel and Related Expenses, "Entertainment Expenses")**

Excise Tax on Investment Income of Private Colleges and Universities – Effective for tax years beginning in 2018, the Tax Cuts and Jobs Act (TCJA) imposes a 1.4% excise tax on the net investment income of private tax-exempt colleges and universities that have at least 500 tuition-paying students (50% of which are located in the U.S.). Also, the applicable college or university must have had an aggregate fair market value of assets (other than those used directly in carrying out the college or university's tax-exempt purpose) at the end of the preceding tax year of at least $500,000 per student. Generally, such assets include assets held by related organizations, including supporting organizations controlled by the school and the applicable net investment income on which the excise tax is imposed is derived from those assets. The number of students is based on the daily average number of full-time equivalent students (full-time students and part-time students on an equivalent basis). Net investment income is gross investment income minus expenses to produce the investment (but disallowing the use of accelerated depreciation methods or percentage depletion).

Unrelated Business Income Tax (UBIT) – Even though an organization is recognized as a tax- exempt organization, it still may be liable for taxes in accordance with the unrelated business income tax (UBIT) rules, because some Income earned by nonprofits may not be tax-exempt. A tax-exempt organization may be subject to UBIT if it has income from a trade or business that is regularly carried on and unrelated to its exempt purpose, and if this is the case, the organization must annually file Form 990-T, "Exempt Organization Business Income Tax

Return."

Tax-exempt organizations should not fear having unrelated business income (UBI), but it is important to recognize when it might arise so the appropriate IRS (and state, if applicable) filings are made. By planning for UBI, and recognizing under which circumstances it might appear, organizations can effectively manage it in accordance with regulations. Income usually does not threaten an organization's tax-exempt status, and in many cases provides a more stable and predictable source of funding than contributions, grants or other forms of exempt income. However, there might be consequences if the income from the activity is significant and it is determined that the organization is no longer organized and operated exclusively for an exempt purpose.

www.irs.gov/pub/irs-pdf/f990t.pdf

Beginning in 2018, the Tax Cuts and Jobs Act (TCJA) requires tax-exempt organizations to determine the net unrelated business income tax (UBIT) "separately" for each unrelated trade or business, i.e. gains and losses have to be calculated separately for each unrelated trade or business. A loss by an unrelated trade or business can't be used to offset income from a tax- exempt organization's other unrelated trades or businesses. In addition, net operating loss (NOL) deductions are only allowable to offset income from the same unrelated trade or business from which the loss occurred. This TCJA change does not apply to any NOLs arising in a tax year beginning before January 1, 2018. So, such NOLs can be used to reduce aggregate UBTI for all unrelated trades or businesses of tax-exempt organizations. **(See Non-Taxable Income, "Net Operating Loss (NOL)")**

The TCJA did not provide criteria for determining how to determine when a tax-exempt organization has more than one unrelated trade or business and how to identify them. However, the IRS has released Notice 2018-67 which provides some guidance. The Notice states that when determining if a tax-exempt organization has more than one unrelated trade or business, it may rely on a reasonable, good-faith interpretation of the law, including use of the North American Industry Classification System (NAICS) codes. For example, an organization's advertising activities and related services, reported under the same NAICS code, might be considered one unrelated trade or business activity, regardless of the source of the income. The Notice requires a tax-exempt organization that is a partner in a partnership that conducts a trade or business that is an unrelated trade or business to include in UBTI its distributive share of gross partnership income (and directly connected partnership deductions) from the unrelated trade or business. The IRS intends to issue proposed regulations that would permit aggregation of gross income and directly connected deductions from such "investment activities."

www.irs.gov/pub/irs-drop/n-18-67.pdf

Estates and Trusts

Income Tax Rates for Estates and Trusts – Estates and trusts are recognized as separate taxable entities for tax purposes. Both estates and trusts must file a tax return on Form 1041, "U.S. Income Tax Return for Estates and Trusts," on or before the fifteenth day of the fourth month following the close of the tax year if it has gross income of $600 or more in the year (April 15 for calendar year taxpayers in 2018). However, executors or administrators of estates can obtain an automatic 6-month extension by filing Form 7004, but trusts can only get a maximum 5 ½ month extension by filing Form 7004. Estates may have a fiscal year, which is a taxable year

other than the calendar year, but a trust is generally required to have a calendar tax year. Estates and trusts are conduits of income to beneficiaries, and as such are allowed a deduction for income that is currently distributed to beneficiaries. Form 1041, Schedule K-1 is used to report distributions to beneficiaries, which must be reported and taxed as income to the beneficiaries on their individual tax returns.
www.irs.gov/pub/irs-pdf/f1041.pdf   www.irs.gov/pub/irs-pdf/i1041.pdf   www.irs.gov/pub/irs-pdf/i7004.pdf
www.irs.gov/pub/irs-access/f1041sk1_accessible.pdf   www.irs.gov/pub/irs-pdf/f7004.pdf

Under the Tax Cuts and Jobs Act, the number of income tax brackets for estates and trusts is cut from 5 in 2017 to 4 in 2018 – 2025, with the 37% tax bracket commencing at over $12,500. Following are the 2018 tax brackets for estates and trusts: 0 - $2,550 (10%); $2,551 - $9,150 ($255.00 + 24% of the amount over $2,550); $9,151 - $12,500 ($1,839.00 + 35% of the amount over $9,150); Over $12,500 ($3,011.50 + 37% of the amount over $12,500). Estates and trusts are subject to the 3.8% surtax on the "net investment income" (NII) of estates and trusts. The threshold for the surtax is the dollar amount at which the highest tax bracket for estates and trusts begins for the tax year, which in 2018 is $12,500.

The Affordable Care Act (ACA) adds a 3.8% surtax on the "net investment income" (NII) of estates and trusts. The threshold for the surtax is the dollar amount at which the highest tax bracket for estates and trusts begins for the tax year, which in 2018 is $12,500. Unlike the thresholds for individuals, the thresholds for estates and trusts is adjusted for inflation each year. Grantor trust income flows-through to the grantor; therefore, only non-grantor trusts are required to pay the NII tax. Non-grantor trusts should consider paying distributions to beneficiaries to avoid the 3.8% NII tax, which kicks in for trusts at $12,500 in 2018. **(See "3.8% Net Investment Income Tax")**

Qualifying Beneficiaries of an Electing Small Business Trust (ESBT) – Generally, eligible beneficiaries of an ESBT include individuals, estates, and certain charitable organizations eligible to hold S-corporation stock directly. Prior to the enactment of the Tax Cuts and Jobs Act (TCJA), a nonresident alien individual could not be a shareholder of an S-corporation and could not be a potential current beneficiary of an ESBT. However, effective as of January 1, 2018, the TCJA allows a nonresident alien individual to be a potential current beneficiary of an ESBT. In 2017 and prior years, an ESBT couldn't have a current beneficiary who was a nonresident alien individual. But in accordance with the TCJA, such individuals can now be shareholders of an S-corporation and can be ESBT beneficiaries. This change is effective for 2018 and subsequent years.

As a general rule, trusts cannot be S-corporation shareholders. However, an exception allows electing small business trusts (ESBTs) to be S-corporation shareholders. An electing small business trust (ESBT) is treated as two separate trusts. The portion of an ESBT that consists of stock in one or more S-corporations is treated as one trust. The portion of an ESBT that consists of all the other assets in the trust is treated as a separate trust. The grantor or another person may be treated as the owner of all or a portion of either or both such trusts under subpart E, part I, subchapter J, chapter 1 of the Internal Revenue Code. The ESBT is treated as a single trust for administrative purposes, such as having one taxpayer identification number and filing one tax return. The grantor portion of an ESBT is the portion of the trust that is treated as owned by the grantor or another person under subpart E. The S-corporation portion of an ESBT is the portion of the trust that consists of S-corporation stock and is not treated as owned by the grantor or another person under Subpart E. The non-S-corporation portion of an ESBT is the portion of the trust that consists of all assets other than S-corporation stock that is not treated as owned by the grantor or another person under subpart E.

Charitable Contribution Deduction for Electing Small Business Trusts (ESBTs) – Generally, a trust is allowed a charitable contribution deduction for amounts of gross income, without limitation, which pursuant to the terms of the governing instrument are paid for a charitable purpose. No carryover of excess contributions is allowed. An individual is allowed a charitable contribution deduction limited to certain percentages of adjusted gross income, generally with a 5-year carryforward of amounts in excess of this limitation. For tax years beginning after Dec. 31, 2017, the TCJA provides that the charitable contribution deduction of an ESBT is not determined by the rules generally applicable to trusts but rather by the rules applicable to individuals. Thus, the percentage limitations and carryforward provisions applicable to individuals apply to charitable contributions made by the portion of an ESBT holding S- corporation stock. However, in 2017 and prior years the deduction for charitable contributions was determined by the rules applicable to trusts rather than to the rules applicable to individuals.

Alaskan Native Corporation Payments and Contributions to Settlement Trusts – The TCJA created new possibilities for Alaska Native Settlement Trusts and Alaska Native Corporations. Congress first authorized Native Corporations to establish Settlement Trusts in 1988 "to promote the health, education, and welfare of its beneficiaries and preserve the heritage and culture of Natives." But the Trusts have been relatively underutilized thus far by Native Corporations. Among the changes made by the TCJA was the addition of section 247 to the Internal Revenue Code (I.R.C.), which permits a Native Corporation to make contributions to Settlement TrustS on a tax-deductible basis rather than an after-tax basis. This should make the use of Settlement Trusts more attractive to Native Corporations.

Estate and Gift Tax

Exemption Amount for Estate and Gift Tax and Generation-Skipping Transfer Tax – Under the Tax Cuts and Jobs Act (TCJA), the exemption amount for the Estate and Gift Tax and Generation-Skipping Transfer Tax is doubled for tax years 2018 – 2025, to $11.2 million (indexed for inflation beginning in 2019). The exemption is scheduled to revert back to half of the 2025 adjusted amount in 2026, which would be approximately the exemption amount in 2017 before being doubled. The exemption amount in 2017 was $5.49 million. The top tax rate remains at 40%. With the availability of the "Portability of the Estate Tax Exemption," the Estate and Gift Tax for married couples should only apply to estates in excess of $22.4 million in 2018.

An Estate tax return is filed on Form 706, and a Gift tax return is filed on Form 709. The exemption amount is the same for both Estate and Gift tax purposes, hence making the wealth transfer tax truly a "unified tax." However, beginning in 2012, any unified credit allocated to gifts in prior periods must be re-determined using the current unified tax rate, not the rates in effect for the years when prior gifts were made (the instructions provide a worksheet for making this calculation, and the result is reported on Form 709, Schedule B, Gifts from Prior Periods).
www.irs.gov/pub/irs-pdf/f706.pdf   www.irs.gov/pub/irs-pdf/i706.pdf
www.irs.gov/pub/irs-pdf/f709.pdf   www.irs.gov/pub/irs-pdf/i709.pdf

Alternative Minimum Tax (AMT)

Thresholds for Phase-Out of Alternative Minimum Tax Exemption Amounts – Once the initial AMTI is determined, an exemption amount further reduces AMTI, but the exemption amounts are phased out when the initial AMTI exceeds certain thresholds. The Tax Cuts and Jobs Act (TCJA) sets forth much higher thresholds for phasing out exemption amounts applicable to alternative minimum taxable income (AMTI) in 2018 than were effective in 2017 and prior years. The thresholds for phaseout of AMTI exemption amounts in 2018 are: $1 million for married filing jointly; $500,000 for single, head of household and married filing separately; and $75,000 for estates and trusts. The exemption amounts for 2018 and subsequent years are also more in 2018 than in 2017 and prior years. The exemption amounts are: $109,400 (married filing jointly and surviving spouses); $70,300 (single and head of household); $54,700 (married filing separately); and $22,500 (estates and trusts). The exemption amounts are reduced by 25% of the amount by which the initial AMTI exceeds the thresholds.

- **Example** – If a married couple has an initial AMTI of $1,200,000, the exemption amount of $109,400 is reduced to $59,400 computed as follows: $1,200,000 minus $1,000,000 = $200,000 X 25% = $50,000; $109,400 minus $50,000 = $59,400. So, $59,400 is the reduced exemption amount that is deducted from the married couples initial AMTI to get a final taxable AMTI of $1,140,600.

- **Example** – If a married couple has an initial AMTI of $900,000, the exemption amount of $109,400 is not reduced because the initial AMTI is not over $1 million. So, the married couple's final taxable AMTI is $790,600 ($900,000 – $109,400 = $790,600).

- **Example** – If an estate has a taxable income $100,000, the exemption amount of $22,500 is reduced to $16,250 computed as follows: $100,000 minus $75,000 = $25,000 X 25% = $6,250; $22,500 minus $6,250 = $16,250. So, $16,250 is the reduced exemption amount that is deducted from the estate's final AMTI to get a final taxable AMTI of $83,750.

If your ordinary income tax is greater than the "Tentative Minimum Tax," you are not subject to AMT. However, if your "Tentative Minimum Tax" is higher, the excess is reported as an additional tax on Form 1040. In the first example above, the married couples' Tentative Minimum Tax would be $315,538 ($191,500 X 26% = $49,790; $1,140,600 – $191,500 = $949,100 X 28% = $265,748; $49,790 + $265,748 = $315,538).

www.irs.gov/pub/irs-pdf/f6251.pdf   www.irs.gov/pub/irs-pdf/i6251.pdf

Affordable Care Act (ACA)

All aspects of the ACA remain in effect in 2018, including the 0.9% Medicare Surtax and the 3.8% Net Investment Income Tax, in spite of extensive efforts to repeal and replace the ACA by President Trump and the Republican-majority Congress. However, the individual shared responsibility provision or "Individual Mandate" requiring taxpayers to pay a penalty if they don't have health insurance coverage has been repealed by the Tax Cuts and Jobs Act (TCJA), effective beginning with the 2019 tax year. On Oct. 16, 2017, the IRS informed taxpayers and tax practitioners that it would not accept electronically filed 2017 individual income tax returns unless taxpayers indicated on their tax returns that they and everyone on their return (spouse and all dependents) had health insurance coverage; qualified for an exemption; or were making a shared-responsibility payment (penalty). The 2017 tax year was the first year that the IRS had enforced this requirement, and the requirement will be enforced in 2018. But of course, this requirement (individual mandate) will go away beginning with the 2019 tax year. **(See Payroll Tax, "0.9% Medicare Surtax"); (See "3.8% Net Investment Income Tax")**

Notice 2018-84 that provides guidance on how the suspension of the personal exemption deduction for determining taxable income by the TCJA will affect some of the rules under the ACA for claiming the premium tax credit. **(See Tax Credits, "Affordable Care Act (ACA) Premium Tax Credits")**
https://www.irs.gov/pub/irs-drop/n-18-84.pdf

On October 23, 2018, the Departments of the Treasury, Labor and Human Services issued proposed regulations on HRAs that would increase the usability of HRAs (primarily for large employers) by expanding employers' ability to offer HRAs to their employees and allow HRAs to be used in conjunction with nongroup health insurance coverage (generally coverage on the individual market). **(See Exclusions From Taxable Income, "Health Reimbursement Arrangement (HRA)")**
https://s3.amazonaws.com/public-inspection.federalregister.gov/2018-23183.pdf

On Sept. 14, 2018, it was revealed that the IRS is making it easier for some qualifying individuals to apply for certain hardship exemptions from having to have health insurance coverage in 2018 (the "Individual Mandate"). The new guidance provides that certain hardship exemptions that previously could only be obtained through the "Exchange" can either be obtained by using the existing application process, or on a taxpayer's 2018 federal tax return without presenting documentary evidence or a written explanation. Also, as of 9/12/2018, it was revealed that Congress will vote on a bill that will delay until 2019 the "employer mandate." Additionally, the bill would change the ACA definition of a "full-time worker" to someone who works 40 hours a week rather than the current definition of only 30 hours a week.

Qualified Small Employer Health Reimbursement Arrangement (QSEHRA) – A qualified small employer health reimbursement arrangement (QSEHRA), or small business HRA, is an employer funded tax-free health benefit that allows small businesses with fewer than 50 full-time or full-time-equivalent (FTE) employees to reimburse their employees for individual health care expenses. QSEHRAs were signed into law by the "Twenty-First Century Cures Act" in December 2017. Most stand-alone health reimbursement arrangements (HRAs), which is an HRA that is not offered in conjunction with a group health plan, have been prohibited since 2014 by the Affordable Care Act (ACA). However, the 21st Century Cures Act (Act) allows small employers that do not maintain group health plans to establish stand-alone HRAs that are called QSEHRAs, effective for plan years beginning on or after Jan. 1, 2017. Like all HRAs, a QSEHRA must be funded solely by the employer. Employees cannot make their own contributions to an HRA, either directly or indirectly through salary reduction contributions. Specific requirements apply, including a maximum benefit limit and a notice requirement. For 2018, the maximum reimbursements cannot exceed $5,050 for those with self-only coverage and $10,250 for those with family coverage. In 2017, the QSEHRA contribution limits were $4,950 annually for self-only employees and $10,000 annually for family coverage. For employees who become eligible for the QSEHRA midyear, the limits must be prorated to reflect the total amount of time the employee is eligible. For example, an employee who is eligible for the QSEHRA for 6 months in 2018 can receive up to $2,524.98 through the benefit that year. **(See Exclusions from Taxable Income, "Qualified Small Employer Health**

Reimbursement Arrangement (QSEHRA)")

In calculating whether a QSEHRA provides affordable coverage, an employee determines whether their QSEHRA qualifies as affordable coverage. In 2018, the federal definition of "affordable coverage" is an insurance policy that costs 9.56% or less of a person's household income, which means that for a QSEHRA to be considered affordable coverage, the employee's premium must cost less than 9.56% of the employee's household income. If these conditions are met, the employee has affordable coverage and doesn't qualify for a premium tax credit. If the conditions are not met, the employee may be eligible for a credit.

- **Example** – Alice, an employee at ABC Company, is granted $5,000 a year through her employer's QSEHRA. This is equal to a monthly allowance of $417 a month. If Alice's premium for self-only coverage through the second-lowest cost silver plan on her exchange is $417 or less, she doesn't qualify for a tax credit. If the premium cost is more than that, however, she must subtract the amount of her HRA monthly allowance from that cost. Let's say the exchange premium is $500, and $500 –$417 = $83. If $83 is equal to or less than 9.56% of Alice's income for the month, the QSEHRA is affordable and she doesn't qualify for a premium tax credit. In this example, Alice would not qualify for a premium tax credit if she were earning $868 per month or more. However, if $83 is greater than 9.56% of Alice's monthly income (i.e., Alice is earning $868 per month or less), she "does" qualify for a premium tax credit.

After determining that you qualify for a premium tax credit, you have to calculate the amount of the premium tax credit. You must make sure the amount of the tax credit is adjusted to reflect the monthly HRA allowance. The law requires any premium tax credit to be reduced by the amount of the monthly HRA allowance.

- **Example** – Assume Alice of ABC Company is eligible for a $600 premium tax credit per month. Because she receives a $417 HRA allowance from her company, she must subtract $417 from $600, leaving her with a tax credit of $183 per month. It's possible that an employee's tax credit will be reduced entirely by the HRA allowance; however, it cannot be reduced below zero.

As a small business owner, you may be concerned about the affordability of your HRA offering. However, small business employers are never involved with making premium tax credit calculations for their employees. Not only would that violate the employee's privacy, but it's also nearly impossible to do. An employer cannot know whether an employee has additional sources of income, whether from a spouse, a second job, or property ownership. As for their employees, they must disclose their HRA monthly allowance to the exchange, which will help calculate the employees' eligibility.

2.3% Excise Tax on Medical Devices – The Federal Register Printing Savings Act of 2017 delays until 2020 the 2.3% excise tax on certain medical devices. The new law replaces the previous law – The "Protecting Americans from Tax Hikes Act of 2015" which imposed a 2-year moratorium on the 2.3% excise tax on medical devices (the excise tax was not imposed in tax years 2016 and 2017).

40% Excise Tax on High-Cost Employer-Provided Health Plans ("Cadillac" Health Plans) – The Federal Register Printing Savings Act of 2017 delays until 2022 the "Cadillac" tax on employers for excess employer-sponsored health insurance coverage. The excise tax which has never been imposed in any tax year so far was to be paid by the coverage provider or person who administered the plan benefits. The idea is to give employers that much more reason to avoid expensive insurance policies and thus give insurers that much more reason to hold costs down.

501

503

505

510

514

515

519

27755469R00297